Lecture Notes in Computer Science 11200

Commenced Publication in 1973
Founding and Former Series Editors:
Gerhard Goos, Juris Hartmanis, and Jan van Leeuwen

More information about this series at http://www.springer.com/series/7407

Tiziana Margaria · Susanne Graf ·
Kim G. Larsen (Eds.)

Models, Mindsets, Meta

The What, the How, and the Why Not?

Essays Dedicated to Bernhard Steffen
on the Occasion of His 60th Birthday

 Springer

Editors
Tiziana Margaria
Lero–The Irish Software Research Center
University of Limerick
Limerick, Ireland

Susanne Graf
Verimag Laboratory
Grenoble, France

Kim G. Larsen
Aalborg University
Aalborg, Denmark

ISSN 0302-9743   ISSN 1611-3349   (electronic)
Lecture Notes in Computer Science
ISBN 978-3-030-22347-2   ISBN 978-3-030-22348-9   (eBook)
https://doi.org/10.1007/978-3-030-22348-9

LNCS Sublibrary: SL1 – Theoretical Computer Science and General Issues

Cover illustration: By Tiziana Margaria-Steffen and Barbara Steffen

This Springer imprint is published by the registered company Springer Nature Switzerland AG
The registered company address is: Gewerbestrasse 11, 6330 Cham, Switzerland

Young Bernhard and the Sea – Denmark, 1990 (Private photograph; used with permission)

Foreword

This Festschrift is dedicated to Bernhard Steffen on the occasion of his 60th birthday. The title, *Models, Mindsets, Meta: The What, the How, and the Why Not?*, reflects some of the guiding principles of Bernhard's functioning (in both his professional and his personal life): Once you choose to do something, question everything and generalize, especially when you need to specialize. In that case, generalize the meta-level. His contagious research enthusiasm, witnessed and enjoyed by his many scientific collaborators, is consistently driven by these principles. His scientific credentials are impressive, he initiated a number of novel research directions as well as solving a variety of technically challenging problems and transforming them into software solutions. In addition, Bernhard created "from scratch" an impressive research group at TU Dortmund.

The variety of his contributions is impressive. Always a neat theoretical framework, always made with some application in mind, and most of the time implemented in some software tool that turns out to be useful in practice. Often "in advance of his time": Dataflow analysis as model-checking as a proper semantic framework for program analysis and a starting point for software model-checking, he established a well-founded framework of service-oriented computing and verification before the term existed, model-based program generation as principle, and model extraction for legacy systems via automata learning: if you do not have a specification, then learn it.

Owing to the wide variety of topics in the contributions, reflecting Bernhard's versatile interests, the best way to organize the volume was along Bernhard's journey, by the locations where he met his colleagues, most of whom double as friends. As is seen on the cover image, Bernhard's journey is a may/must KTS, starting in Kiel but open ended. The may part comprises the various diversions to Uppsala, Cantoira, and ISoLA as a META-topos for symposia style inserts (in a sabbatical, on holiday, or at the ninth ISoLA) that combine research components with community and quality of life. The introductory paper by the editors, the 23 refereed full papers, and the two personal contributions showcase the wide recognition of his passion for science and his success in striving for excellence.

November 2018

Tiziana Margaria
Susanne Graf
Kim G. Larsen

Personal Statement

To my dear friend and colleague Bernhard Steffen on the occasion of his 60th birthday!

One of the first emails I received from Bernhard, dated November 29, 1989, started as follows:

Congratulations!! Our paper was rejected! However, it was not rejected because it is bad, no because it is too theoretical. So, I submitted it just to LICS (slightly improved). If it gets accepted there, then I will be able to get over the rejection.

I hope Bernhard does not mind me sharing this with you, but it is really funny and perfectly illustrates his wry sense of humor and his ability to find humor even in the not-so-happy moments. And the good news is that our LICS submission did get accepted and so began our journey into the world of reactive, generative, and stratified models of probabilistic processes. It has been a great ride and I am very proud and happy to call Bernhard my dear friend and collaborator.

Cheers to you Bernhard on this very happy occasion. You are a remarkable person and scientist and I am so happy to have this opportunity to acknowledge you for all you have done.

Yours,
Scott Smolka

A Tribute to Bernhard Steffen

David Schmidt

Computer Science Department, Kansas State University,
Manhattan, KS, USA
das@ksu.edu

It is a pleasure and an honor to congratulate Bernhard Steffen on the occasion of his 60th birthday. Bernhard's contributions are significant and span multiple fields. I have most appreciated Bernhard's support and friendship over the 30 years that I have known him.

I first met Bernhard in the late 1980s, when I was visiting Edinburgh University. Bernhard had come to Edinburgh from Kiel, where he had just completed his PhD. I remember Bernhard's enthusiasm, his impressive command of facts and results, and most importantly, his strong interest in contributing to the research being undertaken at that time in Edinburgh's Lab for Foundations of Computer Science (LFCS). In retrospect, it seems somewhat inevitable that Bernhard would fall in with Rance Cleveland and Joachim Parrow and help develop the Edinburgh Concurrency Workbench.

At that time, what struck me most strongly about my one-day meeting with Bernhard was his search to connect what he already knew well (data-flow analysis) with what the others in LCFS knew well (concurrency theory). It seemed as if Bernhard was on a "search" towards an "enlightenment" that only he could sense: there was a connection between his work and the work of the others, and time would make this clear.

The results of Bernhard's "search" were revealed to me in a surprising way some years later, in 1995: I had sabbatical leave from my position at Kansas State University and I spent one term at Carnegie Mellon University. By chance, Ed Clarke was offering a graduate seminar on model checking. Knowing little about the subject, I followed Ed's lectures. I was impressed by the use of fixed-point semantics and fixed-point calculation algorithms for both defining and checking properties of state-transition systems. The methodology looked familiar, almost uncomfortably familiar, but I couldn't quite explain why I had that feeling.

I wanted to learn more: I spent much of my time that term in the CMU Computer Science library, reading everything I could find on model checking. It was there that I encountered Bernhard's 1993 Science of Computer Programming article, *Generating Data Flow Analysis Algorithms from Modal Specifications*. That paper held the explanation for which I was searching—all the connections that I had sensed between model checking and data-flow analysis were there in that article, neatly expressed in the box-diamond notation of branching-time temporal logic *augmented with reverse modalities*. At that instant, I recalled the discussion I had with Bernhard that one day in Edinburgh—there was indeed an "enlightenment" that Bernhard had sensed and had achieved.

The next step for me was to apply this enlightenment to the area in which I worked. Using abstract-interpretation-based domain theory, I conceived models of behavior trees whose properties could be expressed in box-diamond notation. Using Bernhard's explanation of data-flow-analysis-as-model-checking, I was able to generate abstract interpretations mechanically from the box-diamond formulas I had written. It was also easy to see how the notations could define the classic, equationally-stated forms of data-flow analysis. Here was truly a unified theory of property specification and implementation.

Bernhard's work changed the direction of my research and led to many years of results. I was honored when Bernhard contacted me in 1997 with a critique of my attempts to apply his insights. In a subsequent meeting in Italy in 1998, Bernhard suggested that we work together to develop further lines of research that followed from his work.

The collaboration between Bernhard and me lasted well over a decade, and it expanded to include Bernhard's research group in Dortmund and the programming-languages research group in Kansas. The collaboration went well beyond authorship of jointly developed papers: it became a long-term exchange and development of research directions, perspectives, and goals. The collaboration meant that I made many visits to Dortmund and stayed at Bernhard's and Tiziana Margaria's home. I enjoyed coffee from Bernhard's impressive espresso machine, I took long walks with Tiziana and Bernhard in the forest next to their home, and I watched their children, Barbara and Bruno, grow to adulthood.

My technical expertise expanded greatly from interactions with Tiziana, Markus Müller-Olm, Jens Knoop, and Oliver Rüthing, and the other members of the Dortmund research group. And members of the Kansas group, notably, John Hatcliff and Matt Dwyer, also became part of the research "family," a family that functions to the present day in the *International Journal on Software Tools for Technology Transfer* and the *ISoLA* conference series.

Bernhard has always impressed me with his enthusiasm for work, his unending desire to transfer his results into the technology mainstream, and especially by his sureness of vision. Throughout his career, Bernhard has always followed a path of certainty towards an "enlightenment" of how software specification, analysis, and implementation should be undertaken. It is this sureness of vision that motivates and justifies the tributes that Bernhard now receives on the occasion of his 60th birthday.

Bernhard, congratulations, and may your vision of computer science continue to lead us for years to come!

Contents

Introduction

Models, Mindsets, Meta: The What, the How, and the Why Not?

Tiziana Margaria[1]([⊠]), Susanne Graf[2], and Kim G. Larsen[3]

[1] Chair of Software Systems, University of Limerick and Lero,
Confirm and HRI, Limerick, Ireland
tiziana.margaria@ul.ie
[2] Verimag, Grenoble, France
Susanne.Graf@imag.fr
[3] Department of Computer Science, Aalborg University, Aalborg, Denmark
kgl@cs.aau.dk

1 The Passion

Bernhard Steffen's first major recognition concerned the collaboration on the Concurrency Workbench, but his theoretical and practical work spans the development and implementation of *novel, specific algorithms*, the establishment of *cross-community relationships* with the effect to obtain simpler, yet more powerful solutions, as well as the initiation of *new lines of research*.

Our personal relation with Bernhard is intertwined with the development of CAV. At CAV 1989 in Grenoble, Susanne Graf was heavily involved in the organization of the event. She started the discussions that would lay the basis for their joint Compositional Minimization of Finite State Systems presented by Bernhard at CAV'90. At CAV'90 in Rutgers, at DIMACS, Bernhard met Tiziana, who was presenting a paper on automated test pattern generation for sequential circuits using Ed Clarke's original EMC model checker. And Bernhard, Susanne and Tiziana plus Rance Cleaveland and Ed Brinksma were together at CAV'91 in Aalborg organized by Kim Larsen. CAV'91 turned out to be quite consequential, not only for Bernhard's private life, but also as a prequel to what would become in 1995 the first TACAS: organized in Passau by Bernhard and Tiziana, the first proceedings appeared as LNCS N.1019, co-edited by Ed Brinksma, Rance Cleaveland, Kim Guldstrand Larsen, Tiziana Margaria, and Bernhard Steffen.

Models were Bernhard's first passion, along with building tools for working with models. The Concurrency Workbench (CWB) [9–11], one of the first tools for the process algebra and model checking-based analysis of concurrent systems, initiated a still living trend of tool development which witnesses the step from so called weak formal methods, which remain at the side of specification an manual (interactive) proof to strong formal methods that aim at fully automatic tool support. Bernhard's innate tool-related thinking led him to a number of conceptual breakthroughs like the first linear algorithm for CTL (a subclass of the alternation-free mu-calculus) [27], the logical characterization of behavioural

© Springer Nature Switzerland AG 2019
T. Margaria et al. (Eds.): Steffen Festschrift, LNCS 11200, pp. 3–13, 2019.
https://doi.org/10.1007/978-3-030-22348-9_1

relations as the basis for establishing semantic relations [12, 48], and the first model checkers for infinite state systems [3–7]. These developments were the basis for the Fixpoint Analysis Machine [47] which exploited the Dataflow Analysis and Model Checking paradigm to derive a homogeneous analysis framework capturing even procedural programs.

Bernhard's Dataflow Analysis and Model Checking paradigm (DFAMC) [44–46] can be regarded as the starting point of modern software model checking. DFA-MC based on the abstract view from the model checking world, where algorithmic problems are formulated as collections of logic properties. With this new mindset, it was possible to derive very powerful program analyses [18–22] as layered fact-finding quests, and they became for the first time elegantly and efficiently solvable with just one algorithm: CTL model checking. In particular the lazy code motion algorithm had a strong practical impact: it is implemented in almost every of today's compilers, and as a recognition of this success it received the 2002 PLDI Test of Time Award which is given ten years after publication to the PLDI papers with the highest long term impact.

Both the CWB and the DFAMC developments initiated lines of research which are still alive. In addition, the work on Reactive, Generative, and Stratified Models of Probabilistic Processes with Rob van Glabbeek, Scott Smolka and Chris Tofts [13] set the scene for modelling probabilistic processes and laid the groundwork for a huge bulk of research on quantitative methods. With Hardi Hungar, Harald Raffelt and Oliver Niese [14,17], Bernhard paved the way to bringing the originally very theoretical work of active automata learning into real practice. Practical analyses on telecommunication systems showed the strong impact of this technique on testing: the classical model-based testing approaches are in a sense converted into test-based modelling approaches [14,42]. As an additional benefit, this approach overcame a prohibitive hurdle to model-based testing: the need of a priori availability of a model. Bernhard's work continued with the development of a corresponding learning framework, the LearnLib [41–43], the extension of the methods to data-sensitive models [15], and to an algorithm that optimally refines the abstraction level of a learning scenario to become deterministic, a requirement for efficient learning [16].

On the software engineering side, he co-established a well-founded framework for service-oriented computing (years before this term was coined) [39,40,51,52]. Underlying this framework is a development philosophy which can be regarded as a well-founded way of extreme programming [28,37,38], now called eXtreme Model Driven Development. XMDD in particular aims at the easy integration of external/remote functionality [32,33,53], with the additional benefit of a formal setting that supports analysis, reasoning and synthesis.

2   The Impact

The impact of Bernhard's research career has been multidimensional.

Concerning the **development of frameworks and tools**, the Concurrency Workbench, the Infinite state and Pushdown model checkers, the ABC/jABC saga with the many generations and variants, ETI/jETI and the LearnLib have so far had the most success. More recently, the move towards meta-level DSLs and the generation of entire IDEs for graph based modelling languages has led to the development of the Cinco Meta-IDE and to the easier generation of specialized editors for domain specific modelling languages as so-called Cinco-products.

Concerning **education**, in the over 25 years as a professor in Aachen, Passau and Dortmund Bernhard has taught in many forms and under many titles the concepts and rigour of Formal Methods in System Design. Most recent achievements are his series of books for undegraduates "Grundlagen der Höheren Informatik" [55] with Oliver Rüthing and Malte Isberner, and "Mathematical Foundations of Advanced Informatics" [54] with Michael Huth and Oliver Rüthing. These books are intended to set the mathematical scene for a formal methods-based approach to comprehension, reasoning, and design. The over 51.000 chapter downloads for the German book witness the dissemination success of this textbook.

Concerning **industrial applications**, many projects with leading IT companies like Siemens Nixdorf in telecommunications, Bertelsmann and the European Patent Office, ThyssenKrupp and IKEA in Supply Chain Management, a learning-based testing environment for T-Systems, order management for BASF-IT, the online conference system OCS and its product line for the Springer Verlag are only a few representatives for the direct impact not mediated by public funding.

Concerning the promotion of **tools as first class citizens** in the software engineering for system correctness, Bernhard's impact has been vast and steady. The impact on the culture of tool comparison and challenge started in 1997 with ETI, the Electronic Tool Integration platform born with STTT [53]. The inaugural issue of STTT featured the introduction of UPPAAL in ETI by Kim G. Larsen, Paul Pettersson and Wang Yi [26]. UPPAAL had been presented originally in TACAS'96 [1]. ETI was a clear precursor of today's service-based composition environments. Its HLL (High Level Language) was an own service and workflow composition language (in today's terminology, a coordination-oriented DSL) with rich tool descriptions ranging over taxonomies as lightweight ontologies. ETI's tool integration platform was later instantiated for a number of application domains: FMICS-jETI [23,30,34] for verification tools stemming from the FMICS Working Group of ERCIM, BiojETI [24,25,29] for bioinformatics tools, and Plan-jETI [31] for the automatic synthesis of workflows through various external and own planning tools and techniques. The ETI initiative was followed by many more: the RERS Challenge on Rigorous Examination of Reactive Systems is associated with ISoLA and other events since 2010, the Software Verification Competition (SV-COMP) takes place in association with TACAS since 2012, and also the Toolimpics starting in the 2019 edition of ETAPS. Not only do these initiatives promote the importance of tools as a means to foster the understanding and wider adoption of new algorithms and techniques, they also address how to make tool evaluation and comparison more systematic, objective and fair. Related to this comparison is also the attention to creating, maintaining and evolving adequate benchmarks and benchmark sets [49].

Concerning **the scientific community**, his contributions to establishing and maturing the culture of tools and the dignity of tool building and tool evaluation as fields of research and investigation have spanned over 25 years of success. Bernhard started TACAS, the Int. Conference on Tools and Algorithms for the Construction and Analysis of Systems, with Ed Brinksma, Kim Larsen and Rance Cleaveland. The first TACAS took place in 1995 in Passau [2] and the conference quickly became the largest, highest rated and most impactful of the ETAPS Joint Conferences. STTT, the International Journal on Software Tools for Technology Transfer started in 1997 with Rance Cleaveland and Tiziana Margaria [8] and more recently managed with John Hatcliff and Tiziana Margaria is meanwhile the venue where to publish tool-related papers and case studies. STTT has a high impact factor and since 2006 it publishes 6 issues per year. As editor of Springer's LNCS series, Bernhard has contributed for over a decade to select thousands of monographs and conference proceedings, supporting the wide dissemination of high quality research and indirecting impacting the career of thousands of young and established researchers.

3   The Vision

Bernhard's vision, developed in large part jointly with Tiziana Margaria and shared - with different accents - by Susanne Graf, Kim Larsen and many other contributors to this book, has always been that of injecting formal methods into system and software development environments. Starting with the position statement in 1997 for the 50 years of ACM [50] and with the IN-METAFrame Environment [51], this approach of *lightweight formal methods* has been consistently seen as a pathway towards the improvement of system design and software quality by aiding both the skilled developers who may or may not master the art and discipline of programming, and the skilled "subject matter experts" who mostly know their application domain to a great depth but cannot program nor are they versed in formal languages or methods. As we wrote in [35], *"more than 90% of the software development costs arise worldwide for a rather primitive software development level, during routine application programming or software update, where there are no technological or design challenges. There, the major problem faced is software quantity rather than achievement of very high quality, and automation should be largely possible. AMDD is intended to address (a significant part of) this 90% 'niche'"*. AMDD is now XMDD, and it targets the 95% 'niche' of application developers who are key stakeholders in application and system design. That vision was already embodied in the ideal software development lifecycle depicted in Fig. 1.

Bernhard and his group, as well as many friends and family, worked consistently over his entire career to deliver this vision. The vision pre-dates

– the idea of agility through fast turn-around times in prototype-driven design,
– the idea of service-oriented architectures due to the reusable building blocks that are software (or system) black boxes and run "somewhere", that led to

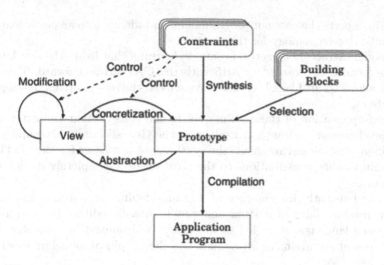

Fig. 1. Application development process in METAFrame (from [51])

the development of the Service Centered Continuous Engineering approach
to evolution-friendly system design,
- the manageability of complex artefacts through the use of abstraction and
perspective (or mindset)-oriented views, that anticipate aspect-oriented programming
- the lifting of application design and execution from the coding level to an
intuitive modelling level, in a move *from the How to the What* as advocated
in [36]. This approach allows a much earlier validation and verification of the
logic of applications and systems, enables model driven design of tests, and
it makes change management and maintenance at the model level faster and
much less costly,
- the use of constraints to guide and check the correctness of the development.
This centrality of constraints and logics puts declarative knowledge (formulated as collection of properties) at the centre of the quality assurance and,
by means of LTL synthesis, also at the centre of automatic synthesis of processes and workflows that are correct by construction. The use of constraints
adds another level of *from the How to the What* above the use of models. It
also allows in many cases to answer *Why not?* questions constructively. This
helps understanding and debugging for example by providing counterexamples to model checking properties, which is an indirect approach to test case
generation, as well as a source of knowledge (an oracle) for the automata
learning approaches. The LTL based constructive approach to workflow synthesis yields a variety of solutions, delivering a set of correct by construction
implementations,
- the use of domain specific languages that are both graphical and operational
transforms the art of application development to a craft manageable also by

domain experts that are not programmers, and ideally into an easily learnable and intuitive technology for the masses,
- the model extraction by active automata learning that led to the development of the LearnLib, awarded in 2015 with the CAV artifact award. This technique allows to lift black box legacy systems to the model driven development paradigm,
- the self-application of these techniques to the construction and extension of the development environment itself, with the Genesis family of compilers, the plugin generation environment, the synthesis of test cases for the MaTRICS, and many other contributions to the creation of a completely model driven tool-suite
- and more recently his embrace of meta-modelling as a means to generate entire product lines of custom and profile specific editors for graph-based modelling languages, that led to the Cinco environment, a generator-driven development environment for domain-specific graphical modeling tools.

If we consider that Bernhard was never a software engineer nor part of the well established software engineering community, this is a remarkable list of fundamental insights. It is even more remarkable that with his group he systematically turned these insights into an impressive collection of coherent achievements that span from fundamental theory to tools construction and to the field practice in industrial and research projects.

4   The Contributions in this Volume

The invited contributions in this volume span the over 30 years of Bernhard Steffen's active research career. Some of the contributing scientists returned specifically for this volume to the topics that were hot at the time of their initial collaboration, while others chose to discuss topics closer to their current interest and activity. We chose therefore not to organize the contributions thematically, but along the main stations of Bernhard's personal activity, each with its specific cultural imprint and relevance to Bernhard's own evolution and maturity.

Kiel 1983-87 with a contribution by

- Hardi Hungar on *Applying Decision Graphs in the Context of Automated Driving*

Edinburgh 1987-89, with contributions by

- Kim Larsen, Bent Thomsen, Lone Leth Thomsen et al. on *Analyzing spreadsheets for parallel execution via model checking*
- Eugenio Moggi et al. on *System Analysis and Robustness*
- Michael Mendler et al. on *Logic Meets Algebra: Compositional Timing Analysis for Synchronous Reactive Multithreading*
- Mariangiola Dezani Ciancaglini et al. on *Intersection Types in Java: back to the future*
- and a personal statement by Scott Smolka

Aarhus 1989-90, with contributions by

- Flemming and Hanne Nielson et al. on *Multi-Valued Logic for Static Analysis and Model Checking*
- Stefania Gnesi, Alessandro Fantechi, Maurice ter Beek et al. on *States and Events in KandISTI: A Retrospective*
- Tiziana Margaria on *Making Sense of Complex Applications: Constructive Design, Features, and Questions*

Aachen 1990-93, with a contribution by

- Gerald Lüttgen et al. on *Interface Automata for Shared Memory*

Passau 1993-97 with contributions by

- Didier Caucal et al. on *Boolean algebras by length recognizability*
- Hubert Garavel and Radu Mateescu with *Reflections on Bernhard Steffen's Physics of Software Tools*
- Sergei Gorlatch on *Toward Structured Parallel Programming: Send-Receive Considered Harmful*
- Klaus Havelund et al. on *Refining the Safety/Lliveness Classification of Temporal Properties According to Monitorability*
- Ulrike Lechner on *Future Security: Processes or Properties? Research Directions in Cybersecurity*

Dortmund 1997 - today with contributions by

- Dimitra Giannakopoulou and Corina Pasareanu et al. on *Statistical Prediction of Failures in Aircraft Collision Avoidance Systems*
- Mike Hinchey et al. on *The ASSL Approach to Formal Specification of Self-Managing Systems*
- Michael Huth on *The Merits of Compositional Abstraction: A Case Study in Propositional Logic*
- Falk Howar et al. on *JConstraints: A Library for Working with Logic Expressions in Java*
- Axel Legay et al. *On the Expressiveness of Joining and Splitting*
- Jakob Rehof et al. on *Fast Verified BCD Subtyping*
- Wolfgang Reisig on *Composition: A Fresh look at an Old Topic*
- Frits Vaandrager et al. on *Benchmarks for Automata Learning and Conformance Testing*
- Jaco van de Pol et al. on *Synchronous or Alternating? LTL Blackbox Checking of Mealy Machines by Combining the LearnLib and LTSmin*
- and a tribute to Bernhard Steffen by Dave Schmidt.

This volume, the talks and the entire B-Day at ISoLA 2018 are a tribute to the first 30 years of Bernhard's passion, impact and vision for many facets of computer science in general and for formal methods in particular. Impact and vision include the many roles that formal methods-supported software development should play in education, in industry and in society. With Bernhard's curiosity and energy as unrelentless drivers, we look forward with great expectations to the next generation of his ideas and initiatives in the years to come.

References

1. Bengtsson, J., Larsen, K.G., Larsson, F., Pettersson, P., Yi, W.: UPPAAL in 1995. In: Margaria, T., Steffen, B. (eds.) TACAS 1996. LNCS, vol. 1055, pp. 431–434. Springer, Heidelberg (1996). https://doi.org/10.1007/3-540-61042-1_66
2. Brinksma, E., Cleaveland, W.R., Larsen, K.G., Margaria, T., Steffen, B. (eds.): TACAS 1995. LNCS, vol. 1019. Springer, Heidelberg (1995). https://doi.org/10.1007/3-540-60630-0
3. Burkart, O., Caucal, D., Moller, F., Steffen, B.: Verification on infinite structures. In: Bergstra, J., Ponse, A., Smolka, S. (eds.) Handbook of Process Algebra, pp. 545–623. Elsevier Science, Amsterdam (2001). http://www.sciencedirect.com/science/article/pii/B9780444828309500278
4. Burkart, O., Steffen, B.: Model checking for context-free processes. In: Cleaveland, W.R. (ed.) CONCUR 1992. LNCS, vol. 630, pp. 123–137. Springer, Heidelberg (1992). https://doi.org/10.1007/BFb0084787
5. Burkart, O., Steffen, B.: Pushdown processes: parallel composition and model checking. In: Jonsson, B., Parrow, J. (eds.) CONCUR 1994. LNCS, vol. 836, pp. 98–113. Springer, Heidelberg (1994). https://doi.org/10.1007/978-3-540-48654-1_9
6. Burkart, O., Steffen, B.: Composition, decomposition and model checking of pushdown processes. Nordic J. Comput. **2**(2), 89–125 (1995). http://dl.acm.org/citation.cfm?id=642068.642070
7. Burkart, O., Steffen, B.: Model checking the full modal mu-calculus for infinite sequential processes. In: Degano, P., Gorrieri, R., Marchetti-Spaccamela, A. (eds.) ICALP 1997. LNCS, vol. 1256, pp. 419–429. Springer, Heidelberg (1997). https://doi.org/10.1007/3-540-63165-8_198
8. Cleaveland, R., Margaria, T., Steffen, B.: Editorial. STTT **1**(1–2), 1–5 (1997). https://doi.org/10.1007/s100090050001
9. Cleaveland, R., Parrow, J., Steffen, B.: A semantics based verification tool for finite state systems. In: Proceedings of the 9th International Symposium on Protocol Specification, Testing and Verification, Enschede, The Netherlands, 6–9 June 1989, pp. 287–302. North-Holland (1989)
10. Cleaveland, R., Parrow, J., Steffen, B.: The concurrency workbench. In: Sifakis, J. (ed.) CAV 1989. LNCS, vol. 407, pp. 24–37. Springer, Heidelberg (1990). https://doi.org/10.1007/3-540-52148-8_3
11. Cleaveland, R., Parrow, J., Steffen, B.: The concurrency workbench: a semantics-based tool for the verification of concurrent systems. ACM Trans. Program. Lang. Syst. **15**(1), 36–72 (1993). http://doi.acm.org/10.1145/151646.151648
12. Cleaveland, R., Steffen, B.: Computing behavioural relations, logically. In: Albert, J.L., Monien, B., Artalejo, M.R. (eds.) ICALP 1991. LNCS, vol. 510, pp. 127–138. Springer, Heidelberg (1991). https://doi.org/10.1007/3-540-54233-7_129
13. van Glabbeek, R.J., Smolka, S.A., Steffen, B., Tofts, C.M.N.: Reactive, generative, and stratified models of probabilistic processes. In: Proceedings of the Fifth Annual Symposium on Logic in Computer Science (LICS 1990), pp. 130–141. LICS, IEEE Computer Society (1990)
14. Hagerer, A., Hungar, H., Niese, O., Steffen, B.: Model generation by moderated regular extrapolation. In: Kutsche, R.-D., Weber, H. (eds.) FASE 2002. LNCS, vol. 2306, pp. 80–95. Springer, Heidelberg (2002). https://doi.org/10.1007/3-540-45923-5_6

15. Howar, F., Steffen, B., Jonsson, B., Cassel, S.: Inferring canonical register automata. In: Kuncak, V., Rybalchenko, A. (eds.) VMCAI 2012. LNCS, vol. 7148, pp. 251–266. Springer, Heidelberg (2012). https://doi.org/10.1007/978-3-642-27940-9_17
16. Howar, F., Steffen, B., Merten, M.: Automata learning with automated alphabet abstraction refinement. In: Jhala, R., Schmidt, D. (eds.) VMCAI 2011. LNCS, vol. 6538, pp. 263–277. Springer, Heidelberg (2011). https://doi.org/10.1007/978-3-642-18275-4_19
17. Hungar, H., Niese, O., Steffen, B.: Domain-specific optimization in automata learning. In: Hunt, W.A., Somenzi, F. (eds.) CAV 2003. LNCS, vol. 2725, pp. 315–327. Springer, Heidelberg (2003). https://doi.org/10.1007/978-3-540-45069-6_31
18. Knoop, J., Rüthing, O., Steffen, B.: Lazy code motion. In: Proceedings of the ACM SIGPLAN 1992 Conference on Programming Language Design and Implementation (PLDI), pp. 224–234. ACM (1992)
19. Knoop, J., Rüthing, O., Steffen, B.: Lazy strength reduction. J. Program. Lang. 1, 71–91 (1993)
20. Knoop, J., Rüthing, O., Steffen, B.: Optimal code motion: theory and practice. ACM Trans. Program. Lang. Syst. 16(4), 1117–1155 (1994)
21. Knoop, J., Rüthing, O., Steffen, B.: Partial dead code elimination. In: Proceedings of the ACM SIGPLAN 1994 Conference on Programming Language Design and Implementation (PLDI), pp. 147–158. ACM (1994)
22. Knoop, J., Steffen, B., Vollmer, J.: Parallelism for free: efficient and optimal bitvector analyses for parallel programs. ACM Trans. Program. Lang. Syst. (TOPLAS) 18(3), 268–299 (1996). http://doi.acm.org/10.1145/229542.229545
23. Kubczak, C., Margaria, T., Nagel, R., Steffen, B.: Plug and play with FMICS-jETI: beyond scripting and coding. ERCIM News 73, 41–42 (2008)
24. Lamprecht, A.L., Margaria, T., Steffen, B.: Bio-jETI: a framework for semantics-based service composition. BMC Bioinform. 10(Suppl 10), S8 (2009)
25. Lamprecht, A.L., Margaria, T., Steffen, B.: From bio-jETI process models to native code. In: 14th IEEE International Conference on Engineering of Complex Computer Systems, ICECCS 2009, Potsdam, Germany, 2–4 June 2009, pp. 95–101. IEEE Computer Society, June 2009. http://www2.computer.org/portal/web/csdl/doi/10.1109/ICECCS.2009.50
26. Larsen, K.G., Pettersson, P., Yi, W.: UPPAAL in a nutshell. STTT 1(1–2), 134–152 (1997). https://doi.org/10.1007/s100090050010
27. Larsen, K.G., Skou, A. (eds.): CAV 1991. LNCS, vol. 575. Springer, Heidelberg (1992). https://doi.org/10.1007/3-540-55179-4
28. Margaria, T., Steffen, B.: Service engineering: linking business and IT. Computer 39(10), 45–55 (2006). http://portal.acm.org/citation.cfm?id=1175939
29. Margaria, T., Kubczak, C., Steffen, B.: Bio-jETI: a service integration, design, and provisioning platform for orchestrated bioinformatics processes. BMC Bioinform. 9(Suppl 4), S12 (2008)
30. Margaria, T., Kubczak, C., Steffen, B., Naujokat, S.: The FMICS-jETI platform: status and perspectives. In: Proceedings of the 2nd International Symposium on Leveraging Applications of Formal Methods, Verification and Validation (ISoLA 2006), pp. 414–418. IEEE Computer Society Press, Paphos, 11 2006
31. Margaria, T., Meyer, D., Kubczak, C., Isberner, M., Steffen, B.: Synthesizing semantic web service compositions with jMosel and golog. In: Bernstein, A., et al. (eds.) ISWC 2009. LNCS, vol. 5823, pp. 392–407. Springer, Heidelberg (2009). https://doi.org/10.1007/978-3-642-04930-9_25

32. Margaria, T., Nagel, R., Steffen, B.: jETI: a tool for remote tool integration. In: Halbwachs, N., Zuck, L.D. (eds.) TACAS 2005. LNCS, vol. 3440, pp. 557–562. Springer, Heidelberg (2005). https://doi.org/10.1007/978-3-540-31980-1_38
33. Margaria, T., Nagel, R., Steffen, B.: Remote integration and coordination of verification tools in JETI. In: Proceedings of 12th IEEE International Conference on the Engineering of Computer-Based Systems, pp. 431–436. IEEE Computer Society, Los Alamitos (2005)
34. Margaria, T., Raffelt, H., Steffen, B., Leucker, M.: The LearnLib in FMICS-jETI. In: ICECCS 2007 Proceedings of the 12th IEEE International Conference on Engineering Complex Computer Systems, pp. 340–352. IEEE Computer Society, Washington, DC (2007)
35. Margaria, T., Steffen, B.: Aggressive model-driven development: synthesizing systems from models viewed as constraints. In: MBEES, pp. 51–62 (2005)
36. Margaria, T., Steffen, B.: From the how to the what. In: Meyer, B., Woodcock, J. (eds.) VSTTE 2005. LNCS, vol. 4171, pp. 448–459. Springer, Heidelberg (2008). https://doi.org/10.1007/978-3-540-69149-5_48
37. Margaria, T., Steffen, B.: Agile IT: thinking in user-centric models. In: Margaria, T., Steffen, B. (eds.) ISoLA 2008. CCIS, vol. 17, pp. 490–502. Springer, Heidelberg (2008). https://doi.org/10.1007/978-3-540-88479-8_35
38. Margaria, T., Steffen, B.: Business process modelling in the jABC: the one-thing-approach. In: Cardoso, J., van der Aalst, W. (eds.) Handbook of Research on Business Process Modeling. IGI Global (2009)
39. Margaria, T., Steffen, B.: Service-orientation: conquering complexity with XMDD. In: Hinchey, M., Coyle, L. (eds.) Conquering Complexity, pp. 217–236. Springer, London (2012). https://doi.org/10.1007/978-1-4471-2297-5_10
40. Margaria, T., Steffen, B., Reitenspieß, M.: Service-oriented design: the roots. In: Benatallah, B., Casati, F., Traverso, P. (eds.) ICSOC 2005. LNCS, vol. 3826, pp. 450–464. Springer, Heidelberg (2005). https://doi.org/10.1007/11596141_34
41. Merten, M., Steffen, B., Howar, F., Margaria, T.: Next generation LearnLib. In: Abdulla, P.A., Leino, K.R.M. (eds.) TACAS 2011. LNCS, vol. 6605, pp. 220–223. Springer, Heidelberg (2011). https://doi.org/10.1007/978-3-642-19835-9_18
42. Raffelt, H., Merten, M., Steffen, B., Margaria, T.: Dynamic testing via automata learning. Int. J. Softw. Tools Technol. Transf. (STTT) 11(4), 307–324 (2009)
43. Raffelt, H., Steffen, B., Berg, T., Margaria, T.: LearnLib: a framework for extrapolating behavioral models. Int. J. Softw. Tools Technol. Transf. (STTT) 11(5), 393–407 (2009)
44. Schmidt, D., Steffen, B.: Program analysis as model checking of abstract interpretations. In: Levi, G. (ed.) SAS 1998. LNCS, vol. 1503, pp. 351–380. Springer, Heidelberg (1998). https://doi.org/10.1007/3-540-49727-7_22. http://portal.acm.org/citation.cfm?coll=GUIDE&dl=GUIDE&id=760066
45. Steffen, B.: Data flow analysis as model checking. In: Ito, T., Meyer, A.R. (eds.) TACS 1991. LNCS, vol. 526, pp. 346–364. Springer, Heidelberg (1991). https://doi.org/10.1007/3-540-54415-1_54. http://www.springerlink.com/content/y5p607674g6q1482/
46. Steffen, B.: Generating data flow analysis algorithms from modal specifications. In: Selected Papers of the Conference on Theoretical Aspects of Computer Software, pp. 115–139. Elsevier Science Publishers B. V., Sendai (1993). http://portal.acm.org/citation.cfm?id=172313
47. Steffen, B., Claßen, A., Klein, M., Knoop, J., Margaria, T.: The fixpoint-analysis machine. In: Lee, I., Smolka, S.A. (eds.) CONCUR 1995. LNCS, vol. 962, pp. 72–87. Springer, Heidelberg (1995). https://doi.org/10.1007/3-540-60218-6_6

48. Steffen, B., Ingólfsdóttir, A.: Characteristic formulae for processes with divergence. Inf. Comput. **110**(1), 149–163 (1994)
49. Steffen, B., Isberner, M., Naujokat, S., Margaria, T., Geske, M.: Property-driven benchmark generation. In: Bartocci, E., Ramakrishnan, C.R. (eds.) SPIN 2013. LNCS, vol. 7976, pp. 341–357. Springer, Heidelberg (2013). https://doi.org/10.1007/978-3-642-39176-7_21
50. Steffen, B., Margaria, T.: Tools get formal methods into practice. ACM Comput. Surv. **28**(4es), 126 (1996). http://doi.acm.org/10.1145/242224.242385
51. Steffen, B., Margaria, T.: METAFrame in practice: design of intelligent network services. In: Olderog, E.-R., Steffen, B. (eds.) Correct System Design. LNCS, vol. 1710, pp. 390–415. Springer, Heidelberg (1999). https://doi.org/10.1007/3-540-48092-7_17
52. Steffen, B., Margaria, T., Braun, V., Kalt, N.: Hierarchical service definition. Ann. Rev. Commun. ACM **51**, 847–856 (1997)
53. Steffen, B., Margaria, T., Braun, V.: The electronic tool integration platform: concepts and design. Int. J. Softw. Tools Technol. Transf. (STTT) **1**(1–2), 9–30 (1997)
54. Steffen, B., Rüthing, O., Huth, M.: Mathematical Foundations of Advanced Informatics, Volume: 1 Inductive Approaches. Springer, Cham (2018). https://doi.org/10.1007/978-3-319-68397-3
55. Steffen, B., Rüthing, O., Isberner, M.: Grundlagen der höheren Informatik - Induktives Vorgehen. Springer Vieweg (2014)

Kiel 1983–1987

Applying Decision Graphs in the Context of Automated Driving

Hardi Hungar[✉]

German Aerospace Center (DLR), Institute of Transportation Systems,
38108 Brunswick, Germany
hardi.hungar@dlr.de

Abstract. Techniques to enable automated driving currently receive a lot of attention in computer science research. Car automation requires realizing several cognitive functions by computers. One important functionality is environment perception. This consists of several sub-tasks which are complex and thus computation intensive when implemented. We propose the use of decision graphs to speed up the execution of a consistency check. This check is applied to the output of a of neural net which classifies regions in an environment image. The check consists in evaluating a set of probabilistic rules. The paper describes how the miAamics approach of pre-computing results of rule evaluations with decision graphs may be profitably used in this application.

Keywords: Decision graphs · Probabilistic knowledge base ·
Markov logic network · Environment perception · Automated driving

1 Introduction

Environment perception is a key functionality of assisted and automated driving. Interpreting an environment image consists in detecting and classifying objects in the image. The following describes an advanced approach to image interpretation combining neural networks and probabilistic logical reasoning from [1].

A camera image is segmented into *regions*. These regions shall correspond to the different objects visible in the image, like traffic participants, road elements, road furniture, and scenery. A neural network performs the segmentation and labels the regions with the kind of object depicted there. This identification process is not perfect. Therefore, the result is subjected to a plausibility check. For that, *rules* are formulated which express knowledge supporting the classification (or hint against it). These rules use the spatial relations between object classes in a street scene. The following two formulas are examples of such rules.

$$\text{Road}(x) \wedge \text{Sky}(y) \wedge \text{Below}(x, y) \rightarrow \text{Consistent}(x) \tag{1}$$

$$\text{Car}(x) \wedge \text{Road}(y) \wedge \text{Inside}(x, y) \rightarrow \text{Consistent}(x) \wedge \text{Consistent}(y) \tag{2}$$

The formulas are intended to capture rules of thumb. The antecedent of (1) will very often, but not always, be true for a correct classification. Also, (2) captures an

T. Margaria et al. (Eds.): Steffen Festschrift, LNCS 11200, pp. 17–23, 2019.
https://doi.org/10.1007/978-3-030-22348-9_2

indication for a correct assignment. But very often, the road region will not surround the car. So this rule applies less often. And sometimes, a car image will be inside a building image. And if the building is wrongly classified as a road, the rule will erroneously apply.

Vague knowledge like that is difficult to formulate in pure predicate logic. Instead, a probabilistic extension of predicate logic is used. To denote the degree of certainty with which a formula holds, a numeric weight is attached to each formula. The higher the weight, the higher the probability that the formula is true for instantiations of the variables with regions in an image. Thus, a rule consists of a formula and a numeric weight.

Such a set of rules is called a *probabilistic knowledge base* (PKB). Its semantics is given by a *Markov Logic Network*. [2]. This semantics gives a probabilistic measure with which a particular setting is a model of the PKB. In our case, the measure gives a consistency estimate, i.e., a figure how much the classification can be trusted. And we will see that the computation of this measure might profit from decision graphs to represent partial evaluations, enabling a (hopefully) real-time consistency check.

2 A Probabilistic Consistency Measure for Object Classifications

2.1 Markov Logic Networks

In the following definition, *groundings* of predicates and formulas are used. Given a set of constants C, the groundings of an n-ary predicate P form the set

$$\text{ground}_c(P) = \{P(c_1, \ldots, c_n) | c_1, \ldots, c_n \in C\}.$$

And the set of groundings of a quantifier-free formula F with variables $\{x_1, \ldots, x_n\}$ are the ground formulas

$$\text{ground}_c(F) = \{F[x_1, \ldots, x_n / c_1, \ldots, c_n] | c_1, \ldots, c_n \in C\}.$$

We assume for simplicity that the formulas in the PKB are quantifier-free. This is true for the rules in our application.

Definition. A *Markov Logic Network* (MLN) L is a set of pairs $\{(F_1, w_1) \ldots, (F_f, w_f)\}$ with first-order formulas F_i and real numbers w_i.

Given a set of constants $C = \{c_1, \ldots, c_s\}$, L defines a *Markov network* $M_{L,C}$ by

(A) The *nodes* of $M_{L,C}$ are all elements of the sets $\text{ground}_c(P)$ for the predicates P appearing in L. These nodes are binary variables which can take values in $\{0,1\}$.

(B) There is an edge between two nodes if the grounded predicates appear in one of the groundings of a formula of L.

(C) $M_{L,C}$ has a *binary feature* for each grounding of each formula F_i of L. A binary feature is a function from the states of the associated node set to $\{0,1\}$. Here, it gives the truth value (0 for *false*, 1 for *true*) of the formula, depending on the values of the associated nodes.

An MLN can be seen as a template for Markov networks. These are undirected graphs, with additional labelings. This graph is a step in assigning a semantics to the MLN for a particular set of constants, given a truth assignment to the nodes of the network, i.e., given an interpretation of the predicates appearing in L for all constants.

Definition. If L is an MLN and C is a set of constants, an *interpretation* I is a function assigning 0 or 1 (for *false* and *true*, resp.) to each node in $M_{L,C}$.

Given I, the binary features provide the truth values of the ground instances of the formulas F_i under the assignment I. I.e., for each $F \in ground_c(F_i)$ with atomic subformulas $P_1, ..., P_n$, there is a binary feature B s.t. $I(F) = B(I(P_1), ..., I(P_n))$. In this way, the Markov networks $M_{L,C}$ introduced above capture the standard semantics of the first-order formulas in the PKB. The probability aspect is introduced by the following definition.

Definition. Let $M_{L,C}$ be a Markov network with interpretation I. Then

$$P(I) = (1/Z) \exp\left(\sum_{i=1}^{f} w_i\, n_i(I)\right) \tag{3}$$

where

$n_i(I)$ is the number true binary features of F_i, and

$Z = \sum_I \left(\exp\left(\sum_{i=1}^{f} w_i\, n_i(I)\right)\right)$, the sum over all interpretations

Thus, each interpretation gets assigned the sum of all weights of all true formula instantiations. This value is turned into a probability by norming it, so that the set of interpretations of atomic predicates over the constant set C forms a discrete probability space. The more formulas (with high weights) are true in an interpretation, the more likely the interpretation is a "true" model of the knowledge base. Though, usually, no interpretation gets a probability of one. The intuition is that no formula needs to be true in a particular domain. But the domain is more likely a model of the knowledge base, if the formulas with positive weights are "mostly" true.

These are (slightly rephrased) the definitions from [2]. They are technically complex, introducing a very explicit semantical domain. Indeed, for our purpose, they could be simplified. The graphical structure of $M_{L,C}$ (namely, clause (B)) is not really relevant, here. It is used in some algorithms working on Markov networks, e.g., probabilistic reasoning. None of these algorithms is used in this paper, though they play a role in the overall classification procedure. We could work on the formulas and groundings and ignore the graphical semantics definition.

2.2 Defining Consistency via Probabilistic Knowledge Bases

In our application to image interpretation, the unary predicates appearing in a rule set L are the possible classifications of the objects in the image, plus the "Consistent" predicate. The binary predicates are the spatial relationships. The constants are region identifiers.

The rules generally have the form of (1) and (2): The antecedent is some proposition about classifications of regions and their spatial relationship. The consequent is a consistency assertion. Weights may be positive and negative. A positive weight means that the antecedent is an indication that the classification is right. A negative weight hints to the opposite.

The consistency check could be formulated as a probabilistic inference problem (for which several algorithms on Markov networks are around). Namely, what is the probability of consistency, given the regions, their spatial relationships, and their classifications as computed by the neural network.

Or, employing the specific form of the rules, just the evidence from the antecedents is computed: Each true antecedent adds to the probability of the consistency expressed in the consequent of the respective rule, for a positive weight. And it discounts from the probability, for a negative weight. This boils down to mainly compute the $n_i(I)$ for the antecedents and multiply it by the respective weight w_i, cf. Eq. (3). From that, by a few additions (number of relevant rules), a consistency figure for a single classification can be computed. Or, by adding all figures, one gets the overall consistency assessment expressed by the PKB.

We will follow the second approach, computing the $n_i(I)$ for the antecedents, in our solution to the plausibility check. The complexity of the task comes from the fact that it is not easy to compute the number of true instantiations of a formula. We will show how decision diagrams can be used to gain online efficiency by offline pre-computation.

3 Decision Diagrams for Fast Evaluation

The following definitions are based on [3].

3.1 Algebraic Decision Diagrams

Definition. An *Algebraic Decision Diagram* (ADD) is a septuple
  $D = (N, T, r, succ_0, succ_1, X, V, var, val)$,
  where

  N is a finite set of nodes
  $r \in N$ is the root
  T is a set of terminal nodes (leaves)
  $succ_0$ and $succ_1$ are functions from N to $N \cup T$
  X is a set of variables
  V is a set of numeric values (e.g., $\mathbb{R}$)
  var and val are labeling functions, var: $N \to X$, val: $T \to V$

such that $N \cup T$ are the nodes of a graph with edges $succ_0$ and $succ_1$, the graph is acyclic, and its root is r.

An ADD is thus a rooted, acyclic graph with uniform degree 2, where each inner node is labeled by a variable, and each leaf carries a value.

Definition. An ADD D defines a function from valuations $I:X \rightarrow \{0,1\}$ to V as follows.

$D(I)(t) = val(t)$ for $t \in T$
$D(I)(n) = $ **if** $I(var(n)) = 1$ **then** $D(I)(succ_1(n))$ **else** $D(I)(succ_0(n))$ for $n \in N$
$D(I) = D(I)(r)$
$D(I)$ is well-defined because of the finiteness and acyclicity of D.

Intuitively, given a valuation of the variables of D, one follows the path from the root, choosing the successor which is indicated by the valuation of the variable at each node on the path. The label of the leaf at the end of the path gives the function value. Thus, given a particular valuation of the variables, the function value is easy to compute.

Definition. An ADD is

- *reduced*, if all nodes define different functions, i.e., for all $n \neq m \in N \cup T$, there is some I s.t. $D(I)(n) \neq D(I)(m)$
- *ordered*, if there is a linear order $<$ on the variable set X, s.t. for all nodes n, m with $m = succ_0(n)$ or $m = succ_1(n)$, $var(n) < var(m)$

RO-ADD denotes the set of reduced, ordered ADDs.

Remark. For each ADD D and each order $<$ on its set of variables X, there is an RO-ADD D' with order $<$ which defines the same function as D. The RO-ADD D' is unique up to isomorphism. I.e., an RO-ADD (given $<$) is a canonical form for a given function.

By eliminating semantically redundant nodes (and redirecting dangling successor pointers), an ADD can be reduced. This is obviously beneficial, as the reduced ADD will have a smaller size. Variable orders are a different matter. They are useful because they greatly simplify the construction of ADDs.

3.2 Applying ADDs

ADDs can efficiently store and retrieve numeric evaluations of weighted sets of logical rules. This is the central idea underlying the patented miAamics machinery [4, 5]. This machinery was developed by Steffen, Margaria, and the author of this paper nearly two decades ago. This machinery can likely be employed in the computation procedure of the consistency check. Somewhat similar to miAamics, we use RO-ADDs to represent rule evaluations. Here, the RO-ADDs give the number of true groundings of antecedents.

Let $\{P_1,\ldots, P_p\}$ be the atomic predicates in the PKB. And let C be constants naming the regions in an image. Only the maximal number of regions is relevant, not the name of the constant denoting a particular region. Let $\{A_1,\ldots, A_f\}$ be the set of antecedents of rules, and let $P_i \leq A_j$ denote that P_i occurs in A_j. Then the set of variables of the RO-ADDs is the union over all $ground_c(P_i)$, and an RO-ADD for A_j will depend on the variables in $ground_c(P_i)$ for $P_i \leq A_j$.

If D_i is an RO-ADD s.t. $D_i(I) = n_i(I)$ for all I, it is easy to compute $n_i(I)$, see above. Such an RO-ADD can be constructed by standard operations on RO-ADDs. The CUDD package, available at https://github.com/sysulic/cudd, offers all necessary functions.

There is, however, a catch. A common obstacle to such usages of decision diagrams is the fact that the size of the graph may explode. In the worst case, an ADD over m variables equals a full binary tree with m + 1 levels (i.e., 2^m-1 nodes and 2^m leaves). And k regions will lead to $2*k + k^2$ variables for the antecedent of (1), which gives an example of a typical, small formula. Though the worst case will not occur for such antecedents, it is not clear that the RO-ADD sizes will be manageable for a reasonable number of regions.

Since we did not perform any experiments with ADD construction for the consistency rules, no definitive answer can currently be given. If a direct encoding in RO-ADDs does not work for all antecedents, there are several ways to cope with that. One is to split the RO-ADD for an antecedent A by replacing A by the following collection of formulas.

$$x = c_1 \wedge A[x/c_1]$$
$$\dots$$
$$x = c_k \wedge A[x/c_k]$$

The set of true groundings of A is the disjoint union of the true groundings of the formulas above. By eliminating one of the variables of a spatial relation predicate in this way, the number of variables on which the corresponding RO-ADD depends is greatly reduced. E.g., there are 440 variables potentially relevant for the antecedent of Formula (1), if there are 20 regions. After splitting the formula as indicated above, there are at most 60 relevant variables for each of the resulting formulas. And splitting can have a large effect on the total space requirements for the RO-ADDs as the combination of two RO-ADDs is often much larger than the sum of their sizes. This way, a complex combinatorial explosion in the pre-computation might be avoided, by committing to a small number of extra additions in the online evaluation.

4 Conclusion

We have presented an approach of using ADDs in the realm of image interpretation. The procedure of segmentation, classification and consistency check is the main topic of the dissertation (in preparation, see also [6]) of Fouopi, a colleague of the author at the DLR. The potential application of the miAamics machinery occurred to the author at a presentation of the consistency check, where its computational complexity was mentioned. The author would like to express his sincere thanks to his colleague for discussing the approach described in this paper.

It should not be difficult to test that approach in practice. Though this has not been done yet, the flexibility of the machinery is likely to enable some profitable usage of it. In any case, the potential benefits should be motivation enough to do this in the near future.

References

1. Pekezou Fouopi, P., Srinivas, G., Knake-Langhorst, S., Köster, F., Niemeijer, J.: Holistische Szenenmodellierung und -Interpretation basierend auf subsymbolischen, symbolischen und probabilistischen Methoden. VDI-Fachkonferenz Umfelderfassung im Fahrzeug (2018)
2. Richardson, M., Domingo, P.: Markov logic networks. Mach. Learn. **62**(1–2), 107–136 (2006)
3. Bahar, R.I., et al.: Algebraic decision diagrams and their applications. Formal Methods Syst. Des. **10**, 171–206 (1997)
4. Kubczak, C., Margaria, T., Steffen, B., Winkler, C., Hungar, H.: An approach to discovery with miAamics and jABC. Semant. Web Serv. Challenge **8**, 217–234 (2009)
5. Hungar, H., Steffen, B., Margaria-Steffen, T.: Methods for generating selection structures, for making selections according to selection structures and for creating selection descriptions. Patent No 9141708 USA, 22 September 2015
6. Lapoehn, S., Pekezou Fouopi, P., Löper, C., Knake-Langhorst, S., Hesse, T.: Semantische Netze als Wissensbasis automatisierter Fahrzeuge. VDI/VW-Gemeinschaftstagung: Fahrassistenzsysteme und automatisiertes Fahren (2016)

Edinburgh 1987–1989

Analyzing Spreadsheets for Parallel Execution via Model Checking

Thomas Bøgholm, Kim G. Larsen, Marco Muñiz, Bent Thomsen[✉],
and Lone Leth Thomsen

Department of Computer Science, Aalborg University, Aalborg, Denmark
bt@cs.aau.dk

Abstract. In this paper we briefly report on work in the Popular Parallel Programming (P3) project where we follow in the footsteps of Bernhard Steffen using the idea of program analysis via model checking and abstract interpretation. The programs we analyze are spreadsheet programs, which for long have been identified as an ideal programming model for parallel execution. We translate spreadsheet programs into Timed Automata Models, which may be analyzed by the UPPAAL model checker and its derivatives, with the purpose of finding schedules for parallel execution. In this paper we mainly focus on the techniques and scalability issues of various variants of UPPAAL, but also report briefly on the performance results achieved through the parallelization.

1 Introduction

Mani Chandy noted as early as in 1985 in his keynote at the fourth annual ACM symposium on Principles of distributed computing (PODC 1985) entitled *Concurrent programming for the masses* that a programming model based on spreadsheets would reach a much wider audience and should be much easier to parallelize than the traditional programming model(s) [7]. However, in the three decades that have passed since this keynote only sporadic efforts have been made in this area [2,4,11,21].

To realize the idea of parallel programming via spreadsheets, it is necessary to adapt and further develop program analysis techniques to the spreadsheet programming model to identify the parts of a program that can be executed in parallel and subsequently find schedules for their execution.

The idea of program analysis via model checking was pioneered by Bernhard Steffen and presented in his 1991 paper entitled *Data Flow Analysis As Model Checking* [20] and further elaborated with David Schmidt in the paper entitled *Program Analysis as Model Checking of Abstract Interpretations* [18].

The Popular Parallel Programming (P3) project[1] set out to follow in the footsteps of Bernhard Steffen by using the idea of program analysis via model

---

[1] https://www.itu.dk/~sestoft/p3/.

© Springer Nature Switzerland AG 2019
T. Margaria et al. (Eds.): Steffen Festschrift, LNCS 11200, pp. 27–35, 2019.
https://doi.org/10.1007/978-3-030-22348-9_3

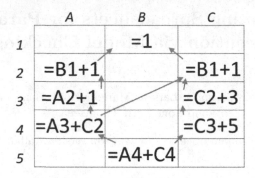

Fig. 1. Example spreadsheet

checking and abstract interpretation to investigate various approaches to parallelizing the execution of spreadsheet programs based on the open source spreadsheets Corecalc and Funcalc[2] implemented in C# and thoroughly described in [19]. The P3 project views spreadsheets as a dataflow language with the purpose of improving compilation of dataflow languages to shared-memory multicore machines, partly by drawing on recent advances in static execution time estimates based on abstract interpretation [6] and scheduling techniques based on timed automata [1,3,5,10,12,16].

2   Spreadsheets and Dataflow

To see how spreadsheets can be viewed as dataflow programs we first look at an example. Figure 1 shows a small spreadsheet with 8 active cells, A2, A3, A4, B1, B5, C2, C3 and C4. Only the formulae are shown, whereas in a normal spreadsheet application the results of the computations would be shown.

B1 is a *data cell*, where the remaining cells are formulae directly or indirectly depending on B1. In a small spreadsheet like this, it is easy to see that the calculation of the value of the formula in cell B4 depends on the value of the formulae in cell A4 and C4. The formula in cell C4 depends on cell C3, which in turn depends on cell C2, depending on cell B1. Similarly cell A4 depends on cell B1 and A3, which depends on A2, which depends on B1. This dependency relationship is depicted by the orange arrows in Fig. 1. Thus to calculate the results presented in Fig. 1 a dataflow in the reverse order of the dependency relationship is needed, i.e. data from cell B1 flows into the formulae in cell A2 and C2. A2 flows into A3. C2 flows into C3 and A4. C3 flows into C4 and finally A4 and C4 flow into B5.

Based on the dependency relationship one can construct a schedule for executing the formulae in parallel on a dual-core machine such that the needed dataflow between cells is upheld. One schedule could be on CPU 1 calculate cell B1. Then in parallel calculate cell A2 on CPU1 and cell C2 on CPU2. Then in

_____
[2] http://www.itu.dk/people/sestoft/funcalc/.

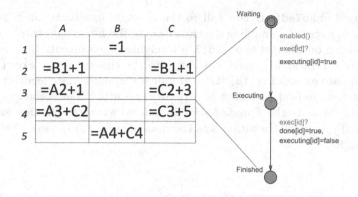

Fig. 2. Example spreadsheet with TA for cell C3

parallel A3 on CPU 1 and B3 on CPU 2, followed by cell A4 on CPU 1 and B4 on CPU2 in parallel. Finally cell B5 can be computed on CPU 1. This schedule would require 5 time units, assuming that the calculation of each cell takes 1 unit. A sequential calculation would require 8 time units.

The example in Fig. 1 is small enough that the dependency relationship and dataflow can be inspected or even constructed manually. However, the relationship quickly becomes difficult to keep track of manually.

3   Generating Timed Automata Models from Spreadsheets

In this section we show various translations from spreadsheet into Timed Automata (TA) which in turn may be analyzed with various variants of the UPPAAL model checker. Timed Automata and extensions such as Priced Timed Automata, together with model checkers, especially the UPPAAL model checker, have for more than a decade been used to solve scheduling problems by a reformulation as reachability problems [1,3,5,10,12,16].

We regard each cell as a task which is translated into a separate process in UPPAAL. Similarly, we generate a process for each computation unit, i.e. CPU, and the scheduling algorithm. These processes are then composed in parallel into a single model. Processes synchronize using channels, and have access to a number of functions, which allows for expressing more complex functionality in a small C-like language.

Figure 2 shows an example spreadsheet with a UPPAAL TA task model for cell C3. The general idea is to translate each cell in a spreadsheet into such models which are then combined into one TA with dependencies between tasks. The task model consists of three locations: *Waiting, Executing, Finished*, which represent the three states of a task. These three states are linked through two edges: The first edge, from *Waiting* to *Executing* contains a *guard, synchronization*, and an *update*.

The guard `enabled(id)` is a call to the function `enabled(job_t id)`, this must evaluate to true for enabling the transition to the *Executing* state. This edge is synchronizing on channel `exec[id]?`, a receiving synchronization indicated by `?`. The `id` of the process is used as index into the channel array `exec[job_t]`. Last, the update `executing[id]=true` atomically updates the executing flag for the current task, indicating that it is currently executing. The second edge from the *Executing* state to the *Finished* state is enabled when the channel `exec[id]` is signaled. Taking this transition sets the done flag for this process and unsets the running flag.

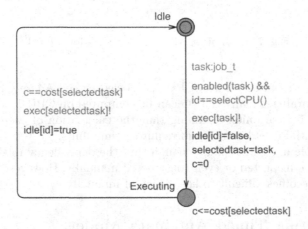

Fig. 3. CPU template

Figure 3 shows the model of a CPU which consists of two locations, *Idle* and *Executing*, representing the two states of a CPU in our model. CPU is a template parameterized with id of type `cid_t`, an integer subtype which ranges from zero to the number of CPUs. Additionally, the CPU template has two locally defined state variables: `clock c`, a clock variable for recording execution time spent in location *Executing*, and `job_t selectedtask`, representing the task this CPU is currently executing. In the *Executing* location, the invariant `c<=cost[selectedtask]` limits the time spent in this location to the execution cost of the selected task.

In UPPAAL the system declarations for the resulting model then consist of:

```
1   Sheet1_A2 = Task(1);
2   Sheet1_A3 = Task(2);
3   Sheet1_A4 = Task(3);
4   Sheet1_B1 = Task(4);
5   Sheet1_B5 = Task(5);
6   Sheet1_C2 = Task(6);
7   Sheet1_C3 = Task(7);
8   Sheet1_C4 = Task(8);
9   Cpus(const cid_t c) = CPU(c);
10
11  system Cpus, Sheet1_A2, Sheet1_A3, Sheet1_A4, Sheet1_B1, Sheet1_B5
        , Sheet1_C2, Sheet1_C3, Sheet1_C4 ;
```

Line 9 creates process instances of the CPU template for each value in *cid_t*, named Cpus. Lines 1–8 create instances for each task, with a name representing the cell in the spreadsheet. Each instance is created separately in order to give identifiable names for each task in the resulting trace. The fastest trace will be the optimal schedule. Here fast refers to lowest global clock value, not the length of the trace, the latter being shortest trace in UPPAAL. The number of clocks in this model is the number of CPUs plus one, for recording the global clock. Unfortunately this approach does not scale beyond toy-like spreadsheets like the one depicted in Fig. 2. This is not surprising as e.g. [13] reports on various task graph scheduling examples with up to 16 tasks. Larger examples quickly run into the state-space explosion problem.

However, often we do not need the optimal schedule, but *a good enough* schedule is sufficient. Such schedules may be explored by UPPAAL-STRATEGO [8] which can be used to model 1 1/2-player games where the opponent is stochastic. Given a game UPPAAL-STRATEGO can synthesize near-optimal strategies for complex systems. It has successfully been used for controlling floor heating systems [14] and controlling traffic lights [9].

In a nutshell UPPAAL-STRATEGO synthesizes near-optimal strategies by: staring with a uniform distribution over the controllable choices, generating runs, evaluating how good are these runs, refining the distribution on the controllable choices via learning algorithms, and iterating.

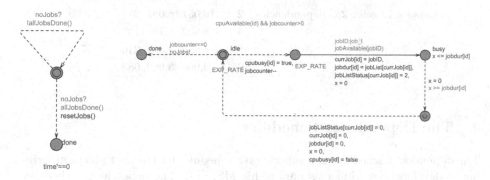

Fig. 4. Stratego model. (Left environment indicating if there are pending jobs Right). CPU-model where controllable choices are among available jobs.

Figure 4 illustrates the UPPAAL-STRATEGO model for 1-CPU. It is a game between the scheduler and the environment which includes the jobs to execute. The solid arrows are the scheduler choices whereas the dashed arrows correspond to the environment choices. Note that the solid arrow has a select statement jobID:job_t which is equivalent to the enumeration of all tasks with one solid arrow for each task. The intuition from the model is as follows. First at location idle a delay is chosen from the exponential distribution with rate EXP_RATE, if there are no jobs left location done is reached, otherwise if a CPU and a job are available a job has to be taken. A job is taken by executing one of the solid arrows induced by jobID:job_t leading to location busy, the CPU stays at this location for the duration of the job. When the job duration has elapsed the environment sets the status of the job to 0 indicating that the job is done, and returns to the initial location. Table 1 shows the results of using UPPAAL-STRATEGO from Fig. 4 in different spreadsheets. In the generated models, all cell computing costs are random values using same initial seed. These costs will in future implementations be replaced by cost inferred based on abstract interpretations of the execution time for cell formula [6].

Table 1. Results for UPPAAL-STRATEGO

Model	CPUs	Cost	Greedy	Time sec	Speedup %
Supportgraph 31 cells 119 dependencies	2	7.047	6.959	42	-1.20
	4	4.884	4.981	45	1.95
	8	4.611	4.611	62	0.00
	16	4.611	4.611	59	0.00
Example 115 cells, 65 dependencies	2	24.890	25.411	1.627	2.05
	4	12.581	13.375	1.373	5.94
	8	6.484	6.993	2.202	7.28
	16	3.450	4.035	199	14.50
Formulacopies 73 cells, 255 dependencies	2	16.051	16.087	253	0,09
	4	8.522	8.181	10	-4,17
	8	4.650	4.307	216	-7,96
	16	3.900	3.982	683	2,06

4   The Dependency Scheduler

The dependency scheduler is a generic task scheduler for the .Net platform, originally developed by Møller as part of his MSc [17]. The dependency scheduler takes as input a set of tasks and a description of their dependencies. The scheduler will then execute these task in such a way that if a task depends on other tasks, it will only execute when these tasks have completed, e.g. if we have three tasks A, B and C, where task A and task B do not have any dependencies and task C is dependent on task B, then the scheduler will execute task A and task B concurrently, and when task B finishes, task C will start. The dependency relationship is described via a dependency graph which may come from a task dependency analysis produced by (various versions of) UPPAAL.

The dependency scheduler uses the thread pool from Microsoft .NET library, which is used to keep track of the threads, managed by .NET. All threads are created from system start up, so no additional time has to be spend on creating new threads during execution.

The dependency scheduler will first start all tasks without dependencies. Tasks will signal when they finish and as soon as tasks dependent on finished tasks are ready for execution, they will be released. Thus a kind of wave of tasks goes through the set of tasks until all tasks have been executed. For spreadsheets, this wave will follow the dataflow based on the schedule of tasks calculated by UPPAAL.

The dependency scheduler has now been fully integrated into the Funcalc platform and can take as input cell formulae wrapped as .Net tasks together with a schedule produced by UPPAAL. For efficiency reasons *null* and *constant data cells* will not be included in the dependency scheduler.

We have carried out a small performance study based on two spreadsheets, the *Building Design benchmark* and the *Ground Water daily benchmark*, from the LibreOffice Benchmarks [15] developed in connection with a study of parallelisation of the LibreOffice spreadsheet on AMD GPUs [4]. These spreadsheets have about one million data cells and about 50.000 formula cells. However, they differ slightly in the complexity of the formulae and the dependencies between cells.

Benchmarks - Spreadsheet Building Design

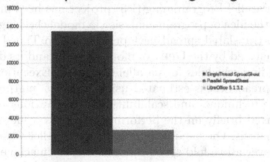

Fig. 5. Benchmarks – building design

Figure 5 shows the average execution time of ten runs of the Building Design benchmark using the original sequential version of Funcalc, the version of Funcalc with the dependency scheduler and an execution with the LibreOffice GPU accelerated version. Lower is better. As can be seen LibreOffice is the fastest executing at 84.86 ms, then Parallel Spreadsheet with 2668.8 ms and then Singlethread with 13463.4 ms. So we obtain approximately a five-fold speedup on a 6 core machine. The benchmark was executed on an I7-5930k 6 core machine with a 3.5 GHz clock and 32 GB DDR4 RAM; the program was executed in 32bit mode limiting memory usage.

Figure 6 shows the average execution time of ten runs of the Ground Water daily benchmark. Again Lower is better. On this benchmark the Parallel Spreadsheet is the fastest at 7142.7 ms, then LibreOffice with 15959.97 ms, then

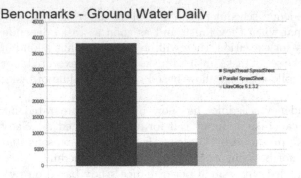

Fig. 6. Benchmark – ground water daily

Singlethread with 38327.9 ms. In this benchmark we see at 5.3 time speedup over the sequential version.

5   Conclusions

The Popular Parallel Programming (P3) project has been inspired by Bernhard Steffen to use the idea of program analysis via model checking and abstract interpretation. We translated spreadsheet programs into Timed Automata Models, which were analyzed by the UPPAAL model checker and its derivatives, with the purpose of finding schedules for parallel execution. Execution time for each formula in the spreadsheet is estimated using abstract interpretation. We mainly focused on the techniques and scalability issues of various variants of UPPAAL, but also reported briefly on the performance results achieved through the parallelization analysis. On some benchmarks the parallel version of Corecalc and Funcalc gain over a five-fold speed up on a six core machine.

References

1. Abdeddaïm, Y., Kerbaa, A., Maler, O.: Task graph scheduling using timed automata. In: Proceedings International Parallel and Distributed Processing Symposium, 2003, p. 8. IEEE (2003)
2. Abramson, D., Roe, P., Kotler, L., Mather, D.: Activesheets: super-computing with spreadsheets. In: 2001 High Performance Computing Symposium (HPC 2001), Advanced Simulation Technologies Conference, pp. 22–26. Citeseer (2001)
3. Alur, R., La Torre, S., Pappas, G.J.: Optimal paths in weighted timed automata. In: Di Benedetto, M.D., Sangiovanni-Vincentelli, A. (eds.) HSCC 2001. LNCS, vol. 2034, pp. 49–62. Springer, Heidelberg (2001). https://doi.org/10.1007/3-540-45351-2_8
4. AMD: Collaboration and open source at amd: Libreoffice (2015). https://developer.amd.com/collaboration-and-open-source-at-amd-libreoffice/

5. Behrmann, G., et al.: Minimum-cost reachability for priced time automata. In: Di Benedetto, M.D., Sangiovanni-Vincentelli, A. (eds.) HSCC 2001. LNCS, vol. 2034, pp. 147–161. Springer, Heidelberg (2001). https://doi.org/10.1007/3-540-45351-2_15

6. Bock, A., Bøgholm, T., Sestoft, P., Thomsen, B., Thomsen, L.L.: Concrete and Abstract Cost Semantics for Spreadsheets. Technical Report, TR-2018-203, IT University, Denmark. https://pure.itu.dk/portal/files/84061527/ITU_TR_2018_203.pdf

7. Chandy, M.: Concurrent programming for the masses (invited address). In: Proceedings of the Fourth Annual ACM Symposium on Principles of Distributed Computing, pp. 1–12. PODC 1985, ACM, New York, NY, USA (1985). https://doi.org/10.1145/323596.323597

8. David, A., Jensen, PGjøl, Larsen, K.G., Mikučionis, M., Taankvist, J.H.: UPPAAL STRATEGO. In: Baier, C., Tinelli, C. (eds.) TACAS 2015. LNCS, vol. 9035, pp. 206–211. Springer, Heidelberg (2015). https://doi.org/10.1007/978-3-662-46681-0_16

9. Eriksen, A.B., et al.: Uppaal stratego for intelligent traffic lights. In: Proceedings of the 12th ITS European Congress, Strasbourg, France, 19–22. June 2017 (2017)

10. Fehnker, A.: Scheduling a steel plant with timed automata. In: rtcsa, p. 280. IEEE (1999)

11. Hirsch, A.: Compiling and optimizing spreadsheets for FPGA and multicore execution. Ph.D. thesis, Massachusetts Institute of Technology (2007)

12. Hune, T., Larsen, K.G., Pettersson, P.: Guided synthesis of control programs using uppaal. Nord. J. Comput. 8(1), 43–64 (2001)

13. Jørgensen, K.Y., Larsen, K.G., Srba, J.: Time-darts: A data structure for verification of closed timed automata. arXiv preprint arXiv:1211.6195 (2012)

14. Larsen, K.G., Mikučionis, M., Muñiz, M., Srba, J., Taankvist, J.H.: Online and compositional learning of controllers with application to floor heating. In: Chechik, M., Raskin, J.-F. (eds.) TACAS 2016. LNCS, vol. 9636, pp. 244–259. Springer, Heidelberg (2016). https://doi.org/10.1007/978-3-662-49674-9_14

15. LibreOffice: Libreoffice benchmarks (2011). https://gerrit.libreoffice.org/gitweb?p=benchmark.git;a=tree

16. Maler, O.: Timed automata as an underlying model for planning and scheduling. In: Proceedings of the 2002 International Conference on Planning for Temporal Domains, pp. 67–70. AAAI Press (2002)

17. Møller, N.K.: Pre-analyses dependency scheduling with multiple threads (2016)

18. Schmidt, D., Steffen, B.: Program analysis as model checking of abstract interpretations. In: Levi, G. (ed.) SAS 1998. LNCS, vol. 1503, pp. 351–380. Springer, Heidelberg (1998). https://doi.org/10.1007/3-540-49727-7_22

19. Sestoft, P.: Spreadsheet Implementation Technology: Basics and Extensions. The MIT Press, Cambridge (2014)

20. Steffen, B.: Data flow analysis as model checking. In: Ito, T., Meyer, A.R. (eds.) TACS 1991. LNCS, vol. 526, pp. 346–364. Springer, Heidelberg (1991). https://doi.org/10.1007/3-540-54415-1_54

21. Wack, A.P.: Partitioning dependency graphs for concurrent execution: a parallel spreadsheet on a realistically modeled message passing environment (1996)

System Analysis and Robustness

Eugenio Moggi[1]([⊠]), Amin Farjudian[2], and Walid Taha[3]

[1] DIBRIS, Genova Univ., Genova, Italy
`moggi@unige.it`
[2] Univ. of Nottingham Ningbo China, Ningbo, China
`amin.farjudian@nottingham.edu.cn`
[3] Halmstad Univ., Halmstad, Sweden
`walid.taha@hh.se`

Abstract. Software is increasingly embedded in a variety of physical contexts. This imposes new requirements on tools that support the design and analysis of systems. For instance, modeling embedded and cyber-physical systems needs to blend discrete mathematics, which is suitable for modeling digital components, with continuous mathematics, used for modeling physical components. This blending of continuous and discrete creates challenges that are absent when the discrete or the continuous setting are considered in isolation. We consider robustness, that is, the ability of an analysis of a model to cope with small amounts of imprecision in the model. Formally, we identify analyses with monotonic maps between complete lattices (a mathematical framework used for abstract interpretation and static analysis) and define robustness for monotonic maps between complete lattices of closed subsets of a metric space.

Keywords: Analyses · Robustness · Domain theory

1 Introduction

The following considerations are taken from the paper "Continuous modeling of real-time and hybrid systems: from concepts to tools" [12] by Steffen et al., which was published in a special section on timed and hybrid systems. They provide the context and motivations for the issues addressed in this short paper.

1. Having served as a successful paradigm in physics and engineering for more than 300 years, starting with the discovery of the differential calculus by Leibniz and Newton at the end of the seventeenth century, **the continuous interpretation of time was overwhelmed by the digital revolution.**
2. The key point of formal description techniques is their mathematical exactness: it is unambiguous how the specified system is going to behave. **Exactness should, however, not be confused with precision**: "the system must respond within at least 1 and up to 20 s" is exact, although one might argue that it is not precise. **Exact specification makes the amount of imprecision explicit.**

© Springer Nature Switzerland AG 2019
T. Margaria et al. (Eds.): Steffen Festschrift, LNCS 11200, pp. 36–44, 2019.
https://doi.org/10.1007/978-3-030-22348-9_4

3. Typically the behavior of the controlled system is given a priori, while the controlling system still needs to be designed in a way guaranteeing a correct overall behavior. ...., for most embedded systems the open system approach is insufficient as **the correctness of the controlling system depends on properties of the environment. Capturing these situations requires modeling the environment as well.**

Imprecision. In a discrete setting one can achieve absolute precision[1], in a continuous setting there are two pervasive and unavoidable sources of imprecision:

1. imprecision in measurements, namely predictions based on a mathematical model and observations on a *real system* can be compared only up to the precision of instruments used for measurements on the real system, and
2. imprecision in representing continuous quantities in computer-assisted tools for modeling and analyzing hybrid/continuous systems.

Thus, a real number $x\colon \mathbb{R}$ in mathematics, becomes $x \pm \epsilon$ in physics, with $\epsilon > 0$ *measurement error*, in theory of computation becomes an interval $[\underline{x}, \overline{x}]$ with $\underline{x}$ and $\overline{x}$ belonging to a subset of $\mathbb{R}$ with exact finite representations (e.g., floating-point or rational numbers) [14][2]. However, any $x\colon \mathbb{R}$ can be **approximated** by *proper rational intervals* $[\underline{x}, \overline{x}]$ with **arbitrarily small imprecision**, i.e., for any $\delta > 0$ there are rational numbers $\underline{x}$ and $\overline{x}$ such that $\underline{x} < x < \overline{x}$ and $0 < \overline{x} - \underline{x} < \delta$.

Approximability extends to continuous maps on $\mathbb{R}$. First, a continuous map f on $\mathbb{R}$ has a Scott continuous *natural extension* $\overline{f}(I) \triangleq \{f(x)|x\colon I\}$ on the cpo $\mathbb{IR}$ of intervals ordered by reverse inclusion. Scott continuity implies that the imprecision of $\overline{f}(I)$ goes to 0 when the imprecision of I goes to 0. Second, $\overline{f}$ can be replaced by a Scott continuous F mapping proper rational intervals to proper rational intervals such that $F([x]) = [f(x)] = \overline{f}([x])$, thus $\overline{f}(I) \subseteq F(I)$. When f is not continuous, one must give up something. Namely, one can find a monotonic F on $\mathbb{IR}$ such that:

1. $\forall x\colon \mathbb{R}.F([x]) = [f(x)]$, but F fails to be Scott continuous, or
2. F is Scott continuous, $\forall I\colon \mathbb{IR}.\overline{f}(I) \subseteq F(I)$, but $\forall x\colon \mathbb{R}.F([x]) = [f(x)]$ fails.

In both cases the property "$F(I)$ converges to $f(x)$ when I converges to x" fails.

Robustness. In [13], we introduced **robustness**, a property of monotonic maps between complete lattices of (closed) subsets in metric spaces. Intuitively, robustness requires that *small changes* to the input I of a map F cause small changes to its output, where the definition of small relies on the metrics. Often, analyses can be identified with monotonic maps between complete lattices. For instance, reachability analysis can be cast as a monotonic map F on the complete lattice $\mathbb{P}(\mathbb{S})$ of subsets of the state space $\mathbb{S}$, that takes a set I of initial states and outputs the set $R(I)$ of states reachable from I, thus $I \subseteq R(I) = R^2(I)$.

---

[1] This does not exclude the possibility of using *imprecise* (aka loose) specifications.
[2] Representing a real with a float, as done in traditional numerical methods, means that the imprecision in computations is either ignored or is tracked manually.

If $\mathbb{S}$ is a metric space, then one has the mathematical framework to measure imprecision. The picture below shows the initial state s of three systems (red, green and blue) consisting of a ball that can move (in a one-dimensional space) under the effect of gravity. We assume that initially the speed is 0, thus from s only s is reachable, i.e., $R_r(\{s\}) = R_g(\{s\}) = R_b(\{s\}) = \{s\}$, but:

- the red ball (top) is *unstable*, i.e., a small change s' to s means that $R_r(\{s'\})$ includes some states far from s;
- the green ball (middle) is *stable*, i.e., a small change s' to s implies that all states in $R_g(\{s'\})$ are close to s;
- the blue ball (bottom) is stable, if a small change s' affects only the position (while the speed remains 0); it is unstable, if the speed can change (and there is no friction).

These claims on s can be recast as follows: R_g is *robust at* $\{s\}$, R_r is not.

Background. We assume familiarity with metric/topological spaces, the notions of open/closed/compact subset of a space [4,10], and make limited use of Category Theory [2,3] and Domain Theory [8]. We may write $x\colon X$ for $x \in X$.

- Every metric space is a topological space whose open subsets are given by unions of open balls $B(x,\delta) \triangleq \{y | d(x,y) < \delta\}$.
- $\mathsf{O}(\mathbb{S})$ is the set of open subsets of a metric/topological space $\mathbb{S}$, $\mathsf{C}(\mathbb{S})$ is the set of closed subsets, and $\mathsf{P}(\mathbb{S})$ is the set of all subsets.
- $\mathbb{P}(\mathbb{S})$ is the complete lattice of all subsets of $\mathbb{S}$ ordered by reverse inclusion, which is the natural *information order* on over-approximations (thus, sups are given by intersections and infs by unions). Similarly, $\mathbb{C}(\mathbb{S})$ is the complete lattice of closed subsets of $\mathbb{S}$ ordered by reverse inclusion (sups are given by intersections, but only finite infs are given by unions).

Contributions. The contributions of this short paper are:

1. A definition of imprecision in the context of metric spaces (Sect. 2), related to the *noise model* in [7] and δ-safety in [11]. The main point is that imprecision makes a subset S of a metric space $\mathbb{S}$ indistinguishable from its closure $\overline{S}$.
2. A notion of robustness [13] (Sect. 3) for monotonic maps $A\colon \mathbb{C}(\mathbb{S}_1) \to \mathbb{C}(\mathbb{S}_2)$, the restriction to closed subsets is due to indistinguishability of S and $\overline{S}$.
3. Results about existence of *best* robust approximations [13] (Sect. 4).

2   Imprecision in Metric Spaces

Definition 1. *Given a metric space $\mathbb{S}$, with distance function d, we define:*

1. *$B(S,\delta) \triangleq \{y | \exists x\colon S.d(x,y) < \delta\}$, where $S\colon \mathsf{P}(\mathbb{S})$ and $\delta > 0$. Intuitively, $B(S,\delta)$ is the set of points in S with imprecision $< \delta$. $B(S,\delta)$ is open, because it is the union of open balls $B(s,\delta)$ with $s\colon S$, moreover $B(B(S,\delta),\delta') \subseteq B(S,\delta+\delta')$.*
2. *$\overline{S}\colon \mathsf{C}(\mathbb{S})$ is the **closure** of $S\colon \mathsf{P}(\mathbb{S})$, i.e., the smallest $C\colon \mathsf{C}(\mathbb{S})$ such that $S \subseteq C$. For $S\colon \mathsf{P}(\mathbb{S})$ and $\delta > 0$ the following holds: $S \subseteq \overline{S} \subseteq B(S,\delta) = B(\overline{S},\delta)$. Thus, in the presence of imprecision, S and $\overline{S}$ are **indistinguishable**.*

3. $S_\delta \stackrel{\Delta}{=} \overline{B(S, \delta)}$ is the δ-**fattening** of S: $\mathsf{P}(\mathbb{S})$. Intuitively, S_δ is the set of points in S with imprecision $\leq \delta$. In fact, $B(S, \delta) \subseteq S_\delta \subseteq B(S, \delta')$ when $0 < \delta < \delta'$. For S: $\mathsf{P}(\mathbb{S})$ the following holds: $\overline{S} = \bigcap_{\delta > 0} B(S, \delta) = \bigcap_{\delta > 0} S_\delta$. Thus, the closure $\overline{S}$ is the set of points that are in S with arbitrarily small imprecision.

We consider some examples of metric spaces motivated by applications.

Example 1 (Discrete). A set $\mathbb{S}$ can be viewed as a **discrete** metric space, i.e., $d(s, s') = 1$ when $s \neq s'$. Any subset S of $\mathbb{S}$ is closed and open. Thus, $\mathsf{C}(\mathbb{S}) = \mathsf{P}(\mathbb{S})$, and $S_\delta = S$ for $\delta \leq 1$. More generally, if $\forall s, s'$: $\mathbb{S}.s \neq s' \implies \delta \leq d(s, s')$, then $\forall S$: $\mathsf{P}(\mathbb{S}).S_\delta = S$, i.e., an imprecision $\leq \delta$ amounts to absolute precision.

Example 2 (Euclidean). Euclidean spaces $\mathbb{R}^n$ (and Banach spaces) are used for modeling continuous and hybrid systems [9]. For C: $\mathsf{C}(\mathbb{R}^n)$, δ-fattening has a simpler alternative definition, namely $C_\delta = \{y | \exists x : C.d(x, y) \leq \delta\}$.

Example 3 (Products, sub-spaces, sums). The product $\mathbb{S}_0 \times \mathbb{S}_1$ of two metric spaces is the product of the underlying sets with metric $d(x, y) \stackrel{\Delta}{=} \max_{i:2} d_i(x_i, y_i)$.

A subset S' of $\mathbb{S}$ inherits the metric, thus can be considered a metric space $\mathbb{S}'$. If S' is also closed, then $\mathsf{C}(\mathbb{S}') \subseteq \mathsf{C}(\mathbb{S})$ and the δ-fattening of S: $\mathsf{P}(\mathbb{S}')$ is $S_\delta \cap S'$.

The sum $\coprod_{i:I} \mathbb{S}_i$ of an I-indexed family of metric spaces is $\{(i, x) | i : I \wedge x : \mathbb{S}_i\}$ with metric $d((i, x), (j, y)) \stackrel{\Delta}{=}$ if $i = j$ then $d_i(x, y)$ else 1. The following hold: $\mathsf{P}(\coprod_{i:I} \mathbb{S}_i) \cong \prod_{i:I} \mathsf{P}(\mathbb{S}_i)$, i.e., a subset in the sum *is* a sum $\coprod_{i:I} S_i$ of subsets. Similarly, $\mathsf{C}(\coprod_{i:I} \mathbb{S}_i) \cong \prod_{i:I} \mathsf{C}(\mathbb{S}_i)$. Moreover, $(\coprod_{i:I} S_i)_\delta = \coprod_{i:I} (S_i)_\delta$ for $\delta \leq 1$.

Remark 1. Usually the state space of a hybrid automaton [1] is a (finite) sum of closed sub-spaces of Euclidean spaces. A hybrid system on a Euclidean space $\mathbb{S}$ is a pair $\mathcal{H} = (F, G)$ of relations on $\mathbb{S}$. Equivalently, $\mathcal{H}$ is a subset $F + G$ of the metric space $\mathbb{S}^2 + \mathbb{S}^2$. Therefore, closure and δ-fattening are applicable to hybrid systems on $\mathbb{S}$ as well as to subsets of $\mathbb{S}$.

3 Analyses and Robustness

We identify analyses with arrows A: $\mathbf{Po}(X, Y)$ in the category $\mathbf{Po}$ of complete lattices and monotonic maps between them. The partial order $\leq$ allows to define over-approximations and compare them. We consider $\leq$ as an information order, thus: $x_0 \leq x$ means that x_0 is an over-approximation of x, $x_1 \leq x_0$ means that x_1 is a bigger over-approximation than x_0 (hence, less informative).

The complete lattice $\bot < \top$ of truth values, usually denoted Σ, is isomorphic to $\mathbb{P}(1)$ with 1 being the singleton set $\{\mathsf{fail}\}$, namely $\top$ (true) corresponds to $\emptyset$ (cannot fail), while $\bot$ (false) corresponds to $\{\mathsf{fail}\}$ (may fail). Safety analyses are arrows A: $\mathbf{Po}(X, \Sigma)$, and over-approximations may give false negatives.

Example 4. Safety analysis for transition systems on $\mathbb{S}$ corresponds to the arrow Sf: $\mathbf{Po}(\mathbb{P}(\mathbb{S}^2) \times \mathbb{P}(\mathbb{S}) \times \mathbb{P}(\mathbb{S}), \Sigma)$ such that $\mathsf{Sf}(R, I, B) = \top \stackrel{\Delta}{\iff} R^*(I)$ and B are disjoint, i.e., the set $R^*(I)$ of states reachable from the set I of initial states by (finitely many) R-transitions is disjoint from the set B of bad states.

Complete lattices do not have the structure to *quantify* imprecision. Thus, we restrict to complete lattices of the form $\mathbb{C}(\mathbb{S})$, with $\mathbb{S}$ a metric space, and use δ-fattening (Sect. 2) to bound imprecision. Namely, given an over-approximation C' of C: $\mathbb{C}(\mathbb{S})$, i.e., $C \subseteq C'$ (or equivalently $C' \leq C$), we say that the imprecision of C' in over-approximating C is $\leq \delta \overset{\Delta}{\Longleftrightarrow} C \subseteq C' \subseteq C_\delta$.

For a metric space $\mathbb{S}$, there is an adjunction in **Po** (Galois connection) between $\mathbb{P}(\mathbb{S})$ and $\mathbb{C}(\mathbb{S})$. In particular, every S: $\mathbb{P}(\mathbb{S})$ has a *best over-approximation* $\overline{S}$: $\mathbb{C}(\mathbb{S})$. In other words, $\mathbb{C}(\mathbb{S})$ is an *abstract interpretation* of $\mathbb{P}(\mathbb{S})$ [5].

Definition 2 (Robustness [13]). *Given A: $\mathbf{Po}(\mathbb{C}(\mathbb{S}_1), \mathbb{C}(\mathbb{S}_2))$ with $\mathbb{S}_1$ and $\mathbb{S}_2$ metric spaces, we say that:*

- *A is **robust** at C $\overset{\Delta}{\Longleftrightarrow} \forall \epsilon > 0. \exists \delta > 0. A(C_\delta) \subseteq A(C)_\epsilon$.*
- *A is **robust** $\overset{\Delta}{\Longleftrightarrow} A$ is robust at every C.*

Robustness is a trivial property of analyses in a discrete setting (Ex 1).

Proposition 1. *If $\mathbb{S}_1$ is discrete, then every A: $\mathbf{Po}(\mathbb{C}(\mathbb{S}_1), \mathbb{C}(\mathbb{S}_2))$ is robust.*

Most analyses are not cast in the right form to ask whether they are robust, but usually one can show that they have the right form up to isomorphisms in **Po**.

Example 5. We consider analyses for (topological) transition systems [6].

1. Reachability Rf_R: $\mathbf{Po}(\mathbb{P}(\mathbb{S}), \mathbb{P}(\mathbb{S}))$ for a transition system R on $\mathbb{S}$ is not a map on closed subsets, but can be replaced by the arrow $C \mapsto \overline{\mathsf{Rf}_R(C)}$ on $\mathbb{C}(\mathbb{S})$. This is the canonical way to turn arrows on $\mathbb{P}(\mathbb{S})$ into arrows on $\mathbb{C}(\mathbb{S})$, but it may fail to be idempotent. A better choice is the *best* idempotent arrow on $\mathbb{C}(\mathbb{S})$ over-approximating Rf_R, denoted Rs_R and called **safe reachability** in [13], i.e., $\mathsf{Rs}_R(C) \overset{\Delta}{=}$ the smallest C': $\mathbb{C}(\mathbb{S})$ such that $C \subseteq C'$ and $R(C') \subseteq C'$.
2. Reachability Rf: $\mathbf{Po}(\mathbb{P}(\mathbb{S}^2) \times \mathbb{P}(\mathbb{S}), \mathbb{P}(\mathbb{S}))$ for transition systems on $\mathbb{S}$. First, we replace $\mathbb{P}(\mathbb{S}^2) \times \mathbb{P}(\mathbb{S})$ with the isomorphic $\mathbb{P}(\mathbb{S}^2 + \mathbb{S})$ (see Example 3). Second, we proceed as done for Rf_R. In particular, we can replace Rf with safe reachability Rs: $\mathbf{Po}(\mathbb{C}(\mathbb{S}^2) \times \mathbb{C}(\mathbb{S}), \mathbb{C}(\mathbb{S}))$ for *closed* transition systems on $\mathbb{S}$.
3. Safety Sf: $\mathbf{Po}(\mathbb{P}(\mathbb{S}^2) \times \mathbb{P}(\mathbb{S}) \times \mathbb{P}(\mathbb{S}), \Sigma)$ is definable in terms of reachability Rf, namely $\mathsf{Sf}(R, I, B) \overset{\Delta}{\Longleftrightarrow} \mathsf{Rf}(R, I) \# B$, where $\#$ is the disjointness predicate. Any replacement for Rf induces a corresponding notion of safety, e.g., safe safety Ss: $\mathbf{Po}(\mathbb{C}(\mathbb{S}^2) \times \mathbb{C}(\mathbb{S}) \times \mathbb{C}(\mathbb{S}), \Sigma)$ is $\mathsf{Ss}(R, I, B) \overset{\Delta}{\Longleftrightarrow} \mathsf{Rs}(R, I) \# B$.

Remark 2. An analysis A: $\mathbf{Po}(\mathbb{C}(\mathbb{S}_1), \mathbb{C}(\mathbb{S}_2))$ is often robust at some C: $\mathbb{C}(\mathbb{S}_1)$, but it is rarely robust at every C. For instance, let R_C be the diagonal relation on C: $\mathbb{C}(\mathbb{R})$, which is a closed transition system on $\mathbb{R}$, then

- Rs_{R_C} is robust, since $\mathsf{Rs}_{R_C}(I) = I$ for every I: $\mathbb{C}(\mathbb{R})$;
- Rs is robust at $(R_\mathbb{N}, I)$ for every I: $\mathbb{C}(\mathbb{R})$, but
- Rs is not robust at $(R_\mathbb{R}, I)$ when $\emptyset \subset I \subset \mathbb{R}$, because $\mathsf{Rs}((R_\mathbb{R})_\delta, I) = \mathbb{R}$.

Time automata are a special case of hybrid automata (e.g., see [12]), and the latter are subsumed by hybrid systems [9]. **Timed transition systems** are an abstraction for all these systems. In particular, there is an abstraction map $\alpha\colon \mathbf{Po}(\mathbb{P}(\mathbb{S}^2 + \mathbb{S}^2), \mathbb{P}(\mathbb{T} \times \mathbb{S}^2))$ from hybrid systems on (the Euclidean space) $\mathbb{S}$ to timed transition systems on (the topological space) $\mathbb{S}$, where $\mathbb{T}$ is the continuous time line, i.e., the space of non negative reals $[0, +\infty)$.

Example 6. Reachability is not appropriate when time matters. For a timed transition system R on $\mathbb{S}$, a better analysis is **evolution** $\mathsf{Ef}_R\colon \mathbf{Po}(\mathbb{P}(\mathbb{S}), \mathbb{P}(\mathbb{T} \times \mathbb{S}))$, which gives the time at which a state is reached, namely $\mathsf{Ef}_R(I) \triangleq$ the smallest $E\colon \mathbb{P}(\mathbb{T} \times \mathbb{S})$ such that $\{0\} \times I \subseteq E$ and $\{(t+d, s')|(t,s)\colon E \wedge (d, s, s')\colon R\} \subseteq E$. By analogy with reachability, one can define $\mathsf{Ef}\colon \mathbf{Po}(\mathbb{P}(\mathbb{T} \times \mathbb{S}^2) \times \mathbb{P}(\mathbb{S}), \mathbb{P}(\mathbb{T} \times \mathbb{S}))$ and safe variants $\mathsf{Es}\colon \mathbf{Po}(\mathbb{C}(\mathbb{T} \times \mathbb{S}^2) \times \mathbb{C}(\mathbb{S}), \mathbb{C}(\mathbb{T} \times \mathbb{S}))$, and cast them in the form required by robustness. Safe evolution can be extended to include asymptotically reachable states $\mathsf{Es}\colon \mathbf{Po}(\mathbb{C}(\mathbb{T} \times \mathbb{S}^2) \times \mathbb{C}(\mathbb{S}), \mathbb{C}(\overline{\mathbb{T}} \times \mathbb{S}))$, where $\overline{\mathbb{T}}$ is $[0, +\infty]$.

4   Best Robust Approximations

Intuitively, when an analysis $A\colon \mathbf{Po}(\mathbb{C}(\mathbb{S}_1), \mathbb{C}(\mathbb{S}_2))$ is robust at C, $A(C)$ is *useful* also in the presence of small amounts of imprecision. This is obvious for analyses $A\colon \mathbf{Po}(\mathbb{C}(\mathbb{S}_1), \Sigma)$, where robustness at C means $A(C_\delta) = A(C)$ when δ is *small*.

Definition 3. *Given* $A\colon \mathbf{Po}(\mathbb{C}(\mathbb{S}_1), \mathbb{C}(\mathbb{S}_2))$, *we say that:*

- $A'\colon \mathbf{Po}(\mathbb{C}(\mathbb{S}_1), \mathbb{C}(\mathbb{S}_2))$ *is a robust approximation of* $A \overset{\triangle}{\Longleftrightarrow}$
  A' *is robust and* $\forall C.A'(C) \leq A(C)$.
- $A^\square\colon \mathbf{Po}(\mathbb{C}(\mathbb{S}_1), \mathbb{C}(\mathbb{S}_2))$ *is a **best robust approximation** of* $A \overset{\triangle}{\Longleftrightarrow}$
  $A^\square$ *is a robust approximation of* A *such that* $A'(C) \leq A^\square(C)$ *for every robust approximation* A' *of* A *and* C.

Every arrow has a *worst* robust approximation, namely the map $C \mapsto \bot$, where $\bot$ is the least element in $\mathbb{C}(\mathbb{S}_2)$. There are $A\colon \mathbf{Po}(\mathbb{C}([0,1]), \mathbb{C}(\mathbb{R}))$ that do not have a best robust approximation (see [13, Ex 4.6]). When $\mathbb{S}_1$ and $\mathbb{S}_2$ are discrete metric spaces, every $A\colon \mathbf{Po}(\mathbb{C}(\mathbb{S}_1), \mathbb{C}(\mathbb{S}_2))$ is robust, thus $A^\square = A$. We give conditions on metric spaces implying existence of best robust approximations. The first result applies to safety analyses and is related to the notion of robustness in [7, Def 2].

Theorem 1. *If $\mathbb{S}_2$ is a finite metric space, then $A\colon \mathbf{Po}(\mathbb{C}(\mathbb{S}_1), \mathbb{C}(\mathbb{S}_2))$ has a best robust approximation $A^\square$ given by $A^\square(C) = \bigcap \{A(C_\delta)|\delta > 0\}$.*

Proof. $\mathbb{C}(\mathbb{S}_2) = \mathbb{P}(\mathbb{S}_2) \cong \Sigma^n$ is a finite complete lattice, when $\mathbb{S}_2$ is a finite (and necessarily discrete) metric space with n points. Therefore, $A'\colon \mathbf{Po}(\mathbb{C}(\mathbb{S}_1), \mathbb{C}(\mathbb{S}_2))$ robust at C means that there exists $\delta > 0$ such that $A'(C) = A'(C_\delta)$.

Since $\{A(C_\delta)|\delta > 0\}$ is a chain in a finite lattice, there exists $\delta > 0$ such that $A(C_{\delta'}) = A(C_\delta)$ when $\delta' < \delta$. Let $\delta(C)$ be the biggest element in $(0, +\infty]$ such that $A(C_{\delta'}) = A(C_\delta)$ when $\delta' < \delta < \delta(C)$. Define $A^\square(C) \triangleq A(C_\delta)$ for $\delta < \delta(C)$, then $A^\square$ is monotonic, since $A^\square(C) = A(C_\delta) \le A(C'_\delta) \le A^\square(C')$ when $C \le C'$ and $\delta < \delta(C)$, and $A^\square$ is a robust approximation of A, since

- $A^\square(C) = A(C_\delta) \le A(C)$ when $\delta < \delta(C)$, and
- $A^\square(C) = A(C_\delta) = A^\square(C_{\delta'})[= A(C_{\delta'})]$ when $\delta' < \delta < \delta(C)$.

Finally, $A^\square$ is the best robust approximation of A, because $A'(C) = A'(C_\delta) \le A(C_\delta) = A^\square(C)$ when A' is a robust approximation of A and δ is small.   □

Table 1. Safe and robust over-approximations of the set of reachable states.

$\mathcal{H}$	S_0	s	S_f	S_s	S_r	S_R	
$\mathcal{H}_E$	$[0,1]$	0	$[0]$	S_f	$\mathbf{S_0}$	S_0	
		$0 < s \le 1$	$[s,1]$	S_f	S_f	S_f	
hs_D	$[0,1]$	0	S_0	S_0	S_0	S_0	
		$0 < s \le 1$	$(0,s]$	$\mathbf{S_0}$	S_0	S_0	
$\mathcal{H}_T$	$\{(x,y)|0 \le x \le y \le 1\}$	$(0,1)$	$S^*(0)$	S_f	S_f	S_f	b=0
		$(0,1)$	$S^*(b)$	$\mathbf{S_f \uplus S(0)}$	S_s	S_s	$0 < b < 1$
		$(0,1)$	$S(1)$	S_f	S_f	$\mathbf{S_0}$	b=1

For $\mathcal{H}_E$ and $\mathcal{H}_D$ we take $\mathcal{H}_0 = (F_0, G_0)$ with $F_0 = [0,1] \times [-1,1]$ and $G_0 = [0,1]^2$. For $\mathcal{H}_T = (F,G)$ we take $\mathcal{H}_0 = (\overline{F}, G_0)$ with $G_0 = \{(y,y)|y:[0,1]\} \times \{(0,y)|y:[0,1]\}$, and we use the notation $S(b) \triangleq [0,b] \times [b]$ and $S^*(b) \triangleq \cup_n S(b^n)$ for subsets of S_0.

The differences in the approximations of the reachable states are highlighted in **bold**.

Theorem 2. *If $\mathbb{S}_1$ and $\mathbb{S}_2$ are compact metric spaces, then $A: \mathbf{Po}(\mathbb{C}(\mathbb{S}_1), \mathbb{C}(\mathbb{S}_2))$ has a best robust approximation $A^\square$ given by $A^\square(C) = \bigcap \{A(C_\delta)|\delta > 0\}$.*

Proof. We refer to [13] for details of the proof. The key points are:

- if $\mathbb{S}$ is a compact metric space, then $\mathbb{C}(\mathbb{S})$ is a continuous lattice;
- if $\mathbb{S}_1$ and $\mathbb{S}_2$ are compact metric spaces, then a map $A': \mathbf{Po}(\mathbb{C}(\mathbb{S}_1), \mathbb{C}(\mathbb{S}_2))$ is robust exactly when it is Scott continuous.   □

5   Examples

We conclude by comparing different reachability analyses for three *deterministic* hybrid systems $\mathcal{H}$ [9]:

$\mathcal{H}_E$ a quantity x grows according to ODE $\dot{x} = x$ when $0 \le x < 1$, and stays constant when it reaches the threshold 1, i.e., $\dot{x} = 0$ when $x = 1$.

$\mathcal{H}_D$ a quantity x decreases according to ODE $\dot{x} = -x$ when $0 < x \leq 1$, and it is *instantaneously* reset to 1 when it is 0, i.e., $x^+ = 1$ when $x = 0$.

$\mathcal{H}_T$ a timer x grows while the timeout y stays constant, i.e., $\dot{x} = 1 \& \dot{y} = 0$ when $0 \leq x < y \leq 1$, when x reaches y it is reset and the timeout updated, i.e., $x^+ = 0 \& y^+ = by$ when $0 < x = y \leq 1$ (with b constant in the interval $[0,1]$), moreover $x^+ = 0 \& y^+ = 1$ when $0 = x = y \leq 1$, i.e., y is reset to 1.

Table 1 gives for each $\mathcal{H}$ above (and initial state s) the following sets:

- $S_f \triangleq \mathsf{Rf}_{\mathcal{H}}(s)$ set of states reachable (from s) in finitely many transitions, S_f is always a subset of the set S of the states reachable in finite time;
- $S_s \triangleq \mathsf{Rs}_{\mathcal{H}}(s)$ superset of S computed by safe reachability;
- $S_r \triangleq \mathsf{Rs}_{\mathcal{H}}^{\square}(s)$ superset of S_s robust w.r.t. over-approximations of s;
- $S_R \triangleq \mathsf{Rs}^{\square}(\overline{\mathcal{H}}, s)$ superset of S_s robust w.r.t. over-approximations of $\overline{\mathcal{H}}$ & s.

Note that S_r depends on a compact subset S_0 (over-approximating s and the *support* of $\mathcal{H}$), and S_R depends also on a compact hybrid system $\mathcal{H}_0$ (with support S_0 and over-approximating $\mathcal{H}$). In particular, $\mathcal{H}_0$ constrains the over-approximations of $\mathcal{H}$. The inclusions $[s \in]S_f[\subseteq S] \subseteq S_s \subseteq S_r \subseteq S_R[\subseteq S_0]$ hold always. We explain why some of these inclusions are strict.

- $\mathcal{H} = \mathcal{H}_E$ & $s = 0$: $S_f = S = S_s \subset S_r$, because any small positive change to s causes the quantity to grow and eventually reach the threshold.
- $\mathcal{H} = \mathcal{H}_D$ & $s > 0$: $S_f = S \subset S_s$, because safe reachability includes 0, which is reachable only asymptotically (not in finite time), and any state in $\mathsf{Rf}_{\mathcal{H}}(0)$.
- $\mathcal{H} = \mathcal{H}_T$ & $s = (0, 1)$ & $0 < b < 1$: $S_f \subset S = S_s$, because the system has a *Zeno behaviour*, namely the state $x = y = 0$ is reachable from $x = y = 1$ in time $b/(1-b)$, but it requires infinitely many updates to the timeout y. Thus S_f computes an under-approximation of what is reachable in finite time.
- $\mathcal{H} = \mathcal{H}_T$ & $s = (0, 1)$ & $b = 1$: $S_f = S = S_r \subset S_R$, because the imprecision in $\mathcal{H}_\delta$ means that y can be updated with any value y^+ in $[\max(0, y - \delta), y]$ when $0 < x = y \leq 1$. Therefore, $x = y = 0$ is reachable in $O(\delta^{-1})$ transitions.

References

1. Alur, R., et al.: The algorithmic analysis of hybrid systems. Theor. Comput. Sci. **138**(1), 3–34 (1995)
2. Asperti, A., Longo, G.: Categories, Types and Scructures: An Introduction to Category Theory for the Working Computer Scientist. MIT Press, Cambridge (1991)
3. Awodey, S.: Category Theory. Oxford University Press, Oxford (2010)
4. Conway, J.B.: A Course in Functional Analysis, 2nd edn. Springer, New York (1990)
5. Cousot, P., Cousot, R.: Abstract interpretation frameworks. J. Logic Comput. **2**(4), 511–547 (1992)
6. Cuijpers, P.J.L., Reniers, M.A.: Topological (bi-) simulation. Electron. Notes Theor. Comput. Sci. **100**, 49–64 (2004)

7. Fränzle, M.: Analysis of hybrid systems: an ounce of realism can save an infinity of states. In: Flum, J., Rodriguez-Artalejo, M. (eds.) CSL 1999. LNCS, vol. 1683, pp. 126–139. Springer, Heidelberg (1999). https://doi.org/10.1007/3-540-48168-0_10
8. Gierz, G., Hofmann, K.H., Keimel, K., Lawson, J.D., Mislove, M.W., Scott, D.S.: Encycloedia of mathematics and its applications. Continuous Lattices and Domains, vol. 93. Cambridge University Press, Cambridge (2003)
9. Goebel, R., Sanfelice, R.G., Teel, A.: Hybrid dynamical systems. IEEE Control Syst. **29**(2), 28–93 (2009)
10. Kelley, J.L.: General Topology. Springer, Berlin (1975)
11. Kong, S., Gao, S., Chen, W., Clarke, E.: dReach: δ-reachability analysis for hybrid systems. In: Baier, C., Tinelli, C. (eds.) TACAS 2015. LNCS, vol. 9035, pp. 200–205. Springer, Heidelberg (2015). https://doi.org/10.1007/978-3-662-46681-0_15
12. Larsen, K.G., Steffen, B., Weise, C.: Continuous modeling of real-time and hybrid systems: from concepts to tools. Int. J. Softw. Tools Technol. Transfer **1**(1–2), 64–85 (1997)
13. Moggi, E., Farjudian, A., Duracz, A., Taha, W.: Safe & robust reachability analysis of hybrid systems. Theor. Comput. Sci. **747C**, 75–99 (2018). https://doi.org/10.1016/j.tcs.2018.06.020
14. Moore, R.E.: Interval Analysis. Prentice-Hall, New Jersey (1966)

Logic Meets Algebra: Compositional Timing Analysis for Synchronous Reactive Multithreading

Michael Mendler[1]([✉]), Joaquín Aguado[1], Bruno Bodin[2], Partha Roop[3], and Reinhard von Hanxleden[4]

[1] Faculty of Information Systems and Applied Computer Sciences,
Bamberg University, Bamberg, Germany
{michael.mendler,joaquin.aguado}@uni-bamberg.de
[2] Department of Computer Science, Edinburgh University, Edinburg, UK
bbodin@inf.ed.ac.uk
[3] Department of Electrical and Computer Engineering, Auckland University,
Auckland, New Zealand
p.roop@auckland.ac.nz
[4] Department of Computer Science, Christian-Albrechts-Universität zu Kiel,
Kiel, Germany
rvh@informatik.uni-kiel.de

Abstract. The intuitionistic theory of the real interval $[0, 1]$, known as Skolem-Gödel-Dummet logic (SGD), generates a well-known Heyting algebra intermediate between intuitionistic and classical logic. Originally of purely mathematical interest, it has recently received attention in Computer Science, notably for its potential applications in concurrency theory. In this paper we show how the logical operators of SGD over the discrete frame $\mathbb{Z}_\infty$, extended by the additive group structure $(\mathbb{Z}, 0, +)$, provides an expressive and yet surprisingly economic calculus to specify the quantitative stabilisation behaviour of synchronous programs. This is both a new application of SGD and a new way of looking at the semantics of synchronous programming languages. We provide the first purely algebraic semantics of timed synchronous reactions which adapts Berry's semantics for Esterel to work on general concurrent/sequential control-flow graphs. We illustrate the power of the algebra for the modular analysis of worst-case reaction time (WCRT) characteristics for time-predictable reactive processors with hardware-supported multi-threading.

1 Introduction

Synchronous control-flow programming (SCP) extends standard imperative programming by deterministic concurrency. This is achieved by forcing threads to execute under the control of a logical clock in lock-step synchronisation, thereby generating a sequence of global *macro steps*, also called *logical instants* or *clock*

© Springer Nature Switzerland AG 2019
T. Margaria et al. (Eds.): Steffen Festschrift, LNCS 11200, pp. 45–67, 2019.
https://doi.org/10.1007/978-3-030-22348-9_5

ticks. During each tick, threads use *signals* to communicate with each other. In contrast to shared variables, signals are accessed using a synchronisation protocol which makes all writes to a signal happen before any read and the value read to be a value uniquely *combined* from the values written. Programs that cannot be scheduled in this way, tick by tick, are detected at compile-time and rejected as *non-constructive.* Synchronous programs can be compiled into sequential C code, hardware circuits for parallel execution or multi-threaded assembly code.

The physical time spent by the running threads to compute the tick reaction is functionally immaterial, because of the clock synchronisation. The functional semantics of SCP is fully captured by the synchronous composition of Mealy machines. The physical timing of a module can be ignored until it is compiled and mapped to an execution architecture. Then it becomes crucial, however, since the *worst-case reaction time* (WCRT) determines the correct physical synchronisation of the compiled modules and the environment. This WCRT value gives the maximal frequency of the clock and the minimal length of a reaction cycle. Assuming an implementation on clocked instruction set processors, the purpose of the WCRT analysis is to determine, at compile time, the maximal number of instruction cycles in any tick.

This paper extends previous work by the authors [1, 21–23, 28] on the WCRT analysis of imperative multi-threaded SCP code running on *Precision-timed (PRET)* architectures. It discusses the Skolem-Gödel-Dummett intuitionistic logic SGD[X] of formal power series for the cycle-accurate modelling of sequential and concurrent program behaviour. Formal power series arise from adjoining an abstract variable X to build polynomials. This is the first time that SGD[X] is presented as a component model, exploring its applications for modular analysis and timing abstractions to trade efficiency and precision. The power of SGD[X] is shown using the Esterel program in Fig. 1 as case study.

We believe the algebraic approach for WCRT analysis of SCP can be an elegant and powerful alternative to other more combinatorial techniques, such as those based on graph traversal [4, 22], state exploration [17, 30], implicit path enumeration with integer linear programming (ILP) solving and iterative narrowing [15, 16, 24, 29] or timed automata [27]. The advantage of SGD[X] algebra over combinatorial definitions of WCRT is that it combines timing and functional specifications in a simple equational calculus. It permits us to study the timed behaviour of SCP employing standard mathematical tools familiar from linear and non-linear system theory. The logical interpretation of SGD[X] supports modular reasoning and timing abstractions at a fine-grained level. Existing WCRT algorithms may be studied as decision procedures for specialised fragments of SGD[X] algebra.

This paper ties up previous work of the authors spread over different publications which have not all used the same mathematical setting. By presenting a single case study, covering all aspects studied separately before, this paper lays out clearly the theoretical background of our approach in a new and uniform way. Regarding the practical usefulness of the approach we refer to our other publications, as cited herein. The relationship with the authors' previous work is discussed both as we go along and in Sect. 6.

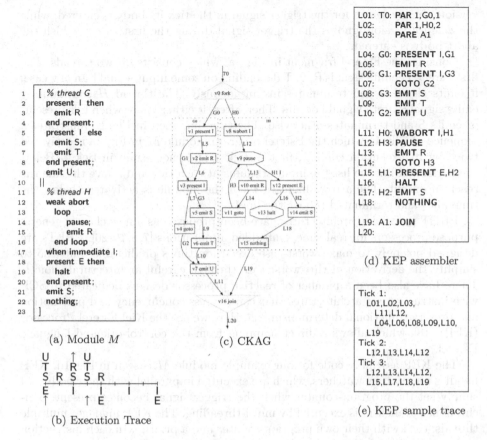

```
1    [ % thread G
2    present I then
3       emit R
4    end present;
5    present I else
6       emit S;
7       emit T
8    end present;
9    emit U;
10   ||
11   % thread H
12   weak abort
13      loop
14         pause;
15         emit R
16      end loop
17   when immediate I;
18   present E then
19      halt
20   end present;
21   emit S;
22   nothing;
23   ]
```

(a) Module M

(c) CKAG

L01: T0:	PAR 1,G0,1
L02:	PAR 1,H0,2
L03:	PARE A1
L04: G0:	PRESENT I,G1
L05:	EMIT R
L06: G1:	PRESENT I,G3
L07:	GOTO G2
L08: G3:	EMIT S
L09:	EMIT T
L10: G2:	EMIT U
L11: H0:	WABORT I,H1
L12: H3:	PAUSE
L13:	EMIT R
L14:	GOTO H3
L15: H1:	PRESENT E,H2
L16:	HALT
L17: H2:	EMIT S
L18:	NOTHING
L19: A1:	JOIN
L20:	

(d) KEP assembler

```
Tick 1:
     L01,L02,L03,
     L11,L12,
     L04,L06,L08,L09,L10,
     L19
Tick 2:
     L12,L13,L14,L12
Tick 3:
     L12,L13,L14,L12,
     L15,L17,L18,L19
```

(e) KEP sample trace

(b) Execution Trace

Fig. 1. A simple Esterel module M with its corresponding control-flow graph and the resulting KEP Assembler (example from [13]).

2   Esterel-Style Multi-threading and WCRT Analysis

A representative example of a high-level SCP language is Esterel [3]. Esterel signals are either *present* or *absent* during one tick. Signals are set to present by the emit statement and signal state is tested with the present test statement. They are reset to absent at the start of each tick. Esterel statements can be either combined in sequence (;) or in parallel (||). The loop statement restarts its body when it terminates. All Esterel statements complete within a single tick, called *(instantaneous) termination*, except for the pause statement, which *pauses* for one tick, and derived statements like halt (= loop pause end), which pauses forever. Esterel supports multiple forms of preemption, e. g., via the abort statement, which simply terminates its body when some trigger signal is present. Abortion can be either weak or strong. *Weak abortion* permits the execution of its body in the tick the trigger signal becomes active, *strong abortion* does not. Both kinds of abortions can be either immediate or delayed. The *immediate* version already senses for the trigger signal in the tick its body is entered, while the *delayed* version ignores the trigger signal during the first tick in which the abort body is entered.

Consider the Esterel fragment in Fig. 1a, which consists of two threads. The first thread G emits signals R, S, T depending on some input signal I. In any case, it emits signal U and terminates instantaneously. The thread H continuously emits signal R, until signal I occurs. Thereafter, it either halts, when E is present, or emits S and terminates otherwise. The time line seen in Fig. 1b illustrates a sequence of ticks in which the Esterel program module M in Fig. 1a is activated twice by its execution context, first in tick 1 and then again in tick 4. Below the horizontal line we list the input stimulus at each tick and above the line the reaction output. The arrows indicate when the module is activated (below the time line) and terminated (above the line).

PRET processing architectures have been proposed as a new class of general purpose processors for real-time, embedded applications [7, 8, 19, 26]. PRETs are designed not only to make worst-case execution times predictable, but also to simplify the derivation of this worst case through careful architectural choices. There have also been a number of reactive processor designs dedicated to SCP with instruction set architectures that can express concurrency and preemption and preserve functional determinism [12]. Here we use the Kiel Esterel Processor (KEP) [18], which allows a direct mapping from the control-oriented language Esterel.

The KEP assembly code for our example module M is seen in Fig. 1d. KEP handles abortion by watchers, which are executed in parallel with their body and simply set the program-counter when the trigger signal becomes present. Synchronous parallelism is executed by multi-threading. The KEP manages multiple threads, each with their own program counter and a priority. In each instruction cycle, the processor determines the active instruction from the thread with the highest priority and executes it. New child threads are initialised by the PAR instruction. The PARE instruction ends the initialisation of parallel threads and sets the program counter of the current thread to the corresponding JOIN. By changing the priorities of the threads, using PRIO instructions, arbitrary interleavings can be specified; the compiler has to ensure that the priorities respect all signal dependencies, *i. e.*, all possible emits of a signal are performed before any testing of the signal. For all parallel threads one join instruction is executed, which checks whether all threads have terminated in the current tick. If this is the case, the whole parallel terminates and the join passes the control to the next instruction. Otherwise the join blocks. On KEP, most instructions, like emit or entering an abort block, are executed in exactly one instruction cycle (ic). The pause instruction is executed both in the tick it is entered, and in the tick it is resumed, to check for weak and strong abortions, respectively. Note that the halt instruction is executed in one ic. Priority changing instructions may be treated like the padding statement nothing, which has no effect other than adding a time delay.

The KEP assembler's control flow is represented in the *concurrent KEP assembler graph (CKAG)* depicted in Fig. 1c. The CKAG is an intermediate representation compiled from the Esterel source Fig. 1a which, due to the nature of the KEP architecture, retains much of the original Esterel program structure. It is important to observe that the CKAG and the KEP assembler have a very close and timing-predictable relationship. Hence, the timing of the KEP can be back-annotated in the CKAG by associating WCRT weights to nodes and edges. We distinguish two kinds of edges, instantaneous and non-instantaneous. Instantaneous edges can be taken immediately when the source node is entered, they reflect control flow starting from instantaneous statements or weak abortions of pre-empted statements. Non-instantaneous edges can only be taken in an instant where the control started in its source node, like control flow from PAUSE statements or strong abortions. The CKAG can be derived from the Esterel program by structural translation. For a given CKAG, the generation of KEP assembler (see Fig. 1c) is straightforward [4]. Most nodes are translated into one instruction, only fork nodes are expanded to multiple instructions to initialise the threads. In our example, the fork v_0 is transformed into three instructions ($L01$–$L03$).

3   Max-Plus Algebra and Skolem-Gödel-Dummet Logic

A standard setting for timing analysis is the discrete max-plus structure over integers $(\mathbb{Z}_\infty, \oplus, \odot, 0, 1)$ where $\mathbb{Z}_\infty =_{df} \mathbb{Z} \cup \{-\infty, +\infty\}$ and $\oplus$ is the maximum and $\odot$ stands for addition. Both binary operators are commutative, associative with the neutral elements $0 =_{df} -\infty$ and $1 =_{df} 0$, respectively, i.e., $x \oplus 0 = x$ and $x \odot 1 = x$. The constant 0 is absorbing for $\odot$, i.e., $x \odot 0 = 0 \odot x = 0$. In particular, $-\infty \odot +\infty = -\infty$. Addition $\odot$ distributes over $\oplus$, i.e., $x \odot (y \oplus z) = x + max(y, z) = max(x + y, x + z) = (x \odot y) \oplus (x \odot z)$. This induces on $\mathbb{Z}_\infty$ a (commutative, idempotent) semi-ring structure. Multiplicative expressions $x \odot y$ are often written $x\,y$ and $\odot$ is assumed to bind more strongly than $\oplus$. Extending $\mathbb{Z}$ to $\mathbb{Z}_\infty$ weakens the ring structure, because the limit values $+\infty$ and $-\infty$ cannot be subtracted. E.g., there is no x such that $x \odot +\infty = 0$. There is, however, a weak form of negation, the *adjugate* $x^* = -x$ which is an involution $(x^*)^* = x$ and antitonic, i.e., $x \leq y$ iff $x^* \geq y^*$. The adjugate satisfies $x \odot x^* \in \{0, 1\}$ and $x \odot x^* = 1$ iff x is *finite*, i.e., $x \in \mathbb{Z}$. The set $\mathbb{Z}_\infty$ is not only an adjugated semi-ring but also a lattice with the natural ordering $\leq$. Meet and join are $x \wedge y = min(x, y)$ and $x \vee y = max(x, y)$, respectively. In fact, with its two limits $-\infty$ and $+\infty$ the order structure $(\mathbb{Z}_\infty, \leq, -\infty, +\infty)$ is a complete lattice. The operators $\oplus$, $\odot$ are monotonic and upper continuous. Note that $\odot$ is upper continuous, $x \odot \bigvee_i y_i = \bigvee_i (x \odot y_i)$, but not lower continuous. Indeed, $+\infty \odot \bigwedge_{i \in \mathbb{Z}} -i = +\infty \odot -\infty = -\infty \neq +\infty = \bigwedge_{i \in \mathbb{Z}} +\infty = \bigwedge_{i \in \mathbb{Z}} (+\infty \odot -i)$.

Max-plus algebra is well-known and widely exploited for discrete event system analysis (see, e.g., [2,10]). What we are going to exploit here, however, is that $\mathbb{Z}_\infty$ also supports logical reasoning, built around the meet (min) operation and the top element of the lattice $(\mathbb{Z}_\infty, \leq)$. The logical view is natural for our application where the values in $\mathbb{Z}_\infty$ represent activation conditions for control flow points, or measure the presence or absence of a signal during a tick. Logical truth, $\top = +\infty$ indicates a signal being *statically present* without giving a definite bound. All other stabilisation values $d \in \mathbb{Z}$ codify *timed presence* which are forms of truth stronger than $\top$. On these multi-valued forms of truth (aka "presence") the meet $\wedge$ acts like logical conjunction while the join $\vee$ is logical disjunction. The bottom element $\bot = -\infty$ corresponding to falsity indicates that a signal is *absent*.

The behaviour of $\bot$ and $\top$, as the truth values for static signals follows the classical Boolean truth tables with respect to $\wedge$ and $\vee$. However, like $\odot$ has no inverse for the limit elements $+\infty$ and $-\infty$, there is no classical complementation for the finite truth values, i.e., those different from $+\infty$ and $-\infty$. For SCP, however, negation is important to model data-dependent branching, priorities and preemption. As it happens, there is a natural *pseudo-complement*, or implication $\supset$, turning the lattice $\mathbb{Z}_\infty$ into an *intuitionistic* logic, or which is the same, a Heyting algebra [5]. The *implication* $\supset$ is the residual with respect to conjunction $\wedge$, i.e, $x \supset y$ is the largest element z such that $x \wedge z \leq y$. It can be directly computed as follows: $x \supset y = y$ if $y < x$ and $x \supset y = +\infty$ if $x \leq y$. Implication internalises the ordering relation in the sense that $x \supset y = \top$ iff $x \leq y$. Taking $x \equiv y$ as an abbreviation of $(x \supset y) \wedge (y \supset x)$, then two values are logically equivalent $x \equiv y = \top$ iff they are identical $x = y$. Implication generates a *pseudo-complement* as $\neg x =_{df} x \supset \bot$ with the property that $\neg x = \top$ if $x = \bot$ and $\neg x = \bot$ if $x > -\infty$. There is also a residual operation $\oslash$ of $\odot$ so that $z \odot x \leq y$ iff $z \leq y \oslash x$. This is a weak form of subtraction so that $y \oslash x = y - x$ if both y and x are finite, $y \oslash x = +\infty$ if $y = +\infty$ or $x = -\infty$ and $y \oslash x = -\infty$ if $-\infty = y < x$ or $y < x = +\infty$. One shows that for all x with $x \odot x^* = \mathbb{1}$ we have $y \oslash x = y \odot x^*$.

The logic $(\mathbb{Z}_\infty, \top, \bot, \wedge, \vee, \supset)$ is isomorphic to the Skolem-Gödel-Dummet logic [6] of the interval $[0, 1] \subset \mathbb{R}$, which is decidable and completely axiomatised by the laws of intuitionistic logic plus the linearity axiom $(x \supset y) \vee (y \supset x)$. This logic, which we name[1] SGD, has played an important role in the study of logics intermediate between intuitionistic and classical logic. It has recently received attention for its applications in Computer Science, notably as a semantics of fuzzy logic [11], dialogue games [9] and concurrent λ-calculus [14].

For our application of SGD, both its semi-ring $(\mathbb{Z}_\infty, \oplus, \odot, \mathbb{0}, \mathbb{1})$ and intuitionistic truth algebra $(\mathbb{Z}_\infty, \bot, \top, \wedge, \vee, \supset)$ structure are equally important. The former to calculate WCRT timing and the latter to express signals and reaction behaviour. To state that a signal a is present with a worst-case delay of 5 ic we can write the equation $a \oplus 5 = 5$ or the formula $a \supset 5$. That c becomes active within 5 ticks of both signals a and b being present is stated by the formula $c \supset (5 \odot (a \vee b))$. Every SGD expression is at the same time the computation of a WCRT and a logical activation condition.

---

[1] Dummett (1959) calls it LC, yet Skolem (1931) and Gödel (1932) studied LC earlier.

4   Max-plus Formal Power Series

To capture the behaviour of a program along sequences of macro ticks, we extend the adjuagated semi-ring $\mathbb{Z}_\infty$ to formal power series. A *(max-plus) formal power series*, *fps*, is an ω-sequence

$$A = \bigoplus_{i \geq 0} a_i X^i = a_0 \oplus a_1 X \oplus a_2 X^2 \oplus a_3 X^3 \cdots \tag{1}$$

with $a_i \in \mathbb{Z}_\infty$ and where exponentiation is repeated multiplication, i.e., $X^0 = \mathbb{1}$ and $X^{k+1} = X X^k = X \odot X^k$. An fps stores an infinite sequence of numbers $a_0, a_1, a_2, a_3, \ldots$ as the scalar coefficients of the base polynomials X^i. An fps A may model the time cost a_i for a thread A to complete each tick i, to reach a given state A or to activate a given signal A. If $a_i = \mathbb{0} = -\infty$ this means that thread A is not executed during the tick i, or that a state A is not reachable. This contrasts with $a_i = \mathbb{1} = 0$ which means A is executed during tick i with zero cost, or that the state A is active at the beginning of the tick. If $a_i > 0$ then thread A is executed taking at most a_i time to finish tick i, or state A is reached within a_i-time during the selected tick. We evaluate A with $X = \mathbb{1}$ for the worst-case time cost $A[\mathbb{1}] = max\{a_i \mid i \geq 0\}$ across all ticks.

Let $\mathbb{Z}_\infty[X]$ denote the set of fps over $\mathbb{Z}_\infty$. For a comprehensive discussion of formal power series in max-plus algebra the reader is referred to [2]. Constants $d \in \mathbb{Z}_\infty$ are naturally viewed as scalar fps $d = d \oplus \mathbb{0}X \oplus \mathbb{0}X^2 \oplus \cdots$. If we want d to be repeated indefinitely, we write an underscore $\underline{d} = d \oplus dX \oplus dX^2 \cdots$. For finite state systems the fps are ultimately periodic. For compactness of notation we write, e.g., $A = \bot{:}2{:}1{:}\underline{4}$ for the ultimately periodic sequence satisfying $A = 2X \oplus 1X^2 \oplus X^3 B$ and $B = 4 \oplus XB$. The semi-ring and logical operations $\star \in \{\oplus, \oslash, \vee, \wedge, \supset, \otimes\}$ are lifted to $\mathbb{Z}_\infty[X]$ in a tick-wise manner, $A \star B = \bigoplus_{i \geq 0}(a_i \star b_i)X^i$ and negation is $\neg A = \bigoplus_{i \geq 0} \neg a_i X^i$. For multiplication $\odot$ there are two ways to lift. First, the tick-wise lifting $A \otimes B = \bigoplus_{i \geq 0}(a_i \odot b_i)X^i$ models multi-threaded parallel composition. It executes A and B synchronously, adding the tick costs to account for the interleaving of instructions. The other "lifting" is *convolution* $A \odot B = \bigoplus_{i \geq 0} \bigoplus_{i=i_1+i_2}(a_{i_1} \odot b_{i_2})X^i$ modelling a form of sequential composition. A special case is *scalar multiplication* $d \odot A = \bigoplus_{i \geq 0}(d \odot a_i)X^i = \underline{d} \otimes A$. The structure $(\mathbb{Z}_\infty[X], \underline{\mathbb{0}}, \underline{\mathbb{1}}, \oplus, \oslash, \otimes, \odot)$ forms a semi-ring for both "multiplications" $\odot$ and $\otimes$ and $(\mathbb{Z}_\infty[X], \bot, \top, \wedge, \vee, \supset, \neg)$ is a tick-wise Skolem-Gödel-Dummett logic. To stress the logical interpretation we will denote both as SGD$[X]$ in the sequel.

5   Equational Specification of Synchronous Control-Flow

We now go on to illustrate the application of SGD$[X]$ to specify the sequential control flow of our running example in Fig. 1a. We first focus on the thread H consisting of the fragment of nodes v_8–v_{15}, seen in Fig. 2. All edges are instantaneous except the edge $L13$ out of v_9, see below.

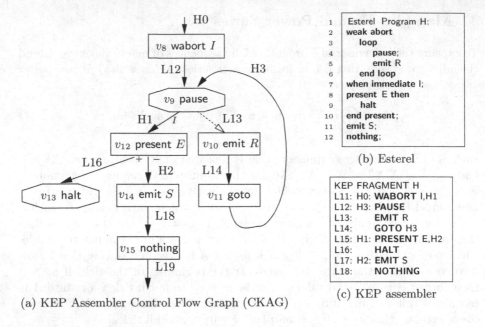

(b) Esterel

(a) KEP Assembler Control Flow Graph (CKAG)

(c) KEP assembler

Fig. 2. The synchronous thread H.

Let us assume that each of the basic instructions take 1 instruction cycle (ic) regardless of how they are entered or exited. This is a simplification of the situation in the KEP processor where the delays may be different. We also generally assume, for convenience, that the code has been checked for causality and that the control flow respects the signal dependencies. This means for the timing of signal communication that input signals may be treated as static booleans, satisfying the axiom $\neg\neg a = a$, or equivalently $a \vee \neg a = \top$, for $a \in \{E, I\}$.

We calculate the time delay to reach a given node A from $H0$ for each tick. More specifically, let $\mathbb{V}$ the set of control primitive variables and $A \in \mathbb{V}$. We identify A with the fps specifying the instants in which the control flow reaches the control point A. The timing value $A[i]$ at tick i then is the maximal waiting time to reach A in tick i. If $A[i] = \bot = -\infty$ then A cannot be reached in this tick. If we are not interested in the time when A is activated but only whether it is reached, then we use the double negation $\neg\neg A$. This abstracts from the absolute costs and reduces A to a purely *boolean clock*. Sometimes it is useful to abstract not to a boolean but an *arithmetic clock* that is $\mathbb{1}$ when A is present and $\bot$ when it is absent. This collapse is done by the operation $tick(A) = \mathbb{1} \wedge \neg\neg A$.

From Fig. 2 we see that edge $L12$ is reached instantaneously in each tick in which control reaches the start edge $H0$, and this is the only way in which $L12$ can be activated. This can be expressed by the equation

$$L12 = 1 \odot H0 = \underline{1} \otimes H0. \tag{2}$$

In each tick, the activation time of $L12$ is 1 instruction cycle (ic) larger than that of the upstream edge $H0$. The conditional branching through node v_{12} depends on the status of (static) signal E. In forward direction, the node v_{12} is:

$$H2 = (1 \odot H1) \wedge \neg E \qquad\qquad L16 = (1 \odot H1) \wedge E \qquad\qquad (3)$$

The left equivalence states that $H2$ is active in a tick at some ic t iff E is absent and $H1$ was active 1 ic earlier. Analogously, $L16$ is active iff $H1$ was active one ic before and E is present. Algebraically, the equalities can be used to compute $H2$ and $L16$ from $H1$ and E.

Next, consider the pause node v_9. It can be entered by two controls, the line number $L12$ and the program label $H3$ and left via two exits, a non-instantaneous edge $L13$ and an instantaneous exit $H1$ (weak abortion). When a thread enters v_9 then either it terminates the current tick inside the node if I is absent or leaves through the weak abort $H1$ if I is present, thereby continuing the current tick, instantaneously. A thread entering v_9 never exits through $L13$ in the same tick. On the other hand, if a thread is started (resumed) from inside the pause node v_9 then control can only exit through $L13$. Algebraically, we specify the pause node as follows:

$$H1 = (1 \odot (L12 \oplus H3)) \wedge I \qquad\qquad (4)$$
$$L13 = 1 \odot X \odot tick(\neg I \wedge \neg\neg(L12 \oplus H3)) \qquad\qquad (5)$$

Equation (4) captures that if a set of schedules activates $H1$ then signal I must be present and one of $L12$ or $H3$ must have been activated 1 ic earlier. Since we are interested in the worst-case we take the maximum. Equation (5) deals with the non-instantaneous exit $L13$ from the pause. The control flow must first pause inside node v_9. This happens in each tick in which one of $L12$ or $H3$ is reached and I is absent. These instants are specified with boolean coefficients by the sub-expression $C = \neg I \wedge \neg\neg(L12 \oplus H3)$. The operator $tick$ translates these pausing instances into the neutral element for sequential composition $\odot$. Specifically, $tick(C) = \underline{1} \wedge \neg\neg C$ forces a coefficient $C = \top = +\infty$ describing presence to become $tick(C) = 0$. On the other hand, $C = \bot = -\infty$ for absence remains unchanged, $tick(C) = \bot$. Finally, the delay $1 \odot X$ shifts the whole time sequence by one instant and adds a unit delay. This unit delay is the cost of exiting the pause node at the start of the next tick.

The second node with memory behaviour in thread H of Fig. 2 is the halt node v_{13}. Once control flow reaches v_{13} it pauses there forever. Using the auxiliary controls $in(v_{13})$ and $out(v_{13})$ for pausing inside v_{13} and resuming from it, respectively, we get

$$in(v_{13}) = 1 \odot (L16 \oplus out(v_{13})) \qquad out(v_{13}) = 1 \odot X \odot tick(in(v_{13})). \qquad (6)$$

The left equation specifies the external entry $L16$ and the fact that exiting the pause immediately re-enters, with 1 ic delay. The right equation states that if the pause is entered it is left in the next tick. Finally, here is the remaining part of H's sequential control flow:

$$L14 = 1 \odot L13 \qquad\qquad H3 = 1 \odot L14 \qquad\qquad\qquad (7)$$

$$L16 = 1 \odot (H1 \wedge E) \qquad L18 = 1 \odot H2 \qquad L19 = 1 \odot L18. \qquad (8)$$

Well, not quite, we are missing the output signals emitted into the environment. Output responses are generated by thread H in nodes v_{10} and v_{14} as implications

$$R \supset 1 \odot L13 \qquad\qquad\qquad S \supset 1 \odot H2 \qquad\qquad\qquad (9)$$

assuming a unit delay between activating the emission statement and the appearance of the signal. The implications express only upper bounds $R \leq L13 + 1$ and $S \leq H2 + 1$ on the emission of signals R and E. This permits other threads concurrent to H also to emit them, possibly at an earlier time.

The Eqs. (2)–(8) form a recursive equation system with independent variables $H0$, I and E. The recursive dependency of variables $L13$, $L14$ and $H3$ on themselves is guarded by the X operator. Hence, for each fixed choice of the independents $H0$, I and E, all the dependents $L12$–$L19$ and $H1$–$H3$ can be solved uniquely. Let us go though the motions to see how this works. To power up the system as in example trace Fig. 1b we activate the start control $H0$ in the first and again in the fourth tick, with initial delay of 3 to account for the upstreaming fork, $H0 = 3{:}\bot{:}\bot{:}3{:}\underline{\bot}$. Signal I is absent initially and then present every second instant, and E is present every fourth tick, $I = \bot{:}\bot{:}(\top \oplus I)$ and $E = \top{:}\bot{:}\bot{:}\bot{:}E$. Note that $\neg I = \top{:}\top{:}(\bot{:}\underline{\top} \wedge \neg I) = \top{:}\top{:}\bot{:}\top{:}(\bot{:}\underline{\top} \wedge \neg I)$. First, it follows $L12 = 1 \odot H0 = 4{:}\bot{:}\bot{:}4{:}\underline{\bot}$. From (7) we get $H3 = 1 \odot L14 = 1 \odot 1 \odot L13 = 2 \odot L13$ and so Eq. (5) becomes

$$L13 = f(L13) = 1 \odot X \odot tick\,(\neg I \wedge \neg\neg(4{:}\bot{:}\bot{:}4{:}\underline{\bot} \oplus (2 \odot L13))). \qquad (10)$$

This is solvable by least fixed point iteration starting with $L13_0 = \bot$ for which we get $L13_1 = f(L13_0) = \bot{:}1{:}\bot{:}\bot{:}1{:}\underline{\bot}$. The second iteration through (10) yields $L13_2 = f(L13_1) = \bot{:}1{:}1{:}\bot{:}1{:}\underline{\bot}$ which is already the fixed point, $L13 = L13_2 = f(L13_2)$. The solution $L13 = \bot{:}1{:}1{:}\bot{:}1{:}\underline{\bot}$ corresponds to the trace in Fig. 1b with the WCRT value guaranteeing $L13$ is always reached 1 ic after the beginning of the tick. The closed solution for $L13$ generates a closed solution for $L14$ and $H3$ by simple substitution, viz. $L14 = 1 \odot L13 = \bot{:}2{:}2{:}\bot{:}2{:}\underline{\bot}$ and $H3 = 1 \odot L14 = \bot{:}3{:}3{:}\bot{:}3{:}\underline{\bot}$. Similarly, we obtain $H1$ from (4), $H1 = 1 \odot (I \wedge (L12 \oplus H3)) = \bot{:}\bot{:}4{:}\bot{:}4{:}\underline{\bot}$. Indeed $H1$ is activated exactly in ticks 2 and 4 with a delay of 4. Since E is absent in tick 2 but present in tick 4, control moves to $H2$ the first time and to $L16$ the second time: The equations give $H2 = 1 \odot (H1 \wedge \neg E) = 1 \odot (\bot{:}\bot{:}4{:}\bot{:}4{:}\underline{\bot} \wedge \bot{:}\top{:}\top{:}\top{:}\neg E) = \bot{:}\bot{:}5{:}\underline{\bot}$. Finally, for $L16$ we have $L16 = 1 \odot (H1 \wedge E) = \bot{:}\bot{:}\bot{:}\bot{:}5{:}\underline{\bot}$.

To sum up, Eqs. (2)–(8) describe the cycle-accurate semantics of thread H in Fig. 2. It is timing and causality sensitive and fully parametric in environment signals. Note that the algebraic specification method outlined in this section is completely uniform and generalises to arbitrary CKAG concurrent control-flow graphs.

5.1   WCRT Component Model

The specification technique described above is
fully expressive for Esterel-style synchronous
control flow. It is compositional at the level
of the primitive controls of the flat control
flow graph. It is not modular, however, as
it does not permit structural abstraction. An
axiomatic specification language that permits
behavioural abstraction for timed synchronous
components, called *(first-order, elementary)*
WCRT-interfaces has been proposed in [22]. It
is based on realisability semantics for constructive logic and was formalised in [21]. These
interfaces capture the purely combinational
behaviour CKAGs, i.e., single ticks. They do

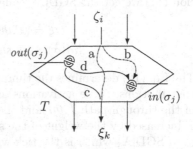

Fig. 3. The four types of thread
paths: through path (a), sink path
(b), source path (c), internal path
(d) (taken from [22]).

not describe the sequential dependencies across sequences of ticks. By translating the model of [21,22] into SGD[X] algebra we now extend WCRT interfaces
for a full semantics of synchronous components.

The key for modularity is to move from primitive control variables $\mathbb{V}$ to a
description based on *(synchronous) reactive blocks*. Figure 3 depicts a program
fragment T abstracted into a reactive block with entry and exit controls. The
paths inside T seen in Fig. 3 illustrate the four ways in which a reactive block
may participate in the execution of a logical tick: Threads may (a) arrive at some
entry control ζ_i, pass straight through the block and leave at some *exit control*
ξ_k; (b) enter through ζ_i but pause inside in some *state control* $in(\sigma_j)$, waiting
there for the next tick; (c) start the tick inside the block from a state $out(\sigma_j)$
and eventually (instantaneously) leave through some exit control ξ_k, or (d) start
and pause inside the block, not leaving it during the current tick. These paths
are called *through paths* (a), *sink paths* (b), *source paths* (c) and *internal paths*
(d), respectively.

Each block T is described by a multi-dimensional WCRT system function in
SGD[X] viewing it as a Mealy automaton over control variables. Let us suppose
for the moment, that the block T has only one entry ζ, one exit ξ and one
state control σ. The system function for such a block is given as a forward
transformation matrix T which connects the logical interface controls in the
$\{\oplus, \otimes\}$-fragment of SGD[X]:

$$\begin{pmatrix} \xi \\ in(\sigma) \end{pmatrix} = T \otimes \begin{pmatrix} \zeta \\ out(\sigma) \end{pmatrix} = \begin{pmatrix} T.thr & T.src \\ T.snk & T.int \end{pmatrix} \otimes \begin{pmatrix} \zeta \\ out(\sigma) \end{pmatrix} \quad (11)$$

All entries of the matrix are logical time series describing the *tick-wise* WCRT
behaviour on the four types of control paths: $T.thr$ for the through path, $T.snk$
for the sink paths, $T.src$ for the source paths and $T.int$ for the internal paths.
Blocks T with more than one entry, exit or state controls have a system matrix

T with more columns and rows, accordingly. Unfolding the matrix multiplication (11) we get the SGD[X] equations

$$\xi = (T.thr \otimes \zeta) \oplus (T.src \otimes out(\sigma)) \tag{12}$$
$$in(\sigma) = (T.snk \otimes \zeta) \oplus (T.int \otimes out(\sigma)) \tag{13}$$

The Eq. (12) determines the timing at exit ξ as the tick-wise worst-case $\oplus$ of two contributions, those activations arriving from entry ζ increased by the weight of the through path $T.thr$ and those arriving from a state control $out(\sigma)$ inside T increased by the weight of the source path $T.src$. The increase is achieved by $\otimes$ in SGD[X] which is the tick-wise addition $\odot$ in SGD. In an analogous way, Eq. (13) captures the activities arriving at the state control $in(\sigma)$ which may also come from entry ξ or a state $out(\sigma)$. It is useful to split (11) column-wise

$$\left(\xi \; in(\sigma)\right)^{\mathsf{T}} = \left(\left(T.thr \; T.snk\right)^{\mathsf{T}} \otimes \zeta\right) \oplus \left(\left(T.src \; T.int\right)^{\mathsf{T}} \otimes out(\sigma)\right). \tag{14}$$

thereby obtaining what are called the *surface* and *depth* behaviours $T.srf = \left(T.thr \; T.snk\right)^{\mathsf{T}}$ and $T.dpt = \left(T.src \; T.int\right)^{\mathsf{T}}$, which can be manipulated separately.

The Eq. (11) expresses the purely combinational behaviour of T. The passage from one tick to the next arises by coupling $out(T)$ and $in(T)$ through the *register equation*

$$out(T) = 1 \odot X \odot tick(in(T)). \tag{15}$$

Note the generality of the pseudo-linear system model (11). All matrix entries $T.thr$, $T.src$, $T.snk$, $T.int$ and the input and output variables ζ, $out(\sigma)$, ξ and $in(\sigma)$ may be arbitrary SGD[X] expressions involving arithmetical and logical operators. For instance, the main thread T of Fig. 1c has state control such as $\neg L11 \wedge in(v_9)$, capturing ticks in which child H is pausing in node v_9 while child G has already terminated in a previous tick, whence $L11$ has value $\bot$, and *a fortiori*, all nodes v in G satisfy $\neg v$, too. In this way, the Eq. (11) can specify both the temporal and the logical behaviour of block T. This will become clear in the next section.

5.2   Module Abstraction

Pseudo-linear specifications like (11) generalise to composite blocks what the Eqs. (2)–(8) do for primitive controls. The vector formulation can be applied as a component model at various levels of abstraction.

For instance, take the pause node v_9 in Fig. 2 as a primitive block with the "forward" Eqs. (4) and (5). It has entry controls $L12$, $H3$ and exit controls $H1$ and $L13$. The auxiliary controls $in(v_9)$ and $out(v_9)$ express conditions for pausing inside the node and for exiting it, respectively. As shown below, Eqs. (4)–(5) induce the surface and depth behaviours $v_9 = \left(v_9.srf \; v_9.dpt\right)$ with

$$\left(H1 \; L13 \; in(v_9)\right)^{\mathsf{T}} = \left(v_9.srf \otimes \left(L12 \; H3\right)^{\mathsf{T}}\right) \oplus \left(v_9.dpt \otimes out(v_9)\right) \tag{16}$$

$$v_9.srf = \begin{pmatrix} \underline{1} \wedge I & \underline{1} \wedge I \\ \bot & \bot \\ \neg I & \neg I \end{pmatrix} \qquad v_9.dpt = \begin{pmatrix} \bot \\ \underline{1} \\ \bot \end{pmatrix}. \tag{17}$$

Notice how the entries combine timing with logical conditions. In particular, the constant $\bot$ indicates where control flows are absent. If we unfold the matrix multiplications in (16) together with (17) we get the following explicit equations:

$$H1 = ((\underline{1} \wedge I) \otimes L12) \oplus ((\underline{1} \wedge I) \otimes H3) \oplus \bot \, out(v_9) \tag{18}$$

$$L13 = \bot \, L12 \oplus \bot \, H3 \oplus \underline{1} \, out(v_9) \tag{19}$$

$$in(v_9) = (\neg I \otimes L12) \oplus (\neg I \otimes H3) \oplus \bot \, out(v_9). \tag{20}$$

slightly simplified using the law $\underline{d} \otimes x = d\,x$. The first Eq. (18) can be seen as logically equivalent to (4) considering a number of laws, such as $\bot \odot x = \bot$, $x \oplus \bot = x$, $(\underline{d} \otimes x) \wedge I = (\underline{d} \wedge I) \otimes x$ for static signal I, and that both $\odot$ and $\wedge$ distribute over $\oplus$. Also one shows that (19) and (20) in combination with the register equation $out(v_9) = 1 \odot X \odot tick(in(v_9))$ is the same as (5).

At a higher level of the component hierarchy we can consider thread H in Fig. 2 as a composite block. Its behaviour is given by the global 3×3 matrix

$$\begin{pmatrix} L19 \\ in(v_9) \\ in(v_{13}) \end{pmatrix} = \begin{pmatrix} \underline{5} \wedge I \wedge \neg E & \underline{7} \wedge I \wedge \neg E & \bot \\ \underline{2} \wedge \neg I & \underline{4} \wedge \neg I & \bot \\ \underline{4} \wedge I \wedge E & \underline{6} \wedge I \wedge E & \underline{1} \end{pmatrix} \otimes \begin{pmatrix} H0 \\ out(v_9) \\ out(v_{13}) \end{pmatrix} \tag{21}$$

which is the exact behavioural description of H equivalent to the Eqs. (2)–(8), solely in terms of the external controls and the internal states v_9 and v_{13}.

From here we may reduce the complexity and precision in various way. For instance, we may abstract from the state information, working with a single state control $in(H) = in(v_9) \oplus in(v_{13})$ and $out(H) = out(v_9) \oplus out(v_{13})$. This collapse is a "base transformation" achieved by pre- and post-multiplication of H with suitable matrices. Specifically, the expansions

$$\begin{pmatrix} L19 \\ in(H) \end{pmatrix} = \begin{pmatrix} 0 & \bot & \bot \\ \bot & \underline{0} & \underline{0} \end{pmatrix} \otimes \begin{pmatrix} L19 \\ in(v_9) \\ in(v_{13}) \end{pmatrix} \qquad \begin{pmatrix} H0 \\ out(v_9) \\ out(v_{13}) \end{pmatrix} \leq \begin{pmatrix} 0 & \bot \\ \bot & \underline{0} \\ \bot & \underline{0} \end{pmatrix} \otimes \begin{pmatrix} H0 \\ out(H) \end{pmatrix}$$

permit us to approximate (21) via a 2×2 matrix H_1

$$\left(L19 \; in(H) \right)^\top \leq H_1 \otimes \left(H0 \; out(H) \right)^\top \tag{22}$$

$$H_1 = \begin{pmatrix} \underline{5} \wedge I \wedge \neg E & \underline{7} \wedge I \wedge \neg E \\ (\underline{2} \wedge \neg I) \oplus (\underline{4} \wedge I \wedge E) & (\underline{4} \wedge \neg I) \oplus (\underline{6} \wedge I \wedge E) \end{pmatrix} \tag{23}$$

Let us suppose we know that input signals E and I are always opposite values. The associated invariant $I = \neg E$ and $\neg I = E$ implies $x \wedge I \wedge \neg E = x \wedge \neg E$ as well as $x \oplus (y \wedge I \wedge E) = x \oplus \bot = x$. In a next step we may decide to give up tracking

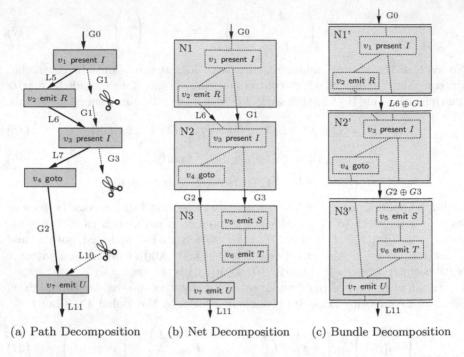

(a) Path Decomposition   (b) Net Decomposition   (c) Bundle Decomposition

Fig. 4. Different structural decompositions of thread G

signal E, abstracting from its value with the over-approximations $x \wedge \neg E \leq x$ and $x \wedge E \leq x$. This yields a sequence of approximated behaviours

$$H \leq H_1 = H_2 =_{df} \begin{pmatrix} \underline{5} \wedge \neg E & \underline{7} \wedge \neg E \\ \underline{2} \wedge E & \underline{4} \wedge E \end{pmatrix} \leq \begin{pmatrix} \underline{5} & \underline{7} \\ \underline{2} & \underline{4} \end{pmatrix} =_{df} H_3. \qquad (24)$$

There are further combinatorial optimisations possible that can be justified algebraically in $\mathrm{SGD}[X]$. For instance, the WCRT algorithm [4] reduces the dimensions of the surface and depth behaviours each by one. This exploits the fact that every schedule reaching $in(H)$ is pausing inside H and thus cannot be extended to a longer instantaneous path of H. In other words, all paths that have length at least $1 \odot in(H)$ must be going through $L19$. Logically, this is the axiom $L19 \oplus d\,in(H) = L19$ for all $d \geq 1$. Under this assumption, the two systems

$$\begin{pmatrix} L19 \\ in(H) \end{pmatrix} = \begin{pmatrix} \underline{5} & \underline{7} \\ \underline{2} & \underline{4} \end{pmatrix} \otimes \begin{pmatrix} H0 \\ out(H) \end{pmatrix} \qquad L19 = (\underline{5}\ \underline{7}) \otimes \begin{pmatrix} H0 \\ out(H) \end{pmatrix}$$

are equivalent. This reduces the WCRT specification further from H_3 to $H_4 = (\underline{5}\ \underline{7})$ without loss of precision. The algorithm [4] exploits this interface optimisation aggressively, at all levels. This renders the analysis of parallel composition particularly efficient, as we shall see in Sect. 5.3.

In more recent work a different abstraction via so-called *tick cost automata (TCA)* has been proposed [28]. It abstracts from signal dependencies like [4], but preserves the dependency on state controls. Also, it is assumed that there are no through paths $T_{thr} = \perp$ (Moore automaton) and the unique entry control ζ is connected to a single state s_0 with zero cost. These restrictions are without loss of generality as they can be achieved by judicious block decomposition. We can understand TCA in terms of $SGD[X]$ using abbreviations $in(s) = (in(s_0)\ in(s_1)\ \cdots\ in(s_{n-1})^\mathsf{T}$

$$\begin{pmatrix} L5 \\ G1 \end{pmatrix} = \begin{pmatrix} \underline{1} \wedge I \\ \underline{1} \wedge \neg I \end{pmatrix} \otimes G0$$

$$L11 = (\underline{1}\ \underline{1}) \otimes \begin{pmatrix} G2 \\ L10 \end{pmatrix}$$

$$\begin{pmatrix} L7 \\ G3 \end{pmatrix} = \begin{pmatrix} \underline{1} \wedge I & \underline{1} \wedge I \\ \underline{1} \wedge \neg I & \underline{1} \wedge \neg I \end{pmatrix} \otimes \begin{pmatrix} L6 \\ G1 \end{pmatrix}$$

$$G2 = \underline{1} \otimes L7$$

$$L6 = \underline{1} \otimes L5$$

$$L9 = \underline{1} \otimes G3$$

$$L10 = \underline{1} \otimes L9$$

Fig. 5. Basic blocks v_1–v_7 of thread G.

and $out(s) = (out(s_0)\ out(s_1)\ \cdots\ out(s_{n-1}))^\mathsf{T}$ for the state controls vectors. The general system equations then are $\xi = T_{exit} \otimes out(s)$, and $in(s) = T_{tick} \otimes out(s)$ together with the entry $in(s_0) = \zeta$ and the register equation $out(s) = X\ tick(in(s))$. These system equations in which T_{exit} and T_{tick} consist of scalars $\mathbb{Z}_\infty$ are solved by numeric fixed point iteration. The work [28] implements these operations using max-plus algebra and explicit normal form TCAs representing the ultimately periodic system solutions.

5.3   Module Composition

$SGD[X]$ permits compositional specifications at different abstraction levels using (max-plus) pseudo-linear transformations. This is the key for dynamic programming techniques and suggests the composition of blocks by matrix multiplication. Depending on how we apply the algebra we can implement different strategies for practical WCRT analysis. We illustrate this for our example program in Fig. 1c. The starting point is the block description of thread G seen in Fig. 5.

Path Decomposition. The naive strategy would be to enumerate all paths from $G0$ to $L11$, sum up the delays on each path and then take the maximum. Each of these paths defines a sub-graph of G with specific side-inputs and side-outputs. For instance, path p_1 as indicated in Fig. 4a has the side-outputs $G1$, $G3$ and side-inputs $G1$, $L10$. Its $SGD[X]$ reaction function $(G1\ G3\ L11)^\mathsf{T} = D_1 \otimes (G0\ L10\ G1)^\mathsf{T}$ has the system matrix in Fig. 6.

The entries measure if and how p_1 connects the respective controls. For instance, the entry $\underline{3} \wedge I \wedge \neg I$ is the delay between input $G0$ and output $G3$. This segment (see Fig. 4a) has delay 3 but is only sensitisable if signal I is simultaneously present and absent. This is impossible since $\underline{3} \wedge I \wedge \neg I = \bot$. The entries $\bot$ in D_1 capture that there is no causal con-

$$D_1 = \begin{pmatrix} \underline{1} \wedge \neg I & \bot & \bot \\ \underline{3} \wedge I \wedge \neg I & \bot & \underline{1} \wedge \neg I \\ \underline{5} \wedge I & \underline{1} & \underline{3} \wedge I \end{pmatrix}$$

Fig. 6. System matrix for path p_1.

trol flow from the corresponding input to the corresponding output line. D_1 can be obtained by successively multiplying (in fps max-plus algebra) the timing matrices of the individual nodes traversed by p_1.

If we are not interested in all combinations of side-inputs and side-outputs we can reduce the matrix D_1. The side-inputs $G1$ and $L10$ are eliminated by selecting only the first column of D_1, i.e., $D_1' = D_1 \otimes \left(\underline{0} \bot \bot \right)^T$, so that $\left(G1 \, G3 \, L11 \right)^T = D_1' \otimes G0$. Getting rid of the side-outputs $G1$ and $G3$ is not so simple. We cannot simply drop the rows and write $L11 = (\underline{5} \wedge I) \otimes G0$. This would be unsound since not every execution of path p_1 exiting from $L11$ must necessarily originate in $G0$ and imply that I is present. What *is* correct, is to say that $L11$ is equivalent to $(\underline{5} \wedge I) \otimes G0$ if neither side-output $G1$ or $G3$ ever becomes active is the set of control flows determining the WCRT. Formally, this is $(\neg G1 \wedge \neg G3) \supset (L11 = (\underline{5} \wedge I) \otimes G0)$. Calculating all other paths through G in a similar fashion finally obtains:

$$p_1 : (\neg G1 \wedge \neg G3) \supset (L11 = D_1'' \otimes G0) \qquad D_1'' = (\underline{5} \wedge I) \qquad (25)$$

$$p_2 : (\neg L5 \wedge \neg G3) \supset (L11 = D_2'' \otimes G0) \qquad D_2'' = (\underline{4} \wedge I \wedge \neg I) \qquad (26)$$

$$p_3 : (\neg G1 \wedge \neg L7) \supset (L11 = D_3'' \otimes G0) \qquad D_3'' = (\underline{6} \wedge I \wedge \neg I) \qquad (27)$$

$$p_4 : (\neg L5 \wedge \neg L7) \supset (L11 = D_4'' \otimes G0) \qquad D_4'' = (\underline{5} \wedge \neg I). \qquad (28)$$

The path schedules (25)–(28) can now be woven together in $\mathrm{SGD}[X]$ algebra to obtain the final result $L11 = D \otimes G0$ where $D = D_1'' \oplus D_2'' \oplus D_3'' \oplus D_4'' = \underline{5}$. For this we exploit, among other laws, that $I \wedge \neg I = \bot$, $I \oplus \neg I = \top$ as well as that $x_i \supset (L11 = y_i)$ implies $\oplus_i x_i \supset (L11 = \oplus y_i)$, and the equation

$$(\neg G1 \wedge \neg G3) \oplus (\neg L5 \wedge \neg G3) \oplus (\neg G1 \wedge \neg L7) \oplus (\neg L5 \wedge \neg L7) \equiv \top.$$

The latter is a consequence of the fact that G is single-threaded: Each activation must make a split decision for either exit $L5$ or $G1$ at node v_1 and for either $L7$ or $G3$ at node v_3.

Weaving Nets. WCRT analysis by path enumeration, though sound, is of worst-case exponential complexity. A more efficient way of going about is to exploit dynamic programming. In the following we illustrate this process in $\mathrm{SGD}[X]$ algebra using the net decomposition of G seen in Fig. 4b. The strategy is to propagate WCRT information forward through G, composing sub-nets $N1$, $N2$, $N3$ rather than paths.

We obtain the system matrix of $N1$ first by combining the matrices of v_1 and v_2 from Fig. 5. To compose them we first lift v_2 as an equation in $L5$ and $G1$ to get $L6 = 1\,L5 \oplus \bot\,G1 = (\underline{1}\,\bot) \otimes (L5\ G1)^\mathsf{T}$. Since $G1 = (\bot\,\underline{0}) \otimes (L5\ G1)^\mathsf{T}$ we can compose with equation v_1:

$$\begin{pmatrix} L6 \\ G1 \end{pmatrix} = \begin{pmatrix} \underline{1} & \bot \\ \bot & \underline{0} \end{pmatrix} \otimes \begin{pmatrix} L5 \\ G1 \end{pmatrix} = \begin{pmatrix} \underline{1} & \bot \\ \bot & \underline{0} \end{pmatrix} \otimes \begin{pmatrix} \underline{1} \wedge I \\ \underline{1} \wedge \neg I \end{pmatrix} G0 = \begin{pmatrix} \underline{2} \wedge I \\ \underline{1} \wedge \neg I \end{pmatrix} G0. \quad (29)$$

In a similar fashion one obtains the specifications of sub-blocks $N2$ and $N3$:

$$\begin{pmatrix} G2 \\ G3 \end{pmatrix} = \begin{pmatrix} \underline{2} \wedge I & \underline{2} \wedge I \\ \underline{1} \wedge \neg I & \underline{1} \wedge \neg I \end{pmatrix} \otimes \begin{pmatrix} L6 \\ G1 \end{pmatrix} \qquad L11 = (\underline{1}\ \underline{3}) \otimes \begin{pmatrix} G2 \\ G3 \end{pmatrix}. \quad (30)$$

If we compose the three sub-nets $N1$, $N2$, $N3$ in sequence, our schedule of G all the way from entry point $G0$ to exit $L11$ is complete:

$$L11 = (\underline{1}\ \underline{3}) \otimes \begin{pmatrix} \underline{2} \wedge I & \underline{2} \wedge I \\ \underline{1} \wedge \neg I & \underline{1} \wedge \neg I \end{pmatrix} \otimes \begin{pmatrix} \underline{2} \wedge I \\ \underline{1} \wedge \neg I \end{pmatrix} G0 = \underline{5}\,G0. \quad (31)$$

This is indeed the weight of the longest path p_3 through G.

Bundling Abstractions. There are of course other ways of arriving at the WCRT, corresponding to different network decompositions of G. It is also possible to condense the timing information by *bundling* the inputs and outputs of $N1$, $N2$, $N3$ *before* they are composed. For instance, one might decide to compress the system equation for $N1$ into a single entry-exit delay $N1'$ specified as $L6 \oplus G1 = d\,G0$ which gives the maximal delay d for an execution entering through $G0$ to come out at $L6$ or $G1$, without distinguishing between paths exiting on $L6$ and those exiting on $G1$. This is applied also to $N2$ and $N3$ as indicated in Fig. 4c.

Algebraically, this compression is justified for $N1$ by pre-composing with $(0\ 0)$ which yields $L6 \oplus G1 = (\underline{0}\ \underline{0}) \otimes (L6\ G1)^\mathsf{T} = (\underline{0}\ \underline{0}) \otimes (\underline{2} \wedge I\ \underline{1} \wedge \neg I)^\mathsf{T} \otimes G0 = (\underline{2} \wedge I \oplus \underline{1} \wedge \neg I) \otimes G0$. For $N2$ and $N3$ we also need compression on the input side. For $N2$ this is possible without losing precision and for $N3$ we need the approximation $(G2\ G3)^\mathsf{T} \leq (\underline{0}\ \underline{0})^\mathsf{T} \otimes (G2 \oplus G3)$. We get approximations $N2'$ and $N3'$ from (29) and (30):

$$G2 \oplus G3 = (\underline{0}\ \underline{0}) \otimes \begin{pmatrix} \underline{2} \wedge I & \underline{2} \wedge I \\ \underline{1} \wedge \neg I & \underline{1} \wedge \neg I \end{pmatrix} \otimes \begin{pmatrix} L6 \\ G1 \end{pmatrix} = (\underline{2} \wedge I \oplus \underline{1} \wedge \neg I)(L6 \oplus G1)$$

$$L11 = (\underline{1}\ \underline{3}) \otimes \begin{pmatrix} G2 \\ G3 \end{pmatrix} \leq (\underline{1}\ \underline{3}) \otimes \begin{pmatrix} \underline{0} \\ \underline{0} \end{pmatrix} (G2 \oplus G3) = 3\,(G2 \oplus G3).$$

Composing $N1'$, $N2'$, $N3'$ is more efficient than composing $N1$, $N2$, $N3$ since it involves only scalars rather than matrices.

Parallel Composition and WCRT Analysis. The main thread T in Fig. 1c is the parallel composition of threads G and H, synchronised by the fork and join nodes v_0 and v_{16}, respectively. Even without reducing threads G and H to their externally observable system functions (21) and (31) we can compose them in parallel. All we need are equations for the fork and join nodes. The fork node v_0 activates both $G0$ and $H0$, when it is reached, taking 3 ics (2 PAR and 1 PARE, see Fig. 1d):

$$(G0 \; H0)^\mathsf{T} = (\underline{3} \; \underline{3})^\mathsf{T} \otimes T0. \tag{32}$$

The join node v_{16} becomes active as soon as one of G or H reaches its termination control. The join finishes its activity in the tick when both have arrived. It then passes control and reactivates the parent at $L20$. At each input $L11$, $L19$ the join behaves like a synchroniser with latching behaviour. We define the operator $\mathsf{sync}(C, R)$, which waits for C to become active at which point it inherits the cost of C. From the next tick onwards it takes a constant cost[2], say 2 ics, until it is reset by R. This leads to the recursive definitions

$$\mathsf{sync}(C, R) = \neg X R \wedge (C \oplus X(\underline{2} \wedge \neg\neg\mathsf{sync}(C, R))) \tag{33}$$

$$L20 = \mathsf{sync}(L11, L20) \otimes \mathsf{sync}(L19, L20) \tag{34}$$

where $L20$ adds up the delays from both threads by $\otimes$ in line with the multi-threading model of execution.

The equations (32)–(34) for fork and join are a surprisingly simple and compositional way of specifying timed concurrent structures. To illustrate let us revisit our sample simulation from Sect. 5 (see also Fig. 1b). The threads G and H arrive at their termination points with $L11 = 6{:}\bot{:}\bot{:}6{:}\bot$ and $L19 = \bot{:}\bot{:}7{:}\bot$, respectively. Thread G terminates in tick 1 and 4 while H finishes only in tick 3. The cost arising from synchronising G is $\mathsf{sync}(L11, L19) = 6{:}2{:}\bot{:}6{:}\underline{2}$ which is 6 at G's first termination time, then 2 while waiting for H, again 6 at the next re-entry in tick 4, when G terminates a second time. But since then H never terminates, the join stays active, generating cost 2 in each subsequent tick. On the other side we have $\mathsf{sync}(L19, L11) = \bot{:}\bot{:}7{:}\bot$, which is the completion time for H. There are no extra cost as H does not need to wait for G. The output of the join has cost $L20 = \bot{:}\bot{:}9{:}\bot$ which at termination in tick 3 combines the 7 ic cost from H plus 2 ic overhead for the join.

We are now nearly complete with our story. The equations tells us for each stimulation environment and control $v \in \mathbb{V}$ if and when v is reachable in any tick. The equations can be used for formal analysis, compiler verification, program transformations, timing-accurate simulation or even directly for implementation.

Here we are interested in obtaining the total WCRT of a program. When concurrency is present, the WCRT of a thread t is not the WCRT of any single control, but the WCRT of a set of controls. It is the worst case cost, over all ticks, of any set of controls that are potentially *concurrent* in t. A set of controls $\mathbb{C} \subseteq \mathbb{V}$ is *concurrent*, written $conc(\mathbb{C})$, if all its elements belong to different child threads. For instance, $\{L11, L14\}$ is concurrent but $\{L6, L11\}$ is not. Concurrent controls

---

[2] In the KEP processor the join is executed at each tick until both threads have terminated, during which time it invokes some constant overhead cost.

execute in independent KEP hardware threads which are interleaved, whence their costs are added. In the search for such $\mathbb{C}$ we may restrict to the *completion controls* $cmpl(t)$ of a thread t. These are the controls in which t may terminate or pause. For instance, $cmpl(G) = \{L11\}$ and $cmpl(H) = \{in(v_9), in(v_{13}), L19\}$. For parent threads these must be included, i.e., we have $cmpl(T) = cmpl(G) \cup cmpl(H) \cup \{L20\}$. The control $L20$ describes the situations in which T terminates. The controls in $cmpl(G)$ are concurrent to those in $cmpl(H)$ and vice versa. None of them is concurrent with $L20$ which happens in their parent.

The worst case reaction time $\mathsf{wcrt}(t)$ of a synchronous program t the maximal sum of WCRT of any set of concurrent completion controls in any tick,

$$\mathsf{wcrt}(t) = max\{(\bigotimes_{v \in \mathbb{C}} v)[1] \mid \mathbb{C} \subseteq cmpl(t), conc(\mathbb{C})\}, \tag{35}$$

where $(\bigotimes_{v \in \mathbb{C}} v)[1] = max\{\bigotimes_{v \in \mathbb{C}} v(i) \mid i \geq 0\} = max\{\sum_{v \in \mathbb{C}} v(i) \mid i \geq 0\}$. Explicit solutions of (35) are non-trivial as it maximises over an infinite number of ticks i and choices of sets $\mathbb{C}$ whose number may grow exponentially with the number of threads. We do not know of any algorithm to solve (35) in its general form, yet solutions exist for special cases.

For normal clock-guarded synchronous programs the fps v are rational and thus can be represented as finite input-output tick cost automata, called IO-BTCA [23]. A given sum $\bigotimes_{v \in \mathbb{C}} v$ of controls can then be obtained by synchronous composition of automata. This is a well-understood construction, though it requires symbolic reasoning on boolean signals and is subject to the state-space explosion problem. The period (number of states) in the fps $v_1 \otimes v_2$ may be the product of the periods of v_1 and v_2. The automata-theoretic approach has been explored in [25] for timed concurrent control flow graphs TCCFGs (similar to CKAGs) using UPPAAL, but it does not scale well.

The situation is simpler for autonomous systems without input signals, which reduce to ultimately periodic sequences over $\mathbb{Z}_\infty$. Any IO-BTCAs can be over-approximated to an autonomous system, called *tick cost automaton* TCA, by eliminating signal dependencies, as discussed in Sect. 5.2, replacing each reference to a signal S or its negation $\neg S$ by $\underline{\top}$. Such approximations are sound but ignore inter-thread communication. The advantage is that the autonomous case of (35) can be translated into an (0/1) ILP. This *implicit path enumeration (IPE)* technique for WCRT analysis yields much better results [29] compared to the automata-theoretic approach.

The IPE approach has been considered the most efficient technique for autonomous approximations until recently, when explicit algebraic solutions for (35) have been attempted. In [23] it is observed that for the natural class of so-called *patient* TCA the computation of the normal form for each v is polynomial. This reduces the problem of computing the tick-wise additions $\bigotimes_{v \in \mathbb{C}} v$ for ultimately periodic sequences v to the *tick alignment problem* studied in [20, 23] which can be solved using graph-theoretic algorithms. This has led to significant speed-up in the original ILP implementation of [29]. Still, even under signal abstraction, the theoretical complexity of computing the periodic normal form of a control $v \in cmpl(T)$ and solving the tick alignment problem remain open problems. Rather interestingly, recent experiments implementing the explicit fixed point construction mentioned in Sect. 5.2 indicate that for autonomous systems both problems may be polynomial in practice [28], despite the theoretical exponential blow-up.

The fastest polynomial algorithm to date for solving (35), unsurprisingly, is also the most over-approximating one. The dynamic programming approach of [4] not only abstracts from signals but also from state dependencies, as explained in Sect. 5.2. It bundles all state controls σ_i of a given program block t into a single pair $out(t) = \oplus_i out(\sigma_i)$, $in(t) = \oplus_i in(\sigma_i)$. The system equation of t then becomes $(\xi \, in(t))^\mathsf{T} = D_t \otimes (\zeta \, out(t))^\mathsf{T}$ where D_t is a matrix of scalar constants. With the register equation $out(t) = X \odot tick(in(t))$ for the feedback, the closed solution is attainable in a single fixed point iteration, in $\mathcal{O}(1)$ time. Moreover, the fps for each control v is of the form $d_0{:}\underline{d_1}$ a delay for the initial tick and all subsequent ones being identical. Hence the calculation of $\bigotimes_{v \in \mathbb{C}} v$ is done in $\mathcal{O}(1)$ time, too. Moreover, the fact that each control has only two entries $v = v(0){:}\underline{v(1)}$ helps greatly in the maximisation over all $\mathbb{C}$: For each given i the tick-wise maximum $\mathsf{wcrt}_i(t) = max\{\bigotimes_{v \in \mathbb{C}} v(i) \mid \mathbb{C} \subseteq cmpl(t), conc(\mathbb{C})\}$ can be obtained bottom-up by induction over the thread hierarchy. The reason is that in the maximum $\mathsf{wcrt}_i(t) = \bigotimes_{v \in \mathbb{C}_{max}} v(i)$ the constituent controls $\mathbb{C}' = \mathbb{C}_{max} \cap cmpl(t')$ for each child t' of t are not only concurrent $conc(\mathbb{C}')$, but necessarily constitute the tick-specific maximum $\mathsf{wcrt}_i(t') = \bigotimes_{v \in \mathbb{C}'} v(i)$ for the child, too.

6   Related Work and Conclusions

A rudimentary version of the WCRT interface model has been proposed originally in [22]. That work focused on the algorithmic aspects of the modular timing analysis of synchronous programs. It was implemented in the backend of a compiler for Esterel, analysing reactive assembly code running on the Kiel Esterel Processor (KEP). A rigorous mathematical definition of the behavioural semantics of the interface models was presented in [21]. The axiomatic approach of [21] highlighted the essentially logical nature of the WCRT interfaces. It was shown how the logical interface language can specify, and relate with each other, standard analysis problems such as shortest path, task scheduling or max-flow problems. However, the logical theory developed by [22] and [21] was still restricted to the modelling of the purely combinational behaviour of a synchronous module, i.e., its reactive behaviour during a single tick. This yields the worst-case timing over *all* states rather than just the *reachable* ones. In general, this is an over-approximation of the exact WCRT. The tick dependency of WCRT behaviour, also called *tick alignment*, was subsequently studied in [23]. It was observed that the combinational timing of single ticks can be modelled in max-min-plus algebra, which is the intuitionistic algebra of SGD. This makes it possible to express the timing behaviour of a synchronous module over arbitrary sequences of clock ticks as formal power series. The composition of synchronous systems arises from the lifting of SGD algebra to formal power series. The paper [23] investigates the tick alignment of timing in its pure form, i.e, without signal communication between concurrent synchronous threads. This induces a form of data abstraction which reduces the WCRT analysis to the maximum weighted clique problem on tick alignment graphs. It is shown in [23] how this reduction permits a considerable speed-up of an existing ILP algorithm that was proposed earlier. By exploiting the logical expressiveness of SGD algebra, formal power series can handle not only tick-dependent timing but also signal communication. This is applied in [1, 28] to obtain the full behavioural semantics of timed and concurrent synchronous control flow graphs in a structural fashion.

In this paper we revisit this earlier work on WCRT interface algebra and in doing so combine, for the first time, the algebraic semantics of [1, 23, 28] with the logical setting of [21, 22]. This is the first timing-enriched and causality-sensitive semantics of SCP which is modular and covers full tick behaviour. The SGD[X] equations constitute a cycle-accurate model and can be used for program analysis and verification. This can also be used to compile Esterel via CKAG control-flow graphs directly into data flow format. In future work it will be interesting to explore the possibility of generating hardware circuits and compare with existing hardware compilation chains for Esterel. On the theoretical side we plan to study algebraic axiomatisation for SGD[X] and its expressiveness, specifically its relationship with ILP.

Dedication

The first author is indebted to Bernhard Steffen for his long continued guidance and encouragement both as a friend and mentor. My first training in academic writing was as a co-author of an article with Bernhard in 1989, when we were both in the LFCS at Edinburgh University. Some years later, I spent a most enjoyable time as a member of the inspiring research environment which Bernhard had created at Passau University. Bernhard's support was not only instrumental for my successful habilitation at Passau. He also ensured, at the right moment, that I would feel pressured to find a secure permanent research job, rather than clinging to yet another limited term position. Talking research, is was him who suggested me to look to synchronous programming as an application for my work on concurrency theory and constructive logic. In this way, the work reported here originally started with a far-sighted vision of Bernhard's.

Acknowledgements. This work was supported by the German Research Council DFG under grant ME-1427/6-2 (PRETSY2).

References

1. Aguado, J., Mendler, M., Wang, J.J., Bodin, B., Roop, P.: Compositional timing-aware semantics for synchronous programming. In: Forum on Specification & Design Languages (FDL 2017), pp. 1–8. IEEE, Verona, September 2017
2. Baccelli, F.L., Cohen, G., Olsder, G.J., Quadrat, J.P.: Synchronisation and Linearity. Wiley, New York (1992)

3. Berry, G., Cosserat, L.: The ESTEREL synchronous programming language and its mathematical semantics. In: Brookes, S.D., Roscoe, A.W., Winskel, G. (eds.) CONCURRENCY 1984. LNCS, vol. 197, pp. 389–448. Springer, Heidelberg (1985). https://doi.org/10.1007/3-540-15670-4_19
4. Boldt, M., Traulsen, C., von Hanxleden, R.: Compilation and worst-case reaction time analysis for multithreaded Esterel processing. EURASIP J. Embed. Syst. **2008**(1), 4 (2008)
5. van Dalen, D.: Intuitionistic logic. In: Gabbay, D., Guenthner, F. (eds.) Handbook of Philosophical Logic, vol. III, chap. 4, pp. 225–339. Reidel, Dordrecht (1986)
6. Dummett, M.: A propositional calculus with a denumerable matrix. J. Symb. Log. **24**, 97–106 (1959)
7. Edwards, S.A., Lee, E.A.: The case for the precision timed (PRET) machine. In: DAC 2007, San Diego, USA, June 2007
8. Edwards, S.A., Kim, S., Lee, E.A., Liu, I., Patel, H.D., Schoeberl, M.: A disruptive computer design idea: architectures with repeatable timing. In: Proceedings of IEEE International Conference on Computer Design (ICCD 2009). IEEE, October 2009
9. Fermüller, C.G.: Parallel dialogue games and hypersequents for intermediate logics. In: Cialdea Mayer, M., Pirri, F. (eds.) TABLEAUX 2003. LNCS (LNAI), vol. 2796, pp. 48–64. Springer, Heidelberg (2003). https://doi.org/10.1007/978-3-540-45206-5_7
10. Geilen, M., Stuijk, S.: Worst-case performance analysis of synchronous dataflow networks. In: CODES+ISSS 2010. ACM, Scottsdale, October 2010
11. Hájek, P.: Metamathematics of Fuzzy Logic. Kluwer, Dordrecht (1998)
12. von Hanxleden, R., Li, X., Roop, P., Salcic, Z., Yoong, L.H.: Reactive processing for reactive systems. ERCIM News **66**, 28–29 (2006)
13. von Hanxleden, R., Mendler, M., Traulsen, C.: WCRT algebra and scheduling interfaces for Esterel-style synchronous multi-threading. Technical report 0807, Christian-Albrechts-Univ. Kiel, Department of Computer Science, June 2008. http://rtsys.informatik.uni-kiel.de/~biblio/downloads/papers/report-0807.pdf
14. Hirai, Y.: A lambda calculus for Gödel–Dummett logic capturing waitfreedom. In: Schrijvers, T., Thiemann, P. (eds.) FLOPS 2012. LNCS, vol. 7294, pp. 151–165. Springer, Heidelberg (2012). https://doi.org/10.1007/978-3-642-29822-6_14
15. Ju, L., Huynh, B.K., Chakraborty, S., Roychoudhury, A.: Context-sensitive timing analysis of Esterel programs. In: Proceedings of 46th Annual Design Automation Conference (DAC 2009), pp. 870–873. ACM, New York (2009)
16. Ju, L., Huynh, B.K., Roychoudhury, A., Chakraborty, S.: Performance debugging of Esterel specifications. Real-Time Syst. **48**(5), 570–600 (2012)
17. Kuo, M., Sinha, R., Roop, P.S.: Efficient WCRT analysis of synchronous programs using reachability. In: Proceedings of 48th Design Automation Conference (DAC 2011), pp. 480–485 (2011)
18. Li, X., von Hanxleden, R.: Multi-threaded reactive programming–the Kiel Esterel Processor. IEEE Trans. Comput. **61**(3), 337–349 (2012)
19. Lickly, B., Liu, I., Kim, S., Patel, H.D., Edwards, S.A., Lee, E.A.: Predictable programming on a precision timed architecture. In: Proceedings of the Conference on Compilers, Architectures, and Synthesis of Embedded Systems (CASES 2008), Atlanta USA, October 2008, pp. 137–146 (2008)
20. Mendler, M., Bodin, B., Roop, P., Wang, J.J.: WCRT for synchronous programs: studying the tick alignment problem. Technical report 95, University of Bamberg, Faculty for Information Systems and Applied Computer Sciences, August 2014

21. Mendler, M.: An algebra of synchronous scheduling interfaces. In: Legay, A., Caillaud, B. (eds.) Proceedings Foundations for Interface Technologies (FIT 2010), EPTCS, Paris, France, vol. 46, pp. 28–48 (2010)
22. Mendler, M., von Hanxleden, R., Traulsen, C.: WCRT algebra and interfaces for Esterel-Style synchronous processing. In: Proceedings of Design, Automation and Test in Europe Conference (DATE 2009), Nice, France, April 2009
23. Mendler, M., Roop, P.S., Bodin, B.: A novel WCET semantics of synchronous programs. In: Fränzle, M., Markey, N. (eds.) FORMATS 2016. LNCS, vol. 9884, pp. 195–210. Springer, Cham (2016). https://doi.org/10.1007/978-3-319-44878-7_12
24. Raymond, P., Maiza, C., Parent-Vigouroux, C., Carrier, F., Asavoae, M.: Timing analysis enhancement for synchronous programs. Real-Time Syst. **51**, 192–220 (2015)
25. Roop, P.S., Andalam, S., von Hanxleden, R., Yuan, S., Traulsen, C.: Tight WCRT analysis of synchronous C programs. In: Proceedings of Compilers, Architecture, and Synthesis for Embedded Systems (CASES 2009), pp. 205–214 (2009)
26. Schoeberl, M.: Time-predictable computer architecture. EURASIP J. Embed. Syst. **2009**, 2:1–2:17 (2009)
27. Waez, M.T.B., Dingel, J., Rudie, K.: A survey of timed automata for the development of real-time systems. Comput. Sci. Rev. **9**, 1–26 (2013)
28. Wang, J., Mendler, M., Roop, P., Bodin, B.: Timing analysis of synchronous programs using WCRT algebra: scalability through abstraction. ACM TECS **16**(5s), 177:1–177:19 (2017)
29. Wang, J.J., Roop, P.S., Andalam, S.: ILPc: a novel approach for scalable timing analysis of synchronous programs. In: CASES 2013, Montreal, Canada, September–October 2013, pp. 20:1–20:10 (2013)
30. Yip, E., Roop, P.S., Biglari-Abhari, M., Girault, A.: Programming and timing analysis of parallel programs on multicores. In: Proceedings on Application of Concurrency to System Design (ACSD 2013), pp. 160–169. IEEE (2013)

Intersection Types in Java:
Back to the Future

Mariangiola Dezani-Ciancaglini[1], Paola Giannini[2([⊠])], and Betti Venneri[3]

[1] Dipartimento di Informatica, Università di Torino, Turin, Italy
`dezani@di.unito.it`
[2] Dipartimento di Scienze e Innovazione Tecnologica,
Università del Piemonte Orientale, Alessandria, Italy
`paola.giannini@uniupo.it`
[3] Dipartimento di Statistica, Informatica, Applicazioni,
Università di Firenze, Florence, Italy
`venneri@unifi.it`

Abstract. In this paper we figure out the future of intersection types in Java developments, based both on the primary meaning of the intersection type constructor and on the present approach in Java. In our vision, the current use of intersection types will be extended in two directions. Firstly, intersections will be allowed to appear as types of fields, types of formal parameters and return values of methods, therefore they will be significantly used as target types for λ-expressions anywhere. Secondly, the notion of functional interface will be extended to any intersection of interfaces, including also several abstract methods with different signatures. Thus a single target type will be able to express multiple, possibly unrelated, properties of one λ-expression.

We formalise our proposal through a minimal Java core extended with these novel features and we prove the type safety property.

1 Introduction

Intersection types have been invented originally for the λ-calculus to increase the set of terms having meaning types [3]. The power of this type system lies on the fact that the set of untyped λ-terms having types is exactly the set of normalising terms, that is terminating programs. This prevents the adoption of this full system in programming languages, but the intuition behind intersection types can be particularly inspiring for language designers looking for mechanisms to improve flexibility of typechecking.

Mariangiola Dezani-Ciancaglini—Partially supported by EU H2020-644235 Rephrase project, EU H2020-644298 HyVar project, IC1402 ARVI and Ateneo/CSP project RunVar.
Paola Giannini—This original research has the financial support of the Università del Piemonte Orientale.

T. Margaria et al. (Eds.): Steffen Festschrift, LNCS 11200, pp. 68–86, 2019.
https://doi.org/10.1007/978-3-030-22348-9_6

The development of the successive versions of Java shows a careful and even more significant entry of intersection types in the shape of intersection (denoted by &) of nominal types. In particular, we remark that the version Java 5 introduced generic types and intersection types later appeared as bounds of generic type variables. It is worth noting that already in the last century Büchi and Weck [2] had proposed to extend Java 1 by allowing intersection types (called there compound types) as parameter types and return types of methods, by showing interesting examples of their use for structuring and reusing code. Java still does not allow these uses of intersections, that are confined to be target types of type-casts. However, one could assume that the proposal of [2] is now realised, in some fashion, in Java with generic types, given that a generic type variable, bounded by an intersection type, can appear as parameter type as well as return type of a method. Unfortunately, the above argument does not fit the case of λ-expressions, which are the key novelty of Java 8, since a generic type variable cannot be instantiated by the type of a λ-expression. Java λ-expressions are *poly expressions* in the sense they can have various types according to context requirements. Each context prescribes the *target type* for the λ-expression used in that context, and Java does not compile when this target type is unspecified. The target type can be either a *functional interface* (i.e., an interface with a single abstract method) or an intersection of interfaces that induces a functional interface. Notably, the λ-expression must match the signature of the unique abstract method of its functional interface. When we cast a λ-expression to an intersection type, this intersection becomes its target type, and so the λ-expression exploits its poly expression nature, having all the types of the intersection. So, in addition to implementing the abstract method, it also acquires all the behaviours that are represented by the default methods defined in the various interfaces forming the intersection. However, when the λ-expression is passed as argument to a method or returned by a method, then its target type cannot be an intersection type. Our proposal wants to free intersection types of all those bindings and restrictions, so that they can appear as types of fields, types of formal parameters and value results of methods, thus playing the role of target types for λ-expressions anywhere these expressions can be used.

The second limitation of Java we want to overcome relates to the definition of functional interface, which must contain one and *only one* abstract method. In Java a λ-expression is able to match multiple headers of abstract methods, with different signatures, but its target type in each context expresses just one of such signatures. This can be frustrating for Java programmers in many situations, where they are compelled to use several copies of the same λ-expression, each one matching a single signature. Completely different, the main idea behind intersection type theory is that an intersection type expresses multiple, possibly unrelated, properties of one term in a single type. The prototypical example is represented by the term $\lambda x.x\,x$, denoting the auto-application function, which can be assigned, for instance, the type $(\alpha\&(\alpha \rightarrow \beta)) \rightarrow \beta$, where α, β are arbitrary types and the arrow denotes the function type constructor. The intersection type $\alpha\&(\alpha \rightarrow \beta)$ says that the parameter must behave both as function and as argument of itself. We can retrieve this powerful feature from intersection type theory to Java, by allowing any intersection of interfaces to be a functional interface having multiple abstract methods. For example, let us consider the method

```
C auto (Arg&Fun x){return x.mFun(x).mArg(new C( ));}
```

where C is any class (without fields for simplicity), Arg and Fun are two Java interfaces with the abstract methods C mArg (C y) and Arg mFun (Arg z), respectively. Although the method is greedy with requirements about its argument, many λ-expressions are ready to match the target type Arg&Fun, first of all the simple identity x->x.

In conclusion, this paper wants to flash forwards to a future development of Java, in which the use of intersection types is extended in the two directions discussed above, in order to study its formal properties. To this end, we formalise the calculus FJP&λ (Featherweight Java with Polymorphic Intersection types and λ-expressions), based on the core language FJ&λ [1], that models the treatment of λ-expressions and intersection types in Java 8. As main result, we prove that FJP&λ preserves type-safety.

2 Syntax

In defining the syntax of FJP&λ we follow the notational convention of [1], recalled here for self-containment. We use A, B, C, D to denote classes, I, J to denote interfaces, T, U to denote nominal pre-types, i.e., either classes or interfaces; f, g to denote field names; m to denote method names; t to denote terms; x, y to denote variables, including the special variable this; τ, σ to denote pre-types as defined below. We use $\overrightarrow{I}$ as a shorthand for the (comma separated) list $I_1, \ldots, I_n$ and $\overline{M}$ as a shorthand for the sequence $M_1 \ldots M_n$ and similarly for the other names. Sometimes order in lists and sequences is unimportant. In rules, we write both $\overline{N}$ as a declaration and $\overrightarrow{N}$ for some name N: the meaning is that a sequence is declared and the list is obtained from the sequence adding commas.

The notation $\overline{\tau f}$; abbreviates $\tau_1 f_1; \ldots \tau_n f_n$; and $\overrightarrow{\tau} \overrightarrow{f}$ abbreviates $\tau_1 f_1, \ldots, \tau_n f_n$ (likewise $\overrightarrow{\tau} \overrightarrow{x}$) and this.$\overline{f} = \overline{f}$; abbreviates this.$f_1 = f_1; \ldots$ this.$f_n = f_n;$. Lists and sequences of interfaces, fields, parameters and methods are assumed

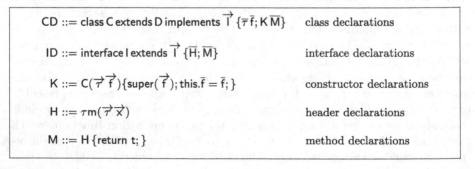

$CD ::= $ class C extends D implements $\overrightarrow{I}$ $\{\overline{\tau f}; K\overline{M}\}$	class declarations
$ID ::= $ interface I extends $\overrightarrow{I}$ $\{\overline{H}; \overline{M}\}$	interface declarations
$K ::= C(\overrightarrow{\tau} \overrightarrow{f})\{super(\overrightarrow{f}); this.\overline{f} = \overline{f}; \}$	constructor declarations
$H ::= \tau m(\overrightarrow{\tau} \overrightarrow{x})$	header declarations
$M ::= H \{return\ t; \}$	method declarations

Fig. 1. Declarations

$$CT(\mathsf{I}) = \mathsf{interface}\,\mathsf{I}\,\mathsf{extends}\,\overrightarrow{\mathsf{I}}\,\{\overline{\mathsf{H}};\overline{\mathsf{M}}\}$$
$$\overline{\mathsf{A\text{-}mh}(\mathsf{I}) = \overrightarrow{\overline{\mathsf{H}}} \uplus \mathsf{A\text{-}mh}(\overrightarrow{\mathsf{I}})}$$

$$CT(\mathsf{I}) = \mathsf{interface}\,\mathsf{I}\,\mathsf{extends}\,\overrightarrow{\mathsf{I}}\,\{\overline{\mathsf{H}};\overline{\mathsf{M}}\} \quad \overline{\mathsf{M}} = \overline{\mathsf{H}'\{\mathsf{return}\,\mathsf{t};\}}$$
$$\overline{\mathsf{D\text{-}mh}(\mathsf{I}) = \overrightarrow{\overline{\mathsf{H}'}} \uplus \mathsf{D\text{-}mh}(\overrightarrow{\mathsf{I}})}$$

$$\mathsf{A\text{-}mh}(\mathsf{I}_1,\ldots,\mathsf{I}_n) = \mathsf{A\text{-}mh}(\mathsf{I}_1\&\ldots\&\mathsf{I}_n) = \mathsf{A\text{-}mh}(\mathsf{C}\&\mathsf{I}_1\&\ldots\&\mathsf{I}_n) = \uplus_{1\le i\le n}\,\mathsf{A\text{-}mh}(\mathsf{I}_i)$$

$$\mathsf{D\text{-}mh}(\mathsf{I}_1,\ldots,\mathsf{I}_n) = \mathsf{D\text{-}mh}(\mathsf{I}_1\&\ldots\&\mathsf{I}_n) = \mathsf{D\text{-}mh}(\mathsf{C}\&\mathsf{I}_1\&\ldots\&\mathsf{I}_n) = \uplus_{1\le i\le n}\,\mathsf{D\text{-}mh}(\mathsf{I}_i)$$
$$\text{if } \mathsf{D\text{-}mh}(\mathsf{I}_j) \cap \mathsf{D\text{-}mh}(\mathsf{I}_\ell) \ne \epsilon \text{ implies either } \mathsf{I}_j <: \mathsf{I}_\ell \text{ or } \mathsf{I}_\ell <: \mathsf{I}_j$$

$$\mathsf{mh}(\mathsf{Object}) = \epsilon$$

$$CT(\mathsf{C}) = \mathsf{class}\,\mathsf{C}\,\mathsf{extends}\,\mathsf{D}\,\mathsf{implements}\,\overrightarrow{\mathsf{I}}\,\{\overline{\tau}\,\overline{\mathsf{f}};\mathsf{K}\,\overline{\mathsf{M}}\} \quad \overline{\mathsf{M}} = \overline{\mathsf{H}\{\mathsf{return}\,\mathsf{t};\}}$$
$$\overline{\mathsf{mh}(\mathsf{C}) = \overrightarrow{\overline{\mathsf{H}}} \uplus \mathsf{mh}(\mathsf{D}) \uplus \mathsf{mh}(\overrightarrow{\mathsf{I}})}$$

$$\mathsf{mh}(\overrightarrow{\mathsf{I}}) = \mathsf{A\text{-}mh}(\overrightarrow{\mathsf{I}}) \uplus \mathsf{D\text{-}mh}(\overrightarrow{\mathsf{I}}) \qquad \text{if } \mathsf{A\text{-}mh}(\overrightarrow{\mathsf{I}}) \cap \mathsf{D\text{-}mh}(\overrightarrow{\mathsf{I}}) = \epsilon$$

$$\mathsf{mh}(\mathsf{I}_1\&\ldots\&\mathsf{I}_n) = \mathsf{mh}(\mathsf{I}_1,\ldots,\mathsf{I}_n) \qquad \mathsf{mh}(\mathsf{C}\&\mathsf{I}_1\&\ldots\&\mathsf{I}_n) = \mathsf{mh}(\mathsf{C}) \uplus \mathsf{mh}(\mathsf{I}_1,\ldots,\mathsf{I}_n)$$

Fig. 2. Functions A-mh, D-mh and mh

to contain no duplicate names. The keyword super, used only in constructor's body, refers to the superclass constructor. Figure 1 gives declarations: CD ranges over class declarations; ID ranges over interface declarations; K ranges over constructor declarations; H ranges over method header (or abstract method) declarations; M ranges over method (or concrete method) declarations.

A main novelty of FJP&λ with respect to Java is that the types of fields, parameters and return terms are intersections instead of nominal types. The syntax of FJP&λ is obtained from the syntax of FJ&λ with default methods of [1] by replacing everywhere nominal pre-types by arbitrary pre-types. As usual a class declaration specifies the name of the class, its superclass and the implemented interfaces. A class has fields $\overline{\mathsf{f}}$, a single constructor K and methods $\overline{\mathsf{M}}$. The instance variables $\overline{\mathsf{f}}$ are added to the ones of its superclasses and should have names disjoint from these. An interface declaration lists the extended interfaces, the method headers, and the default methods (omitting the keyword default). The arguments of the constructors correspond to the immutable values of the class fields. The inherited fields are initialised by the call to super, while the new fields are initialised by assignments. Headers relate method names with result and parameter pre-types. Methods are headers with bodies, i.e., return expressions. We omit implements and extends when the lists of interfaces are empty.

Object is a special class without fields and methods, does not require a declaration and it is the top of the class hierarchy.

A *class table CT* is a mapping from nominal types to their declarations. A *program* is a pair (CT, t). In the following we assume a fixed class table.

Pre-types (ranged over by τ, σ) are either nominal types or intersections of:
- interfaces or
- a class (in leftmost position) and any number of interfaces.

Using ι to denote either an interface or an intersection of interfaces we define:

$$\tau ::= C \mid \iota \mid C\&\iota \quad \text{where} \quad \iota ::= I \mid \iota\&I$$

The notation $C[\&\iota]$ means either the class C or the pre-type $C\&\iota$.

Types are pre-types whose method declarations are consistent. To define consistency we use the partial functions A-mh, D-mh and mh that map pre-types to lists of method headers, considered as sets, see Fig. 2. As in [1], A-mh and D-mh collect abstract and default methods in interfaces, whereas the function mh collects all method headers of interfaces and classes. We use ϵ for the empty list. With $\uplus$ we denote the set-theoretic union of lists of method headers, that is defined only if the same method name does not occur with different pre-types.

For example C mArg(C x) $\uplus$ Arg mFun(Arg x) is defined, while

C mArg(C x) $\uplus$ Arg mArg(Arg x)

is not defined.

As we can see from the penultimate line of Fig. 2, function mh is defined for a list of interfaces only if the same method name is not declared both as abstract and default method, see page 292 of [6].

Definition 1 (Types). *A pre-type τ is a type if* mh(τ) *is defined.*

For example, if we consider
interface Arg {C mArg(C x);} and interface Fun {Arg mFun(Arg x);}
then Arg&Fun is a type; whereas if we define
interface ArgD {D mArg(D x);}
where the class D differs from the class C, then the pre-type Arg&ArgD is not a type, since mh(Arg) $\uplus$ mh(ArgD) is not defined.

Notice that the present definition of type coincides with that in [1], and therefore all types here are Java types.

In the following we will always restrict $T, U, \tau, \sigma, \iota$ to range over types. The typing rules for classes and interfaces (see Fig. 11) assure that all nominal pre-types in a well-formed class table are types.

Terms are defined in Fig. 3. Terms are a subset of Java terms, with the addition that λ-*expressions* may or may not be *decorated by intersections* of interfaces. The intersection of interfaces decorating a λ-expression represents its *target type*. *Values*, ranged over by v, u, are either proper values or pure λ-expressions. *Proper values*, ranged over by w, are either objects or decorated λ-expressions. Pure λ-expressions are written by the user, whereas decorated λ-expressions are generated by reduction. A parameter p of a λ-expression can

$t ::=$		terms	$v ::=$		values
	v	value		w	proper value
	x	variable		$\overrightarrow{p} \to t$	pure λ-expression
	$t.f$	field access	$w ::=$		proper values
	$t.m(\overrightarrow{t})$	method invocation		$\text{new } C(\overrightarrow{V})$	object
	$\text{new } C(\overrightarrow{t})$	object		$(\overrightarrow{p} \to t)^\iota$	decorated λ-expression
	$(\tau)\,t$	cast	$p ::=$		parameters
				x	untyped
				$\tau\,x$	typed

Fig. 3. Terms

$$\frac{CT(C) = \text{class } C \text{ extends } D \text{ implements } \overrightarrow{I}\ \{\overrightarrow{\tau\,f}; K\,\overline{M}\}}{C <: D \quad C <: I_j \quad \forall I_j \in \overrightarrow{I}}\ [<: C]$$

$$\frac{CT(I) = \text{interface } I \text{ extends } \overrightarrow{I}\ \{\overline{H}; \overline{M}\}}{I <: I_j \quad \forall I_j \in \overrightarrow{I}}\ [<: I] \qquad \tau <: \text{Object} \ [<: \text{Object}]$$

$$\frac{\tau <: T_i \quad \text{for all } 1 \le i \le n}{\tau <: T_1 \& \ldots \& T_n}\ [<: \&R] \qquad \frac{T_i <: \tau \quad \text{for some } 1 \le i \le n}{T_1 \& \ldots \& T_n <: \tau}\ [<: \&L]$$

Fig. 4. Subtyping

be either untyped or typed, but typing rules forbid to mix untyped and typed parameters in the same λ-expression. A difference with [1] is the freedom of decorating λ-expression with interfaces and intersections of interfaces without requiring exactly one abstract method as in Java (see [6], page 321).

We use t_λ to range over pure λ-expressions.

The *subtype relation* $<:$ is the reflexive and transitive closure of the relation induced by the rules of Fig. 4. It takes into account both the hierarchy between nominal types induced by the class table and the set theoretic properties of intersection. Rule [$<: \&R$] formalises the statement in the last two lines of page 677 in [6].

Our definition of intersection types is consistent with the requirements of the Java Language Specification [6] (pages 70–71). In particular, on one side from Definition 1, τ is a type if "$\text{mh}(\tau)$ defined", and therefore we can define a nominal class that is a subtype of τ. On the other, the existence of a nominal class which is a subtype of τ assures $\text{mh}(\tau)$ defined since rule [$C\ OK$] in Fig. 11 requires $\text{mh}(C)$ defined and $\text{mh}(\tau) \subseteq \text{mh}(C)$, see the proof of Lemma 1(2).

Notice that $\iota <: \text{Object} \& \iota <: \iota$ for all ι, but these types cannot be considered equivalent, since ι can be the target type of a λ-expression whereas $\text{Object} \& \iota$ cannot.

3   Operational Semantics

For the evaluation and typing rules we need the auxiliary definitions of Figs. 5 and 6. The fields of a class C, dubbed fields(C), are specified by a list of pairs associating names and types of the fields that are defined in C or in one of its superclasses. To give the signature of methods, i.e. the parameters and result types, we specify method name and type. Moreover, it is useful to distinguish between abstract and default method in interfaces. Therefore, we have three lookup functions: A-mtype(m; τ), D-mtype(m; τ) and mtype(m; τ). Their definition uses the functions given in Fig. 2.

$$\text{fields(Object)} = \epsilon$$

$$\frac{CT(C) = \text{class C extends D implements } \overrightarrow{\text{I}} \ \{\overline{\tau}\, \overline{f}; K\, \overline{M}\} \qquad \text{fields(D)} = \overrightarrow{\sigma}\, \overrightarrow{g}}{\text{fields(C)} = \overrightarrow{\sigma}\, \overrightarrow{g}, \overrightarrow{\tau}\, \overrightarrow{f}}$$

$$\frac{\sigma\, m(\overrightarrow{\sigma}\, \overrightarrow{x}) \in \text{A-mh}(\tau)}{\text{A-mtype}(m;\tau) = \overrightarrow{\sigma} \to \sigma} \qquad \frac{\sigma\, m(\overrightarrow{\sigma}\, \overrightarrow{x}) \in \text{D-mh}(\tau)}{\text{D-mtype}(m;\tau) = \overrightarrow{\sigma} \to \sigma} \qquad \frac{\sigma\, m(\overrightarrow{\sigma}\, \overrightarrow{x}) \in \text{mh}(\tau)}{\text{mtype}(m;\tau) = \overrightarrow{\sigma} \to \sigma}$$

Fig. 5. Lookup fields and method types

The body of a method m for a type τ is specified by mbody(m; τ) of Figure 6. If τ is a class C, we first look for a definition of m in C, then in its superclass, and, if not found, we look for a default method with name m in the interfaces $\overrightarrow{\text{I}}$ implemented by C. The fact that the function D-mh(τ) of Fig. 2 (used by D-mtype(m; $\overrightarrow{\text{I}}$) of Fig. 5) is defined ensures that, if there is more than one definition of m, then there is a most specific one which is the one returned. This is enforced by the rules for mbody(m; $\overrightarrow{\text{I}}$) and mbody(m; $l_1 \& \ldots \& l_n$).

In typing the source code, Java uses for λ-expressions the types prescribed by the contexts enclosing them. These types are called *target types*. This means that λ-expressions are *poly expressions*, i.e. they can have different types in different contexts, see page 93 of [6]. More precisely:

(1) the target type of a λ-expression that occurs as a actual parameter of a constructor call is the type of the field in the class declaration;
(2) the target type of a λ-expression that occurs as a actual parameter of a method call is the type of the parameter in the method declaration;
(3) the target type of a λ-expression that occurs as a return term of a method is the result type in the method declaration;
(4) the target type of a λ-expression that occurs as the body of another λ-expression is the result type of the target type of the external λ-expression;
(5) the target type of a λ-expression that occurs as argument of a cast is the cast type.

$$CT(\mathsf{C}) = \text{class } \mathsf{C} \text{ extends } \mathsf{D} \text{ implements } \overrightarrow{\mathsf{I}} \, \{\overline{\tau}\,\overline{\mathsf{f}}; \mathsf{K}\,\overline{\mathsf{M}}\}$$
$$\sigma\mathsf{m}(\overrightarrow{\sigma}\overrightarrow{\mathsf{x}})\{\text{return } \mathsf{t};\} \in \overrightarrow{\mathsf{M}}$$
$$\rule{8cm}{0.4pt}$$
$$\mathtt{mbody}(\mathsf{m};\mathsf{C}) = (\overrightarrow{\mathsf{x}}, \mathsf{t})$$

$$CT(\mathsf{C}) = \text{class } \mathsf{C} \text{ extends } \mathsf{D} \text{ implements } \overrightarrow{\mathsf{I}} \, \{\overline{\tau}\,\overline{\mathsf{f}}; \mathsf{K}\,\overline{\mathsf{M}}\}$$
$$\mathsf{m} \text{ is not defined in } \overrightarrow{\mathsf{M}} \quad \mathtt{mbody}(\mathsf{m};\mathsf{D}) \text{ is defined}$$
$$\rule{8cm}{0.4pt}$$
$$\mathtt{mbody}(\mathsf{m};\mathsf{C}) = \mathtt{mbody}(\mathsf{m};\mathsf{D})$$

$$CT(\mathsf{C}) = \text{class } \mathsf{C} \text{ extends } \mathsf{D} \text{ implements } \overrightarrow{\mathsf{I}} \, \{\overline{\tau}\,\overline{\mathsf{f}}; \mathsf{K}\,\overline{\mathsf{M}}\}$$
$$\mathsf{m} \text{ is not defined in } \overrightarrow{\mathsf{M}} \quad \mathtt{mbody}(\mathsf{m};\mathsf{D}) \text{ is not defined}$$
$$\rule{8cm}{0.4pt}$$
$$\mathtt{mbody}(\mathsf{m};\mathsf{C}) = \mathtt{mbody}(\mathsf{m};\overrightarrow{\mathsf{I}})$$

$$CT(\mathsf{I}) = \text{interface } \mathsf{I} \text{ extends } \overrightarrow{\mathsf{I}} \, \{\overline{\mathsf{H}}; \overline{\mathsf{M}}\} \quad \tau\mathsf{m}(\overrightarrow{\tau}\overrightarrow{\mathsf{x}})\{\text{return } \mathsf{t};\} \in \overrightarrow{\mathsf{M}}$$
$$\rule{8cm}{0.4pt}$$
$$\mathtt{mbody}(\mathsf{m};\mathsf{I}) = (\overrightarrow{\mathsf{x}}, \mathsf{t})$$

$$CT(\mathsf{I}) = \text{interface } \mathsf{I} \text{ extends } \overrightarrow{\mathsf{I}} \, \{\overline{\mathsf{H}}; \overline{\mathsf{M}}\} \quad \mathsf{m} \text{ is not defined in } \overrightarrow{\mathsf{M}}$$
$$\rule{8cm}{0.4pt}$$
$$\mathtt{mbody}(\mathsf{m};\mathsf{I}) = \mathtt{mbody}(\mathsf{m};\overrightarrow{\mathsf{I}})$$

$$\mathtt{mbody}(\mathsf{m};\mathsf{I}_1,\ldots,\mathsf{I}_n) = \mathtt{mbody}(\mathsf{m};\mathsf{I}_1 \& \ldots \& \mathsf{I}_n) = \mathtt{mbody}(\mathsf{m};\mathsf{I}_j)$$
$$\text{if } \mathtt{mbody}(\mathsf{m};\mathsf{I}_\ell) \text{ defined implies } \mathsf{I}_j <: \mathsf{I}_\ell$$

$$\mathtt{mbody}(\mathsf{m};\mathsf{C}\&\mathsf{I}_1\& \ldots \&\mathsf{I}_n) = \begin{cases} \mathtt{mbody}(\mathsf{m};\mathsf{C}) & \text{if defined} \\ \mathtt{mbody}(\mathsf{m};\mathsf{I}_1,\ldots,\mathsf{I}_n) & \text{otherwise} \end{cases}$$

Fig. 6. Method body lookup

According to [6] (page 602): "It is a compile-time error if a lambda expression occurs in a program in someplace other than an assignment context, an invocation context (like (1), (2), (3) and (4) above), or a casting context (like (5) above)."

FJP&λ extends Java allowing any intersection of interfaces as target type, while Java requires exactly one abstract method.

Following [1] the reduction rules assure that the pure λ-expressions are decorated by their target types in the evaluated terms. The mapping $(\mathsf{t})^{?\tau}$ defined as follows:

$$(\mathsf{t})^{?\tau} = \begin{cases} (\mathsf{t})^\tau & \text{if } \mathsf{t} \text{ is a pure } \lambda\text{-expression,} \\ \mathsf{t} & \text{otherwise} \end{cases}$$

decorates with τ pure λ-expressions, whereas leaves all the other terms unchanged. This mapping is used in propagating the type expected for λ-expressions in constructor and method calls and in casts. The typing rules assure that if t is a pure λ-expression, then τ is an interface or an intersection of interfaces, i.e. reducing well-typed terms we only get decorated terms of the shape $(t_\lambda)^\iota$.

As usual $[x \mapsto t]$ denotes the substitution of x by t and it generalises to an arbitrary number of variables/terms as expected.

The notation $\overrightarrow{x} \mapsto (\overrightarrow{v})^{?\overrightarrow{\tau}}$ is short for $x_1 \mapsto (v_1)^{?\tau_1}, \ldots, x_n \mapsto (v_n)^{?\tau_n}$.

$$\frac{\tau\, f_j \in \texttt{fields}(C)}{\texttt{new}\, C(\overrightarrow{v}).f_j \longrightarrow (v_j)^{?\tau}} \text{ [E-ProjNew]} \qquad \frac{C <: \tau}{(\tau)\, \texttt{new}\, C(\overrightarrow{v}) \longrightarrow \texttt{new}\, C(\overrightarrow{v})} \text{ [E-CastNew]}$$

$$\frac{\texttt{mbody}(m;C) = (\overrightarrow{x},t) \quad \texttt{mtype}(m;C) = \overrightarrow{\tau} \to \tau}{\texttt{new}\, C(\overrightarrow{v}).m(\overrightarrow{u}) \longrightarrow [\overrightarrow{x} \mapsto (\overrightarrow{u})^{?\overrightarrow{\tau}}, \texttt{this} \mapsto \texttt{new}\, C(\overrightarrow{v})](t)^{?\tau}} \text{ [E-InvkNew]}$$

$$\frac{\texttt{A-mtype}(m;\iota) = \overrightarrow{\tau} \to \tau}{(\overrightarrow{y} \to t)^\iota.m(\overrightarrow{v}) \longrightarrow [\overrightarrow{y} \mapsto (\overrightarrow{v})^{?\overrightarrow{\tau}}](t)^{?\tau}} \text{ [E-InvkλU-A]}$$

$$\frac{\texttt{A-mtype}(m;\iota) = \overrightarrow{\tau} \to \tau}{(\overrightarrow{\tau}\,\overrightarrow{y} \to t)^\iota.m(\overrightarrow{v}) \longrightarrow [\overrightarrow{y} \mapsto (\overrightarrow{v})^{?\overrightarrow{\tau}}](t)^{?\tau}} \text{ [E-InvkλT-A]}$$

$$\frac{\texttt{mbody}(m;\iota) = (\overrightarrow{x},t) \quad \texttt{D-mtype}(m;\iota) = \overrightarrow{\tau} \to \tau}{(t_\lambda)^\iota.m(\overrightarrow{v}) \longrightarrow [\overrightarrow{x} \mapsto (\overrightarrow{v})^{?\overrightarrow{\tau}}, \texttt{this} \mapsto (t_\lambda)^\iota](t)^{?\tau}} \text{ [E-Invkλ-D]}$$

$$(\iota)\, t_\lambda \longrightarrow (t_\lambda)^\iota \text{ [E-Castλ]} \qquad \frac{\iota <: \iota'}{(\iota')\,(t_\lambda)^\iota \longrightarrow (t_\lambda)^\iota} \text{ [E-CastλTarget]}$$

Fig. 7. Computational rules

The reduction rules are given in Figs. 7 and 8. The rules for method calls decorate actual parameters and bodies that are λ-expressions with the expected types. This is also the case for the rule of field access and the rule for cast of λ-expressions. It is easy to verify that all pure λ-expressions being actual parameters or resulting terms in the l.h.s. are decorated by their target types in the r.h.s. We only comment the rules regarding method calls when the receivers are λ-expressions, since the others are obvious. A decorated λ-expression implements all the abstract methods declared in the interfaces of its target type, so in rules [E-InvkλU-A] and [E-InvkλT-A] the call of one of such methods reduces to the body of the λ-expression in which the formal parameters are substituted by the actual ones. In case the method called is one of the default methods with body t, the λ-expression acts as the object on which the method is called. Then the call reduces to t in which the (decorated) λ-expression replaces this and the actual parameters replace the formal ones. In this way we follow Java 8 specification [6] (page 480), but for the decoration of the λ-expression.

The reduction rules in Fig. 8 specify the (standard) execution strategy.

For example, assuming that the method auto of the Introduction is defined in class AutoApp we get

$$\frac{t \longrightarrow t'}{t.f \longrightarrow t'.f} \text{ [E-Field]} \qquad \frac{t \longrightarrow t'}{(\tau)\,t \longrightarrow (\tau)\,t'} \text{ [E-Cast]}$$

$$\frac{t \longrightarrow t'}{t.m(\overrightarrow{t}) \longrightarrow t'.m(\overrightarrow{t})} \text{ [E-Invk-Recv]}$$

$$\frac{t \longrightarrow t'}{w.m(\overrightarrow{v}, t, \overrightarrow{t}) \longrightarrow w.m(\overrightarrow{v}, t', \overrightarrow{t})} \text{ [E-Invk-Arg]}$$

$$\frac{t \longrightarrow t'}{\text{new } C(\overrightarrow{v}, t, \overrightarrow{t}) \longrightarrow \text{new } C(\overrightarrow{v}, t', \overrightarrow{t})} \text{ [E-New-Arg]}$$

Fig. 8. Congruence rules

$$\text{new AutoApp().auto(x->x)} \longrightarrow (\text{x->x})^{\text{Arg\&Fun}}.\text{mFun}((\text{y->y})^{\text{Arg\&Fun}}).\text{mArg(new C())}$$
$$\longrightarrow (\text{y->y})^{\text{Arg\&Fun}}.\text{mArg(new C())}$$
$$\longrightarrow \text{new C()}$$

where in duplicating the parameter of auto we used two renamings of the identity $(\text{x->x})^{\text{Arg\&Fun}}$ and $(\text{y->y})^{\text{Arg\&Fun}}$ to clarify that they have different roles.

4   Typing Rules

FJP&λ generalises FJ&λ allowing to use intersections everywhere and avoiding the restriction that target types must have a single abstract method. We start discussing the rules for terms shown in Fig. 9. The typing judgment is $\Gamma \vdash t : \tau$, where an environment Γ is a finite mapping from variables to types.

Field access is well typed, rule [T-FIELD], if the type is an intersection with at least one class (our interfaces cannot have fields) and the class contains the required field. In rules [T-INVK] and [T-NEW] the actual parameters are typed with the type judgement $\vdash^*$ which behaves differently depending on the fact that the term is a pure λ-expression or any other term. The judgment $\vdash^*$ is defined as follows

$$\frac{\Gamma \vdash t : \sigma \quad \sigma <: \tau}{\Gamma \vdash^* t : \tau} \qquad \frac{\Gamma \vdash (t_\lambda)^\iota : \iota}{\Gamma \vdash^* t_\lambda : \iota}$$

and taking advantage of the notation $(\ )^?$, can be synthesised by:

$$\frac{\Gamma \vdash (t)^{?\tau} : \sigma \quad \sigma <: \tau}{\Gamma \vdash^* t : \tau} \text{ [}\vdash \vdash^*\text{]}$$

As usual $\Gamma \vdash^* \overrightarrow{t} : \overrightarrow{\tau}$ is short for $\Gamma \vdash^* t_1 : \tau_1, \ldots, \Gamma \vdash^* t_n : \tau_n$.

According to the judgment $\vdash^*$, actual parameters that are not pure λ-expressions can have any type which is a subtype of the type of the matching parameter, whereas pure λ-expression can only have the type required by the context, which is the type of the matching parameter. The premise of the rule $\vdash^*$ for pure λ-expressions requires that we derive for λ-expressions decorated with their target type exactly their target type. The rules for typing decorated λ-expressions are [T-λU], if the parameters are untyped, and [T-λT], if they are typed. Note that, in the type system $\vdash$ there is no typing rule for pure λ-expressions, since we expect each λ-expression to be decorated with its target type. Rule [T-λU] requires that the body of the λ-expression be well typed for all the headers of the abstract methods declared in the interfaces occurring in its target type. The body of the λ-expression is typed by means of $\vdash^*$ to use the correct typing judgement for pure λ-expressions and other terms. In addition to the requirements of [T-λU], when the types of the parameters are specified, rule [T-λT] prescribes that they coincide with the types of the parameters of all the abstract methods declared in the interfaces occurring in the target type of the λ-expression. We observe that rules [T-λU] and [T-λT] can give type to any λ-expression when $\texttt{A-mh}(\iota)$ is the empty list. This is consistent with our formal setting, where we use any λ-expression just for calling default methods in the absence of abstract methods.

$$\frac{x : \tau \in \Gamma}{\Gamma \vdash x : \tau} \text{ [T-VAR]} \qquad \frac{\Gamma \vdash t : C[\&\iota] \quad \tau f \in \texttt{fields}(C)}{\Gamma \vdash t.f : \tau} \text{ [T-FIELD]}$$

$$\frac{\Gamma \vdash t : \tau \quad \texttt{mtype}(m; \tau) = \vec{\sigma} \to \sigma \quad \Gamma \vdash^* \vec{t} : \vec{\sigma}}{\Gamma \vdash t.m(\vec{t}) : \sigma} \text{ [T-INVK]}$$

$$\frac{\texttt{fields}(C) = \vec{\tau}\vec{f} \quad \Gamma \vdash^* \vec{t} : \vec{\tau}}{\Gamma \vdash \texttt{new } C(\vec{t}) : C} \text{ [T-NEW]}$$

$$\frac{\tau m(\vec{\tau}\,\vec{x}) \in \texttt{A-mh}(\iota) \text{ implies } \Gamma, \vec{y} : \vec{\tau} \vdash^* t : \tau}{\Gamma \vdash (\vec{y} \to t)^\iota : \iota} \text{ [T-}\lambda\text{U]}$$

$$\frac{\Gamma \vdash (\vec{y} \to t)^\iota : \iota \quad \tau m(\vec{\sigma}\,\vec{x}) \in \texttt{A-mh}(\iota) \text{ implies } \vec{\sigma} = \vec{\tau}}{\Gamma \vdash (\vec{\tau}\,\vec{y} \to t)^\iota : \iota} \text{ [T-}\lambda\text{T]}$$

Fig. 9. Syntax directed typing rules

$$\frac{\Gamma \vdash^* t : \tau}{\Gamma \vdash (\tau) t : \tau} \text{ [T-UCAST]}$$

$$\frac{\Gamma \vdash t : \tau \quad \tau \sim C[\&\iota] \quad \sigma \sim D[\&\iota'] \quad \tau \not<: \sigma \quad \text{either } C <: D \text{ or } D <: C}{\Gamma \vdash (\sigma) t : \sigma} \text{ [T-UDCAST]}$$

Fig. 10. Cast typing rules

The rules for type casts in Fig. 10 are as in [1]. We use $\tau' \sim \sigma'$ as short for $\tau' <: \sigma'$ and $\sigma' <: \tau'$. The condition $\tau \not<: \sigma$ forbids to apply rule [T-UDCAST] when rule [T-UCAST] can be used instead.

A type derivation for the term reduced at the end of Sect. 3 is:

$$\frac{\vdash \texttt{new AutoApp()} : \texttt{AutoApp} \quad \texttt{mtype(AutoApp; auto)} = \texttt{Arg\&Fun} \to \texttt{C} \quad \Delta}{\vdash \texttt{new AutoApp().auto(x->x)} : \texttt{C}}$$

where Δ is the derivation:

$$\frac{\dfrac{\texttt{A-mh(Arg\&Fun)} = \{\texttt{C mArg(C x), Arg mFun(Arg x)}\} \quad \texttt{y:C} \vdash \texttt{y : C} \quad \texttt{y:Arg} \vdash \texttt{y : Arg}}{\vdash \texttt{(y->y)}^{\texttt{Arg\&Fun}} : \texttt{Arg\&Fun}}}{\vdash^* \texttt{(y->y)} : \texttt{Arg\&Fun}}$$

Finally, we define the rules for checking that method, class and interface declarations are well formed. Note the use of the judgement $\vdash^*$ for typing the bodies of the methods. For methods the key difference with respect to the corresponding rule of FJ&λ is the presence of intersection types in place of nominal types.

$$\frac{\vec{\mathsf{x}} : \vec{\tau}, \mathsf{this} : \mathsf{T} \vdash^* \mathsf{t} : \tau \quad \tau\,\mathsf{m}(\vec{\tau}\,\vec{\mathsf{x}}) \in \mathsf{mh(T)}}{\tau\,\mathsf{m}(\vec{\tau}\,\vec{\mathsf{x}})\{\mathsf{return\ t};\}\ \mathit{OK}\ \mathsf{in}\ \mathsf{T}} \quad [\text{M } \mathit{OK} \text{ in T}]$$

$$\frac{\mathsf{K} = \mathsf{C}(\vec{\sigma}\,\vec{g}, \vec{\tau}\,\vec{f})\{\mathsf{super}(\vec{g}); \mathsf{this}.\vec{f} = \vec{f};\} \quad \mathsf{fields(D)} = \vec{\sigma}\,\vec{g} \quad \vec{\mathsf{M}}\ \mathit{OK}\ \mathsf{in}\ \mathsf{C}}{\mathsf{mh(C)}\ \mathsf{defined} \quad \mathsf{mtype(m; C)}\ \mathsf{defined}\ \mathsf{implies}\ \mathsf{mbody(m; C)}\ \mathsf{defined}}{\mathsf{class\ C\ extends\ D\ implements}\ \vec{\mathsf{I}}\ \{\vec{\tau}\,\vec{\mathsf{f}}; \mathsf{K}\,\vec{\mathsf{M}}\}\ \mathit{OK}} \quad [\text{C } \mathit{OK}]$$

$$\frac{\vec{\mathsf{M}}\ \mathit{OK}\ \mathsf{in}\ \mathsf{I} \quad \mathsf{mh(I)}\ \mathsf{defined}}{\mathsf{interface\ I\ extends}\ \vec{\mathsf{I}}\ \{\vec{\mathsf{H}}; \vec{\mathsf{M}}\}\ \mathit{OK}} \quad [\text{I } \mathit{OK}]$$

Fig. 11. Method, class and interface declaration typing rules

To sum up, the program (CT, t) is well typed if the class table CT is well formed and for some τ we have that $\vdash \mathsf{t} : \tau$, using the declarations and the subtyping of CT.

5   Subject Reduction and Progress

The subject reduction proof of FJP&λ extends that of FJ&λ taking into account the replacement of nominal types by intersection types and the generalisation of target types.

As usual our type system enjoys *weakening*, i.e., $\Gamma \vdash \mathsf{t} : \tau$ implies $\Gamma, \mathsf{x} : \sigma \vdash \mathsf{t} : \tau$ and $\Gamma \vdash^* \mathsf{t} : \tau$ implies $\Gamma, \mathsf{x} : \sigma \vdash^* \mathsf{t} : \tau$.

Lemma 1. *(1) If* $C[\&\iota]$ <: $D[\&\iota']$, *then* $\texttt{fields}(D) \subseteq \texttt{fields}(C)$.
(2) If $\texttt{mtype}(m; \tau) = \overrightarrow{\rho} \to \rho$, *then* $\texttt{mtype}(m; \sigma) = \overrightarrow{\rho} \to \rho$ *for all* $\sigma <: \tau$.

Proof. (1) Assume that ι and ι' are present and D is not $\texttt{Object}$, the proof in the other cases is simpler. From $C\&\iota$ <: $D\&\iota'$ and rule $[<: \&R]$ of Fig. 4 we get $C\&\iota$ <: D. Therefore, since ι <: D cannot hold, from rule $[<: \&L]$ of Fig. 4 we have that C <: D.
(2) By induction on the derivation of $\sigma <: \tau$ it is easy to prove $\texttt{mh}(\tau) \subseteq \texttt{mh}(\sigma)$.

Lemma 2 (Substitution).

(1) If $\Gamma, \mathsf{x}: \sigma \vdash^* t: \tau$ *and* $\Gamma \vdash^* v: \sigma$, *then* $\Gamma \vdash^* [\mathsf{x} \mapsto (v)^{?\sigma}] t: \tau$.
(2) If $\Gamma, \mathsf{x}: \sigma \vdash t: \tau$ *and* $\Gamma \vdash^* v: \sigma$, *then* $\Gamma \vdash [\mathsf{x} \mapsto (v)^{?\sigma}] t: \rho$ *for some* $\rho <: \tau$.

Proof. (1) and (2) are proved by simultaneous induction on type derivations.
(1). If $\Gamma, \mathsf{x}: \sigma \vdash^* t: \tau$, then the last rule applied is $[\vdash \vdash^*]$. We consider first the case of t being a pure λ-expression, and then t being any of the other terms.
Case $t = \overrightarrow{\mathsf{y}} \to t'$. The premise of rule $[\vdash \vdash^*]$ must be $\Gamma, \mathsf{x}: \sigma \vdash (\overrightarrow{\mathsf{y}} \to t')^\tau: \tau$. By part (2) of the induction hypothesis we have that $\Gamma \vdash ([\mathsf{x} \mapsto (v)^{?\sigma}](\overrightarrow{\mathsf{y}} \to t'))^\tau: \rho$ for some $\rho <: \tau$. Since the last rule applied in the derivation is [T-λU], we get $\rho = \tau$. Using rule $[\vdash \vdash^*]$ we conclude $\Gamma \vdash^* [\mathsf{x} \mapsto (v)^{?\sigma}](\overrightarrow{\mathsf{y}} \to t'): \tau$. The proof for the case $t = \overrightarrow{\tau}\,\overrightarrow{\mathsf{y}} \to t'$ is similar.
Case t **not a pure** λ**-expression.** The premise of rule $[\vdash \vdash^*]$ is $\Gamma, \mathsf{x}: \sigma \vdash t: \rho$ for some $\rho <: \tau$. By part (2) of the induction hypothesis $\Gamma \vdash [\mathsf{x} \mapsto (v)^{?\sigma}] t: \rho'$ for some $\rho' <: \rho$. The transitivity of <: gives $\rho' <: \tau$. Applying rule $[\vdash \vdash^*]$ we conclude $\Gamma \vdash^* [\mathsf{x} \mapsto (v)^{?\sigma}] t: \tau$.
(2). By cases on the last rule used in the derivation of $\Gamma, \mathsf{x}: \sigma \vdash t: \tau$.
Case [T-VAR]. $\Gamma, \mathsf{x}: \sigma \vdash \mathsf{x}: \tau$ implies $\sigma = \tau$. The judgment $\Gamma \vdash^* v: \tau$ must be obtained by applying rule $[\vdash \vdash^*]$ with premise $\Gamma \vdash (v)^{?\tau}: \rho$ for some $\rho <: \tau$, as required.
Case [T-FIELD]. In this case $t = t'.f$ and

$$\frac{\Gamma, \mathsf{x}: \sigma \vdash t': C\&\iota \quad \tau f \in \texttt{fields}(C)}{\Gamma, \mathsf{x}: \sigma \vdash t'.f: \tau}$$

(the case in which $\&\iota$ is missing is easier). The induction hypothesis implies $\Gamma \vdash [\mathsf{x} \mapsto (v)^{?\sigma}] t': \rho$ for some $\rho <: C\&\iota$. The subtyping rules of Fig. 4 give $\rho = D[\&\iota']$ for some D and ι'. By Lemma 1(1) we have that $\texttt{fields}(C) \subseteq \texttt{fields}(D)$ and then $\tau f \in \texttt{fields}(D)$. Therefore applying rule [T-FIELD] we conclude $\Gamma \vdash [\mathsf{x} \mapsto (v)^{?\sigma}] t'.f: \tau$.
Case [T-INVK]. In this case $t = t'.m(\overrightarrow{t})$ and

$$\frac{\Gamma, \mathsf{x}: \sigma \vdash t': \rho \quad \texttt{mtype}(m; \rho) = \overrightarrow{\tau} \to \tau \quad \Gamma, \mathsf{x}: \sigma \vdash^* \overrightarrow{t}: \overrightarrow{\tau}}{\Gamma, \mathsf{x}: \sigma \vdash t'.m(\overrightarrow{t}): \tau}$$

From $\Gamma, \mathsf{x}: \sigma \vdash^* \overrightarrow{t}: \overrightarrow{\tau}$ we get $\Gamma \vdash^* [\mathsf{x} \mapsto (v)^{?\sigma}]\overrightarrow{t}: \overrightarrow{\tau}$ by part (1) of the induction hypothesis. By induction hypothesis on $\Gamma, \mathsf{x}: \sigma \vdash t': \rho$ we have that $\Gamma \vdash [\mathsf{x} \mapsto (v)^{?\sigma}] t': \rho'$ for some $\rho' <: \rho$. Lemma 1(2) gives $\texttt{mtype}(m; \rho') = \overrightarrow{\tau} \to \tau$. Applying rule [T-INVK] we conclude $\Gamma \vdash [\mathsf{x} \mapsto (v)^{?\sigma}](t'.m(\overrightarrow{t})): \tau$.

Case [T-NEW]. By part (1) of the induction hypothesis on the judgments for the parameters.

Case [T-λU]. In this case $t = (\overrightarrow{y} \to t')^\tau$ and

$$\frac{\rho(\overrightarrow{m}\,\overrightarrow{\rho})x \in \text{A-mh}(\tau) \text{ implies } \Gamma, x : \sigma, \overrightarrow{y} : \overrightarrow{\rho} \vdash^* t' : \rho}{\Gamma, x : \sigma \vdash (\overrightarrow{y} \to t')^\tau : \tau}$$

By part (1) of the induction hypothesis we have that $\rho(\overrightarrow{m}\,\overrightarrow{\rho})x \in \text{A-mh}(\tau)$ implies $\Gamma, \overrightarrow{y} : \overrightarrow{\rho} \vdash^* [x \mapsto (v)^{?\sigma}]t' : \rho$. Applying rule [T-$\lambda$U] we conclude

$$\Gamma \vdash ([x \mapsto (v)^{?\sigma}](\overrightarrow{y} \to t'))^\tau : \tau$$

Case [T-λT]. In this case $t = (\overrightarrow{\tau}\,\overrightarrow{y} \to t')^\tau$ and

$$\frac{\Gamma, x : \sigma \vdash (\overrightarrow{y} \to t')^\tau : \tau \quad \rho\,m(\overrightarrow{\rho}\,\overrightarrow{x}) \in \text{A-mh}(\iota) \text{ implies } \overrightarrow{\rho} = \overrightarrow{\tau}}{\Gamma, x : \sigma \vdash (\overrightarrow{\tau}\,\overrightarrow{y} \to t')^\tau : \tau}$$

By induction hypothesis we have that $\Gamma \vdash ([x \mapsto (v)^{?\sigma}](\overrightarrow{y} \to t'))^\tau : \tau$. Applying rule [T-$\lambda$T] we conclude $\Gamma \vdash ([x \mapsto (v)^{?\sigma}](\overrightarrow{\tau}\,\overrightarrow{y} \to t'))^\tau : \tau$.

Lemma 3. *If* $\text{mtype}(m; \tau) = \overrightarrow{\sigma} \to \sigma$ *and* $\text{mbody}(m; \tau) = (\overrightarrow{x}, t)$*, then*

$$\overrightarrow{x} : \overrightarrow{\sigma}, \text{this} : T \vdash^* t : \sigma \text{ for some } T \text{ such that } \tau <: T.$$

Proof. Let $\tau = C\&\iota$, the other cases being simpler. By definition of mbody method m must be declared in:

– class C or
– some interface in ι or
– some class or interface from which either C or an interface in ι inherits.

In all cases rule [M *OK* in C] or [M *OK* in I] of Fig. 11 gives the desired typing judgement.

Lemma 4. *If* $\Gamma \vdash^* t : \tau$*, then* $\Gamma \vdash (t)^{?\tau} : \sigma$ *for some* $\sigma <: \tau$.

Proof. The judgment $\Gamma \vdash^* t : \tau$ must be obtained by applying rule $[\vdash \vdash^*]$ with premise $\Gamma \vdash (t)^{?\tau} : \sigma$ for some $\sigma <: \tau$, as required.

Theorem 1 (Subject Reduction). *If* $\Gamma \vdash t : \tau$ *without using rule* [T-UDCAST] *and* $t \longrightarrow t'$*, then* $\Gamma \vdash t' : \sigma$ *for some* $\sigma <: \tau$.

Proof. By induction on a derivation of $t \longrightarrow t'$, with a case analysis on the final rule. We only consider interesting cases.

Case $\dfrac{\tau f_j \in \text{fields}(C)}{\text{new } C(\overrightarrow{v}).f_j \longrightarrow (v_j)^{?\tau}}$ [E-ProjNew]

The l.h.s. is typed as follows:

$$\dfrac{\dfrac{\text{fields}(C) = \overrightarrow{\tau}\,\overrightarrow{f} \quad \Gamma \vdash^* \overrightarrow{v} : \overrightarrow{\tau}}{\Gamma \vdash \text{new } C(\overrightarrow{v}) : C} \quad \tau f_j \in \text{fields}(C)}{\Gamma \vdash \text{new } C(\overrightarrow{v}).f_j : \tau}$$

From Lemma 4 and $\Gamma \vdash^* \overrightarrow{v} : \overrightarrow{\tau}$ we derive that

$$\Gamma \vdash (v_j)^{?\tau} : \sigma \text{ for some } \sigma <: \tau.$$

Case $\dfrac{\text{mbody}(m;C) = (\overrightarrow{x},t'') \quad \text{mtype}(m;C) = \overrightarrow{\tau} \to \tau}{\text{new } C(\overrightarrow{v}).m(\overrightarrow{u}) \longrightarrow [\overrightarrow{x} \mapsto (\overrightarrow{u})^{?\overrightarrow{\tau}}, \text{this} \mapsto \text{new } C(\overrightarrow{v})](t'')^{?\tau}}$ [E-InvkNew]

The l.h.s. is typed as follows:

$$\frac{\Gamma \vdash \text{new } C(\overrightarrow{v}) : C \quad \text{mtype}(m;C) = \overrightarrow{\tau} \to \tau \quad \Gamma \vdash^* \overrightarrow{u} : \overrightarrow{\tau}}{\Gamma \vdash \text{new } C(\overrightarrow{v}).m(\overrightarrow{u}) : \tau}$$

By Lemma 3 $\text{mbody}(m;C) = (\overrightarrow{x}, t'')$ implies $\overrightarrow{x} : \overrightarrow{\tau}, \text{this} : T \vdash^* t'' : \tau$ with
$C <: T$ for some T. Let $\Gamma' = \overrightarrow{x} : \overrightarrow{\tau}, \text{this} : T$. By Lemma 4 $\Gamma' \vdash (t'')^{?\tau} : \rho$ for
some $\rho <: \tau$ and by weakening $\Gamma, \Gamma' \vdash (t'')^{?\tau} : \rho$. From $\Gamma \vdash \text{new } C(\overrightarrow{v}) : C$ and
$C <: T$ we get $\Gamma \vdash^* \text{new } C(\overrightarrow{v}) : T$. From $\Gamma \vdash^* \overrightarrow{u} : \overrightarrow{\tau}$ and $\Gamma \vdash^* \text{new } C(\overrightarrow{v}) : T$
and $\Gamma, \Gamma' \vdash (t'')^{?\tau} : \rho$ and Lemma 2(2) we get

$$\Gamma \vdash [\overrightarrow{x} \mapsto (\overrightarrow{u})^{?\overrightarrow{\tau}}, \text{this} \mapsto \text{new } C(\overrightarrow{v})](t'')^{?\tau} : \sigma \text{ for some } \sigma <: \rho.$$

Finally by transitivity of $<:$ we have $\sigma <: \tau$.

Case $\dfrac{\text{A-mtype}(m; \iota) = \overrightarrow{\tau} \to \tau}{(\overrightarrow{y} \to t'')^\iota.m(\overrightarrow{v}) \longrightarrow [\overrightarrow{y} \mapsto (\overrightarrow{v})^{?\overrightarrow{\tau}}](t'')^{?\tau}}$ [E-InvkλU-A]

The l.h.s. is typed as follows:

$$\frac{\dfrac{\pi n(\overrightarrow{\pi}\,\overrightarrow{x}) \in \text{A-mh}(\iota) \text{ implies } \Gamma, \overrightarrow{y} : \overrightarrow{\pi} \vdash^* t'' : \pi}{\Gamma \vdash (\overrightarrow{y} \to t'')^\iota : \iota} \quad \text{mtype}(m; \iota) = \overrightarrow{\tau} \to \tau \quad \Gamma \vdash^* \overrightarrow{v} : \overrightarrow{\tau}}{\Gamma \vdash (\overrightarrow{y} \to t'')^\iota.m(\overrightarrow{v}) : \tau}$$

The premise of rule [E-InvkλU-A] implies $\Gamma, \overrightarrow{y} : \overrightarrow{\tau} \vdash^* t'' : \tau$. By Lemma 4
$\Gamma, \overrightarrow{y} : \overrightarrow{\tau} \vdash (t'')^{?\tau} : \rho$ for some $\rho <: \tau$. By Lemma 2(2) we derive

$$\Gamma \vdash [\overrightarrow{y} \mapsto (\overrightarrow{v})^{?\overrightarrow{\tau}}](t'')^{?\tau} : \sigma \text{ for some } \sigma <: \rho$$

Finally by transitivity of $<:$ we have $\sigma <: \tau$.

Case $\dfrac{\text{mbody}(m; \iota) = (\overrightarrow{x}, t'') \quad \text{D-mtype}(m; \iota) = \overrightarrow{\tau} \to \tau}{(t_\lambda)^\iota.m(\overrightarrow{v}) \longrightarrow [\overrightarrow{x} \mapsto (\overrightarrow{v})^{?\overrightarrow{\tau}}, \text{this} \mapsto (t_\lambda)^\iota](t'')^{?\tau}}$ [E-Invkλ-D]

The l.h.s. is typed as follows:

$$\frac{\Gamma \vdash (t_\lambda)^\iota : \iota \quad \text{mtype}(m; \iota) = \overrightarrow{\tau} \to \tau \quad \Gamma \vdash^* \overrightarrow{v} : \overrightarrow{\tau}}{\Gamma \vdash (t_\lambda)^\iota.m(\overrightarrow{v}) : \tau}$$

By Lemma 3 $\text{mbody}(m; \iota) = (\overrightarrow{x}, t'')$ implies $\overrightarrow{x} : \overrightarrow{\tau}, \text{this} : T \vdash^* t'' : \tau$ with $\iota <: T$
for some T. Let $\Gamma' = \overrightarrow{x} : \overrightarrow{\tau}, \text{this} : T$. By Lemma 4 $\Gamma' \vdash (t'')^{?\tau} : \rho$ for some
$\rho <: \tau$ and by weakening $\Gamma, \Gamma' \vdash^* (t'')^{?\tau} : \rho$. From $\Gamma \vdash (t_\lambda)^\iota : \iota$ and $\iota <: T$ by
rule [$\vdash \vdash^*$] we derive $\Gamma \vdash^* (t_\lambda)^\iota : T$. Therefore, by Lemma 2(2) we derive

$$\Gamma \vdash [\overrightarrow{x} \mapsto (\overrightarrow{v})^{?\overrightarrow{\tau}}, \text{this} \mapsto (t_\lambda)^\iota](t'')^{?\tau} : \sigma \text{ where } \sigma <: \rho$$

The transitivity of $<:$ implies $\sigma <: \tau$.

Case $\dfrac{t \longrightarrow t'}{\text{w.m}(\overrightarrow{v}, t, \overrightarrow{t}) \longrightarrow \text{w.m}(\overrightarrow{v}, t', \overrightarrow{t})}$ [E-Invk-Arg]

The l.h.s. is typed as follows:

$$\dfrac{\varGamma \vdash w : \rho \quad \texttt{mtype}(m; \rho) = \overrightarrow{\tau} \to \tau \quad \varGamma \vdash^* \overrightarrow{v} : \overrightarrow{\tau_v} \quad \varGamma \vdash^* t : \sigma \quad \varGamma \vdash^* \overrightarrow{t} : \overrightarrow{\tau_t}}{\varGamma \vdash \text{w.m}(\overrightarrow{v}, t, \overrightarrow{t}) : \tau}$$

where $\overrightarrow{\tau} = \overrightarrow{\tau_v}, \sigma, \overrightarrow{\tau_t}$. By Lemma 4 $\varGamma \vdash^* t : \sigma$ implies $\varGamma \vdash (t)^{?\sigma} : \sigma'$ for some $\sigma' <: \sigma$. Since $t \longrightarrow t'$ implies that t cannot be a λ-expression we get $(t)^{?\sigma} = t$. By induction hypothesis $\varGamma \vdash t' : \rho'$ for some $\rho' <: \sigma'$. Being $\rho' <: \sigma$ applying rule $[\vdash \vdash^*]$ we derive $\varGamma \vdash^* t' : \sigma$. Therefore using the typing rule [T-INVK] we conclude

$$\varGamma \vdash \text{w.m}(\overrightarrow{v}, t, \overrightarrow{t}) : \tau$$

Rule [T-UDCAST] breaks subject reduction already for FJ, as shown in [8] (Sect. 19.4). Following [8] we can recover subject reduction by erasing the condition "either C <: D or D <: C" in rule [T-UDCAST]. In this way the rule becomes:

$$\dfrac{\varGamma \vdash t : \tau \quad \tau \not<: \sigma}{\varGamma \vdash (\sigma) t : \sigma}\ \text{[T-STUPIDCAST]}$$

The closed terms that are typed without using rule [T-UDCAST] enjoy the standard progress property. This can be easily proven by just looking at the shapes of well-typed irreducible terms.

Theorem 2 (Progress). *If $\vdash^* t : \tau$ without using rule [T-UDCAST] and t cannot reduce, then t is a proper value.*

Using rule [T-UDCAST] we can type casts of proper values which cannot be reduced, for example, $(C)\,(\texttt{new Object}())$ with C different from $\texttt{Object}$. An example involving a λ-expression is $(C)\,(\epsilon \to \texttt{new Object}())^I$, where I is the interface with the only signature $\texttt{Object}\,m()$. This term can be obtained by reducing $(C)\,(I)\,(\epsilon \to \texttt{new Object}())$.

To characterise the stuck terms, i.e., the irreducible terms which can be obtained by reducing typed terms and are not values, we resort to the notion of evaluation context, as done in [8] (Theorem 19.5.4). *Evaluation contexts $\mathcal{E}$ are defined as expected:*

$$\mathcal{E} ::= [\,] \mid \mathcal{E}.f \mid \mathcal{E}.m(\overrightarrow{t}) \mid \text{w.m}(\overrightarrow{v}, \mathcal{E}, \overrightarrow{t}) \mid \text{new } C(\overrightarrow{v}, \mathcal{E}, \overrightarrow{t}) \mid (\tau)\mathcal{E}$$

Stuck terms are evaluation contexts with holes filled by casts of typed proper values which cannot reduce, i.e., terms of the shapes $(\tau)\,\texttt{new } C(\overrightarrow{v})$ with $C \not<: \tau$ and $(\tau)\,(t_\lambda)^\iota$ with $\iota \not<: \tau$. Notice that $(A[\&\iota])\,\texttt{new } C(\overrightarrow{v})$ cannot be typed when A, C are unrelated classes. Instead rule [T-UDCAST] allows us to type all terms of the shape $(\tau)\,(t_\lambda)^\iota$, when $(t_\lambda)^\iota$ has a type.

6 Type Inference

Our type system naturally uses the technique of *bidirectional checking* [4,9]. In fact the judgments ⊢ operate in synthesis mode, propagating typing upward from subexpressions, while the judgments ⊢* operate in checking mode, propagating typing downward from enclosing expressions.

We assume a given class table to compute the lookup functions and the subtype relation. The partial function $\mathtt{tInf}(\Gamma; \mathtt{t})$ gives (if any) the type τ such that $\Gamma \vdash \mathtt{t} : \tau$. It is defined by mutual recursion with the predicate $\mathtt{tCk}(\Gamma; \mathtt{t}; \tau)$ which is true if $\Gamma \vdash^* \mathtt{t} : \tau$. So, according to rule [⊢ ⊢*]:

$$\mathtt{tCk}(\Gamma; \mathtt{t}; \tau) \quad \text{if} \quad \mathtt{tInf}(\Gamma; (\mathtt{t})^{?\tau}) = \sigma \text{ and } \sigma <: \tau$$

This asserts that, if we can infer the type of an expression, then we can check that it has this type, and, in case it is not a λ-expression, also all its supertypes. We write $\mathtt{tCk}(\Gamma; \overrightarrow{\mathtt{t}}; \overrightarrow{\tau})$ as short for $\mathtt{tCk}(\Gamma; \mathtt{t}_1; \tau_1), \ldots, \mathtt{tCk}(\Gamma; \mathtt{t}_n; \tau_n)$. Figure 12 gives $\mathtt{tInf}$. The definition is an algorithmic reading of the rules of Figs. 9 and 10. The definition of $\mathtt{tInf}$ uses the predicate $\mathtt{tCk}$ (on subexpressions) to check the types of actual parameters, type casts, and bodies of decorated λ-expressions against the types expected from the contexts. As we can see, $\mathtt{tInf}$ is undefined for pure λ-expressions.

$\mathtt{tInf}(\Gamma; \mathtt{x})$	$= \tau$ if $\mathtt{x} : \tau \in \Gamma$
$\mathtt{tInf}(\Gamma; \mathtt{t.f})$	$= \tau$ if $\mathtt{tInf}(\Gamma; \mathtt{t}) = \mathtt{C}[\&\iota]$ and $\tau \mathtt{f} \in \mathtt{fields}(\mathtt{C})$
$\mathtt{tInf}(\Gamma; \mathtt{new\,C}(\overrightarrow{\mathtt{t}}))$	$= \mathtt{C}$ if $\mathtt{fields}(\mathtt{C}) = \overrightarrow{\tau}\overrightarrow{\mathtt{f}}$ and $\mathtt{tCk}(\Gamma; \overrightarrow{\mathtt{t}}; \overrightarrow{\tau})$
$\mathtt{tInf}(\Gamma; \mathtt{t.m}(\overrightarrow{\mathtt{t}}))$	$= \tau$ if $\mathtt{tInf}(\Gamma; \mathtt{t}) = \sigma$ and $\mathtt{mtype}(\mathtt{m}; \sigma) = \overrightarrow{\tau} \to \tau$
	 and $\mathtt{tCk}(\Gamma; \overrightarrow{\mathtt{t}}; \overrightarrow{\tau})$
$\mathtt{tInf}(\Gamma; (\tau)\,\mathtt{t})$	$= \tau$ if one of the following conditions holds
	• $\mathtt{tCk}(\Gamma; \mathtt{t}; \tau)$
	• $\tau = \mathtt{C}[\&\iota]$ and $\mathtt{tInf}(\Gamma; \mathtt{t}) = \mathtt{D}[\&\iota']$
	 and either $\mathtt{C} <: \mathtt{D}$ or $\mathtt{D} <: \mathtt{C}$
$\mathtt{tInf}(\Gamma; (\overrightarrow{\mathtt{y}} \to \mathtt{t})^\iota)$	$= \iota$ if $\mathtt{tCk}(\Gamma, \overrightarrow{\mathtt{y}} : \overrightarrow{\tau}; \mathtt{t}; \tau)$ for all $\tau\mathtt{m}(\overrightarrow{\tau}\overrightarrow{\mathtt{x}}) \in \mathtt{A\text{-}mh}(\iota)$
$\mathtt{tInf}(\Gamma; (\overrightarrow{\tau}\overrightarrow{\mathtt{y}} \to \mathtt{t})^\iota)$	$= \iota$ if $\mathtt{tCk}(\Gamma, \overrightarrow{\mathtt{y}} : \overrightarrow{\sigma}; \mathtt{t}; \tau)$ and $\overrightarrow{\sigma} = \overrightarrow{\tau}$ for all $\tau\mathtt{m}(\overrightarrow{\sigma}\overrightarrow{\mathtt{x}}) \in \mathtt{A\text{-}mh}(\iota)$

Fig. 12. Type inference function

$\mathtt{OK}(\tau\mathtt{m}(\overrightarrow{\tau}\overrightarrow{\mathtt{x}})\{\mathtt{return\ t}; \}, \mathsf{T})$	if $\tau\mathtt{m}(\overrightarrow{\tau}\overrightarrow{\mathtt{x}}) \in \mathtt{mh}(\mathsf{T})$ and
	$\mathtt{tCk}(\Gamma, \overrightarrow{\mathtt{x}} : \overrightarrow{\tau}, \mathtt{this} : \mathsf{T}; \mathtt{t}; \tau)$
$\mathtt{OK}(\mathtt{class\ C\ extends\ D\ implements}\ \overrightarrow{\mathsf{I}}\ \{\overline{\tau}\overline{\mathtt{f}}; \mathtt{K}\,\overline{\mathsf{M}}\})$ if	
	$\mathtt{K} = \mathtt{C}(\overrightarrow{\sigma}\overrightarrow{\mathtt{g}}, \overrightarrow{\tau}\overrightarrow{\mathtt{f}})\{\mathtt{super}(\overrightarrow{\mathtt{g}}); \mathtt{this}.\overline{\mathtt{f}} = \overline{\mathtt{f}}; \}$
	and $\mathtt{fields}(\mathtt{D}) = \overrightarrow{\sigma}\overrightarrow{\mathtt{g}}$ and $\mathtt{OK}(\overline{\mathsf{M}}, \mathtt{C})$
	and $\mathtt{mh}(\mathtt{C})$ def. and for any $\mathtt{m}$
	$\mathtt{mtype}(\mathtt{m}; \mathtt{C})$ def. impl. $\mathtt{mbody}(\mathtt{m}; \mathtt{C})$ def.
$\mathtt{OK}(\mathtt{interface\ I\ extends}\ \overrightarrow{\mathsf{I}}\ \{\overline{\mathsf{H}}; \overline{\mathsf{M}}\})$	if $\mathtt{OK}(\overline{\mathsf{M}}, \mathsf{I})$ and $\mathtt{mh}(\mathsf{I})$ def.
$\mathtt{OK}(\overrightarrow{\mathtt{C}}\,\overrightarrow{\mathsf{I}})$	if $\mathtt{OK}(\overrightarrow{\mathtt{C}})$ and $\mathtt{OK}(\overrightarrow{\mathsf{I}})$

Fig. 13. Well-formedness function

Building on Fig. 11, Fig. 13 defines a predicate OK which tests well-formedness of class tables, i.e. of classes, interfaces and methods.

We use the following abbreviations: def. for defined, impl. for implies, $\mathsf{OK}(\overrightarrow{\mathsf{M}}, \mathsf{T})$ for $\mathsf{OK}(\mathsf{M}_1, \mathsf{T}), \ldots, \mathsf{OK}(\mathsf{M}_n, \mathsf{T})$, and $\mathsf{OK}(\overrightarrow{\mathsf{M}})$ for $\mathsf{OK}(\mathsf{M}_1), \ldots, \mathsf{OK}(\mathsf{M}_n)$.

7 Conclusion and Related Works

The core language presented here is essentially based on FJ&λ [1], which in turn extends [7]. Our objective was to investigate how to extend the present use of intersection types in Java through a formal account. As a main result, we proved that the cross fertilisation between intersection types and λ-expressions can be further enhanced, getting a more interesting usability of Java λ-expressions while preserving the language type safety. Notably, nominal intersection types are used everywhere, and the functional interface of a λ-expression can provide more than one abstract method (hence, an intersection type for the function). In this way, a λ-expression can be used with different types in different contexts, similarly to what happens in a functional language.

We refer to [1] for a wide survey of the works that are related to this topic, concerning both intersection type theory and the modelling of object-oriented features by intersection types. We refer to Oracle documentation [6] for Java with λ-expressions and intersections.

This paper concentrates mostly on the formal foundation of our proposal. Concerning feasibility of its implementation, in ongoing work we are devising a translation from our calculus into FJ&λ which exactly models the present Java approach. Moreover, we want to investigate how programming methodologies can benefit from these novel features, that seem to be very promising for avoiding the application of *design patterns* [5] and getting a reduced amount of code.

Acknowledgements. We would like to thank the anonymous referees for their helpful comments.

References

1. Bettini, L., Bono, V., Dezani-Ciancaglini, M., Giannini, P., Venneri, B.: Java & lambda: a featherweight story. Logical Meth. Comput. Sci. **14**(3) (2018)
2. Büchi, M., Weck, W.: Compound types for Java. In: Freeman-Benson, B.N., Chambers, C. (eds.) OOPSLA, pp. 362–373. ACM (1998)
3. Coppo, M., Dezani-Ciancaglini, M., Venneri, B.: Functional characters of solvable terms. Math. Logic Q. **27**(2–6), 45–58 (1981)
4. Davies, R., Pfenning, F.: Intersection types and computational effects. In: Odersky, M., Wadler, P. (eds.) ICFP, pp. 198–208. ACM (2000)
5. Gamma, E., Helm, R., Johnson, R., Vlissides, J.: Design Patterns: Elements of Reusable Object-oriented Software. Addison-Wesley, Reading (1995)
6. Gosling, J., Joy, B., Steele, G.L., Bracha, G., Buckley, A.: The Java Language Specification, Java SE 8 Edition. Oracle (2015)

7. Igarashi, A., Pierce, B.C., Wadler, P.: Featherweight Java: a minimal core calculus for Java and GJ. ACM Trans. Program. Lang. Syst. **23**(3), 396–450 (2001)
8. Pierce, B.C.: Types and Programming Languages. MIT Press, Cambridge (2002)
9. Pierce, B.C., Turner, D.N.: Local type inference. ACM Trans. Program. Lang. Syst. **22**(1), 1–44 (2000)

Aarhus 1989–1990

Multi-valued Logic for Static Analysis and Model Checking

Flemming Nielson[1(✉)], Hanne Riis Nielson[1], and Fuyuan Zhang[2]

[1] Department of Mathematics and Computer Science,
Technical University of Denmark, 2800 Kgs. Lyngby, Denmark
{fnie,hrni}@dtu.dk
[2] Division of Physics and Applied Physics,
School of Physical and Mathematical Sciences, Nanyang Technological University,
21 Nanyang Link, Singapore 637371, Singapore
fuyuanzhang@163.com

Abstract. We extend Alternation-Free Least Fixed Point Logic to be based on Belnap logic, while maintaining the close correspondence between static analysis and model checking pioneered by Bernhard Steffen, and opening up for handling access control policies central to the construction of secure IT systems.

1 Introduction

Static Analysis. A variety of techniques are used to ensure properties of programs before they are being deployed for execution. The area of static analysis covers techniques like the use of type and effect systems, data flow analysis, constraint based analysis, and abstract interpretation. Much of the early work of Bernhard Steffen was in the area of data flow analysis for 'optimizing' the implementation of programming languages [15,32–34].

Traditionally data flow analyses are presented in equational form and are classified with respect to two criteria. One is whether they present a forward flow of information (in the direction of normal execution) or a backward flow of information (in the opposite direction of normal execution). The other is how to combine data flow information when paths merge, whether to take a union (or least upper bound) or an intersection (or greatest lower bound). The latter criterion tends to also determine whether one desires least or greatest solutions to the dataflow equations.

Static Analysis as Model Checking. The more complex static analyses involve several sets of data flow equations that need to interact and a key consideration is how best to do so. Bernhard Steffen was the first to realise that some of the program logics were useful for expressing this interaction and subsequently that many static analysis problems could be recast as model checking [29,31]. At the conceptual level this opened up for an understanding of the interplay between

© Springer Nature Switzerland AG 2019
T. Margaria et al. (Eds.): Steffen Festschrift, LNCS 11200, pp. 89–109, 2019.
https://doi.org/10.1007/978-3-030-22348-9_7

static analysis and model checking and how developments in one area could facilitate advances in the other.

At the practical level the areas continued to develop largely independently, however, and to some extent this was due to the different focus of the two areas. Static analyses generally aims for approximative answers (due to undecidability of the precise answers when dealing with infinite state systems) that can be obtained in polynomial time with respect to the size of the programs; model checking generally aims for precise answers (on finite state systems) that seem to require exponential time with respect to the size of programs. Combinations of static analysis and model checking were considered in [8].

Model Checking as Static Analysis. The interplay between static analysis and model checking is more intimate than the work of Bernhard Steffen would suggest. It is not only possible to reduce many static analysis problems to model checking [29,31] but it is in fact also possible to reduce some model checking problems to static analysis [19,35]. This insight builds on the use of a generalisation of Datalog, called Alternation-Free Least Fixed Point Logic, originally employed for the development of static analysis for process calculi [22,23,25].

Beyond Two-Valued Logic. The approximative nature of static analysis means that if a static analysis provides a boolean answer then at most one of the answers can be precise; usually static analyses are formulated so that a negative answer can be trusted whereas a positive answer can be the result of overapproximation. In contrast, the nature of model checking is such that both the negative and positive answers can be precise (but the models need to be sufficiently simple). This suggests that two-valued logics are not the best way to describe the results of static analyses, and some work on heap analyses have already been using Kleene's three-valued logic to get the precision required [28]. Also in model checking there has been interest in studying modal transition systems [17] and corresponding three-valued versions of computation tree logic [2,3,10]. Finally, when studying security properties of programs it is clear that the proper modelling of access control decisions require considerably more than two logical values [4,5,13,27]: as is evident from the 'eXtensible Access Control Markup Language' (XACML) composite policies not only may grant or deny access but can also be inapplicable and even contradictory.

This motivates the development of the present paper, of presenting a logical approach to static analysis that builds on multi-valued logics, and of showing its ability to deal with model checking of modal transition systems.

2   Multi-valued Logic

There are a multitude of multi-valued logics and our treatment cannot be comprehensive. One that arises naturally also from the considerations of static analysis, is the four-valued Belnap logic, and one that has been used for pointer analysis is Kleene's three-valued logic.

Belnap Logic as a Bilattice. Belnap logic [1,9] generalises the two standard logical values t and f to also include two non-standard logical values: $\bot$ that denotes *unknown*, and $\top$ that denotes *conflict*. It is standard to write Four = $\{\bot, t, f, \top\}$.

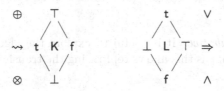

Fig. 1. The knowledge order (Four, $\leadsto$) and the logical order (Four, $\Rightarrow$).

Belnap logic is equipped with a partial order $\leadsto$ called the *knowledge order* (or information order) and depicted in the left part of Fig. 1. The partial order illustrates the point that $\top$ presents conflicting information in that both t and f seem possible, whereas $\bot$ presents the absence of any information. The partial order (Four, $\leadsto$) is in fact a complete lattice with binary greatest lower bound denoted $\otimes$ and binary least upper bound denoted $\oplus$. Clearly the operators $\otimes$ and $\oplus$ are commutative, associative, idempotent and monotonic with respect to the knowledge order.

In the context of static analysis this partial order naturally arises when considering booleans. The set of booleans is Two = $\{t, f\}$ and for static analysis it would be natural to use an analysis domain $(\mathcal{P}(\mathsf{Two}), \subseteq)$ that is the powerset of Two ordered under subset inclusion. It is immediate that the partial order is isomorphic to the partial order (Four, $\leadsto$) introduced above.

Belnap logic is also equipped with a partial order $\Rightarrow$ called the *logical order* (or truth order) and depicted in the right part of Fig. 1. The partial order illustrates how Four contains the traditional logical values ordered under classical implication. The partial order (Four, $\Rightarrow$) is also a complete lattice with binary greatest lower bound denoted $\wedge$ and binary least upper bound denoted $\vee$. Clearly the operators $\wedge$ and $\vee$ are commutative, associative, idempotent and monotonic with respect to the logical order.

We can extend negation $\neg$ from Two to Four by setting $\neg(\bot) = \bot$, $\neg(t) = f$, $\neg(f) = t$, and $\neg(\top) = \top$. Similarly we can define conflation $\sim$ by setting $\sim(\bot) = \top$, $\sim(t) = t$, $\sim(f) = f$, and $\sim(\top) = \bot$.

Belnap Logic is Interlaced. For the purposes of static analysis it is essential that the transfer functions (i.e. the analysis version of the semantic functions) are monotonic because we usually rely on Tarski's fixed point theorems for ensuring that a static analysis has a best (usually least) solution. These considerations usually only consider the knowledge order but here we shall extend the considerations to also consider the logical order. The following facts show that Belnap logic nicely intertwines the monotonicity considerations of the two partial orders.

Fact 1. *The operators* $\otimes$, $\wedge$, $\oplus$, $\vee$ *are monotonic with respect to the knowledge order* $(\rightsquigarrow)$ *as well as the logical order* $(\Rightarrow)$.

Fact 2. *Negation* $(\neg)$ *is monotonic with respect to the knowledge order* $(\rightsquigarrow)$ *but anti-monotonic with respect to the logical order* $(\Rightarrow)$. *Conflation* $(\sim)$ *is monotonic with respect to the logical order* $(\Rightarrow)$ *but anti-monotonic with respect to the knowledge order* $(\rightsquigarrow)$.

Belnap Logic is Distributive. It is useful to explore the algebraic laws enjoyed by the Belnap operators as this allows rephrasing the transfer functions of static analysis.

Fact 3. *All the distributive laws*

$$(f_1 \ \mathsf{op}_1 \ f_2) \ \mathsf{op}_2 \ f_3 = (f_1 \ \mathsf{op}_2 \ f_3) \ \mathsf{op}_1 \ (f_1 \ \mathsf{op}_2 \ f_3)$$

hold for all choices of $f_1, f_2, f_3 \in$ Four *and for all choices of* $\mathsf{op}_1, \mathsf{op}_2 \in \{\otimes, \wedge, \oplus, \vee\}$.

Fact 4. *We have the following version of De Morgan's laws:*

$$\neg(f_1 \vee f_2) = (\neg f_1) \wedge (\neg f_2) \quad \neg(f_1 \wedge f_2) = (\neg f_1) \vee (\neg f_2)$$
$$\neg(f_1 \oplus f_2) = (\neg f_1) \oplus (\neg f_2) \quad \neg(f_1 \otimes f_2) = (\neg f_1) \otimes (\neg f_2)$$
$$\sim(f_1 \vee f_2) = (\sim f_1) \vee (\sim f_2) \quad \sim(f_1 \wedge f_2) = (\sim f_1) \wedge (\sim f_2)$$
$$\sim(f_1 \oplus f_2) = (\sim f_1) \otimes (\sim f_2) \quad \sim(f_1 \otimes f_2) = (\sim f_1) \oplus (\sim f_2)$$

Kleene's Three-Valued Logic. Kleene's three-valued logic has already been used extensively for static analysis of heap structures [28]. It is often presented as Three $= \{0, \frac{1}{2}, 1\}$ and is partially ordered by the usual 'less than or equal to' on the numbers. The number 0 corresponds to falsity, the number 1 to truth, and the number $\frac{1}{2}$ to an undecided truth value. It is clear that Kleene's three-valued logic can be seen as a fragment of (Four, $\Rightarrow$) by mapping 0 to f, 1 to t, and $\frac{1}{2}$ to either $\perp$ or $\top$. In this case $\Rightarrow$ generalises ordinary implication to Kleene's three-valued logic.

Taking the knowledge order into account the traditional approach [9] (also taken in [35, Chapter 4]) is to map $\frac{1}{2}$ to $\perp$ indicating that the undecided truth value arises due to lack of information. But a number of papers on static analysis (e.g. [28] and including our own [18,21]) instead map $\frac{1}{2}$ to $\top$ as this better indicates that the truth value arises due to conflicting information. In this paper we shall be using the notation from Four so as to avoid any confusion as to which embedding is intended.

3   Alternation-Free Least Fixed Point Logic

We shall introduce a version of Alternation-Free Least Fixed Point Logic (*ALFP*) [22,23,25] based on Belnap logic in a simplified form that makes the semantic treatment more succinct.

In the following let $\mathcal{U}$ be a non-empty and finite universe of values with u as a typical element, let $\mathcal{C} \subseteq \mathcal{U}$ be a finite and non-empty set of constants with c as a typical element, let $\mathcal{V}$ be a finite and non-empty set of variables with x as a typical element, let $\mathcal{R}$ be a finite and non-empty set of relation symbols with R as a typical element, let v be a typical element of $\mathcal{C} \cup \mathcal{V}$, and let f be a typical element of Four. We shall write $\overline{v}$ is a shorthand for a non-empty list $v_1, \cdots, v_n$.

The syntax of ALFP based on Belnap logic is based on clauses cl and pre-conditions pre defined by the following grammar:

$$\text{cl} :: = \text{true} \mid \text{cl} \wedge \text{cl} \mid \forall x : \text{cl} \mid \text{pre} \rightsquigarrow R(\overline{v}) \mid \text{pre} \Rightarrow R(\overline{v})$$
$$\text{pre} :: = f \mid R(\overline{v}) \mid \neg R(\overline{v}) \mid {\sim} R(\overline{v}) \mid \text{pre op pre} \mid \text{OP}\, x.\,\text{pre}$$
$$\text{op} :: = \vee \mid \wedge \mid \oplus \mid \otimes$$
$$\text{OP} :: = \exists \mid \forall \mid \bigoplus \mid \bigotimes$$

At the clause level we have some standard constructions from two-valued predicate logic and we have two base clauses: pre $\rightsquigarrow R(\overline{v})$ and pre $\Rightarrow R(\overline{v})$. The intention is that pre will evaluate to an element of Four as will $R(\overline{v})$ and we then check the appropriate order between them.

At the precondition level we have constants in Four and we have three base queries: $R(\overline{v})$, $\neg R(\overline{v})$, and ${\sim} R(\overline{v})$. (The limited placement of negation and conflation is no restriction thanks to Fact 4.) Preconditions can be combined using the operators $\vee$, $\wedge$, $\oplus$, and $\otimes$ that denote the binary lattice operations associated with Four. The binary lattice operations extend to general least upper bound and greatest lower bound operations; we prefer to write them in logical form as a form of quantifiers denoted $\exists$, $\forall$, $\bigoplus$, and $\bigotimes$. The semantics will make it clear that when $\mathcal{U} = \{u_1, \cdots, u_N\}$ then OP $x.\,R(x)$ will be equivalent to $R(u_1) \text{op} \cdots \text{op} R(u_N)$ for corresponding choices of OP and op.

Stratified ALFP. So far the syntax is too liberal and allows writing clauses like $\neg R(c_1) \Rightarrow R(c_2)$ that would seem to have no least solution (when $c_1 \neq c_2$). We therefore introduce a notion of stratification ensuring that relations cannot be defined non-monotonically on themselves.

Stratification is based on a mapping $\cdot^{\sharp} : \mathcal{R} \to \mathsf{N}_0$ that gives a non-negative *rank* to each relation and we shall assume that relations of rank 0 are predefined (and hence cannot be defined in clauses) and write $\mathcal{R}_0 = \{R \in \mathcal{R} \mid R^{\sharp} = 0\}$. Since we are based on Belnap logic we shall also need a mapping $\cdot^{\flat} : \mathsf{N}_1 \to \{\mathsf{K}, \mathsf{L}\}$ that associates each positive rank with an *order* that is either the knowledge order or the logical order.

Definition 1. *A clause* cl *is* closed *when it contains no free variables from* $\mathcal{V}$. *A clause* cl *is* stratified *when it satisfies the following two conditions:*

- *In each subclause* pre $\rightsquigarrow R(\overline{v})$ *occurring in* cl *we have* $R^{\sharp} > 0$ *and* $R^{\sharp\flat} = \mathsf{K}$ *as well as for each base query* $R'(\overline{v}')$ *occurring in* pre *we have* $R'^{\sharp} \leq R^{\sharp}$, *for each base query* $\neg R'(\overline{v}')$ *occurring in* pre *we have* $R'^{\sharp} \leq R^{\sharp}$, *and for each base query* ${\sim} R'(\overline{v}')$ *occurring in* pre *we have* $R'^{\sharp} < R^{\sharp}$.

– *In each subclause* pre $\Rightarrow R(\overline{v})$ *occurring in* cl *we have* $R^\sharp > 0$ *and* $R^{\sharp b} = $ L *as well as for each base query* $R'(\overline{v}')$ *occurring in* pre *we have* $R'^\sharp \leq R^\sharp$, *for each base query* $\neg R'(\overline{v}')$ *occurring in* pre *we have* $R'^\sharp < R^\sharp$, *and for each base query* $\sim R'(\overline{v}')$ *occurring in* pre *we have* $R'^\sharp \leq R^\sharp$.

This means that $\neg R'(c_1) \Rightarrow R(c_2)$ and $\sim R'(c_1) \rightsquigarrow R(c_2)$ are stratified only if the rank of R' is strictly smaller than that of R, and hence that neither $\neg R(c_1) \Rightarrow R(c_2)$ nor $\sim R(c_1) \rightsquigarrow R(c_2)$ can be stratified.

When we define the semantics below it will become clear that Facts 1 and 2 then ensure that the definition of a relation only depends monotonically on itself as will be exploited in the proof of Theorem 1.

Semantics. An interpretation of a relation R will be a mapping from tuples of elements of the universe into Four. We shall dispense with the bookkeeping needed to keep track of the intended arity of each relation R (and we did not do so above) but we cannot merely let R be a mapping in $\mathcal{U}^* \to$ Four from the set of all tuples of elements of the universe into Four because $\mathcal{U}^*$ is infinite even when $\mathcal{U}$ is finite. Hence we shall assume that there is a maximal arity a of relations (as can be read off from the clause considered) and let R be a mapping $\mathcal{U}^{\leq a} \to$ Four where $\mathcal{U}^{\leq a}$ denotes the set of tuples of length between 1 and a.

The semantics of ALFP amounts to defining when an interpretation

$$\rho \in \mathsf{Int} = (\mathcal{R} \to \mathcal{U}^{\leq a} \to \mathsf{Four})$$

of relations and a partial interpretation

$$\sigma : \mathcal{V} \hookrightarrow \mathcal{U}$$

of variables satisfy a given clause cl, written

$$(\rho, \sigma) \models \mathsf{cl}$$

and producing an ordinary truth value in Two, and this requires defining the semantics of a precondition pre, written

$$[\![\mathsf{pre}]\!](\rho, \sigma)$$

and producing a value in Four.

We shall extend $\sigma : \mathcal{V} \hookrightarrow \mathcal{U}$ to a mapping $\sigma : (\mathcal{V} \cup \mathcal{C})^{\leq a} \hookrightarrow \mathcal{U}^{\leq a}$ by setting $\sigma(c) = c$ and $\sigma(v_1, \cdots, v_n) = (\sigma(v_1), \cdots, \sigma(v_n))$. The definitions are then rather straightforward and given in Fig. 2. It is immediate that $(\rho, [\,]) \models \mathsf{cl}$ is a well-defined boolean value (in Two) whenever the clause cl is closed and stratified.

Lexicographic Order. It is useful to be able to relate interpretations of relations by means of a lexicographic order. In order to cut down on the length of the definitions we shall write $\sqsubseteq^\mathsf{K}$ for $\rightsquigarrow$ and $\sqsubseteq^\mathsf{L}$ for $\Rightarrow$ and extend the orderings on Four to $\mathcal{U}^{\leq a} \to$ Four in the standard way, i.e. $\mathbf{R}_1 \sqsubseteq^o \mathbf{R}_2$ iff $\forall \overline{u} \in \mathcal{U}^{\leq a} : \mathbf{R}_1(\overline{u}) \sqsubseteq^o \mathbf{R}_2(\overline{u})$.

$$[\![R(\bar{v})]\!](\rho, \sigma) = \rho(R)(\sigma(\bar{v}))$$
$$[\![\neg R(\bar{v})]\!](\rho, \sigma) = \neg(\rho(R)(\sigma(\bar{v})))$$
$$[\![\sim R(\bar{v})]\!](\rho, \sigma) = \sim(\rho(R)(\sigma(\bar{v})))$$
$$[\![\mathsf{pre}_1 \text{ op } \mathsf{pre}_2]\!](\rho, \sigma) = [\![\mathsf{pre}_1]\!](\rho, \sigma) \text{ op } [\![\mathsf{pre}_2]\!](\rho, \sigma)$$
$$[\![\mathsf{OP}\, x.\, \mathsf{pre}]\!](\rho, \sigma) = \mathsf{OP}_{u \in \mathcal{U}} \, [\![\mathsf{pre}]\!](\rho, \sigma[x \mapsto u])$$
$$[\![f]\!](\rho, \sigma) = f$$

$$(\rho, \sigma) \models \mathsf{true}$$
$$(\rho, \sigma) \models \mathsf{cl}_1 \wedge \mathsf{cl}_2 \text{ iff } ((\rho, \sigma) \models \mathsf{cl}_1) \wedge ((\rho, \sigma) \models \mathsf{cl}_2)$$
$$(\rho, \sigma) \models \forall x : \mathsf{cl} \text{ iff } \forall u \in \mathcal{U} : (\rho, \sigma[x \mapsto u]) \models \mathsf{cl}$$
$$(\rho, \sigma) \models \mathsf{pre} \rightsquigarrow R(\bar{v}) \text{ iff } [\![\mathsf{pre}]\!](\rho, \sigma) \rightsquigarrow \rho(R)(\sigma(\bar{v}))$$
$$(\rho, \sigma) \models \mathsf{pre} \Rightarrow R(\bar{v}) \text{ iff } [\![\mathsf{pre}]\!](\rho, \sigma) \Rightarrow \rho(R)(\sigma(\bar{v}))$$

Fig. 2. The Belnap semantics of ALFP: $[\![\mathsf{pre}]\!](\rho, \sigma)$ is an element in Four, and $(\rho, \sigma) \models \mathsf{cl}$ is an element in Two.

Definition 2. *The lexicographic order $\rho_1 \sqsubseteq \rho_2$ is defined by:*

$$\rho_1 \sqsubseteq \rho_2 \text{ iff } \rho_1 = \rho_2 \vee \rho_1 \sqsubset \rho_2$$

$$\rho_1 \sqsubset \rho_2 \text{ iff } \exists k > 0 : \begin{cases} \exists R \in \mathcal{R} : R^\sharp = k \wedge \rho_1(R) \neq \rho_2(R) \wedge \\ \forall R \in \mathcal{R} : \begin{cases} R^\sharp < k \Rightarrow \rho_1(R) = \rho_2(R) \wedge \\ R^\sharp = k \Rightarrow \rho_1(R) \sqsubseteq^{k^\flat} \rho_2(R) \end{cases} \end{cases}$$

For an interpretation $\rho : \mathcal{R} \to \mathcal{U}^{\leq a} \to \mathsf{Four}$ write $\rho|_0 : \mathcal{R}_0 \to \mathcal{U}^{\leq a} \to \mathsf{Four}$ for the interpretation defined by $\rho|_0(R) = \rho(R)$ whenever $R^\sharp = 0$. Next write $\mathsf{Int}[\varrho] = \{\rho \in \mathsf{Int} \mid \forall R \in \mathcal{R}_0 : \rho(R) = \varrho(R)\}$ whenever $\varrho : \mathcal{R}_0 \to \mathcal{U}^{\leq a} \to \mathsf{Four}$.

Lemma 1. *The lexicographic order $\sqsubseteq$ is a partial order. Furthermore, for each choice of $\varrho : \mathcal{R}_0 \to \mathcal{U}^{\leq a} \to \mathsf{Four}$, the set $\mathsf{Int}[\varrho]$ is a complete lattice.*

Proof. To show that $\sqsubseteq$ is a partial order we first note that $\sqsubseteq$ is reflexive. For anti-symmetry suppose by way of contradiction that $\rho_1 \neq \rho_2$, that $\rho_1 \sqsubseteq \rho_2$ (which gives a number $k_1 > 0$) and $\rho_2 \sqsubseteq \rho_1$ (which gives a number $k_2 > 0$); since $\mathcal{U}^{\leq a} \to \mathsf{Four}$ is a complete lattice (under either one of $\rightsquigarrow$ and $\Rightarrow$) this gives a contradiction both when $k_1 = k_2$ and when $k_1 \neq k_2$. For transitivity suppose that ρ_1, ρ_2, ρ_3 are distinct (as otherwise the result will be trivial) and $\rho_1 \sqsubseteq \rho_2$ (which gives a number $k_1 > 0$) and $\rho_2 \sqsubseteq \rho_3$ (which gives a number $k_2 > 0$); choosing k to be the smaller of k_1 and k_2 establishes the result.

To see that $\mathsf{Int}[\varrho]$ is a complete lattice it suffices to consider an arbitrary subset M_0 and construct its greatest lower bound. Define ρ_0 such that $\rho_0(R) = \varrho(R)$ when $R^\sharp = 0$ and arbitrary otherwise. We proceed inductively by defining ρ_{i+1} to give the proper interpretation to relations of rank at most $i + 1$ using that ρ_i does so for relations of rank strictly less than $i + 1$. Given M_i and ρ_i define the set of interpretations $M_{i+1} \subseteq M_i$ relevant for the extension of ρ_i to ρ_{i+1} by

$$M_{i+1} = \{\rho \in M_i \mid \forall R \in \mathcal{R} : R^\sharp \leq i \Rightarrow \rho(R) = \rho_i(R)\}$$

and next define ρ_{i+1} as an extension of ρ_i on relations of rank $i+1$ (making an arbitrary definition for relations of higher rank just to ensure that we have a total function) by

$$\rho_{i+1}(R) = \begin{cases} \rho_i(R) \text{ if } R^\sharp \leq i \\ \bigsqcap_{\rho \in M_{i+1}}^{(i+1)^\flat} \rho(R) \text{ if } R^\sharp = i+1 \\ \bot^{R^{\sharp\flat}} \text{ if } R^\sharp > i+1 \end{cases}$$

where $\bigsqcap_{\rho \in M_{i+1}}^{\mathsf{L}}$ is $\bigwedge_{\rho \in M_{i+1}}$, $\bigsqcap_{\rho \in M_{i+1}}^{\mathsf{K}}$ is $\bigotimes_{\rho \in M_{i+1}}$, $\bot^{\mathsf{L}}$ is $\lambda \bar{v}.\mathsf{f}$, and $\bot^{\mathsf{K}}$ is $\lambda \bar{v}.\bot$. Note that for relations of rank $i+1$ the appropriate order (L or K) is given by $o = (i+1)^\flat$ and $\bigsqcap_{\rho \in M_{i+1}}^{(i+1)^\flat} \rho(R) = \bigsqcap^o M_{i+1}$ gives the proper interpretation of R by taking the appropriate greatest lower bound ($\bigwedge$ or $\bigotimes$) of M_{i+1}.

Since $\mathcal{R}$ is finite there will be a maximal rank k and ρ_k is the desired greatest lower bound of M_0.

Algebraic Laws. In the AFLP approach to static analysis the transfer functions are encoded as preconditions and it is useful to have algebraic laws that allow rearranging these. We are free to use the algebraic laws from Facts 3 and 4 as they preserve stratification and closedness as well as the semantics of preconditions and clauses. At the clause level we can use the usual logical properties of conjunction and quantification, e.g. that conjunction is associative and commutative.

Additionally we can combine distinct clauses into one. The two clauses

$$(\mathsf{pre}_1 \Rightarrow R(\bar{v})) \wedge \cdots \wedge (\mathsf{pre}_n \Rightarrow R(\bar{v}))$$
$$(\mathsf{pre}_1 \vee \cdots \vee \mathsf{pre}_n) \Rightarrow R(\bar{v})$$

are equivalent as are the two clauses

$$(\mathsf{pre}_1 \rightsquigarrow R(\bar{v})) \wedge \cdots \wedge (\mathsf{pre}_n \rightsquigarrow R(\bar{v}))$$
$$(\mathsf{pre}_1 \oplus \cdots \oplus \mathsf{pre}_n) \rightsquigarrow R(\bar{v})$$

Moore Families. Recall that a *Moore family* is a subset of a complete lattice that is closed under greatest lower bounds (and hence is non-empty). In the abstract interpretation approach to static analysis [6,7,20] the establishment of a Moore family result shows that there is a least solution to the static analysis problem, in our case $\bigsqcap\{\rho \in \mathsf{Int}[\varrho] \mid (\rho, []) \models \mathsf{cl}\}$, for the analysis problem that cl expresses.

Theorem 1. *For each choice of an interpretation* $\varrho : \mathcal{R}_0 \to \mathcal{U}^{\leq a} \to \mathsf{Four}$ *and a closed and stratified clause* cl, *the set* $\{\rho \in \mathsf{Int}[\varrho] \mid (\rho, []) \models \mathsf{cl}\}$ *is a Moore family.*

Proof. Using the algebraic laws we can rewrite cl into the equivalent formula $\mathsf{true} \wedge \mathsf{cl}_1 \wedge \cdots \wedge \mathsf{cl}_k$ such that cl_i defines only relations of rank i. Let $\rho_0, \cdots, \rho_k$ be the construction of the greatest lower bound ρ_k of $M_0 = \{\rho \in \mathsf{Int}[\varrho] \mid (\rho, []) \models \mathsf{cl}\}$ as in the proof of Lemma 1. We shall prove by induction on i that $(\rho_i, []) \models \mathsf{true} \wedge \mathsf{cl}_1 \wedge \cdots \wedge \mathsf{cl}_i$ and the base case $i = 0$ is immediate.

For the inductive case write Int_{i+1} for the set of interpretations of relations of rank $i + 1$, and write $\rho_i[\rho]$ for the interpretation that uses ρ on relations of rank $i + 1$ and uses ρ_i otherwise. It follows from the induction hypothesis that $(\rho_i[\rho], [\,]) \models \mathsf{true} \wedge \mathsf{cl}_1 \wedge \cdots \wedge \mathsf{cl}_i$ for all ρ and in particular $(\rho_{i+1}, [\,]) \models \mathsf{true} \wedge \mathsf{cl}_1 \wedge \cdots \wedge \mathsf{cl}_i$. We can define a function $F_{i+1} : \mathsf{Int}_{i+1} \to \mathsf{Int}_{i+1}$ such that $(\rho_i[\rho], [\,]) \models \mathsf{cl}_{i+1}$ is equivalent to $F_{i+1}(\rho) \sqsubseteq^{(i+1)^b} \rho$ which we shall abbreviate to $F_{i+1}(\rho) \sqsubseteq \rho$. By Facts 1 and 2 and Definition 1 this is a monotonic function. Then $\{\rho \in \mathsf{Int}_{i+1} \mid F_{i+1}(\rho) \sqsubseteq \rho\}$ is a Moore family, as $F_{i+1}(\bigsqcap M) \sqsubseteq F_{i+1}(\rho) \sqsubseteq \rho$ for each $\rho \in M$ and hence $F_{i+1}(\bigsqcap M) \sqsubseteq \bigsqcap M$. It follows that $(\rho_{i+1}, [\,]) \models \mathsf{true} \wedge \mathsf{cl}_1 \wedge \cdots \wedge \mathsf{cl}_i \wedge \mathsf{cl}_{i+1}$.

4   Model Checking as Static Analysis

Modal Transition Systems. There are many three-valued formulations of transition systems in the literature. Examples include *Partial Kripke structures* [3], *Modal transition systems* (MTSs [16,17]), and *Kripke modal transition systems* (Kripke MTSs) [11,14,30]. It has been shown in [12] that these approaches are equally expressive and we shall follow the approach of [30] in this section.

Definition 3 (Kripke Modal Transition Systems). *A Kripke Modal Transition System (Kripke MTS) over a finite atomic propositions set P is a tuple $M = (S, S_0, \overset{must}{\longrightarrow}, \overset{may}{\longrightarrow}, L)$, where S is a nonempty finite set of states, $S_0 \subseteq S$ is a set of initial states, $\overset{may}{\longrightarrow} \subseteq S \times S$ and $\overset{must}{\longrightarrow} \subseteq S \times S$ are transition relations such that both $\overset{may}{\longrightarrow}$ and $\overset{must}{\longrightarrow}$ are total and $\overset{must}{\longrightarrow} \subseteq \overset{may}{\longrightarrow}$, and $L : S \times P \to \{\mathsf{t}, \top, \mathsf{f}\}$ is an interpretation that associates a truth value in $\{\mathsf{t}, \top, \mathsf{f}\}$ with each atomic proposition in P for each state in S.*

Transitions in $\overset{must}{\longrightarrow}$ (resp. $\overset{may}{\longrightarrow}$) are *must* transitions (resp. *may* transitions), and we write $s \overset{must}{\longrightarrow} s'$ (resp. $s \overset{may}{\longrightarrow} s'$) to denote $(s, s') \in \overset{must}{\longrightarrow}$ (resp. $(s, s') \in \overset{may}{\longrightarrow}$). State s' is a must (resp. may) successor of s if $s \overset{must}{\longrightarrow} s'$ (resp. $s \overset{may}{\longrightarrow} s'$). Totality means that all states always have at least one successor.

A *must* (resp. *may*) path from state s is an infinite sequence of states $\pi = s_0, s_1 \ldots$, where $s = s_0$ and we have $s_i \overset{must}{\longrightarrow} s_{i+1}$ (resp. $s_i \overset{may}{\longrightarrow} s_{i+1}$) for each consecutive pair of states s_i, s_{i+1} in π. We use $\Pi(s)_{must}$ (resp. $\Pi(s)_{may}$) to represent the set of must (resp. may) paths from state s. For an infinite path $\pi = s_0, s_1 \ldots$, we use $\pi[k]$ for $0 \leq k$ to denote the $(k+1)$th state s_k of π.

Three-Valued Computation Tree Logic (CTL). Reasoning about properties of Kripke MTSs entails the use of a three-valued logical formalism, where we can characterize uncertainties of system behaviors using the truth value $\top$, denoting that it is *unknown* whether the formula holds or not. We consider a fragment of the game-based three-valued CTL studied in [30] (that used $\bot$ instead of $\top$ but this does not relate well to the meaning of the knowledge order of Belnap logic.).

This amounts to defining CTL state formulas ϕ based on a set of propositions **P**, with p as a typical element, as follows:

$$\phi ::= \mathbf{true} \mid p \mid \neg\phi \mid \phi_1 \wedge \phi_2 \mid \phi_1 \vee \phi_2 \mid \mathbf{E}\psi \mid \mathbf{A}\psi$$

where ψ are CTL path formulas. CTL path formulas are defined as follows, where ϕ are CTL state formulas:

$$\psi ::= \mathbf{X}\phi \mid \phi_1\mathbf{U}\phi_2 \mid \mathbf{F}\phi \mid \mathbf{G}\phi$$

We give the semantics of three-valued CTL with respect to Kripke MTSs in Fig. 3. The semantics is obtained from [30], and we derived the case for the **F** operator by using that $\mathbf{F}\phi$ is a shorthand for $\mathbf{true}\mathbf{U}\phi$, and the case for the **G** operator by using that $\mathbf{G}\phi$ is a shorthand for $(\neg\mathbf{true})\mathbf{V}\phi$.

Least Fixed Point CTL. We show in Appendix B that the following fragment suffices to define the full CTL:

$$\phi ::= \mathbf{true} \mid p \mid \neg\phi \mid \phi_1 \wedge \phi_2 \mid \phi_1 \vee \phi_2 \mid \mathbf{EX}\phi \mid \mathbf{AX}\phi \mid \mathbf{E}[\phi_1\mathbf{U}\phi_2] \mid \mathbf{AF}\phi$$

Results like these are standard in traditional two-valued model checking where it is more common to use Existential Normal Form with $\mathbf{EG}\phi$ instead of the dual $\mathbf{AF}\phi$, but to better relate to the ALFP development below we chose an operator for which the least fixed point is desired.

In preparation for the encoding in ALFP we establish two facts on unfolding that are standard in the two-valued setting but also hold in our setting. We say that two CTL formulae are *equivalent*, written $\phi_1 \equiv \phi_2$, whenever $[(M, s) \models \phi_1] = [(M, s) \models \phi_2]$ for all M and s.

Fact 5. *The equivalence* $\mathbf{E}[\phi_1\,\mathbf{U}\phi_2] \equiv \phi_2 \vee (\phi_1 \wedge \mathbf{EX}\mathbf{E}[\phi_1\,\mathbf{U}\phi_2])$ *holds in three-valued CTL.*

Fact 6. *The equivalence* $\mathbf{AF}\phi \equiv \phi \vee \mathbf{AX}\mathbf{AF}\phi$ *holds in three-valued CTL.*

Three-Valued CTL Encoded in Multi-Valued ALFP. We now show that the semantics of least fixed point CTL can be encoded in ALFP.

To encode a Kripke MTS $(S, S_0, \overset{must}{\longrightarrow}, \overset{may}{\longrightarrow}, L)$ into three-valued ALFP, we take the universe $\mathcal{U}$ to be S and define corresponding relations in ϱ as follows:

- for each atomic proposition p over **P**, we define a relation P_p such that $\varrho(P_p)(s) = L(s, p)$,
- we define a transition relation T such that $\varrho(T)(s, s') = \mathsf{t}$ if $(s, s') \in\overset{must}{\longrightarrow}$, $\varrho(T)(s, s') = \top$ if $(s, s') \in\overset{may}{\longrightarrow}$ but $(s, s') \notin\overset{must}{\longrightarrow}$, and $\varrho(T)(s, s') = \mathsf{f}$ otherwise.

Our approach follows the syntax-directed approach of flow logic tradition [24, 26]. For each CTL formula ϕ, we define a corresponding relation R_ϕ, and we define a judgement of the form $\mathbf{R} \vdash \phi$ that is intended to ensure that $[(M, s) \models \phi'] =$

$$[(M, s) \models \mathbf{true}] \quad = \mathsf{t}$$

$$[(M, s) \models p] \quad\quad = L(s, p)$$

$$[(M, s) \models \neg\phi] \quad\; = \neg[(M, s) \models \phi]$$

$$[(M, s) \models \phi_1 \vee \phi_2] = [(M, s) \models \phi_1] \vee [(M, s) \models \phi_2]$$

$$[(M, s) \models \phi_1 \wedge \phi_2] = [(M, s) \models \phi_1] \wedge [(M, s) \models \phi_2]$$

$$[(M, s) \models \mathbf{E}\psi] \quad = \begin{cases} \mathsf{t} & \text{if } \exists \pi \in \Pi(s)_{must} : [(M, \pi) \models \psi] = \mathsf{t} \\ \mathsf{f} & \text{if } \forall \pi \in \Pi(s)_{may} : [(M, \pi) \models \psi] = \mathsf{f} \\ \top & \text{otherwise} \end{cases}$$

$$[[(M, s) \models \mathbf{A}\psi] \quad = \begin{cases} \mathsf{t} & \text{if } \forall \pi \in \Pi(s)_{may} : [(M, \pi) \models \psi] = \mathsf{t} \\ \mathsf{f} & \text{if } \exists \pi \in \Pi(s)_{must} : [(M, \pi) \models \psi] = \mathsf{f} \\ \top & \text{otherwise} \end{cases}$$

$$[(M, \pi) \models \mathbf{X}\phi] \quad = \begin{cases} \mathsf{t} & \text{if } [(M, \pi[1]) \models \phi] = \mathsf{t} \\ \mathsf{f} & \text{if } [(M, \pi[1]) \models \phi] = \mathsf{f} \\ \top & \text{otherwise} \end{cases}$$

$$[(M, \pi) \models \phi_1 \mathbf{U}\phi_2] = \begin{cases} \mathsf{t} & \exists\, 0 \leq k : ([(M, \pi[k]) \models \phi_2] = \mathsf{t} \wedge \forall\, 0 \leq j < k : \\ & \quad [(M, \pi[j]) \models \phi_1] = \mathsf{t}) \\ \mathsf{f} & \forall\, 0 \leq k : ((\exists\, 0 \leq j < k : [(M, \pi[j]) \models \phi_1] = \\ & \quad \mathsf{f}) \vee [(M, \pi[k]) \models \phi_2] = \mathsf{f}) \\ \top & \text{otherwise} \end{cases}$$

$$[(M, \pi) \models \mathbf{F}\phi] \quad = \begin{cases} \mathsf{t} & \exists\, 0 \leq k : [(M, \pi[k]) \models \phi] = \mathsf{t} \\ \mathsf{f} & \forall\, 0 \leq k : [(M, \pi[k]) \models \phi] = \mathsf{f} \\ \top & \text{otherwise} \end{cases}$$

$$[(M, \pi) \models \mathbf{G}\phi] \quad = \begin{cases} \mathsf{t} & \forall\, 0 \leq k : [(M, \pi[k]) \models \phi] = \mathsf{t} \\ \mathsf{f} & \exists\, 0 \leq k : [(M, \pi[k]) \models \phi] = \mathsf{f} \\ \top & \text{otherwise} \end{cases}$$

Fig. 3. Three-valued semantics for CTL.

$\rho(R_{\phi'})(s)$ holds in the least model for all subformulas ϕ' of ϕ. (Here $\mathbf{R}$ denotes a family of relations that includes $R_{\phi'}$ whenever ϕ' is a subformula of ϕ.) The ALFP clauses defining the judgement $\mathbf{R} \vdash \phi$ in Fig. 4 impose the constraints needed to ensure that the *least solution* (in the manner of Theorem 1) to the constraint system provides the correct value of $R_{\phi'}$ for all subformulas ϕ' of ϕ. If a subformula ϕ' occurs in several places in ϕ we will be generating the same constraints several times but this does not affect the set of solutions.

Equivalence. It is immediate that Fig. 4 defines a closed formula $\mathbf{R} \vdash \phi$ of ALFP whenever ϕ is a formula of CTL. To obtain stratification, we let $\mathcal{R}_0 = \{T\} \cup \{P_p \mid p \in \mathbf{P}\}$, and we define $R_{\phi'}^{\sharp}$ such that $R_{\phi'}^{\sharp} < R_{\phi''}^{\sharp}$ whenever ϕ' is a subformula of ϕ'', and finally we take the order to be always L.

$$R \vdash \textbf{true} \qquad \underline{\text{iff}} \ [\forall s : \mathsf{t} \Rightarrow R_{true}(s)]$$

$$R \vdash p \qquad \underline{\text{iff}} \ [\forall s : P_p(s) \Rightarrow R_p(s)]$$

$$R \vdash \phi_1 \vee \phi_2 \quad \underline{\text{iff}} \ R \vdash \phi_1 \wedge R \vdash \phi_2 \wedge$$
$$[\forall s : R_{\phi_1}(s) \vee R_{\phi_2}(s) \Rightarrow R_{\phi_1 \vee \phi_2}(s)]$$

$$R \vdash \neg \phi \qquad \underline{\text{iff}} \ R \vdash \phi \wedge$$
$$[\forall s : \neg R_\phi(s) \Rightarrow R_{\neg \phi}(s)]$$

$$R \vdash \textbf{EX}\phi \qquad \underline{\text{iff}} \ R \vdash \phi \wedge$$
$$[\forall s : [\exists s' : T(s, s') \wedge R_\phi(s')] \Rightarrow R_{\textbf{EX}\phi}(s)]$$

$$R \vdash \textbf{AX}\phi \qquad \underline{\text{iff}} \ R \vdash \phi \wedge$$
$$[\forall s : [\forall s' : \neg T(s, s') \vee R_\phi(s')] \Rightarrow R_{\textbf{AX}\phi}(s)]$$

$$R \vdash \textbf{E}[\phi_1 \textbf{U} \phi_2] \ \underline{\text{iff}} \ R \vdash \phi_1 \wedge R \vdash \phi_2 \wedge$$
$$[\forall s : R_{\phi_2}(s) \Rightarrow R_{\textbf{E}[\phi_1 \textbf{U} \phi_2]}(s)] \wedge$$
$$[\forall s : [\exists s' : T(s, s') \wedge R_{\phi_1}(s) \wedge R_{\textbf{E}[\phi_1 \textbf{U} \phi_2]}(s')]$$
$$\Rightarrow R_{\textbf{E}[\phi_1 \textbf{U} \phi_2]}(s)]$$

$$R \vdash \textbf{AF}\phi \qquad \underline{\text{iff}} \ R \vdash \phi \wedge$$
$$[\forall s : R_\phi(s) \Rightarrow R_{\textbf{AF}\phi}(s)] \wedge$$
$$[\forall s : [\forall s' : \neg T(s, s') \vee R_{\textbf{AF}\phi}(s')] \Rightarrow R_{\textbf{AF}\phi}(s)]$$

Fig. 4. Least fixed point CTL encoded in multi-valued ALFP.

We then have the following theorem (motivated by [35, Chapter 4]) saying that the best analysis result of our flow logic approach to the analysis of Kripke MTSs coincides with the solutions for the model checking problem for three-valued CTL with respect to Kripke MTSs.

Theorem 2. *The interpretation ρ given by $\forall s \in S : \rho(R_\phi)(s) = [(M, s) \models \phi]$ is obtained by defining $\rho = \bigsqcap \{\rho' \in \mathsf{Int}[\varrho] \mid (\rho', []) \models (R \vdash \phi)\}$.*

Proof. For the relation R_{true} corresponding to the CTL formula **true**, $\rho(R_{true})$ should map each state s to t and this is guaranteed by the ALFP clause $\forall s : \mathsf{t} \Rightarrow R_{true}(s)$.

For the atomic proposition p we make use of the predefined relation P_p and impose the constraint $\forall s : P_p(s) \Rightarrow R_p(s)$ such that in the least solution $\rho(R_p)$ maps a state s to the same truth value as $\varrho(P_p)$ does.

The clauses for boolean operators $\vee, \wedge$ and $\neg$ follow the same pattern so we just explain one of them, namely disjunction $\phi_1 \vee \phi_2$. The judgements $R \vdash \phi_1$ and $R \vdash \phi_2$ ensure that for the relations $R_{\phi'}$ corresponding to subformulas ϕ' of ϕ_1 or ϕ_2, $\rho(R_{\phi'})$ map states to truth values correctly. The clause $\forall s : R_{\phi_1}(s) \vee R_{\phi_2}(s) \Rightarrow R_{\phi_1 \vee \phi_2}(s)$ requires that $R_{\phi_1 \vee \phi_2}(s)$ is mapped to t if $R_{\phi_1}(s)$ or $R_{\phi_2}(s)$ is mapped to t, and allows that $R_{\phi_1 \vee \phi_2}(s)$ is mapped to f if both $R_{\phi_1}(s)$ and $R_{\phi_2}(s)$ are mapped to f, and otherwise allows $R_{\phi_1 \vee \phi_2}(s)$ to be mapped to $\top$.

In the case of **EX**ϕ, the first conjunct ensures that for the relations $R_{\phi'}$ corresponding to subformulas of ϕ, $\rho(R_{\phi'})$ maps states to truth values correctly. The second conjunct requires that if there is a *must* transition from s to s', i.e. $\varrho(T)(s, s')$ equals t, and $R_\phi(s')$ is mapped to t, then $R_{\textbf{EX}\phi}(s)$ is mapped to t. Conversely, if $R_{\textbf{EX}\phi}(s)$ is forced to be mapped to t there must be a *must* transition from s to some s' where $R_\phi(s')$ is mapped to t. Also, if for all *may* transitions from s to s', i.e. $\varrho(T)(s, s')$ equals either t or $\top$, $R_\phi(s')$ is mapped to f, then $R_{\mathbf{EX}\phi}(s)$ is allowed to be mapped to f. Conversely, if $R_{\mathbf{EX}\phi}(s)$ is allowed to be mapped to f then all *may* transitions from s to s' must have that $R_\phi(s')$ is mapped f. This ensures that the least solution to the clauses generated treats the **EX** operator in accordance with Fig. 3.

In the case of $\mathbf{AX}\phi$, the first conjunct plays the same role as in the case of $\mathbf{EX}\phi$. The second conjunct requires that if for all *may* transitions from s to s', i.e. $\varrho(T)(s, s')$ equals either t or $\top$, $R_\phi(s')$ is mapped to t, then $R_{\mathbf{AX}\phi}(s)$ is mapped to t. Conversely, if $R_{\mathbf{AX}\phi}(s)$ is forced to be mapped to t then for each *may* transition from s to some s' it must be the case that $R_\phi(s')$ is mapped to t. Also, if there is a *must* transition from s to s', i.e. $\varrho(T)(s, s')$ equals t, and $R_\phi(s')$ is mapped to f, then $R_{\mathbf{AX}\phi}(s)$ is allowed to be mapped to f. Conversely, if $R_{\mathbf{AX}\phi}(s)$ is allowed to be mapped to f there must be a *must* transition from s to some s' such that $R_\phi(s')$ is mapped to f. This ensures that the least solution to the clauses generated treats the **AX** operator in accordance with Fig. 3.

In the case of $\mathbf{E}[\phi_1 \mathbf{U} \phi_2]$, the judgements $\mathbf{R} \vdash \phi_1$ and $\mathbf{R} \vdash \phi_2$ play the same role as in the case of $\phi_1 \vee \phi_2$. Using the algebraic laws of Sect. 3 the remaining two conjuncts can be reformulated as the equivalent

$$\forall s : \left(R_{\phi_2}(s) \vee [\exists s' : T(s, s') \wedge R_{\phi_1}(s) \wedge R_{\mathbf{E}[\phi_1 \mathbf{U} \phi_2]}(s')] \right) \Rightarrow R_{\mathbf{E}[\phi_1 \mathbf{U} \phi_2]}(s)$$

and for the least solution we then have that

$$\forall s : [\![R_{\phi_2}(s) \vee [\exists s' : T(s, s') \wedge R_{\phi_1}(s) \wedge R_{\mathbf{E}[\phi_1 \mathbf{U} \phi_2]}(s')]]\!] = [\![R_{\mathbf{E}[\phi_1 \mathbf{U} \phi_2]}(s)]\!]$$

which is in agreement with Fact 5, where also the least solution is intended.

In the case of $\mathbf{AF}\phi$, the first conjunct plays the same role as in the case of $\mathbf{EX}\phi$. Using the algebraic laws of Sect. 3 the remaining two conjuncts can be reformulated as the equivalent

$$\forall s : (R_\phi(s) \vee [\forall s' : \neg T(s, s') \vee R_{\mathbf{AF}\phi}(s')]) \Rightarrow R_{\mathbf{AF}\phi}(s)$$

and for the least solution we then have

$$\forall s : [\![R_\phi(s) \vee [\forall s' : \neg T(s, s') \vee R_{\mathbf{AF}\phi}(s')]]\!] = [\![R_{\mathbf{AF}\phi}(s)]\!]$$

which is in agreement with Fact 6, where also the least solution is intended.

5   Access Control

Access control is a security mechanism that intends to ensure the confidentiality and integrity of data by placing restrictions on whom can read and modify data. It is usually implemented by a reference monitor that inspects each request for reading or modifying data and determines whether or not to grant the operation based on the access control policy in place. Access control policies can be quite complex and to control the complexity it is usually necessary to construct them in a compositional manner.

Access control decisions are basically two-valued: either the request is *granted* or it is *denied*. However, a two-valued logic is insufficient for a compositional approach as policies may be inapplicable or even provide conflicting advice. Researchers have therefore proposed the use of compositional policy languages based on Belnap logic [4,5,13] and this is the approach we shall be taking in the present section. Realistic access control languages like XACML 3.0 actually require going beyond having four truth values [27].

Policies and Their Semantics. In this paper we are inspired by the development of [13] and we shall define a policy language that embeds the Belnap operators introduced in Sect. 2; it is given by the following syntax

$$pol :: = f \mid bpol \mid \neg pol \mid \sim pol \mid pol \wedge pol \mid pol \vee pol \mid pol \otimes pol \mid pol \oplus pol$$

where $f \in$ Four and $bpol$ is the basic policies.

The basic policies will be matched against the actions of the system of interest and we shall pay special interest to the actions requesting access to data and leave the remaining ones unspecified:

$$act:: = \mathsf{read}(s, o, t) \mid \mathsf{write}(s, o, t) \mid \cdots$$

Here $\mathsf{read}(s, o, t)$ is an action where the subject s requests read access to an object of type t owned by o, and $\mathsf{write}(s, o, t)$ is an action where the subject s requests write access to an object of type t owned by o.

The semantics of the basic policies is given by a function $[\![bpol]\!]$ that given an action will evaluate to a value in Four with the idea being that t means that the action is allowed, f that it is denied, $\perp$ that the policy does not apply, and $\top$ that we have conflicting information. Examples of such basic policies and their semantics is given in Fig. 5 and will be explained in more detail shortly. This function is then lifted to general policies in a straightforward manner by taking:

$$
\begin{aligned}
[\![f]\!](act) &= f \\
[\![op\ pol]\!](act) &= op([\![pol]\!](act)) &&\text{for } op \in \{\neg, \sim\} \\
[\![pol_1\ op\ pol_2]\!](act) &= [\![pol_1]\!](act)\ op\ [\![pol_2]\!](act) &&\text{for } op \in \{\wedge, \vee, \otimes, \oplus\}
\end{aligned}
$$

When specifying policies it is often useful to be able to specify that one policy takes priority over another, written $pol_1 > pol_2$, and meaning that the intended policy is pol_2 whenever pol_1 is not applicable and otherwise it is pol_1. The priority operator on Four is traditionally [13] defined as:

$$(f_1 > f_2) = \begin{cases} f_2 \text{ if } f_1 = \perp \\ f_1 \text{ if } f_1 \neq \perp \end{cases}$$

However, it turns out to be a derived operator in our setting:

Fact 7. *All multi-argument functions over* Four *are derived operators; in particular,* $(f_1 > f_2) = f_1 \oplus (f_2 \otimes \sim (f_1 \oplus (\neg f_1)))$.

$$[\![\mathsf{READ_{own}}]\!](act) = \begin{cases} \mathsf{EQ}(s,o) & \text{if } act = \mathsf{read}(s,o,t) \\ \bot & \text{otherwise} \end{cases}$$

$$[\![\mathsf{WRITE_{own}}]\!](act) = \begin{cases} \mathsf{EQ}(s,o) & \text{if } act = \mathsf{write}(s,o,t) \\ \bot & \text{otherwise} \end{cases}$$

$$[\![\mathsf{READ_{doc}}]\!](act) = \begin{cases} \mathsf{AC}(s,o,t,\mathsf{r}) & \text{if } act = \mathsf{read}(s,o,t) \wedge \mathsf{D}(s) \wedge \mathsf{P}(o) \\ \bot & \text{otherwise} \end{cases}$$

$$[\![\mathsf{READ_{ns}}]\!](act) = \begin{cases} \mathsf{AC}(s,o,t,\mathsf{r}) & \text{if } act = \mathsf{read}(s,o,t) \wedge \mathsf{N}(s) \wedge \mathsf{P}(o) \\ \bot & \text{otherwise} \end{cases}$$

$$[\![\mathsf{WRITE_{doc}}]\!](act) = \begin{cases} \mathsf{AC}(s,o,t,\mathsf{w}) \wedge \mathsf{EQ}(t,\mathsf{mr}) & \text{if } act = \mathsf{write}(s,o,t) \wedge \mathsf{D}(s) \wedge \mathsf{P}(o) \\ \bot & \text{otherwise} \end{cases}$$

$$[\![\mathsf{WRITE_{ns}}]\!](act) = \begin{cases} \mathsf{AC}(s,o,t,\mathsf{w}) \wedge \mathsf{EQ}(t,\mathsf{cp}) & \text{if } act = \mathsf{write}(s,o,t) \wedge \mathsf{N}(s) \wedge \mathsf{P}(o) \\ \bot & \text{otherwise} \end{cases}$$

$$[\![\mathsf{WRITE_{pat}}]\!](act) = \begin{cases} \mathsf{f} & \text{if } act = \mathsf{write}(s,o,t) \wedge \mathsf{P}(s) \wedge s = o \wedge t \neq \mathsf{ps} \\ \bot & \text{otherwise} \end{cases}$$

Fig. 5. Basic policies and their semantics.

Example Scenario. Let us consider a hospital scenario where three boolean data bases D, N and P indicate whether or not principals are doctors, nurses or patients, respectively. An access control matrix AC governs the access to the patient records and following [13] we shall assume that it contains three types of information: medical records (mr), care plans (cp) and patient surveys (ps). Given a subject s, an object o and a type t we write $\mathsf{AC}(s,o,t,\mathsf{r}) \in \mathsf{Two}$ for whether or not read access is permitted, and $\mathsf{AC}(s,o,t,\mathsf{w})$ for whether or not write access is permitted.

Figure 5 gives a number of examples of basic policies. The first two are examples of general policies saying that anyone should be able to read and write their own data. Here we use EQ for an equality predicate. As an example the policy READ$_{\mathsf{own}}$ only applies to a read action and it will check whether the subject equals the object; if the action is not a read action the policy simply evaluates to $\bot$ as it is not applicable.

In the hospital context the access control matrix will allow doctors and nurses to read the different kinds of patient records; this is expressed by the basic policies READ$_{\mathsf{doc}}$ and READ$_{\mathsf{ns}}$ specified in Fig. 5. The boolean data bases D, N and P are used to check the relevant roles of the subjects and objects and only in that case the access control matrix AC is consulted to check the rights. Using the priority operator we can express the combined policy

$$\mathsf{READ_{own}} > (\mathsf{READ_{doc}} \oplus \mathsf{READ_{ns}})$$

that ensures that the patient has the right to read his own data but at the same time the doctors and nurses have access to the patient records.

In the scenario of [13] only doctors may write medical records whereas nurses only are allowed to write care plans; this is expressed by the basic policies $WRITE_{doc}$ and $WRITE_{ns}$ of Fig. 5. The main difference from before is that extra checks are inserted on the type of information being accessed. In analogy with above we can form the policy:

$$WRITE_{own} > (WRITE_{doc} \oplus WRITE_{ns})$$

However, this is too permissive as it will permit the patient to write his own medical records and care plans. To prevent this we make use of the policy $WRITE_{pat}$ that only applies if the patient attempts to write anything but a patient survey in his/her patient records and it will prevent that from happening. The overall policy can then be formulated as

$$WRITE_{pat} > (WRITE_{own} > (WRITE_{doc} \oplus WRITE_{ns}))$$

Thus if the patient attempts to write, say a medical record, then $WRITE_{pat}$ evaluates to f and the access will be denied. On the other hand if he/she attempts to write a patient survey then $WRITE_{pat}$ does not apply and the general policy $WRITE_{own}$ will grant the access.

Our requirement to the overall policy HOSPITAL for the hospital therefore is that it incorporates all of the above ingredients. To this end define

$$HOSPITAL = \begin{array}{l} (READ_{own} > (READ_{doc} \oplus READ_{ns})) \oplus \\ (WRITE_{pat} > (WRITE_{own} > (WRITE_{doc} \oplus WRITE_{ns}))) \end{array}$$

To connect this to our development of Alternation-Free Least Fixed Point Logic we proceed as follows.

The reference monitor will grant or deny access based on a basic policy RefMon. Given an action act this gives us a value $[\![RefMon]\!](act) \in$ Four but access control decisions will either *grant* the access or *deny* it and hence we need to map values in Four to values in Two. There are several approaches for this and we shall take what is known as the *liberal approach*: access is denied if some evidence suggests so and otherwise it is granted. This amounts to defining

$$deny(f) = f \rightsquigarrow f$$
$$grant(f) = f \rightsquigarrow t$$

Thus the decision made by the reference monitor is $grant([\![RefMon]\!](act)) \in$ Two.

To express that the decisions of the reference monitor should be faithful to the intended policy we may write

$$\forall act : [\![HOSPITAL]\!](act) \rightsquigarrow [\![RefMon]\!](act)$$

and this produces a closed clause of ALFP when 'partially evaluating' the definitions of the basic policies. It is a stratified clause when we take the order to be always K and let AC and EQ have rank 0 and RefMon have rank 1.

6   Conclusion

We believe that the use of logical formalisms for static analysis provides a stable framework for allowing complex analyses to interact. Our previous work on Flow Logic (including [24,26]) have shown how a logical approach can provides a general framework for developing static analyses for a variety of programming languages and process calculi. The development of the Succinct Solver [23] for clauses in two-valued Alternation-Free Least Fixed Point Logic proved to be a sound and powerful implementation strategy for many of these analyses.

In this paper we have shown how to extend Alternation-Free Least Fixed Point Logic to be based on Belnap logic, while maintaining the close correspondence between static analysis and model checking pioneered by Bernhard Steffen, and opening up for handling security policies central to the construction of secure IT systems.

We leave the generalisations and extensions to future papers but conclude by briefly sketching some of them. In fact we can freely choose complete lattices and transfer functions for each stratum, ensuring that we change statum whenever we use non-monotonic functions, and imposing suitable well-formedness conditions using a simple type system.

While we did not establish an algorithm for computing the solution guaranteed by Theorem 1, it is possible to adapt the development of the Succinct Solver to obtain an implementation taking time that is only exponential in the nesting depth of quantifiers and the maximal arities of relations but otherwise essentially linear in the size of clauses and the universe. Alternatively, using ideas in [35, Chapter 4] clauses using Belnap logic can be translated to only linearly larger clauses using classical logic and then the Succinct Solver can be applied directly.

A   Proofs of Key Facts

Proof of Fact 1. There is an easy graphical proof of the interesting cases. First observe that the Hasse diagram for $\Rightarrow$ in Fig. 1 is obtained from the Hasse diagram for $\rightsquigarrow$ by rotating it 90° clockwise. Next observe that in the Hasse diagram for $\Rightarrow$ the operator $\otimes$ 'moves to the left' whereas the operator $\oplus$ 'moves to the right'. Similarly observe that the Hasse diagram for $\rightsquigarrow$ in Fig. 1 is obtained from the Hasse diagram for $\Rightarrow$ by rotating it 90° anti-clockwise. Next observe that in the Hasse diagram for $\rightsquigarrow$ the operator $\wedge$ 'moves to the right' whereas the operator $\vee$ 'moves to the left'.

Proof of Fact 3. The interesting cases are when $op_i \in \{\otimes, \oplus\}$ and $op_{3-i} \in \{\wedge, \vee\}$ (for $i \in \{1, 2\}$) as the other cases follow since (Four, $\rightsquigarrow$) and (Four, $\Rightarrow$) are distributive lattices. It is straightforward to validate the remaining eight interesting cases.

Proof of Fact 4. There is an easy graphical proof of these laws. For the first two we observe that negation ($\neg$) is also the dualisation operator on (Four, $\Rightarrow$) where $\wedge$ is greatest lower bound and $\vee$ is least upper bound. For the next two observe that negation ($\neg$) works 'sideways' on $(\mathsf{Four}, \rightsquigarrow)$. The remaining four laws are analogous.

Proof of Fact 7. We first show the equation $(f_1 > f_2) = f_1 \oplus (f_2 \otimes \sim(f_1 \oplus (\neg f_1)))$ by considering two cases for the value of f_1. If $f_1 = \bot$ we note that $(f_1 \oplus (\neg f_1)) = \bot$ and hence that $f_1 \oplus (f_2 \otimes \sim(f_1 \oplus (\neg f_1))) = \bot \oplus (f_2 \otimes \top) = f_2$ as desired. If $f_1 \neq \bot$ we note that $(f_1 \oplus (\neg f_1)) = \top$ and hence that $f_1 \oplus (f_2 \otimes \sim(f_1 \oplus (\neg f_1))) = f_1 \oplus (f_2 \otimes \bot) = f_1$ as desired.

For the general result, it follows from [1, Proposition 17] that all multi-argument functions over Four are expressible in terms of $\neg$, $\oplus$, $\bot$ and $\supset$ defined by

$$(f_1 \supset f_2) = \begin{cases} f_2 \text{ if } \mathsf{t} \rightsquigarrow f_1 \\ \mathsf{t} \text{ otherwise} \end{cases}$$

Define $S[f] = (f \wedge \top) \otimes (\neg(f \wedge \top))$ and note that

$$S[f] = \begin{cases} \top \text{ if } \mathsf{t} \rightsquigarrow f \\ \bot \text{ otherwise} \end{cases} = \begin{cases} \top \text{ if } f \in \{\mathsf{t}, \top\} \\ \bot \text{ if } f \in \{\mathsf{f}, \bot\} \end{cases}$$

so that is suffices to verify that $(f_1 \supset f_2) = (f_2 \otimes (S[f_1])) \oplus (\mathsf{t} \otimes (\sim S[f_1]))$.

B   Least Fixed Point CTL Suffices for CTL

We need to show that the following CTL operators can be defined using the least fixed point fragment of CTL: $\mathbf{A}[\phi_1 \mathbf{U} \phi_2]$, $\mathbf{EF}\phi$, $\mathbf{AG}\phi$ and $\mathbf{EG}\phi$. This is standard in the two-valued setting but also holds in our setting as expressed by the following facts (where we dispense with the proofs). We begin with two facts on path formulas.

Fact 8. *For any M and π, $[(M, \pi) \models \mathbf{F}\phi] = [(M, \pi) \models \mathbf{true} \mathbf{U} \phi]$.*

Fact 9. *For any M and π, $[(M, \pi) \models \mathbf{G}\phi] = \neg[(M, \pi) \models \mathbf{F}\neg\phi]$.*

We continue with four facts on state formulas. (One may check that we have the equivalence $\mathbf{AX}\phi \equiv \neg\mathbf{EX}\neg\phi$ but the explicit presence of $\mathbf{AX}$ in least fixed point CTL is helpful for our development.)

Fact 10. *The equivalence $\mathbf{EF}\phi \equiv \mathbf{E}[\mathbf{true} \mathbf{U} \phi]$ holds in three-valued CTL.*

Fact 11. *The equivalence $\mathbf{EG}\phi \equiv \neg\mathbf{AF}\neg\phi$ holds in three-valued CTL.*

Fact 12. *The equivalence $\mathbf{AG}\phi \equiv \neg\mathbf{EF}\neg\phi$ holds in three-valued CTL.*

Fact 13. *The equivalence $\mathbf{A}[\phi_1 \mathbf{U} \phi_2] \equiv \neg\mathbf{E}[\neg\phi_2 \mathbf{U}(\neg\phi_1 \wedge \neg\phi_2)] \wedge \mathbf{AF}\phi_2$ holds in three-valued CTL.*

References

1. Arieli, O., Avron, A.: The value of the four values. Artif. Intell. **102**(1), 97–141 (1998)
2. Bruns, G., Godefroid, P.: Model checking partial state spaces with 3-valued temporal logics. In: Halbwachs, N., Peled, D. (eds.) CAV 1999. LNCS, vol. 1633, pp. 274–287. Springer, Heidelberg (1999). https://doi.org/10.1007/3-540-48683-6_25
3. Bruns, G., Godefroid, P.: Generalized model checking: reasoning about partial state spaces. In: Palamidessi, C. (ed.) CONCUR 2000. LNCS, vol. 1877, pp. 168–182. Springer, Heidelberg (2000). https://doi.org/10.1007/3-540-44618-4_14
4. Bruns, G., Huth, M.: Access-control policies via Belnap logic: effective and efficient composition and analysis. In: Proceedings of the 21st IEEE Computer Security Foundations Symposium, pp. 163–176. IEEE Computer Society (2008)
5. Bruns, G., Huth, M.: Access control via Belnap logic: intuitive, expressive, and analyzable policy composition. ACM Trans. Inf. Syst. Secur. **14**(1):9:1–9:27 (2011)
6. Cousot, P., Cousot, R.: Abstract interpretation: a unified lattice model for static analysis of programs by construction or approximation of fixpoints. In: Proceedings of the 4th Annual ACM SIGPLAN-SIGACT Symposium on Principles of Programming Languages (POPL 1977), pp. 238–252. ACM (1977)
7. Cousot, P., Cousot, R.: Systematic design of program analysis frameworks. In: Conference Record of the Sixth Annual ACM SIGPLAN-SIGACT Symposium on Principles of Programming Languages (POPL 1979), pp. 269–282. ACM (1979)
8. Cousot, P., Cousot, R.: Refining model checking by abstract interpretation. Autom. Softw. Eng. **6**(1), 69–95 (1999)
9. Fitting, M.: Kleene's three valued logics and their children. Fundam. Inform. 20(1/2/3), 113–131 (1994)
10. Godefroid, P., Huth, M., Jagadeesan, R.: Abstraction-based model checking using modal transition systems. In: Larsen, K.G., Nielsen, M. (eds.) CONCUR 2001. LNCS, vol. 2154, pp. 426–440. Springer, Heidelberg (2001). https://doi.org/10.1007/3-540-44685-0_29
11. Godefroid, P., Jagadeesan, R.: Automatic abstraction using generalized model checking. In: Brinksma, E., Larsen, K.G. (eds.) CAV 2002. LNCS, vol. 2404, pp. 137–151. Springer, Heidelberg (2002). https://doi.org/10.1007/3-540-45657-0_11
12. Godefroid, P., Jagadeesan, R.: On the expressiveness of 3-valued models. In: Zuck, L.D., Attie, P.C., Cortesi, A., Mukhopadhyay, S. (eds.) VMCAI 2003. LNCS, vol. 2575, pp. 206–222. Springer, Heidelberg (2003). https://doi.org/10.1007/3-540-36384-X_18
13. Hankin, C., Nielson, F., Nielson, H.R.: Advice from Belnap policies. In: Proceedings of the 22nd IEEE Computer Security Foundations Symposium, CSF 2009, pp. 234–247. IEEE Computer Society (2009)
14. Huth, M., Jagadeesan, R., Schmidt, D.: Modal transition systems: a foundation for three-valued program analysis. In: Sands, D. (ed.) ESOP 2001. LNCS, vol. 2028, pp. 155–169. Springer, Heidelberg (2001). https://doi.org/10.1007/3-540-45309-1_11
15. Knoop, J., Rüthing, O., Steffen, B.: Lazy code motion. In: Proceedings of the ACM SIGPLAN'92 Conference on Programming Language Design and Implementation (PLDI), pp. 224–234. ACM (1992)
16. Larsen, K.G.: Modal specifications. In: Proceedings of the International Workshop on Automatic Verification Methods for Finite State Systems, Grenoble, France, pp. 232–246 (1989)

17. Larsen, K.G., Thomsen, B.: A modal process logic. In: Proceedings of the Third Annual Symposium on Logic in Computer Science (LICS 1988), pp. 203–210. IEEE Computer Society (1988)

18. Nielson, F., Nanz, S., Nielson, H.R.: Modal abstractions of concurrent behavior. ACM Trans. Comput. Log. **12**(3), 18:1–18:40 (2011)

19. Nielson, F., Nielson, H.R.: Model checking *Is* static analysis of modal logic. In: Ong, L. (ed.) FoSSaCS 2010. LNCS, vol. 6014, pp. 191–205. Springer, Heidelberg (2010). https://doi.org/10.1007/978-3-642-12032-9_14

20. Nielson, F., Nielson, H.R., Hankin, C.: Principles of Program Analysis. Springer, Heidelberg (2005). https://doi.org/10.1007/978-3-662-03811-6

21. Nielson, F., Nielson, H.R., Sagiv, S.: Kleene's logic with equality. Inf. Process. Lett. **80**(3), 131–137 (2001)

22. Nielson, F., Nielson, H.R., Seidl, H.: Cryptographic analysis in cubic time. Electr. Notes Theor. Comput. Sci. **62**, 7–23 (2001)

23. Nielson, F., Seidl, H., Nielson, H.R.: A succinct solver for ALFP. Nord. J. Comput. **9**(4), 335–372 (2002)

24. Nielson, H.R., Nielson, F.: Flow logic: a multi-paradigmatic approach to static analysis. In: Mogensen, T.Æ., Schmidt, D.A., Sudborough, I.H. (eds.) The Essence of Computation. LNCS, vol. 2566, pp. 223–244. Springer, Heidelberg (2002). https://doi.org/10.1007/3-540-36377-7_11

25. Nielson, H.R., Nielson, F., Buchholtz, M.: Security for mobility. In: Focardi, R., Gorrieri, R. (eds.) FOSAD 2001. LNCS, vol. 2946, pp. 207–265. Springer, Heidelberg (2004). https://doi.org/10.1007/978-3-540-24631-2_6

26. Nielson, H.R., Nielson, F., Pilegaard, H.: Flow logic for process calculi. ACM Comput. Surv. **44**(1), 3:1–3:39 (2012)

27. Ramli, C.D.P.K., Nielson, H.R., Nielson, F.: The logic of XACML. Sci. Comput. Program. **83**, 80–105 (2014)

28. Sagiv, S., Reps, T.W., Wilhelm, R.: Parametric shape analysis via 3-valued logic. In: Proceedings of the 26th ACM SIGPLAN-SIGACT Symposium on Principles of Programming Languages, POPL 1999, pp. 105–118. ACM (1999)

29. Schmidt, D., Steffen, B.: Program analysis *as* model checking of abstract interpretations. In: Levi, G. (ed.) SAS 1998. LNCS, vol. 1503, pp. 351–380. Springer, Heidelberg (1998). https://doi.org/10.1007/3-540-49727-7_22

30. Shoham, S., Grumberg, O.: A game-based framework for CTL counter examples and 3-valued abstraction-refinement. ACM Trans. Comput. Log. **9**(1), 1 (2007)

31. Steffen, B.: Data flow analysis as model checking. In: Ito, T., Meyer, A.R. (eds.) TACS 1991. LNCS, vol. 526, pp. 346–364. Springer, Heidelberg (1991). https://doi.org/10.1007/3-540-54415-1_54

32. Steffen, B., Knoop, J.: Finite constants: characterizations of a new decidable set of constants. In: Kreczmar, A., Mirkowska, G. (eds.) MFCS 1989. LNCS, vol. 379, pp. 481–491. Springer, Heidelberg (1989). https://doi.org/10.1007/3-540-51486-4_94

33. Steffen, B., Knoop, J., Rüthing, O.: The value flow graph: a program representation for optimal program transformations. In: Jones, N. (ed.) ESOP 1990. LNCS, vol. 432, pp. 389–405. Springer, Heidelberg (1990). https://doi.org/10.1007/3-540-52592-0_76

34. Steffen, B., Knoop, J., Rüthing, O.: Efficient code motion and an adaption to strength reduction. In: Proceedings of the International Joint Conference on Theory and Practice of Software Development, Volume 2, TAPSOFT 1991. LNCS, vol. 494, pp. 394–415. Springer (1991)
35. Zhang, F.: Model checking as static analysis. Ph.D. thesis, The Technical University of Denmark (DTU) (2012). Supervised by Flemming Nielson and Hanne Riis Nielson

States and Events in KandISTI
A Retrospective

Maurice H. ter Beek[1], Alessandro Fantechi[1,2], Stefania Gnesi[1(✉)],
and Franco Mazzanti[1]

[1] ISTI–CNR, Pisa, Italy
{terbeek,gnesi,mazzanti}@isti.cnr.it
[2] University of Florence, Florence, Italy
alessandro.fantechi@unifi.it

Abstract. Early work on automated formal verification produced pioneering model-checking algorithms, in which system computations were
modelled either as sequences of distinguished states in which the system
evolves or as sequences of events or actions occurring during the system's state transitions. In both cases, automata-like structures generally
known as transition systems were exploited to capture all possible computations, but still either state-based or event-based. Many years later,
both views were combined in descriptions of computations as the evolution between distinguished states by means of transitions characterised
by the occurrence of events, and verification tools were adapted to this
more general setting. Meanwhile, the most important drive in improving
verification tools concerned the complexity of models, which was attacked
by algorithms capable of minimising the information needed for deciding
the verification questions. One of the outcomes of this quest was local,
on-the-fly model checking. Both of these lines of research, pioneered by
Bernhard Steffen, are discussed in this paper in a general retrospective on
state-based and event-based models of transition systems and temporal
logics, followed by an overview of how this is exploited in the KandISTI
model-checking environment.

1 Introduction

The development of expressive models of transitions systems that are capable
of efficiently supporting formal verification by means of model-checking algorithms has been one of the concerns of Bernhard Steffen's career in research.
The traditional model for the interpretation of modal and state-based logics, i.e.
a Kripke structure [1], in which states are labelled by atomic propositions, was
adopted by the early model-checking algorithms for CTL and LTL (cf. [2] and
the references therein). On the other hand, Labelled Transition Systems (LTS),
in which transitions instead are labelled with events, emerged as the most appropriate semantic model for process algebrae and process calculi [3,4]. In search
for more expressivity and flexibility, the work by Bernhard Steffen and others

© Springer Nature Switzerland AG 2019
T. Margaria et al. (Eds.): Steffen Festschrift, LNCS 11200, pp. 110–128, 2019.
https://doi.org/10.1007/978-3-030-22348-9_8

has addressed models in which both states and transitions are labelled, such as Doubly-Labelled Transition Systems [5], Kripke Transition Systems [6], and Labelled Kripke Structures [7].

It is well known that model checking is affected by the state-space explosion problem, for which realistic system models may require an exponential number of states (which may not fit the available computer memory). Or, as Cleaveland puts it in [8], "Consequently, while the best traditional model-checking algorithms [9–12] are linear in the number of states of a system, their applicability is severely restricted by the prohibitive number of states systems can have." Bernhard Steffen has made seminal contributions to the efficiency of model-checking algorithms [10,13]. To mitigate the state-space explosion problem, local, on-the-fly model-checking algorithms [14–16] can be of help. While these have the same worst-case complexity, they generally perform better in the many cases in which only a subset of the system states, generated 'on demand', needs to be analysed to determine whether a system model satisfies a formula. Local model checking moreover may provide results for infinite state spaces. Bernhard Steffen has made several important contributions also to this development (cf., e.g., [17,18]). In this paper, we list some models and logics that combine state and transition labelling and show how the KandISTI model-checking environment [19] and its rich logic, presented in this paper, exploit these features and thus relate to the aforementioned contributions of Bernhard Steffen.

KandISTI[1] is a family of model checkers developed at ISTI–CNR for over two decades now, which includes UMC [20], CMC [21], VMC [22], and FMC [23]. Each tool allows the efficient verification, by means of explicit-state on-the-fly model checking, of functional properties expressed in a state-based and event-based branching-time temporal logic, which builds upon the family of logics based on ACTL [24–26], i.e. action-based versions of CTL [9,27]. The KandISTI model checkers allow on-the-fly model checking with a complexity that is linear with respect to the size of the model and the size of the formula[2].

This paper is organised as follows. Sections 2 and 3 introduce transition system models and temporal logics, respectively, that explicitly combine state-based and event-based information. Section 4 discusses how KandISTI exploits states and events in a rich modelling and verification environment based on a comprehensive temporal logic, and highlights some of its more interesting features. Section 5 concludes the paper.

2 Modelling Structures for Reasoning on both State-Based and Event-Based Properties

In the literature, one can find several variants of graph structures that have information associated with both their nodes and their edges, used as models for state/event-based logical specifications.

---

[1] Available online at http://fmt.isti.cnr.it/kandisti.

[2] When ignoring the fixed point operators and the parametric aspects of the logic.

One of the first structures that comes to mind is the one adopted for the propositional μ-calculus [28]. These models are constituted by a set of states, a set of *propositional constants* and a set of *program constants*. From a semantic point of view, the interpretation of a propositional constant is a set of states. Therefore each (control) state might have several state labels. The interpretation of a program constant, instead, is a transition relation (i.e. edges associated with exactly one label).

In the *Doubly-Labelled Transition Systems (L^2TS)* introduced by De Nicola and Vaandrager [5], the same concept was reshaped by explicitly assigning to each state a set of *atomic propositions*, and by describing the (now unique) transition relation as a set of triples of the form ⟨source state, observable or silent *event*, target state⟩. No constraints are explicitly imposed on the finiteness or absence of internal structure of atomic propositions and events.

Lawford, Ostroff and Wonham [29] introduced so-called *State-Event Labeled Transition Systems (SELTS)*, which are equivalent to the underlying model of the state/event systems of Graf and Loiseaux [30], in which a model is described by a countable set of states, a finite set of binary relations on the states, an initial state, and a mapping from the states to sets of atomic predicates (i.e. edges are still associated with precisely one label).

In 1999, together with Müller–Olm and Schmidt, Bernhard Steffen coined the term *Kripke Transition System (KTS)* [6]. In a KTS, states are labelled with sets of *atomic propositions* and transitions are labelled with sets of *events*. No constraint is imposed on the absence of internal structure of the labels, nor on the totality of the transition relation, and the presence of an explicit initial state is allowed (i.e. *rooted* structures). The authors point out that edge labellings can be encoded by node labellings and vice versa, such that theoretical analyses typically study one form of labelling. Nevertheless, we very much agree with their motivation for introducing KTS: "For modeling purposes, however, it is often natural to have *both* kinds of labeling available."

In 2004, Chaki et al. introduced *Labelled Kripke Structures (LKS)* [7], which are characterised by a finite set of states, an initial subset of states, a finite set of atomic state propositions, a finite set of events and a binary transition relation among states. The transition relation is no longer required to be total. A state-labelling function associates each state with a set of state propositions, and a transition-labelling function associates each pair of ⟨source, target⟩ states with a set of events (i.e. we cannot have two transitions between the same two states with different labellings).

In 2006, Pecheur and Raimondi use *Mixed Transition Systems* [31], not to be confused with Larsen's Modal Transition Systems [32–34], to denote a generalisation of both state-based models (Kripke structures) and action-based models (LTS) into a common super-structure very similar to L^2TS, which is characterised by a set of states (a subset of which can be qualified as initial states), a transition relation defined as a set of triples of the form ⟨source state, event, target state⟩ and two interpretation functions that associate each state and event with a set of *propositional atoms* over states and events, respectively.

3   Temporal Logics for Reasoning on both State-Based and Event-Based Properties

As already apparent form the previous section, state- and event-based models have been proposed often together with specific temporal logics having those models as interpretation structures.

We already mentioned the propositional μ-calculus [28], which is an extension of modal logic with propositions and fixed point operators [35]. Atomic propositions can be satisfied by single states. Modal operators are indexed by events that label the transitions. Fixed point operators are then introduced to extend the meaning of logic formulae over full, possibly infinite, computations.

Next to the Boolean constants *false* and *true*, the μ-calculus contains *atomic propositions*, logical connectives and the *diamond* and *box* operators $\langle \rangle$ and $[]$ of modal logic. The *least* and *greatest fixed point* operators μ and ν provide recursion used for 'finite' and 'infinite' looping, respectively.

Kindler and Vesper [36] introduced the *Event-and-State-based Temporal Logic (ESTL)* to reason over events and states of Petri nets, which are a typical example of a formal model for reasoning over states (places) and events (transitions). ESTL is a linear-time logic based on four basic temporal operators, namely *eventually* and *once* (eventually in the past), working on state properties, and *sometime* and *sometime in the past*, working on transition properties. From these operators, four dual operators called *always, so far, every-time* and *every-time in the past* can be derived. We refer to [36] for their precise meaning.

Also the logic interpreted over the LKS introduced in [7], called SE-LTL, is a linear-time logic. This logic is based on the X (*next*), G (*always*), F (*eventually*) and U (*until*) linear-time operators, which can be applied both to state and to transition properties.

The Mixed Transition Systems introduced in [31] serve as interpretation model for the *Action-Restricted CTL (ARCTL)* logic, which extends CTL but is less expressive than ACTL from [24]. In fact, ARCTL is instead a branching-time logic over mixed state/event models introduced as a generalisation of CTL. ARCTL has the same temporal operators as CTL, except that they can be restricted to paths whose actions satisfy a given action formula.

Among the various state- and event-based logics proposed in the literature, UCTL [20] was designed to include both the branching-time action-based logic ACTL [24,25] and the branching-time state-based logic CTL [27,37], with the aim to reason over UML state diagram specifications and L^{2}TS. The logic UCTL is *adequate* with respect to strong bisimulation equivalence on L^{2}TS [38]. Adequacy [39], as also investigated by Bernhard Steffen in [40], means that two L^{2}TS A_1 and A_2 are strongly bisimilar if and only if $F_1 = F_2$, where $F_i = \{ \psi \in UCTL \mid A_i \models \psi \}$ for $i = 1, 2$. In other words, adequacy implies that if there is a formula that is not satisfied by one of the L^{2}TS but satisfied by the other L^{2}TS, then the two L^{2}TS are not bisimilar, and—on the other hand—if two L^{2}TS are not bisimilar, then there must exist a distinguishing formula.

The UCTL logic initially was supported by the UMC v3.3[3] model checker, which later evolved into the KandISTI family of model checkers, as explained in the next section.

4 Exploiting States and Events in KandISTI

In this section, we first introduce the KandISTI tool and we show how it exploits states and events in a rich modelling and verification environment, based on a comprehensive temporal logic interpreted over L^2TS, after which we discuss some of its more interesting features in more detail.

4.1 KandISTI

For over more than two decades, we are developing the KandISTI family of model checkers, each one based on a different specification language, but all sharing a common temporal logic and verification engine. The main objective of KandISTI is to provide formal support in the design phase of a software system, especially in its early stages, i.e. when a design is still likely to be incomplete and contain mistakes. The main features of KandISTI focus on the possibility to (i) explore the evolution of a system and generate a summary of its behaviour; (ii) investigate abstract system properties using a temporal logic supported by an on-the-fly model checker; and (iii) obtain a clear explanation of the model-checking results, in terms of possible evolutions of the specific specification model.

While the specification models supported by KandISTI are rather different, ranging from UML statecharts to various process algebrae, its verification engine is unique and based on a common temporal logic which encompasses the specific logics initially associated to the specific tools: ACTL for FMC, UCTL for UMC, SocL for CMC and v-ACTL for VMC. This is feasible by separating state-space generation (which depends on the underlying specification model) from L^2TS analysis, and by the introduction of an explicit abstraction mechanism that allows to specify the details of the model that should be observable as labels on the states and transitions of the L^2TS. Another essential characteristic of KandISTI is the on-the-fly structure of the model-checking algorithm: the L^2TS corresponding to the specification model is generated on demand, following the incremental needs of the verification engine. Given a state of an L^2TS, the validity of a logic formula on that state is evaluated by analysing the transitions allowed in that state, and by analysing the validity of the necessary sub-formulae possibly in some of the necessary next reachable states, and all this recursively.

Hence, each tool consists of two separate, interacting components: a tool-specific L^2TS generator engine and a common logical verification engine. The L^2TS generator engine is again structured in two components: a ground evolutions generator, strictly based on the operational semantics of the specification language, and an abstraction mechanism which allows to associate abstract observable events to system evolutions and abstract atomic propositions to the system states. The overall structure of KandISTI is depicted in Fig. 1.

---

[3] Still available online at http://fmt.isti.cnr.it/umc/legacy/V3.3.

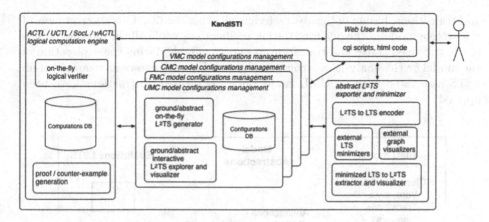

Fig. 1. The architecture of the KandISTI framework (from [41])

All KandISTI model checkers offer a downloadable command-line version of the tool as well as an online GUI through http://fmt.isti.cnr.it/kandisti. Detailed descriptions of the model-checking algorithms and architecture underlying KandISTI are beyond the scope of this paper, but they can be found in [20,21,41–43].

4.2   Modelling with KandISTI

The structure of the models underlying the KandISTI framework (still called L^2TS) is very similar to the KTS of Bernhard Steffen and colleagues and to the L^2TS of De Nicola and Vaandrager, in the sense that both states and transitions can be labelled with finite sets of predicates or events, and a unique initial state is explicitly required. None of the domains of states, predicates and events is required to be finite, and a matching function is required to evaluate whether an event expression or state predicate is satisfied by the set of labels associated to the states or transitions.

Very few model-checking tools provide support for sets of structured labels associated with the edges of a model's evolution graphs. KandISTI, for what we know, is the only publicly available framework that supports this. The tool of the KandISTI framework that better allows to exploit the doubly-labelling feature is UMC. In UMC, a model describes the possible evolutions of a set of UML-like state machines. The state labels of the abstract model contain the relevant state information that we want to observe (typically the values of a subset of the local variables of the state machines), while the transition labels contain the relevant information that we want to observe concerning the occurrence of events during system evolution.

The KandISTI framework allows an abstract view (in terms of an L^2TS) to be associated with the basic operational model of the specification language. So-called "abstraction rules" need to be defined by the user to associate a set of abstract observable (composite) state and event predicates with relevant states and transitions, hiding in the abstract view all other details. This abstract view of the system model is the one used during verification, while all the internal details of the traversed states and transitions remain available during the exploration of the model or the analysis of a counterexample. Figure 2 shows an example of an L^2TS associated with an UML model once the desired abstractions have been applied.

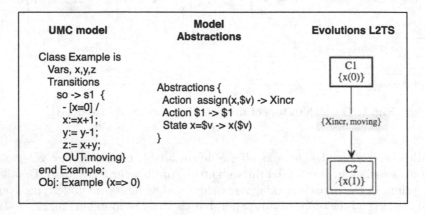

Fig. 2. From UMC model + abstractions to L^2TS

4.3 Verification with KandISTI

Figure 3 provides the syntax of the logic supported by the KandISTI framework. It encompasses the various logics of the individual model-checking tools, ranging from UCTL (cf. Sect. 3) to the most recent addition, v-ACTL, for the analysis of so-called Modal Transition Systems with variability constraints (MTSv) [43]. The logic of KandISTI includes the following rich set of features:

- Parametric state predicates (represented by the state labels of the L^2TS), e.g. $pred1(arg1, arg2)$, $pred2$, and $pred3(*, arg3)$, where $*$ means 'don't care'.
- Parametric event formulae (represented by Boolean expressions over the transition labels (events) of the L^2TS), e.g. $(act1(arg1, arg2) \lor act2)$ and $\neg act3(arg3, *, *)$.
- Classical diamond and box modalities from Hennessy–Milner logic [44], e.g. $[act1] (pred1 \rightarrow \langle act2 \rangle true)$.
- Classical high-level CTL operators (e.g. *next*, *always*, *eventually*, *globally*, *until*, and *weak until*) in their state-based, action-based as well as mixed modality flavours, e.g. $EX\,pred1$, $A\,[pred1(arg1)\ U\ pred2]$, $AG\,EF\,pred1$, and $E\,[pred1(arg1)\ W\ pred2]$.
- High-level ACTL-like operators (i.e. action-based variants of above CTL operators), e.g. $EX_{act1}\,true$, $A\,[pred1(arg1)\ _{act1}U_{act2}\ pred2]$, $AG\,EF_{act1}\,pred1$, and $E\,[\,pred1(arg1)\ _{act1}W\ pred2\,]$.

KandISTI logic

State predicates

$$p ::= \ell \mid \ell(e, \ldots)$$
$$\ell ::= id$$
$$e ::= val \mid * \mid \%var$$

Event formulae

$$\chi ::= true \mid false \mid \ell \mid \ell(e,\ldots) \mid \tau \mid \neg\chi \mid \chi \wedge \chi' \mid \chi \vee \chi'$$
$$\ell ::= id \mid * \mid \$var \mid \%var$$
$$e ::= val \mid * \mid \$var \mid \%var$$

State fomulae

$$\phi ::= rel \mid true \mid false \mid P \mid (\phi) \mid \neg\phi \mid \phi \wedge \phi' \mid \phi \vee \phi' \mid \phi \rightarrow \phi' \mid$$
$$\langle\chi\rangle\phi \mid \langle\chi\rangle^{\square}\phi \mid [\chi]\phi \mid [\chi]^{\square}\phi \mid E\pi \mid A\pi$$
$$rel ::= \%var\ relop\ \%var \mid \%var\ relop\ val$$
$$relop ::= \leq \mid < \mid = \mid \neq \mid > \mid \geq$$

Path fomulae

$$\pi ::= X_\chi\phi \mid X_\chi^{\square}\phi \mid [\phi_\chi U_{\chi'}\phi'] \mid [\phi_\chi U\phi'] \mid [\phi_\chi W_{\chi'}\phi'] \mid [\phi_\chi W\phi'] \mid$$
$$F\phi \mid F_\chi\phi \mid F^{\square}\phi \mid F_\chi^{\square}\phi \mid G\phi \mid G_\chi\phi \mid G^{\square}\phi \mid G_\chi^{\square}\phi$$

$\%var$ denotes a bound variable, whereas $\$var$ denotes a free variable, and it may only occur inside certain contexts (viz. next, diamond, box, eventually, and on the right side of the until operators) but not inside Boolean disjunctions or negations of event formulae.

Fig. 3. Full syntax of the KandISTI logic. Actually, the logic of the KandISTI framework supports also (not optimised) versions of the least and greatest fixed-point operators μ and ν from the μ-calculus (cf. Sect. 3), to be written as `min` and `max`, respectively.

- Parametric formulae expressing data correlations among actions and subformulae, e.g. $[act1(\$1, \$2)]\ AF_{act2(\%1,\%2)}\ true$ and $EF_{\$1}\ EF_{\%1}\ true$.
- Deontic variants of some of the above operators (which allow to reason on classical Modal Transition Systems (MTS) [32,34,43], whose transitions are partitioned into mandatory and optional transitions), e.g. $\langle act1 \rangle^{\square}\ true$ and $EF_{act1}^{\square}\ pred1$.
- Special-purpose predefined state predicates, e.g. $PRINT(msg, arg1, arg2)$ (prints the current state and the message msg each time it is evaluated), $DEPTH\_LT\_n$ (returns $TRUE$ if when evaluated the current evaluation depth is less than n), and $FINAL$ (shorthand for a final state).

The latter category of special-purpose predefined state predicates allows a better control and understanding of the ongoing evaluation process. Indeed, model checking is a technique that can be used for a variety of goals. On one side we have pure validation of a system design which is supposed to be correct with a high probability, as a final result of a development phase. In this case, the design of the verification tools is often focussed on techniques that contrast the state-space explosion problems (e.g. minimising memory requirements), often at the expense of a clear, easily understandable explanation when the validation fails.

On the opposite side we have the goal of an easy but exhaustive analysis/debugging of an initial (likely wrong) design. In this case, the focus of the tool can be more oriented to the collection and preservation of all the diagnostic information that might be useful to explain a negative result, even at the cost of an increased or less efficient usage of the resources.

Our KandISTI framework falls in this second class of verification environments. During the (on-the-fly) evaluation process all the local information of the generated states and transitions is preserved, to be eventually used when an explanation of the evaluation result is requested. The exploitation of this approach is made possible by the *lazy, left-to-right* evaluation approach for Boolean operators, and the *top-down* evaluation process with respect to the formula structure.

In the KandISTI framework, the logical verification engine shared by all the tools observes the underlying model as an abstract L^2TS. This L^2TS is independent from the operational semantics of the particular specification language adopted by the various tools, thanks to the intermediate set of abstraction rules associated to the specification itself. We do not provide the full semantics in this paper, but instead refer to its exhaustive (incremental) treatment in [20,21,43].

We note that not all KandISTI model checkers are able to fully exploit all features of the logic. For instance, VMC and FMC specifications do not support state labelling (and therefore neither state predicates), whereas variability-related aspects (e.g. the deontic 'boxed' operators) are fully supported only by VMC specifications (but partially supported by FMC and UMC specifications).

The actual usage of the logic in the KandISTI framework exploits a machine-friendly, ASCII-only, syntax. In particular, the silent event τ must be written as `tau`; the propositional connectives $\neg$, $\wedge$, $\vee$, and $\rightarrow$ must be written as `not` (or $\sim$), `and` (or `&` or `&&`), `or` (or `|` or `||`), and `implies`; the relational operators $\leq$, $\neq$, and $\geq$ must be written as `<=`, `!=` (or `\=`), and `>=`, respectively (and $=$ may also be written as `==`); the 'boxed' variants $\langle\chi\rangle^\square$, $[\chi]^\square$, $X^\square$, $F^\square$, and $G^\square$ of the modal and temporal operators $\langle\chi\rangle$, $[\chi]$, X, F, and G, respectively, must be written by appending `#` to the operators (e.g. `<>#` and `F#`); finally, the event-based variants of the temporal operators U, W, X, F, and G must be written by (prefixing and) suffixing the operators with the event formulae between curly brackets (e.g. `{e1} U {e2}` and `X {e}`).

In the following sections, we focus in detail on two particular features that have allowed KandISTI to cope with specialised formal verification tasks.

4.4   Variable Binding

In certain cases, it is useful to express the fact that an event expression that appears in a formula can make use of variable names (e.g. $\$var$), which can either be free variables or variables bound to a value by a previous binding operator in the same formula. This data extraction feature from transition labels can be found also in other μ-calculus-based languages, like for example MCL [45].

The contexts in which a variable name is allowed to appear are only the next operator X, the diamond and box operators $\langle\rangle$ and $[\,]$, the *eventually* operator F, and on the right side of the *(weak) until* operators W and U. Moreover, in these contexts, the event expression can only have the form of a *basic event predicate*, or a *conjunction* of basic event predicates, and the variable name can only appear in the place of the *event name* or the place of an *event argument*. Here are some examples of legal occurrences of variable names:

$$[\$event]\ldots,\quad \langle aa(\$1,\$2)\rangle\ldots,\quad E[\ldots U_{\$event(\$var,123)}\ldots],$$
$$EF_{event(\$var)\wedge\neg event(11)}\cdots,\quad AF_{\$var}\cdots$$

When such an event expression is evaluated with respect to a set of transition labels, if the expression matches the labels, then a set of variable bindings occurs, and the obtained bound values can be referred inside the subsequent part of the formula by using the $\%var$ notation. Let us consider the L^2TS shown in Fig. 4a.

With the following formula we can express the property that along any path, any event may occur at most once (the formula is true in the L^2TS of Fig. 4a).

$$AG\,[\$event]\,\neg EF_{\%event}$$

The next formula, instead, states that whenever an event of the form $cc(arg1, arg2)$ occurs, its arguments differ (the formula is true in the L^2TS of Fig. 4a).

$$AG\,[cc(\$1,\$2)]\,(\%1\neq\%2)$$

The following formula states the existence of a path in which an aa event with one argument is always eventually followed by a cc event with two arguments, where the second argument of cc is equal to the first argument of aa (again, the formula is true in the L^2TS of Fig. 4a).

$$EF_{aa(\$1)}\,AF_{cc(*,\%1)}$$

Finally, below formula, instead, expresses that for all the transitions that contain the event aa with an argument that is different from the value 3 lead to a state from which it is possible to perform a cc event with two arguments, of which the first one is equal to the argument of aa and the second one is greater than the first one (also this formula is true in the L^2TS of Fig. 4a).

$$[aa(\$1)\wedge\neg aa(3)]\,\langle cc(\%1,\$2)\rangle\,(\%1<\%2)$$

Note that this formula might have been encoded in an equivalent way as follows.

$$[aa(\$1)]\,(\,(\%1\neq 3)\to\langle cc(\%1,\$2)\rangle\,(\%1<\%2)\,)$$

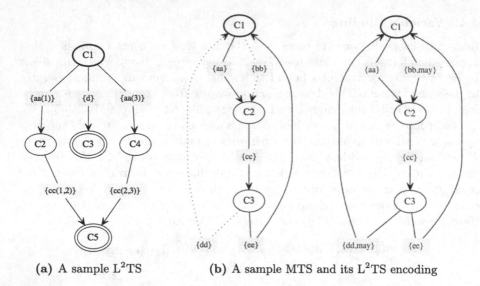

(a) A sample L²TS   (b) A sample MTS and its L²TS encoding

Fig. 4. Sample L²TS and MTS

Note that the presence of the bound value notation %*var* introduces also the possibility of a new class of basic state predicates that have the form of a simple relation, where a bound value is compared with another bound value or literal.

4.5 MTS Model Checking

The VMC, UMC, and FMC tools of the KandISTI framework exploit another interesting use of the composite labelling of a model's transitions. In this case, the model is defined by a sequential algebraic process, and the first parameter of the events, if corresponding to the "may" literal, indicates the optionality of the corresponding evolution. This allows a direct encoding of an aforementioned MTS as an L²TS, using the additional "may" label to denote the deonticity of the evolution. When displayed to the user (cf. Fig. 5), the corresponding graphical view of the L²TS simply removes the optional "may" labels and shows this information via a dashed representation of the transition edge.

One of the purposes of MTS is to describe families of implementations, where edges may be associated with an 'optional' flavour that explicitly pinpoints the variability allowed among the possible implementation variants. In Fig. 4b, we show an example of an MTS and its L²TS encoding, which will be used to show the way in which our KandISTI logical engine allows to reason on this kind of systems. Figure 6 depicts the four implementation variants that constitute the family represented by the MTS of Fig. 4b.

Now suppose we try to evaluate the formula EX_{bb} *true* on the MTS/L²TS of Fig. 4b. The formula will appear to be satisfied by the MTS because actually there is an initial transition that satisfies the event expression *bb*. However, it

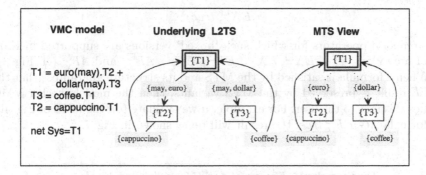

Fig. 5. From VMC model to L²TS (MTS)

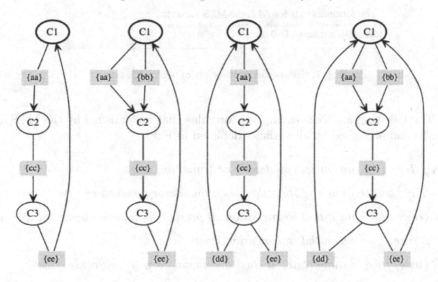

Fig. 6. All four implementation variants of the MTS of Fig. 4b

is also clear that it is not true that this formula holds for all the MTS variants. This means that a *TRUE* result returned by the EX_{act} operator on an MTS, might in general not be preserved by all the implementation variants of the MTS. Note, instead, that a negation of a next operator that returns a *FALSE* result is indeed preserved by all the allowed variants (i.e. EX_{cc} *true* is does not hold on the MTS and neither on all its implementation variants). If we want to verify the existence of a next transition in all the variants, by checking a formula on the MTS, e.g. the existence of an initial *aa* transition, then we should verify the following formula.

$$EX_{aa \wedge \neg may} \ true$$

The KandISTI logic allows to simplify the writing of formulae like the above (making use of implicit $\ldots \wedge \neg may$ event expressions) by offering 'boxed' versions of most temporal operators. The above formula can hence be written as follows.

$$EX_{aa}^{\Box} \; true$$

The temporal operators for which such 'boxed' versions are supported in KandISTI are $\langle \chi \rangle^{\Box}$, $[\chi]^{\Box}$, $EX^{\Box}$, $EX_{\chi}^{\Box}$, $EF^{\Box}$, $EF_{\chi}^{\Box}$, $AF^{\Box}$, and $AF_{\chi}^{\Box}$ (cf. Fig. 3).

When a formula is satisfied by the MTS and its structure guarantees that the *TRUE* result is preserved by the MTS variants, then the model checker VMC notifies this fact to the user. For example, if we evaluate (on the MTS of Fig. 4b) the formula $AG \; EF_{cc}^{\Box} \; true$, the result will be as shown in Fig. 7.

The Formula: *AG E[true {not may} U {cc and not may}true]*
is TRUE

The formula holds for ALL the MTS variants

(evaluation time= 0.060 sec.)

Fig. 7. Successful evaluation of $AG \; EF_{cc}^{\Box} \; true$

The following are some exemplary formulae that are satisfied by the MTS of Fig. 4b and preserved by all variants depicted in Fig. 6:

$EX_{aa}^{\Box} \; true$ *an initial mandatory aa transition exists*

$AG \; EF_{cc}^{\Box} \; true$ *from any state there is a mandatory path to cc*

$[bb] \, \langle cc \rangle^{\Box} \; true$ *an initial bb transition, if present, is followed by cc transition*

$\neg \langle cc \rangle \; true$ *no initial cc transition exists*

$AG \, \langle true \rangle^{\Box} true$ *in any state, at least one mandatory transition is possible*

The general rule, proved in [43], is that a *TRUE* result of any of the operators

$$\langle \chi \rangle^{\Box}, \; [\chi], \; EX^{\Box}, \; EX_{\chi}^{\Box}, \; EF^{\Box}, \; EF_{\chi}^{\Box}, \; AF^{\Box}, \; AF_{\chi}^{\Box}, \; AG$$

is preserved by all the variants when appearing in a context without negations (or under an even number of negations), whereas a *FALSE* result of the operators

$$\langle \chi \rangle, \; [\chi]^{\Box}, \; EX, \; EX_{\chi}, \; EF, \; EF_{\chi}, \; AF, \; AF_{\chi}$$

is preserved by all the variants when appearing in a context under an odd number of negations.

If we observe closely the MTS of Fig. 4b, we immediately see that it satisfies a particular property, namely that all its nodes are the source of at least one mandatory (i.e. not labelled with *may*) transition. A node that satisfies this property or which is final (i.e. without outgoing edges) is called *live* and an MTS is called *live* if all its nodes are. Under these circumstances, we have the additional property that also AF and AF_χ formulae, if $TRUE$, preserve their validity in all the implementation variants [43].

For example, we can verify that the MTS of Fig. 4b (and therefore all its variants depicted in Fig. 6) satisfies the property that any path from any state (in any variant) will eventually and necessarily reach a cc event. The property can be expressed by the following formula.

$$AG\ AF_{cc}\ true$$

One of the tools of the KandISTI framework, namely the variability model checker VMC [22, 46], is explicitly tailored for the verification of behavioural models of so-called (software) product families in the form of MTS with variability constraints (MTSv) [43]. One of the particular features supported by VMC is the possibility to express variability constraints that allow to fine-tune the set of valid implementation variants, and in particular allow to extend further the notion of *live* nodes.

Let us consider the MTSv shown in Fig. 8. The constraint aa ALT bb allows to specify that we consider as valid variants (products) of the MTSv only those variants that either have the aa event or the bb event, but not both of them, nor none of them (i.e. equivalent to a logical xor). Therefore there exist precisely two valid implementations, for both of which the formula AF_{cc} *true* holds. This property can be checked directly on the MTSv, because the specified variability constraint has the effect of transforming the C1 node into a *live* node.

The second constraint aa OR bb, instead, allows to specify that we consider as valid variants (products) of the MTSv only those variants that have either the aa event or the bb event, and possibly both of them, but not none of them (i.e. equivalent to a logical or). In this case, we end up with three valid LTS variants,

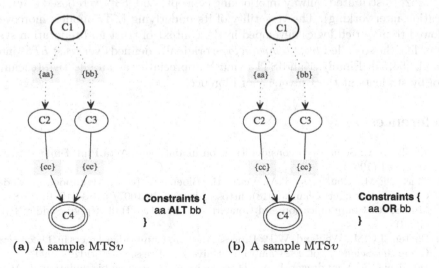

(a) A sample MTSv (b) A sample MTSv

Fig. 8. Sample MTSv with different variability constraints

and the formula AF_{cc} *true* continues to hold. Also in this case the effect of the variability constraint is to change the status of the node C1 into a *live* node, thus allowing the verification of the above formula directly on the MTSv with the guarantee the *TRUE* result is preserved by all the valid variants.

5 Conclusion

The KandISTI family of model checkers fully exploits the expressive power of the underlying L^2TS models. The framework plays the role of an experimental workbench, targeted mainly at teaching and research activity, without having in mind verification efficiency as its major aim.

The capability to navigate the state space both at the concrete and at an abstract level, together with useful debugging-oriented tools allow easy but exhaustive analysis/debugging of an initial (likely wrong) system design: in such cases, the focus of the tool is oriented to the collection and preservation of all the information that might be useful to explain a negative result, even at the cost of an increased or less efficient usage of the resources. Indeed, during the (on-the-fly) evaluation process all the local information of the generated states and transitions is preserved, to be possibly used once an explanation of the evaluation result is requested. Moreover, a small set of basic state predicates is defined, which allows to better control and understand the ongoing evaluation. The exploitation of this approach is made possible by the *lazy, left-to-right* evaluation approach for Boolean operators and the *top-down* (with respect to the formula structure and initial root state) evaluation process.

The characteristics of the KandISTI framework outlined in this paper have favoured its use in numerous exploratory studies, such as those in [47, 48] (intelligent domotic environments), [49–51] (deadlock avoidance in train scheduling), [52] (distributed railway interlocking concept) and [53] (web-based communication interworking). The versatility of its underlying L^2TS models moreover allowed to map rich logics developed in the context of trust and reputation systems, like the so-called *trust temporal logic* originally defined over *trust LTS*, onto UCTL [54, 55]. Finally, KandISTI is much appreciated as an effective teaching tool by students at the University of Florence.

References

1. Kripke, S.A.: Semantical considerations on modal logic. Acta Phil. Fennica **16**(5–6), 83–94 (1963)
2. Clarke, E.M., Henzinger, T.A., Veith, H., Bloem, R. (eds.): Handbook of Model Checking. Springer, Cham (2018). https://doi.org/10.1007/978-3-319-10575-8
3. Milner, R.: Communication and Concurrency. Prentice Hall, Upper Saddle River (1989)
4. Baeten, J.C.M., Weijland, W.P.: Process Algebra, Cambridge Tracts in Theoretical Computer Science, vol. 18. Cambridge University Press, Cambridge (1990)
5. De Nicola, R., Vaandrager, F.W.: Three logics for branching bisimulation. J. ACM **42**(2), 458–487 (1995)

6. Müller-Olm, M., Schmidt, D., Steffen, B.: Model-checking: a tutorial introduction. In: Cortesi, A., Filé, G. (eds.) SAS 1999. LNCS, vol. 1694, pp. 330–354. Springer, Heidelberg (1999). https://doi.org/10.1007/3-540-48294-6_22

7. Chaki, S., Clarke, E.M., Ouaknine, J., Sharygina, N., Sinha, N.: State/Event-based software model checking. In: Boiten, E.A., Derrick, J., Smith, G. (eds.) IFM 2004. LNCS, vol. 2999, pp. 128–147. Springer, Heidelberg (2004). https://doi.org/10.1007/978-3-540-24756-2_8

8. Cleaveland, R.: Pragmatics of model checking: an STTT special section. Int. J. Softw. Tools Technol. Transf. **2**(3), 208–218 (1999). https://doi.org/10.1007/s100090050030

9. Clarke, E.M., Emerson, E.A., Sistla, A.P.: Automatic verification of finite-state concurrent systems using temporal logic specifications. ACM Trans. Program. Lang. Syst. **8**(2), 244–263 (1986). https://doi.org/10.1145/5397.5399

10. Cleaveland, R., Steffen, B.: A linear-time model-checking algorithm for the alternation-free modal Mu-Calculus. Form. Method. Sys. Design **2**(2), 121–147 (1993). https://doi.org/10.1007/BF01383878

11. Queille, J.P., Sifakis, J.: Specification and verification of concurrent systems in CESAR. In: Dezani-Ciancaglini, Mariangiola, Montanari, Ugo (eds.) Programming 1982. LNCS, vol. 137, pp. 337–351. Springer, Heidelberg (1982). https://doi.org/10.1007/3-540-11494-7_22

12. Vardi, M.Y., Wolper, P.: An automata-theoretic approach to automatic program verification. In: Proceedings Symposium on Logic in Computer Science (LICS 1986), pp. 332–344. IEEE (1986)

13. Cleaveland, R., Klein, M., Steffen, B.: Faster model checking for the modal Mu-Calculus. In: von Bochmann, G., Probst, D.K. (eds.) CAV 1992. LNCS, vol. 663, pp. 410–422. Springer, Heidelberg (1993). https://doi.org/10.1007/3-540-56496-9_32

14. Bhat, G., Cleaveland, R., Grumberg, O.: Efficient on-the-fly model checking for CTL*. In: Proceedings 10th Symposium on Logic in Computer Science (LICS 1995), pp. 388–397. IEEE (1995). https://doi.org/10.1109/LICS.1995.523273

15. Mateescu, R., Sighireanu, M.: Efficient on-the-fly model-checking for regular alternation-free mu-calculus. Sci. Comput. Program. **46**(3), 255–281 (2003). https://doi.org/10.1016/S0167-6423(02)00094-1

16. Holzmann, G.J.: The SPIN Model Checker: Primer and Reference Manual. Addison-Wesley, Reading (2003)

17. Burkart, O., Steffen, B.: Model checking for context-free processes. In: Cleaveland, W.R. (ed.) CONCUR 1992. LNCS, vol. 630, pp. 123–137. Springer, Heidelberg (1992). https://doi.org/10.1007/BFb0084787

18. Hungar, H., Steffen, B.: Local model checking for context-free processes. In: Lingas, A., Karlsson, R., Carlsson, S. (eds.) ICALP 1993. LNCS, vol. 700, pp. 593–605. Springer, Heidelberg (1993). https://doi.org/10.1007/3-540-56939-1_105

19. ter Beek, M.H., Gnesi, S., Mazzanti, F.: From EU projects to a family of model checkers. In: De Nicola, R., Hennicker, R. (eds.) Software, Services, and Systems. LNCS, vol. 8950, pp. 312–328. Springer, Cham (2015). https://doi.org/10.1007/978-3-319-15545-6_20

20. ter Beek, M.H., Fantechi, A., Gnesi, S., Mazzanti, F.: A state/event-based model-checking approach for the analysis of abstract system properties. Sci. Comput. Program. **76**(2), 119–135 (2011). https://doi.org/10.1016/j.scico.2010.07.002

21. Fantechi, A., Gnesi, S., Lapadula, A., Mazzanti, F., Pugliese, R., Tiezzi, F.:
A logical verification methodology for service-oriented computing. ACM Trans.
Softw. Eng. Methodol. **21**(3), 16:1–16:46 (2012). https://doi.org/10.1145/2211616.
2211619

22. ter Beek, M.H., Mazzanti, F., Sulova, A.: VMC: a tool for product variability
analysis. In: Giannakopoulou, D., Méry, D. (eds.) FM 2012. LNCS, vol. 7436, pp.
450–454. Springer, Heidelberg (2012). https://doi.org/10.1007/978-3-642-32759-
9_36

23. ter Beek, M.H., Fantechi, A., Gnesi, S., Mazzanti, F.: Using FMC for family-based
analysis of software product lines. In: Proceedings 19th International Software
Product Line Conference (SPLC 2015), pp. 432–439. ACM (2015). https://doi.
org/10.1145/2791060.2791118

24. De Nicola, R., Vaandrager, F.: Action versus state based logics for transition systems. In: Guessarian, I. (ed.) LITP 1990. LNCS, vol. 469, pp. 407–419. Springer,
Heidelberg (1990). https://doi.org/10.1007/3-540-53479-2_17

25. De Nicola, R., Fantechi, A., Gnesi, S., Ristori, G.: An action based framework
for verifying logical and behavioural properties of concurrent systems. In: Larsen,
K.G., Skou, A. (eds.) CAV 1991. LNCS, vol. 575, pp. 37–47. Springer, Heidelberg
(1992). https://doi.org/10.1007/3-540-55179-4_5

26. Fantechi, A., Gnesi, S., Mazzanti, F., Pugliese, R., Tronci, E.: A symbolic model
checker for ACTL. In: Hutter, D., Stephan, W., Traverso, P., Ullmann, M. (eds.)
FM-Trends 1998. LNCS, vol. 1641, pp. 228–242. Springer, Heidelberg (1999).
https://doi.org/10.1007/3-540-48257-1_14

27. Clarke, E.M., Emerson, E.A.: Design and synthesis of synchronization skeletons
using branching time temporal logic. In: Kozen, D. (ed.) Logic of Programs 1981.
LNCS, vol. 131, pp. 52–71. Springer, Heidelberg (1982). https://doi.org/10.1007/
BFb0025774

28. Kozen, D.: Results on the propositional mu-Calculus. Theoret. Comput. Sci. **27**,
333–354 (1983). https://doi.org/10.1016/0304-3975(82)90125-6

29. Lawford, M., Ostroff, J.S., Wonham, W.M.: Model reduction of modules for state-
event temporal logics. In: Proceedings IFIP TC6 WG6.1 International Conference
on Formal Description Techniques IX/Protocol Specification, Testing and Verification XVI (FORTE/PSTV'96). IFIP Conference Proceedings, vol. 69, pp. 263–278.
Chapman & Hall, Ltd. (1996)

30. Graf, S., Loiseaux, C.: Property preserving abstractions under parallel composition.
In: Gaudel, M.-C., Jouannaud, J.-P. (eds.) CAAP 1993. LNCS, vol. 668, pp. 644–
657. Springer, Heidelberg (1993). https://doi.org/10.1007/3-540-56610-4_95

31. Pecheur, C., Raimondi, F.: Symbolic model checking of logics with actions. In:
Edelkamp, S., Lomuscio, A. (eds.) MoChArt 2006. LNCS (LNAI), vol. 4428, pp.
113–128. Springer, Heidelberg (2007). https://doi.org/10.1007/978-3-540-74128-
2_8

32. Larsen, K.G., Thomsen, B.: A modal process logic. In: Proceedings 3rd Symposium
on Logic in Computer Science (LICS 1988), pp. 203–210. IEEE (1988). https://
doi.org/10.1109/LICS.1988.5119

33. Antonik, A., Huth, M., Larsen, K.G., Nyman, U., Wąsowski, A.: 20 years of modal
and mixed specifications. Bull. EATCS **95**, 94–129 (2008)

34. Křetínský, J.: 30 years of modal transition systems: survey of extensions and anal-
ysis. In: Aceto, L., Bacci, G., Bacci, G., Ingólfsdóttir, A., Legay, A., Mardare,
R. (eds.) Models, Algorithms, Logics and Tools. LNCS, vol. 10460, pp. 36–74.
Springer, Cham (2017). https://doi.org/10.1007/978-3-319-63121-9_3

35. Bradfield, J.C., Stirling, C.: Modal logics and μ-Calculi: an introduction. In: Bergstra, J.A., Ponse, A., Smolka, S.A. (eds.) Handbook of Process Algebra, pp. 293–330. Elsevier (2001). https://doi.org/10.1016/B978-044482830-9/50022-9

36. Kindler, E., Vesper, T.: ESTL: a temporal logic for events and states. In: Desel, J., Silva, M. (eds.) ICATPN 1998. LNCS, vol. 1420, pp. 365–384. Springer, Heidelberg (1998). https://doi.org/10.1007/3-540-69108-1_20

37. Clarke, E.M., Grumberg, O., Peled, D.A.: Model Checking. The MIT Press, Cambridge (1999)

38. ter Beek, M.H., Fantechi, A., Gnesi, S., Mazzanti, F.: An action/state-based model-checking approach for the analysis of communication protocols for service-oriented applications. In: Leue, S., Merino, P. (eds.) FMICS 2007. LNCS, vol. 4916, pp. 133–148. Springer, Heidelberg (2008). https://doi.org/10.1007/978-3-540-79707-4_11

39. Pnueli, A.: Linear and branching structures in the semantics and logics of reactive systems. In: Brauer, W. (ed.) ICALP 1985. LNCS, vol. 194, pp. 15–32. Springer, Heidelberg (1985). https://doi.org/10.1007/BFb0015727

40. Steffen, B., Ingólfsdóttir, A.: Characteristic formulae for processes with divergence. Inf. Comput. **110**(1), 149–163 (1994). https://doi.org/10.1006/inco.1994.1028

41. Gnesi, S., Mazzanti, F.: An abstract, on the fly framework for the verification of service-oriented systems. In: Wirsing, M., Hölzl, M. (eds.) Rigorous Software Engineering for Service-Oriented Systems. LNCS, vol. 6582, pp. 390–407. Springer, Heidelberg (2011). https://doi.org/10.1007/978-3-642-20401-2_18

42. ter Beek, M.H., Mazzanti, F., Gnesi, S.: CMC-UMC: a framework for the verification of abstract service-oriented properties. In: Proceedings 24th Symposium on Applied Computing (SAC 2009), pp. 2111–2117. ACM (2009). https://doi.org/10.1145/1529282.1529751

43. ter Beek, M.H., Fantechi, A., Gnesi, S., Mazzanti, F.: Modelling and analysing variability in product families: model checking of modal transition systems with variability constraints. J. Log. Algebr. Meth. Program. **85**(2), 287–315 (2016). https://doi.org/10.1016/j.jlamp.2015.11.006

44. Hennessy, M., Milner, R.: Algebraic laws for nondeterminism and concurrency. J. ACM **32**(1), 137–161 (1985). https://doi.org/10.1145/2455.2460

45. Mateescu, R., Thivolle, D.: A model checking language for concurrent value-passing systems. In: Cuellar, J., Maibaum, T., Sere, K. (eds.) FM 2008. LNCS, vol. 5014, pp. 148–164. Springer, Heidelberg (2008). https://doi.org/10.1007/978-3-540-68237-0_12

46. ter Beek, M.H., Mazzanti, F.: VMC: recent advances and challenges ahead. In: Proceedings 18th International Software Product Line Conference (SPLC 2014), vol. 2, pp. 70–77. ACM (2014). https://doi.org/10.1145/2647908.2655969

47. Corno, F., Sanaullah, M.: Design time methodology for the formal verification of intelligent domotic environments. ISAmI 2011. AINSC, vol. 92, pp. 9–16. Springer, Heidelberg (2011). https://doi.org/10.1007/978-3-642-19937-0_2

48. Corno, F., Sanaullah, M.: Formal verification of device state chart models. In: Proceedings 7th International Conference on Intelligent Environments (IE 2011), pp. 66–73. IEEE (2011). https://doi.org/10.1109/IE.2011.36

49. Mazzanti, F., Spagnolo, G.O., Della Longa, S., Ferrari, A.: Deadlock avoidance in train scheduling: a model checking approach. In: Lang, F., Flammini, F. (eds.) FMICS 2014. LNCS, vol. 8718, pp. 109–123. Springer, Cham (2014). https://doi.org/10.1007/978-3-319-10702-8_8

50. Mazzanti, F., Spagnolo, G.O., Ferrari, A.: Designing a deadlock-free train sched-uler: a model checking approach. In: Badger, J.M., Rozier, K.Y. (eds.) NFM 2014. LNCS, vol. 8430, pp. 264–269. Springer, Cham (2014). https://doi.org/10.1007/978-3-319-06200-6_22

51. Mazzanti, F., Ferrari, A., Spagnolo, G.O.: Towards formal methods diversity in railways: an experience report with seven frameworks. Int. J. Softw. Tools Technol. Transf. **20**(3), 263–288 (2018). https://doi.org/10.1007/s10009-018-0488-3

52. Fantechi, A., Haxthausen, A.E., Nielsen, M.B.R.: Model checking geographically distributed interlocking systems using UMC. In: Proceedings 25th Euromicro Inter-national Conference on Parallel, Distributed and Network-Based Processing (PDP 2017), pp. 278–286. IEEE (2017). https://doi.org/10.1109/PDP.2017.66

53. Paganelli, F., Ambra, T., Fantechi, A., Giuli, D.: Formalizing REST APIs for web-based communication and SIP interworking. Telecommun. Syst. **66**(1), 75–93 (2017). https://doi.org/10.1007/s11235-016-0271-2

54. Aldini, A.: Modeling and verification of trust and reputation systems. Secur. Comm. Netw. **8**(16), 2933–2946 (2015). https://doi.org/10.1002/sec.1220

55. Aldini, A.: Design and verification of trusted collective adaptive systems. ACM Trans. Model. Comput. Simul. **28**(2), 9:1–9:27 (2018). https://doi.org/10.1145/3155337

Making Sense of Complex Applications: Constructive Design, Features, and Questions

Tiziana Margaria[✉]

Chair of Software Systems, University of Limerick, and Lero, Limerick, Ireland
tiziana.margaria@ul.ie

Abstract. We highlight how concepts of constructive design help in the comprehension of complex systems, using the history and evolution of the Online Conference Service (OCS) and its product line, including the Online Journal Service for journal management, as examples for the needs and solutions of how to master design of systems with complex behaviour. They nicely summarize over 20 years of evolution of one of the most exciting and long lived joint research streams with Bernhard Steffen and our research group. The constructive design concepts we found most useful include the use of features to make large and complex systems more manageable, properties to formulate behavioural requirements on the models' functionality as well as policies and access rights, and the role of questions as model checking problems as well as test-driven exploration.

1 The Online Conference Service (OCS) over the Years

The Online Conference Service (OCS) was first designed in 1998-99 [14,17,20], in a collaboration with Springer Verlag that continues until this day, and in a time where we had successfully embraced the service oriented culture prevalent in Intelligent Network (IN) Services in those years. Following the collaboration with Siemens in their INXpress product in 1994-96 [41], we had successfully transported the same culture of service orientation into the METAFrame development framework described in [40]. We transported it from the telecommunication into the internet domain, with initial collaborations with Bertelsmann's Telemedia for the METACatalogue online shop [36]. At about the same time, we used the same service-oriented and model driven technology to integrate printed and online information in a pioneering multiplatform mashup that included the very first QR codes, based on IDOCs, the NeoMedia Technologies' Intelligent Document Solutions. This Online Integrated Print Service (IPS) was presented in cooperation with Springer Verlag at the CeBIT 1998 [5].

The OCS (see [17,19]) proactively helped authors, Program Committee chairs, Program Committee members, and reviewers to cooperate efficiently during their collaborative handling of the composition of a conference program. Its strength in terms of adaptation to the needs of each conference and community

T. Margaria et al. (Eds.): Steffen Festschrift, LNCS 11200, pp. 129–148, 2019.
https://doi.org/10.1007/978-3-030-22348-9_9

was its customization ability: it was in fact flexibly reconfigurable online at any time for each role, for each conference, and for each user [15].

The original OCS was extremely successful: it formed a Software Product Line with the Online Journal Service (OJS), the Management Overview System (MOS), and the LNCS Proposal Service for the LNCS Editors (this last service hosted by Springer Verlag in Heidelberg). This initial OCS implementation served hundreds of conferences, mostly in non-CS domains, and today this OJS is still in use for STTT, Springer's International Journal on Software Tools for Technology Transfer. An example of OCS's continued use was presented in [20], where we analyzed its use and discussed its effectiveness in the ETAPS joint federated conferences, that widely adopted it in the early 2000s.

Together, these online decision systems formed a family of services sharing the same concept of role-based management of user rights. These services have been successfully used over the last 8 years for a number of collaborative editorial processes revolving around the management of scientific publications for conferences and journals. With increasingly complex access management tasks within the family of services, we needed to accommodate both flexible roles and flexible exception handling which led us gradually towards a web-based, model driven Role Management Service. Such reconfigurability at runtime in this type of system was innovative when it was created 10 years earlier.

The next generation of the OCS [32] has been built in jABC4 [33] and in a model-driven and service-oriented online fashion that led to an agile, phase-oriented and role-driven organization of the software. This organisation lent itself to a large variety of analyses by means of formal methods model checking of the emerging global behavior that resulted as emergent property from the collaboration (and coordination) of the basic features. We reconstructed the global behavior models via active automata learning, with successive validation of these global models for global properties.

This generation of OCS services has supported hundreds of conferences for the Springer Verlag, and it is available as well for FoMaC, the LNCS Transactions on Foundations for Managing Change [1,37].

The current generation of OCS, called Equinocs, is being completely redesigned in a DSL-meta-modelling supported fashion. The meta-model based design approach covered initially the data models and persistency management in DyWA [31]. In Equinocs it covers now the complete web application design thanks to DIME [3], the DyWA Integrated Modelling Environment, the most advanced and comprehensive CINCO-product [30].

In this paper, we summarize the service and feature-based design of the OCS software product line (SPL) in Sect. 2, highlighting in particular how thinking in terms of units of functionality naturally led to the adoption of a feature based development. The adoption of a feature-oriented service description that goes beyond the traditional concept stemming from the Intelligent Network systems is further detailed in Sect. 3. The user-centric model based on intents adopted in the New OCS1 is described in Sect. 4, as well as the use of automata learning technologies to reconstruct the emerging global behaviour and to make it

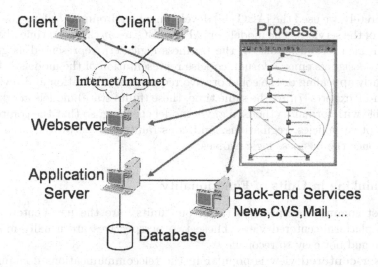

Fig. 1. Client/Server architecture of the OCS

amenable to model checking. The new meta-modelling approaches that underlie the design of the third and current generation of the OCS and similar applications, DyWA and DIME, are sketched in Sect. 5. Finally, Sect. 6 concludes the paper and identifies a new challenge related to behavioural synthesis.

2   Service and Feature-Based Design of the OCS Software Product Line

The OCS, like the OJS, exhibited a typical Client-Server Architecture (see Fig. 1) with a distributed backend. It ran on an application server that executed the whole workflow of the application. The back-end services comprised Database, News, CVS, and Mail services, and they were running on separate servers accessible by the OCS. The database was used to store the article's meta data and service specific data, e.g. user profiles, roles, and reports, whereas the article files and sources were handled by the CVS version control system. All the services and their functionalities were accessible to the users via the common internet browsers without the need to install any software on the client side.

The OCS was designed as a process controlled system whose business logic was consistently designed in an eXtreme Model Driven paradigm [26] according to the Lightweight Process Coordination approach [25]. A central advantage of this model driven development style is the agility at the business process modelling level: decoupling the design of the logic from the implementation level we achieved a high degree of reuse of features inside the services. This organisation in features was a central asset when transitioning to a family of services.

Concretely, we used the jABC [44] development environment[1] along the whole lifecycle of the services. The models in jABC/ABC are at the same time abstract, coarse grained formal models of the business logic [17], represented as graphs. This way, designers enjoy a visual, concise representation of the models, which is particularly appealing or the collaborative requirement elicitation and reviewing with non-IT experts [7]. At the same time, these (finite state) models are directly analyzable with formal methods, e.g. via model checking, so that the compliance to descriptive policies, regulations, and constraints can be proven, and easily checked once the business logic evolves.

2.1   Thinking in Units of Functionality

The most common perspectives taken on "units" are the user-centered view and the platform-centered view. These two perspectives are usually mutually exclusive and not easy to reconcile.

A **user-centered** view is popular in the telecommunications domain: it is embodied by the "idea" of a SIB, a Service Independent Building Block that is defined by the use one can make (which meaningful service does it offer to me?) and not by its implementation. The library of SIBs for Intelligent Network services was itself standardized [10], leading to a well-defined set of capabilities that defined the DSL available to a library user (here an IN application designer). This standardization "from the outside" ensured the interoperation between functionalities offered by the different vendors, independently of the technology, platform, operating system, programming language chosen by any particular member of this complex ecosystem.

A **platform-centered** model is native to the Service Component Architecture (SCA) [13] idea of a service, and provides a completely different take on the concept of service: it is the inside-out perspective from the point of view of a provider. It is the same perspective that underlies other architectural perspectives popular in software engineering: the "unit" is a static building block that offers its many and articulated capabilities to an environment that must know how to use it. The concept of "use" is here the static composability with other components, not what functionality it provides to the users.

We follow the principle that *form follows function*: first we determine a use, and then we see how best to cater to that use. So architecture, granularity, interfaces and implementations must follow the use, and not the other way around. In view of continuous evolution of software systems, change management process is ubiquitous. Change comes in terms of maintenance and upgrade, for example with extension of the SIB palettes, in new implementations of the same SIBs, and in the evolution of the classification of the SIB palettes along a domain specific organization in taxonomies [23].

Already back then we were thinking semantically. Simple but powerful semantic descriptions in terms of atomic propositions ranging over taxonomies were

---

[1] The releases prior to 2005 were realized in the ABC [38], the C++ predecessor of the jABC.

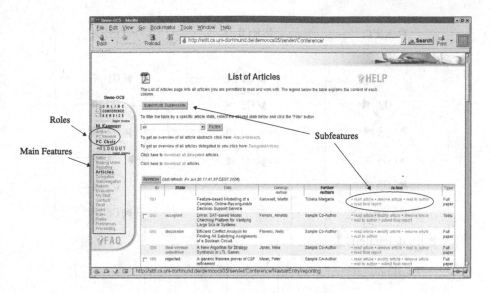

Fig. 2. Role-based management in the OCS: the user's view

attached to the SIBs and used to express properties. Our CTL model checker and the LTL synthesis algorithm were able to use these properties to check the SLG models or to build property-compliant workflows.

2.2 Feature Model in the OCS

The service's capabilities are grouped in *features*, which are assigned to specific *roles*, described in more details in [17]. Figure 2 shows the feature structure for the management of the List of Articles from the service user's point of view. In the OCS, a single user may be assigned many roles: e.g., a PC Chair could be also a PC Member, thus do reviews, or a PC Member may be allowed to submit papers and thus be simultaneously Author. Users can switch between their roles at any time during a working session. In the snapshot of Fig. 2 the user has selected the PC Chair role This is the main role of the service providing the full access on the necessary service components for managing the conference. A fine granular roles and rights management system takes care of the adequate admin-istration of the context, role and user-specific permissions and restrictions. We distinguish between Main Features in the navigation bar and their Subfeatures placed in the content page. The navigation bar provides a set of first level features according to the active role of the user. Users in different roles cooperate during the lifetime of a PC's operations and make use of the OCS capabilities which are provisioned at the feature level. It is through the cooperation of its features that the OCS provides timely, transparent, and secure handling of the papers and the related submission, review, report and decision management tasks.

From the point of view of the user and role management, features are seen as a collection of functionalities of the service which can be switched on and off

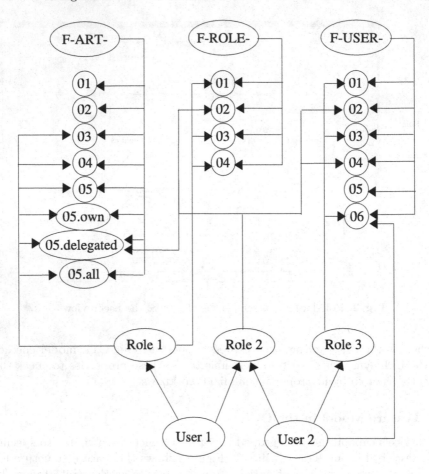

Fig. 3. The user-role-rights relations

for single roles and for single users. Figure 3 shows a schematic example of the relations between the users, roles, and rights.

3   Feature-Oriented Service Description: Beyond IN

The definition of feature depends heavily on their use as well as on the context. We learned to know and use features in the context of Intelligent Networks [9,39,43]. In IN services, the base system was large: a switch that offered POTS (plain old telephone service) functionality. The features were comparatively small extensions of that behaviour, as implemented in our environment for the creation of Intelligent Network Services [41] and in the original METAFrame'95 environment [40].

Our own notion of OCS features has been more general and more similar to a DSL in order to capture services that tend to have a *lean* basis service that deals with session, user, and role-rights management, and a collection of very rich features. This different balance and organisation brings a different perspective on the role and purpose of features.

Definition 1 (Feature). *(see [28])*

1. A feature *is a piece of (optional) functionality built on top of a base system.*
2. *It is* monotonic, *in the sense that each feature* extends *the base system by an* increment *of functionality.*
3. *The description of each feature* may *consider or require other features, additionally to the base system.*
4. *It is defined from an* external *point of view, i.e., by the viewpoint of* users and/or providers *of* services.
5. *Its granularity is determined by* marketing *or* provisioning *purposes.*

To support the complex evolution of services, we adopted a *multilevel organization* of features whereby more specialistic features build upon the availability of other, more basic, functionalities. In order to keep this structure manageable and the behaviours easily understandable, we restrict our focus to *monotonic* features which are guaranteed to add behaviour. Restricting behaviour, which is also done via features in other contexts (e.g. [6]), is done in an orthogonal way in our setting, via constraints at the requirements level.

The definition of the feature-based architecture of our systems was already back then based on

- DSLs where the SIBs are the domain specific primitives, and features as SLGs, available both as descriptions (services) and implementations, and
- knowledge about the properties of SIB and feature behaviours expressed as constraints.

Definition 2 (Feature-oriented Description). *(see [28])*

1. *A* feature-oriented service description *of a complex service specifies the behaviours of a* base system *and a* set of *optional features.*
2. *The behaviour of each feature and of the basic system are given by means of Service Logic Graphs (SLGs) [43].*
3. *The realization of each SLG bases on a library of* reusable components *called Service Independent Building-Blocks (SIBs).*
4. *The feature-oriented service description includes also a set of* abstract requirements *that ensure that the intended purposes are* met.
5. Interactions *between features are regulated* explicitly *and are usually expressed via* constraints.
6. *Any* feature composition *is allowed that does not violate any constraint.*

We distinguish the description of the feature's behaviour from that of the legal use of a feature. Restrictions on behaviours are expressed at a different level, i.e. at the requirements level. They are part of an aspect-oriented description of properties that we want to be able to check automatically, using formal verification methods.

Thinking in features was essential to mastering the complexity of the OCS and its transformation into a Product Line: although we never published the feature models of these systems, they share not only portions of code (as common in code-based reuse) but entire SLG palettes and SLGs themselves. In fact, the article, delegation, and report management are similar to those of the OCS and can be reused without problems. What changes in this approach is the decision structure: a journal has an asynchronous, noncompetitive evaluation of single papers, rather than the synchronous, competitive evaluation of a set of submissions for a conference. Features like the discussion forums for single papers are seldom used. Instead there is a more sophisticated status and progress management, the management of several cycles of revision for a submission, and a number of management roles that cover different aspects (Editor, Editor in Chief, Guest Editor, Editorial Office for the manuscript management, ...). Due to the longer life of the OJS instances, the personal situation of single users is usually subject to changes and compartmentation, requiring a finer grained management of the roles and rights. This fine grained management could be done via exception handling within an OCS-style role management, though this solution does not scale elegantly.

We chose instead to introduce an additional personalisation layer to the role management concept to handle the individual differences from the norm [15]. Personalization is added to the OJS dynamically via an additional user permission concept that is implemented by a user-role-rights modifier to the OCS-style role management. We extended the user/role management and made it possible to assign rights to single users. Such properties were model checkable as shown in [15] and amounted to a dynamic extension of a RBAC model as shown in [16]. Having well exceeded the approximately 2500 nodes and 3500 edges of the original OCS, this organization form was not able to master the model complexity and the related system complexity. A new User-centric mindset provided the solution.

4   The User-Centric Model in the New OCS

Changing the perspective from a system construction mindset to a user-centric mindset that expresses the point of view and the experience of any user, with one or more roles, brought us to approach the design of the new the OCS as the design of a reactive system with a graphical user interface that is provided as a web application. Users decide autonomously when they execute their tasks, which typically consist of small workflows. In case of multiple tasks, they also choose the order in which they want to process or perhaps reject a task. The potential interactions offered by the OCS application strongly depend on the specific phase (submission, reviewing, discussion, ...) of the evaluation process, which has a control-oriented character. Considering the high degree of freedom in choosing individual tasks and the large number of involved actors, we moved away from modeling this coordination directly, in terms of control-oriented graph structures. This decision was made due to the complexity of a prescriptive logic for such

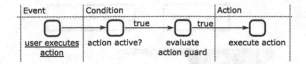

Fig. 4. ECA rule for the declarative aspects of the new OCS (from [32])

coordination mechanisms. As seen with the previous design, direct coordination indirectly reintroduced at the SLG and feature level a coordination-style state explosion problem [4]. We decided instead to adopt a hybrid modeling approach comprised of

- a collection of individual models for each business entity (like conference, paper, ...) organized and synchronized by means of events and resource sharing,
- individual models in terms of control-flow graph-like structures, expressing the stepwise evolution of the individual processes for each of the involved business objects within the overall evaluation process, which consist of
- states embedding Event-Condition-Action-rules. As shown in Fig. 4, ECA-rules model the potential of user interactions as a set of rules which can be accessed concurrently, and which are selected according to a current event and an associated condition. They declaratively express the alternative behaviors that the system offers in each state.

In practice, we did not have anymore a predefined SLG structure, but rather a collection of individual models for the various business entities that could be verified by means of techniques like model checking [32]. At this time we had also built the LearnLib [29,35] that had become an efficient and scalable automata learning platform. We dealt with the overall correctness of the evaluation processes along an alternative approach: we used automata learning to build via guided experimentation the overall behavioral model from the real implementation, and then model checked that inferred automaton w.r.t the desired properties. The charm of this approach is that it suppresses all the internal details of the complex design models as well as the difficulty of dealing with the complex communication and synchronization methods in modern enterprise architectures, and clearly focussed on the primary issue: the user level correctness. Figure 5 sketches how we proceeded. We started with some local models describing for example the overall evaluation pattern for conference proceedings and the lifecycle of papers from the user's perspective. These models can then be model checked for essential properties, comprising security aspects, progress properties, or simply the intended causality. Subsequently, these 'local' models were semi-automatically combined and transformed to run on an enterprise platform using complex communication and synchronization primitives, like event handling, process creation, etc. In particular, this means that we did not construct a global model of the OCS. We gave instead full freedom for the above-mentioned transformation, which we then complemented by automata learning techniques

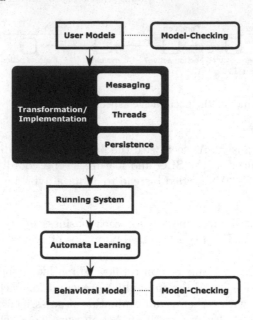

Fig. 5. Procedure model for the model-driven development approach for the new OCS (from [32])

to retrospectively infer a global model. Key to the global validation of the corresponding emergent behavior is the experimental exploration of and behavioral model construction for the system via automata learning.

4.1   Intent-Oriented Decomposition: Declarative Meets Prescriptive

Figure 6 depicts the user model of a conference paper's behavior as a hybrid graph. Syntactically, the first state is the 'Start' node and the control flows along the edges. Edge labels represent events (either system events or user interactions) that trigger the transition to a successor state. For example, system events occur when a deadline expires and cause the system to transition to a different phase (state) with a different behavior. The available actions in a given state are recognizably modeled as ECA rules. It is not uniquely determined what of the rich control structure is best captured as control structure and what as ECA rule: this is clearly a matter of design. In fact, if one wishes less states and more compact graphs it is possible to introduce more preconditions than just those defined by the state and the role.

4.2   Learning and Validating Emerging Global Behaviour

Automata learning [8,34] has the potential to infer or extrapolate approximations and views of a user process via systematic experimentation with the application running on an enterprise platform. The arising models can then be used

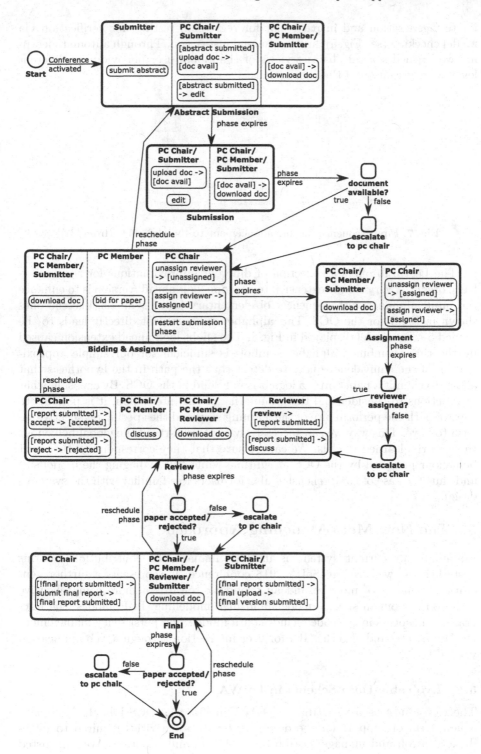

Fig. 6. The hybrid user model of a paper's behavior in the new OCS (from [32])

for test generation and in particular for regression testing, for verification via model checking (see Fig. 5), and for manual inspection. Through automata learning we learned several abstract views of the global user behaviour at different levels of aggregation of the user actions.

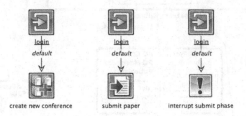

Fig. 7. Input sequences as an enhancement to the alphabet (from [32])

The LearnLib offers a collection of different approximations for the equivalence oracle. A very simple extension to the 'one look-ahead' version is to enhance the input alphabet with sequences of elementary input symbols, like the ones shown in Fig. 7 for the OCS. This alphabet enhancement directly leads to the refined 5-state model displayed in Fig. 8. The slight look-ahead extension caused by the three combined alphabet symbols is sufficient for our simple approximation of the equivalence query to detect that the path in the hypothesis that allows to submit a paper after a logout is not valid in the OCS. By choosing what user actions to consider and the granularity of the interaction, it is possible to control both the performance of the learning step and the specific perspective we wish to have. This way we can successively explore parts of the global behaviour through the learned models. We can be sure that they correspond to the exact behaviour provided by the OCS at runtime while still managing the model size and thus the ease of comprehension also for users less familiar with the system's design.

5   The New Meta-Modelling Approach

Equinocs, our current system, is used to manage the contributions to this Festschrift as well as the ISoLA 2018 conference. It represents a further generational change of mindset and an evolution towards a more comprehensive adoption of domain specific models and metamodelling. In Equinocs, the integration of aspects in the code includes data models and persistency management via DyWA [31] and also the GUI for user interaction through a web application via DIME [3].

5.1   Evolvable Data Schema in DyWA

The case study used to introduce DyWA in [31] was OCS-Lite. It showcased a new form of support for the design of business activities required to introduce, control, and manage new business objects and resources. We contrasted

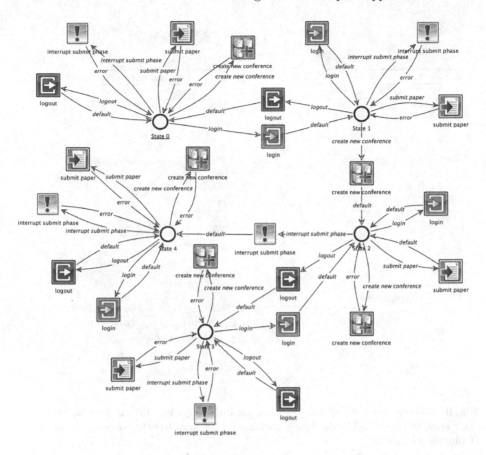

Fig. 8. Learned Mealy automaton with symbol sequences (Fig. 7) (from [32])

the standard BPM approaches, focused on the business logic only, with DyWA's ease of definition and management for the data and objects that occur in the applications. We demonstrated its efficient and robust support for evolution and change. The name DyWA stands for Dynamic Web Application, where the "dynamics" concern the ease of evolution and change of the data architecture and data schema, a holy grail in traditional software maintenance. We introduced the Online Conference Service (OCS)-lite as a small case study, modelled its types in DyWA, created the necessary processes in jABC, and exported them back into DyWA in order to offer to the end users a running web application obtained entirely without manual coding. We then changed the requirements, impacting both the data types and the business logic of the application, and showed how the application was evolved by users accordingly without writing new code. The power of DyWA is connected with behavioral model-driven design as auspicated in [21] and [22]: the original DyWA was for the user a web-based definition facility for the type schema of any application domain of choice.

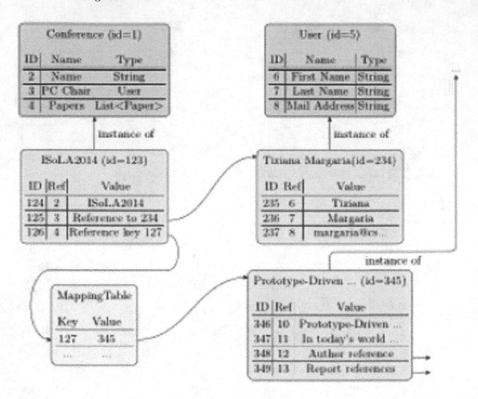

Fig. 9. Schematic layout of the OCS-lite business objects. Objects (green) reference their specific types and fields (blue), and hold references to other objects. (From [31]) (Color figure online)

Coupled with the defined types is the automatic generation of corresponding Create, Read, Update, Delete (CRUD) operations, so that application experts are able to model domain specific business processes which are directly executable in our modelling environment. Upon change, the prototype can be augmented or modified stepwise by acting on one or more types in the type schema, the corresponding data-objects, and the executable process models, while maintaining executability at all times. As every step is automated via a corresponding code generator, no manual coding is required.

As shown in Fig. 9, the web application runs on a meta schema that describes data in terms of *MS-types* and *MS-objects*, both stored in the meta schema database. A MS-type is used to model the concrete types and associations of an application domain, whereas MS-objects hold the actual data of the application and thus constitute instantiations of the respective MS-Types. Objects are linked to a type, yielding a concept of typed domain specific data. This organization allows to save domain unspecific, arbitrary data as long as they can be described with the type schema. The concrete basic types are the Java types. This design decision greatly simplifies the ORM aspects because referen-

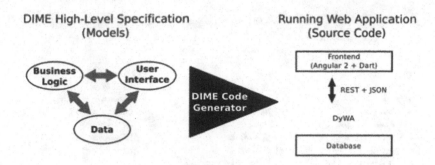

Fig. 10. The DIME concept: full generation of web applications from abstract model specifications (From [3])

tial integrity is guaranteed by design, independently from the names of types and fields. As a consequence, the further goal of independence from the kind of database is easily achievable. Indeed, the DyWA design is mappable to a large variety of persistence paradigms, e.g., to a NoSQL, relational, or any other class of database.

5.2 Evolvable Web Applications in DIME

Equinocs is implemented in DIME, the DyWA Integrated Modeling Environment [3] that allows the integrated modelling of all the aspects needed for the design of a complete web application in terms of Graphical Domain-Specific Languages (GDSLs). Figure 11 shows that models capture the control flow as so far happened in the Service Logic Graphs, but we have additionally also data models and UI models in the same IDE. All these models are interdependently connected, shaping the 'one thing' in a manner which is formal, yet easy to understand and to use. The continuous and model driven deployment cycle is simplified to the extent that its code can be one-click-generated and deployed as a complete and ready to run web application. This happens along the process sketched in Fig. 10.

We did not yet report on Equinocs, but we have used the same DIME technology to design a smaller service for the matchmaking of students with Final Year Project topics proposed by supervisors in the Computer Science and Information Systems Department in Limerick, called the *CSIS FYP* service. This service is used as a common case study for applied XMDD in the 5 modules taught to 3rd semester Computer Science bachelor students. The students learn the various kinds of models supported by DIME, compare them with the UML standard, E-R diagrams, and other state-of-the-art techniques for modelling and OOP design/development. They apply requirement engineering methods to the description of the system "as-is" and identify ways to extend or improve it along the wishes of various stakeholders they interview. The generative approach in DIME is compared with the manual modelling + coding approach taught in

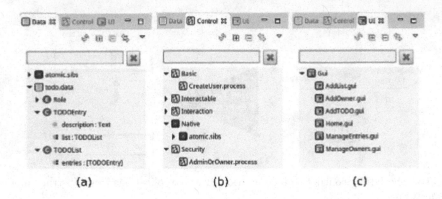

Fig. 11. Model component views in DIME: (a) Data (b) Control (c) UI (From [3])

Object Oriented Development. The DyWA is compared to the standard relational database design and use. As a different approach to Software Quality, they also apply model checking to the models, building upon the knowledge of CTL gained in the first semester and using the GEAR model checker they used on the first semester projects [2]. Finally, we use the active automata learning approach based on LearnLib [24] and specifically the ALEX front-end [27] in order to extract a complete and checkable model from the running system, compare it to the design models, and generate both model driven and model based test suites in the Software Testing module.

6   Conclusions and Perspectives

Constructive design, tied to executable systems and "living" models, proved to significantly support the comprehension of complex systems. For example, during this semester we have used all these papers and material to teach the new module *Software Requirements and Modelling* at the University of Limerick. The concepts of traditional model driven design vs. XMDD, the use and role of properties for constraint-guarded vs. constraint-based design [12], the essence of features as a means to organise and reuse, and the feature interaction problem [11]. Properties were used to formulate verifiable behavioural requirements on the models' functionality as well as policies and access rights, and we explored the role of "questions" both as model checking problems as well as for test-driven exploration of the final system.

Although working in practice with the modern CSIS FYP service, a web application designed in DIME and thus from the point of view of the OCS evolution, at the leading edge of our current technology, the research papers about the older versions of the OCS served excellently as a scaffolding support. The students were able to compare the much smaller FYP service with the "logic" of the concrete design and the design principles of the previous generations, retracing the evolution and development of the concepts, the IDEs, and the corresponding capabilities. They could better appreciate the interplay between all these capabilities. Making sense of a complex system is greatly aided by the organisation along intents in a user-centred way.

Considering the 20 years of our technology journey embodied by the various stages of the OCS, we see that we did not yet include the synthesis of new behaviours by using model construction [42], e.g. using PROPHETS [18], which would constitute the ultimate level of automation: constructing new portions of the system directly from questions, at the borderline between declarative and prescriptive. We look forward to tackling this further challenge with Bernhard Steffen.

Acknowledgements. Thanks for years of excellent collaboration along the OCS adventure are due to Martin Karusseit, Johannes Neubauer, Stefan Naujokat and Steve Boßelmann: it has been an exciting journey!

This work was supported, in part, by Science Foundation Ireland grants 13/RC/2094 and 16/RC/3918 and co-funded under the European Regional Development Fund through the Southern & Eastern Regional Operational Programme to Lero - the Irish Software Research Centre (www.lero.ie) and Confirm, the Centre for Smart Manufacturing (www.confirm.ie)

References

1. Steffen, B. (ed.): Transactions on Foundations of Mastering Change. Springer, Heidelberg (2016). https://doi.org/10.1007/978-3-319-46508-1
2. Bakera, M., Margaria, T., Renner, C., Steffen, B.: Tool-supported enhancement of diagnosis in model-driven verification. Innov. Syst. Softw. Eng. **5**, 211–228 (2009). https://doi.org/10.1007/s11334-009-0091-6
3. Boßelmann, S., et al.: DIME: a programming-less modeling environment for web applications. In: Margaria, T., Steffen, B. (eds.) ISoLA 2016, Part II. LNCS, vol. 9953, pp. 809–832. Springer, Cham (2016). https://doi.org/10.1007/978-3-319-47169-3_60
4. Clarke, E.M., Grumberg, O., Peled, D.: Model Checking. MIT Press, Cambridge (2001)
5. Friese, T., Margaria, T., Hofmann, A.: Integrating printed and online information. STTT **2**(2), 202 (1998). https://doi.org/10.1007/s100090050028
6. Harris, H., Ryan, M.: Theoretical foundations of updating systems. In: International Conference on Automated Software Engineering, p. 291 (2003)
7. Hörmann, M., Margaria, T., Mender, T., Nagel, R., Steffen, B., Trinh, H.: The jABC approach to rigorous collaborative development of SCM applications. In: Margaria, T., Steffen, B. (eds.) ISoLA 2008. CCIS, vol. 17, pp. 724–737. Springer, Heidelberg (2008). https://doi.org/10.1007/978-3-540-88479-8_52
8. Hungar, H., Steffen, B.: Behavior-based model construction. STTT Int. J. Softw. Tools Technol. Transf. **6**(1), 4–14 (2004)
9. ITU: general recommendations on telephone switching and signaling intelligent network: introduction to intelligent network capability set 1. In: Recommendation Q.1211, Telecommunication Standardization Sector of ITU, Geneva, March 1993

10. ITU-T: recommendation q.1204. In: Distributed Functional Plane for Intelligent Network Capability Set 2: Parts 1–4, September 1997
11. Jonsson, B., Margaria, T., Naeser, G., Nyström, J., Steffen, B.: Incremental requirement specification for evolving systems. Nordic J. Comput. **8**, 65–87 (2001). http://dl.acm.org/citation.cfm?id=774194.774199
12. Jörges, S., Lamprecht, A.L., Margaria, T., Schaefer, I., Steffen, B.: A constraint-based variability modeling framework. Int. J. Softw. Tools Technol. Transf. (STTT) **14**(5), 511–530 (2012)
13. Jung, G., Margaria, T., Nagel, R., Schubert, W., Steffen, B., Voigt, H.: SCA and jABC: bringing a service-oriented paradigm to web-service construction. In: Margaria, T., Steffen, B. (eds.) ISoLA 2008. CCIS, vol. 17, pp. 139–154. Springer, Heidelberg (2008). https://doi.org/10.1007/978-3-540-88479-8_11
14. Karusseit, M., Margaria, T.: Feature-based modelling of a complex, online-reconfigurable decision support service. In: 1st International Workshop Automated Specification and Verification of Web Sites, WWV 2005, eNTCS 1132, March 2005
15. Karusseit, M., Margaria, T.: A web-based runtime-reconfigurable role management service. In: 2nd International Workshop on Automated Specification and Verification of Web Systems, WWV 2006, pp. 53–60. IEEE (2007)
16. Karusseit, M., Margaria, T., Willebrandt, H.: Policy expression and checking in XACML, WS-policies, and the jABC. In: Proceedings of Workshop on Testing, Analysis, and Verification of Web Services and Applications, held in conjunction with the ISSTA 2008, TAV-WEB 2008, Seattle, Washington, USA, pp. 20–26. ACM (2008)
17. Karusseit, M., Margaria, T.: Feature-based modelling of a complex, online-reconfigurable decision support service. Electr. Notes Theor. Comput. Sci. **157**(2), 101–118 (2006)
18. Lamprecht, A.L., Naujokat, S., Margaria, T., Steffen, B.: Synthesis-based loose programming. In: Proceedings of the 7th International Conference on the Quality of Information and Communications Technology (QUATIC 2010), Porto, Portugal, pp. 262–267. IEEE, September 2010
19. Lindner, B., Margaria, T., Steffen, B.: Ein personalisierter internetdienst für wissenschaftliche begutachtungsprozesse. In: Proceedings of GI-VOI-BITKOM-OCG-TeleTrusT Konferenz on Elektronische Geschäftsprozesse (eBusiness Processes), Universität Klagenfurt (2001)
20. Margaria, T., Karusseit, M.: Community usage of the online conference service: an experience report from three CS conferences. In: 2nd IFIP Conference on E-Commerce, E-Business, E-Government (I3E 2002), Towards The Knowledge Society: eCommerce, eBusiness, and eGovernment, Lisbon, Portugal. IFIP Conference Proceedings, I3E 2002, vol. 233, pp. 497–511. Kluwer (2002)
21. Margaria, T.: Knowledge management for inclusive system evolution. In: Steffen, B. (ed.) Transactions on Foundations for Mastering Change I. LNCS, vol. 9960, pp. 7–21. Springer, Cham (2016). https://doi.org/10.1007/978-3-319-46508-1_2
22. Margaria, T.: Generative model driven design for agile system design and evolution: a tale of two worlds. In: Howar, F., Barnat, J. (eds.) FMICS 2018. LNCS, vol. 11119, pp. 3–18. Springer, Cham (2018). https://doi.org/10.1007/978-3-030-00244-2_1
23. Margaria, T., Bakera, M., Kubczak, C., Naujokat, S., Steffen, B.: Automatic generation of the SWS-challenge mediator with jABC/ABC. In: Petrie, C., Margaria, T., Zaremba, M., Lausen, H. (eds.) Semantic Web Services Challenge. Results from the First Year, vol. 8, pp. 119–138. Springer, Boston (2008). https://doi.org/10.1007/978-0-387-72496-6_7

24. Margaria, T., Raffelt, H., Steffen, B.: Knowledge-based relevance filtering for efficient system-level test-based model generation. Innov. Syst. Softw. Eng. **1**(2), 147–156 (2005)
25. Margaria, T., Steffen, B.: Lightweight coarse-grained coordination: a scalable system-level approach. Softw. Tools Technol. Transf. **5**(2–3), 107–123 (2004)
26. Margaria, T., Steffen, B.: Service-orientation: conquering complexity with XMDD. In: Hinchey, M., Coyle, L. (eds.) Conquering Complexity, pp. 217–236. Springer, London (2012). https://doi.org/10.1007/978-1-4471-2297-5_10
27. Margaria, T., Steffen, B. (eds.): ISoLA 2016, Part II. LNCS, vol. 9953. Springer, Cham (2016). https://doi.org/10.1007/978-3-319-47169-3
28. Margaria, T., Steffen, B., Reitenspieß, M.: Service-oriented design: the roots. In: Benatallah, B., Casati, F., Traverso, P. (eds.) ICSOC 2005. LNCS, vol. 3826, pp. 450–464. Springer, Heidelberg (2005). https://doi.org/10.1007/11596141_34
29. Merten, M., Steffen, B., Howar, F., Margaria, T.: Next generation LearnLib. In: Abdulla, P.A., Leino, K.R.M. (eds.) TACAS 2011. LNCS, vol. 6605, pp. 220–223. Springer, Heidelberg (2011). https://doi.org/10.1007/978-3-642-19835-9_18
30. Naujokat, S., Lybecait, M., Kopetzki, D., Steffen, B.: CINCO: a simplicity-driven approach to full generation of domain-specific graphical modeling tools. Softw. Tools Technol. Transf. **20**, 327–354 (2017)
31. Neubauer, J., Frohme, M., Steffen, B., Margaria, T.: Prototype-driven development of web applications with DyWA. In: Margaria, T., Steffen, B. (eds.) ISoLA 2014, Part I. LNCS, vol. 8802, pp. 56–72. Springer, Heidelberg (2014). https://doi.org/10.1007/978-3-662-45234-9_5
32. Neubauer, J., Margaria, T., Steffen, B.: Design for verifiability: the OCS case study. In: Formal Methods for Industrial Critical Systems: A Survey of Applications, chap. 8, pp. 153–178. Wiley-IEEE Computer Society Press, March 2013
33. Neubauer, J., Steffen, B., Margaria, T.: Higher-order process modeling: product-lining, variability modeling and beyond. Electron. Proc. Theor. Comput. Sci. **129**, 259–283 (2013)
34. Raffelt, H., Steffen, B., Berg, T., Margaria, T.: LearnLib: a framework for extrapolating behavioral models. STTT **11**(5), 393–407 (2009)
35. Raffelt, H., Steffen, B., Berg, T., Margaria, T.: LearnLib: a framework for extrapolating behavioral models. Int. J. Softw. Tools Technol. Transf. (STTT) **11**(5), 393–407 (2009)
36. Steffen, B., Margaria, T., Braun, V.: Coarse-granular model checking in practice. In: Dwyer, M. (ed.) SPIN 2001. LNCS, vol. 2057, pp. 304–311. Springer, Heidelberg (2001). https://doi.org/10.1007/3-540-45139-0_20. http://dl.acm.org/citation.cfm?id=380921.380949
37. Steffen, B. (ed.): Transactions on Foundations for Mastering Change I. LNCS, vol. 9960. Springer, Cham (2016). https://doi.org/10.1007/978-3-319-46508-1
38. Steffen, B., Margaria, T.: METAFrame in practice: design of intelligent network services. In: Olderog, E.-R., Steffen, B. (eds.) Correct System Design. LNCS, vol. 1710, pp. 390–415. Springer, Heidelberg (1999). https://doi.org/10.1007/3-540-48092-7_17
39. Steffen, B., Margaria, T., Braun, V., Kalt, N.: Hierarchical service definition. Ann. Rev. Commun. ACM **51**, 847–856 (1997)
40. Steffen, B., Margaria, T., Claßen, A., Braun, V.: The METAFrame'95 environment. In: CAV, pp. 450–453 (1996)

41. Steffen, B., Margaria, T., Claßen, A., Braun, V., Reitenspieß, M.: an environment for the creation of intelligent network services. In: Intelligent Networks: IN/AIN Technologies, Operations, Services and Applications - A Comprehensive Report, pp. 287–300. IEC: International Engineering Consortium (1996)
42. Steffen, B., Margaria, T., Freitag, B.: Module configuration by minimal model construction. Technical report, Fakultät für Mathematik und Informatik, Universität Passau (1993)
43. International Telecommunication Union: Intelligent network - global functional plane architecture. In: Recommendation Q.1203 (1992)
44. Universität Dortmund: jABC Website. http://www.jabc.de

Aachen 1990–1993

Interface Automata for Shared Memory

Johannes Gareis[1], Gerald Lüttgen[1(✉)], Ayleen Schinko[2], and Walter Vogler[2]

[1] Software Technologies Research Group, University of Bamberg, Bamberg, Germany
{johannes.gareis,gerald.luettgen}@swt-bamberg.de
[2] Institut für Informatik, University of Augsburg, Augsburg, Germany
{ayleen.schinko,walter.vogler}@informatik.uni-augsburg.de

Abstract. Interface theories based on *Interface Automata* (IA) are formalisms for the component-based specification of concurrent systems. Extensions of their basic synchronization mechanism permit the modelling of data, but are studied in more complex and expressive settings involving modal transition systems, imply severe restrictions such as determinacy, or do not abstract from internal computation.

In this paper, we show how de Alfaro and Henzinger's original IA theory can be conservatively extended by shared memory data, without sacrificing simplicity or imposing restrictions. Our extension *IA for shared Memory* (IAM) decorates transitions with pre- and post-conditions over arithmetic expressions on shared variables, which are taken into account by IA's notion of component compatibility. Simplicity is preserved as IAM can be embedded into IA and, thus, accurately lifts IA's compatibility concept to shared memory. We also provide a ground semantics for IAM that demonstrates that our abstract handling of data within IA's open systems view is faithful to the standard treatment of data in closed systems.

1 Introduction

Behavioural types [8,16] play an increasingly important role when developing and verifying software systems. For object-oriented software, behavioural types are specified as *contracts* [22], annotating methods and classes with pre- and post-conditions and invariants, resp. For distributed software, *session types* are employed [12,18] to describe communication interactions and their progression.

More general interface theories for concurrent systems are frequently founded on de Alfaro and Henzinger's *Interface Automata* (IA) [2,3], which model system components as labelled transition systems that distinguish a component's input and output actions. Parallel component composition assumes that a component may wait on inputs but never on outputs, implying that a component's output must be consumed immediately, or a communication error occurs. In case no system environment may restrict the system components' behaviour

Research support provided by the DFG (German Research Foundation) under grant nos. LU 1748/3-2 and VO 615/12-2.

T. Margaria et al. (Eds.): Steffen Festschrift, LNCS 11200, pp. 151–166, 2019.
https://doi.org/10.1007/978-3-030-22348-9_10

so that all errors are avoided, the components are deemed to be incompatible. To support refinement during software development, IA is equipped with an *alternating simulation* preorder so that one may substitute an abstract component by a concrete one, provided the concrete component offers no fewer inputs and no more outputs than the abstract component. Because this implies that outputs cannot be enforced, researchers have based IA-inspired interface theories on the more expressive *Modal Transition Systems* (MTS) and *modal refinement* [7,9,14,19,25].

To enable the modelling of richer classes of concurrent systems and software, IA has been extended in various ways to capture data in addition to control [1,4–6,11,13,17,24]. Except for [17], most of these works focus on the shared memory paradigm, which gets much attention with today's shift towards multi-core computing. Doyen et al. [13] study a basic interface theory with shared memory concurrency, but their parallel composition permits only limited communication. This is in contrast to de Alfaro et al.'s *Sociable Interfaces* [1], where scoping and non-interference conditions ensure that interfaces can participate in sophisticated n-to-n communication schemes on global variables. However, this leads to a rather difficult to grasp setting with an arguably complex game semantics. Bauer et al. [4–6] introduce data by employing pre-and post-conditions in a contract style, but within the more expressive MTS setting. They also restrict themselves to a pessimistic view on component compatibility, where components are already deemed to be incompatible if there *exists* a system environment that triggers a communication error, counter to the optimistic view adopted by IA. The authors of [11,24] stick to the simpler IA setting, but introduce technical mistakes, inaccuracies and unnecessary limitations in their work. In addition, most approaches above do not abstract from internal computation [1,4–6,11,13,24], and some impose stronger restrictions on determinacy than the input determinacy of IA, at least for some of their results [6,13].

This paper shows that IA nevertheless permits a *simple* and *faithful* extension to shared memory data, which does neither increase expressiveness nor introduce unnecessary complexities. To do so, we develop *Interface Automata for Shared Memory* (IAM) which, as in [4–6,11,24], abstractly specify data manipulations via pre- and post-conditions attached to transitions (Sect. 2). In contrast to [11,24], pre-conditions act as transition guards, whereby the post-conditions of an output-transition and a matching input-transition describe an assumption and guarantee, resp., on the data state obtained after the synchronization. Similar to [1], an output transition may be understood as invoking an operation associated with the transition's action, whereas the matching input transition describes how this operation manipulates the system's data state. Hence, one may think of the input transition to actually perform the operation. We adopt the point-to-point, handshake communication model of IA that is inspired by the process algebra CCS [23]. A communication error occurs if either, as in IA, an output is not expected in the current system state, or if the new data state after synchronization does not obey the output transition's assumption.

We conservatively extend the concepts of parallel composition and alternating refinement to IAM, while preserving compositionality, abstracting from internal computation and refraining from stricter determinacy requirements (Sect. 3). Then, we formally prove that IAM can be embedded into IA, which implies that one can reason finitely about component compatibility in IA even when infinite data domains are involved (Sect. 4); this is an important aspect not considered in related work. We also demonstrate that our abstract treatment of data via pre- and post-conditions, where data states are implicit, is faithful to the concrete treatment known from closed systems. To do so, we give closed IAM interfaces a *ground semantics*, in which data states are explicit and which is bisimilar to our IAM semantics (Sect. 5). Hence, IA does indeed offer a natural encoding of shared memory data, without requiring a more complex setting.

Interfaces were also studied by Bernhard Steffen to whom this Festschrift is dedicated. Steffen applied reactive interfaces for the compositional minimization of finite state systems [15], using a reduction technique not unlike the pruning employed when composing IA interfaces in parallel. He also investigated the frequent problems that off-the-shelf components do not come with descriptions of their interface behaviour, showing that these can be extracted from components via active automata learning [27], and that provided interface descriptions are under-specified and must be strengthened to be useful in practice [21].

2 The IAM Setting

This and the following section present our extension of IA for shared memory.

IA in a Nutshell. An IA interface P specifies a system component as a transition system over some input and output alphabets I and O, resp., where a transition is labelled either with an input action $a?$, an output action $a!$ or the internal action τ. Two interfaces P and Q may be composed in parallel, whereby P and Q synchronize on actions a that are in the input alphabet of one automaton and in the output alphabet of the other, resulting in an internal τ-transition, and they interleave on all other actions. However, if one interface, say P, outputs an action at a state p, which Q cannot receive in its current state q but on which it must synchronize (due to the action being in Q's input alphabet), a communication error occurs. The parallel composition prunes all such error states $\langle p, q \rangle$ as well as those states from which an error state can be reached autonomously via output and internal transitions, i.e., from which the environment of $P \parallel Q$ can no longer prevent the system from entering an error state. This consideration of errors makes the IA interface theory suitable for reasoning about *component compatibility*.

IA also supports the compositional refinement of systems via a notion of *alternating simulation*: P refines Q if the input transitions of Q can be simulated by P and, vice versa, the output transitions of P can be simulated by Q. For a component R, the parallel composition of P with R has no more communication errors than that of Q with R. Indeed, for the input-deterministic IA interfaces, alternating simulation is a pre-congruence for parallel composition.

The Extension IAM of IA. To capture shared memory in IA, our extension IAM additionally labels transitions of an interface by *pre-* and *post-conditions*, similar to [1,5,6]. These allow us to abstractly specify and reason about manipulations of *global variables*, without explicitly modelling data states. Formally, pre- and post-conditions are predicates over a set V of variables that represent the shared memory, ranged over by $x, y, \ldots$, i.e., propositional formulas over arithmetic expressions over V that employ the usual propositional operators $\neg, \vee, \wedge, \Rightarrow$ and arithmetic operators such as $<, =$ and $\geq$. The universe of such predicates is denoted by $Pred(V)$, with representatives $\varphi, \varphi', \ldots$ used for pre-conditions and $\psi, \psi', \ldots$ for post-conditions. A *data state* σ is a valuation $\sigma : V \rightarrow \mathbb{D}$ over a domain $\mathbb{D}$ of values. The set of all data states over V is denoted by $[\![V]\!]$, and we define $[\![\varphi]\!] =_{df} \{\sigma \in [\![V]\!] \mid \sigma \models \varphi\}$.

Intuitively, a pre-condition acts as a guard for a transition. An output transition labelled $(\varphi, a!, \psi)$ specifies that it is only executable when the system's implicit data state satisfies pre-condition φ and expects that the system environment, upon synchronizing on a, leaves the system in a data state respecting post-condition ψ. Similarly, an input transition labelled $(\varphi, a?, \psi)$ is executable in data states satisfying φ and guarantees that it implicitly manipulates variables only in ways such that the resulting data state satisfies post-condition ψ. In other words, post-conditions are employed in output transitions to express assumptions and in input transitions to give guarantees on data states resulting from a synchronization. Similar to communication mismatches, an assumption of an output transition that is not met by a synchronizing input transition also gives rise to an error in the parallel composition (see Sect. 3).

Definition 1 (Interface Automata for Shared Memory). *An* Interface Automaton for Shared Memory *(IAM) is a tuple* $(P, I, O, \rightarrow)$, *where*

- *P is the* state set;
- $A =_{df} I \cup O$ *is the* alphabet *consisting of disjoint sets I and O of* input *and* output actions, *resp., not containing the distinguished* internal action τ;
- $\rightarrow \subseteq P \times Pred(V) \times (A \cup \{\tau\}) \times Pred(V) \times P$ *is the* transition relation. *For a transition* $(p, \varphi, \alpha, \psi, p') \in \rightarrow$, *written* $p -(\varphi, \alpha, \psi)\rightarrow p'$ *for simplicity, its pre-condition* φ *and its post-condition* ψ *must be satisfiable, denoted by* φ sat *and* ψ sat, *resp. Moreover,* $\rightarrow$ *is required to be* data deterministic *for input actions, i.e., for all* $p \in P$ *and different transitions* $p -(\varphi, a?, \psi)\rightarrow p'$ *and* $p -(\varphi', a?, \psi')\rightarrow p''$ *with* $a? \in I$, *the conjunction* $\varphi \wedge \varphi'$ *is unsatisfiable.*

Note that this definition coincides with the one of IA [2] in case only the tautology true, written *tt*, is allowed as pre- and post-condition. In particular, the normally finer notion of data determinism is then the same as *input determinism*, which is needed for achieving compositionality for parallel composition (see Theorem 6 below). In the sequel, we simply write P for an IAM $(P, I, O, \rightarrow)$, and use $a, a?, a!, \alpha, \alpha?$ and $\alpha!$ as representatives of the sets $A, I, O, A \cup \{\tau\}$, $I \cup \{\tau\}$ and $O \cup \{\tau\}$, resp. In figures, pre- and post-conditions are set in square brackets.

We now adapt the notion of (weak) *alternating simulation* from IA to IAM. First observe that a single IAM transition may represent many transitions when explicitly considering the underlying data state. This implies that the behaviour of a transition in one IAM might need to be matched by multiple transitions in another IAM, i.e., by a *family* (a countable set) of transitions. For example, the behaviour of a transition labelled with pre-condition $x \geq 0$ may only be covered by two transitions with pre-conditions $x = 0$ and $x > 0$, resp., where the former transition matches the behaviour for data states in which x has value 0 and the latter in which x has a strictly positive value. In the following, families of transitions are indexed over some countable index set with representative i, and a weak transition $\overset{\varepsilon}{\Rightarrow}$ stands for a finite and possibly empty sequence of τ-transitions labelled with arbitrary but satisfiable pre- and post-conditions. Moreover, the symbol $\Rightarrow$ is also used for logical implication on predicates, where $\psi_i \Rightarrow \psi$ means that ψ_i *implies* ψ is valid.

Definition 2 (Alternating Simulation). *For IAMs P, Q, relation $\mathcal{R} \subseteq P \times Q$ is an* alternating simulation *if the following holds for all $p\mathcal{R}q$ and φ, a, ψ:*

(i) $q \,\text{--}(\varphi, a?, \psi) \!\!\rightarrowtail_Q q'$ *implies that there exists a family $p \,\text{--}(\varphi_i, a?, \psi_i)\!\!\rightarrowtail_P p'_i$ with $\varphi \Rightarrow \bigvee_i \varphi_i$ and, for all i, $\psi_i \Rightarrow \psi$ and $p'_i \mathcal{R} q'$.*

(ii) $p \,\text{--}(\varphi, a!, \psi)\!\!\rightarrowtail_P p'$ *implies that there exists a family $q_i \,\text{--}(\varphi_i, a!, \psi_i)\!\!\rightarrowtail_Q q'_i$ with $\varphi \Rightarrow \bigvee_i \varphi_i$ and, for all i, $q \overset{\varepsilon}{\Rightarrow}_Q q_i$, $\psi_i \Rightarrow \psi$ and $p' \mathcal{R} q'_i$.*

(iii) $p \,\text{--}(\varphi, \tau, \psi)\!\!\rightarrowtail_P p'$ *implies that there exists a q' with $q \overset{\varepsilon}{\Rightarrow}_Q q'$ and $p' \mathcal{R} q'$.*

We write $p \sqsubseteq_{IAM} q$ and say that p IAM-refines q, if there exists an alternating simulation $\mathcal{R}$ such that $p\mathcal{R}q$.

Here and in the following, whenever we refer to properties on states such as $p \sqsubseteq_{IAM} q$, we consider these properties in their 'global' context of the IAMs P and Q with $p \in P$ and $q \in Q$.

It can be shown that $\sqsubseteq_{IAM}$ is reflexive and transitive, and thus a preorder. As in alternating simulation $\sqsubseteq_{IA}$ for IA [2], inputs must be matched immediately in $\sqsubseteq_{IAM}$, i.e., leading or trailing τs are not allowed. Cond. (i) shows that, additionally in IAM, pre-conditions are weakened while post-conditions are strengthened. The weakening of a pre-condition keeps in line with IA in that refinement may introduce additional inputs. The strengthening in the post-conditions ensures that refinement does not loosen guarantees, i.e., strengthening prevents the refined system from reaching more data states than specified. Note that, as Cond. (i) covers input actions, the pre-conditions φ_i are pairwise disjoint due to data determinism. Outputs are matched the other way around as specified in Cond. (ii) which is analogous to Cond. (i) except that, as in $\sqsubseteq_{IA}$, leading τs are permitted when matching output transitions. Cond. (iii) reflects that τ-transitions are treated similarly to output transitions, but pre- and post-conditions do not matter for τ-transitions (see Sect. 5). Despite the fact that $\sqsubseteq_{IA}$ does not consider families when matching transitions, our alternating simulation $\sqsubseteq_{IAM}$ for IAM coincides with $\sqsubseteq_{IA}$ when considering only IAMs, where all pre- and post-conditions are *tt*. For such IAMs, it does not matter with which family member a transition is matched, any one family member would do.

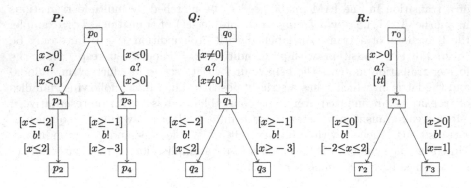

Fig. 1. Refinement $P \sqsubseteq_{IAM} Q \sqsubseteq_{IAM} R$.

An example illustrating alternating refinement is depicted in Fig. 1, where IAMs P, Q, R are defined over shared variable set $V = \{x\}$ with domain $\mathbb{R}$, such that $P \sqsubseteq_{IAM} Q \sqsubseteq_{IAM} R$. The input transition $r_0 \, \text{--}(x > 0, a?, tt) \rightarrow r_1$ of the most abstract interface R is matched by transition $q_0 \, \text{--}(x \neq 0, a?, x \neq 0) \rightarrow q_1$ of Q, where the pre-condition is weakened and the post-condition strengthened. This transition is in turn matched by the family $p_0 \, \text{--}(x > 0, a?, x < 0) \rightarrow p_1$ and $p_0 \, \text{--}(x < 0, a?, x > 0) \rightarrow p_3$ of P. The reasoning for the output transitions is similar, observing that transition $q_1 \, \text{--}(x \geq -1, b!, x \geq -3) \rightarrow q_3$ of Q must also be matched by a family of transitions in R, namely $r_1 \, \text{--}(x \leq 0, b!, -2 \leq x \leq 2) \rightarrow r_2$ and $r_1 \, \text{--}(x \geq 0, b!, x = 1) \rightarrow r_3$. Note that R has overlapping pre-conditions in r_1; unlike for inputs, data determinism is not required for outputs in IAM.

3   Parallel Composition

This section extends the parallel operator of IA [2], as outlined in the introduction to the previous section, to IAM. Two IAMs P, Q can be composed, if the actions that are in the alphabets of both, are an output action in one IAM and an input action in the other. When the overall system is in data state σ and P is in (control) state p with $p \, \text{--}(\varphi, a!, \psi) \rightarrow_P p'$ such that $\sigma \models \varphi$, then P can perform action $a!$. If Q has action $a?$ and is in (control) state q with $q \, \text{--}(\varphi', a?, \psi') \rightarrow_Q q'$ such that $\sigma \models \varphi'$, it provides a new data state σ' with $\sigma' \models \psi'$. If σ' meets the expectation of P, i.e., $\sigma' \models \psi$, the data state changes from σ to σ' and the components jointly move from state $\langle p, q \rangle$ to $\langle p', q' \rangle$. Otherwise, we have a communication mismatch, and $\langle p, q \rangle$ is an error state. This also holds if there is no transition $q \, \text{--}(\varphi', a?, \psi') \rightarrow_Q q'$ with $\sigma \models \varphi'$. In the parallel composition P and Q, all error states as well as those states are pruned, from which reaching an error cannot be prevented by any system environment.

This intuition is formalized by the following definitions. First, we define the *parallel product* $P \otimes Q$ that synchronizes and interleaves the transitions of two *composable* IAMs P, Q. Then, *error states* are formally introduced, so that the *parallel composition* $P \parallel Q$ may be obtained from $P \otimes Q$ via *pruning*.

Definition 3 (Parallel Product). *IAMs* $(P, I_P, O_P, \to_P)$, $(Q, I_Q, O_Q, \to_Q)$ *are* composable *if* $O_P \cap O_Q = \emptyset = I_P \cap I_Q$. *The product* $P \otimes Q$ *is defined as* $(P \times Q, I, O, \to)$, *where* $I =_{df} (I_P \cup I_Q) \setminus (A_P \cap A_Q)$, $O =_{df} (O_P \cup O_Q) \setminus (A_P \cap A_Q)$, *and the transition relation* $\to$ *is the least relation satisfying the following rules:*

(P1-) $\langle p, q \rangle -\!(\varphi_P, \alpha, \psi_P) \mapsto \langle p', q \rangle$ *if* $p -\!(\varphi_P, \alpha, \psi_P) \mapsto p'$ *and* $\alpha \notin A_Q$;

(P?!) $\langle p, q \rangle -\!(\varphi_P \wedge \varphi_Q, \tau, \psi_P) \mapsto \langle p', q' \rangle$ *if* $\varphi_P \wedge \varphi_Q$ *sat,* $p -\!(\varphi_P, a?, \psi_P) \mapsto p'$, $q -\!(\varphi_Q, a!, \psi_Q) \mapsto q'$ *and* $\psi_P \Rightarrow \psi_Q$.

There are also Rules (P-2) and (P!?) symmetric to (P1-) and resp. (P?!), i.e., with the roles of P *and* Q *being exchanged.*

Rules (P1-) and (P-2) model the asynchronous interleaving of autonomous transitions of P and Q. Rules (P?!) and (P!?) govern the synchronizations between P and Q, where the resulting synchronized transition is an internal τ-transition. Its pre-condition is the conjunction of the pre-conditions of the two involved transitions, as both must be fulfilled in the system's current data state for P and Q to engage in their transitions. As part of the synchronization, the input transition may alter the data state but, in doing so, must respect the post-condition of the output transition. This explains the implication $\psi_P \Rightarrow \psi_Q$ between the post-conditions of the involved transitions in Rule (P?!), whereby the synchronized transition is labelled with the stronger post-condition ψ_P.

Additional constraints on pre-/post-conditions for consecutive transitions are not needed for the open systems studied here. This is because a system's environment may arbitrarily interfere with data states and, thus, make a pre-condition of a transition true even if it contradicts the post-condition of the preceding transition. The situation changes, however, when considering closed systems as we do in Sect. 5.

Definition 4 (Parallel Composition). *Given a parallel product* $P \otimes Q$ *of IAMs* P, Q, *a state* $\langle p, q \rangle$ *is an* error state *if at least one of the following holds:*

(E!?φ) $p -\!(\varphi_P, a!, \psi_P) \mapsto p'$ *with* $a? \in I_Q$, *and there exists* σ *such that* $\sigma \models \varphi_P$ *but* $\sigma \not\models \varphi_Q$ *for all transitions* $q -\!(\varphi_Q, a?, \psi_Q) \mapsto q'$;

(E!?ψ) $p -\!(\varphi_P, a!, \psi_P) \mapsto p'$ *and there exists a transition* $q -\!(\varphi_Q, a?, \psi_Q) \mapsto q'$ *such that* $\varphi_P \wedge \varphi_Q$ *sat and* $\psi_Q \not\Rightarrow \psi_P$, *i.e.,* $[\![\psi_Q]\!] \not\subseteq [\![\psi_P]\!]$.

Rules (E?!φ) and (E?!ψ), not shown above, are symmetric to (E!?φ) and (E!?ψ), resp. The set $E \subseteq P \times Q$ *of* illegal states *is the least set containing all error states and those states* $\langle p, q \rangle$ *for which there exists a transition* $\langle p, q \rangle -\!(\varphi, \alpha!, \psi) \mapsto \langle p', q' \rangle$ *with* $\langle p', q' \rangle \in E$. *The parallel composition* $P \parallel Q$ *can then be computed by* pruning *the illegal states, i.e., by removing all states in* E *and their incoming and outgoing transitions. If* $\langle p, q \rangle \in P \parallel Q$, *then states* p *and* q *are* compatible, *written* $p \parallel q$; *one also says that* $p \parallel q$ *is defined.*

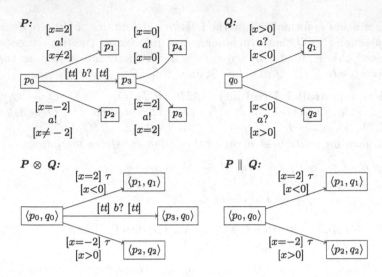

Fig. 2. Parallel composition of IAMs P, Q, where $I_P=\{b\}$, $O_P=I_Q=\{a\}$ and $O_Q=\emptyset$.

Observe that this definition coincides with the corresponding one for IA, if we consider IAMs where only tt occurs as pre- and post-condition. Figure 2 shows an example for computing the parallel product of two IAMs P, Q and applying pruning so as to obtain $P\|Q$. Synchronisation takes place on action a, which is shared among the components, while action b of P is interleaved. Observe that P's output transition $p_0 -(x = 2, a!, x \neq 2) \rightarrow p_1$ may synchronize with the upper transition $q_0 -(x > 0, a?, x < 0) \rightarrow q_1$ of Q, because the data state where x has value 2 fulfills both pre-conditions $x = 2$ and $x > 0$ and, regarding the post-conditions, $x < 0$ implies $x \neq 2$. This results in transition $\langle p_0, q_0 \rangle -(x = 2, \tau, x < 0) \rightarrow \langle p_1, q_1 \rangle$ being part of $P \otimes Q$. A synchronization of P's same transition with Q's lower transition is impossible, because the pre-conditions $x = 2$ and $x < 0$ contradict each other, and the necessary implication on the post-conditions would also not hold. Similar considerations can be made for the other two potential synchronizations between P in state p_0 and Q in state q_0 on action a. Thus, $\langle p_0, q_0 \rangle$ is not an error state: each output transition in p_0 can properly synchronize with at least one input transition in q_0. The b?-transition of P in p_0 is asynchronously interleaved, because Q is not aware of this action. Afterwards, p_3 tries to synchronize again with Q on action a, but $p_3 -(x = 0, a!, x = 0) \rightarrow p_4$ cannot be matched with any input transition of q_0 due to their unfitting pre- and post-conditions. Hence, $\langle p_3, q_0 \rangle$ is an error state by either Rule (E!?φ) or (E!?ψ), implying that transition $\langle p_0, q_0 \rangle -(tt, b?, tt) \rightarrow \langle p_3, q_0 \rangle$ in $P \otimes Q$ is pruned and not part of $P \| Q$.

Proposition 5 (Associativity & Commutativity). *Let P, Q, R be IAMs with $A_P \cap A_Q \cap A_R = \emptyset$, $p \in P$, $q \in Q$ and $r \in R$. Parallel composition is associative in the sense that, if $(p \| q) \| r$ is defined, then $p \| (q \| r)$ is defined and both are isomorphic. It is commutative in the analogous sense.*

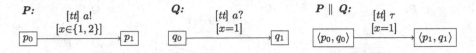

Fig. 3. IAMs P, Q and their parallel composition $P \parallel Q$.

Preorder $\sqsubseteq_{IAM}$ is compositional wrt. parallel composition, which follows directly from the properties of our embedding of IAM to IA in the next section:

Theorem 6 (Compositionality). *Let P, Q, R be IAMs and $p \sqsubseteq_{IAM} q$, for some $p \in P$, $q \in Q$. Further assume that Q and R are composable. Then, (i) P and R are composable; (ii) $p \parallel r \sqsubseteq_{IAM} q \parallel r$, and $p \parallel r$ is defined if $q \parallel r$ is.*

4 Embedding IAM into IA

This section shows that, while IAM adds shared memory data to the IA interface theory, it does not alter IA's concept of component compatibility and refinement. IAM is rather an intuitive (finite) abstraction for reasoning about (infinite) data, which maintains IA's simplicity that has made IA popular. Because we need to compare IAM and IA interfaces and IA considers initial states [2], we fix an initial state for every IAM P. Let p_0 and q_0 be the initial states of IAMs P and Q, resp. Then, $\langle p_0, q_0 \rangle$ is the initial state of the parallel product $P \otimes Q$ (cf. Definition 3). If this initial state is *illegal* according to Definition 4, i.e., $\langle p_0, q_0 \rangle \in E$, then P and Q are called *incompatible* and the parallel composition $P \| Q$ is undefined. We write $P \sqsubseteq_{IAM} Q$ if $p_0 \mathcal{R} q_0$ for some alternating simulation $\mathcal{R}$ (cf. Definition 2).

In the following, we develop a translation from IAM to IA such that behaviour is preserved and our parallel composition and refinement match exactly those of IA. Intuitively, the behaviour of an IAM P with initial state p_0 consists of runs of the form $(\sigma_0, p_0) \xrightarrow{\alpha_0} (\sigma_0', p_1)(\sigma_1, p_1) \xrightarrow{\alpha_1} (\sigma_1', p_2) \cdots (\sigma_{n-1}, p_{n-1}) \xrightarrow{\alpha_{n-1}} (\sigma_{n-1}', p_n)$, for transitions $p_i -\!(\varphi_i, \alpha_i, \psi_i)\!\rightarrow p_{i+1}$ with $\sigma_i \models \varphi_i$ and $\sigma_i' \models \psi_i$, for all $0 \le i < n$. Note that σ_i' and σ_{i+1} might well be different, because interface theories consider open systems and P's environment can always interleave and arbitrarily modify the data state; we consider this further in Sect. 5.

For our translation, one might consider to integrate data states into actions, so that the above run gives rise to $\alpha_0(\sigma_0, \sigma_0') \cdots \alpha_{n-1}(\sigma_{n-1}, \sigma_{n-1}')$, now as a sequence of actions, i.e., each $\alpha_i(\sigma_i, \sigma_i')$ is taken to be an (atomic) action. However, this translation does not work in general. Consider IAMs P, Q of Fig. 3, where $V = \{x\}$ and $\mathbb{D} = \{1, 2\}$. By the above idea, P would have transition $p_0 \xrightarrow{a(x=1, x=2)!} p_1$ in the resp. IA, as shown in Fig. 4. The only possible match in the IA for Q would be $q_0 \xrightarrow{a(x=1, x=1)?} q_1$; thus, $\langle p_0, q_0 \rangle \in E$, i.e., P and Q are incompatible. But there is no communication mismatch in the operational reality, because Q decides about the new data state when answering the request of P. In other words, P would take the transition $p_0 \xrightarrow{a(x=1, x=1)!} p_1$.

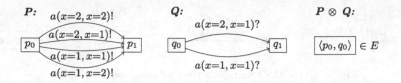

Fig. 4. Intuitive, direct but wrong translation of P and Q into IA.

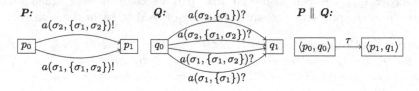

Fig. 5. Correct translation of P and Q into IA.

To resolve this problem, we translate output transition $p -\!(\varphi, a!, \psi)\!\rightarrowtail p'$ of IAM P to multiple IA transitions $\{p \xrightarrow{a(\sigma, M)!} p' \mid \sigma \models \varphi,\ M \supseteq [\![\psi]\!]\}$, and analogously for input transitions. The final IA translation of the above example can be found in Fig. 5, where now σ_1 and σ_2 denote the data states that assign value 1 and 2 to x, resp. The previous conflict is prevented, resulting in a well-formed IA $P \parallel Q$ that matches our translation. The crucial action for detecting errors is $a(\sigma, [\![\psi]\!])$, reflecting what P knows when choosing the above transition in (control) state p and data state σ. Even this is not truthful wrt. the data states reached in a parallel composition: these are determined by the resp. input transition and often form a proper *subset* of $[\![\psi]\!]$. This is not a problem as we ignore the target data states anyway; however, it explains why the $a(\sigma, M)$-transitions with larger set $M \supseteq [\![\psi]\!]$ do not disturb as is evidenced by Theorem 8.

Definition 7 (Embedding of IAM in IA). *An IAM P with initial state p_0 is translated to the IA $IA(P) =_{df} (P, I', O', \rightarrow_{IA(P)})$ with initial state p_0, where $I' =_{df} \{a(\sigma, M) \mid a \in I, \sigma \in [\![V]\!], M \subseteq [\![V]\!]\}$, $O' =_{df} \{a(\sigma, M) \mid a \in O, \sigma \in [\![V]\!], M \subseteq [\![V]\!]\}$, and $\rightarrow_{IA(P)}$ is obtained from $\rightarrow_P$ according to the following rules:*

- $p -\!(\varphi, a, \psi)\!\rightarrowtail p'$ *implies* $p \xrightarrow{a(\sigma, M)}_{IA(P)} p'$, *whenever* $\sigma \models \varphi$ *and* $M \supseteq [\![\psi]\!]$;
- $p -\!(\varphi, \tau, \psi)\!\rightarrowtail p'$ *implies* $p \xrightarrow{\tau}_{IA(P)} p'$.

This embedding satisfies two important properties: it is a homomorphism for parallel composition and monotonic wrt. alternating simulation.

Theorem 8 (Homomorphism & Monotonicity). *For all IAMs P, Q, the IA interface $IA(P \parallel Q)$ is isomorphic to $IA(P) \parallel IA(Q)$, due to the identity mappings on state pairs and actions. Moreover, $P \sqsubseteq_{IAM} Q$ iff $IA(P) \sqsubseteq_{IA} IA(Q)$.*

Theorem 6, i.e., the compositionality of parallel composition for IAM, now follows directly from the corresponding property for IA [2] and the above theorems.

5   Ground Semantics

Communication via shared memory works efficiently only for a limited number of processes that are locally close to each other. In practical applications, one has a cluster of processes that communicate among each other via shared memory, and with the environment, e.g., via message passing [17]. To sketch the use of our framework for designing shared memory systems, we assume that the latter communication is by synchronizing on common actions, i.e., the environment sees the cluster as an IA, and the cluster is originally specified by an IA. The final cluster P is then a closed system in the sense that the shared memory is inaccessible from the outside. So far, we have assumed that a state p of P can be entered while being in some data state σ' and then left because of a data state σ different from σ'. In a closed system, there is no environment that can change σ' to σ in-between. Hence, our ground semantics requires that p can only be left via a transition whose pre-condition is satisfied not only by σ but also by σ'.

States of the ground semantics are again pairs $\langle p, \sigma \rangle$, where p is a (control) state and σ a data state. A transition of p vanishes if σ does not satisfy the pre-condition. In an open IAM, pre- and post-conditions are irrelevant for τ-transitions, as the environment can change the data states arbitrarily before and after engaging in the internal transition. Once we close the system, however, all pre- and post-conditions become relevant and must be taken into account.

The ground semantics of a closed IAM P, denoted by $c(P)$, describes the behaviour of P as seen from the environment, given some *initial data state* σ_0. The $c(P)$ is essentially an IA without pre- and post-conditions, but it might violate input determinism when several data states satisfy a pre-condition. In this section, we call such IA-like systems *quasi-IAs*. Similarly, a system that is an IAM except for data determinism is a *quasi-IAM*.

Definition 9 (Ground Semantics). *A closed IAM P is a tuple $(P, I, O, \rightarrow_P, p_0, \sigma_0)$, where $(P, I, O, \rightarrow_P, p_0)$ is an IAM with initial state p_0 and σ_0 is the initial data state. The* ground semantics *of P is the quasi-IA $c(P) =_{df} (P \times [\![V]\!], I, O, \rightarrow_{c(P)}, \langle p_0, \sigma_0 \rangle)$ such that $\langle p, \sigma \rangle \xrightarrow{\alpha}_{c(P)} \langle p', \sigma' \rangle$ if there is a transition $p -(\varphi, \alpha, \psi) \rightarrow_P p'$ with $\sigma \models \varphi$ and $\sigma' \models \psi$.*

Usually, we are only interested in the reachable part of $c(P)$. This may be infinite even for finite P, because the domain $\mathbb{D}$ is infinite in most cases.

For describing how the development of a closed shared memory cluster fits the IA approach, we first consider the final IAM P, which usually is a composition of IAMs. We define a quasi-IA that properly reflects the behaviour of P wrt. the ground semantics, but is *finite* whenever P is. This quasi-IA is based on an IAM to which we refer as the *reduction* of P; it has the same ground semantics as P.

Definition 10 (Reduction). *Given a closed IAM* $(P, I, O, \rightarrow_P, p_0, \sigma_0)$*, assume that every* $p \in P$ *has countably many outgoing transitions, indexed over* J*, with pre-conditions* φ_j*. For each* $J' \subseteq J$*, let* $\varphi_{J'}$ *be* $\bigwedge_{j \in J'} \varphi_j \wedge \bigwedge_{j \notin J'} \neg\varphi_j$*. Set* J' *is called* p*-index set if* $\varphi_{J'}$ *is satisfiable. The reduction of* P *is the closed quasi-IAM* $(red(P), I, O, \rightarrow_{red(P)}, \langle p_0, \varphi_0 \rangle, \sigma_0)$ *with the following properties:*

- *State set* $red(P) \subseteq P \times Pred(V)$ *consists of states* $\langle p, \varphi_J \rangle$*, for a* p*-index set* J*.*
- *If* $p - (\varphi_j, \alpha, \psi) \mapsto_P p'$ *and there are* p*- and* p'*-index sets* J *and* J'*, resp., with* $j \in J$ *and* $\psi \wedge \varphi_{J'}$ *sat, then* $\langle p, \varphi_J \rangle - (\varphi_J, \alpha, \psi \wedge \varphi_{J'}) \mapsto_{red(P)} \langle p', \varphi_{J'} \rangle$*.*
- *Predicate* φ_0 *in the initial state* $\langle p_0, \varphi_0 \rangle$ *is* φ_{J_0}*, where* J_0 *is the* p_0*-index set* $\{j \mid \sigma_0 \models \varphi_j\}$*.*

All states $\langle p, \varphi_\emptyset \rangle$ can be identified with a new state *dead*, because they have no outgoing transitions. Observe that, for each (control) state p and data state σ, there is a unique p-index set J with $\sigma \models \varphi_J$; for this J, data state σ satisfies φ_i above if and only if $i \in J$. Furthermore, if two transitions numbered i and j concern the same input $a?$, pre-conditions φ_i and φ_j contradict each other due to data determinism. Thus, a p-index-set J can contain at most one index of an $a?$-transition for a fixed $a?$, i.e., there is at most one $p - (\varphi, a?, \psi) \mapsto_P p'$ that gives rise to $a?$-transitions from $\langle p, \varphi_J \rangle$. Observe that the formulas φ_J are finite for finite P.

Now, we show that $c(red(P))$ is essentially identical to $c(P)$; note again that the former's advantage over the latter is that $c(red(P))$ is finite whenever P is, even though $c(P)$ may be infinite. We call a state $\langle\langle p, \varphi_J \rangle, \sigma \rangle$ of $c(red(P))$ *data consistent* if $\sigma \models \varphi_J$. In other words, φ_J is an invariant for data consistent states $\langle\langle p, \varphi_J \rangle, \sigma \rangle$. All reachable states in $c(red(P))$ are data consistent: the initial state is data consistent, because φ_0 is defined such that $\sigma_0 \models \varphi_0$. Furthermore, if σ satisfies the post-condition of a transition leading to $\langle p', \varphi_{J'} \rangle$ in $red(P)$, then $\sigma \models \varphi_{J'}$, i.e., the resp. state $\langle\langle p', \varphi_{J'} \rangle, \sigma \rangle$ of $c(red(P))$ is data consistent.

Theorem 11 (Data Consistency). *Let* P *be a closed IAM. Each reachable state of* $c(red(P))$ *is data consistent. The quasi-IA induced by data consistent states is isomorphic to* $c(P)$ *due to the isomorphism* $\iota : \langle\langle p, \varphi_J \rangle, \sigma \rangle \mapsto \langle p, \sigma \rangle$ *where* $\sigma \models \varphi_J$*. The reachable parts of* $c(red(P))$ *and* $c(P)$ *are isomorphic due to the resp. restriction of* ι*.*

This theorem shows that $red(P)$ and P have the same behaviour as seen from the environment. We now define a simple translation of IAM P to a quasi-IA $ia(P)$. It turns out that $ia(red(P))$ has essentially the same behaviour as $c(P)$.

Definition 12 (Quasi-IA). *Quasi-IA* $ia(P)$ *is obtained from IAM* P *by deleting all pre- and post-conditions.*

The quasi-IA $ia(P)$ is only IA-like, because we do not necessarily get an input deterministic system. Input determinism is implied by data determinism in combination with P being unambiguous, i.e., for an IAM P, the post-conditions ψ of input transitions of $red(P)$ leading to some $\langle p', \_ \rangle$ do not satisfy $\psi \wedge \varphi_{J'}$ for more than one p'-index-set J'. The notion of similar behaviour as used here is (strong) bisimilarity, which is clearly much stronger than mutual IA refinement.

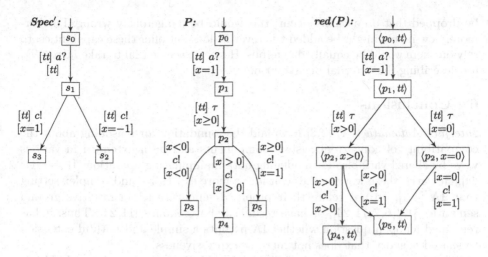

Fig. 6. Example illustrating IAM's application context.

Theorem 13 (Correctness). *$ia(red(P))$ and $c(P)$ are bisimilar for all closed IAMs P. They are equivalent wrt. $\sqsubseteq_{IA}$ if they are IAs.*

We now work out the scenario described at the beginning of this section, where one wants to extend a given IA specification *Spec* by shared memory. This can be done by decorating each transition with *tt* as pre- and post-condition, except for the post-conditions of output transitions. As first design choices, we select an initial data state σ_0 and, for each output transition, a single expected σ. A possible resulting IAM *Spec'* is given in Fig. 6; the essential point is that $ia(Spec')$ is indeed *Spec*. To get a working implementation, one typically refines specification *Spec'* by a parallel composition that is implemented component-wise; Fig. 6 shows a realisation P of *Spec'*, i.e., P is the parallel composition of the final cluster. One can show that, if P, as in Fig. 6, is input-deterministic and each postcondition of an input transition is satisfied by only one data state, $ia(P)$ is an IA, and by $P \sqsubseteq_{IAM} Spec'$, one can conclude $ia(P) \sqsubseteq_{IA} ia(Spec') = Spec$. These conditions also guarantee that $ia(red(P)) \sqsubseteq_{IA} ia(P)$. So, the design process ends with a closed composition P of IAMs; the outside behaviour of P is exactly described by $ia(red(P))$, which IA-refines *Spec*.

Figure 6 also shows $red(P)$. State p_2 in P has transitions with overlapping pre-conditions. This leads to three satisfiable conditions φ_J, which are equivalent to $x < 0$, $x > 0$ and $x = 0$. As $x < 0$ is always invalid after the τ-transition in P, state p_2 results in two reachable states in $red(P)$; the post-conditions of the two τ-transitions are suitably adapted. The left-hand state inherits the two c-transitions where $x > 0$ is allowed, the right-hand state only the c-transition where $x = 0$ is allowed; the pre-conditions are adapted.

Finally, observe that also $ia(P) \sqsubseteq_{IA} Spec$, but $ia(P)$ might have outputs that cannot ever occur, i.e., outputs for which the environment does not have to care. However, when taking just an IA-refinement of $ia(P)$, some other outputs could be dropped that do actually occur; this would be dangerously wrong. Furthermore, new inputs might be added wherever P does not offer these capabilities; to rely on them would be equally dangerous. Hence, it is essential to take $ia(red(P))$ for describing the external behaviour of P.

6 Conclusions

Interface Automata (IA) [2,3] have laid the foundation for reasoning about the compatibility of concurrent system components and been extended in various ways by shared variables for modelling data manipulating operations [1,4–7,11, 24]. However, these works either consider a more expressive and complex setting than IA [4–7], do not relate their proposed semantics to an intuitive ground semantics [1,4,6,7,11,24], or have technical shortcomings [11,24]. Thus, it has remained an open question whether IA permits a simple and faithful extension to shared memory that does not increase expressiveness.

This paper answered this question positively. Our interface theory IAM is a conservative extension of IA by shared memory. Similar to [4,5,11,24], we decorated action-labelled transitions with pre- and post-conditions constraining data states. A pre-condition acts as the transition's guard, and a post-condition of an output (input) transition specifies an assumption (guarantee) on the data state reached when executing the transition. We extended IA's concepts of compatibility, refinement and parallel composition to this setting, and provided a translation from IAM to IA. The latter shows that IAM accurately lifts IA's concepts to shared memory, while attaining finiteness when reasoning about potentially infinite data domains. In this sense, IAM does not increase expressiveness, and keeps the simplicity that has made IA increasingly popular in the formal methods community. To prove that IAM treats shared variables faithfully, we provided a ground semantics for closed IAMs; this makes the data states, which are implicit in an IAM, explicit within a closed IA, and is not unlike the implementation semantics of [5].

Future Work. We propose to extend IAM with features enhancing its practicality. Firstly, we wish to add scoping for actions and data. Action scoping can be realised by pruning inputs and hiding outputs [10]. Data scoping requires us to introduce an access control to IAM's global variables [1,4–6]. Secondly, IAM currently cannot capture operations such as *integer increment*, for which a 'prime' variant of each variable would be needed to relate values before and after an operation. This needs further investigation as it impacts our embedding and ground semantics. Thirdly, a conjunction operator should be added to IAM. This is not as easy as for IA [20], where two interfaces always have a common refinement so that contradictions cannot occur. In IAM, contradictions may arise due to transitions with conflicting post-conditions. Finally, we want to attach data invariants to IAM states. The idea is that, while a component is in a state, a compatible environment can only alter data in ways respecting the invariant. This restricts the environments with which a component can be composed, thus making shared variables more meaningful wrt. an open systems view.

Acknowledgements and Dedication. We thank the anonymous reviewers for their thorough comments that have helped us to improve the paper's presentation.

The second author wishes to dedicate this paper to Bernhard Steffen, on the occasion of his 60th birthday. I first met Bernhard when he was a young professor at RWTH Aachen University and I was his student. At a time when I feared that software development is primarily based on experience, he showed me the mathematical beauty of computer programs and the possibilities this offers for advancing software engineering. He was a refreshing lecturer and introduced his students to the latest advances in concurrency theory, program analysis and automated verification. As my PhD advisor, I got to admire Bernhard's outstanding intuition that often led him to gain deep insights between fields, as is evidenced, e.g., in his works on *data-flow analysis as model checking* [26]. He taught me the foundations of process algebras and compositional semantics, which fired my scientific curiosity and led to my dissertation and ultimately to this Festschrift contribution. Bernhard, I thank you for your support, your patience and your trust, and wish you many more fruitful years full of scientific curiosity and achievement.—Gerald

References

1. de Alfaro, L., da Silva, L.D., Faella, M., Legay, A., Roy, P., Sorea, M.: Sociable interfaces. In: Gramlich, B. (ed.) FroCoS 2005. LNCS (LNAI), vol. 3717, pp. 81–105. Springer, Heidelberg (2005). https://doi.org/10.1007/11559306_5
2. de Alfaro, L., Henzinger, T.A.: Interface automata. In: ESEC/FSE, pp. 109–120. ACM (2001)
3. de Alfaro, L., Henzinger, T.A.: Interface-based design. In: Broy, M., Grünbauer, J., Harel, D., Hoare, T. (eds.) Engineering Theories of Software Intensive Systems. NSS, vol. 195, pp. 83–104. Springer, Dordrecht (2005). https://doi.org/10.1007/1-4020-3532-2_3
4. Bauer, S.S., Hennicker, R., Bidoit, M.: A modal interface theory with data constraints. In: Davies, J., Silva, L., Simao, A. (eds.) SBMF 2010. LNCS, vol. 6527, pp. 80–95. Springer, Heidelberg (2011). https://doi.org/10.1007/978-3-642-19829-8_6
5. Bauer, S.S., Hennicker, R., Wirsing, M.: Interface theories for concurrency and data. Theoret. Comput. Sci. **412**(28), 3101–3121 (2011)
6. Bauer, S.S., Guldstrand Larsen, K., Legay, A., Nyman, U., Wąsowski, A.: A modal specification theory for components with data. In: Arbab, F., Ölveczky, P.C. (eds.) FACS 2011. LNCS, vol. 7253, pp. 61–78. Springer, Heidelberg (2012). https://doi.org/10.1007/978-3-642-35743-5_5
7. Bauer, S.S., Mayer, P., Schroeder, A., Hennicker, R.: On weak modal compatibility, refinement, and the MIO workbench. In: Esparza, J., Majumdar, R. (eds.) TACAS 2010. LNCS, vol. 6015, pp. 175–189. Springer, Heidelberg (2010). https://doi.org/10.1007/978-3-642-12002-2_15
8. Benveniste, A., et al.: Contracts for system design. Found. Trends EDA **12**(2–3), 124–400 (2018)
9. Bujtor, F., Fendrich, S., Lüttgen, G., Vogler, W.: Nondeterministic modal interfaces. Theoret. Comput. Sci. **642**(C), 24–53 (2016)
10. Chilton, C., Jonsson, B., Kwiatkowska, M.: An algebraic theory of interface automata. Theoret. Comput. Sci. **549**, 146–174 (2014)

11. Chouali, S., Mountassir, H., Mouelhi, S.: An I/O automata-based approach to verify component compatibility: application to the CyCab car. ENTCS **238**(6), 3–13 (2010)
12. Dardha, O., Giachino, E., Sangiorgi, D.: Session types revisited. Inf. Comput. **256**, 253–286 (2017)
13. Doyen, L., Henzinger, T.A., Jobstmann, B., Petrov, T.: Interface theories with component reuse. In: EMSOFT, pp. 79–88. ACM (2008)
14. Fendrich, S., Lüttgen, G.: A generalised theory of interface automata, component compatibility and error. Acta Inf. (2018). https://doi.org/10.1007/s00236-018-0319-8
15. Graf, S., Steffen, B., Lüttgen, G.: Compositional minimisation of finite state systems using interface specifications. Formal Asp. Comput. **8**(5), 607–616 (1996)
16. Hatcliff, J., Leavens, G.T., Leino, K.R.M., Müller, P., Parkinson, M.: Behavioral interface specification languages. ACM Comput. Surv. **44**(3), 16:1–16:58 (2012)
17. Holík, L., Isberner, M., Jonsson, B.: Mediator synthesis in a component algebra with data. In: Meyer, R., Platzer, A., Wehrheim, H. (eds.) Correct System Design. LNCS, vol. 9360, pp. 238–259. Springer, Cham (2015). https://doi.org/10.1007/978-3-319-23506-6_16
18. Honda, K., Yoshida, N., Carbone, M.: Multiparty asynchronous session types. SIG-PLAN Not. **43**(1), 273–284 (2008)
19. Larsen, K.G., Nyman, U., Wąsowski, A.: Modal I/O automata for interface and product line theories. In: De Nicola, R. (ed.) ESOP 2007. LNCS, vol. 4421, pp. 64–79. Springer, Heidelberg (2007). https://doi.org/10.1007/978-3-540-71316-6_6
20. Lüttgen, G., Vogler, W.: Modal interface automata. LMCS **9**(3:4) (2013)
21. Margaria, T., Sistla, A.P., Steffen, B., Zuck, L.D.: Taming interface specifications. In: Abadi, M., de Alfaro, L. (eds.) CONCUR 2005. LNCS, vol. 3653, pp. 548–561. Springer, Heidelberg (2005). https://doi.org/10.1007/11539452_41
22. Meyer, B.: Applying design by contract. IEEE Comput. **25**(10), 40–51 (1992)
23. Milner, R.: Communication and Concurrency. Prentice Hall, Upper Saddle River (1989)
24. Mouelhi, S., Chouali, S., Mountassir, H.: Refinement of interface automata strengthened by action semantics. ENTCS **253**(1), 111–126 (2009)
25. Raclet, J.-B., Badouel, E., Benveniste, A., Caillaud, B., Legay, A., Passerone, R.: A modal interface theory for component-based design. Fundam. Inform. **108**(1–2), 119–149 (2011)
26. Steffen, B.: Data flow analysis as model checking. In: Ito, T., Meyer, A.R. (eds.) TACS 1991. LNCS, vol. 526, pp. 346–364. Springer, Heidelberg (1991). https://doi.org/10.1007/3-540-54415-1_54
27. Steffen, B., Howar, F., Isberner, M.: Active automata learning: from DFAs to interface programs and beyond. In: ICGI. JMLR, vol. 21, pp. 195–209 (2012). JMLR.org

Passau 1993–1997

Boolean Algebras by Length Recognizability

Didier Caucal$^{(\boxtimes)}$ and Chloé Rispal

CNRS, LIGM, University Paris-Est, Paris, France
{caucal,rispal}@u-pem.fr

Abstract. We present a simple approach to define Boolean algebras on languages. We proceed by inverse deterministic and length-preserving morphisms on automata whose vertices are words. We give applications for context-free languages and context-sensitive languages.

1 Introduction

The family of regular languages is closed under many operations. Those closure properties give an easy way to work with this family and specially the closure under Boolean operations. Some of these Boolean closure properties are not satisfied at the next level of the Chomsky hierarchy: the family of context-free languages is not closed under complementation and intersection, and the subfamily of deterministic context-free languages is not closed under union and intersection. A standard way to get Boolean algebras is by recognizability by inverse morphism. This notion has been extended to many finite structures (see [10] among others) and also to infinite automata [5].

An automaton is a set of labeled edges with some initial and final vertices. A morphism f from an automaton G into an automaton H is a mapping from the vertices of G to the vertices of H such that for any edge $s \xrightarrow{a} t$ of G, $f(s) \xrightarrow{a} f(t)$ is an edge of H and for s initial/final in G, $f(s)$ is initial/final in H. The recognizability by an automaton H according to an automata family $\mathcal{F}$ is defined as the set of languages accepted by the automata of $\mathcal{F}$ that can be mapped by morphism into H.

A good way to obtain Boolean algebras of context-free languages is by structural recognizability [5]. Considering a family of automata such that each labeled transition $\xrightarrow{a}$ is a binary relation on a set $\mathcal{R}$, the morphism has to be a relation of $\mathcal{R}$. This structural notion, together with a natural notion of determinism on morphisms defines Boolean subalgebras of many language families. Nevertheless, those Boolean algebras can be too restrictive. For instance, the set of visibly pushdown languages [1] can not be obtained by structural recognizability.

In this paper, we consider the length recognizability for automata whose vertices are words: the morphisms are still deterministic but we replace the structural condition by the length-preserving property. We define natural conditions

© Springer Nature Switzerland AG 2019
T. Margaria et al. (Eds.): Steffen Festschrift, LNCS 11200, pp. 169–185, 2019.
https://doi.org/10.1007/978-3-030-22348-9_11

on automata families such that this length recognizability defines Boolean sub-algebras. The closure under intersection is given by the length synchronization, a natural and usual parallelization operation on word automata. To get the closure under difference, we introduce a new operation: the length superposition. When an automata family is closed under these two operations and under simple conditions, we get a Boolean algebra of languages accepted by automata which are deterministically length recognized by an unambiguous automaton (see Theorems 1 and 2). We give applications for sub-families of context-free languages and of context-sensitive languages. In particular, the family of visibly pushdown languages can be defined by length recognizability.

2   Word Automata

We consider finite and infinite automata having words as vertices. In this section, we give basic notations and definitions, and recall the notions of determinism and unambiguity.

Let N, T be countable sets of symbols called respectively *non-terminals* and *terminals*. We take a set $C = \{\iota, o\}$ of two *colors*.

A word *automaton* G is a subset of $N^* \times T \times N^* \cup C \times N^*$ of *vertex* set

$$V_G = \{ u \mid \exists a, v \ (u,a,v) \in G \vee (v,a,u) \in G \} \cup \{ u \mid \exists c \in C \ (c,u) \in G \}$$

such that the following sets are finite:

$$N_G = \{ x \in N \mid \exists u,v \in N^* \ uxv \in V_G \} \text{ the set of non-terminals of } G,$$
$$T_G = \{ a \in T \mid \exists u,v \ (u,a,v) \in G \} \text{ the set of terminals or } labels \text{ of } G.$$

We denote by $I_G = \{ s \mid (\iota, s) \in G \}$ the set of *initial vertices* and by $F_G = \{ s \mid (o, s) \in G \}$ the set of *final vertices* of G. Any triple $(s, a, t) \in G$ is an *edge* labeled by a from *source* s to *goal* t; it is also denoted by $s \xrightarrow{a}_G t$ i.e. $\xrightarrow{a}_G = \{ (s,t) \mid s \xrightarrow{a}_G t \}$ is the *a-transition* of G. Any couple $(c, s) \in G$ is a vertex s *colored* by $c \in C$; it is denoted by $c\, s \in G$ and $\xrightarrow{c}_G = \{ (s,s) \mid c\, s \in G \}$ is the *c-transition* of G. Taking symbols $|$, κ, and a triple (T_{-1}, T_0, T_1) of disjoint finite subsets of T, we define the *input-driven automaton*:

$$\mathrm{Inp}(T_{-1}, T_0, T_1) = \{ \, |^n\kappa \xrightarrow{a} |^{n+i}\kappa \mid i \in \{-1, 0, 1\} \wedge a \in T_i \wedge n, n+i \geq 0 \, \}$$
$$\cup \{\iota\kappa\} \cup \{o|^n\kappa \mid n \geq 0 \, \}.$$

The automaton $\mathrm{Inp}(\{b\}, \{c\}, \{a\})$ is represented below.

Let $\longrightarrow_G$ be the unlabeled edge relation *i.e.* $s \longrightarrow_G t$ if $s \xrightarrow{a}_G t$ for some $a \in T$. The *accessibility* relation $\longrightarrow^*_G$ is the reflexive and transitive closure under composition of $\longrightarrow_G$. A graph G is *accessible* (resp. *co-accessible*) from $P \subseteq V_G$ if for any $s \in V_G$, there is $r \in P$ such that $r \longrightarrow^*_G s$ (resp. $s \longrightarrow^*_G r$).

An automaton G is *trimmed* if it is accessible from I_G and co-accessible from F_G. The previous automaton is trimmed. The *restriction* $G_{|P}$ of an automaton G to a vertex subset P is the automaton induced by P:

$$G_{|P} \ = \ \{ \, (u,a,v) \in G \mid u, v \in P \, \} \cup \{ \, (c,u) \in G \mid u \in P \, \}.$$

The *trimmed automaton* of G is $G_{\iota,o} \ = \ G_{|\{ s \mid \exists i \in I_G \ \exists f \in F_G \ (i \longrightarrow^*_G s \longrightarrow^*_G f) \}}$ the restriction of G to the vertices accessible from I_G and co-accessible from F_G. Thus $G_{\iota,o}$ is trimmed and $L(G_{\iota,o}) = L(G)$. Similarly, the *accessible automaton* of G is $G_\iota \ = \ G_{|\{ s \mid \exists i \in I_G \ (i \longrightarrow^*_G s) \}}$. Recall that a *path* is a sequence $s_0 \xrightarrow{a_1} s_1 \ldots s_{n-1} \xrightarrow{a_n} s_n$ of consecutive transitions; this path leads from the *source* s_0 to the *goal* s_n and is labeled by $u = a_1 \ldots a_n \in T^*$ and we write $s_0 \xrightarrow{u}_G s_n$. We also write $\iota \xrightarrow{u}_G s, s \xrightarrow{v}_G o, \iota \xrightarrow{u}_G o$ if there exists $i \in I_G$ and $f \in F_G$ such that we have respectively $i \xrightarrow{u}_G s, s \xrightarrow{v}_G f, i \xrightarrow{u}_G f$. A path is *accepting* if its source is initial and its goal is final. The *language accepted* by an automaton G is the set $L(G) \ = \ \{ \, u \in T^* \mid \iota \xrightarrow{u}_G o \, \}$ of labels of its accepting paths. For instance, the previous automaton $\mathrm{Inp}(\{b\}, \{c\}, \{a\})$ accepts the language

$$L(\mathrm{Inp}(\{b\}, \{c\}, \{a\})) \ = \ \{ \, u \in \{a,b,c\}^* \mid \forall \, v \leq u, \ |v|_a \geq |v|_b \, \}$$

of prefixes of well-parenthesed words (a the open parenthesis and b the close one). An automaton G is *deterministic* if it has at most one initial vertex: $\iota s, \iota t \in G \implies s = t$, and if for any vertex r and any label $a \in T$, there exists at most one transition starting from r and labeled by a: $(r \xrightarrow{a}_G s \wedge r \xrightarrow{a}_G t) \implies s = t$. More generally, an automaton G is *unambiguous*, if any two accepting paths have distinct labels. The previous automaton $\mathrm{Inp}(T_{-1}, T_0, T_1)$ is deterministic. Any deterministic automaton is unambiguous. Here is an unambiguous automaton Un which is not deterministic.

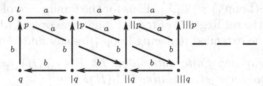

3   Recognizability

In order to get Boolean subalgebras of many language families, the recognizability by inverse morphism [6] has been extended to infinite automata [5]. We recall this notion as well as the definition of a deterministic morphism.

A *morphism* f from an automaton G into an automaton H is a mapping $f : V_G \longrightarrow V_H$ such that for any $s, t \in V_G$, $a \in T_G$ and $c \in C$,

$$s \xrightarrow{a}_G t \implies f(s) \xrightarrow{a}_H f(t) \quad \text{and} \quad cs \in G \implies cf(s) \in H$$

we write $G \xrightarrow{f} H$ or $G \longrightarrow H$ and we say that G is *reducible* into H. Any word accepted by an automaton is by morphism accepted by the image automaton.

Lemma 1. *Let* $G \longrightarrow H$. *We have*

$$L(G) \subseteq L(H) \text{ and } G' \longrightarrow H' \text{ for any } G' \subseteq G \text{ and } H \subseteq H'.$$

Let us give uniqueness conditions of a morphism between automata.

Lemma 2. *There is at most one morphism from a trimmed automaton into an unambiguous automaton.*

Proof. Let $G \xrightarrow{g} H$ and $G \xrightarrow{h} H$ with G trimmed and H unambiguous.

Let s be any vertex of G. As G is trimmed, there exists $u, v \in T^*$ such that $\iota \xrightarrow{u}_G s \xrightarrow{v}_G o$. As g and h are morphisms, we have

$$\iota \xrightarrow{u}_H g(s) \xrightarrow{v}_H o \text{ and } \iota \xrightarrow{u}_H h(s) \xrightarrow{v}_H o.$$

As H is unambiguous, $g(s) = h(s)$.   □

For families $\mathcal{F}$ of automata, we want to get Boolean subalgebras of

$$\mathcal{L}(\mathcal{F}) = \{\, L(G) \mid G \in \mathcal{F} \,\}.$$

Recall that a language family $\mathcal{L}$ is a *Boolean algebra relative to* a language $L \in \mathcal{L}$ if for any $P, Q \in \mathcal{L}$, $P \subseteq L$ and $L - P, P \cap Q \in \mathcal{L}$.

A first approach is to take an automata family $\mathcal{F}$ and a *recognizer* $H \in \mathcal{F}$ to define the set of languages accepted by all possible automata of $\mathcal{F}$ which are reducible to H:

$$\mathrm{Rec}_{\mathcal{F}}(H) = \{\, L(G) \mid G \in \mathcal{F} \wedge G \longrightarrow H \,\}.$$

For any finite subset $A \subset T$, we define the trimmed and deterministic automaton Loop_A with a unique vertex κ and the loops labeled by each letter of A:

$$\mathrm{Loop}_A = \{\, \kappa \xrightarrow{a} \kappa \mid a \in A \,\} \cup \{\iota\kappa, o\kappa\}.$$

For any family $\mathcal{F}$ of automata labeled in A, each automaton is reducible to Loop_A hence $\mathrm{Rec}_{\mathcal{F}}(\mathrm{Loop}_A) = \mathcal{L}(\mathcal{F})$. Thus for the family $\mathcal{F}in$ of finite automata, $\mathrm{Rec}_{\mathcal{F}in}(\mathrm{Loop}_A)$ is the set $\mathrm{Reg}(A^*)$ of regular languages over A which is a Boolean algebra. This can be extended replacing Loop_A by any finite automaton.

Proposition 1. *For any finite automaton* H, $\mathrm{Rec}_{\mathcal{F}in}(H) = \{L \subseteq L(H) \mid L \text{ regular}\}$ *is a Boolean algebra relative to* $L(H)$.

However $\mathcal{L}(\mathcal{F})$ is not in general a Boolean algebra. To get Boolean algebras by recognizability, we introduce simple conditions on the morphisms.

In order to preserve by inverse the determinism, we say that a morphism $G \xrightarrow{f} H$ is a *deterministic morphism* and we write $G \xrightarrow{f}_d H$ if

$$\iota s, \iota t \in G \wedge f(s) = f(t) \implies s = t$$
$$r \xrightarrow{a}_G s \wedge r \xrightarrow{a}_G t \wedge f(s) = f(t) \implies s = t.$$

Any morphism from a deterministic automaton is a deterministic morphism:

$$G \xrightarrow{f} H \wedge G \text{ deterministic} \implies G \xrightarrow{f}_d H. \tag{1}$$

Any deterministic morphism preserves by inverse determinism and unambiguity.

Lemma 3. *Let* $G \xrightarrow{f}_d H$ *with* H *unambiguous (resp. deterministic). Then* G *is unambiguous (resp. deterministic) and*

$$(\iota \xrightarrow{u}_G s \wedge u \in L(G) \wedge o\,f(s) \in H) \implies os \in G.$$

Proof. Let $G \xrightarrow{f}_d H$ with H unambiguous.

(i) Let us check that G is unambiguous. Let

$$s_0 \xrightarrow{a_1}_G s_1 \ldots s_{n-1} \xrightarrow{a_n}_G s_n \text{ and } t_0 \xrightarrow{a_1}_G t_1 \ldots t_{n-1} \xrightarrow{a_n}_G t_n$$

with $\iota\,s_0, \iota\,t_0, o\,s_n, o\,t_n \in G$. As f is a morphism,

$$f(s_0) \xrightarrow{a_1}_H f(s_1) \ldots f(s_{n-1}) \xrightarrow{a_n}_H f(s_n) \text{ with } \iota\,f(s_0)\,o\,f(s_n) \in H$$
$$f(t_0) \xrightarrow{a_1}_H f(t_1) \ldots f(t_{n-1}) \xrightarrow{a_n}_H f(t_n) \text{ with } \iota\,f(t_0), o\,f(t_n) \in H.$$

As H is unambiguous, we have $f(s_0) = f(t_0), \ldots, f(s_n) = f(t_n)$.
As f is a deterministic morphism, we get $s_i = t_i$ by induction on $0 \le i \le n$.
(ii) Assume that H is deterministic. Let us check that G is deterministic.
Case 1: let $\iota\,s, \iota\,t \in G$.
    As f is a morphism, $\iota\,f(s), \iota\,f(t) \in H$. As H is deterministic, $f(s) = f(t)$.
    As f is a deterministic morphism, $s = t$.
Case 2: let $r \xrightarrow{a}_G s$ and $r \xrightarrow{a}_G t$.
    As f is a morphism, $f(r) \xrightarrow{a}_G f(s)$ and $f(r) \xrightarrow{a}_G f(t)$.
    As H is deterministic, $f(s) = f(t)$. As f is a deterministic morphism, $s = t$.
(iii) Let $s_0 \xrightarrow{a_1}_G s_1 \ldots \xrightarrow{a_n}_G s_n$ with $\iota\,s_0 \in G, o\,f(s_n) \in H$ and $a_1 \ldots a_n \in L(G)$.
Let us check that $o\,s_n \in G$.
As $a_1 \ldots a_n \in L(G)$, there exists $t_0 \xrightarrow{a_1}_G t_1 \ldots \xrightarrow{a_n}_G t_n$ with $\iota\,t_0, o\,t_n \in G$.
Thus $f(s_0) \xrightarrow{a_1}_H f(s_1) \ldots \xrightarrow{a_n}_H f(s_n)$ and $f(t_0) \xrightarrow{a_1}_H f(t_1) \ldots \xrightarrow{a_n}_H f(t_n)$
with $\iota\,f(s_0), \iota\,f(t_0), o\,f(s_n), o\,f(t_n) \in H$.
As H is unambiguous, we have $f(s_i) = f(t_i)$ for every $0 \le i \le n$.
As f is deterministic, we get $s_i = t_i$ for every $0 \le i \le n$.
Thus $o\,s_n = o\,t_n \in G$.   □

When restricting to deterministic morphisms in $\text{Rec}_{\mathcal{F}}(H)$, we define

$$\text{dRec}_{\mathcal{F}}(H) = \{\, L(G) \mid G \in \mathcal{F} \wedge G \longrightarrow_d H \,\}.$$

Let $\mathcal{F}_{\text{det}} = \{\, G \in \mathcal{F} \mid G \text{ deterministic} \,\}$. By (1) and Lemma 3, we have

$$\text{dRec}_{\mathcal{F}}(H) = \text{Rec}_{\mathcal{F}_{\text{det}}}(H) \text{ for any } H \in \mathcal{F}_{\text{det}}.$$

Thus $\text{dRec}_{\mathcal{F}}(\text{Loop}_A) = \mathcal{L}(\mathcal{F}_{\text{det}})$ is not in general a Boolean algebra. We now specialize the previous notions by vertex length restriction.

4   Recognizability by Length

To get Boolean algebras, the recognizability for infinite automata has been used with a structural condition [5]. In the following, we replace it by a length-preserving condition. When the morphisms are deterministic and under simple conditions on the automata family, this gives less restrictive Boolean subalgebras.

A word automaton G is *length-deterministic* if it satisfies the conditions:

$$(\iota\, s,\, \iota\, t \in G \wedge |s| = |t|) \implies s = t$$
$$(r \xrightarrow{a}_G s \wedge r \xrightarrow{a}_G t \wedge |s| = |t|) \implies s = t.$$

Thus the structure $(\mathbb{N}, 0, <)$ is described by the length-deterministic automaton:

More generally any automaton without two vertices of the same length is length-deterministic. We also say that a morphism $G \xrightarrow{f} H$ is *length-preserving* if $|f(u)| = |u|$ for any $u \in V_G$; we write $G \xrightarrow{f}_\ell H$ and we say that G is *length-reducible* to H. Note that

$$(G \longrightarrow_{\ell d} H \text{ and } H \text{ length-deterministic}) \implies G \text{ length-deterministic}.$$

Let us particularize the subfamilies $\mathrm{Rec}_{\mathcal{F}}(H)$ and $\mathrm{dRec}_{\mathcal{F}}(H)$ by restriction to length-preserving morphisms: for any automata family $\mathcal{F}$ and any $H \in \mathcal{F}$, let

$$\ell\mathrm{Rec}_{\mathcal{F}}(H) = \{\, \mathrm{L}(G) \mid G \in \mathcal{F} \wedge G \longrightarrow_\ell H \,\}$$
$$\ell\mathrm{dRec}_{\mathcal{F}}(H) = \{\, \mathrm{L}(G) \mid G \in \mathcal{F} \wedge G \longrightarrow_{\ell d} H \,\}.$$

We have the following inclusions:

$$\mathrm{dRec}_{\mathcal{F}}(H)$$
$$\ell\mathrm{dRec}_{\mathcal{F}}(H) \qquad\qquad \mathrm{Rec}_{\mathcal{F}}(H)$$
$$\ell\mathrm{Rec}_{\mathcal{F}}(H)$$

As $\emptyset \longrightarrow_{\ell d} H$ and $H \longrightarrow_{\ell d} H$, we have $\emptyset, \mathrm{L}(H) \in \ell\mathrm{dRec}_{\mathcal{F}}(H)$. We prove that $\ell\mathrm{dRec}_{\mathcal{F}}(H)$ is a Boolean algebra relative to $\mathrm{L}(H)$ for H unambiguous and $\mathcal{F}$ closed under two simple operations that we introduce now, namely the synchronization by length for the closure under intersection and the superposition by length for the closure under difference.

5   Synchronization by Length

We define a binary parallelization operation $\|$ on word automata according to the vertex length. We show that $\ell\mathrm{Rec}_{\mathcal{F}}(H)$ is closed under intersection when H is unambiguous and $\mathcal{F}$ is closed under $\|$ (cf. Proposition 2). To get the closure of $\ell d\mathrm{Rec}_{\mathcal{F}}(H)$ under intersection, $\mathcal{F}$ has to be closed under restriction by accessibility from the initial vertices and co-accessibility from the final vertices (cf. Proposition 3).

Let $\Delta_N = \{ (u,v) \in N^* \times N^* \mid |u| = |v| \}$ be the set of couples of words over N of same length. The *length synchronization* is the bijection $\| : \Delta_N \longrightarrow (N \times N)^*$ defined by

$$a_1 \ldots a_n \parallel b_1 \ldots b_n = (a_1, b_1) \ldots (a_n, b_n) \text{ for any } n \geq 0, \ a_1, b_1, \ldots, a_n, b_n \in N.$$

We also consider the *first projection* π_1 and the *second projection* π_2 as the surjective mappings $(N \times N)^* \longrightarrow N^*$ defined by $\pi_1(u,v) = u$ and $\pi_2(u,v) = v$.

Given word automata G and G' with an injective alphabetic morphism ϕ from $N_G \times N_{G'}$ into N, we define their *length synchronization* $G \parallel_\phi G'$ as the following word automaton:

$$G \parallel_\phi G' = \{ \phi(u \parallel u') \xrightarrow{\ a\ } \phi(v \parallel v') \mid u \xrightarrow{\ a\ }_G v \wedge u' \xrightarrow{\ a\ }_{G'} v' \}$$
$$\cup \ \{ c\phi(u \parallel u') \mid cu \in G \wedge cu' \in G' \}.$$

Since the coding ϕ is not essential, it will usually be omitted. Note that

$$G, G' \text{ deterministic} \implies G \parallel G' \text{ deterministic}$$
$$V_G, V_{G'} \text{ regular} \implies V_G \parallel V_{G'} \text{ regular}.$$

As an example, consider the following respective two graphs G and G':

Their length synchronization $G \parallel G'$ is the following graph:

The length synchronization gives the closure under intersection.

Lemma 4. *For any automata G, G', H, we have the following properties:*

(a) $G \parallel G' \xrightarrow{\pi_1}_\ell G$ *and* $G \parallel G' \xrightarrow{\pi_2}_\ell G'$,
(b) $L(G \parallel G') \subseteq L(G) \cap L(G')$,
(c) $(G \longrightarrow_\ell H, G' \longrightarrow_\ell H, H \text{ unambiguous}) \implies L(G \parallel G') = L(G) \cap L(G')$.

Let us give basic properties on the vertices of length synchronized automata.

Lemma 5. *Let* $G \xrightarrow{f}_\ell H$ *and* $G' \xrightarrow{f'}_\ell H$. *We have*

(a) $(u \parallel u' \in V_{(G \parallel G')_\iota}$ *and* H *length-deterministic*$) \implies f(u) = f'(u')$
(b) $(u \parallel u' \in V_{(G \parallel G')_{\iota,o}}$ *and* H *unambiguous*$) \implies f(u) = f'(u')$.

Let us apply Lemma 4 (c) to the intersection closure by length recognizability.

Proposition 2. *The language family* $\ell\mathrm{Rec}_\mathcal{F}(H)$ *is closed under intersection when* H *is unambiguous and* $\mathcal{F}$ *is closed under* $\|$.

This proposition is not suitable for the family $\ell\mathrm{dRec}_\mathcal{F}(H)$ because Lemma 4 (a) cannot be extended to deterministic reductions: for instance,

$$G = \{\varepsilon \xrightarrow{a} 0,\, \varepsilon \xrightarrow{a} 1,\, 1 \xrightarrow{a} 10,\, \iota\varepsilon,\, o\,0,\, o\,10\}$$

is a trimmed and unambiguous automaton but $G \parallel G \not\longrightarrow_d G$ since

$$G \parallel G = \{\, \varepsilon \xrightarrow{a} (0,0),\, \varepsilon \xrightarrow{a} (0,1),\, \varepsilon \xrightarrow{a} (1,0),\, \varepsilon \xrightarrow{a} (1,1),$$
$$(1,1) \xrightarrow{a} (1,1)(0,0),\, \iota\varepsilon,\, o\,(0,0),\, o\,(1,1)(0,0)\,\}.$$

Nevertheless $(G \parallel G)_{\iota,o} \longrightarrow_{\ell d} G$. This property can be generalized.

Lemma 6. *We have* $(G \longrightarrow_\ell H \;\vee\; G' \longrightarrow_\ell H) \implies G \parallel G' \longrightarrow_\ell H$
$(G \longrightarrow_{\ell d} H, G' \longrightarrow_{\ell d} H, H \text{ unambiguous}) \implies (G \parallel G')_{\iota,o} \longrightarrow_{\ell d} H.$

We say that an automata family $\mathcal{F}$ is closed under ιo-*restriction* if $G_{\iota,o} \in \mathcal{F}$ for any $G \in \mathcal{F}$. Let us apply Lemmas 4 and 6.

Proposition 3. *The language family* $\ell\mathrm{dRec}_\mathcal{F}(H)$ *is closed under intersection when* H *is unambiguous and* $\mathcal{F}$ *is closed under* $\|$ *and* ιo-*restriction.*

Now we study the closure of $\ell\mathrm{dRec}_\mathcal{F}(H)$ under the difference operation.

6   Superposition by Length

We define a binary superposition operation $/\!/$ on word automata according to vertex lengths. When $\mathcal{F}$ is an automata family closed under $/\!/$, we obtain simple conditions for $\ell\mathrm{dRec}_\mathcal{F}(H)$ to be closed under difference (cf. Proposition 5). Then we obtain two general ways to get $\ell\mathrm{dRec}_\mathcal{F}(H)$ as a Boolean algebra relative to $L(H)$ (Theorems 1 and 2).

We say that a word automaton G is ε-*free* if ε is not a vertex of G: $\varepsilon \notin V_G$.

For $L \subseteq N^*$, we write $u \leq L$ if u is prefix of a word of L: $\exists\, v\, (uv \in L)$. Given ε-free automata G and H with an injection $\phi : N_G{\times}N_H \longrightarrow N$ and a non-terminal $\# \in N - N_G$, we define the *length superposition* $G /_{\phi,\#} H$ of G on H as the following word automaton:

$\quad G /_{\phi,\#} H$
$= \{\, \phi(u\|x) \xrightarrow{a} \phi(v\|y) \mid u \xrightarrow{a}_G v \wedge x \xrightarrow{a}_H y \,\}$
$\cup \{\, \iota\,\phi(u\|x) \mid \iota u \in G \wedge \iota x \in H \,\}$
$\cup \{\, o\,\phi(u\|x) \mid u \in V_G \wedge ou \notin G \wedge ox \in H \,\}$
$\cup \{\, \phi(u\|x) \xrightarrow{a} \phi(v\#\|y) \mid x \xrightarrow{a}_H y \wedge u \in V_G \wedge$
$\qquad\qquad\qquad\qquad\qquad \neg\exists\, w\,(u \xrightarrow{a}_G w \wedge |w| = |y|) \wedge v \leq u\,\#^* \,\}$
$\cup \{\, \phi(u\#^{|x|-|u|}\|x) \xrightarrow{a} \phi(v\#\|y) \mid x \xrightarrow{a}_H y \wedge u \leq V_G \wedge |x| > |u| \wedge v \leq u\,\#^* \,\}$
$\cup \{\, o\,\phi(u\#^{|x|-|u|}\|x) \mid ox \in H \wedge u \leq V_G \wedge |x| > |u| \,\}$
$\cup \{\, \iota\,\phi(\#^{|x|}\|x) \mid \iota x \in H \wedge \forall\, \iota u \in G,\, |u| \neq |x| \,\}.$

Since the coding ϕ is not essential, it will usually be omitted. Moreover, we will assume that # is always a new non-terminal. The definition of G/H is done in order to follow in parallel and by length the paths of G and H. When a transition of H can not be length synchronized by G, a transition of G/H leads to a copy of H by marking the vertices by #. Note that

$$G, H \text{ deterministic} \implies G/H \text{ deterministic.}$$

As an example, we have $G \xrightarrow{\ f\ }_{\ell d} H$ for the following ε-free deterministic automaton G:

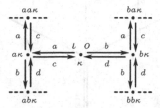

for the morphism $f(u\kappa) = ||^{|u|}\kappa$ for any $u \in \{a, b\}^*$ and for the following automaton H:

$$\iota \bullet \underset{\kappa}{\overset{O \quad a,b}{\rightleftarrows}} \bullet \underset{|\kappa}{\overset{a,b}{\underset{c,d}{\rightleftarrows}}} \bullet \underset{||\kappa}{\overset{a,b}{\underset{c,d}{\rightleftarrows}}} \bullet \underset{|||\kappa}{\overset{a,b}{\underset{c,d}{\rightleftarrows}}} \bullet \ -\ -\ -$$

We represent below $(G/H)_{\iota,o}$ where any vertex u stands for the word $u \, || \, ||^{|u|-1}\kappa$.

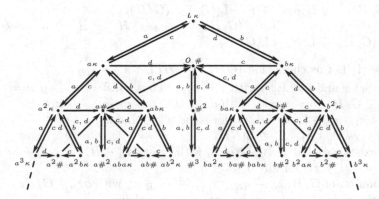

In order to avoid crossing edges, one can also represent this automaton by the following 'Happy Birthday' picture:

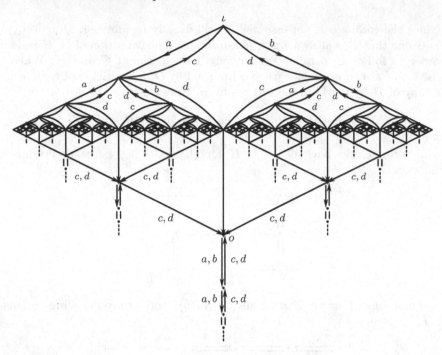

The length superposition gives the closure under difference.

Lemma 7. *For any ε-free automata G, H, we have*

(a) $(G/H) \xrightarrow{\pi_2}_{\ell} H$ and $L(H) - L(G) \subseteq L(G/H)$.

(b) $(G \longrightarrow_{\ell} H, \quad (G/H) \xrightarrow{\pi_2}_{d} H, \quad H \quad unambiguous)$
$\implies L(G/H) \subseteq L(H) - L(G)$.

Proof.   (i) Let us check that $(G/H) \xrightarrow{\pi_2} H$. Let $s \xrightarrow{a}_{G/H} t$.

So $s = u \| x$ and $t = v \| y$ with $x \xrightarrow{a}_H y$. Thus $\pi_2(s) = x \xrightarrow{a}_H y = \pi_2(t)$.
Let $cs \in G/H$. So $s = u \| x$ with $cx \in H$. Thus $c\pi_2(s) = cx \in H$.

(ii) Let $a_1 \ldots a_n \in L(H) - L(G)$ for some $n \geq 0$ and $a_1, \ldots, a_n \in T$.
Let us show that $a_1 \ldots a_n \in L(G/H)$.
There exists $x_0 \xrightarrow{a_1}_H x_1 \ldots \xrightarrow{a_n}_H x_n$ with $\iota x_0, o x_n \in H$.
Let $z_i = (\#^{|x_i|}, x_i)$ for any $0 \leq i \leq n$.
By definition of G/H, $z_0 \xrightarrow{a_1}_{G/H} z_1 \ldots \xrightarrow{a_n}_{G/H} z_n$ with $o z_n \in G/H$.
We distinguish the two complementary cases below.
Case 1: $\neg \exists u_0 (\iota u_0 \in G \wedge |u_0| = |x_0|)$.
So $\iota z_0 \in G/H$ hence $a_1 \ldots a_n \in L(G/H)$.
Case 2: $\exists u_0 (\iota u_0 \in G \wedge |u_0| = |x_0|)$. Let $0 \leq m \leq n$ maximal such that

$$u_0 \xrightarrow{a_1}_G u_1 \ldots \xrightarrow{a_m}_G u_m \text{ with } |u_1| = |x_1|, \ldots, |u_m| = |x_m|.$$

Thus $u_0 \| x_0 \xrightarrow{a_1}_{G/H} u_1 \| x_1 \ldots \xrightarrow{a_m}_{G/H} u_m \| x_m$ and $\iota (u_0 \| x_0) \in G/H$.
Case 2.1: $m = n$. As $a_1 \ldots a_n \notin L(G), o u_n \notin G$.
Thus $o(u_n \| x_n) \in G/H$ hence $a_1 \ldots a_n \in L(G/H)$.

Case 2.2: $m < n$. There exists $u'_{m+1}, \ldots, u'_n$ such that

$$u_m \,\|\, x_m \overset{a_{m+1}}{\longrightarrow}_{G/H} u'_{m+1}\# \,\|\, x_{m+1} \cdots \overset{a_m}{\longrightarrow}_{G/H} u'_n\# \,\|\, x_n \,.$$

As $o\,x_n \in H$, we have $o\,(u'_n\# \,\|\, x_n) \in G/H$ hence $a_1 \ldots a_n \in L(G/H)$.

(iii) Assume that $G \overset{f}{\longrightarrow}_{\ell} H$ and $(G/H) \overset{\pi_2}{\longrightarrow}_d H$ with H unambiguous.
Let $w \in L(G/H)$. Let us check that $w \in L(H) - L(G)$.
By Lemma 1, $w \in L(H)$. Assume that $w \in L(G)$.
There exists a path $u \overset{w}{\longrightarrow}_G v$ with $\iota u, o v \in G$.
Thus $f(u) \overset{w}{\longrightarrow}_H f(v)$ with $\iota f(u), o f(v) \in H$. As f is length-preserving,

$$u \,\|\, f(u) \overset{w}{\longrightarrow}_{G \,\|\, H} v \,\|\, f(v) \ \text{ with } \ \iota\,(u \,\|\, f(u)), o\,(v \,\|\, f(v)) \in G \,\|\, H.$$

Thus $u \,\|\, f(u) \overset{w}{\longrightarrow}_{G/H} v \,\|\, f(v)$ with $\iota\,(u \,\|\, f(u)) \in G/H$.
Furthermore $o\,\pi_2(v \,\|\, f(v)) = o\,f(v) \in H$.
By Lemma 3, $o\,(v \,\|\, f(v)) \in G/H$. Thus $o\,v \notin G$ which is a contradiction.

$\square$

Let us apply Lemma 7 restricted to deterministic automata with Proposition 2.

Proposition 4. *The family* $\ell\mathrm{dRec}_{\mathcal{F}}(H) = \ell\mathrm{Rec}_{\mathcal{F}_{\det}}(H)$ *is closed under difference when H is deterministic and ε-free, and $\mathcal{F}$ is closed under $\|$ and $/$.*

In general, the condition $(G/H) \overset{\pi_2}{\longrightarrow}_d H$ is necessary in Lemma 7. For instance, let us consider the following ε-free unambigous automaton H:

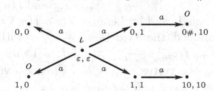

Here is $(H/H)_\iota$ where any vertex u, v represents $\perp u \,\|\, \perp v$.

Thus H/H is not deterministically reducible into H and $L(H/H) = L(H) = \{a, aa\}$. In order to accept $L(H) - L(G)$ by length superposition when $G \longrightarrow_{\ell d} H$, we have to restrict to vertices of the trimmed automaton $G \,\|\, H$ and to vertices of the copies of H. We define the *restricted length superposition* $G/\!/H$ by

$$G/\!/H = (G/H)_{|P} \ \text{ for } \ P = V_{(G \,\|\, H)_{\iota,o}} \cup \{\, u\#^n \,\|\, x \mid n > 0 \wedge u \le V_G \wedge x \in V_H \,\}.$$

For the previous automaton H, the automaton $(H/\!/H)_\iota$ is the following:

We get that $L(H/\!/H) = \emptyset = L(H) - L(H)$. Such an example can be generalized.

Lemma 8. *For any ε-free automata G, H such that $G \longrightarrow_{\ell d} H$, we have*

(a) H *unambiguous* $\Longrightarrow$ $(G/\!/H) \longrightarrow_{\ell d} H$
(b) H *unambiguous* $\Longrightarrow$ $\mathrm{L}(G/\!/H) \subseteq \mathrm{L}(H) - \mathrm{L}(G)$
(c) G *trimmed and H length-deterministic* $\Longrightarrow$ $\mathrm{L}(H) - \mathrm{L}(G) \subseteq \mathrm{L}(G/\!/H)$.

Proof. Let us prove implications (b) and (c).

(i) Suppose H is unambiguous. Let us prove that $\mathrm{L}(G/\!/H) \subseteq \mathrm{L}(H) - \mathrm{L}(G)$.
Let $w \in \mathrm{L}(G/\!/H)$. By Lemma 7 (a) and 1, $w \in \mathrm{L}(H)$.
Assume that $w \in \mathrm{L}(G)$. There exists $u \xrightarrow{w}_G v$ with $\iota u, o v \in G$.
So $u \parallel f(u) \xrightarrow{w}_{G/\!/H} v \parallel f(v)$ with $\iota (u \parallel f(u)) \in G/\!/H$.
Furthermore $o\,\pi_2(v \parallel f(v)) = o\,f(v) \in H$.
By (a) and Lemma 3, $o\,(v \parallel f(v)) \in G/\!/H$ which is a contradiction.
(ii) Suppose that G is trimmed and H is length-deterministic.
Let us prove that $\mathrm{L}(H) - \mathrm{L}(G) \subseteq \mathrm{L}(G/\!/H)$.
Let $a_1 \ldots a_n \in \mathrm{L}(H) - \mathrm{L}(G)$ for some $n \geq 0$ and $a_1, \ldots, a_n \in T$.
Let us show that $a_1 \ldots a_n \in \mathrm{L}(G/\!/H)$.
There exists $x_0 \xrightarrow{a_1}_H x_1 \ldots \xrightarrow{a_n}_H x_n$ with $\iota x_0, o x_n \in H$.
Let $z_i = (\#^{|x_i|}, x_i)$ for any $0 \leq i \leq n$.
By definition of $G/\!/H$, $z_0 \xrightarrow{a_1}_{G/\!/H} z_1 \ldots \xrightarrow{a_n}_{G/\!/H} z_n$ with $o z_n \in G/\!/H$.

We distinguish the two complementary cases below.
Case 1: $\neg \exists\, u_0\, (\iota u_0 \in G \wedge |u_0| = |x_0|)$.
  So $\iota z_0 \in G/\!/H$ hence $a_1 \ldots a_n \in \mathrm{L}(G/\!/H)$.
Case 2: $\exists\, u_0\, (\iota u_0 \in G \wedge |u_0| = |x_0|)$. Let $0 \leq m \leq n$ maximal such that

$$u_0 \xrightarrow{a_1}_G u_1 \ldots \xrightarrow{a_m}_G u_m \text{ with } |u_1| = |x_1|, \ldots, |u_m| = |x_m|.$$

Thus $u_0 \parallel x_0 \xrightarrow{a_1}_{G \parallel H} u_1 \parallel x_1 \ldots \xrightarrow{a_m}_{G \parallel H} u_m \parallel x_m$ and $\iota (u_0 \parallel x_0) \in G \parallel H$.
As H is length-deterministic and by Lemma 5 (a), $f(u_i) = id(x_i) = x_i$ for any
$0 \leq i \leq m$. As G is trimmed, there exists $u_m \longrightarrow^*_G u'$ with $o u' \in G$.
Thus $(u_m \parallel x_m) = (u_m \parallel f(u_m)) \longrightarrow^*_{G \parallel H} (u' \parallel f(u'))$ with $o (u' \parallel f(u')) \in G \parallel H$.
It follows that $u_m \parallel x_m$ is a vertex of $(G \parallel H)_{\iota,o}$ hence a vertex of $G/\!/H$.
Case 2.1: $m = n$. As $a_1 \ldots a_n \notin \mathrm{L}(G), o u_n \notin G$.
  Thus $o(u_n \parallel x_n) \in G/\!/H$ hence $a_1 \ldots a_n \in \mathrm{L}(G/\!/H)$.
Case 2.2: $m < n$. There exists $u'_{m+1}, \ldots, u'_n$ such that

$$u_m \parallel x_m \xrightarrow{a_{m+1}}_{G/\!/H} u'_{m+1}\# \parallel x_{m+1} \ldots \xrightarrow{a_m}_{G/\!/H} u'_n\# \parallel x_n.$$

As $o x_n \in H$, we have $o\,(u'_n\# \parallel x_n) \in G/\!/H$ hence $a_1 \ldots a_n \in \mathrm{L}(G/\!/H)$. $\qquad\square$

Let us apply Lemma 8 with Proposition 3.

Proposition 5. *The language family $\ell d\mathrm{Rec}_{\mathcal{F}}(H)$ is closed under difference when H is unambiguous, ε-free and length-deterministic, and $\mathcal{F}$ is closed under ιo-restriction, $\parallel$ and $/\!/$.*

Propositions 3 and 5 give Boolean algebras by length-preserving deterministic recognizability.

Theorem 1. *The language family $\ell dRec_{\mathcal{F}}(H)$ is a Boolean algebra relative to $L(H)$ for any automata family $\mathcal{F}$ closed under the operations $\|$ and $/\!/$ and ιo-restriction, and for any automaton H in $\mathcal{F}$ which is unambiguous, ε-free and length-deterministic.*

The closure under ιo-restriction is not satisfied for general automata families since the closure under accessibility and co-accessibility is required. This can be avoided by restricting to deterministic automata through Propositions 2 and 4.

Theorem 2. *The language family $\ell dRec_{\mathcal{F}}(H) = \ell Rec_{\mathcal{F}_{\det}}(H)$ is a Boolean algebra relative to $L(H)$ for any automata family $\mathcal{F}$ closed under the operations $\|$ and $/$, and for any automaton H in $\mathcal{F}$ which is deterministic and ε-free.*

We apply these two theorems for general automata families.

7 Boolean Algebras of Context-Free Languages

A general way of accepting context-free languages is through suffix automata. We prove that this automaton family is closed under previous operations to get Boolean algebras of context-free languages by Theorem 1.

An *elementary suffix automaton* is of the form: for $a \in T \cup \{\iota, o\}$,
$$W(u \xrightarrow{a} v) = \{ wu \xrightarrow{a} wv \mid w \in W \} \text{ where } W \in Reg(N^*) \text{ and } u, v \in N^*.$$
A *suffix automaton* is a finite union of elementary suffix automata. The family $\mathcal{S}tack$ of suffix automata defines the family $\mathcal{L}(\mathcal{S}tack)$ of context-free languages.

For instance, the previous 'Happy Birthday' automaton HB is in $\mathcal{S}tack$. In fact by denoting (κ, κ) by κ, $(\#, \kappa)$ by $\#_\kappa$, and $(x, |)$ by x for any $x \in \{a, b, \#\}$, HB is the union of the following elementary suffix automata:

$$
\begin{array}{lll}
\{a,b\}^*(\kappa \xrightarrow{a} a\kappa) & \{a,b\}^*(\kappa \xrightarrow{b} b\kappa) & \{\varepsilon\}(\kappa \xrightarrow{\iota} \kappa) \\
\{a,b\}^*(a\kappa \xrightarrow{c} \kappa) & \{a,b\}^*(b\kappa \xrightarrow{d} \kappa) & \{\varepsilon\}(\# \xrightarrow{o} \#) \\
\{a,b\}^*(b\kappa \xrightarrow{c} \#_\kappa) & \{a,b\}^*(a\kappa \xrightarrow{d} \#_\kappa) & \{a,b\}^*\#^*(\#_\kappa \xrightarrow{a,b} \#\#_\kappa) \\
\{a,b\}^*(a\#_\kappa \xrightarrow{c,d} \#_\kappa) & \{a,b\}^*(b\#_\kappa \xrightarrow{c,d} \#_\kappa) & \{a,b\}^*\#^*(\#\#_\kappa \xrightarrow{c,d} \#_\kappa)
\end{array}
$$

This automata family is closed under the previous operations.

Lemma 9. *The family $\mathcal{S}tack$ is closed under ιo-restriction, $\|$, $/$ and $/\!/$.*

Proof. (i) $\mathcal{S}tack$ is closed under regular restriction which is distributive over union and
$$W(u \xrightarrow{a} v)_{|P} = (W \cap Pu^{-1} \cap Pv^{-1})(u \xrightarrow{a} v)$$
where $Pu^{-1} = \{ v \mid vu \in P \}$ is the *right residual* of $P \subseteq N^*$ by $u \in N^*$.
Given G in $\mathcal{S}tack$ and a letter $\star$ in T, the graph $\{ u \xrightarrow{\star} v \mid u \longrightarrow_G^* v \}$ is in $\mathcal{S}tack$ (Proposition 3.18 in [3]). So $\longrightarrow_G^*$ is a rational relation: it is recognized by a finite transducer. Thus, the set of vertices deriving from or to a regular vertex

subset remains regular. Hence $\mathcal{S}$tack is closed under ιo-restriction.

(ii) $\mathcal{S}$tack is closed under $\parallel$ since this operation is distributive over union and

$$W(u \xrightarrow{a} v) \parallel Z(x \xrightarrow{a} y)$$
$$= \{ (wu \parallel zx) \xrightarrow{a} (wv \parallel zy) \mid w \in W \wedge z \in Z \wedge (|wu| = |zx| \wedge |wv| = |zy|) \}$$
$$= \{ (wu \parallel zx) \xrightarrow{a} (wv \parallel zy) \mid w \in W \wedge z \in Z \wedge$$
$$(|u| - |x| = |z| - |w| = |v| - |y|) \}.$$

So $W(u \xrightarrow{a} v) \parallel Z(x \xrightarrow{b} y) = \emptyset$ if $a \neq b$ or $|u| - |v| \neq |x| - |y|$, otherwise is

$$\bigcup_{s \in N^{|x|-|u|}} (Ws^{-1} \parallel Z).((su \parallel x) \xrightarrow{a} (sv \parallel y)) \quad \text{for } |u| \leq |x|$$

$$\bigcup_{s \in N^{|u|-|x|}} (W \parallel Zs^{-1}).((u \parallel sx) \xrightarrow{a} (v \parallel sy)) \quad \text{for } |u| > |x|.$$

Furthermore for $G, G' \in \mathcal{S}$tack, $I_{G \parallel G'} = I_G \parallel I_{G'}$ remains regular and is described by the rule $(I_G \parallel I_{G'}).(\varepsilon \xrightarrow{\iota} \varepsilon)$. It is the same for $O_{G \parallel G'} = O_G \parallel O_{G'}$.

(iii) Let us show that $\mathcal{S}$tack is closed under $/$. As $G/(H \cup H') = G/H \cup G/H'$, it remains to consider $G / Z(x \xrightarrow{a} y)$ for $G = \bigcup_{i=1}^{n} W_i(u_i \xrightarrow{a_i} v_i)$. Let us define the language

$$L = \bigcup \{ W_i.u_i \mid 1 \leq i \leq n \wedge a_i = a \wedge |u_i| - |v_i| = |x| - |y| \}.$$

Let us check that $(V_G - L) \parallel Zx$ is equal to

$$\{ s \parallel zx \mid s \in V_G \wedge z \in Z \wedge |s| = |zx| \wedge \neg \exists t (s \xrightarrow{a}_G t \wedge |t| = |zy|) \}.$$

Let $s \in V_G$ and $z \in Z$ such that $|s| = |zx|$. We have to show that

$$s \in L \iff \exists t (s \xrightarrow{a}_G t \wedge |t| = |zy|).$$

$\Longrightarrow$: Assume that $s \in L$. There exists $1 \leq i \leq n$ and $w \in W_i$ such that

$$s = wu_i \text{ and } a_i = a \text{ and } |u_i| - |v_i| = |x| - |y|.$$

Hence $s \xrightarrow{a} wv_i$ with $|wv_i| = |w| + |u_i| + |y| - |x| = |s| + |y| - |x| = |zy|$.

$\Longleftarrow$: Suppose there exists t such that $s \xrightarrow{a}_G t$ and $|t| = |zy|$. So there exists $1 \leq i \leq n$ and $w \in W_i$ such that $a_i = a$, $s = wu_i$, $t = wv_i$. As $|zx| = |s|$ and $|zy| = |wv_i|$, we get $|wv_i| - |y| = |z| = |s| - |x|$. Thus $|wv_i x| = |sy| = |wu_i y|$ i.e. $|u_i y| = |v_i x|$. So $s = wu_i \in L$. Thus the following subgraph of G/H: the set of $u \parallel x \xrightarrow{a} v\# \parallel y$ such that

$$x \xrightarrow{a}_H y \wedge u \in V_G \wedge \neg \exists w (u \xrightarrow{a}_G w \wedge |w| = |y|) \wedge v \leq u \#^*$$

is equal to the following suffix automaton:

$$(V_G - L).(\varepsilon \xrightarrow{a} \#^{|y|-|x|}) \parallel Z.(x \xrightarrow{a} y) \quad \text{for } |x| < |y|$$

otherwise $|x| \geq |y|$ and by union on $1 \leq i \leq n$ with $W = W_i$ and $u \in \{u_i, v_i\}$, if $|u| > |x| - |y|$ we take the suffix automaton:

$$(W - Lu^{-1}).(u \xrightarrow{a} v\#) \parallel Z.(x \xrightarrow{a} y) \quad \text{for } v < u \text{ and } |u| - |v\#| = |x| - |y|$$

and if $|u| \leq |x| - |y|$, having $|u| = |x|$ we get $y = \varepsilon$ and we take the suffix automaton:

$$(W - Lu^{-1})s^{-1}.(su \xrightarrow{a} \#) \parallel Z.(x \xrightarrow{a} \varepsilon) \quad \text{for any suffix letter } s \text{ of } W.$$

Similarly denoting by P_G the set of prefixes of V_G, the subgraph of G/H:

$$\{ u\#^n \| x \xrightarrow{a} v\#\|y \mid x \xrightarrow{a}_H y \wedge n > 0 \wedge u \leq V_G \wedge v \leq u\#^* \}$$

is equal to the following suffix automaton:

$$P_G \#^+.(\varepsilon \xrightarrow{a} \#^{|y|-|x|}) \parallel Z.(x \xrightarrow{a} y) \quad \text{for } |x| \leq |y|$$

otherwise $|x| > |y|$ and the automaton is the unions of the following automata:

$$(P_G \#^+)u^{-1}.(u \xrightarrow{a} \#) \parallel Z.(x \xrightarrow{a} y) \quad \text{for } u \in N_G^*\#^+ \text{ and } |u| = |x| - |y| + 1.$$

Finally, the other subgraphs of G/H are described as before.
With (i), it follows that $\mathcal{S}$tack is also closed under $\|$.   □

Let us apply Theorem 1 with Lemma 9.

Proposition 6. *The family $\ell d\mathrm{Rec}_{\mathcal{S}\text{tack}}(H)$ is a Boolean algebra relative to* $\mathrm{L}(H)$ *for any unambiguous, ε-free and length-deterministic automaton H.*

In particular, we obtain again that $\ell d\mathrm{Rec}_{\mathcal{S}\text{tack}_{\text{det}}}(H)$ for H deterministic, is a relative Boolean algebra [8]. A well-known relative Boolean algebra is the family $\ell d\mathrm{Rec}_{\mathcal{S}\text{tack}}(\mathrm{Inp}(T_{-1}, T_0, T_1))$ of input-driven languages according to the triple (T_{-1}, T_0, T_1) of finite disjoint subsets of T [7].
Adding the loops labeled in T_{-1} on the initial vertex κ of $\mathrm{Inp}(T_{-1}, T_0, T_1)$, we get the *visibly automaton*

$$\mathrm{Vis}(T_{-1}, T_0, T_1) = \mathrm{Inp}(T_{-1}, T_0, T_1) \cup \{ \kappa \xrightarrow{a} \kappa \mid a \in T_{-1} \}$$

accepting $\mathrm{L}(\mathrm{Vis}(T_{-1}, T_0, T_1)) = (T_{-1} \cup T_0 \cup T_1)^*$, and the Boolean algebra $\ell d\mathrm{Rec}_{\mathcal{S}\text{tack}}(\mathrm{Vis}(T_{-1}, T_0, T_1))$ is the family of visibly pushdown languages according to (T_{-1}, T_0, T_1) [1]. Note that we can enhance the visibility of pushdown automata by taking a mapping $\| \ \|$ from a finite subset $T_{\| \|} \subset T$ to $\mathbb{Z}$, by taking $|, \kappa \in N$, and by defining the following automaton:

$$\mathrm{Vis}_{\| \|} = \{ |^n\kappa \xrightarrow{a} |^{\max(0, n + \|a\|)} \mid n \geq 0 \wedge a \in T_{\| \|} \} \cup \{ \iota\kappa \} \cup \{ o|^n\kappa \mid n \geq 0 \}$$

In particular $\mathrm{Vis}(T_{-1}, T_0, T_1) = \mathrm{Vis}_{\| \|}$ for $T_{\| \|} = T_{-1} \cup T_0 \cup T_1$ with $\|a\| = i$ for any $a \in T_i$ and $i \in \{-1, 0, 1\}$. For any $\| \ \|$, $\mathrm{L}(\mathrm{Vis}_{\| \|}) = T_{\| \|}^*$ and $\ell d\mathrm{Rec}_{\mathcal{S}\text{tack}}(\mathrm{Vis}_{\| \|}) = \ell\mathrm{Rec}_{\mathcal{S}\text{tack}_{\text{det}}}(\mathrm{Vis}_{\| \|})$ is a Boolean algebra.
We further increase the pushdown visibility by taking $|, \dagger, \kappa \in N$ and the recognizer

$$2\mathrm{Vis}_{\| \|} = \{ |^n\kappa \xrightarrow{a} |^{n + \|a\|} \mid n \in \mathbb{Z} \wedge a \in T_{\| \|} \} \cup \{ \iota\kappa \} \cup \{ o|^n\kappa \mid n \in \mathbb{Z} \}$$

where $|^{-n} = \dagger^n$ for any $n > 0$. Thus $\ell d\mathrm{Rec}_{\mathcal{S}\text{tack}}(\mathrm{Vis}_{\| \|})$ is still a Boolean algebra.
Note that Proposition 6 also applies to non-deterministic recognizers like the unambiguous automaton Un (defined at the end of Sect. 2) which is also ε-free and length-deterministic.
Proposition 6 may also be restricted to the family of counter automata.

8   Boolean Algebras of Context-Sensitive Languages

A simple way to define context-sensitive languages is through the synchronized relations of bounded length difference.

An *elementary bounded synchronized automaton* is an automaton of the form:

$$R(u \xrightarrow{a} v) = \{ \ xu \xrightarrow{a} yv \mid (x,y) \in R \ \} \text{ for } R \in Reg((N{\times}N)^*) \text{ and } u,v \in N^*$$

where $a \in T \cup \{\iota, o\}$. A *bounded synchronized automaton* is a finite union of elementary bounded synchonized automata. The family $\mathcal{S}$ync of bounded synchronized automata accepts the family $\mathcal{L}(\mathcal{S}$ync$)$ of context-sensitive languages [9].

Similarly to the proof of Lemma 9, we get that $\mathcal{S}$ync is closed under $\|$ and $/$. However, $\mathcal{S}$ync is not closed under ιo-restriction, nor closed under $/\!/$ because the set of vertices accessible from a given vertex for a bounded synchronized automaton is not necessarily regular (also not effective). Nevertheless and by restricting to deterministic recognizers, we can apply Theorem 2.

Proposition 7. *The family* $\ell\mathrm{dRec}_{\mathcal{S}\mathrm{ync}}(H) = \ell\mathrm{Rec}_{\mathcal{S}\mathrm{ync}_{\mathrm{det}}}(H)$ *is a Boolean algebra relative to* $\mathrm{L}(H)$ *for any deterministic and ε-free automaton H.*

Thus $\ell\mathrm{dRec}_{\mathcal{S}\mathrm{ync}}(\mathrm{Inp}(T_{-1}, T_0, T_1))$ defines the relative Boolean algebra of *bounded synchronized input-driven languages* w.r.t. to (T_{-1}, T_0, T_1). Likewise we have the Boolean algebra $\ell\mathrm{dRec}_{\mathcal{S}\mathrm{ync}}(\mathrm{Vis}_{\|\,\|})$ of *bounded synchronized visibly languages* w.r.t. $\|\,\|$. Theorem 2 can be applied to many other automata families, such as the family of vector addition systems (or Petri nets) with regular contexts.

Deterministic length recognizability allows to obtain Boolean algebras using automata families and recognizers. We have applied it to suffix automata and bounded synchronized automata but one can use it on any automata family closed under length synchronization, length superposition and trimmed restriction. For instance, it is suitable for families of automata defined by sequentiality and parallelism operations such as the families studied among others by Bernhard Steffen [2].

References

1. Alur, R., Madhusudan, P.: Visibly pushdown languages. In: Babai, L. (ed.) 36th STOC ACM Proceedings, pp. 202–211 (2004)
2. Burkart, O., Caucal, D., Moller, F., Steffen, B.: Verification on infinite structures. In: Handbook of Process Algebra, pp. 545–623 (2001)
3. Caucal, D.: On infinite transition graphs having a decidable monadic theory. In: Meyer, F., Monien, B. (eds.) ICALP 1996. LNCS, vol. 1099, pp. 194–205. Springer, Heidelberg (1996). https://doi.org/10.1007/3-540-61440-0_128
4. Caucal, D.: Boolean algebras of unambiguous context-free languages. In: Hariharan, R., Mukund, M., Vinay, V. (eds.) 28th FSTTCS, Dagstuhl Research Server (2008)
5. Caucal, D., Rispal, C.: Recognizability for automata. In: Hoshi, M., Seki, S. (eds.) DLT 2018. LNCS, vol. 11088, pp. 206–218. Springer, Cham (2018). https://doi.org/10.1007/978-3-319-98654-8_17

6. Eilenberg, S.: Algèbre catégorique et théorie des automates, Institut H. Poincaré (1967). and Automata, languages and machines, Vol. A, Academic Press (1974)
7. Mehlhorn, K.: Pebbling mountain ranges and its application to DCFL-recognition. In: de Bakker, J., van Leeuwen, J. (eds.) ICALP 1980. LNCS, vol. 85, pp. 422–435. Springer, Heidelberg (1980). https://doi.org/10.1007/3-540-10003-2_89
8. Nowotka, D., Srba, J.: Height-Deterministic Pushdown Automata. In: Kučera, L., Kučera, A. (eds.) MFCS 2007. LNCS, vol. 4708, pp. 125–134. Springer, Heidelberg (2007). https://doi.org/10.1007/978-3-540-74456-6_13
9. Rispal, C.: The synchronized graphs trace the context-sensitive languages. Electr. Notes Theor. Comput. Sci. **68**(6), 55–70 (2002)
10. Thomas, W.: Uniform and nonuniform recognizability. Theoretical Computer Science **292**, 299–316 (2003)

Reflections on Bernhard Steffen's Physics of Software Tools

Hubert Garavel[✉] and Radu Mateescu

Univ. Grenoble Alpes, Inria, Cnrs, Lig, 38000 Grenoble, France
{hubert.garavel,radu.mateescu}@inria.fr

Abstract. Many software tools have been developed to implement the concepts of formal methods, sometimes with great success, but also with an impressive tool mortality and an apparent dispersion of efforts. There has been little analysis so far of such tool development as a whole, in order to make it more coherent, efficient, and useful to the society. Recently, however, Bernhard Steffen published a paper entitled "The Physics of Software Tools: SWOT Analysis and Vision" that precisely proposes such a global vision. We highlight the key ideas of this paper and review them in light of our own experience in designing and implementing the CADP toolbox for the specification and analysis of concurrent systems.

1   Introduction

The present article was written in honour of Bernhard Steffen and included in a collective Festschrift book offered to him at the occasion of his 60th birthday, in addition to another Festschrift article [18], jointly dedicated to Susanne Graf and Bernhard Steffen.

In a recent position statement entitled *The Physics of Software Tools: SWOT Analysis and Vision* [49], Bernhard Steffen analyzes the current situation of software tools implementing the concepts of formal methods and suggests directions for organizing the development of these tools in a more coherent and efficient way. This analysis is rooted in Bernhard Steffen's double experience in developing software tools (including ETI [7,50], jETI [35], LearnLib [24,42,44] and CINCO [43]) and managing the research community in formal methods (notably with the launch of the TACAS conference[1], of the STTT journal[2], and the RERS challenge[3]). The position statement [49] is written in a lively style, enriched with insightful anecdotes. Despite its seemingly simple form, it puts forward many diverse ideas that freely spring from all parts of the text.

We believe that global debates on the present and future of formal methods are essential, and Bernhard Steffen's position statement is a most welcome contribution in this respect. The present article exposes the key ideas of this position

---

[1] http://tacas.info.
[2] http://sttt.cs.uni-dortmund.de.
[3] http://rers-challenge.org.

© Springer Nature Switzerland AG 2019
T. Margaria et al. (Eds.): Steffen Festschrift, LNCS 11200, pp. 186–207, 2019.
https://doi.org/10.1007/978-3-030-22348-9_12

statement in an orderly way, each idea being first illustrated with citations from [49] (written in italics), then commented and discussed by us, with examples borrowed from process calculi and model checking, based on our own experience in designing and implementing the CADP toolbox [17] for the specification and analysis of concurrent systems.

The present article is organized as follows. Section 2 gives an overview of the current status of software tools that implement the concepts of formal methods and summarizes the main difficulties often faced by the users of these tools. Section 3 analyzes some human factors that can be seen as subjective causes of these difficulties. Section 4 proposes remedies and action points that could be taken, both at the individual level of each tool developer and at the collective level of the research community as a whole, to improve the situation. Finally, Sect. 5 makes concluding remarks.

2   Current status and difficulties

In [49], the current landscape of software tools is characterized by eight ideas.

Definition of formal tools.

"We focus our attention here on formal methods-based software tools like as they are addressed by STTT. — the software tools that are meant to help controlling the way software is developed — a means for supporting the design, construction, and analysis of (large-scale) systems"

The analysis of Bernhard Steffen does not consider all kinds of software on Earth but, more concretely, the particular class of software tools intended to assist the design of software and software-intensive systems. As examples of such tools, he cites static analyzers, model checkers, theorem provers, SAT and SMT solvers, automata learning tools, model-based test generation tools, etc. Such tools are also referred to as "formal-methods based tools", but specific terminology (e.g., "software development tools", "meta software tools", or "higher-order software") would be possible. In the remainder of this article, we will call "formal tools" those software tools addressed by Bernhard Steffen, even if some of them implement learning techniques, which are not fully predictable from a formal point of view.

Formal tools are successful.

"Formal methods-based tools had a lot of success stories in recent years. — The success of these tools is due to many factors, whereby Moore's law can be regarded as a general enabler. — Many solutions are impressive for very particular cases, and we have seen many publications about such success stories."

As examples of formal methods for which successful tools have been developed, Bernhard Steffen mentions: static analysis, symbolic execution, model checking, statistical model checking, SAT and SMT solvers, systems synthesis, automata learning, and model-based testing. A complementary list can be found in [14, Sect. 1.3.4], which provides a list of 30 success stories in formal methods, one per year between 1982 and 2011. Certain formal tools are indeed successful, considering, e.g., the list of 190+ case studies tackled using the CADP toolbox[4].

However, the global picture is more contrasted, as the success of formal methods in some application domains does not mean a uniform acceptance of these methods in all branches of computer science and software design activities. One starts seeing mathematical theories that are formally checked using proof assistants, but, on the other hand, most of the distributed algorithms published so far are neither formally specified nor verified beyond simple testing. A few companies use formal methods when it is required by safety regulations (e.g., avionics, railways, etc.) or when design errors not caught by conventional validation are too expensive to patch after release (e.g., hardware design), but most companies do not use formal methods, certifying the design process rather than the final product and relying instead on agile methodologies and testing techniques that give little assurance as the complexity of software increases.

As a consequence, one faces a massive problem with software quality, resulting in abnormally high numbers of failures and security breaches. Although end-users might develop tolerance for quality degradation, the ever-growing dependency of modern societies on improper software is worrying. It is fair to admit that, so far, formal methods did not handle this issue satisfactorily.

Formal tools are complex.

"The complexity of software systems, even though man made, often crosses the border of what can be fully controlled and reasoned about via mathematical reasoning. — These tools have become so complex and so special that they are no longer just a means for supporting the development of reliable systems, but an object of study in their own right. — Software tools [...] become so complex that each of them turns into a reality of their own, with its own 'physics', that needs to be studied in its own right. — The complexity of the individual tools has grown so enormously that tool developers risk to devote their entire intuition to their specific 'tool world'."

Software projects are among the most involved creations of human mind. This is especially true of formal tools, which, even though they do not have a huge volume of code[5], contain highly complex algorithms that have been difficult to design and are still difficult to understand and make evolve. Such difficulty often arises from the fact that these tools try to provide partial solutions to generally undecidable problems, or implement computationally-expensive algorithms as efficiently as possible to make them affordable in practice. Recently, a new dimension of complexity has appeared with the introduction of learning techniques, the correctness of which is validated empirically but difficult to demonstrate formally (see, e.g., [45]).

The traditional concerns about the so-called "software crisis" are still there, and even more relevant for formal tools. The development of usable tools required the efforts of many high-profile scientists, continuously working for

---

[4] http://cadp.inria.fr/case-studies.
[5] We believe that most formal tools are less than one million lines of code.

several decades. For instance, the early steps of theorem proving can be traced back to the 1960s (see, e.g., [32]), and the first verification tools based on state-space exploration for concurrent systems appeared in the 1970s [52] [46]. As time passed, the amount of knowledge accumulated in mainstream formal tools has grown so largely that it would be difficult, today, to design a new theorem prover or model checker from scratch. We thus agree with Bernhard Steffen that such tools are worth being studied in their own right: they are a valuable technical heritage that should be preserved and studied (as carefully as, e.g., operating systems and network protocols) in order to remain available for the next generations.

Formal tools are fragmented.

"*The landscape of software tools considered here is extremely heterogeneous and fragmented. — More and more impressive individual tool landscapes have evolved, exploiting parallelization, sometimes even the structure of GPUs, while also comprising numerous dedicated heuristics either directly implemented in their special individual algorithms or imported through powerful SAT and SMT solvers, and more recently the integration of machine-learning technology. Thus the situation became even more diverse.*"

Heterogeneity and fragmentation are indeed present and have multiple causes. At the top level is the existence of three main approaches to verification: static analysis, theorem proving, and model checking, which rely upon very different principles, although they may overlap in concrete applications. Then, each of these main approaches is itself fragmented into many, often incompatible variants. Considering only, as an example, the landscape of model checkers for concurrent systems, heterogeneity comes from the modelling formalisms (e.g., message-passing vs shared-memory models, automata vs Petri nets vs process calculi, timed vs untimed, etc.), from the logical property formalisms (e.g., state-based vs action-based models, linear-time vs branching-time properties, temporal logics vs μ-calculus, etc.), from the verification algorithms used (e.g., explicit-state vs symbolic model checking), and from the implementation techniques used (e.g., C/C++ vs Java vs OCaml, Unix vs Windows, mono-core vs multi-cores vs clusters vs GPUs, etc.). An individual tool developer or even a large research team cannot feasibly explore all these aspects simultaneously: choices must be made that select certain aspects and restrict others, leading to "specialized" formal tools that may indeed not interoperate well with other tools designed to address similar or related problems. Another impressive example of fragmentation is the large collection of tools dealing with quantitative verification of automata-based models: for this setting, known as the "quantitative automata zoo" [23], not less than 74 formal tools have been developed in academia[6].

Formal tools are difficult to learn.

"*The adoption of tools is very cumbersome. Thus users, having become acquainted with one tool, are typically reluctant to change, [...] a phenomenon*

---

[6] http://cadp.inria.fr/resources/zoo.

hindering innovation. — Many formal methods tools are very hard to use and therefore scare users away, and only very few users master more than one of the more complex tools."

There are several reasons hindering the adoption of formal tools. Perhaps, the main reason is that these tools rely upon complex mathematical theories that, in many cases, must be assimilated by users to fully exploit the tool capabilities [11]. A second reason is that, in the fragmented landscape of formal tools, there is almost no standard language for describing models and properties: each tool has its own input languages, different from those of other tools providing similar functionality. A third reason is that, more often than not, these languages closely reflect the particular algorithms implemented in the tool, the limitations of these algorithms, and the personal preferences of tool developers; for many users, these languages are felt as intricate notations, too far from the classical background of computer programmers and system designers. Finally, one should also mention tools implementing a wealth of algorithms on equal footing, forcing users to learn and try dozens of options to determine which ones are useful for solving a given problem.

The applicability of formal tools is hard to estimate.

"It is often difficult to judge whether a certain tool would fit a given purpose, even if it is specifically designed for the intended programming language. Judging how easy it would be to adapt a certain tool to some purpose is typically even much more difficult due to feature interaction effects: How does a certain new kind of analysis interfere with the current analyses, optimizations, representations, approximations, and transformations? This question is so difficult that often even the core developers of a tool are unable to answer it or even radically fail in assessing their tool's profile. — Prospective users therefore have a hard time to orient themselves in the current tool landscape, and even experts typically only have very partial knowledge."

The aforementioned fragmentation, which makes the tool landscape vast and densely populated, is the first reason for the situation accurately described by Bernhard Steffen. Another cause is the lack of standardized criteria for characterizing the functionality and scope of formal tools. In the 80s and early 90s, there was a naive expectation that formal methods would spread everywhere and solve most issues of software development; practitioners then discovered that the applicability of formal methods was much more limited than stated by their proponents, and this disillusion blocked for years the dissemination of formal methods in many industries. Today, many formal tools come with a catalog of demo examples; however, such catalogs are often limited to a handful of relatively small examples that have been successfully tackled. To better determine the applicability of formal tools, one would need larger collections of industrial-size models in open source, together with usage metadata, such as the time and cost spent in these models; one would also need reports about problems and failures using particular tools. Because such information is scarcely available, the prevailing way to know about the applicability of a formal tool is to acquire self-experience with this tool, which is long, expensive, and not necessarily compatible with most industrial agendas.

The performance of formal tools is hard to predict.

"The true effects of combining methodologies as diverse as classical static analysis, model checking, SAT and SMT solving, and dynamic methods like simulation, runtime verification, testing, and learning, with their dedicated means of optimizations in terms of, e.g., BDD coding, parallelization, and various forms of abstraction and reduction, are very dependent on the particular tools and typically hardly predictable. — The BDD encoding of Boolean functions [...] showed impressive practical results, but may also perform extremely poorly, and we are still far from understanding when it performs well. Imagine in comparison how difficult it must be to predict the performance of today's software tools."

The performance of formal tools is also crucial for their applicability, as a formal tool that is theoretically sound and suitable for certain problems may be useless if it delivers poor performance in practice. The difficulty to predict the performance of formal tools arises, on the one hand, from the lack of predictability of the basic engines (Bernhard Steffen mentions BDDs, but the same holds for SAT, SMT, BES[7], or PBES[8] solvers), and, on the other hand, from the lack of compositionality (there are few theoretical results enabling one to infer the performance of a composed system from that of its components). Also, the quality of tool implementation should also be taken into account, as programming skills sometimes make a significant difference.

Formal tools are hard to analyze objectively.

"Peculiarities of tools may have a major impact on the evaluation process, and [...] tool-based observations may well be dominated by special implementation effects. — It is sometimes hard to distinguish which of the presented results about the applied technology can be generalized, and which are merely a view through the glasses of a particular implementation. — Experimental investigations [...] provide interesting indications about the applied technology, but typically fail to provide sufficient evidence to transfer results to other settings and tools. Moreover, implementation-specific details often dominate the observed effects which thereby become invalid for drawing conceptual conclusions. — Working with a particular such analysis tool forces one to live in its dedicated artificial world with its own 'physics'. The tools' ecosystems may impose quite a strong bias when trying to observe the power of analysis technologies via case studies, even to the point that the observed effects are dominated by tool-imposed implementation details. Do [the observations] reflect the object of study, or are they imposed by the particularities of the used tool? Like in the case of physics, this may make the difference between a cause to rethink the entire conceptual framework (i.e., change the established laws), or just a hint towards a side-effect of a

---

[7] Boolean equation systems [33].
[8] Parameterized Boolean equation systems [22,38].

particular implementation detail of (or even an error in) the tool (i.e., a flaw in the experimental setup).".

The concern that experimental observations may be biased by tool-specific aspects is a driving idea expressed many times in Bernhard Steffen's paper. Three potential risks are pointed out: over-interpretation of the obtained results, corruption of scientific knowledge (*"biases [...] may enter corresponding publications without being noticed"*), and misleading impact on scientists (*"[it] may end up steering research agendas in wrong directions"*).

Although such dangers exist, we believe that they should not be exaggerated, as the well-established scientific approach provides effective countermeasures. It is indeed true that a poor programmer may disqualify a valuable algorithm for some time, but if the algorithm sounds interesting, other scientists will try to implement it and come up with different experimental results. Also, publications containing invalid observations or conclusions have always been part of science, but sooner or later, if the topic is still of interest, they are detected and corrected (see, e.g., [21] vs [51] on the comparative assessment of term rewrite engines).

Finally, we observe that individual and collective research agendas are not exclusively based on experimental results published in scientific literature; many other factors play a role: public funding policies, marketing plans from private companies, research agendas of other research institutions and countries, etc. There is also an intellectual inertia factor: conformance with mainstream approaches (usually, those with the largest number of publications) and adherence to influential scientists (skillfully mixing objective facts and subjective preferences) often play a greater role than the cold examination of experimental results. We give here three examples, all taken from the model-checking world: (i) state-based approaches are still predominating, although action-based approaches have better theoretical properties (abstraction, composition, etc.) and are easier to store and exchange as computer files; (ii) linear-time temporal logics, despite the exponential complexity of their algorithms, are often preferred to branching-time temporal logics, whose algorithms have linear complexity; (iii) symbolic model checking was claimed to definitely outperform explicit-state model checking, but recent experiments [29, Sect. 4.3] show that it is not the case.

3   Analysis of human factors

Having discussed the objective causes for the complexity and fragmentation of formal tools, Bernhard Steffen also considers subjective causes related to human behaviour, especially two of them, which we now review in the present section.

Academia seeks for novelty rather than consolidation.

"People prefer to strive for something new and, in contrast to, e.g., physics, there is no established culture of control and consolidation."

This statement can be understood in two ways. Bernhard Steffen issued it to suggest that, in the formal tool community, scientists do not spend enough effort to refute misconceptions resulting from a wrong interpretation of observations. This would require independent scientists to redo published experiments, carefully analyzing all assumptions and experimental conditions to make sure that the stated conclusions are valid. It is true that, usually, experimental results concerning formal tools are heavily scrutinized before publication, and very lightly after. The main reason why computer science differs from physics in this respect is that formal tools are living artifacts: by the time one wants to redo the experiments, the tools may have been abandoned[9], replaced with newer versions, or turned into commercial products.

But the above statement about novelty vs consolidation can also be given, we believe, a more general meaning. In the formal tool community, the standard practice is, given a new idea, to develop a tool prototype, to experiment it on a few well-chosen case studies, publish the results, and move on to the next challenging idea. Quite often, many concrete problems are left unsolved in this approach, and the tool prototypes quickly developed for proof-of-concept experiments are never maintained any further. As Bernhard Steffen points out, the need for consolidated tools that could be reused by others does not outweigh the fascination for novel ideas, driven by the industrial challenges of the digital revolution, whose ultimate goal appears to be the design, for each human activity, of a computer system capable of performing this activity autonomously. One thus observes a growing gap between, on the one hand, increasingly complex theories and formalisms combining paradigms such as concurrency, mobility, cyberphysics, uncertainty, autonomy, learning, etc. and, on the other hand, a fragmented landscape of formal tools that only address one or a few of these paradigms, only in a partial manner and with major scalability issues. Consequently, a second gap is expanding between, on the one hand, the increasing ambition and complexity of industrial systems and, on the other hand, the capabilities of formal tools to analyze such systems. A pessimistic account of this discrepancy can be found in [48], with the worrying prospect that autonomous systems require enginers to throw away all established guidelines for producing safe and secure computing systems, announcing an era where potentially dangerous machines will be out of control. The role of ethics is often to curb opportunities made possible by science; in this case, ethics will face opportunities that science, at present, cannot master.

Tool developers focus too much on their own tools.

"The main threat to establishing a global tool experimentation and exchange platform is individualism. Individual developers or small teams currently working on tools typically integrate whatever functionality they consider interesting into their own dedicated tool landscape rather than investing into a global infrastructure aiming at making these functionalities available to everybody. This seems easier, and it currently also generates higher rewards. Experimental results concerning a certain setting or tool are welcome in many conferences, and optimizing

---

[9] See, e.g., http://cadp.inria.fr/resources/zoo or http://rewriting.loria.fr/systems. html to observe the impressive mortality of formal tools.

*one's own tool for a certain benchmark is a completely different matter than sys-
tematically establishing conceptually new approaches with a stable and predictive
performance profile."*

To a large extent, these observations are correct. As mentioned already, the
landscape of formal tools is fragmented. If we omit small prototypes with no
follow-through, the remaining larger, mature tools tend to organize themselves
as complete software stacks or platforms, with the goal of providing all the
functionalities that end users can expect. This often leads to the well-known
"silo effect" of software engineering, making it difficult to combine and compare
the functionalities of separate tools.

Apart from the technical reasons for fragmentation exposed in Sect. 2, Bernhard Steffen points out the role of human factors: individualism, academic evaluation criteria, and also the *"not-developed-here syndrome"* [49, Sect. 5]. It seems
indeed that certain decisions with no objective justification can only be explained
by such subjective factors. For instance, in the early 90s, the concurrency theory
community certainly missed an historical opportunity by not widely adopting
the international standard LOTOS [25], continuing instead to spend resources
on older languages (e.g., CCS and CSP) or even the definition of new ones (e.g.,
PSF and μCRL), and undertaking the development of separate model checkers
for all these languages[10]; such dispersion of efforts on several languages that
were similar to, but incompatible with LOTOS prevented this community from
reaching the critical mass required for a large industrial acceptance.

There are cases, however, where a duplication of efforts is not a waste of
resources, in particular when several tools, developed independently and offering
comparable functionalities, share the same input language. Examples are BDD
packages, SAT solvers, model checkers for Petri nets, etc. In such cases, the
competition between different tool developers leads to faster progress, and the
redundancy provided by independent implementations can be useful for high-
assurance certification purposes.

4   Actions and remedies

Having described the current situation of formal tools and its causes, Bernhard
Steffen suggests directions for improvement. These can be divided into *individual
actions*, which should locally guide the development of each formal tool, and
collective actions, which should be globally undertaken by the community of
formal tool developers and users.

---

[10] Scientific literature sometimes reflects, many years later, such rivalries from the past:
for instance, the *Handbook of Process Algebra* [3] cites LOTOS only two times in
1356 pages, and, in the *Handbook of Model Checking*, the 47-page chapter on process
algebra [9] does not mention LOTOS nor the CADP tools, although these are the
historically first and most widely used model checkers for process algebra.

4.1   Individual actions

Tool developers are the main stakeholders who can improve the current situation. To this aim, Bernhard Steffen lists three expectations that developers should fulfill.

Formal tools should be modular.

"Even better would be the possibility to access implemented tool functionality more selectively — bundling (tool) functionality so that it can easily be used by others — [and] openly exchanged, thus tearing down the boundaries between the individual tools — [allowing] cross-tool combinations of individual tool functionalities. — The need for a more systematic approach to establish the profiles of tools and methods is obvious. — Even the core developers of a tool [...] radically fail in assessing their tool's profile."

In order to avoid the aforementioned "silo effect", one should indeed promote the design of modular tools, divided into software components that can be reused separately. These components should have clean interfaces and their functionalities should be properly documented. Bernhard Steffen does not mention the need for common formats or converters between formats, but this is implicitly required for information exchange and tool interoperability. Notice also that open source and modular design are two orthogonal aspects, the former never being a substitute for the latter.

We all the more agree with Bernhard Steffen that, since its origins, our CADP model checking toolbox has been carefully architected around generic software components providing distinct, well-defined functionalities with documented interfaces for external use. Such building blocks have proven successful for the rapid construction of new tools: at present, not less than 94 formal tools[11] have been developed by reusing the software components of CADP. For example, the most recent of these tools is TESTOR [37], which generates conformance tests on the fly and is almost entirely built using three generic technologies of CADP: the BCG environment for on-disk storage of labelled transition systems, the OPEN/CÆSAR environment for on-the-fly exploration of labelled transition systems, and the CÆSAR_SOLVE library for solving Boolean equation systems.

Formal tools should be correct.

"Software tool providers are responsible to establish technology that is trusted. — Due to the very high complexity of today's tools, [errors] are deemed to be quite frequent. In fact, it is still quite rare that validation tools are themselves developed with the technology they are intended to provide."

It is a fact that formal tools may contain errors. In the case of the CADP toolbox, we fix defects in almost every monthly release. Many errors are minor, but some can be severe and corrupt the verification results[12]. To avoid such

---

[11] http://cadp.inria.fr/software.

[12] See, e.g., the TLA+ model checker bug found in 2018, which could prevent reachable state spaces from being entirely explored (http://lamport.azurewebsites.net/tla/toolbox-1-5-5.html).

issues, formal tools should be properly designed according to software engineering principles, extensively validated, and regularly maintained.

The traditional validation approach consists in thorough testing. This approach, which is used for the CADP toolbox, requires one to build large collections of test cases, a problem that will be further addressed in Sect. 4.2. Such collections can be used for non-regression testing, for cross-checking different tools, and for perfoming sanity checks (e.g., checking that any labelled transition system is bisimilar to itself, etc.). Software competitions (see Sect. 4.2 below) are also effective in detecting bugs in formal tools. In any case, the potential presence of errors should not be an excuse to avoid formal tools, because the more they are used, the more errors are detected and fixed.

There exist more ambitious approaches, in which formal tools (e.g., a static analyzer [27] or a Lustre compiler [5]) are themselves formally verified. On the long run, this will certainly become the standard approach; in the meantime, such approaches, because they demand time and effort, can only be applied to formal tools that are already mature and stable.

Bernhard Steffen goes one step further by suggesting that formal tools could be *"themselves developed with the technology they are intended to provide"*. Maybe this is going too far: there is no reason, for instance, why a BDD package should be verified using itself, whereas proof techniques for pointer manipulation algorithms are clearly more appropriate. However, we can mention, in the case of CADP, three examples that sustain Bernhard Steffen's intuition about "circular use" of formal tools: (i) The CÆSAR.ADT compiler [12], which translates LOTOS abstract data types to C, is used to bootstrap itself and to build the XTL model checker [39], both tools being mostly written using LOTOS abstract data types; (ii) Similarly, the LNT language [19], as implemented by the TRAIAN compiler, serves as a basis for implementing the LNT2LOTOS translator for LNT, as well as a dozen of compilers/translators for other languages [16]; (iii) The DLC compiler [10], which translates LNT concurrent descriptions with multiway rendezvous [20] into distributed POSIX processes communicating using TCP sockets, enables formal validation, as its inputs and outputs, both expressed in LNT, can be compared against each other modulo safety equivalence.

Formal tools should be user-friendly.

"Software tool providers are responsible to establish technology that is trusted and accepted, and eventually widely used. This does not only comprise correctness but also usability of the tools, a feature often underestimated and therefore a weakness of many tools. — Many tools offer so many options that users have a hard time dealing with the standard features. — The ultimate success of these technologies is when they turn into commodity and are used without the users actually being aware of them. — Many techniques are embedded into development environments (IDEs), typically in such a way that users do not really recognize them — [and get] fast feedback that can be understood without knowing the underlying technology."

We already echoed Bernhard Steffen's concern that formal tools are hard to learn (see Sect. 2 above). This problem can be addressed in, at least, three complementary ways.

A first way, mentioned by Bernhard Steffen, consists in making the use of formal techniques transparent, by hiding their complexity from the end users. This is the old concept of "lightweight" [26], "invisible" or "disappearing" [47] formal methods. Static analysis, for instance, is a particularly successful technique in this respect. Unfortunately, such simplified approaches cannot cover all user needs.

A second way, also evoked by Bernhard Steffen, consists in reducing the excessive number of options offered by some tools. A wealth of options can be useful to expert users for finely tuning the performance of formal analyses, by exploiting the particularities of the problem under investigation. The aforementioned recommendation of making formal tools modular also contributes to the growth in the number of components, and of options for these components. For most users, however, the existence of many options is a problem in itself, possibly leading to a combinatorial explosion in the number of option combinations. To enhance the user-friendliness of formal tools, it is thus important to reduce the set of options by systematically applying Occam's razor principle[13], and to properly identify the default options, which should be the most effective ones on the largest number of problems. The quest for simplicity must also concern graphical user interfaces and high-level scripting languages (such as the SVL language [15] of CADP), which abstract away many low-level details from the users.

A third way consists in curbing the complexity of the languages used by formal tools, e.g., the languages used to describe the system under study, to express the properties to be verified, to specify strategies and tactics for achieving formal proofs, etc. Most of these languages have a steep learning curve and tricky semantic details that require time to be fully understood. We observe two long-term trends to address this problem: (i) There are attempts to get rid of such "abstract" languages, by replacing them with the more "concrete" languages actually used by implementers; this is the case, for instance, of static analysis and software model checking, which bypass high-level formal specification languages to directly operate on lower-level, possibly ambiguous, programming languages; (ii) Alternative approaches, still keeping formal specification languages, strive to make them as user-friendly as possible, especially by replacing mathematical formalism with simpler notations more acceptable by industry engineers; for instance, in the realm of model checking, "pattern libraries"[14] provide catalogs of usual properties, thus alleviating the use of full-fledge temporal logic formulas; similarly, the LNT language [19], which supersedes old-fashioned process calculi such as ACP, CCS, and CSP [9], has an intuitive syntax inspired from functional- and imperative-programming languages that makes this language

---

[13] This makes it also easier to check the correctness of formal tools.

[14] See, e.g., http://patterns.projects.cs.ksu.edu, http://cadp.inria.fr/resources/evaluator/actl.html, and http://cadp.inria.fr/resources/evaluator/rafmc.html.

significantly easier [40] and accessible to engineers without formal methods background [6].

4.2 Collective actions

Individual actions, although desirable, cannot be sufficient, and Bernhard Steffen also considers collective actions to be undertaken, at a larger level, by the scientific community interested in formal tools, encompassing both tool developers and tool users. We hereafter review these collective actions, whose main goal is to fight the fragmentation issue, which Bernhard Steffen calls *"tool individualism"*.

Tool and benchmark repositories.

"What is required for a true success is to establish a corresponding open source community which contributes to the tool and benchmark repositories — making existing tools and benchmarks adequately available to the public — establishing a truly global and open repository."

These are three distinct ideas that need to be considered separately. We analyze each of them in turn, taking into account the lessons to be learnt from (at least) four initiatives targeting these stated goals, namely: the original ETI (Electronic Tool Integration) [7,50] launched in the 90s by Bernhard Steffen and colleagues, the jETI [35] followup project[15] launched in the mid-2000s, the VSR (Verified Software Repository) [1,4] project, well-specified but not fully implemented[16], and the CPS-VO (Cyber-Physical Systems Virtual Organization) project[17] launched in the early 2010s, the only one running and available today.

First, the wish for a global repository containing all formal tools raises cost/benefit and feasibility questions. Today, there is no major problem in downloading a formal tool from the Web site of its developers and installing this tool on one's local machine; thus, the added value of such a repository could be: (i) to provide an exhaustive catalog of formal tools and (ii) to deliver SaaS (Software as a Service) by enabling the remote execution of formal tools not installed on one's local machine. Point (i) takes significant time, as we learnt it ourselves when building a catalog of formal tools for quantitative verification[18]; moreover, catalogs need to be updated regularly, as new tools appear and old tools disappear. Point (ii) takes time and money, since providing such a service to everyone has a cost, not only in acquisition of hardware servers or cloud computing resources, but also in daily maintenance, to keep track of the latest versions of each tool, to ensure interoperability between ever-changing tools, and to carefully address security issues. This is confirmed by Bernhard Steffen: *"The ETI initiative failed, for two main reasons: the manual integration effort at the ETI site in Dortmund exceeded our expectations, [and] tool providers were*

---

[15] http://eti.cs.uni-dortmund.de.
[16] http://vsr.sourceforge.net.
[17] http://cps-vo.org.
[18] http://cadp.inria.fr/resources/zoo.

(correctly) worried that ETI would not be able to keep up with upgrades and new versions"; therefore, the revised jETI platform adopted an alternative approach, by remotely coordinating formal tools hosted and maintained at their developers' sites.

Second, the requirement for open source seems to contradict the wish for a truly global repository, since prominent commercial tools used in industry to design real systems (e.g., development tools for synchronous languages, static analyzers, hardware verification tools, etc.) are not open source and would be thus excluded from the repository. Moreover, the open source requirement (even combined with free software) does not solve the fragmentation issue: GitHub, for instance, hosts many dead formal tool prototypes, all in open source with free licenses. Finally, this requirement would make it harder to find a proper business model for running the repository: users might accept being charged a fee for remotely executing commercial tools, but may be reluctant to pay for merely using free software. It is worth noticing that the CPS-VO repository has a more flexible policy[19] allowing various degrees of tool integration.

Third, having a global benchmark repository would be certainly helpful to the research community, since it would provide a central point where all (or most) formal models designed in the world could be obtained. Such benchmarks are useful to ensure that experiments can be reproduced, to test formal tools and evaluate their performance, and, for high-level models readable by humans, to teach users how formal tools should be employed. At present, many collections of such benchmarks are available, from multiple sources: (i) Almost every major formal tool comes with a library of demo examples[20], usually encoded in the particular input format(s) required by this tool; (ii) Software competitions tend to accumulate, year after year, many models for benchmarking purpose[21]; (iii) There also exist independent collections of benchmarks, such as the VLTS (Very Large Transition Systems)[22] collection developed by CWI and INRIA; (iv) Many articles in scientific conferences and journals report about industrial case studies tackled using formal tools, but it is very rare to find the complete models mentioned in these publications, excepted in dedicated venues, such as the MARS (Modelling and Analysis of Real Systems) workshops that manages a public repository of formal models[23] in parallel to its workshop proceedings. Because these collections of benchmarks are heterogeneous and distributed at many places, it would be indeed desirable to access them from a central point; this would also provide an incentive for exchanging all the benchmarks that, at the moment, are not shared, such as the test cases written for a specific tool and the test cases captured by formal tools running as Web applications.

---

[19] http://cps-vo.org/group/tools.
[20] See for instance http://cadp.inria.fr/demos in the case of the CADP toolbox.
[21] See http://mcc.lip6.fr/models.php in the case of the Model Checking Contest.
[22] http://cadp.inria.fr/resources/vlts.
[23] http://www.mars-workshop.org/repository.html.

Let us finally suggest that a global benchmark repository could also record, whenever possible, economical information (such as time spent, cost, manpower, return on investment, etc.) about case studies done using formal tools.

Artifact evaluations.

"Recent requirements to make tools available (open source) and the newly established trend to establish artifact evaluations [...] are welcome measures to address th[e tool individualism] threat. They naturally impose a certain level of usability and maturity, as reviewers (and other users) start to repeat the experiments and to play with variations of the considered scenarios. In the longer term this should lead to a maturity level."

An increasing number of software conferences have indeed set up artifact evaluation committees to evaluate software tools and deliver verified artifact certificates [30]. Such initiatives increase the reproducibility of experimental results. However, we disagree with Bernhard Steffen on two points: (i) Artifact evaluations do not fight tool individualism, they fight improper claims about the capabilities of software tools, i.e., cheating and overselling; (ii) Open source and artifact evaluations are two different notions; open source is not always required for artifact evaluations[24].

Tool competitions.

"Experimental investigations, today [are] often supported by diverse and frequent tool challenges. — Even tool competitions and challenges, certainly events intended to support knowledge exchange and establishing global tool knowledge, nevertheless reinforce [tool individualism]. Of course, the more direct comparison of different tools that they impose supports tool development as a whole, but winners are typically associated with individual tools, most frequently operated by their developers."

Software competitions, together with studies that systematically evaluate various formal tools on the same set of problems (e.g., [40,41] for a comparison of model checkers or [21] for a performance assessment of term rewrite engines) primarily aim at benchmarking the capability and performance of formal tools. Software competitions and such comparative studies also have three additional merits: (i) They increase tool interoperability, either with the design of common formats or interfaces that each tool has to support, or with the development of translators between the various input languages accepted by the tools; (ii) They are nowadays the main setting in which large collections of diverse, complex benchmarks are being produced; (iii) They reveal bugs in formal tools and impose the correction of these bugs[25]. We therefore believe that the credits given to competition winners and the potential reinforcement of tool individualism are a low price to pay for the high benefits of software competitions.

---

[24] http://www.artifact-eval.org/guidelines.html.

[25] For instance, the average confidence rate of all tools participating in the Model Checking Contest increases every year: 89.65% in 2015, 94.20% in 2016, and 97.34% in 2017 [29, Sect. 4.2].

Collaborative projects.

"The situation became even more diverse, despite all the efforts aiming at exchange like various tool competitions and overarching projects."

Collaborative projects, such as those supervised by national or European research funding agencies, allocate resources to scientists and encourage their cooperation with industry. So far, collaborative projects failed to prevent the fragmentation issue for formal tools, even though, from time to time, some projects enabled the development of interconnections between different tools.

Most collaborative projects have two characteristics: they fund short-term activities (usually, 3–5 years) and they ask for groundbreaking research results. This does not fit well with the situation of formal tools, which require longer-term efforts for significant progress. Indeed, the mainstream formal tools available today have taken decades to produce, and their efficiency does not only lie in major scientific breakthroughs, but also in hundreds or thousands of minor enhancements, the accumulation of which really makes a difference. Also, global repositories, such as the aforementioned ETI/jETI and CPS-VO, are long-term platforms that are out of scope for most project calls.

All in one, the outcome of collaborative projects is often limited. In general, these projects help to undertake the development of new formal tools but fail to consolidate them on the long run, unless perhaps for those tools whose technical leaders show outstanding communication skills.

Relaunching the ETI/jETI exchange platform.

"This is an ideal situation tò re-launch the ETI initiative. — With today's Internet infrastructure and technology, which fosters truly service-oriented approaches, [ETI's] ambitions are now more than realistic, yet still require a concerted community effort to align and integrate the employed technologies as well as their means of communication and exchange in order to leverage the individual strengths. The ETI initiative could be an exciting corresponding challenge and opportunity for the tool community to support synergies, help to pinpoint tool/technology profiles, and ease the exchange of knowledge and benchmarks in a tangible way. — In a first step, the new ETI could be built just by making existing tools and benchmarks adequately available to the public and exploiting the ETI's mediator technology to support cross tool combination. In a further step, ETI itself could turn into a domain-specific open source IDE for tool development which directly supports the development of tool functionalities in a fashion suitable to be openly exchanged, thus tearing down the boundaries between the individual tools and establishing a truly global and open repository."

When ETI was launched in 1997, it was a novel, exciting concept and CADP, thanks to its modular architecture and well-defined interfaces, was one of the very first tools to be integrated in ETI [8,34,36,50].

Today, the situation is different. There have been already two attempts at implementing the ETI idea; yet, as Bernhard Steffen points out: *"the ETI idea has still not turned into reality"*. Could a third attempt succeed better than the two former ones? We have no definite answer, but we can mention several risk factors to be considered.

Twenty years after its inception, a new ETI would now face fierce competitors for most of its features, e.g., CPS-VO, which is a close approximation of what a reloaded ETI could be, GitHub, which offers a worldwide repository of open source software, Figshare[26], which hosts benchmarks and research outputs of many academic institutions, Eclipse[27], which is the reference platform for open source IDEs, etc. We already evoked the difficulties to get funding for academic collaborative platforms running over a long period of time, and the eventuality that such funding might be even harder to obtain in a strict open-source context.

The relevance of Web technologies for interconnecting formal tools can also be questioned. From our experience in model checking, we know how much performance matters when dealing with huge state spaces and repeating basic operations over billions of states and transitions. To this aim, we designed specific cross-tool technologies, such as the BCG file format, in which every bit is optimized, and the OPEN/CÆSAR framework [13], in which all memory allocations are carefully controlled. In comparison, for the same tasks, Web protocols and services, although they support secure communications between remote machines owned by different users, would be considerably slower and resource-consuming.

Division of labour.

"We envision tool developers that, rather than spending significant time to integrate their ideas into their own complex tool infrastructure, concentrate on their specific expertise and directly contribute to the repository for open exchange and experimentation. This would allow a clear division of labour, where the developers of tool functionality profit from the providers of benchmarks and the maintainers of the ETI infrastructure for open exchange, and vice versa."

From an economical perspective, the division of work proposed by Bernhard Steffen sounds rational, as it suggests that each actor will focus on the reduced number of tasks for which he is the most competent and productive.

Yet, a relaunched ETI would require tool developers to abandon some of the technologies they designed and/or are familiar with (e.g., user interfaces, file formats, etc.), and to adapt their formal tools, so as to use instead other technologies selected and prescribed by the maintainers of the ETI infrastructure. This is a difficult point, as history shows that generic cross-tool technologies (such as CASE tools, software buses, coordination languages, etc.) are not easily accepted by tool developers unless they see tangible benefits in doing so.

First, this raises the question of what would be the concrete incentives for developers to forget about tool individualism and to adhere to the discipline of the new ETI platform. The traditional incentive, i.e., financial rewards for producing quality software components (e.g., software-as-a-service in cloud computing or application stores for smartphones) is ruled out by the stated open-source policy. An alternative incentive relies in the scientists' sense of collective purpose, but it is unsure whether calls to rationality and goodwill are enough to convince the best developers to renounce their design freedom. Another incentive

---

[26] http://figshare.com.
[27] http://www.eclipse.org.

mentioned by Bernhard Steffen is that developers would get access to numerous benchmarks through ETI, but this would only work if benchmark providers make the effort of depositing their data in ETI, and would work better if such benchmarks are exclusively available via ETI.

Second, because the new ETI intends to become a truly global, centralized platform and substitute itself to existing parts (e.g., user interfaces) of many formal tools, one cannot exclude the eventuality of ETI becoming a single point of failure. In order to integrate very diverse formal tools, the architects of the new ETI should either design common formats and interfaces, or make open calls for such technologies and select the best candidates; these are difficult decisions, with a strong impact on the complexity and performance of the entire platform and its attractiveness for tool developers. Moreover, such decisions are likely to trigger lengthy discussions, or even conflicts, about technical choices; this can only be solved by adopting proper rules and arbitration procedures, at the risk of turning the project into a bureaucratic entity generating frustration and disinterest for some tool developers. Thus, the success of the ETI platform will also crucially depend on the skills of its administrators.

Finally, we would like to advocate for tool individualism, which is sharply, perhaps excessively, criticized by Bernhard Steffen. Quite often, tool individualism leads to a dispersion of efforts, but it can also have a positive role: some major tool sets (e.g., CADP, LTSmin [28], PRISM [31], UPPAAL [2], etc.) make real efforts to combine multiple scientific advances into a coherent framework. Even if these tool sets do not fully implement the ETI concept of central repository, they are nevertheless partial, yet valuable integration and exchange platforms.

5 Conclusion

The needs for safe and secure computer systems are still far from being satisfied, and made even more elusive by the recent trends towards intelligent and autonomous systems. Formal methods can address parts of the problem, but the current situation of software tools implementing formal methods is all but optimal, with a fragmented landscape that prevents one from inferring fundamental knowledge from experimental results.

While many scientists focus their research on particular technical problems, Bernhard Steffen is one of the rare voices calling for a global awareness. In a recent, dense paper [49], he accurately analyzes the status of formal tools and proposes remedy actions. Because we believe that his vision deserves consideration, the present article highlighted the key ideas of [49] and discussed them in detail, based on our experience in formal verification and model checking. The topic is far from being exhausted, and we expect that other developers of formal tools will participate in the debate, bringing complementary opinions and expertise.

So far, research in formal methods has produced a wealth of approaches, methodologies, and algorithms. It might be that most low-hanging fruits have been picked, and that the scientific agenda for the next decades could be different, with the emphasis not so much on further discovering new results than revisiting the foundations to blend all existing results into coherent theories and tools.

Acknowledgements. We are grateful to Lian Apostol and Wendelin Serwe, who proofread this manuscript, and to the anonymous reviewers for their helpful comments and suggestions.

References

1. Arenas, A.E., Bicarregui, J., Margaria, T.: The FMICS view on the verified software repository. J. Integr. Des. Process Sci. (IDPT) **10**(4), 47–54 (2006)
2. Behrmann, G., David, A., Larsen, K.G., Pettersson, P., Yi, W.: Developing UPPAAL over 15 Years. Softw. Pract. Experience **41**(2), 133–142 (2011)
3. Bergstra, J.A., Ponse, A., Smolka, S.A. (eds.): Handbook of Process Algebra. Elsevier, Amsterdam (2001)
4. Bicarregui, J., Hoare, C.A.R., Woodcock, J.C.P.: The verified software repository: a step towards the verifying compiler. Formal Aspects Comput. **18**(2), 143–151 (2006)
5. Bourke, T., Brun, L., Dagand, P.E., Leroy, X., Pouzet, M., Rieg, L.: A formally verified compiler for Lustre. In: Cohen, A., Vechev, M.T. (eds.) Proceedings of the 38th ACM SIGPLAN Conference on Programming Language Design and Implementation (PLDI 2017), Barcelona, Spain. pp. 586–601. ACM, June 2017
6. Bouzafour, A., Renaudin, M., Garavel, H., Mateescu, R., Serwe, W.: Model-checking synthesizable system verilog descriptions of asynchronous circuits. In: Krstic, M., Jones, I.W. (eds.) Proceedings of the 24th IEEE International Symposium on Asynchronous Circuits and Systems (ASYNC 2018), Vienna, Austria. IEEE, May 2018
7. Braun, V., Kreileder, J., Margaria, T., Steffen, B.: The ETI online service in action. In: Cleaveland, R. (ed.) TACAS 1999. LNCS, vol. 1579, pp. 439–443. Springer, Heidelberg (1999). https://doi.org/10.1007/3-540-49059-0_31
8. Braun, V., Margaria, T., Weise, C.: Integrating tools in the ETI platform. Int. J. Softw. Tools Technol. Transf. (STTT) **1–2**(1), 31–48 (1997)
9. Cleaveland, R., Roscoe, A.W., Smolka, S.A.: Process algebra and model checking. Handbook of Model Checking, pp. 1149–1195. Springer, Cham (2018). https://doi.org/10.1007/978-3-319-10575-8_32
10. Evrard, H., Lang, F.: Automatic distributed code generation from formal models of asynchronous processes interacting by multiway rendezvous. J. Log. Algebraic Meth. Program. **88**, 121–153 (2017)
11. Finney, K.: Mathematical notation in formal specification: too difficult for the masses? IEEE Trans. Softw. Eng. **22**(2), 158–159 (1996)
12. Garavel, H.: Compilation of LOTOS abstract data types. In: Vuong, S.T. (ed.) Proceedings of the 2nd International Conference on Formal Description Techniques FORTE 1989, Vancouver B.C., Canada, pp. 147–162. North-Holland, December 1989
13. Garavel, H.: OPEN/CÆSAR: an open software architecture for verification, simulation, and testing. In: Steffen, B. (ed.) TACAS 1998. LNCS, vol. 1384, pp. 68–84. Springer, Heidelberg (1998). https://doi.org/10.1007/BFb0054165
14. Garavel, H., Graf, S.: Formal methods for safe and secure computers systems. BSI Study 875, Bundesamt für Sicherheit in der Informationstechnik, Bonn, Germany, December 2013

15. Garavel, H., Lang, F.: SVL: a scripting language for compositional verification. In: Kim, M., Chin, B., Kang, S., Lee, D. (eds.) Proceedings of the 21st IFIP WG 6.1 International Conference on Formal Techniques for Networked and Distributed Systems (FORTE 2001), Cheju Island, Korea. pp. 377–392. Kluwer Academic Publishers, August 2001. full version available as INRIA Research Report RR-4223

16. Garavel, H., Lang, F., Mateescu, R.: Compiler construction using LOTOS NT. In: Horspool, R.N. (ed.) CC 2002. LNCS, vol. 2304, pp. 9–13. Springer, Heidelberg (2002). https://doi.org/10.1007/3-540-45937-5_3

17. Garavel, H., Lang, F., Mateescu, R., Serwe, W.: CADP 2011: a toolbox for the construction and analysis of distributed processes. Int. J. Softw. Tools Technol. Transf. (STTT) **15**(2), 89–107 (2013)

18. Garavel, H., Lang, F., Mounier, L.: Compositional verification in action. In: Howar, F., Barnat, J. (eds.) FMICS 2018. LNCS, vol. 11119, pp. 189–210. Springer, Cham (2018). https://doi.org/10.1007/978-3-030-00244-2_13

19. Garavel, H., Lang, F., Serwe, W.: From LOTOS to LNT. In: Katoen, J.-P., Langerak, R., Rensink, A. (eds.) ModelEd, TestEd, TrustEd. LNCS, vol. 10500, pp. 3–26. Springer, Cham (2017). https://doi.org/10.1007/978-3-319-68270-9_1

20. Garavel, H., Serwe, W.: The unheralded value of the multiway rendezvous: illustration with the production cell benchmark. In: Hermanns, H., Höfner, P. (eds.) Proceedings of the 2nd Workshop on Models for Formal Analysis of Real Systems (MARS 2017), Uppsala, Sweden. Electronic Proceedings in Theoretical Computer Science, vol. 244, pp. 230–270, April 2017

21. Garavel, H., Tabikh, M.-A., Arrada, I.-S.: Benchmarking implementations of term rewriting and pattern matching in algebraic, functional, and object-oriented languages – The 4th rewrite engines competition. In: Rusu, V. (ed.) WRLA 2018. LNCS, vol. 11152, pp. 1–25. Springer, Cham (2018). https://doi.org/10.1007/978-3-319-99840-4_1

22. Groote, J.F., Willemse, T.A.C.: Parameterised boolean equation systems. Theor. Comput. Sci. **343**, 332–369 (2005)

23. Hartmanns, A., Hermanns, H.: In the quantitative automata zoo. Sci. Comput. Program. **112**, 3–23 (2015)

24. Isberner, M., Howar, F., Steffen, B.: The open-source LearnLib – A framework for active automata learning. In: Kroening, D., Păsăreanu, C.S. (eds.) CAV 2015. LNCS, vol. 9206, pp. 487–495. Springer, Cham (2015). https://doi.org/10.1007/978-3-319-21690-4_32

25. ISO/IEC: LOTOS - A Formal Description Technique Based on the Temporal Ordering of Observational Behaviour. International Standard 8807, International Organization for Standardization - Information Processing Systems - Open Systems Interconnection, Geneva, September 1989

26. Jackson, D., Wing, J.: Lightweight formal methods. IEEE Comput. **29**, 21–22 (1996)

27. Jourdan, J.H., Laporte, V., Blazy, S., Leroy, X., Pichardie, D.: A formally-verified C static analyzer. In: Rajamani, S.K., Walker, D. (eds.) Proceedings of the 42nd Annual ACM SIGPLAN-SIGACT Symposium on Principles of Programming Languages (POPL 2015), Mumbai, India, pp. 247–259. ACM, January 2015

28. Kant, G., Laarman, A., Meijer, J., van de Pol, J., Blom, S., van Dijk, T.: LTSmin: high-performance language-independent model checking. In: Baier, C., Tinelli, C. (eds.) TACAS 2015. LNCS, vol. 9035, pp. 692–707. Springer, Heidelberg (2015). https://doi.org/10.1007/978-3-662-46681-0_61

29. Kordon, F., et al.: MCC'2017 – the seventh model checking contest. In: Koutny, M., Kristensen, L.M., Penczek, W. (eds.) Transactions on Petri Nets and Other Models of Concurrency XIII. LNCS, vol. 11090, pp. 181–209. Springer, Heidelberg (2018). https://doi.org/10.1007/978-3-662-58381-4_9

30. Krishnamurthi, S.: Artifact evaluation for software conferences. SIGPLAN Not. **48**(4S), 17–21 (2013)

31. Kwiatkowska, M., Norman, G., Parker, D.: PRISM 4.0: verification of probabilistic real-time systems. In: Gopalakrishnan, G., Qadeer, S. (eds.) CAV 2011. LNCS, vol. 6806, pp. 585–591. Springer, Heidelberg (2011). https://doi.org/10.1007/978-3-642-22110-1_47

32. Loveland, D.W.: Automated theorem proving: a quarter century review. In: Bledsoe, W.W., Loveland, D.W. (eds.) Automated Theorem Proving - After 25 Years, Contemporary Mathematics, vol. 29, pp. 1–45. American Mathematical Society (1984)

33. Mader, A.: Verification of modal properties using boolean equation systems. In: VERSAL 8, Bertz Verlag, Berlin (1997)

34. Margaria, T., Braun, V., Kreileder, J.: Interacting with ETI: a user session. Int. J. Softw. Tools for Technol. Transf. (STTT) **1–2**(1), 49–63 (1997)

35. Margaria, T., Nagel, R., Steffen, B.: jETI: a tool for remote tool integration. In: Halbwachs, N., Zuck, L.D. (eds.) TACAS 2005. LNCS, vol. 3440, pp. 557–562. Springer, Heidelberg (2005). https://doi.org/10.1007/978-3-540-31980-1_38

36. Margaria, T., Steffen, B.: LTL guided planning: revisiting automatic tool composition in ETI. In: Proceedings of the 31st IEEE/NASA Software Engineering Workshop (SEW 2007), Columbia, USA, pp. 214–226. IEEE Computer Society Press, March 2007

37. Marsso, L., Mateescu, R., Serwe, W.: TESTOR: a modular tool for on-the-fly conformance test case generation. In: Beyer, D., Huisman, M. (eds.) TACAS 2018. LNCS, vol. 10806, pp. 211–228. Springer, Cham (2018). https://doi.org/10.1007/978-3-319-89963-3_13

38. Mateescu, R.: Local model-checking of an alternation-free value-based modal mu-calculus. In: Bossi, A., Cortesi, A., Levi, F. (eds.) Proceedings of the 2nd International Workshop on Verification, Model Checking and Abstract Interpretation (VMCAI 1998), Pisa, Italy. University Ca' Foscari of Venice, September 1998

39. Mateescu, R., Garavel, H.: XTL: a meta-language and tool for temporal logic model-checking. In: Margaria, T. (ed.) Proceedings of the International Workshop on Software Tools for Technology Transfer (STTT 1998), Aalborg, Denmark, pp. 33–42. BRICS, July 1998

40. Mazzanti, F., Ferrari, A.: Ten diverse formal models for a CBTC automatic train supervision system. In: Gallagher, J.P., van Glabbeek, R., Serwe, W. (eds.) Proceedings of the 3rd Workshop on Models for Formal Analysis of Real Systems and the 6th International Workshop on Verification and Program Transformation (MARS/VPT 2018), Thessaloniki, Greece. Electronic Proceedings in Theoretical Computer Science, vol. 268, pp. 104–149, April 2018

41. Mazzanti, F., Ferrari, A., Spagnolo, G.O.: Towards formal methods diversity in railways: an experience report with seven frameworks. Int. J. Softw. Tools Technol. Transf. (STTT) **20**(3), 263–288 (2018)

42. Merten, M., Steffen, B., Howar, F., Margaria, T.: Next generation LearnLib. In: Abdulla, P.A., Leino, K.R.M. (eds.) TACAS 2011. LNCS, vol. 6605, pp. 220–223. Springer, Heidelberg (2011). https://doi.org/10.1007/978-3-642-19835-9_18

43. Naujokat, S., Lybecait, M., Kopetzki, D., Steffen, B.: CINCO: a simplicity-driven approach to full generation of domain-specific graphical modeling tools. Int. J. Softw. Tools Technol. Transf. (STTT) **20**(3), 327–354 (2018)
44. Raffelt, H., Steffen, B., Berg, T., Margaria, T.: LearnLib: a framework for extrapolating behavioral models. Int. J. Softw. Tools Technol. Transf. (STTT) **11**(5), 393–407 (2009)
45. Ruan, W., Huang, X., Kwiatkowska, M.: Reachability analysis of deep neural networks with provable guarantees. In: Proceedings of the 27th International Joint Conference on Artificial Intelligence (IJCAI 2018), Stockholm, Sweden, pp. 2651–2659, July 2018
46. Rudin, H., West, C.H., Zafiropulo, P.: Automated protocol validation: one chain of development. Comput. Netw. **2**, 373–380 (1978)
47. Rushby, J.: Disappearing formal methods. In: Proceedings of the 5th IEEE International Symposium on High-Assurance Systems Engineering (HASE 2000), Albuquerque, NM, USA, pp. 95–96. IEEE Computer Society, November 2000
48. Sifakis, J.: System design in the era of IoT - meeting the autonomy challenge. In: Bliudze, S., Bensalem, S. (eds.) Proceedings of the 1st International Workshop on Methods and Tools for Rigorous System Design (MeTRiD 2018), Thessaloniki, Greece. Electronic Proceedings in Theoretical Computer Science, vol. 272, pp. 1–22, April 2018
49. Steffen, B.: The physics of software tools: SWOT analysis and vision. Int. J. Softw. Tools Technol. Transf. (STTT) **19**(1), 1–7 (2017)
50. Steffen, B., Margaria, T., Braun, V.: The electronic tool integration platform: concepts and design. Int. J. Softw. Tools Technol. Transf. (STTT) **1–2**(1), 9–30 (1997)
51. van Weerdenburg, M.: An account of implementing applicative term rewriting. Electron. Not. Theor. Comput. Sci. **174**(10), 139–155 (2007)
52. West, C.H.: General technique for communications protocol validation. IBM J. Res. Dev. **22**(4), 393–404 (1978)

Toward Structured Parallel Programming:
Send-Receive Considered Harmful

Sergei Gorlatch[✉]

University of Muenster, Münster, Germany
gorlatch@uni-muenster.de

Abstract. During the software crisis of the 1960s, Dijkstra's famous thesis *"goto considered harmful"* paved the way for structured programming. In this paper that is a modified version of the short communication [10], we suggest that many current difficulties of parallel programming based on message passing are caused by poorly structured communication, which is a consequence of using low-level *send-receive* primitives. We argue that, like *goto* in sequential programs, *send-receive* should be avoided as far as possible and replaced by *collective operations* in the setting of message passing. We dispute some widely held opinions about the apparent superiority of low-level, pairwise primitives over collective operations, and we present substantial theoretical and empirical evidence to the contrary in the context of MPI (Message Passing Interface).

We also briefly mention our recent results obtained in the broader context of programming for modern many-core parallel systems.

Keywords: Programming methodology · Parallel systems · Structured programming · Message Passing Interface (MPI)

1 Introduction

The development of software for modern parallel and distributed systems is still a challenging and difficult task. One of the obvious reasons for this unsatisfactory situation is that today's programmers rely mostly on the programming culture of the 1980s and '90s, the Message Passing Interface (MPI) [15] still being the programming tool of choice for demanding applications.

The main advantage of MPI is that in the 1980s it integrated and standardized parallel constructs that were proven in practice. This put an end to the unacceptable previous situation when every hardware vendor provided its own set of communication primitives, and those primitives sometimes differed even between different brands of the same machine.

In order to enable high performance, MPI's communication management based on low-level primitives *send* and *receive* results in a complicated programming process. Several attempts were made to overcome this (e.g. HPF and OpenMP). However, despite reported success stories, these approaches have

© Springer Nature Switzerland AG 2019
T. Margaria et al. (Eds.): Steffen Festschrift, LNCS 11200, pp. 208–217, 2019.
https://doi.org/10.1007/978-3-030-22348-9_13

never achieved the popularity of MPI, mostly because they make the performance of parallel programs less understandable and difficult to predict.

A similar "software crisis" occurred in the sequential setting in the 1960s. The breakthrough was made by Dijkstra in his famous letter *"goto* considered harmful" [5], in which the finger of blame was pointed at the *goto* statement. By that time, [3] had formally demonstrated that programs could be written without any *goto* statements, in terms of only three control structures – sequence, selection and repetition. The notion of so-called *structured programming* [4] became almost synonymous with "goto elimination".

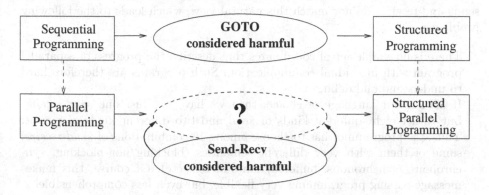

Fig. 1. As *goto* in the sequential case, *send-receive* complicates parallel programming.

Bernhard Steffen et al. [21] demonstrated that structured, rigorous programming greatly improves the formal analyses of important properties of parallel programs. In order to benefit from the experience in structured programming, we should answer the question: Which concept/construct plays a similar harmful role to that of *goto* in the parallel setting? As shown in Fig. 1 and demonstrated from Sect. 2 onwards, we suggest *send-receive* statements to be "considered harmful" and avoided as far as possible in parallel MPI programs.

The thrust of this paper is:

Parallel programming based on message passing can be improved by expressing communication in a structured manner, without using send-receive statements.

We demonstrate the advantages of collective operations over *send-receive* in five areas: simplicity, expressiveness, programmability, performance and predictability. This paper is a slightly modified version of [10]. The structured approach has been recently extended in different areas of parallel programming. In particular, novel parallel architectures like multi-core CPUs and many-core GPUs (Graphics Processing Units) require structured parallel programming at the node level, as an alternative to the low-level CUDA and OpenCL approaches, while message passing considered in this paper remains relevant for parallelizing across nodes. For our recent results, we refer the reader to the survey on algorithmic skeletons [11], the SkelCL library [26], skeleton-based transformations [16], and the LIFT approach [17].

2   The Challenge of Simplicity

Myth: Send-receive primitives are a simple way of specifying communication in parallel programs.

To reason effectively about a parallel program comprising hundreds or thousands of processes, one needs a suitable abstraction level. Programmers usually think in terms of how data has to be distributed to allow local computation: there is a stage (phase) of computation followed by a stage of communication, these stages being either synchronized, as in the BSP model [28], or not. Collectives neatly describe data redistributions between two stages, while individual sends and receives do not match this natural view, which leads to the following problems:

- There is no simple set of coordinates that describe the progress of a parallel program with individual communication. Such programs are therefore hard to understand and debug.
- If MPI is our language of choice, then we have not just one *send-receive*, but rather eight different kinds of *send* and two different kinds of *receive*. Thus, the programmer has to choose among 16 combinations of *send-receive*, some of them with very different semantics (blocking/non-blocking, synchronous/asynchronous, buffered/non-buffered, etc). Of course, this makes message-passing programming very flexible, but even less comprehensible!
- The last but not least problem is the size of programs. For example, a program for data broadcasting using MPI_Bcast may have only three instead of its *send-receive* equivalent's 31 lines of code [9, 23].

Reality: The apparent simplicity of *send-receive* turns out to be the cause of large program size and complicated communication structure, which make both the design and debugging of parallel programs difficult.

3   The Challenge of Programmability

Myth: The design of parallel programs is so complicated that it will probably always remain an *ad hoc* activity rather than a systematic process.

The structure of programs with collective operations (a.k.a. collectives) as a sequence of stages facilitates high-level program transformations. A possible kind of transformation fuses two consecutive collective operations into one.

This is illustrated in Fig. 2 for a program with p processes, where each process either follows its own control flow, depicted by a down-arrow, or participates in a collective operation, depicted by a shaded area. Fusing two collective operations into one may imply a considerable saving in execution time; more on that in Sect. 6.

A particular fusion rule (1) states that, if operators op1 and op2 are associative and op1 distributes over op2, then the following transformation of a composition of scan and reduction is applicable.

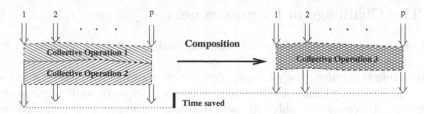

Fig. 2. The idea of fusing collective operations by a transformation like (1).

Here, function `Make_pair` duplicates its arguments, thus creating a pair, and `Take_first` yields the first component of a pair. Both functions are executed without interprocessor communication. The binary operator `f(op1,op2)` on the right-hand side works on pairs of values and is built using the operators from the left-hand side of the transformation. The precise definition of `f`, as well as other similar transformations, can be found in [8].

$$
\begin{bmatrix} \texttt{MPI\_Scan (op1);} \\ \texttt{MPI\_Reduce (op2);} \end{bmatrix} \implies \begin{bmatrix} \texttt{Make\_pair;} \\ \texttt{MPI\_Reduce (f(op1,op2));} \\ \texttt{if my\_pid==ROOT then Take\_first;} \end{bmatrix}
$$

(1)

Rule (1) and other rules from [8] have the advantage that they are (a) proved formally as theorems, (b) parameterized by the occurring operators, e.g. `op1` and `op2`, and therefore customizable for a particular application, (c) valid for all possible implementations of collective operations, and (d) applicable independently of the parallel target architecture, and (e) suitable for automation.

Besides fusion rules, there are also transformations that decompose one collective operation into a sequence of smaller operations. Composition and decomposition rules can sometimes be applied in sequence, thus leading to more complex transformations, for example:

$$
\begin{bmatrix} \texttt{MPI\_Scan(op1);} \\ \texttt{MPI\_Allreduce(op2);} \end{bmatrix} \implies \begin{bmatrix} \texttt{Make\_pair;} \\ \texttt{MPI\_Reduce-scatter(f(op1,op2));} \\ \texttt{Take\_first;} \\ \texttt{MPI\_Allgather;} \end{bmatrix}
$$

Profound results have been achieved with formalisms for the verification of concurrent and message-passing programs (see [25] for a very good overview of the state of the art). With collective operations, we take a different approach: we design message-passing programs in a stepwise manner (see [8]) by applying semantically sound transformations like (1). In Sect. 6, we show that such design process can be geared to predicting and improving performance.

Reality: Collective operations facilitate high-level program transformations that can be applied in a systematic program-design process.

4   The Challenge of Expressiveness

Myth: Collective operations are too inflexible and, therefore, unable to express many important applications.

To refute this quite widely held opinion, we present in Table 1 several important applications, which according to the recent literature were implemented using collective operations only, without notable performance loss compared with their counterparts using *send-receive*.

Table 1. Applications expressed using collective operations only

Application	Communication/Computation Pattern
Polynomial Multiplication	Bcast (group); Map; Reduce; Shift
Polynomial Evaluation	Bcast; Scan; Map; Reduce
Fast Fourier Transform	Iter (Map; All-to-all (group))
Molecular Simulation	Iter (Scatter; Reduce; Gather)
N-Body Simulation	Iter (All-to-all; Map)
Matrix Multiplication (SUMMA)	Scatter; Iter (Scatter; Bcast; Map); Gather
Matrix Multiplication (3D)	Allgather (group); Map; All-to-all; Map

Here, Map stands for local computations performed in the processes without communication; Shift is a cyclic, unidirectional exchange between all processes; Iter denotes repetitive action; (group) means that the collective operation is applied not to all processes of the program, but rather to an identified subset of processes (in MPI, it can be specified by a communicator).

Additional confirmation of the expressive power of collective operations is provided by the PLAPACK package for linear algebra [7], which has been implemented entirely without individual communication primitives.

Moreover, in one of the best textbooks on parallel algorithms [22], the whole methodology centres on implementing and then composing collective operations.

In paper [6], we proved the Turing universality of a programming language based on just two recursive collective patterns – anamorphisms and catamorphisms. This fact can be viewed as a counterpart to the "structured program theorem" by Böhm and Jacopini [3] for parallel programming.

Reality: A broad class of communication patterns found in important parallel applications is covered by collective operations.

5   The Challenge of Performance

Myth: Programs using *send-receive* are, naturally, faster than their counterparts using collective operations.

The usual performance argument in favour of individual communication is that collective operations are themselves implemented in terms of individual *send-receive* and thus cannot be more efficient than the latter. However, there are two important aspects here that are often overlooked:

1. The implementations of collective operations are written by the implementers, who are much more familiar with the parallel machine and its network than an application programmer can be. Recent algorithms for collective communication [24] take into account specific characteristics of the interprocessor network, which can then be considered during the compilation phase of the communication library. The MagPIe library is geared to wide-area networks of clusters [20]. In [27], the tuning for a given system is achieved by conducting a series of experiments on the system. When using *send-receive*, the communication structure would probably have to be re-implemented for every new kind of network.
2. Very often, collective operations are implemented not via *send-receive*, but rather directly in the hardware, which is simply impossible at the user level. This allows all machine resources to be fully exploited and sometimes leads to rather unexpected results: e.g. a simple bidirectional exchange of data between two processors using *send-receive* on a Cray T3E takes twice as long as a version with two broadcasts [1]. The explanation for this phenomenon is that the broadcast is implemented directly on top of the shared-memory support of the Cray T3E.

Below, we dispute some other commonly held opinions about the performance superiority of *send-receive*, basing our arguments on empirical evidence from recent publications.

- It is not true that non-blocking versions of *send-receive*, MPI_Isend and MPI_Irecv, are invariably fast owing to the overlap of communication with computation. As demonstrated by [1], these primitives often lead to slower execution than the blocking version because of the extra synchronization.
- It is not true that the flexibility of *send-receive* allows faster algorithms than the collective paradigm. Research has shown that many designs using *send-receive* eventually lead to the same high-level algorithms as obtained by the "batch" approach [14]. In fact, batch versions often run faster [18].
- It is not true that the routing of individual messages over a network offers fundamental performance gains as compared with the routing for collective operations. As shown formally in [28], the performance gap in this case becomes, with large probability, arbitrarily small for large problem sizes.

Reality: There is strong evidence that *send-receive* does not offer fundamental performance advantages over collective operations. The latter offer machine-tuned, efficient implementations without changing the applications themselves.

6   The Challenge of Predictability

Myth: Reliable performance data for parallel programs can only be obtained *a posteriori*, i.e. by actually running the program on a particular machine configuration.

Performance predictability is, indeed, often even more difficult to achieve than absolute performance itself. Using collective operations, not only can we design programs by means of the transformations presented in Sect. 3; we can also estimate the impact of every single transformation on the program's performance. Table 2 contains a list of transformations from [12], together with the conditions under which these transformations improve performance.

Table 2. Impact of transformations on performance

Composition rule	Improvement if
Scan_1; Reduce_2 → Reduce	always
Scan; Reduce → Reduce	$t_s > m$
Scan_1; Scan_2 → Scan	$t_s > 2m$
Scan; Scan → Scan	$t_s > m(t_w + 4)$
Bcast; Scan → Comcast	always
Bcast; Scan_1; Scan_2 → Comcast	$t_s > m/2$
Bcast; Scan; Scan → Comcast	$t_s > m(\frac{1}{2}t_w + 4)$
Bcast; Reduce → Local	always
Bcast; Scan_1; Reduce_2 → Local	always
Bcast; Scan; Reduce → Local	$t_w + \frac{1}{m} \cdot t_s \geq \frac{1}{3}$

In the above table, a binomial-tree implementation of collective operations is presumed, our cost model having the following parameters: start-up/latency t_s, transfer time t_w and block size m, with the time of one computation operation assumed as the unit. These parameters are used in the conditions listed in the right column of the table. The estimates were validated in experiments on a Cray T3E and a Parsytec GCel 64 (see [8] for details).

Since the performance impact of a particular transformation depends on the parameters of both the application and the machine, there are alternatives to choose from in a particular design. Usually, the design process can be captured as a tree, one example of which is given in Fig. 3.

The best design decision is obtained by checking the design conditions, which depend either on the problem properties, e.g. the distributivity of operators, or on the characteristics of the target machine (number of processors, latency and bandwidth, etc.). For example, if the distributivity condition holds, it takes us from the root into the left subtree in Fig. 3. If the block size in an application is small, Condition 1 (defined in [8]) yields "no", and we thus end up with the second (from left to right) design alternative, where op3= f(op1,op2) according to rule (1). Note that the conditions in the tree of alternatives may change for a different implementation of the collective operations involved.

Arguably, *send-receive* allows a more accurate performance model than collective operations do. Examples of well-suited models for finding efficient implementations are LogP and LogGP [19]. However, these models are overly detailed

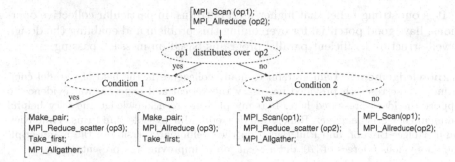

Fig. 3. The tree of design alternatives with decisions made in the nodes.

and difficult for an application programmer to use, as demonstrated by a comparison with batch-oriented models [2, 13].

Reality: Collective operations contribute to the challenging goal of predicting program characteristics during the design process, i.e. without actually running the program on a machine. The use of *send-receive* obviously makes the program's performance much less predictable. Furthermore, the predictablity of collective operations greatly simplifies the modelling task at the application level, as compared with models like LogP.

7   Conclusion

This short communication proposes – perhaps somewhat polemically – viewing the *send-receive* primitives as harmful and, consequently, trying to avoid them in parallel programming.

We demonstrate the advantages of collective operations over *send-receive* in five major areas, which we call challenges: simplicity, expressiveness, programmability, performance and predictability. Based on recent publications in the field and our own research, we present hard evidence that many widely held opinions about *send-receive* vs. collective operations are mere myths.

Despite the success of structured programming, *goto* has not gone away altogether, but has either been hidden at lower levels of system software or packaged into safe language constructs. Similarly, there are parallel applications where non-determinism and low-level communication are useful, e.g. a taskqueue-based search. This motivates the development of "collective design patterns" or skeletons which should provide more complex combinations of both control and communication than the currently available collective operations of MPI.

We conclude by paraphrasing Dijkstra's famous letter [5], which originally inspired our work. Applied to message passing, it might read as follows:

> The various kinds and modes of send-receive used in the MPI standard, *buffered, synchronous, ready, (non-)blocking*, etc., are just too primitive; they are too much an invitation to make a mess of one's parallel program.

It is our strong belief that higher-level patterns, in particular collective operations, have good potential for overcoming this problem and enabling the design of well-structured, efficient parallel programs based on message passing.

Acknowledgements. I am grateful to many colleagues in the field of parallel computing, whose research provided necessary theoretical and experimental evidence to support the ideas presented here. It is my pleasure to acknowledge the very helpful comments of Chris Lengauer, Robert van de Geijn, Murray Cole, Jan Prins, Thilo Kielmann, Holger Bischof, and Phil Bacon on the preliminary version of the manuscript. The anonymous referees of [10] did a great job in improving the presentation.

References

1. Bernaschi, M., Iannello, G., Lauria, M.: Experimental results about MPI collective communication operations. In: Sloot, P., Bubak, M., Hoekstra, A., Hertzberger, B. (eds.) HPCN-Europe 1999. LNCS, vol. 1593, pp. 774–783. Springer, Heidelberg (1999). https://doi.org/10.1007/BFb0100638
2. Bilardi, G., Herley, K., Pietracaprina, A., Pucci, G., Spirakis, P.: BSP vs. LogP. In: Eighth ACM Symposium on Parallel Algorithms and Architectures, pp. 25–32 (1996)
3. Böhm, C., Jacopini, G.: Flow diagrams, Turing machines and languages with only two formation rules. Commun. ACM **9**, 366–371 (1966)
4. Dahl, O.J., Dijkstra, E.W., Hoare, C.A.: Structured Programming. Academic Press, London (1975)
5. Dijkstra, E.W.: Go To statement considered harmful. Commun. ACM **11**(3), 147–148 (1968)
6. Fischer, J., Gorlatch, S.: Turing universality of morphisms for parallel programming. In: Gorlatch, S., Lengauer, C. (eds.) Third Int. Workshop on Constructive Methods for Parallel Programming (CMPP 2002). Forschungsberichte der Fakultät IV - Elektrotechnik und Informatik, vol. 2002/07, pp. 81–98. Technische Universität Berlin, June 2002
7. van de Geijn, R.: Using PLAPACK: Parallel Linear Algebra Package. Scientific and Engineering Computation Series. MIT Press, Cambridge (1997)
8. Gorlatch, S.: Towards formally-based design of message passing programs. IEEE Trans. Softw. Eng. **26**(3), 276–288 (2000). http://wwwmath.uni-muenster.de/pvs/publikationen/papers/GorTSE.ps.gz
9. Gorlatch, S.: Send-recv considered harmful? myths and truths about parallel programming. In: Malyshkin, V. (ed.) PaCT 2001. LNCS, vol. 2127, pp. 243–257. Springer, Heidelberg (2001). https://doi.org/10.1007/3-540-44743-1_24
10. Gorlatch, S.: Send-receive considered harmful: myths and realities of message passing. ACM TOPLAS **26**(1), 47–56 (2004)
11. Gorlatch, S.: Parallel skeletons. In: Padua, D. (ed.) Encyclopedia of Parallel Computing, pp. 1417–1422. Springer, Boston, MA (2011). https://doi.org/10.1007/978-0-387-09766-4_24
12. Gorlatch, S., Wedler, C., Lengauer, C.: Optimization rules for programming with collective operations. In: Atallah, M. (ed.) Proceeding of the IPPS/SPDP 1999, pp. 492–499. IEEE Computer Society Press (1999)
13. Goudreau, M.W., Lang, K., Rao, S.B., Suel, T., Tsantilas, T.: Towards efficiency and portablility. Programming with the BSP model. In: Eighth ACM Symposium on Parallel Algorithms and Architectures, pp. 1–12 (1996)

14. Goudreau, M., Rao, S.: Single-message vs. batch communication. In: Heath, M., Ranade, A., Schreiber, R. (eds.) Algorithms for Parallel Processing, pp. 61–74. Springer, New York (1999)
15. Gropp, W., Lusk, E., Skjellum, A.: Using MPI: Portable Parallel Programmingwith the Message Passing. MIT Press, Cambridge (1994)
16. Hagedorn, B., Steuwer, M., Gorlatch, S.: A transformation-based approach to developing high-performance GPU programs. In: Petrenko, A.K., Voronkov, A. (eds.) PSI 2017. LNCS, vol. 10742, pp. 179–195. Springer, Cham (2018). https://doi.org/10.1007/978-3-319-74313-4_14
17. Hagedorn, B., Stoltzfus, L., Steuwer, M., Gorlatch, S., Dubach, C.: High performance stencil code generation with Lift. In: Proceedings ACM CGO 2018, pp. 100–112 (2018). Best paper award
18. Hwang, K., Xu, Z.: Scalable Parallel Computing. McGraw Hill, New York (1998)
19. Kielmann, T., Bal, H.E., Gorlatch, S.: Bandwidth-efficient collective communication for clustered wide area systems. In: Parallel and Distributed Processing Symposium (IPDPS 2000), pp. 492–499 (2000)
20. Kielmann, T., Hofman, R.F., Bal, H.E., Plaat, A., Bhoedjang., R.A.: MagPIe: MPI's collective communication operations for clustered wide area systems. In: Proceedings of the ACM PPoPP, pp. 131–140 (1999)
21. Knoop, J., Steffen, B., Vollmer, J.: Parallelism for free: efficient and optimal bitvector analyses for parallel programs. ACM TOPLAS 18(3), 268–299 (1996)
22. Kumar, V., et al.: Introduction to Parallel Computing. Benjamin/Cummings Publ, Redwood City (1994)
23. Pacheco, P.: Parallel Programming with MPI. Morgan Kaufmann Publ, San Francisco (1997)
24. Park, J.Y.L., Choi, H.A., Nupairoj, N., Ni, L.M.: Construction of optimal multicast trees based on the parameterized communication model. In: Proceedings of the International Conference on Parallel Processing (ICPP), vol. I, pp. 180–187 (1996)
25. Schneider, F.B.: On Concurrent Programming. Springer-Verlag, New York (1997). https://doi.org/10.1007/978-1-4612-1830-2
26. Steuwer, M., Gorlatch, S.: Skelcl: A high-level extension of OpenCL formulti-GPU systems. J. Supercomput. 69(1), 25–33 (2014). https://doi.org/10.1007/s11227-014-1213-y
27. Vadhiyar, S.S., Fagg, G.E., Dongarra, J.: Automatically tuned collective communications. In: Proceedings of the Supercomputing 2000. Dallas, TX, November 2000
28. Valiant, L.G.: General purpose parallel architectures. In: Handbook of Theoretical Computer Science, vol. A, Chap. 18, pp. 943–971. MIT Press (1990)

Refining the Safety–Liveness Classification of Temporal Properties According to Monitorability

Doron Peled[1][(✉)] and Klaus Havelund[2][(✉)]

[1] Department of Computer Science, Bar Ilan University, Ramat Gan, Israel
doron.peled@gmail.com
[2] Jet Propulsion Laboratory, California Institute of Technology, Pasadena, USA
klaus.havelund@jpl.nasa.gov

Abstract. Runtime verification is the topic of analyzing execution traces using formal techniques. It includes monitoring the execution of a system against temporal properties, commonly to detect violations. Not every temporal property is fully monitorable however: in some cases, the correctness of the execution does not depend on any finite prefix. We study the connection between monitorability and Lamport's classification of properties to safety and liveness and their dual classes. We refine the definition of monitorability and provide algorithms to check which verdicts can be expected, a priori and during runtime verification.

1 Introduction

Runtime verification facilitates the direct monitoring of the execution of a system, checking it against a formal specification. This can be useful for many applications, including testing a system before it is deployed, as well as monitoring the system after deployment. This approach can be applied to improve the reliability of safety critical and mission critical systems, including safety as well as security aspects, and can more generally be applied for processing streaming information. Often, the stream of information is not a priori limited to a specific length, and the monitored property is supposed to follow the execution for as long as it is running.

Monitoring properties are often given in linear temporal logic (LTL) [22]. These properties are traditionally interpreted over infinite execution sequences (the monitored system keeps emitting events). But for runtime verification to

---

D. Peled—The research performed by this author was partially funded by Israeli Science Foundation grant 2239/15: "Runtime Measuring and Checking of Cyber Physical Systems".
K. Havelund—The research performed by this author was carried out at Jet Propulsion Laboratory, California Institute of Technology, under a contract with the National Aeronautics and Space Administration.

© Springer Nature Switzerland AG 2019
T. Margaria et al. (Eds.): Steffen Festschrift, LNCS 11200, pp. 218–234, 2019.
https://doi.org/10.1007/978-3-030-22348-9_14

be useful, it is necessary to be able to provide information after observing only finite execution sequences, also referred to as *prefixes*. For example, the property $\Box p$ (for some atomic proposition p), which asserts that p always happens, can be refuted by a runtime monitor if p does not hold in some observed event. At this point, no matter which way the execution is extended, the property will not hold, resulting in a negative verdict. However, no finite prefix of an execution can establish that $\Box p$ holds. In a similar way, the property $\Diamond p$ cannot be refuted, since p may appear at any time in the future; but once p happens, we know that the property is satisfied, independent on any continuation, and we can issue a positive verdict. For the property $(\Box p \vee \Diamond q)$ we may not have a verdict at any finite time, in the case where all the observed events satisfy both p and $\neg q$. On the other hand, we may never "lose hope" to have such a verdict, as a later state satisfying q will result in a positive verdict; at this point we can abandon the monitoring, since the property cannot be further violated. On the other hand, for the property $\Box \Diamond p$ we can never provide a verdict in finite time: for whatever happens, p can still appear an infinite number of times, and we cannot guarantee or refute that this property holds when observing any finite prefix of an execution. The problem of monitorability of a temporal property was studied in [5,10,25], basically requiring that at any point of monitoring we still have a possibility to obtain a finite positive or negative verdict.

We refine here the study of LTL monitorability, distinguishing cases where *some* verdicts are always possible during runtime, *no* verdicts are expected, or some verdicts are possible *a priori*, but may not be available later, depending on the monitored prefix. We extend Lamport's safety and liveness classification of temporal properties with guarantee, which is the dual of safety, and morbidity, which we define as the dual of liveness. To complete this classification to cover all possible temporal specifications, we add another class, which we term quaestio. We study the relationship between this classification and monitorability. In particular, the safety class includes the properties whose failure can be detected after a finite prefix, and the liveness properties are those where one can never conclude a failure after a finite prefix.

We suggest some variants for runtime verification algorithms that take the refined notions of monitorability into account before and during runtime verification. Equipped with these algorithms, we can check what kind of verdicts one can expect a priori from monitoring an execution against a given temporal specification, and can also update this expectation during runtime when some verdicts are not possible anymore. In addition, these algorithms can be used to decide whether a given specification is a safety, guarantee, liveness, or morbidity property.

Related Work. Alpern and Schneider [1] formalized Lamport's definition of safety and liveness, Sistla [27] showed a PSPACE algorithm for checking safety, and an EXPSPACE algorithm for checking liveness. Checking liveness was shown to be in EXPSPACE-complete in [18]. Drissi-Kaitouni and Jard [8], as well as Kupferman and Vardi [19] studied the problem of monitoring LTL properties for an execution sequence. Pnueli and Zaks [25] proposed constructing compositional testers for runtime verification. They also considered the issue of monitorability of a property, requiring that any finite prefix can be extended in a finite manner such that a positive or negative verdict can be reported in finite time. Finally, they provided a tester based algorithm for checking whether an observed finite prefix can be extended in a finite way to obtain a positive or a negative verdict. Fernandez, Jard, Jéron and Viho supported checking for availability of future verdicts for a given test objective in the TGV test case generator [11]. Bauer, Leucker and Schallhart defined prefixes that cannot be finitely extended to obtain a verdict for a temporal specification as *ugly* prefixes; then they defined a property to be monitorable if it has no ugly prefixes. They showed that safety and guarantee properties are monitorable, but there are some other monitorable properties that are not in these classes. Diekert and Leucker [7] studied monitorability and its connection to safety and liveness using topological characterizations. Falcone, Fernandez and Mounier [9] considered the Manna-Pnueli hierarchy of properties and showed that some of the classes of this hierarchy have both monitorable and non-monitorable properties.

Contribution. We revisit the classification of properties according to safety, guarantee and liveness after completing it to cover all the temporal properties. We add new classes of properties. The first one we call *morbidity*; it is the dual class to liveness, i.e., a negation of a liveness property is a morbidity property and vice versa. To complete the space of temporal properties, we add another class called quaestio.

We provide an alternative definition for these classes that is based on the possible results one can obtain during runtime monitoring; this depends on whether one can always/sometimes/never obtain a positive or a negative verdict based on a finite trace. Then we study a refinement of runtime monitorability with respect to these classes and their intersections.

We propose an assortment of algorithms for runtime verification, which extend the classical LTL runtime verification algorithm. These variants allow us to decide a priori what kind of verdicts are expected from a property, and update the possibilities as the monitored execution unfolds. Because of the close connection between the discussed classification and notions of monitorability, they can also be used to identify the class of a given LTL specification.

Overview of Paper. The paper is organized as follows. Section 2 provides some preliminary introductions to selected concepts, including runtime verification and linear temporal logic. Section 3 presents our refinement of Lamport's classification of temporal properties. Section 4 introduces algorithms for determining monitorability and classification of temporal properties. Finally, Sect. 5 concludes the paper.

2 Preliminaries

2.1 Runtime Verification

Runtime verification (RV) [2,13] very generally refers to the use of rigorous (formal) techniques for *processing* execution traces emitted by a system being observed. The purpose is, again generally viewed, to evaluate the state of the observed system. Since only single executions (or collections thereof) are analyzed, RV scales well compared to more comprehensive formal methods, but of course at the cost of coverage. Nonetheless, RV can be useful due to the rigorous methods involved. Note that in runtime verification one is not concerned with how to obtain various executions, as in e.g. test case generation. This reflects a focus of attention (research) rather than a judgment of utility – test case generation is of course of critical importance.

An execution trace is generated by the observed executing system, typically by instrumenting the system to generate events when important transitions take place. Instrumentation can be manual by inserting logging statements in the code, or it can be automated using instrumentation software, such as e.g. aspect-oriented programming frameworks. In the extreme case, an event can represent a complete view of the internal state of the system. Processing can take place on-line, as the system executes, or off-line, by processing log files produced by the system. In the case of on-line processing, observations can be used to control the monitored system.

Processing can take numerous forms. We focus here on *specification-based* runtime verification, where an execution trace is checked against a property expressed in a formal (usually temporal) logic. More formally, assume an observed system S, and assume further that a finite execution of S up to a certain point is captured as an execution trace $\xi = e_1.e_2.\ \ldots\ .e_n$, which is a sequence of observed events. Each event e_i captures a snapshot of S's execution state. Assume the type $\mathbb{E}$ of events; then the RV problem can be formulated as constructing a program $M : \mathbb{E}^* \to D$, which when applied to the trace ξ, as in $M(\xi)$, returns some data value $d \in D$ in a domain D of interest. In specification-based RV, typically M is generated from a formal specification, given e.g. as a temporal logic formula, a state machine, or a regular expression, and d is a *verdict* in the Boolean domain ($d \in \mathbb{B}$), or some extension of the Boolean domain as discussed in [4], indicating whether the execution trace conforms with the specification.

However, the field should be perceived broadly, e.g. d can be a visualization of the execution trace, a learned specification (specification mining), statistical information about the trace, an action to perform on the running system S, etc. The problem can be even further generalized to computing a result from multiple traces, as e.g. done in specification learning [15–17,24] and statistical model checking [21], giving M the type $M : 2^{\mathbb{E}^*} \to D$.

That execution trace is often unbounded in length, representing the fact that the observed system "keeps running", without a known termination point. Hence it is important that the monitoring program is capable of producing verdicts based on finite prefixes of the execution trace observed so far. The remainder of the paper discusses what kind of verdicts can be produced from finite prefixes given a specific property.

2.2 Linear Temporal Logic

The classical definition of linear temporal logic is based on future operators [22]:

$$\varphi ::= true \,|\, p \,|\, (\varphi \wedge \varphi) \,|\, \neg\varphi \,|\, (\varphi \, \mathcal{U} \, \varphi) \,|\, \bigcirc \varphi$$

where p is a proposition from a finite set of propositions P, with $\mathcal{U}$ standing for *until*, and $\bigcirc$ standing for *next-time*. One can also write $(\varphi \vee \psi)$ instead of $\neg(\neg\varphi \wedge \neg\psi)$, $(\varphi \rightarrow \psi)$ instead of $(\neg\varphi \vee \psi)$, $\Diamond\varphi$ (*eventually* φ) instead of $(true \, \mathcal{U} \, \varphi)$ and $\Box\varphi$ (*always* φ) instead of $\neg\Diamond\neg\varphi$.

LTL formulas are interpreted over an infinite sequence of events[1] $\xi = e_0.e_1.e_2\ldots$, where $e_i \subseteq P$ for each $i \geq 0$. These are the propositions that *hold* in that event. We denote by ξ_i the suffix $e_i.e_{i+1}.e_{i+2}\ldots$ of ξ. LTL semantics is defined as follows:

- $\xi_i \models true$.
- $\xi_i \models p$ iff $p \in e_i$.
- $\xi_i \models \neg\varphi$ iff not $\xi_i \models \varphi$.
- $\xi_i \models (\varphi \wedge \psi)$ iff $\xi_i \models \varphi$ and $\xi_i \models \psi$.
- $\xi_i \models \bigcirc\varphi$ iff $\xi_{i+1} \models \varphi$.
- $\xi_i \models (\varphi \, \mathcal{U} \, \psi)$ iff for some $j \geq i$, $\xi_j \models \psi$, and for all $i \leq k < j$, $\xi_k \models \varphi$.

Then $\xi \models \varphi$ when $\xi_0 \models \varphi$.

An LTL property can be translated into a nondeterministic Büchi automaton [12,30]. The translation can incur an exponential blowup. This nondeterministic automaton can be used directly for model checking, but requires determinization [26], e.g., for the purpose of synthesizing a reactive system from the temporal property. Unfortunately, determinization results here in additional exponential explosion. This sums up to a double exponential blowup of the translation from the LTL property to the deterministic (Rabin, Street) automaton that accepts the same language. It turns out that we also need (a different kind of) determinization for runtime verification [19].

Past time LTL (PLTL) is interpreted over finite sequences, looking backwards from the current event. PLTL has the back mirror operators of LTL's modal operators.

Bauer, Leucker and Schallhart [5] define three categories of prefixes of execution sequences over 2^P for a temporal property φ.

- A *good* prefix is one where all its extensions (infinite sequences of elements from 2^P) satisfy φ.
- A *bad* prefix is one where none of its infinite extensions satisfies φ.
- An *ugly* prefix cannot be extended into a good or a bad prefix.

---

[1] The classical interpretation of LTL is over states [22], but in the context of RV, we monitor a sequence of events that are reported by the instrumentation.

3 Characterizing Temporal Properties

Safety and liveness temporal properties were defined informally on infinite execution sequences by Lamport [20] as *something bad cannot happen* and *something good will happen*. These informal definitions were later formalized by Alpern and Schneider [1]. Guarantee properties where used in an orthogonal characterization by Manna and Pnueli [22]. Guarantee properties are the dual of safety properties, that is, the negation of a safety property is a guarantee property and vice versa. We add to this picture morbidity properties, which is the dual class of liveness properties.

safety A property φ is a *safety* property, if for every execution that does not satisfy it, there is a finite prefix such that completing it in any possible way into an infinite sequence would not satisfy φ.

guarantee (co-safety) A property φ is a *guarantee* property, if for every execution satisfying it, there is a finite prefix such that completing it in any possible way into an infinite sequence satisfies φ.

liveness A property φ is a *liveness* property if every finite prefix can be extended to satisfy φ.

morbidity (co-liveness) A property φ is a *morbidity* property if every finite prefix can be extended to violate φ.

Online runtime verification of LTL properties inspects finite prefixes of the execution. Hence, it may sometimes provide only a partial verdict on the satisfaction and violation of the inspected property [4,23]. This motivates providing three kinds of verdicts:

failed when the current prefix cannot be extended in any way into an execution that satisfies the specification,

satisfied when any possible extension of the current prefix satisfies the specification, and

undecided when the current prefix can be extended to satisfy the specification but also extended to satisfy its negation.

Tracing a *safety* property, we can provide an indication as soon as it fails. Correspondingly, we can report on the satisfaction of a *guarantee* property as soon as a finite prefix satisfies it. The only property that is both a safety and a liveness (and a guarantee) property is *true*.

Each temporal property is a conjunction of a liveness and a safety property [1]. Due to the connection between safety and guarantee and between liveness and morbidity, we immediately obtain that every temporal property is a disjunction of a guarantee and a morbidity property. Manna and Pnueli characterized syntactically the temporal safety properties as $\square\varphi$, and the guarantee properties as $\lozenge\varphi$, where φ is a PLTL property.

Safety, guarantee, liveness and morbidity can be seen as characterizing finite monitorability of temporal properties: if a safety property is violated, there will be a finite prefix witnessing it; on the other hand, for a liveness property, one can never provide such a finite negative evidence. We suggest the following alternative definitions of classes of temporal properties.

AFR (safety) Always Finitely Refutable: when the property does not hold on an infinite execution, refutation can be identified after a finite (bad) prefix.
AFS (guarantee) Always Finitely Satisfiable: when the property is satisfied on an infinite execution, satisfaction can be identified after a finite (good) prefix.
NFR (liveness) Never Finitely Refutable: Refutation (i.e., a bad prefix) can never be identified after a finite prefix.
NFS (morbidity) Never Finitely Satisfiable: Satisfaction (i.e., a good prefix) can never be identified after a finite prefix.

It is easy to see that the definitions of the classes AFR and safety are the same and so are those for AFS and guarantee. We will show the correspondence between NFR and liveness. A liveness property φ is defined to satisfy that any finite prefix can be extended to an execution that satisfies φ. The definition of the class NFR only mentions prefixes of executions that do not satisfy φ; but for prefixes of executions that satisfy φ this trivially holds. The correspondence between NFS and morbidity is shown in a symmetric way.

The above four classes of properties, however, do not cover the entire set of possible temporal properties, independent of the actual formalism that is used to express them. The following two classes complete the classification.

SFR Sometimes Finitely Refutable: for some infinite executions that violate the property, refutation can be identified after a finite prefix; for other infinite executions violating the property, this is not the case.
SFS Sometimes Finitely Satisfiable: for some infinite executions that satisfy the property, satisfaction can be identified after a finite prefix; for other infinite executions satisfying the property, this is not the case.

Let *Prop* be the set of all properties expressible in some temporal formalism, e.g., LTL or Büchi automata. Then it is clear that *Prop* = AFR ∪ SFR ∪ NFR. The only property that is mutual to two of these classes is *true*, which holds both for AFR and for NFR. It also holds that *Prop* = AFS ∪ SFS ∪ NFS. The only temporal property that is mutual to two of these classes (AFS and NFS) is *false*. Every temporal property must belong then to a class XFR, where X stands for A, S or N, and also to a class XFS, again with X is A, S or N. We call it the FR/FS classification. The FR/FS classification refines the classification of properties as safety, guarantee, liveness and morbidity, in the sense of further dividing these into sub-classes as shown in Fig. 1. Specifically, it identifies the intersections between these classes. Below we give examples for the nine combinations of XFR and XFS, appearing in clockwise order in Fig. 1.

- SFR ∩ NFS: $(\Diamond p \wedge \Box q)$
- AFR ∩ NFS: $\Box p$
- AFR ∩ SFS: $(p \vee \Box q)$
- AFR ∩ AFS: $\bigcirc p$

- SFR ∩ AFS: $(p \wedge \Diamond q)$
- NFR ∩ AFS: $\Diamond p$
- NFR ∩ SFS: $(\Box p \vee \Diamond q)$
- NFR ∩ NFS: $\Box \Diamond p$
- SFR ∩ SFS: $((p \vee \Box \Diamond p) \wedge \bigcirc q)$

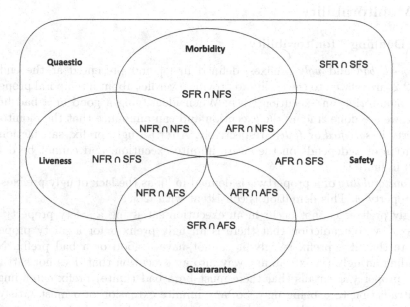

Fig. 1. Classification of properties: safety, guarantee, liveness, morbidity and quaestio.

The set of all properties *Prop* is not covered by safety, guarantee, liveness and morbidity. The missing properties are in SFR ∩ SFS. We call the class of such properties **Quaestio** (Latin for *question*).

Observe that for AFR ∩ AFS we gave an example of a property with only the nexttime operator ○. We show that for LTL, any property φ in AFR ∩ AFS can be written with only the nexttime and the Boolean operators. To see this, consider a tree whose edges are labeled with elements from 2^P; every finite path from the root down is labeled with a prefix of a *minimal* good prefix[2] for φ. That is, if a prefix is good then the path terminates in a leaf node. This is a finitely branching tree, since the number of successors of each node are at most $2^{|P|}$. Assume that this tree has an infinite path. This path must satisfy φ, as, being a safety property, if this path does not satisfy φ, it has a bad prefix, which cannot be extended to satisfy φ. So assume that this path satisfies φ. But φ is also a guarantee property, hence it must have a finite good prefix. But according to the construction, a good prefix leads to a leaf node and is not extended in the tree,

---

[2] A finite extension of a good (bad or ugly) prefix remains good (bad or ugly, respectively).

contradicting the assumption that the tree has an infinite path. Since the tree is finite, it is easy to see that one can express φ in LTL based on the finitely many good paths in the tree using $\bigcirc$ and the Boolean operators[3]. The converse also holds: any property that is expressible in this way corresponds to such a finite tree, and thus is in the intersection of a safety and liveness.

4   Monitorability

4.1   Defining Monitorability

The *good*, *bad* and *ugly* prefixes, defined in [5] and presented at the end of Sect. 2.2, are related to the ability to provide a verdict about a temporal property when monitoring an execution trace. When identifying a good or a bad finite prefix, we are done tracing the execution and can announce that the monitored property is *satisfied* or *failed*, respectively. After an ugly prefix, satisfaction or refutation of φ depends on the entire infinite execution, and cannot be determined in finite time.

Monitorability of a property φ is defined in [5] as the lack of ugly prefixes for the property φ. This definition is consistent with [25].

Ugly prefixes cannot occur in an execution satisfying a safety property [5]. Suppose by contradiction that there is an ugly prefix σ for a safety property φ. Note that if a prefix is ugly, it cannot have a good or a bad prefix. Now extending an ugly prefix σ in any way into an execution that does not satisfy a safety property φ entails that there must be a bad (finite) prefix extending σ, a contradiction to σ being ugly. So, any infinite extension of σ must satisfy φ. But then σ itself must be a good prefix, a contradiction again to σ being ugly. Thus, every safety property is monitorable. Because guarantee properties are the negations of safety properties, one obtains using a symmetric argument that every guarantee property is also monitorable.

4.2   Runtime Verification Algorithms for Monitorability

We present four algorithms. The first one is a classical algorithm for runtime verification of LTL (or Büchi automata) properties. The second algorithm can be used to check during run time what kind of verdicts can still be produced given the current prefix. The third algorithm can be used to check whether the property is monitorable, and also be used under the refinement of monitorability that we present in the next section. The fourth algorithm can be used to check the class of a given temporal property under the extension of Lamport's safety/liveness characterization given in this paper.

---

[3] One can also use other operators to express the same property, e.g., by adding a trivial disjunct, as in $(\varphi \vee (\Box p \wedge \Diamond \neg p))$.

Algorithm 1. Monitoring Sequences Using Automata

Kupferman and Vardi [19] provide an algorithm for detecting good and bad prefixes. For good prefixes, start by constructing a Büchi automaton $\mathcal{A}_{\neg\varphi}$ for $\neg\varphi$, e.g., using the translation in [12]. Note that this automaton is not necessarily deterministic [29]. States of $\mathcal{A}_{\neg\varphi}$, from which one cannot reach a cycle that contains an accepting state, are deleted. Checking for a positive verdict for φ, one keeps for each monitored prefix the set of states that $\mathcal{A}_{\neg\varphi}$ would be after observing that input. One starts with the set of initial states of the automaton $\mathcal{A}_{\neg\varphi}$. Given the current set of successors S and an event $e \in 2^P$, the next set of successors S' is set to the successors of the states in S according to the transition relation Δ of $\mathcal{A}_{\neg\varphi}$. That is, $S' = \{s'|s \in S \wedge (s, e, s') \in \Delta\}$. Reaching the empty set of states, the monitored sequence is good, and the property must hold since the current prefix cannot be completed into an infinite execution satisfying $\neg\varphi$.

This is basically a *subset construction* for a deterministic automaton $\mathcal{B}_\varphi$, whose initial state is the set of initial states of $\mathcal{A}_{\neg\varphi}$, accepting state is the empty set, and transition relation as described above. The size of this automaton is $O(2^{2^{|P|}})$, resulting in double exponential explosion from the size of the checked LTL property. But in fact, we do not need to construct the entire automaton $\mathcal{B}_\varphi$ in advance, and can avoid the double exponential explosion by calculating its current state on-the-fly, while performing runtime verification. Thus, the incremental processing per each event is exponential in the size of the checked LTL property. Unfortunately, a single exponential explosion is unavoidable [19].

Checking for a *failed* verdict for φ is done with a symmetric construction, translating φ into a Büchi automaton $\mathcal{A}_\varphi$ and then the deterministic automaton $\mathcal{B}_{\neg\varphi}$ (or calculating its states on-the-fly) using a subset construction as above. Note that $\mathcal{A}_{\neg\varphi}$ is used to construct $\mathcal{B}_\varphi$ and $\mathcal{A}_\varphi$ is used to construct $\mathcal{B}_{\neg\varphi}$. Runtime verification of φ uses both automata for the monitored input, reporting a *failed* verdict if $\mathcal{B}_{\neg\varphi}$ reaches an accepting state, a *satisfied* verdict if $\mathcal{B}_\varphi$ reaches an accepting state, and an *undecided* verdict otherwise. The algorithm guarantees to report a positive or negative verdict on the *minimal* good or bad prefix that is observed.

Algorithm 2. Checking Availability of Future Verdicts

We alter the above runtime verification algorithm to check whether positive or negative verdicts can still be obtained after the current monitored prefix at runtime. Applying DFS on $\mathcal{B}_\varphi$, we search for states from which one cannot reach the accepting state. Then we replace these states with a single state $\perp$ with a self loop, obtaining the automaton $\mathcal{C}_\varphi$. Reaching $\perp$, after monitoring a finite prefix σ with $\mathcal{C}_\varphi$ happens exactly when we will not have a good prefix anymore. This means that after σ, a *satisfied* verdict cannot be issued anymore for φ.

Similarly, we perform BFS on $\mathcal{B}_{\neg\varphi}$ to find all the states in which the accepting state is not reachable, then replace them by a single state $\top$ with a self loop, obtaining $\mathcal{C}_{\neg\varphi}$. Reaching $\top$ after monitoring a prefix means that we will not be able again to have a bad prefix, hence a *failed* verdict cannot be issued anymore for φ.

We can perform runtime verification while updating the state of both automata, C_φ and $C_{\neg\varphi}$ on-the-fly, upon each input event. However, we need to be able to predict if, from the current state, an accepting state is not reachable. While this can be done in space exponential in φ, it makes an incremental calculation whose time complexity is doubly exponential in the size of φ, as is the algorithm for that by Pnueli and Zaks [25]. This is hardly a reasonable complexity for the incremental calculation performed between successive monitored events for an on-line algorithm. Hence, a pre-calculation of these two automata before the monitoring starts is preferable, leaving the incremental time complexity exponential in φ, as in Algorithm 1.

Algorithm 3. Checking Monitorability

A small variant on the construction of C_φ and $C_{\neg\varphi}$ allows checking if a property is monitorable. The algorithm is simple: construct the product $C_\varphi \times C_{\neg\varphi}$ and check whether the state $(\bot, \top)$ is reachable. If so, the property is non-monitorable, since there is a prefix that will transfer the product automaton to this state and thus it is ugly. It is not sufficient to check separately that C_φ can reach $\top$ and that $C_{\neg\varphi}$ can reach $\bot$. In the property $(\neg(p \wedge r) \wedge ((\neg p\, \mathcal{U}(r \wedge \Diamond q)) \vee (\neg r\, \mathcal{U}(p \wedge \Box q))))$: both $\bot$ and $\top$ can be reached, separately, depending on which of the predicates r or p happens first. But in either case, there is still a possibility for a good or a bad extension, hence it is a monitorable property.

If the automaton $C_\varphi \times C_{\neg\varphi}$ consists of only a single state $(\bot, \top)$, then there is no information whatsoever that we can obtain from monitoring the property.

The above algorithm is simple enough to construct, however its complexity is doubly exponential in the size of the given LTL property. This may not be a problem, as the algorithm is performed off-line and the LTL specifications are often quite short.

We show that checking monitorability is in EXPSPACE-complete. The upper bound is achieved by a binary search version of this algorithm[4]. For the lower bound we show a reduction from checking if a property is (not) a liveness property, a problem known to be in EXPSPACE-complete [18,27].

- We first neutralize bad prefixes. Now, when ψ is satisfiable, then $\Diamond\psi$ is monitorable (specifically, any prefix can be completed into a *good* prefix) iff ψ has a good prefix.
- Checking satisfiability of a property ψ is in PSPACE-complete [28][5].
- ψ has a good prefix iff ψ is not a morbidity property, i.e., if $\varphi = \neg\psi$ is not a liveness property.
- Now, φ is *not* a liveness property iff either φ is unsatisfiable or $\Diamond\neg\varphi$ is monitorable.

---

[4] To show that a property is not monitorable, one needs to guess a state of $\mathcal{B}_\varphi \times \mathcal{B}_{\neg\varphi}$ and check that (1) it is reachable, and (2) one cannot reach from it an empty component, both for $\mathcal{B}_\varphi$ and for $\mathcal{B}_{\neg\varphi}$. (There is no need to construct C_φ or $C_{\neg\varphi}$.)

[5] Proving that liveness was PSPACE-hard was shown in [3].

Algorithm 4. Identifying the Class of a Property

We can identify the classes of properties AFS (guarantee), SFS, NFS (morbidity), AFR (safety), SFR and NFR (liveness) for any given temporal property. Thus, we can also identify if a property is in an intersection of two of these classes.

For the classes AFS, SFS and NFS, we reverse acceptance in C_φ, i.e., all states are accepting except for the empty state, obtaining $\widehat{C}_\varphi$. We take now the product $\widehat{C}_\varphi \times \mathcal{A}_\varphi$ and check its emptiness. We can apply a procedure that performs model checking with the property φ and the state space of $\widehat{C}_\varphi$, see [6]. The language (accepted sequences) of $\widehat{C}_\varphi \times \mathcal{A}_\varphi$ consists exactly of the executions that satisfy the property φ and do not have a good prefix. For such executions it is never sufficient to observe a finite prefix in order to decide that the property is satisfied. We apply a similar construction for AFR, SFR, NFR, removing the accepting state from $C_{\neg\varphi}$ to obtain $\mathcal{D}_{\neg\varphi}$, and taking the product $\widehat{C}_{\neg\varphi} \times \mathcal{A}_{\neg\varphi}$.

We then have the following conditions for identifying the different classes:

AFR (safety) $\widehat{C}_{\neg\varphi} \times \mathcal{A}_{\neg\varphi} = \emptyset$.

Because in this case, executions satisfying $\neg\varphi$, i.e., not satisfying φ, cannot avoid having a bad state.

NFR (liveness) The automaton $C_{\neg\varphi}$ consists of a single state $\top$.

Because the automaton $C_{\neg\varphi}$ consists of a single state $\top$ exactly when we will never observe a bad prefix.

SFR $\widehat{C}_{\neg\varphi} \times \mathcal{A}_{\neg\varphi} \neq \emptyset$ and $C_{\neg\varphi}$ does not consist of a single state $\top$.

Because in this case, there is an execution that avoids having any bad state, but there are still prefixes that are bad.

AFS (guarantee) $\widehat{C}_\varphi \times \mathcal{A}_\varphi = \emptyset$.

Because in this case, executions satisfying φ cannot avoid having a good state.

NFS (morbidity) The automaton C_φ consists of a single state $\bot$.

Because the automaton C_φ consists of a single state $\bot$ exactly when we can never observe a good prefix.

SFS: $\widehat{C}_\varphi \times \mathcal{A}_\varphi \neq \emptyset$ and C_φ does not consist of a single state $\bot$.

Because in this case, there is an execution that avoids having any good state, but there are still prefixes that are good.

For a more efficient algorithm for checking if an LTL formula is a safety (AFR) see [27]. There, an algorithm, based on a binary search on the construction of $\mathcal{A}_\varphi$ and $\mathcal{A}_{\neg\varphi}$ is presented. That algorithm is polynomial space in the size of the property φ. Hence the problem of checking safety is in PSPACE. A lower bound, showing that the problem is in PSPACE-complete is also given in [27]: one can check whether φ is valid (a problem known to be in PSPACE-complete) exactly when $\varphi \vee \Diamond p$ is a safety property, where p is a proposition that does not appear in φ. Thus, the same result applies to checking if an LTL formula is a guarantee property.

Checking liveness (NFR) was shown to be in EXPSPACE-complete in [18]. Thus, checking that a property is in SFR is also in EXPSPACE-complete, since SFR complements AFR $\cup$ NFR, hence is equivalent to checking that the property is neither safety, nor liveness. For the same reasons, these complexity results also apply to the dual classes: by checking the negation of the given property, we have that guarantee (AFS) is in PSPACE-complete, and that morbidity (NFS) and SFS are in EXPSPACE-complete. This agrees with the complexity of the binary search based algorithms given above.

4.3 Refining Monitorability

We first look at the relationship between the above classification of properties and monitorability. Any property that is in AFR (safety) or in AFS (guarantee) is monitorable as identified in [5,10]. A property that is NFR $\cap$ NFS is non-monitorable. In fact no verdict is ever expected on any sequence that is monitored against such a property. This leaves the three classes SFR $\cap$ SFS, SFR $\cap$ NFS and NFR $\cap$ SFS, for which some properties are monitorable and others are not. This is demonstrated in the following table.

Class	Monitorable example	Non-monitorable example
SFR $\cap$ SFS	$((\Diamond r \vee \Box \Diamond p) \wedge \bigcirc q)$	$((p \vee \Box \Diamond p) \wedge \bigcirc q)$
SFR $\cap$ NFS	$(\Diamond p \wedge \Box q)$	$(\Box \Diamond p \wedge \bigcirc q)$
NFR $\cap$ SFS	$(\Box p \vee \Diamond q)$	$(\Box \Diamond p \vee \bigcirc q)$

We propose that RV can still be applied for non-monitorable properties if initially some verdicts can be made. We refine the definition of monitorability into the following categories:

- A property is *monitorable* if it cannot have an ugly prefix. This corresponds to the definition of monitorability in [5,25]. Safety and guarantee properties are universally monitorable. But as demonstrated above, some of the properties in SFR $\cap$ SFS, SFR $\cap$ NFS and NFR $\cap$ SFS are also monitorable.

Checking monitorability can be done using Algorithm 3. In Fig. 2, the light gray areas correspond to properties that are monitorable.
- A property has *zero monitoring information* if there is no information that can be obtained by monitoring it any finite amount of time. The properties in the intersection of liveness and morbidity are those that have zero monitoring information. The black area in Fig. 2 correspond to properties with zero monitoring information. Checking that a property has zero monitoring information can be done by applying algorithm 3 (or Algorithm 4 for checking that the property is both in NFR and in NFS).

- A property is *weakly monitorable* if there exist ugly prefixes, but not all the finite prefixes are ugly. In this case, there is still information that we can obtain by monitoring it, but at times, we may observe an ugly prefix, from which no interesting information can be concluded in finite amount of time. Algorithm 3 can be used to check that a property is non-monitorable, yet also not in zero monitoring information. In this case, instead of using Algorithm 1 for performing the runtime verification, one can use Algorithm 2 to also check whether *some* verdict is still possible for the current prefix, abandoning the runtime verification when this is not the case. The dark gray areas in Fig. 2 represent the weakly monitorable properties.

Consider the property $(p \lor (\neg q \; \mathcal{U} \; (p \land \Box \Diamond r)))$. This property is in quaestio. It is non-monitorable, as demonstrated by the ugly prefix $\{\}.\{p\}$ (i.e., all the propositions are false in the first event, and only p is true in the second event), after which no verdict can be given. We consider it to be weakly monitorable. A priori, we can expect both a positive or a negative verdict: if p holds in the first event, then a positive verdict is given; if q holds before p, then a negative verdict is given. Algorithm 3 can identify the fact that this property is both non-monitorable but is not a zero monitoring information property.

This calls for using Algorithm 2 rather than Algorithm 1 to perform the runtime verification. Suppose now that the first event is $\{q\}$. Since p does not hold in the first event, we still have to satisfy the right disjunct $(\neg q \; \mathcal{U} \; (p \land \Box \Diamond r))$. Algorithm 2 can inform that from now on, one can expect only a negative verdict. If the next event is $\{\}$, Algorithm 2 will inform that no further verdict can be given, hence monitoring can be aborted.

5   Conclusion

Temporal specification is often focused on infinite execution sequences. This abstracts the idea that the correctness requirements for a system should not depend on its bounded execution. Although model checking is capable of checking such properties for finite state systems, one can never exhaustively test an infinite execution. Runtime verification offers an alternative approach to model checking. It can be applied directly to the system itself, and it can help with testing the system when its state space is prohibitively high. On the other hand, runtime verification is limited to observing at any point only a finite portion of the execution.

The notion of monitorability identifies the kinds of verdicts that one can obtain from observing finite prefixes of an execution. Monitorability deals with the ability to obtain a verdict, positive or negative, given a finite prefix of an execution. In particular, non-monitorability characterizes situations where it may not be worthy anymore to wait for a verdict. However, we argued that the definition of monitorability needs to be refined, allowing to monitor properties where a priori there are some useful verdicts that may be observed, even if after observing some prefix of the execution these verdicts are not available anymore.

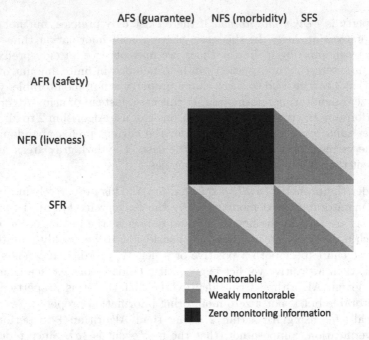

Fig. 2. Classification of properties according to monitorability.

We studied here the connection between monitorability and Lamport's classification of properties as safety and liveness. To do that we needed to extend this classification using the dual classes, guarantee and morbidity, and complete the picture with another property that we termed quaestio.

We also provided algorithms for checking whether a property is monitorable or not, whether it belongs to a certain monitorability class, and what kind of verdict (positive or negative) we can expect after monitoring a certain prefix against a given property. This is useful to decide whether one should apply runtime verification for a given temporal property given expected verdicts, and what kind of verdicts one can still obtain after a given monitored prefix. It also allows to recognize when, during runtime verification, there is no further interesting information that we can expect, consequently abandoning the monitoring.

References

1. Alpern, B., Schneider, F.B.: Recognizing safety and liveness. Distrib. Comput. **2**(3), 117–126 (1987)
2. Bartocci, E., Falcone, Y., Francalanza, A., Reger, G.: Introduction to runtime verification. In: Bartocci, E., Falcone, Y. (eds.) Lectures on Runtime Verification. LNCS, vol. 10457, pp. 1–33. Springer, Cham (2018). https://doi.org/10.1007/978-3-319-75632-5_1
3. Basin, D.A., Jiménez, C.C., Klaedtke, F., Zalinescu, E.: Deciding safety and liveness in TPTL. Inf. Process. Lett. **114**(12), 680–688 (2014)

4. Bauer, A., Leucker, M., Schallhart, C.: The good, the bad, and the ugly, but how ugly is ugly? In: Sokolsky, O., Taşıran, S. (eds.) RV 2007. LNCS, vol. 4839, pp. 126–138. Springer, Heidelberg (2007). https://doi.org/10.1007/978-3-540-77395-5_11
5. Bauer, A., Leucker, M., Schallhart, C.: Runtime verification for LTL and TLTL. ACM Trans. Softw. Eng. Method. **20**(4), 14:1–14:64 (2011)
6. Clarke, E.M., Grumberg, O., Peled, D.: Model Checking. MIT Press, Cambridge (2000)
7. Diekert, V., Leucker, M.: Topology, monitorable properties and runtime verification. Theor. Comput. Sci. **537**, 29–41 (2014)
8. Drissi-Kaitouni, O., Jard, C.: Compiling temporal logic specifications into observers, INRIA Research Report RR-0881 (1988)
9. Falcone, Y., Fernandez, J.-C., Mounier, L.: Runtime verification of safety-progress properties. In: Bensalem, S., Peled, D.A. (eds.) RV 2009. LNCS, vol. 5779, pp. 40–59. Springer, Heidelberg (2009). https://doi.org/10.1007/978-3-642-04694-0_4
10. Falcone, Y., Fernandez, J.-C., Mounier, L.: What can you verify and enforce at runtime? STTT **14**(3), 349–382 (2012)
11. Fernandez, J.-C., Jard, C., Jéron, T., Viho, C.: An experiment in automatic generation of test suites for protocols with verification technology. Sci. Comput. Program. **29**(1–2), 123–146 (1997)
12. Gerth, R., Peled, D.A., Vardi, M.Y., Wolper, P.: Simple on-the-fly automatic verification of linear temporal logic. In: Dembiński, P., Średniawa, M. (eds.) PSTV 1995. IFIPAICT, pp. 3–18. Springer, Boston (1996). https://doi.org/10.1007/978-0-387-34892-6_1
13. Havelund, K., Reger, G., Thoma, D., Zălinescu, E.: Monitoring events that carry data. In: Bartocci, E., Falcone, Y. (eds.) Lectures on Runtime Verification. LNCS, vol. 10457, pp. 61–102. Springer, Cham (2018). https://doi.org/10.1007/978-3-319-75632-5_3
14. Havelund, K., Roşu, G.: Synthesizing monitors for safety properties. In: Katoen, J.-P., Stevens, P. (eds.) TACAS 2002. LNCS, vol. 2280, pp. 342–356. Springer, Heidelberg (2002). https://doi.org/10.1007/3-540-46002-0_24
15. Isberner, M., Howar, F., Steffen, B.: The TTT algorithm: a redundancy-free approach to active automata learning. In: Bonakdarpour, B., Smolka, S.A. (eds.) RV 2014. LNCS, vol. 8734, pp. 307–322. Springer, Cham (2014). https://doi.org/10.1007/978-3-319-11164-3_26
16. Isberner, M., Howar, F., Steffen, B.: Learning register automata: from languages to program structures. Mach. Learn. **96**(1–2), 65–98 (2014)
17. Isberner, M., Howar, F., Steffen, B.: The open-source LearnLib. In: Kroening, D., Păsăreanu, C.S. (eds.) CAV 2015. LNCS, vol. 9206, pp. 487–495. Springer, Cham (2015). https://doi.org/10.1007/978-3-319-21690-4_32
18. Kupferman, O., Vardi, G.: On relative and probabilistic finite counterability. Formal Meth. Syst. Des. **52**(2), 117–146 (2018)
19. Kupferman, O., Vardi, M.Y.: Model checking of safety properties. Formal Meth. Syst. Des. **19**(3), 291–314 (2001)
20. Lamport, L.: Proving the correctness of multiprocess programs. IEEE Trans. Softw. Eng. **3**(2), 125–143 (1977)
21. Larsen, K.G., Legay, A.: Statistical model checking: past, present, and future. In: Margaria, T., Steffen, B. (eds.) ISoLA 2016. LNCS, vol. 9952, pp. 3–15. Springer, Cham (2016). https://doi.org/10.1007/978-3-319-47166-2_1
22. Manna, Z., Pnueli, A.: The Temporal Logic of Reactive and Concurrent Systems - Specification. Springer, New York (1992)

23. Meredith, P.O., Jin, D., Griffith, D., Chen, F., Rosu, G.: An overview of the MOP runtime verification framework. Int. J. Softw. Tools Technol. Transf. **14**, 249–289 (2011)

24. Peled, D., Vardi, M.Y., Yannakakis, M.: Black box checking. In: Wu, J., Chanson, S.T., Gao, Q. (eds.) Formal Methods for Protocol Engineering and Distributed Systems. IAICT, vol. 28, pp. 225–240. Springer, Boston, MA (1999). https://doi.org/10.1007/978-0-387-35578-8_13

25. Pnueli, A., Zaks, A.: PSL model checking and run-time verification via testers. In: Misra, J., Nipkow, T., Sekerinski, E. (eds.) FM 2006. LNCS, vol. 4085, pp. 573–586. Springer, Heidelberg (2006). https://doi.org/10.1007/11813040_38

26. Baier, C., Bertrand, N., Größer, M.: The effect of tossing coins in omega-automata. In: Bravetti, M., Zavattaro, G. (eds.) CONCUR 2009. LNCS, vol. 5710, pp. 15–29. Springer, Heidelberg (2009). https://doi.org/10.1007/978-3-642-04081-8_2

27. Sistla, A.P.: Safety, liveness and fairness in temporal logic. Formal Aspects Comput. **6**(5), 495–512 (1994)

28. Sistla, A.P., Clarke, E.M.: The complexity of propositional linear temporal logics. In: STOC 1982, pp. 159-168 (1982)

29. Thomas, W.: Automata on infinite objects, handbook of theoretical computer science. In: Formal Models and Semantics, vol. B, pp. 133–192 (1990)

30. Vardi, M.Y., Wolper, P.: Automata-theoretic techniques for modal logics of programs. J. Comput. Syst. Sci. **32**(2), 183–221 (1986)

Future Security: Processes or Properties?—Research Directions in Cybersecurity

Ulrike Lechner[✉]

Fakultät für Informatik, Universität der Bundeswehr München,
Neubiberg, Germany
Ulrike.Lechner@unibw.de

Abstract. Security in critical infrastructures is a highly relevant topic and as the level of security of critical infrastructures needs to be increased the need for adequate methods and tools is apparent. "Processes and their properties" is the analysis perspective through which we revisit empirical data from our research on critical infrastructures to identify future research directions in security.

Keywords: Critical infrastructures · IT security · Case studies · Processes

1 Introduction and Motivation

Public perception of Cybersecurity is being associated with trendy hackers penetrating IT systems and cool guys who detect and analyze malware on the fly. "I can do more damage on my laptop sitting in my pajamas before my first cup of Earl Grey than you can do in a year in the field" – this is how the new, young, cool Q describes his Cyber skills to the more traditional 007 in the scene in which the new quartermaster Q and James Bond meet for the first time in Skyfall. The atmosphere in this first meeting is mellow as Q and Bond discuss that youth is no guarantee for innovation and age no guarantee for efficiency and Q hands over a -traditional- tool for the upcoming mission that includes a solid amount of Cyber. This meeting kicks off the joint endeavor to protect the critical infrastructure of the modern society.

In fact, safety of critical infrastructures, and in particular IT security in critical infrastructures is one of today's major challenges. "Critical infrastructures (CI, KRITIS) are organizational and physical structures and facilities of such vital importance to a nation's society and economy that their failure or degradation would result in sustained supply shortages, significant disruption of public safety and security, or other dramatic consequences." [1] The increasing use of information and communication technology creates new areas of vulnerability and dependencies [1] and current geopolitical developments heighten the levels of risk.

Critical infrastructure providers need to increase the level of security and they also need to meet – in our case – requirements from German and European legislation as, e.g., the German IT Security Act [2]. According to the German IT Security Act (IT Sicherheitsgesetz, Gesetz zur Erhöhung der Sicherheit informationstechnischer Systeme) Critical infrastructures need to adhere to the state of the art in IT security and

T. Margaria et al. (Eds.): Steffen Festschrift, LNCS 11200, pp. 235–246, 2019.
https://doi.org/10.1007/978-3-030-22348-9_15

have an information security management system including risk management. Every two years, CIs need to validate their security standards. Increasing the level of security and validating and certifying security measures is an enormous effort – given the complexity of the technical infrastructures of CIs. Think e.g. of energy plants, transportation infrastructure or hospitals with countless components. Note that the situation is similar in other countries as, e.g. the NIS directive requires the EU member states to have minimum capabilities and standards in IT security. Also, nations as US, Russia or China issued regulations to increase the security levels of their CIs (for a comparison of national cybersecurity regulations see, e.g. [3]).

Given the effort that information security management takes, it is apparent that both innovation, effectiveness and efficiency are needed. This is the start point of the endeavor to revisit established methods for processes and properties to increase security of critical infrastructures. A lot of research is done in, e.g., technologies to monitor networks, to identify threats or in endpoint security while all the processes pose a huge potential for method and tool support as well as for innovation. This "world of processes" is our particular focus. We argue that the domain of cybersecurity is a universe of processes. There are

- business processes and workflows in production and service provisioning, facilitated by information systems and networked ICT infrastructures,
- attack chains, i.e. processes with various process steps and complex structures that can adapt themselves to components and architectures of the targeted systems,
- processes and workflows of IT service and IT security management in production and service provisioning.

Moreover, these three kinds of processes interact with implications for vulnerabilities and security levels (cf. e.g. [4]). Formal and semi-formal methods have been employed to increase dependability of cyber-physical systems or of workflows and processes. It seems however, that little of this knowledge, methods and tools is utilized in the process and workflow systems in information security management systems of critical infrastructures. Critical infrastructures with their industrial control systems can be seen as reactive systems according to [5]. We are particularly interested in formal methods as, e.g. [6–9] on the analysis of processes and the design of workflows that guarantee properties as e.g. security and safety properties. This is where we start with our endeavor to explore research directions and first step in this journey is about the human factor.

2   Risk Perception and Reaction - the Human Factor

Humans are considered to be a weak spot in security and safety and one of the weaknesses is risk perception and risk response: We asked IT security experts in the two studies Monitor and Monitor 2.0 [10] of IT security in critical infrastructures for an assessment of the threat level of their own organization, of their industrial sector and for economic region Germany (Fig. 1) and distinguish all participants, KRITIS, i.e. the participants that are German critical infrastructure according to the German IT Security Act and small and medium sized enterprises (SMEs). The Monitor 2.0 study had 69 study participants and Monitor 1.0 had 79 participants. Participants were invited to the study via email, via multiplicators and by individual telephone acquisition. More information about method and demographics is available at monitor.itskritis.de.

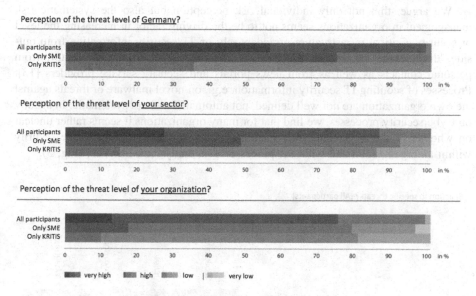

Fig. 1. Threat level perception [10]

There is a distinctive pattern in the answers to these questions. On average, study participants rate the threat level to their own organization lower than the risk to their sector and this threat level again lower than threat level for Germany (Fig. 1). For the ability to defend against cyberattacks the converse applies [11]: the capabilities of their own organization are rated higher than the capabilities of the sector and these capabilities are again higher than the capabilities of the economic region Germany.

This pattern in risk perception is known in literature: people in general estimate their own risk rather optimistic – a phenomenon known as optimism bias [12]. That such perception of individual risks is a deeply rooted human trait illustrates the Nobel Memorial Prize in Economic Sciences 2017 that was awarded to Richard Thaler for his work in behavioral economics [12].

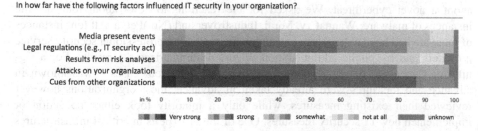

Fig. 2. Impact factors on IT security in an organization [10]

We asked for the influences on security in an organization. We find (cf. Fig. 2) that attacks against the organization and regulations have the strongest impact on IT security measures in an organization while the impact of risk analysis on IT security in an organization seems to be weaker.

We argue, that not only individual risk perception but also the systematic risk management in organizations seems not to be the driving factor in increasing the level of security. Critical infrastructure providers rely on IT security information from outside: they source information from public administration, from their sector, from personal contacts as well as from news portals and security service providers [13]. Processes of scouting IT security information, e.g., on novel malware or threats against the own organization are not well defined, not automated and not systematic. In a study on Cybersecurity processes, we find that for many organizations it seems rather unclear on whether IT security related information to the outside contributes to the security within an organization and what the processes eventually look like [11] (Fig. 3).

Reaction to specific threats? (All particpants)

	Wannacry	Mirai	Industroyer	(Not)Petya
The threat was known in advance and measures could be taken	51%	26%	20%	38%
No measures were taken	13%	30%	30%	20%
New measures were taken	18%	7%	7%	12%
Existing measures were checked	62%	39%	37%	50%
I do not know	7%	23%	25%	15%

Fig. 3. Reactions of an organization to specific threats [10].

A Litmus test for the level of perceived risk are the activities, when there is news about a novel cyberthreat. We asked for the reactions to news about four specific instances of malware: WannaCry, Mirai, Industroyer and (Not)Petya. All four instances of malware had been extensively covered in the media, by professional security service providers and by public administration. Figure 4 summarizes the results. For a significant percentage of organizations, the threat – in all four cases – was known in advance and measures were already taken in advance, most organizations however reviewed their existing measures, while only a minority took either no action or implemented new IT security measures. One of the IT experts in critical infrastructures commented on that figure that – "yes, for every new malware we look what that means for our processes".

This illustrates on the one hand that critical infrastructure providers take their responsibility seriously and scrutinize their IT security measures and their processes whenever novel malware appears on stage. Note that critical infrastructure providers, i.e. that are categorized as Kritis according to the German IT Security Act are in general more active – they review processes more often and they take more often new measures than providers of (non-critical) infrastructures [10]. This reaction to novel threats can be seen as an indicator it seems that more support in "high level understanding of the process landscape" could be beneficial for security.

To sum up this brief impression on the human factor in IT security: It is a deeply human trait to be optimistic, to underestimate risks and threats in particular to oneself of one's organization, to respond not rationally to abstract risks in the future. There are indicators that the institutionalized systematic risk management as part of the information security management in organizations is not the main driving factor and that better understanding of the process landscape could contribute to make IT security less tedious. The Nobel laureate Richard Thaler suggests that it takes smart decision architectures and a nudge strategy to ensure that humans make the right, the safe and future oriented decisions [12]. Nudge is a concept in behavioral science, political theory and economics which proposes positive reinforcement and indirect suggestions as ways to influence the behavior and decision making of groups or individuals. Nudging contrasts with other ways to achieve compliance, such as education, legislation or enforcement [12]. This means, we need to understand the conflicts in decision making about security and safety to look for smart decision architectures and for rigorous methods in the analysis of processes and the level of security. A study of real world cases provides insights in the challenges.

3   Security and Processes – the Case Study Series Case Kritis Revisited

IT security in critical infrastructures requires a balance for human, organizational and technical security measures and has to do with conflicting goals of different stakeholders. This part in our considerations on processes and properties, revisits the Case Kritis case study series [14, 15].

Case studies are considered to be a method to study complex, real world phenomena [16] and therefore a suitable method to study IT security measures in critical infrastructures. Our approach is inspired by the eXperience method for case studies [17] with its holistic approach to business strategy, processes and implementation and the inductive development of theory from case studies [18]. The case studies were conducted from 2015 to 2017 and the cross case study was done in 2017 and 2018.

Particular to this case study series is the focus on processes, more precisely on business processes together with other models of deployment views and network structure together with risk and cost considerations. The notation for modeling processes is the Event Driven Process Chain.

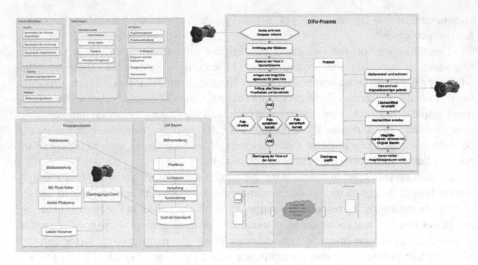

Fig. 4. Examples for process models in the case studies [14, 15]

The nine cases with organization, title, case study authors and the case type (successful project, technology or organizational culture) together with a cross case analysis are summarized in Table 1. Note that one case study (Dairy) is anonymized due to the sensitivity of the topic for the organization. The cases are presented briefly below.

Table 1. The case studies

Key	Title (Original Title)	Authors
Bundeswehr	Working Group IT-SecAsBw – How a working ground fosters IT Security Awareness inland and abroad (*AG IT-SecAwBw – Wie eine Arbeitsgruppe IT-Security Awareness im In- und Ausland fördert*)	A. Rieb, G. Opper
genua gmbh	Remote Maintenance in Critical Infrastructures (*Fernwartung Kritischer Infrastrukturen*)	A. Rieb
itWatch GmbH	A Secure Standard Process for Digital Crime Scene Photography with DeviceWatch (*Ein sicherer Standardprozess für die Digitale Tatortfotografie mit DeviceWatch*)	S. Lücking, S. Dännart
kbo	Balanced Risk Management for Sustainable Security (*Ausgewogenes Risikomanagement für nachhaltige Sicherheit*)	T. Kehr, S. Dännart
Dairy	IT Security in a Dairy: Family Tradition and High Availability (IT-Sicherheit in der Molkerei: Familientradition und Hochverfügbarkeit)	S. Dännart
PREVENT	IT Security for Business Processes in the Financial Sector: The Management Solution PREVENT (*IT-Sicherheit für Geschäftsprozesse im Finanzsektor: die Managementlösung PREVENT*)	S. Rudel, T. Bollen

(continued)

Table 1. (*continued*)

Key	Title (Original Title)	Authors
SAP SE	Information Security at SAP SE: The Longest Human Firewall in the World (*Informationssicherheit bei SAP SE: Die längste Human Firewall der Welt*)	U. Lechner, T. Gurschler, A. Rieb
Stadt Gera	Coordination Center East Thuringia: IT-Security in a Coordination Center (*Zentrale Leitstelle Ostthüringen: IT-Sicherheit in einer Leitstelle*)	T. Gurschler, A. Rieb, M. Hofmeier
ugarbe software	Information Security with ClassifyIt: Information Security through Digital Classification of Documents and Emails (*Informationssicherheit durch ClassifyIt: Informationssich. durch gestützte Klassifizierung von Dokumenten und E-Mails*)	A. Rieb

The case "**Working Group IT-SecAsBw – How a working ground fosters IT Security Awareness inland and abroad**" is about an IT security awareness campaign: Key visual of the campaign is a power plug with the symbol of a face – a symbol that IT security is both about technology measures and the human factor alike. The PIA campaign exemplifies a collaborative, longitudinal IT security activity with a tradition to engage IT security staff and with a minimum of dedicated resources.

Case "**Remote Maintenance in Critical Infrastructures**" tackles with remote access for maintenance one of the 10 most relevant IT security topics in Critical Infrastructures according to BSI [19]. The remote, secure login for maintenance purposes is the core process considered in the case study. Remote access via a single interface, the functionality to control and monitor "sessions" for remote maintenance increases the security level of critical infrastructures. The single interface for all maintenance service providers and all service operation decreases complexity in securing remote access while the solution is easy to integrate in existing IT landscape in a critical infrastructure.

The case "**A Secure Standard Process for Digital Crime Scene Photography**" presents an innovative secure-by-design solution for crime scene photography and the handling of digital crime scene photos in police work. Police officers may use any digital camera, the photos are watermarked with a signature when transferred in the police information system such that authenticity of pictures is maintained throughout police work. Amortization took only three years and the new process is considered to be modern as well as user friendly as it saves time and resources.

Case "**Balanced Risk Management for Sustainable IT Security**" analyses the reaction to ransomware threats against hospitals. While the first reaction to an imminent ransomware was a complete separation of the hospital from the Internet, the hospital established to a more refined strategy later with a considerable speed up of IT security processes and an increased priority for IT security investments. The novel process of security incident response includes all stakeholders in the hospital as well as external service providers. Joint responsibility for IT security measures as well as a proved and tested communication policy rounds up the process. A few months after the process was first implemented in the reaction to the ransomware threat: the hospital group was successful in the defense against a considerable threat.

Case **"IT Security in the Food Industry: Tradition and High Availability"** reports on a safety and security culture of a family owned dairy in a rural area. The processing of sensitive primary products as raw milk requires high availability of production lines. The case is about the strategy of the CIO – he integrates traditional organizational and modern IT security measures in a successful digitalization strategy. Cornerstone of his strategy are close relations to IT staff, the integration of IT staff and technicians into one team with uniform IT processes, training of staff and the loyalty of staff over generations to the company as the main employer in town. Employees practice essential IT security routines as e.g., restoring data from backups in their daily work, new IT technology is only implemented when staff feels confident to handle disruptions and IT staff is encouraged to identify and experiment with potentially useful IT innovations. The case explores also IT security measures to ensure high availability as real time backups of the core SAP system or VLan encapsulation of production lines.

The case **"IT Security for Business Processes in the Financial Sector – The Management Solution PREVENT"** demonstrates real-life complexity of a comprehensive enterprise level risk management. In this case study, the business process is the unit of analysis in risk management. The underlying business case is a (fictitious) computing center of a bank that provides business processes as a service to several (fictitious) client banks. The risk management approach comprises a unified way to source all risk relevant data and a collection of tools (simulations, analytic methods) for risk analysis. The case exemplifies the novel risk management approach which an analysis of interdependencies between infrastructure, information system and business process level. The case argues about the advantages such a comprehensive risk management and the business models for which such a comprehensive risk management is a prerequisite.

"Information Security at SAP SE: The Longest Human Firewall in the World" is a case study on the information security campaign at SAP SE. Key visual of the campaign is a chain of SAP employees with a group handshake with crossed arms – a symbol for the joint effort to protect the company. Employees take part in an individual (mandatory) information security training and can then become part of the human firewall with a picture and an individual statement on information security. The case study highlights the pivotal role of employees in information security and that information security eventually benefits from "fun" but also from perseverance.

Case study **"Coordination Center East Thuringia: IT-Security in a Coordination Center"** discusses availability of emergency services: The alarm process from an emergency call to alerting the emergency services need to be available despite outage of IT components. The case study presents fallbacks and redundancies as well as IT security concepts to ensure highest availability of the emergency number 112 with emergency services. It addresses questions in the further development of information and communication technologies in a coordination center of emergency services. Success factors are the volition of staff not only to use but to understand the infrastructure with its technologies and to get to the bottom of any problem to solve it.

Case **"Information Security by Digital Classification of Documents and E-Mails"** is about a tool to ensure confidentiality of information. ClassifyIt is a PlugIn for Microsoft Office that support users in the classification of documents and emails. Together with a firewall it ensures that only documents and emails with adequate classification can leave the organization and that encryption that is adequate for the document is used for sending it via email. The software is distributed via standard software distribution tools, and it can be customized individually, interfaces for users and administrators are perceived to be user friendly and it needs no Internet connection.

The cases illustrate that IT security in critical infrastructures illustrate the relevance of processes for the implementation of IT security in critical infrastructure. More security adds new process steps and new processes or innovates existing processes. In our motivating example, Q suggests a traditional tool to master the cyber-challenge. The next section reviews formal methods to contribute to the new field of cybersecurity.

4   Towards Future Research Directions

This analysis revisits the cases and goes beyond the formal cross case-analysis as presented in [14]. Our observations on processes and IT security management are:

- Processes play a pivotal role in implementation of security.
- Management of complexity is important: The case "PREVENT" exemplifies the complexity of a comprehensive risk assessment and that IT security management needs a dedicated approach to data collection and analysis with adequate tool support. The SAP case illustrates that measurements of the level of IT security can be relatively simple (SAP uses only a couple of questions) – what matters is perseverance over several years to see how the level of security changes over time. All measures are bundled in one Web-portal and interference with other parts of the processes is limited.
- Several cases illustrate strategies in the decisions and tradeoffs to be made in IT security for successful solutions. In the cases of on "Balanced Risk Management" illustrates that more security requires more complex processes in IT administration with additional steps and with more stakeholders. The case on the Coordination Center East Thuringia exemplifies how availability and IT security need to be balanced: the coordination center needs to maintain availability and short response times. IT security measures are challenged whether they eventually decrease availability by, e.g. reducing redundancy and introducing new, single point of failures.
- The cases on IT security products (Remote Maintenance, ClassifyIt) argue that integration in the existing IT landscape of these technologies takes little effort – the security technologies are seamless to integrate and require limited investments in trainings. They integrate in existing processes and standardize processes.
- The case on the novel process of crime scene photography illustrates the advantages of an innovative, secure-by-design solution - the new process is more modern, more efficient than the old, analogous way of handling photographs.

The cases illustrate strategies in practice and the implications of increasing the level of security in critical infrastructures – security tends to add complexity. IT Security in Critical Infrastructure is about processes – the "process and properties" perspective guides our analysis with the aim to take advantage of methods and tools for the new field of IT security of critical infrastructures. We identify four themes:

Our first point is about *agility*. IT security is reactive – every novel threat requires to review the processes (cf. Sect. 2) and the systematic risk management within an organization seems not to be the main driver for developments. Agility is one of the core themes in digitalization as products and services need to be adapted to strategic changes in business models and in services [20]. So, it needs to be "easy" to transform business processes and IT security likewise according to both strategic and security needs. We argue that knowing the process landscape, understanding its key properties is prerequisite in business transformation in case of elevated levels of security. Model checking processes as in e.g. [7, 21] would help to identify and validate key properties to facilitate more agility.

Retrofitting existing infrastructures is – in practice – a challenge and necessity, black box methods as described in [22] an instrument to add security by not interfering with the core properties of a system and the interfaces of existing infrastructure. Given that many of such infrastructures use protocols from the pre-IP-era and the interfaces may not tolerate novel IT security measures as penetration testing and could be damaged by malware then such methods could contribute to security.

Scalability is the second concern that needs to be addressed in the field of IT-security for critical infrastructures. Standard processes with variations are important to maintain complexity when adding new (security systems). From our joint research with critical infrastructure providers in ITS|KRITIS we understand that architectures and various applications, as, e.g., identity and access management solutions are designed with security requirements and reduce complexity by using standard processes. We also understand that a plethora of novel security applications needed to be integrated in critical infrastructures. Each application should come with a plug-and-play interface to be easily integrated, e.g., in a workbench. From a security management and point of view, every application should come also with a plug-and-play process model to be able to validate the properties of the process landscape – yet for different kind of processes than that what is being studied in [6, 23]. Also, each application needs to come with a plug-and-play risk model such that the risk model of the enterprise, e.g. in form of stochastic processes can be updated as easy as the IT infrastructure.

Also, critical for security is the *scheduling of processes* – the security of process landscape with operational processes, security process and maintenance processes crucially depends on the schedule of maintenance and security processes. Also, the predictability of schedule could be an issue in case of advanced persistent threats. Canzani et al. demonstrate on basis of system dynamics and game theory that the dynamics of attacker-defender games and the interdependencies of critical infrastructure require rigorous methods [4]. Here, more research would contribute to security and also to a more efficient use of resources and more efficient responses in security. The work of B. Steffen exemplifies the feasibility of advanced, mathematical methods in scheduling [24].

5 A Discussion on Future Security

IT security in critical infrastructures needs a next generation approach – we argue that the methods of scheduling, formal methods or checking properties will advance the field of IT security in critical infrastructures as they facilitate better designs of the processes in IT security and in critical infrastructures. We also argue, that IT security is in the domain of Critical Infrastructure is both about novel security technology and about processes and smart decision architectures. We identify agility, retrofitting, scalability and scheduling as future research topics.

Security is a question of both innovation and security – similar to the discussion between Bond and Q – traditional tools many help to master the cyber-challenges in novel future security approaches. We hope that the journey does not stop here and that we initiate a discussion for new research directions.

Acknowledgements. This research is funded by the German Federal Ministry of Education and Research under grant number FKZ: 16KIS0213K. I would also like to thank all authors and coauthors and co-editors of the case study series, all case study partners and interviewees for the insights as well as our project partners from VeSiKi and our fellow projects from ITS|KRITIS for the support of the case study series. We also thank the anonymous reviewers for their valuable comments.

References

1. Federal Office for Information Security: Recommendation for critical information infrastructure protection. Website about the protection of critical infrastructure maintained in cooperation by the BBK and the BSI. www.bsi.bund.de/EN/Topics/Criticalinfrastructures/criticalinfrastructures_node.html
2. Bundesgesetzblatt: Gesetz zur Erhöhung der Sicherheit informationstechnischer Systeme (IT-Sicherheitsgesetz, Bundesgesetzblatt Jahrgang 2015 Teil I Nr. 31) (2015)
3. Kipker, D.-K., Müller, S.: Internationale Cybersecurity-Regulierung (2018)
4. Canzani, E., Kaufmann, H., Lechner, U.: An operator-driven approach for modeling interdependencies in critical infrastructures based on critical services and sectors. In: Havarneanu, G., Setola, R., Nassopoulos, H., Wolthusen, S. (eds.) CRITIS 2016. LNCS, vol. 10242, pp. 308–320. Springer, Cham (2017). https://doi.org/10.1007/978-3-319-71368-7_27
5. Jähnichen, S., Wirsing, M.: Rigorous engineering of collective adaptive systems track introduction. In: Margaria, T., Steffen, B. (eds.) ISoLA 2016. LNCS, vol. 9952, pp. 535–538. Springer, Cham (2016). https://doi.org/10.1007/978-3-319-47166-2_37
6. Howar, F., Isberner, M., Merten, M., Steffen, B., Beyer, D., Păsăreanu, C.S.: Rigorous examination of reactive systems. Int. J. Softw. Tools Technol. Transf. **16**, 457–464 (2014)
7. Boelmann, S., Neubauer, J., Naujokat, S., Steffen, B.: Model driven design of secure high assurance systems: an introduction to the open platform from the user perspective. In: Proceedings of the International Conference on Security and Management, p. 145 (2016)
8. Kunnappilly, A., Legay, A., Margaria, T., Seceleanu, C., Steffen, B., Traonouez, L.-M.: Analyzing ambient assisted living solutions: a research perspective. In: 12th International Conference on Design Technology of Integrated Systems in Nanoscale Era. S., pp. 1–7 (2017)

9. Varriale, A., Di Natale, G., Prinetto, P., Steffen, B., Margaria, T.: SEcube™: an open security platform - general approach and strategies. In: International Conference on Security and Management (SAM 16). S. pp. 131–137 (2016)
10. Lechner, U.: Monitor 2.0 IT-Sicherheit Kritischer Infrastrukturen (2018)
11. Bhanu, Y., et al.: A cyberthreat search process and service. In: ICISSP 2016 - Proceedings of the 2nd International Conference on Information Systems Security and Privacy (2016)
12. Thaler, R.H., Sunstein, C.R.: Nudge: Improving Decisions About Health, Wealth, and Happiness. Yale Univ Pr (2008)
13. Sorbi, M.J., Mak, S.B., Houtveen, J.H., Kleiboer, A.M., van Doornen, L.J.P., Sorbil, M.J.: Mobile Web-based monitoring and coaching: feasibility in chronic migraine. J. Med. Internet Res. **9**, 14–23 (2007)
14. Lechner, U., Dännart, S., Rieb, A., Rudel, S.: IT-Sicherheit in Kritischen Infrastrukturen: Fallstudien zur IT-Sicherheit in Kritischen Infrastrukturen. Logos Verlag, Berlin (2018)
15. Dännart, S., Diefenbach, T., Hofmeier, M., Rieb, A., Lechner, U.: IT-Sicherheit in Kritischen Infrastrukturen – eine Fallstudien-basierte Analyse von Praxisbeispielen. In: Drews, P., Burkhardt, F., Niemeyer, P., und Xie, L. (Hrsg.) Konferenzband Multikonferenz Wirtschaftsinformatik 2018: Data driven X - Turning Data into Value. Leuphana Universität Lüneburg, Lüneburg (2018)
16. Yin, R.K.: The case study crisis: some answers. Adm. Sci. Q. **26**, 58–65 (1981)
17. Schubert, P., Wölfle, R.: The experience methodology for writing IS case studies. In: Americas Conference on Information Systems, pp. 19–30 (2006)
18. Eisenhardt, K.M.: Building theories from case study research. Acad. Manag. Rev. **14**(4), 532–550 (1989)
19. BSI: Industrial Control System Security: Top 10 Bedrohungen und Gegenmaßnahmen 2016 (2016)
20. Margaria, T., Steffen, B.: Service engineering: linking business and IT. Computer **39**, 45–55 (2006)
21. Hähnle, R., Steffen, B.: Constraint-based behavioral consistency of evolving software systems. BT - Machine Learning for Dynamic Software Analysis: Potentials and Limits - International Dagstuhl Seminar 16172, Dagstuhl Castle, Germany, 24–27 April 2016 (2016). Revised Papers, https://doi.org/10.1007/978-3-319-96562-8_8
22. Nissen, V., Stelzer, D., Straßburger, S., Hrsg, D.F.: Volker Nissen, Dirk Stelzer, Steffen Straßburger und Daniel Fischer (Hrsg.) Multikonferenz Wirtschaftsinformatik (MKWI) 2016 Band II. (2016)
23. Jasper, M., et al.: The RERS 2017 challenge and workshop (invited paper). In: BT - Proceedings of the 24th ACM SIGSOFT International SPIN Symposium on Model Checking of Software, Santa Barbara, CA, USA, July 10–14, 2017, (2017). http://doi.acm.org/10.1145/3092282.3098206
24. Chadli, M., et al.: High-level frameworks for the specification and verification of scheduling problems. Int. J. Softw. Tools Technol. Transf. **20**, 397–422 (2018)

Dortmund 1997 – Today

Statistical Prediction of Failures
in Aircraft Collision Avoidance Systems

Yuning He[1]([⊠]), Dimitra Giannakopoulou[1], and Johann Schumann[2]

[1] NASA Ames, Moffett Field, CA 94035, USA
{yuning.he,dimitra.giannakopoulou}@nasa.gov
[2] SGT, NASA ARC, Moffett Field, CA 94035, USA
johann.m.schumann@nasa.gov

Abstract. ACAS X is the next generation onboard collision avoidance system aimed at replacing the current standard TCAS for commercial aircraft. On-board collision avoidance systems are designed to help avoid dangerous Near Mid-Air Collision (NMAC) scenarios. Despite the fact that such systems can be very efficient in doing so, NMACs may still occur under rare circumstances. In this paper, we study the high dimensional time-series state space for encounters of aircraft equipped with ACAS X. We describe statistical modeling and learning techniques for predicting whether and when NMAC situations may occur. An iterative variable selection algorithm identifies the most influential variables for NMAC attribution. We also present a methodology for finding safety-boundaries, characterized as geometrical objects, that separate safe operational regions from dangerous ones where NMACs can occur. Even though our approach is presented in the context of ACAS X, it can be easily extended to numerous other domains including robotics, autonomous spacecraft, or self-driving cars.

1 Introduction

Maintaining safe separation among aircraft in the air space is extremely important. Despite careful planning of the flight paths and supervision by air-traffic control, situations can arise where aircraft come dangerously close to each other (termed Near Mid-Air Collisions, or NMACs). A high density of aircraft and the increased use of Unmanned Aerial Vehicles (UAVs) exacerbate the problem.

Onboard collision avoidance systems predict whether an NMAC might occur in less than one minute and produce "advisories", i.e., recommended maneuvers for the pilot to avoid the situation. The current collision avoidance standard, TCAS [1], is required on all large passenger and cargo aircraft worldwide, and has been successful in preventing mid-air collisions. To increase robustness and safety, the Federal Aviation Administration (FAA) has been developing a new system, ACAS X, which uses probabilistic models to represent uncertainty. Even though this novel approach leads to a significant improvement in safety and operational performance, it is not able to completely eliminate NMACs under

© Springer Nature Switzerland AG 2019
T. Margaria et al. (Eds.): Steffen Festschrift, LNCS 11200, pp. 249–267, 2019.
https://doi.org/10.1007/978-3-030-22348-9_16

all possible circumstances. More generally, algorithms designed to operate in highly autonomous environments (e.g., UAVs or swarms of UAVs), may, under rare conditions, fail to produce the desired outcome.

The aim of this work is to predict if/when autonomous algorithms fail, as well as to characterize their unsafe regions (often called "coffin corners" [2] in aircraft dynamics); once the system is in such a region, it will inevitably cause the algorithm to eventually produce an undesirable outcome. Even though our work is applicable to a variety of algorithms, we focus our study on ACAS X, both because of its relevance, but also because we have worked with it in the past. In ACAS X, the description of the movements of the two aircraft, pilot reaction, and advisories issued produce high-dimensional time series. In principle, the prediction of NMACs can be done through forward simulation of the system, but its high dimensionality causes severe scalability issues.

We have developed a framework based on statistical techniques for prediction of specific events and characterization of safety boundaries for high dimensional time series data. We use a novel iterative algorithm for the reduction of the number of variables, which makes the prediction algorithm much more efficient. Our algorithm for the detection and characterization of time-variant boundaries uses Bayesian techniques and advanced active learning for high efficiency and quality. We have applied this framework to ACAS X to specifically answer the following questions: (a) given a current state of both aircraft, can we predict if an NMAC will occur within the next 50 s and if so, how far in the future will the NMAC occur; and (b) what are the boundaries between safe behavior versus unsafe behavior in the aircraft state space?

Our framework has several applications in practice. For algorithm design and improvement, variable reduction provides a detailed and statistically founded understanding of which variables to focus on. For test-case generation, our statistical prediction models and safety boundaries can guide stress testing tools towards "rewarding" regions of the state space. For example, Adastress [3] uses reinforcement learning to generate high probability NMAC scenarios for ACAS X. Our models could be used to guide Adastress in a more targeted fashion. Safety regions can lead to a substantial reduction of generated test cases, as it might be sufficient to test for only one scenario in a specific region.

Finally, during runtime, statistical models can monitor a system and warn about unexpected undesirable situations. In scenarios where missions of different value are flown, such models could additionally assist with determining corrective actions. For example, in the case of air taxi versus packet delivery by a UAS, the packet delivery could be aborted to avoid loss of human life. Similarly, dynamic monitoring against safety boundaries provides an efficient means of steering the system away from dangerous coffin corners.

The remainder of the paper is structured as follows: Sect. 2 discusses related work, and Sect. 3 briefly describes the ACAS X system and our data sets. Sections 4 and 5 present our approach for NMAC prediction, and safety boundary learning, respectively, together with associated experiments. Section 6 summarizes the paper and discusses future work.

2   Related Work

Our work on prediction of NMACs in ACAS X uses and customizes existing techniques developed for time-series data; an overview is provided in [4].

Modeling safety boundaries in a high-dimensional space requires effective sampling techniques. Our work builds on approaches based upon active learning, e.g., Active Learning MacKay (ALM, [5]) and Active Learning Cohn (ALC, [6]). Such sampling techniques compare favorably to more traditional Markov-Chain Monte-Carlo (MCMC) based alternatives. We also incorporate a heuristic for the selection of candidate sampling points based on expected improvement (EI) statistics. The general approach, first presented in [7], cannot be directly used for boundary computation. Our work defines an EI function that effectively explores the sampling space to discover boundaries.

Our work contributes to several efforts for the verification and validation of the safety-critical ACAS X system. Essen and Giannakopoulou [8,9] developed the Verica tool and applied probabilistic verification and synthesis to an early version of ACAS X. Their aim was to study the impact of design issues such as model discretization and the selection of costs for the dynamic programming. Jeannin et al. [10] analyzed ACAS X using hybrid approaches. They performed analysis on hybrid models of the system. They then used the KeYmaera tool to compute safe regions for restricted types of encounters and for a single advisory. Safe regions characterize the types of advisories that are safe for the corresponding encounter. ACAS X advisories for specific encounters can then be compared against their corresponding safe regions. The advantage of taking a hybrid approach is that it does not require discretization. However, the entire hybrid model for ACAS X is prohibitively large, which forced the authors to work with a restricted number of scenarios.

In [11], the authors define conformance relations to explore the relationship of abstract models that are used the in the design of ACAS X and the real world. Lee et al. [3] have developed Adastress, a tool that uses reinforcement learning to generate high probability NMAC aircraft encounters. In addition, Adastress uses grammar-based techniques to explain characteristics of generated NMAC encounters at a higher level. Finally, [12] uses the Reluplex method for the formal analysis of a trained neural network that implements an ACAS X variant for unmanned aircraft.

Note that NMAC events only occur very infrequently in practice. To be able to build better predictive models, we used Adastress to create a dataset that includes a high enough percentage of NMAC scenarios. Alternatively, one could use rare event modeling techniques such as [13].

3   The ACAS X System

This section provides background information on the ACAS X system, and the relevant data that we used in our study.

The on-board collision avoidance system ACAS X [14] aims at preventing catastrophic midair collisions between commercial transport aircraft by alerting the pilots and suggesting evasive maneuvers. It models aircraft encounters with a Markov Decision Process (MDP) and uses dynamic programming to obtain optimal decision tables for on-board processing. ACAS X models uncertainties in pilot behavior as well as environmental influences as statistical noise. We use the term loss of horizontal separation (LHS) to describe the situation where two aircraft are within 500 ft from each other ignoring their altitude difference. A Near Mid-Air Collision (NMAC) occurs when the altitude difference between the two aircraft is less than 100 ft when the LHS occurs.

This work targets actual and simulated flight data, as opposed to data obtained from the MDP that ACAS X is based on. ACAS X monitors the entire airspace in the vicinity of an aircraft and resolves conflicts by iteratively analyzing pairs of aircraft, within a time horizon of 50 s. We therefore consider encounters of length 50 s, between two aircraft equipped with ACAS X. Note that an NMAC may or may not occur during this time frame. In fact, NMAC scenarios are rare in actual flight and simulation tests.

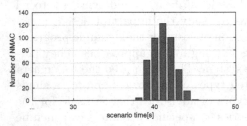

Fig. 1. Histogram of NMAC times in the data set. All NMACs occur between $t = 38$ s and 45 s.

We used the Adastress tool [3] to generate a synthetic data set with a high percentage of NMAC scenarios (around 8%), which allowed us to better develop our prediction and safety boundary models. The data set consists of a total of 28,738 scenarios, where two aircraft, each equipped with ACAS X, are converging. Of these scenarios, 2,410 scenarios lead to an NMAC situation. In these cases, the NMAC occurred at around 40 s into the scenario as shown in Fig. 1.

Each scenario is a 77 dimensional time series representing the state of the two aircraft, pilots, and the two ACAS X systems. Details about these state variables can be found in [14]. A visualization of selected variables of such a high-dimensional data stream is shown in Fig. 2. The figure depicts the trajectories of two aircraft in a horizontal and vertical projection. The aircraft start flying toward each other with a decreasing horizontal and vertical distance. At some point, ACAS X detects the dangerous situation and issues an advisory to one aircraft (marked in yellow). The advisory to climb is executed by the pilot. However, this evasive maneuver is not sufficient to avoid an NMAC, which occurs at $t = 35$ s (vertical line in Panel B).

4   Prediction of NMAC Events

In this paper, we address the prediction of potentially dangerous NMAC events. Generally speaking, given the past trajectories of both aircraft, issued advisories, and pilot reaction, we want to learn models that predict, whether an NMAC event will occur in the future and when it will occur.

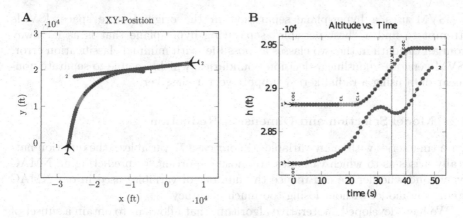

Fig. 2. Example Encounter (see [11]) between two aircraft shown horizontally (A) and in terms of difference in altitude h (B). Despite evasive actions (yellow and red), an NMAC occurs at $t = 35$ s. (Color figure online)

Our approach to model-learning is based on Support Vector Machines and develops novel methods for model selection and dimension reduction, which will be described in the rest of this section.

4.1 The Learning Model

Support vector machines (SVMs) [15] are supervised learning models for data classification. To make classification easier, SVMs typically use transformations to map data points to another space, as illustrated in Fig. 3. The picture is in 2D for simplicity to allow easy visual intuition, but the data may be high dimensional, as is the case for our problem. In this paper, scenarios are classified as 'NMAC', or 'no NMAC'.

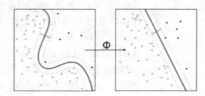

Fig. 3. SVM for separation of data

The SVM objective function uses a generalized dot product named kernel $K(x, y) = \langle \Phi(x), \Phi(y) \rangle$ to measure the similarity between data points x and y at high dimensional spaces. In this paper, we explore two standard choices of kernels K: (i) linear SVM (lSVM) with $K(x, y) = \langle x, y \rangle$, and (ii) radial SVM (rSVM) with $K(x, y) = exp(-a||x - y||^2)$.

lSVM uses a hyper-plane separation in the original state space. lSVMs attempt to find a "best possible" separating hyper-plane that is as far away from all the data in the two classes as possible, with minimal classification error. rSVM generates non-linear decision boundaries, which are able to separate non-linear data using a radial kernel support vector classifier.

4.2   Model Selection and Dimension Reduction

For a time series with many variables (in our case 77 variables), the question naturally arises as to which variables are most important for predicting an NMAC event, and whether we can reduce the number of variables used in our NMAC prediction model without losing too much accuracy.

We have developed an iterative algorithm that allows us to obtain a subset of variables that are most influential for the prediction. To evaluate our algorithm, we use typical metrics of the quality of prediction models, based the following numbers: TP/FP (true/false positives) describe the number of times our model correctly/incorrectly predicts an NMAC, respectively. Similarly, TN/FN (true-/false negatives) describe the number of times the model correctly/incorrectly predicts the absence of an NMAC, respectively. Recall $R = TP/(TP + FN)$ denotes the ratio of the correctly predicted NMAC observations to all NMAC observations in the data set. Precision $P = TP/(TP + FP)$ is the ratio of correctly predicted positive NMAC observations to the total predicted positive observations. Finally, the F1 metric provides a value balancing the capabilities of the model with respect to recall and precision [16].

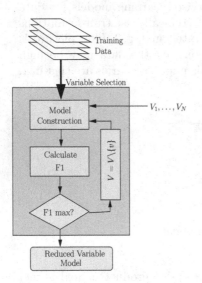

We use a fixed data set for our experiments, split into two separate sets for training and testing. Our greedy selection algorithm, illustrated in Fig. 4, starts by training a model based on the full set of time series variables $V = \{V_1, V_2, \ldots, V_N\}$ and computing the F1 metric of this model. It then evaluates, for each variable $v \in V$, the effect of removing it from V. It does that by training and evaluating a new model based on $V \backslash \{v\}$. It then selects as less influential, the variable v that results in the highest F1 score; when removing this variable, our overall prediction accuracy remains as high as possible. When a variable is removed, the algorithm constructs a new SVM model and calculates its F1 score. This is repeated until the prediction accuracy of the new model is not acceptable in the context of a particular application. Note that for ACAS X, removal of variables resulted in an increase in F1 score.

Fig. 4. Iterative variable selection and model generation

Our algorithm is not guaranteed to produce an optimal solution, but it provides system designers with valuable help in reducing the dimensionality of a problem in a systematic way. It operates in the original as opposed to a projected space, to make its results more understandable to system designers.

4.3   Experiments and Results

Our work builds NMAC prediction models to classify scenarios as involving an NMAC or not. For NMAC classified scenarios, we build time-of-NMAC (T_{NMAC}) prediction models to predict when NMACs occur.

To build NMAC prediction models, we split the data set of 28,738 scenarios obtained from Adastress into 80%/20% chunks as training and test data, respectively. To build T_{NMAC} prediction models, we use the subset of 2,410 NMAC scenarios, similarly split into 80%/20% chunks.

We consider two cases based on the information that is used to make the prediction: (1) *intervals*: given information from the start of the scenario to some time t, predict whether and when an NMAC occurs in the interval $[t + 1, 50]$; (2) *sliding-window*: given information within a window $[t_0, t_1]$ of length Δ_t time steps (i.e., $t_1 - t_0 = \Delta_t$), predict whether and when an NMAC occurs in the interval $[t_1 + 1, 50]$. Our analysis considers fixed-length sliding windows where $1 \leq t_0 \leq 50 - \Delta_t$.

Learning the Model on Intervals. Given data from a time interval $[1, t]$, where $t = 1, \ldots, 37$ s, we set up models to predict if there is an NMAC later in the scenario. In order to also analyze the effect of the length of the history, we compared the results to only using data from the last 10 s, i.e., from the interval $[t - 9 s, t]$.

We report on the application of radial SVM on all 77 variables, because it performed better than linear SVM. The performance metrics (Recall, Precision, and F1) for all $t = 1, \ldots, 37$ s are shown in Fig. 5A. Solid lines correspond to experiments using $[t - 9 s, t]$, dashed lines to experiments using $[1, t]$ as inputs. The Error Rate comparison is shown in Fig. 5B.

The trends of using longer history are qualitatively similar to the results obtained for prediction using only the last 10 time steps $[t - 9 s, t]$, with Recall and F1 increasing and the Error Rate decreasing with increasing t. It is obviously easier to accurately predict an NMAC as the time t gets closer to the actual NMAC time, and the predictive power is poor when the current time t is far away from the occurrence of NMAC.

The Precision results are noisier with a spike from $t = 8 s$ to $t = 10 s$. That far away from any NMAC event (NMACs start to occur at $t = 38 s$ and later), the Radial SVM method is usually hesitant to predict any NMACs. At times $t = 8 s, 9 s$, and 10 s, our method predicted 1, 1, and 2 NMACs, respectively and these happened to be correct. So the precision is 1 for these three times. For all other times in the range of $[1 s, 19 s]$, the Radial SVM method predicted 0 NMACs, resulting in an undefined Precision (plotted as 0 in the figures), so

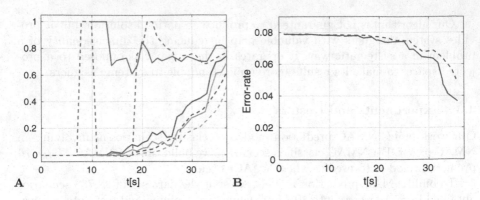

Fig. 5. A: Comparing the F1 (blue), Recall (green), and Precision (red) for predicting NMAC using 10 history steps $[t - 9\,\mathrm{s}, t]$ (solid) and using all history $[1, t]$ (dashed). **B**: Comparing the Error Rate for predicting NMAC using 10 history steps $[t - 9\,\mathrm{s}, t]$ (solid) and using all history $[1, t]$ (dashed). The models were constructed using Radial SVM on all 77 variables. (Color figure online)

there appears to be a spike from $t = 8\,\mathrm{s}$ to $t = 10\,\mathrm{s}$. Starting from time $t = 20\,\mathrm{s}$, the Precision remains roughly constant (especially for times $t = 25\,\mathrm{s}$ onward). This is also qualitatively similar to the 10-step history Precision results. Note that the 10-step history model does not provide any data for $t < 10\,\mathrm{s}$ since there are not enough history steps for such early times.

One might guess that the $[t - 9\,\mathrm{s}, t]$ predictions should always be worse than the $[1, t]$ predictions, because the former is using less data than the latter. But that was not the case in our experimental results. The 10-step history predictions were in fact always better than the full history predictions for the Recall, F1, and Error Rate measures. This could be because the older data (older than 10 time step in this case) are not helpful in the prediction and the SVM fitting has a hard time learning to ignore those older data and focusing on the small amount of data near the current time t that is relevant for predicting future NMAC events.

Prediction Using a Sliding Window. For this experiment, we used both linear and radial SVM. As a sanity check, we compared them to a trivial baseline model (BL) that predicts NMAC if and only if that NMAC occurs within the scope $[t_0, t_1]$ of the sliding window.

Table 1 (left) shows the results for $[t_0, t_1] = [31\,\mathrm{s}, 40\,\mathrm{s}]$. As most of the NMACs occur after $t_1 = 40\,\mathrm{s}$, the detection baseline model BL has quite limited recall of NMAC events. The Linear SVM model was able to predict some NMACs outside of $[t_0, t_1] = [31\,\mathrm{s}, 40\,\mathrm{s}]$, but performed by far not as well as the Radial SVM. The Radial SVM model had excellent results with 83% recall and 80% precision and thus significantly outperformed Linear SVM, which in turn outperformed BL.

All NMACs in our test set occur at $t = 38\,\mathrm{s}$ or later. We therefore also carried out a pure prediction experiment with $[t_0, t_1] = [26\,\mathrm{s}, 35\,\mathrm{s}]$, illustrated

Table 1. Comparison of performance for different algorithms to predict NMAC in the interval [31 s, 40 s] (left) and in the interval [26 s, 35 s] (right). Numbers obtained by running a test set of 5748 scenarios (=20% of all scenarios).

Interval	[31 s, 40 s]			[26 s, 35 s]		
Metric	Baseline	lSVM	rSVM	Baseline	lSVM	rSVM
true positives TP	167	322	379	0	0	277
false negatives FN	287	132	75	454	454	177
false positives FP	0	135	92	0	0	61
true negatives TN	5294	5159	5202	5294	5294	5233
Precision P	1.0	0.7	0.80	–	–	0.82
Recall R	0.37	0.71	0.83	0	0	0.61
F1	0.54	0.71	0.82	–	–	0.70
Error rate e	0.050	0.046	0.029	0.079	0.079	0.041

in Table 1(right). For this experiment, neither BL (Column 1) nor linear SVM (Column 2) were able to predict any NMACs (Column 1 and Column 2). On the other hand, radial SVM was able to predict 61.0% of the NMACs, the earliest of which were 3 time steps later than t1 = 35 s. Finally, Table 2 shows results for Radial SVM for different intervals between the two cases discussed above.

Table 2. Comparison of performance for three different prediction intervals using Radial SVM

$[t_0, t_1] =$	[26 s, 35 s]	[27 s, 36 s]	[28 s, 37 s]
true positives TP	277	282	312
false negatives FN	177	172	142
false positives FP	61	61	77
true negatives TN	5233	5233	5217
Precision P	0.82	0.82	0.80
Recall R	0.61	0.62	0.69
F1	0.70	0.71	0.74
Error rate e	0.041	0.041	0.038

Predicting T_{NMAC}. In our initial experiment, we trained models to predict the time T_{NMAC} at which the first NMAC after the start of a scenario will occur. This experiment only uses data in the interval $[t_0, t_1] = [28 s, 37 s]$. As evident from Fig. 1 this defines an interval, which is located before any NMACs have actually occurred in the training or test data but that is still relatively close in time to actual NMAC occurrences.

For this experiment, we used only important variables, namely the slant range s, which is the line-of-sight distance between the two aircraft, and Δ_z, the absolute vertical distance between the two aircraft. We selected these two variables based on our understanding and previous experience with ACAS X. The importance of these variables was also confirmed by the variable selection algorithm described in Sect. 4.2.

We built a radial SVM-based learning model for classification and performed regression to give us a continuous valued T_{NMAC} prediction. This model was trained on our data set of 1956 scenarios. When tested with the 454 runs from the test set, the absolute prediction error was only 0.27 s. To make an integer time step prediction for when an NMAC occurs, we rounded the predictions of our model to the nearest integer and checked the prediction performance. The average absolute prediction error using rounded predictions is defined as

$$E = |\text{round}(\hat{T}_{NMAC}) - T_{NMAC}|$$

where $\hat{T}_{NMAC}$ is the predicted and T_{NMAC} the actual (integral) time when the NMAC occurs. Over our 454 test runs, the absolute error E is less than 0.10 s. After rounding the real-valued predictions obtained directly from our model, 410 of the 454 test predictions (90.3%) were exactly the correct NMAC time step.

Iterative Variable Selection. For this experiment, we started with the rSVM model to predict NMACs in the time interval [28 s, 37 s] (see Table 2) and used the variable elimination algorithm described in Sect. 4.2. We might expect that the model accuracy should decrease as fewer variables are used since less information is provided to help discriminate between scenarios with an NMAC and non-NMAC scenarios.

During the first iteration of the algorithm, variable v_{66} with the name tds^2 is removed, but the F1 score of the radial SVM model using all 77 variables except variable number 66 is larger than the radial SVM model using all 77 variables (0.771 versus 0.740). Table 3 shows the details. Variables with superscript 1 are values observed by aircraft 1, those with superscript 2 are observed by aircraft 2. Usually these variables are correlated, but there can be differences due to noise and data errors.

In fact, this trend continues through Step 11 where each time we remove another variable, the F1 score of the radial SVM model increases. The radial SVM model fitting procedure does not seem to be able to ignore the "extra" variables and instead the additional information causes some confusion in the model.

Subsequently, 60 variables are removed (Steps 11 through 70), whose absence does not change the F1 score (or Precision or Recall) of the model, which remains constant at 0.913. There appears to be a lot of highly correlated variables in the dataset. Figure 6 shows how the F1 metric develops during the run of the algorithm.

Table 3. Individual steps of the iterative variable selection, showing how Precision, Recall, and F1 develop after iteratively removing variables v_i.

Step	Precision	Recall	F1	v_i removed	Variable name
0	0.802	0.687	0.740	–	–
1	0.821	0.727	0.771	66	tds^2
2	0.812	0.905	0.856	29	tds^1
...					
68	0.866	0.965	0.913	68	R^2_{stay}
69	0.866	0.965	0.913	69	R^2_{follow}
70	0.866	0.965	0.913	70	R^2_{timer}
71	0.864	0.965	0.912	5	s^1
72	0.855	0.963	0.906	22	r^1_{target}
73	0.848	0.945	0.894	2	v^1_{vert}
74	0.859	0.949	0.902	39	v^2_{vert}
75	0.855	0.949	0.900	59	r^2_{target}
76	0.833	0.936	0.882	42	s^2
					Δ_z

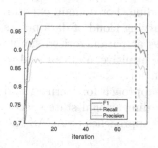

Fig. 6. Development of F1, Recall, and Precision during the iterative variable selection algorithm

The optimal set of variables is selected, when after an initial rise of F1 during the algorithm, F1 starts dropping again (dashed line in Fig. 6). In our case, only seven variables, numbered 5, 22, 2, 39, 59, 42, and 76, remain. These are the slant range s^1, s^2 (as observed by each aircraft) between the two aircraft, their difference in altitude Δ^1_{alt}, their relative vertical speed (as observed by each aircraft) v^1_{vert}, v^2_{vert}, the target range r^2_{target}, and the absolute value of the altitude difference between both aircraft, Δ_z. With this small subset of variables we achieve a radial SVM model with Precision, Recall, and F1 performance of 86.6% Precision, 96.5% Recall, and F1 = 0.913. This is a significant improvement over our previous best model that used all 77 variables with 80.2% Precision and 68.7% Recall. Table 4 summarizes the results.

5 Timeseries Safety Boundary Learning and Characterization

Given the safety-critical nature of ACAS X, a question that arises naturally is how "far" an aircraft is from a "safe" region, where no NMAC can happen.

Table 4. Model performance with iterative dimension reduction

Model	Precision	Recall	F1
77 variables	0.802	0.687	0.740
7 variables	0.866	0.965	0.913
1 variable Δ_z	0.833	0.936	0.882

In general, a safe region is an area in a potentially high-dimensional state space, where the probability P of an adverse event happening is very low (typically around 10^{-9} in the aerospace domain). Designers and pilots are interested to remain in such safe regions. Boundaries to unsafe regions, where a dangerous event is likely to happen, are of particular interest.

In the context of ACAS X, aircraft can climb, descend, or fly level based upon pilot actions and advisories issued by ACAS X. Safety boundaries are therefore not fixed within a high-dimensional state space of position, speeds, and headings, amongst others. Rather, they change over time as the scenario develops. Detection and characterization of such time-series safety boundaries is quite challenging.

In general, as a null hypothesis, one can define a safety boundary as the set of points x in the state space such that $P(x = safe) = 0.5$. Such a safety boundary can, for example, be visualized as an elevation line on a map, separating safe areas from lower-lying areas, which are prone to flooding. For domain experts, however, a representation of a boundary as a time-varying cloud of data points is not helpful. A characterization of safety-boundaries as parameterized simple geometrical objects (e.g., plane, sphere, cone) is more intuitive, and can lead to better analysis and understanding of the system behavior.

In the remainder of this section, we present our approach for learning and characterizing time-series safety boundaries for high dimensional state spaces. We then present results from the application of these approaches to ACAS X.

5.1   Learning

Learning of a safety-boundary in a high-dimensional state space requires a huge number of data points, which increases exponentially with the number of dimensions. In the context of ACAS X, each data point corresponds to one simulation run. Even with the simulation running faster than real time, a systematic exploration of scenarios would require too much time.

We therefore use an active learning algorithm for learning and characterization of the safety boundaries. This algorithm starts with a small set of labeled data points $D = \{\langle X_i, y_i \rangle\}$ for $1 \leq i \leq M$ (here, $M = 50$). The iterative algorithm uses the information gathered so far to find a new candidate point X_c that is close to the suspected boundary, because we are most interested in this area. Then, the ACAS X simulator is executed on X_c and returns y_c indicating whether there has been an NMAC or not. This data point is then added $D = D \cup \{X_c\}$ and a new iteration occurs.

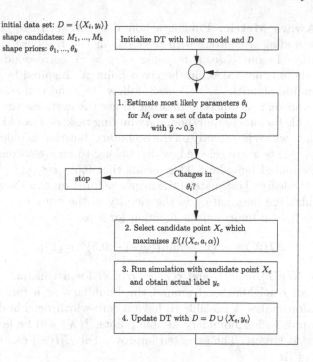

Fig. 7. Algorithm for safety boundary active learning and shape characterization

The flow-chart of the detailed algorithm is shown in Fig. 7. It combines three different ingredients, which will be described in detail below: DynaTrees [17] are used for storage and iterative updates of the data D as well as for the efficient estimation of the boundary surface in high dimensions, a boundary-aware metric to find candidate points X_c that are close to the suspected safety boundary, and a Bayesian technique to estimate the most likely parameters Θ for the geometric shape M_i of the boundary.

DynaTrees. Dynamic regression trees (DynaTrees) [17] are regression and classification learning models with complicated response surfaces in on-line application settings. DynaTrees create a sequential tree model whose state changes over time with the accumulation of new data, and provide particle learning algorithms that allow for the efficient on-line posterior filtering of tree-states.

A major advantage of DynaTrees is that they allow for the use of very simple models within each partition. The models also facilitate a natural division in sequential particle-based inference: tree dynamics are defined through a few potential changes that are local to each newly arrived observation, while global uncertainty is captured by the ensemble of particles.

DynaTree uses both constant and linear mean functions at the tree leaves, along with multinomial leaves for classification problems, and allows for prediction to be integrated over all model parameters conditional on a given tree.

Boundary-Aware Metric. Finding a boundary between two classes can be considered as finding a contour with $a = 0.5$ in the response surface of the system response. In our case, a response of $y = 1$ corresponds to NMAC; $y = 0$ means there is no NMAC in the given point X. Inspired by [7] and work on contour finding algorithms, we loosely follow [18], and define our heuristics by using an improvement function. In order to use the available resources as efficiently as possible for our contour/boundary finding task, one would ideally select candidate points which lie directly on the boundary, but that is unknown. Therefore, new trial points x are selected, which belong to an ϵ-environment around the current estimated boundary. This means that $0.5 - \epsilon \leq \hat{y}(x) \leq 0.5 + \epsilon$ for $\epsilon > 0$. $\hat{y}(x)$ is the learned estimate of the response function at x. New data points should maximize the information in the vicinity of the boundary. Following [7] and [18], we define an improvement function for x as

$$I(X) = \epsilon^2(x) - \min\{(y(x) - 0.5)^2, \epsilon^2(x)\} \tag{1}$$

here, $y(x) \sim N(\hat{y}(x), \sigma^2(x))$, and $\epsilon(x) = \alpha\,\sigma(x)$ for a constant $\alpha \geq 0$. This term defines an ϵ-neighborhood around the boundary as a function of $\sigma(x)$. This formulation makes it possible to have a zero-width neighborhood around existing data points. For boundary sample points, $I(X)$ will be large when the predicted $\sigma(x)$ is largest. The expected improvement $E[I(x)]$ can be calculated easily following [18] as

$$
\begin{aligned}
E[I(x)] = - \int_{0.5-\alpha\sigma(x)}^{0.5+\alpha\sigma(x)} (y - \hat{y}(x))^2 \phi\left(\frac{y-\hat{y}(x)}{\sigma(x)}\right) dy \\
+ 2(\hat{y}(x) - 0.5)\sigma^2(x)\left[\phi(z_+(x)) - \phi(z_-(x))\right] \\
+ (\alpha^2\sigma^2(x) - (\hat{y}(x) - 0.5)^2)\left[\Phi(z_+(x)) - \Phi(z_-(x))\right],
\end{aligned}
\tag{2}
$$

where $z_\pm(x) = \frac{0.5-\hat{y}(x)}{\sigma(x)} \pm \alpha$, and ϕ and Φ are the standard normal density and cumulative distribution, respectively. Each of these three terms are instrumental in different areas of the space. The first term summarizes information from regions of high variability within the ϵ-band. The integration is performed over the ϵ-band as $\epsilon(x) = \alpha\,\sigma(x)$. The second term is concerned with areas of high variance farther away from the estimated boundary. Finally, the third term is active close to the estimated boundary. After the expected improvement has been calculated, the candidate point is selected as the point, which maximizes the expected improvement.

Boundary Shape Characterization. The overall problem can be formulated as: given a classifier P_n based on a data set D_n consisting of n data points. We want to fit simple, parameterized shapes (from a dictionary provided by experts) to areas of high entropy that approximate the boundaries between the two classes. We also will select new data points that support the fitting process.

Suppose there are m shape classes $M_1, \ldots, M_m$ with $m \geq 1$ which are parameterized by $\Theta_1, \ldots, \Theta_m$. The task is to fit l shapes $S_1, \ldots, S_l, l \geq 1$, where

$S_1 = (i_1, \Theta_1), \ldots, S_l = (i_l, \Theta_l)$ and i_j denotes the shape class for the jth shape with $i_j \in \{M_1, \ldots, M_m\}$. Several of the i_j can be the same to accommodate more than one shape belonging to the same class. The Θ_i should be different since we do not want to represent the same boundary shape twice.

For example, we may consider the $m = 2$ shape classes $M_1 = hyperplane$ and $M_2 = sphere$ in R^d. Hyper-planes are represented as $a_1 x_1 + \cdots + a_d x_d + a_{d+1} = 0$ with parameter vector $\Theta_1 = (a_1, \ldots, a_d, a_{d+1}) \in R^{d+1}$. In the same d-dimensional space, a sphere of radius r with center $c = (c_1, \ldots, c_d)$ is described by $(x_1 - c_1)^2 + \cdots + (x_d - c_d)^2 = r^2$ with parameter vector $\Theta_2 = (c, r) \in R^{d+1}$. Now suppose we are in the plane ($d = 2$) and that the true class boundaries are described by the line $5x + y - 0.1 = 0$ (a hyper-plane in R^2), the circle $(x-0.3)^2 + (y-0.4)^2 = 0.2^2$ (a sphere in R^2), and the vertical line $x + 0y - 0.7 = 0$. This is represented in our model as $l = 3$ with the specific shapes $S_1 = (i_1 = hyperplane, \Theta_1 = (5, 1, -0.1))$, $S_2 = (i_2 = sphere, \Theta_2 = (0.3, 0.4, 0.2))$, and $S_3 = (i_3 = hyperplane, \Theta_3 = (1, 0, -0.7))$.

Given n data points D_n, we want to find the l shapes $S_1, \ldots, S_l$ that approximate the boundaries between classes in the classifier C_n fit to D_n. That is we are interested in shape sets $\mathcal{S} = (S_1, \ldots, S_l)$ that give large posterior probabilities $P(S_1, \ldots, S_l | D_n)$. We will sample from the posterior shape set $\arg\max_{\mathcal{S}} P(\mathcal{S} | D_n)$ as the number of data points increases.

5.2 Experiments and Results

To evaluate our safety-boundary approach on ACAS X, we focus only on the 7 variables in our data set that were identified as most influential by our Iterative Variable Selection procedure (see Table 3). Because high-dimensional time-series boundaries are difficult to visualize, we first look at the temporal development of the relevant variables during the last 10 s before an NMAC, $[T_{NMAC} - 9, T_{NMAC}]$. Figure 8 shows the variables as measured by aircraft 2: $v_{vert}^2, s^2, r_{target}^2, \Delta_z$. Red dots belong to scenarios leading to an NMAC, green dots to scenarios without an NMAC.

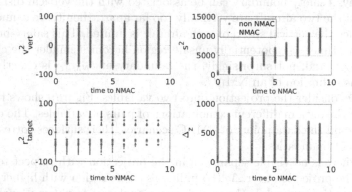

Fig. 8. Temporal development for variables $v_{vert}^2, s^2, r_{target}^2, \Delta_z$ for NMAC (red) and non-NMAC (green) scenarios. (Color figure online)

These plots correspond to an individual projection of the high dimensional space onto one selected variable over time. The behavior of the variables v_{vert}^2 and s^2 for the NMAC and non-NMAC cases are very similar, shown as a very high overlap of red and green dots in the top two panels of Fig. 8. This indicates that there does not exist a significant boundary.

In contrast, for the target rate r_{target}^2, regions can be identified that only contain red or only green dots, which indicates that a safety boundary can be associated with this variable. If the absolute value of the target rate is large enough, i.e., $r_{target}^2 > 50$ over the last 5 s, then the scenario will lead to NMAC. This boundary has a high correlation with the safety boundary that our algorithm found, as shown in Fig. 10 on the next page.

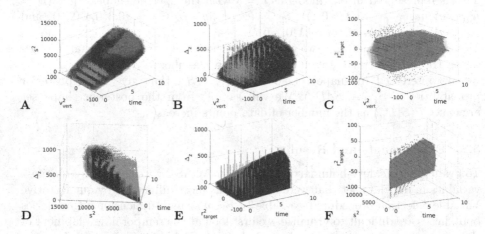

Fig. 9. Boundaries for pairs of variables (NMAC (red) and non-NMAC (green) scenarios). (Color figure online)

Similarly, a safety boundary can be associated with the vertical distance Δ_z over time: if the two aircraft are vertically too far apart, then there cannot be an NMAC, since the vertical speed of each aircraft is limited. This safety-boundary changes over time—the potentially unsafe region becomes smaller the closer we get to t_{NMAC}, and, not surprisingly, the boundary at t_{NMAC} is exactly 100 ft, which is the definition of an NMAC.

We now consider the projection onto two variables. Figure 9 shows the visualization of the data in different combinations of pairs of variables. The dark-red "cones" shroud the data points of NMAC scenarios; their surfaces correspond to projections of boundaries.

While there is no visible separation in the projection with respect to s^2 and v_{vert} (A), the projection over Δ_z (B) indicates a safe region with higher vertical distance near the time when the two aircraft are closest together. Panels E and F show similar boundaries as in the panels above.

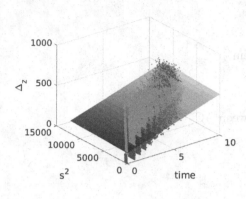

Fig. 10. Projection of temporal state space onto two variables with characterized boundary.

In Panel C, a safe region (shrouded in dark green) is surrounded by NMAC situations, in particular in conjunction with a high target rate r^2_{target} and low vertical speed, and we can see a clear separation.

Running our active learning algorithm, we obtained a safety boundary characterized as a plane defined by the equation: $37.68(t - t_{NMAC}) - \Delta_z + 0.0024s^2 + 128.7 = 0$. Figure 10 shows its projection onto s^2 and Δ_z over time as a colored surface. Red dots correspond to NMAC scenarios, green dots correspond to safe scenarios, where no NMAC occurs.

6   Conclusions

We have presented statistical modeling and learning techniques for predicting whether and when a dangerous situation may occur. We also developed a methodology for modeling safety-boundaries, characterized as geometrical objects, that separate safe operational regions from dangerous ones. Our approach was demonstrated on the ACAS X system, but can be extended to numerous other domains including robotics, autonomous spacecraft, or self-driving cars.

We specifically studied the high-dimensional time-series state space for encounters of aircraft equipped with the airborne collision avoidance system ACAS X where, under rare circumstances dangerous NMACs can occur. We demonstrated that our methods can reliably predict if and when an NMAC will occur in the imminent future, based upon a small temporal interval of the high-dimensional time-series data.

Our iterative variable selection algorithm revealed that most of the 77 variables in the data set carry information that is unimportant for the prediction task. The algorithm selected seven variables, which resulted in a prediction model with a substantially higher performance than using all 77. Using our active-learning approach, we modeled a safety boundary among the relevant variables and characterized it.

Acknowledgements. We thank Ritchie Lee for providing the dataset for our experiments. The work presented has been performed under NASA's System-Wide Safety Project.

Nomenclature

AC	Aicraft
ACAS-X	AC Collision Avoidance System
ALC	Active Learning Cohn
ALM	Active Learning MacKay
Δ^i_{alt}	difference in altitude $i = 1, 2$
Δ_z	absolute vertical distance between AC
DynaTree	Dynamic Regression Tree
$E[\ldots]$	Expectation
F1	weighted average of P and R
FAA	Federal Aviation Authority
FN	False Negative
FP	False Positive
$I(X)$	Improvement
LHS	Least Horizontal Separation
NMAC	Near Mid-Air Collision
P	Precision
R	Recall
r^i_{target}	target range AC_i, $i = 1, 2$
s	slant range
SVM	Support Vector Machine
T_{NMAC}	Time to NMAC event
TCAS	Traffic Collision Avoidance System
TN	True Negative
TP	True Positive
UAV	Unmanned Aerial Vehicle
v^i_{vert}	vertical speed for AC_i, $i = 1, 2$

References

1. Kuchar, J., Drumm, A.C.: The traffic alert and collision avoidance system. Linc. Lab. J. **16**(2), 277 (2007)
2. Hynes, C., Hardy, G., Sherry, L.: Synthesis from design requirements of a hybrid system for transport aircraft longitudinal control. Technical report NASA/TP-2007-213475, NASA (2007)
3. Lee, R., Kochenderfer, M.J., Mengshoel, O.J., Brat, G.P., Owen, M.P.: Adaptive stress testing of airborne collision avoidance systems. In: 2015 IEEE/AIAA 34th Digital Avionics Systems Conference (DASC), pp. 6C2–1. IEEE (2015)
4. Rao, T.S. (ed.): Time Series Analysis: Methods and Applications. Elsevier, Amsterdam (2012)
5. MacKay, D.J.C.: Information-based objective functions for active data selection. Neural Comput. **4**(4), 589–603 (1992)
6. Cohn, D.A.: Neural network exploration using optimal experimental design. Adv. Neural Inf. Process. Syst. **6**(9), 679–686 (1996)
7. Jones, D., Schonlau, M., Welch, W.J.: Efficient global optimization of expensive black box functions. J. Glob. Optim. **13**, 455–492 (1998)

8. von Essen, C., Giannakopoulou, D.: Probabilistic verification and synthesis of the next generation airborne collision avoidance system. STTT **18**(2), 227–243 (2016)
9. von Essen, C., Giannakopoulou, D.: Analyzing the next generation airborne collision avoidance system. In: Ábrahám, E., Havelund, K. (eds.) TACAS 2014. LNCS, vol. 8413, pp. 620–635. Springer, Heidelberg (2014). https://doi.org/10.1007/978-3-642-54862-8_54
10. Jeannin, J.-B., et al.: A formally verified hybrid system for the next-generation airborne collision avoidance system. In: Baier, C., Tinelli, C. (eds.) TACAS 2015. LNCS, vol. 9035, pp. 21–36. Springer, Heidelberg (2015). https://doi.org/10.1007/978-3-662-46681-0_2
11. Giannakopoulou, D., Guck, D., Schumann, J.: Exploring model quality for ACAS X. In: Fitzgerald, J., Heitmeyer, C., Gnesi, S., Philippou, A. (eds.) FM 2016. LNCS, vol. 9995, pp. 274–290. Springer, Cham (2016). https://doi.org/10.1007/978-3-319-48989-6_17
12. Katz, G., Barrett, C., Dill, D., Julian, K., Kochenderfer, M.: Reluplex: an efficient SMT solver for verifying deep neural networks. ArXiv e-prints, February 2017
13. Madigan, S.E.D.: A flexible bayesian generalized linear model for dichotomous response data with an application to text categorization. Inst. Math. Stat. **91**(54), 76 (2007)
14. Kochenderfer, M.J., Chryssanthacopoulos, J.P.: Robust airborne collision avoidance through dynamic programming. Project Report ATC-371, Massachusetts Institute of Technology, Lincoln Laboratory (2011)
15. Chen, Y., Councill, I.G.: An introduction to support vector machines: a review. AI Mag. **24**, 105–107 (2003)
16. Powers, D.M.W.: Evaluation: from precision, recall and F-measure to ROC, informedness, markedness and correlation. J. Mach. Learn. Technol. **2**(1), 37–63 (2011)
17. Taddy, M.A., Gramacy, R.B., Polson, N.G.: Dynamic trees for learning and design. J: Am. Stat. Assoc. **106**(493), 109–123 (2011)
18. Ranjan, P., Bingham, D., Michailidis, G.: Sequential experiment design for contour estimation from complex computer codes. Technometrics **50**(4), 527–541 (2008)

The ASSL Approach to Formal Specification of Self-managing Systems

Emil Vassev[1] and Mike Hinchey[2(✉)]

[1] Concordia University, Montreal, Canada
emil@vassev.com
[2] Lero-The Irish Software Research Centre, University of Limerick,
Limerick, Ireland
mike.hinchey@lero.ie

Abstract. ASSL (Autonomic System Specification Language) is a framework dedicated to the development of self-managing systems whereby developers are helped with problem formation, system design, system analysis and evaluation, and system implementation. The bottom line is a special multi-tier approach to specification exposing a rich set of constructs allowing a system to be modeled by emphasizing different key aspects, but centering the model around special self-management policies. This article presents in detail the aforementioned mechanism together with the underlying semantics. As a case study, we also present ASSL specifications of self-managing behavior of prospective autonomous NASA space exploration missions.

Keywords: Autonomic computing · Formal specification

1 Introduction

Complexity is widely recognized as one of the biggest challenges information technology faces today. To respond to this threat, many initiatives, such as Autonomic Computing (AC) [1–3], have been started to deal with complexity in contemporary computerized systems. AC is a rapidly growing field that promises a new approach to developing large-scale complex systems capable of self-management. The phrase "autonomic computing" came into the popular consciousness at the AGENDA 2001 conference where Paul Horn from IBM presented the new computing paradigm by likening computer systems to the human Autonomic Nervous System [1]. The idea behind this is that software systems must manage themselves, as the human body does, or they risk being crushed under their own complexity. Many major software vendors, such as IBM, HP, Sun, and Microsoft have started research programs to create self-managing computer systems. However, their main research efforts are mainly to make individual components of particular systems more self-managing rather than providing a complete solution to the problem of autonomic system development. As a result, ten years later after the AC initial announcement, there is still much to be done in making the transition to "autonomic culture" [4] and we still need programming techniques and technologies that emphasize the AC paradigm and provide us with programming concepts for implementing autonomic systems.

T. Margaria et al. (Eds.): Steffen Festschrift, LNCS 11200, pp. 268–296, 2019.
https://doi.org/10.1007/978-3-030-22348-9_17

This article presents the formalism of the Autonomic System Specification Language (ASSL) [5, 6], a dedicated to AC formal tool that emerges as a formal approach to developing autonomic systems. Providing both a formal notation and tools that support modeling and specification, validation and code generation of autonomic systems, ASSL has been successfully used in a variety of projects targeting functional prototypes of autonomous NASA space exploration missions [7, 8], autonomic pattern-recognition systems [9], home-automation sensor networks [10], etc. Note that a good understanding of the ASSL formalism and mastering the same were of major importance for the success of these endeavors. This paper gives an overview of the ASSL operational semantics and through formal semantics definitions it presents the operational behavior of some of the ASSL specifications for space exploration missions [7, 8]. This approach helps ASSL developers conceive an explicit understanding of the ASSL formalism.

The rest of this article is organized as follows. In Sect. 2, we discuss different formalisms for autonomic systems. Section 3 describes the ASSL specification model. Section 4 presents the ASSL operational semantics, which is used in Sect. 5 to enlighten ASSL specifications of NASA space exploration missions. Section 5 also presents some test results and Sect. 6 gives a brief overview of the ASSL's formal verification mechanisms. Finally, Sect. 7 concludes the article with summary remarks.

2 Formalism for Autonomic Systems

Conceptually, any formalism aims to assist the development of computer systems by providing formal notations that can be used to specify desirable system concepts (e.g. functionality). Usually, formal notations help developers precisely describe with the logical underpinning of mathematics features of the system under consideration at a higher level of abstraction than the one provided by implementation. However, a requirement is that developers should be able to move in a logical way from a formal specification of a system to implementation.

2.1 Formal Approaches to AC

Autonomic systems are special computer systems that emphasize *self-management* through *context awareness* and *self-awareness* [1–4]. Therefore, an AC formalism should not only provide a means of description of system behavior but also should tackle the vital for autonomic systems self-management and awareness issues. Moreover, an AC formalism should provide a well-defined semantics that makes the AC specifications a base from which developers may design, implement, and verify autonomic systems.

Formalisms dedicated to AC have been targeted by a variety of industrial and university projects. IBM Research developed a framework called Policy Management for Autonomic Computing (PMAC) [14, 15]. The PMAC formalism emphasizes the specification of self-management policies encompassing the scope under which those policies are applicable. A PMAC policy specification includes: (1) conditions to which a policy is in conformance (or not); (2) a set of resulting actions; (3) goals; and (4) decisions that need to be taken.

The so-called Specification and Description Language (SDL) is an object-oriented, formal language defined by the International Telecommunications Union – Telecommunications Standardization Sector (ITU-T) [16]. SDL is dedicated to real-time systems, distributed systems, and generic event-driven systems. The basic theoretical model of an SDL system consists of a set of extended finite state machines, running in parallel and communicating via discrete signals, thus making SDL suitable for the specification of self-management behavior.

Cheng et al. talk in [17] about a specification language for self-adaptation based on the ontology from system administration tasks and built over the underlying formalism of *utility theory* [18]. In this formalism, special self-adaptation actions are described as architectural operators, which are provided by the architectural style of the target system. A script of actions corresponds to a sequence of architectural operators. This sequence forms the so-called *adaptation tactic* defined in three parts: (1) the conditions of applicability; (2) a sequence of actions; and (3) a set of intended effects after execution. The definition of a tactic is similar to the "design by contract" interface definition [19].

Another formalism for Autonomic Systems (Ass) is provided by the *chemical programming* approach (represented by the Gamma Formalism [20]) which uses the chemical reaction metaphor to express the coordination of computations. The Gama Formalism describes computation in terms of chemical reactions (described as rules) in solutions (described as multisets of elements). When applied to AS specifications, the Gama Formalism captures the intuition of a collection of cooperative components that evolve freely according to some predefined constraints (rules). System self-management arises as a result of interactions between components, in the same way as "intelligence" emerges from cooperation in colonies of biological agents.

In [21], Andrei and Kirchner present a biologically inspired formalism for AC called Higher-Order Graph Calculus (HOGC). This approach extends the Gama Formalism with high-level features by considering a graph structure for the molecules and permitting control on computations to combine rule applications. HOGC borrows various concepts from graph theory, in particular from *graph transformations* [22], and use representations for graphs that have been already intensively formalized.

2.2 The ASSL Formalism

ASSL is a *declarative* specification language for autonomic systems with well-defined semantics. It implements modern programming language concepts and constructs like inheritance, modularity, type system, and high abstract expressiveness. Being a formal language designed explicitly for specifying autonomic systems (ASs) ASSL copes well with many of the AS aspects [1–4]. Moreover, specifications written in ASSL present a view of the system under consideration, where specification and design are intertwined. Conceptually, ASSL is defined through formalization tiers (see Sect. 3). Over these tiers, ASSL provides a *multi-tier specification model* that is designed to be scalable and exposes a judicious selection and configuration of infrastructure elements and mechanisms needed by an AS. In order to determine the level of ASSL formalism, we investigated in the vast field of formal specification languages. Srivas and Miller in [11] refer to *constructive* versus *descriptive* style of specification (also known as *model-oriented* versus *property-oriented*). The constructive or model-oriented style is typically associated with the use of definitions, whereas the descriptive or property-oriented style is generally associated with the use of axioms [12]. ASSL benefits from both styles, by using a property-oriented axiomatization as a top-level specification style and introducing a suitable number of specification layers with increasingly detailed model-oriented descriptions. As a formal language, ASSL defines a neutral, implementation-independent representation for ASs. Similar to many formal notations, ASSL enriches the underlying logic with modern programming concepts and constructs thereby increasing the expressiveness of the formal language while retaining the precise semantics of the underlying logic. For example, the ASSL formalism for self-management policies (see Sect. 3) is based on *event calculus* [13], whose formalism is enriched to fit in the ASSL mechanism for specifying self-management policies [5, 6].

To the best of our knowledge, the ASSL formalism is currently the only complete solution to the problem of AS specification. Although other solutions do exist, they emphasize individual AC aspects (e.g. self-management policies), which is far from what ASSL is proposing with its reach multi-tier specification model. Moreover, the ASSL framework together with the powerful formalism provides mature tools that allow ASSL specifications to be edited and formally validated. Finally, an operational Java application may be generated from any valid ASSL specification.

3 ASSL Specification Model

The ASSL formal notation is based on a specification model exposed over hierarchically organized *formalization tiers* [5, 6]. This specification model provides both infrastructure elements and mechanisms needed by an AS. ASSL defines ASs with special *self-managing policies*, *interaction protocols* (IPs), and *autonomic elements* (AEs), where the ASSL tiers and their sub-tiers describe different aspects of the AS under consideration.

Table 1 presents the ASSL specification model. As shown, it decomposes an AS in two directions - (1) into levels of functional abstraction; and (2) into functionally related sub-tiers. The first decomposition presents the system from three different perspectives (three major tiers) [5, 6]:

(1) a *general and global AS perspective*, where we define the general *system rules* (providing AC behavior), *architecture*, and global *actions*, *events*, and *metrics* applied in these rules;
(2) an *interaction protocol perspective*, where we define the means of communication between AEs within an AS;
(3) a *unit-level perspective*, where we define interacting sets of individual computing elements (AEs) with their own AC behavior rules, actions, events, metrics, etc.

The second decomposition presents the major tiers AS, ASIP, and AE as composed of functionally related sub-tiers, where new AS properties emerge at each sub-tier. This allows for different approaches to AS specification. For example, we may start with a global perspective of the system by specifying the AS service-level objectives and self-management policies and by digging down to find the needed metrics at the very detail

Table 1. ASSL multi-tier specification model

AS	AS Service-level Objectives	
	AS Self-management Policies	
	AS Architecture	
	AS Actions	
	AS Events	
	AS Metrics	
ASIP	AS Messages	
	AS Channels	
	AS Functions	
AE	AE Service-level Objectives	
	AE Self-management Policies	
	AE Friends	
	AEIP	AE Messages
		AE Channels
		AE Functions
		AE Managed Elements
	AE Recovery Protocols	
	AE Behavior Models	
	AE Outcomes	
	AE Actions	
	AE Events	
	AE Metrics	

level of AE sub-tiers. Alternatively, we may start working at the detail level of AE sub-tiers and build our AS bottom-up. Finally, we can work on both abstract and detail level sides by constantly synchronizing their specification.

3.1   ASSL Tiers

The AS Tier specifies an AS in terms of *service-level objectives* (AS SLOs), *self-management policies*, *architecture topology*, *actions*, *events*, and *metrics* (see Table 1). The AS SLOs are a high-level form of behavioral specification that help developers establish system objectives such as performance. The self-management policies could be any of (but not restricted to) the four so-called self-CHOP policies defined by the AC IBM blueprint [2]: *self-configuring*, *self-healing*, *self-optimizing*, and *self-protecting*. These policies are driven by *events* and trigger the execution of *actions* driving an AS in critical situations. The metrics constitute a set of parameters and observables controllable by an AS. At the ASIP Tier, the ASSL framework helps developers specify an AS-level interaction protocol as a public communication interface, expressed with special *communication channels*, *communication functions*, and *communication messages*. At the AE Tier, the ASSL formal model exposes specification constructs for the specification of the system's AEs. Note that AEs are considered to be analogous to software agents able to manage their own behavior and their relationships with other AEs.

Note that ASSL targets only the AC features of a system and helps developers clearly distinguish the *AC features* from the *system-service features*. This is possible, because with ASSL we model and generate special *AC wrappers* in the form of ASs that embed the components of non-AC systems [5, 6]. The latter are considered as *managed elements* controlled by the AS in question. Conceptually, a managed element can be any software or hardware system (or sub-system) providing services. Managed elements are specified per AE (see Table 1) where the emphasis is on the *interface* needed to control a managed element. It is important also to mention that the ASSL tiers and sub-tiers are intended to specify different aspects of an AS, but it is not necessary to employ all of them in order to model such a system. For a simple AS we need to specify (1) the AEs providing self-managing behavior intended to control the managed elements associated with an AE; and (2) the communication interface. Here, self-management policies must be specified to provide such self-managing behavior at the level of AS (the AS Tier) and at the level of AE (AE Tier). The following sub-sections briefly present some of the ASSL sub-tiers.

Self-management Policies. The self-management behavior of an ASSL-developed AS is specified with the self-management policies. These policies are specified with special ASSL constructs termed *fluents* and *mappings* [5, 6]. A fluent is a state where an AS enters with fluent-activating events and exits with fluent-terminating events. A mapping connects fluents with particular actions to be undertaken. Usually, an ASSL specification is built around self-management policies, thus making such a specification AC-driven. Self-management policies are driven by events and actions determined deterministically. The following ASSL code presents a sample specification of a self-healing policy.

```
ASSELF_MANAGEMENT {
    SELF_HEALING {
        FLUENT inLosingSpacecraft {
            INITIATED_BY { EVENTS.spaceCraftLost }
            TERMINATED_BY { EVENTS.earthNotified }
        }
        MAPPING {
            CONDITIONS { inLosingSpacecraft }
            DO_ACTIONS { ACTIONS.notifyEarth }
        }
    }
} // ASSELF_MANAGEMENT
```

ASSL Events. ASSL aims at event-driven autonomic behavior. Hence, to specify self-management policies, we need to specify appropriate events (see Sect. 3.1). Here, we rely on the reach set of event types exposed by ASSL [5, 6]. To specify ASSL events, one may use logical expressions over SLOs, or may relate events with metrics (see the ASSL code below), other events, actions, time, and messages. Moreover, ASSL allows for the specification of special conditions that must be stated before an event is prompted.

```
EVENT newAsteroidDetected {
    ACTIVATION {
        CHANGED { AS.METRICS.numberOfAsteroids }
    }
}
```

ASSL Metrics. For an AS, one of the most important success factors is the ability to sense the environment and react to sensed events. Together with the rich set of events, ASSL imposes metrics as a means of determining dynamic information about external and internal points of interest. Although four different types of metric are allowed [5, 6], the most important are the so-called *resource metrics* because those are intended to measure special *managed element* quantities. The following ASSL code demonstrates the ASSL specification of a resource metric (**noObstacle**) related to a managed element (**OBSTACLE_SENSOR**).

```
METRIC noObstacle {
    METRIC_TYPE { RESOURCE }
    METRIC_SOURCE { AEIP.MANAGED_ELEMENTS.OBSTACLE_SENSOR.isClean }
    THRESHOLD_CLASS { Boolean [ true ] }
}
```

Managed Elements. An AE typically controls *managed elements*. In an ASSL-developed AS, a managed element is specified with a set of special interface functions intended to provide control functionality over that managed element. Note that ASSL can specify and generate interfaces controlling a managed element (generated as a stub), but not the real implementation of these interfaces. This is just fine for prototyping, however when deploying an AS prototype the generated interfaces must be manually programmed to deal with the controlled system (or sub-system).

```
MANAGED_ELEMENT meReceptor {
    INTERFACE_FUNCTION reset ()
    INTERFACE_FUNCTION getRadiationLevel {
        PARAMETERS { DECIMAL xCoord; DECIMAL yCoord; DECIMAL zCoord }
        RETURNS { DECIMAL }
        TRIGGERS { AS.EVENTS.newRadiationLevel }
        ONERR_TRIGGERS { AS.EVENTS.cannotGetRadiationLevel }
    }
}
```

Interaction Protocols. ASSL *interaction protocols* provide a means of communication interface expressed with *messages* that can be exchanged among AEs, *communication channels* and *communication functions*. Thus, by specifying an ASSL interaction protocol we develop an embedded messaging system needed to connect the AEs of an AS. In a basic communication process ongoing in such a system, an AE relies on a communication function to receive a message over an *incoming* communication channel, changes its internal state and sends some new messages over an *outgoing* channel [5, 6].

```
ASIP {
    MESSAGES { MESSAGE msgHello { SENDER { AES.ae2 }  RECEIVER { AES.ae1 } } }
    CHANNELS {
        CHANNEL chnIIO { ACCETS { ANY }  ACCESS { SEQUENTIAL }  DIRECTION { INOUT } }
    }
    FUNCTIONS {
        FUNCTION sendHello {
            PARAMETERS { BOOLEAN hasSpeed; BOOLEAN hasDirection }
            DOES { MESSAGES.msgHello >> CHANNELS.chnIIO }
        }
    }
}
```

4 ASSL Notation and Semantics

ASSL is a declarative specification language for ASs with well-defined semantics [5, 6]. The language provides a powerful formal notation that enriches the underlying logic with modern programming language concepts and constructs such as *inheritance*, *modularity*, *type system*, and *abstract expressiveness*. As a formal language, ASSL defines a *neutral* (i.e., implementation-independent) representation for ASs described as a set of interacting AEs. The following is a generic meta-grammar in Extended Backus-Naur Form (BNF) [23] presenting the syntax rules for specifying ASSL tiers. Note that this meta-grammar is an abstraction of the ASSL grammar, which cannot be presented here due to the complex structure of the ASSL specification model (see Sect. 3), where each tier has its own syntax and semantic rules. The interested reader is advised to refer to [5] for the complete ASSL grammar expressed in BNF and for the semantics of the language.

```
GroupTier →   FINAL? ASSLGroupTierId { Tier+ }
Tier →   FINAL? ASSLTierId TierName? { Data* TierClause+ }
TierClause →   FINAL? ASSLClauseId ClauseName? { Data* }
Data →   TypeDecl* | VarDecl* | CllctnDecl* | Statement*
TypeDecl →   CustTypeIdentifier
VarDecl →   Type VarIdentifier
CllcntDecl →   Type CustCllctnIdentifier
Type →   CustType | PredefType
Statement →   Assign-Stmnt | Loop | If-Then-Else | Cllctn-Stmnt
Loop →   Foreach-Stmnt | DoWhile-Stmnt | WhileDo-Stmnt
```

As shown in the grammar above, an ASSL tier is syntactically specified with an ASSL *tier identifier*, an optional *name* and a *content block* bordered by curly braces.

Moreover, we distinguish two syntactical types of tier: *single tiers* (*Tier*) and *group tiers* (*GroupTier*), where the latter comprise a set of single tiers. Each single tier has an optional *name* (*TierName*) and comprises a set of special *tier clauses* (*TierClause*) and optional *data* (*Data*). The latter is a set of *data declarations* and *statements*. Data declarations could be: (1) *type declarations*; (2) *variable declarations*; and (3) *collection declarations*. Statements could be: (1) *loop statements*; (2) *assignment statements*; (3) *if-then-else statements*; and (4) *collection statements*. Statements can comprise *Boolean* and *numeric expressions*. In addition, although not shown in the grammar above, note that identifiers participating in ASSL expressions are either simple, consisting of a single identifier, or qualified, consisting of a sequence of identifiers separated by "." tokens.

4.1 ASSL Operational Semantics

The formal evaluation of the operational behavior of ASSL specification models is a stepwise evaluation of the specified ASSL tiers, where the latter are evaluated as state transition models in which operations cause a current state to evolve to a new state [5]. Thus, if we use the convention for semantic function in which σ states for a current state and σ' states for a new state then the state evolution caused by an operation Op is denoted as:

$$\sigma \xrightarrow{Op(x_1, x_2, \ldots, x_n)} \sigma'$$

where the operation $Op(x_1, x_2, \ldots, x_n)$ is an abstraction of a *transition operation* performed by the framework which potentially takes n arguments. All the arguments are evaluated to their expression value first, and then the operation is performed. Here, Op is a transition operation of type O^{trans} (see the set definition below).

$$O^{trans} \{ DegradSLO, NormSLO, FluentIn, FluentOut, \\ ActionMap, Action, Function, MsgRcvd, MsgSent, Event, \\ EventOver, Metric, ChangeStruct, CreateAE, ExtClass, \\ RcvryProtocol, BhvrModel, MngRsrcFunction, Outcome \}$$

In addition, the operational semantics of the ASSL tiers introduces the notion of *tier environment* ρ presenting the *host tier* of the sub-tiers or clauses under evaluation. Thus, we write $\rho \vdash_\sigma$ to mean that ρ is evaluated in context σ and $\rho \vdash_\sigma e \rightarrow e'$ to mean that, in a given tier environment ρ (host tier for the expression e) one step of the evaluation of expression e in the context σ results in the expression e'. Here, the context σ is defined by the tier content, i.e., sub-tiers, tier clauses, etc. Note that the ASSL tiers may participate in expressions where they are presented by their *TierName*. For example, AS/AE SLO, AS/AE policies, fluents, AS/AE events, and AS/AE metrics can participate in Boolean expressions, where they are evaluated as **true** or **false** in the context of their host tier based on their performance.

The following subsections present two algorithms implemented by the ASSL framework for operational evaluation of ASSL actions and self-management policies.

4.2   Operational Evaluation of ASSL Actions

From operational semantics perspective, the AS/AE Action tier is the most important and the most complex ASSL tier. The following is a partial EBNF grammar presenting syntactically that tier.

Action-Decl → ***ACTION IMPL****? Action-Name { Action-Decl-Seqnce }*
Action-Decl-Seqnce → *Params-Decl? Returns-Decl? Guards-Decl? Ensures-Decl?*
        Var-Decl-Seqnce? Does-Decl OnErr-Does-Decl? Trigs-Decl? OnErr-Trigs-Decl?

ASSL actions comprise the tier clauses: *PARAMETERS {...}, RETURNS {...}, GUARDS {...}, ENSURES {...}, DOES {...}, ONERR_DOES {...}, TRIGGERS {...},* and *ONERR_TRIGGERS {...}.* Note that only the *DOES {...}* clause is mandatory. The operational evaluation of an ASSL action follows the following algorithm:

I. Map the arguments, if any, from the action call to the parameters (*PARAMETERS {...}* clause).
II. Process the action guards, if any (*GUARDS {...}* clause):

- If the guards are held then perform the action.
- Otherwise, deny the action.

III. Evaluate the variable declarations, if any.
IV. Process the *DOES {...}* clause:

- If a return statement is hit, then stop the action and return a result.
- Else, process all the statements until the end of the *DOES {...}* clause.

V. If the *DOES {...}* clause is evaluated correctly, then evaluate the *ENSURES {...}* clause (in respect to the *TRIGGERS {...}* clause):

- If the *ENSURES {...}* clause is held then trigger notification events via the *TRIGGERS {...}* clause and exit the action normally.
- Else, process the *ONERR_DOES {...}* clause and trigger error events via the *ONERR_TRIGGERS {...}* clause.

VI. If an error occurs while evaluating the action clauses, then stop the evaluation process and:

- Process the *ONERR_DOES {...}* clause (similar to the evaluation of the *DOES {...}* clause), if any.
- Trigger error events via the *ONERR_TRIGGERS {...}* clause, if any.

4.3   Operational Evaluation of ASSL Policies

ASSL specifies policies with *fluents* and *mappings* (see Sect. 3.1). Whereas the former are considered as specific policy conditions, the latter map these conditions to appropriate actions. A partial presentation of the fluent grammar is the following:

> Fluent-Decl → **FLUENT** Fluent-Name { Fluent-Inner-Decl }
> Fluent-Name → **Bool-Identifier**
> Fluent-Inner-Decl → Initiates-Sqnce Terminates-Sqnce
> Fluent-Inner-Decl → Initiates-Sqnce
> Initiates-Sqnce → **INITIATED_BY** { Event-Names }
> Terminates-Sqnce → **TERMINATED_BY** { Event-Names }

> Map-Decl → **MAPPING** { Mapping-Inner-Decl }
> Mapping-Inner-Decl → Condition-Sqnce Action-Sqnce
> Condition-Sqnce → **CONDITIONS** { Fluent-Names }
> Action-Sqnce → **DO_ACTIONS** { Action-Calls ; Action-Calls-Forall }

An ASSL policy is evaluated based on its fluents. The operational evaluation of a fluent follows the following algorithm:

If an event has occurred in the system then:

I. Process the *INITIATED_BY { ...}* clause to check if that event can initiate the policy fluent f and if so, initiate that fluent:

- If the policy fluent f has been initiated then process only the policy *MAPPING {....}* clauses comprising the fluent f in their *CONDITIONS {....}* clause.
- Evaluate the *CONDITIONS {....}* clause and if the stated conditions are held then evaluate the *DO_ACTIONS {....}* clause to perform the actions listed there.

II. Process the *TERMINATED_BY { ...}* clause to check if that event can terminate the previously-initiated policy fluent f and if so, terminate it.

The semantic rules 1 through to 2 present the operational semantics that cope with the algorithm stated above. In these rules, each premise is a system transition operation (see Sect. 4.1) such as *Event(ev)*, *FluentIn(f, ev)*, *FluentOut(f, ev)*, and *ActionMap(f, a)*.

(1)
$$\frac{\sigma \xrightarrow{Event(ev)} \sigma'}{f \vdash_{\sigma'} \textbf{\textit{INITIATED\_BY}}\{ev_1, \ldots, ev_n\} \xrightarrow{FluentIn(f,ev)} \sigma''} ev \in \{ev_1, \ldots, ev_n\}$$

(2)
$$\frac{\sigma \xrightarrow{FluentIn(f,ev)} \sigma' \quad \sigma' \xrightarrow{Event(ev)} \sigma''}{f \vdash_{\sigma''} \textbf{\textit{TERMINATED\_BY}}\{ev_1, \ldots, ev_n\} \xrightarrow{FluentOut(f,ev)} \sigma'''} ev \in \{ev_1, \ldots, ev_n\}$$

(3)
$$\frac{\sigma \xrightarrow{FluentIn(f,ev)} \sigma'}{map \vdash_{\sigma'} \textbf{\textit{CONDITIONS}}\{f_1, \ldots, f_n\} \xrightarrow{ActionMap(f,a)} \sigma''} f \in \{f_1, \ldots, f_n\}$$

(4)
$$\frac{\sigma \xrightarrow{ActionMap(f,a)} \sigma'}{map \vdash_{\sigma'} \textbf{\textit{DO\_ACTIONS}}\{a_1, \ldots, a_n\} \xrightarrow{\forall a \in \{a_1, \ldots, a_n\} \bullet Action(a)} \sigma''} a \in A^\sigma$$

Here, A^σ is the finite set of actions in the context σ. The first premise in rule 2 evaluates whether the fluent f is initiated, i.e., only initiated fluents can be terminated.

5 Case Study - ASSL Specifications for NASA ANTS

5.1 Nasa Ants

The Autonomous Nano-Technology Swarm (ANTS) concept sub-mission PAM (Prospecting Asteroids Mission) is a novel approach to asteroid belt resource exploration that provides for extremely high autonomy, minimal communication requirements with Earth, and a set of very small explorers with a few consumables [24]. These explorers forming the swarm are pico-class, low-power, and low-weight spacecraft, yet capable of operating as fully autonomous and adaptable units. The units in a swarm are able to interact with each other, thus helping them to self-organize based on the emergent behavior of the simple interactions. Figure 1 depicts the ANTS concept mission. A transport spacecraft launched from Earth to carries a laboratory that assembles tiny spacecraft. Once it reaches a point in space, termed L1 (the Earth-Moon Lagrangian point), where gravitational forces on small bodies are balanced, the transport releases the assembled swarm, which will head for the asteroid belt. Each spacecraft is equipped with a solar sail for power; thus it relies primarily on power from the sun, using only tiny thrusters to navigate independently. Moreover, each spacecraft also has onboard computation, artificial intelligence, and heuristics systems for control at the individual and team levels.

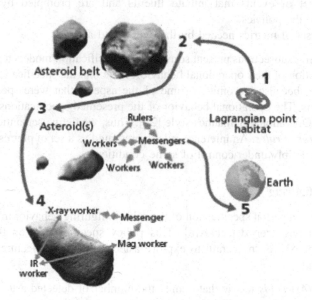

Fig. 1. ANTS mission concept [24]

As Fig. 1 shows, there are three classes of spacecraft—*rulers*, *messengers* and *workers*. Sub-swarms are formed to explore particular asteroids in an ant colony analogy. Hence, ANTS exhibits self-organization since there is no external force directing its behavior and no single spacecraft unit has a global view of the intended macroscopic behavior. The internal organization of a swarm depends on the global task to be performed and on the current environmental conditions. In general, a swarm consists of several sub-swarms, which are temporal groups organized to perform a particular task. Each swarm group has a group leader (*ruler*), one or more *messengers*, and a number of *workers* carrying a specialized instrument. The messengers are needed to connect the team members when they cannot connect directly, due to a long distance or a barrier.

5.2   Specifying ANTS with ASSL

In our endeavor to specify ANTS with ASSL, we emphasized modeling ANTS self-management policies such as self-configuring [8], self-healing [25], self-scheduling [26] and emergent self-adapting [27]. In addition, we proposed a specification model for the ANTS safety requirements [8]. To specify the ANTS safety requirements, we used the AS/AE SLO tier specification structures, and to specify the self-management policies we used ASSL tiers and clauses as following:

- self-management policy tiers to specify the self-management policies under consideration through a finite set of *fluents* and *mappings*.
- *actions*—a finite set of actions that can be undertaken by ANTS in response to certain conditions, and according to the self-management policies.
- *events*—a set of events that initiate fluents and are prompted by the actions according to the policies.
- *metrics*—a set of metrics needed by the events and actions.

The following subsections present some ASSL specification models together with a formal presentation of their operational behavior. Note that the specifications presented here are partial, because we omitted some of the aspects that were specified due to space limitations. The operational behavior of the presented specifications is presented in a Structural Operational Semantics style [28]. Thus, we define semantics definitions formed by *inference rules*. An inference rule is presented as a set of premises deducting a conclusion, possibly under control of some condition.

5.3   Self-configuring

Figure 2 presents a partial specification of the self-configuring behavior in ANTS when a new asteroid has been detected [8]. This policy specifies the "on the fly" team configuration of ANTS spacecraft, to explore asteroids. The key features of the proposed model are:

- a *numberOfAsteroids* metric that counts the number of detected asteroids;
- an *inANTSReconfigurationForNewAsteroid* fluent that takes place when the swarm detects a new asteroid;

- a *reconfigureANTS* action that performs the ANTS reconfiguration;
- a *newAsteroidDetected* event that initiates the fluent above and is prompted by the *numberOfAsteroids* metric when the latter changes its value.

```
AS ANTS {
  ASSELF_MANAGEMENT {
    SELF_CONFIGURING {
      FLUENT inANTSReconfigurationForNewAsteroid {
        INITIATED_BY { EVENTS.newAsteroidDetected }
        TERMINATED_BY {EVENTS.reconfigurationForNewAsteroidDone }
      }
      MAPPING { // force ANTS reconfiguration
        CONDITIONS { inANTSReconfigurationForNewAsteroid }
        DO_ACTIONS { ACTIONS.reconfigureANTS }
      }
    }
  } // ASSELF_MANAGEMENT
  ACTIONS {
    ACTION IMPL reconfigurationForNewAsteroid { TRIGGERS { EVENTS.reconfigurationForNewAsteroidDone }

    ACTION reconfigureANTS {
      GUARDS { ASSELF_MANAGEMENT.SELF_CONFIGURING.inANTSReconfigurationForNewAsteroid }
      ENSURES { EVENTS.reconfigurationForNewAsteroidDone }
      DOES { call IMPL ACTIONS.reconfigurationForNewAsteroid }
      ONERR_TRIGGERS { EVENTS.reconfigurationForNewAsteroidDenied }
    }
  } // ACTIONS
  EVENTS {
    EVENT newAsteroidDetected {    ACTIVATION { CHANGED { AS.METRICS.numberOfAsteroids } } }
    EVENT reconfigurationForNewAsteroidDone { }
    EVENT reconfigurationForNewAsteroidDenied { }
  }
  METRICS {
    METRIC numberOfAsteroids {
      METRIC_TYPE { RESOURCE }
      DESCRIPTION { "the number of detected asteroids during the ANTS lifecycle" }
      THRESHOLD_CLASS { DECIMAL [0 ~ } } //open range: from 0 to ....
    }
  }
} // AS ANTS
```

Fig. 2. ASSL specification: self-configuring

Operational Behavior. We consider two main states in this specification model— ANTS "in" and ANTS "not in" the *inANTSReconfigurationForNewAsteroid* fluent; i.e. ANTS performing self-configuring and ANTS not performing self-configuring. While operating, ANTS workers can discover a new asteroid. This increases the number of detected asteroids; i.e. the metric *numberOfAsteroids* changes its value, this causing the framework to perform the *Metric*(numberOfAsteroids) *transition operation*. The latter consecutively prompts the *newAsteroidDetected* event, which is attached to that metric (the event is prompted when the metric has changed its value). Rule 5 presents the operational evaluation of the *newAsteroidDetected* event:

$$(5) \quad \frac{\langle ANTS \rangle \xrightarrow{\textit{Metric}(\text{numberOfAsteroids})} \langle ANTS \rangle'}{ev \vdash_\sigma \textbf{\textit{CHANGED}} \ \{\text{numberOfAsteroids}\} \xrightarrow{\textit{Event}(\text{newAsteroidDetected})} \sigma'}$$

where *ev* is the tier environment exposed by that event and the transition operation *Event*(newAsteroidDetected) denotes that the event has been prompted. Subsequently, that transition operation initiates the *inANTSReconfigurationForNewAsteroid* fluent. Inference rules 6 through 9 enforce a definite strategy for evaluating that fluent's clauses in their host tier context σ and in the context π of the **SELF_CONFIGURING** policy. These semantic rules follow the algorithm presented in Sect. 4.3. Thus,

$$(6) \quad \frac{\langle ANTS \rangle \xrightarrow{\textit{Event}(\text{newAsteroidDetected})} \langle ANTS \rangle'}{f \vdash_{\sigma,\pi} \textbf{\textit{INITIATED\_BY}}\{\text{newAsteroidDetected}\} \xrightarrow{\textit{FluentIn}(f,\text{newAsteroidDetected})} \sigma',\pi'}$$

$$(7) \quad \frac{ANTS \xrightarrow{\textit{Event}(\text{reconfigurationForNewAsteroidDone})} ANTS' \quad \pi \vdash_\sigma \text{inANTSReconfigurationForNewAsteroid} \to \textbf{\textit{true}}}{f \vdash_{\sigma,\pi} \textbf{\textit{TERMINATED\_BY}}\{\text{reconfigurationForNewAsteroidDone}\} \xrightarrow{\textit{FluentOut}(f,\text{reconfigurationForNewAsteroidDone})} \sigma',\pi'}$$

$$(8) \quad \frac{f \vdash_{\sigma,\pi} \textbf{\textit{INITIATED\_BY}}\{\text{newAsteroidDetected}\} \xrightarrow{\textit{FluentIn}(f,\text{newAsteroidDetected})} \sigma',\pi'}{map \vdash_{\sigma',\pi'} \textbf{\textit{CONDITIONS}}\{\text{inANTSReconfigurationForNewAsteroid}\} \xrightarrow{\textit{ActionMap}(f,\text{reconfigureANTS})} \sigma'',\pi''}$$

$$(9) \quad \frac{map \vdash_{\sigma',\pi'} \textbf{\textit{CONDITIONS}}\{\text{inANTSReconfigurationForNewAsteroid}\} \xrightarrow{\textit{ActionMap}(f,\text{reconfigureANTS})} \sigma'',\pi''}{map \vdash_{\sigma'',\pi''} \textbf{\textit{DO\_ACTIONS}}\{\text{reconfigureANTS}\} \xrightarrow{\textit{Action}(\text{reconfigureANTS})} \sigma''',\pi'''}$$

where f is the tier environment exposed by the *inANTSReconfigurationForNewAsteroid* fluent and *map* is the tier environment exposed by the **MAPPING** {...} clause (see Fig. 2). Here, *FluentIn*(f, newAsteroidDetected) is a transition operation denoting that the **SELF_CONFIGURING** policy has entered that fluent (initiated by the *newAsteroidDetected* event) and *FluentOut*(f, reconfigurationForNew AsteroidDone) is a transition operation denoting that the **SELF_CONFIGURING** policy has exited the same fluent (terminated by the *reconfigurationForNew AsteroidDone* event) (see rules 6 and 7). In addition, *ActionMap*(f, reconfigureANTS) is a transition operation denoting that the **SELF_CONFIGURING** policy has mapped the *reconfigureANTS* action to that fluent.

Rules 10 through 17 present the operational evaluation of the *reconfigureANTS* action, thus following the algorithm presented in Sect. 4.2. This evaluation is triggered by the *Action*(reconfigureANTS) transition operation, which is performed by the framework when the *inANTSReconfigurationForNewAsteroid* fluent is mapped to the *reconfigureANTS* action (see Rule 9). This causes the state transition $\langle ANTS \rangle \xrightarrow{Action(\text{reconfigureANTS})} \langle ANTS \rangle'$. Thus, in the given *reconfigureANTS* action tier environment a defined in the tier context σ we evaluate the operational action clauses.

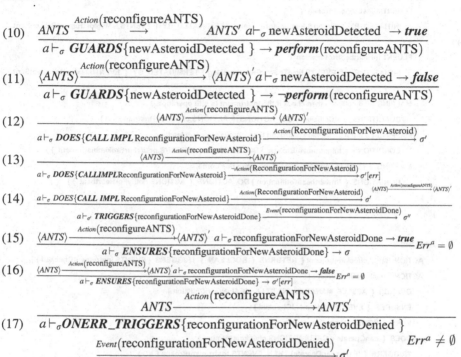

$$
(10) \quad \frac{ANTS \xrightarrow{Action(\text{reconfigureANTS})} ANTS' \quad a \vdash_\sigma \text{newAsteroidDetected} \rightarrow \textbf{\textit{true}}}{a \vdash_\sigma \textbf{\textit{GUARDS}}\{\text{newAsteroidDetected}\} \rightarrow \textbf{\textit{perform}}(\text{reconfigureANTS})}
$$

$$
(11) \quad \frac{\langle ANTS \rangle \xrightarrow{Action(\text{reconfigureANTS})} \langle ANTS \rangle' \quad a \vdash_\sigma \text{newAsteroidDetected} \rightarrow \textbf{\textit{false}}}{a \vdash_\sigma \textbf{\textit{GUARDS}}\{\text{newAsteroidDetected}\} \rightarrow \neg\textbf{\textit{perform}}(\text{reconfigureANTS})}
$$

$$
(12) \quad \frac{\langle ANTS \rangle \xrightarrow{Action(\text{reconfigureANTS})} \langle ANTS \rangle'}{a \vdash_\sigma \textbf{\textit{DOES}}\{\textbf{\textit{CALL IMPL}}\,\text{ReconfigurationForNewAsteroid}\} \xrightarrow{Action(\text{ReconfigurationForNewAsteroid})} \sigma'}
$$

$$
(13) \quad \frac{\langle ANTS \rangle \xrightarrow{Action(\text{reconfigureANTS})} \langle ANTS \rangle'}{a \vdash_\sigma \textbf{\textit{DOES}}\{\textbf{\textit{CALLIMPL}}\,\text{ReconfigurationForNewAsteroid}\} \xrightarrow{\neg Action(\text{ReconfigurationForNewAsteroid})} \sigma'[err]}
$$

$$
(14) \quad \frac{a \vdash_\sigma \textbf{\textit{DOES}}\{\textbf{\textit{CALL IMPL}}\,\text{ReconfigurationForNewAsteroid}\} \xrightarrow{Action(\text{ReconfigurationForNewAsteroid})} \sigma' \quad \langle ANTS \rangle \xrightarrow{Action(\text{reconfigureANTS})} \langle ANTS \rangle'}{a \vdash_{\sigma'} \textbf{\textit{TRIGGERS}}\{\text{reconfigurationForNewAsteroidDone}\} \xrightarrow{Event(\text{reconfigurationForNewAsteroidDone})} \sigma''}
$$

$$
(15) \quad \frac{\langle ANTS \rangle \xrightarrow{Action(\text{reconfigureANTS})} \langle ANTS \rangle' \quad a \vdash_\sigma \text{reconfigurationForNewAsteroidDone} \rightarrow \textbf{\textit{true}}}{a \vdash_\sigma \textbf{\textit{ENSURES}}\{\text{reconfigurationForNewAsteroidDone}\} \rightarrow \sigma} \; Err^a = \emptyset
$$

$$
(16) \quad \frac{\langle ANTS \rangle \xrightarrow{Action(\text{reconfigureANTS})} \langle ANTS \rangle' \, a \vdash_\sigma \text{reconfigurationForNewAsteroidDone} \rightarrow \textbf{\textit{false}}}{a \vdash_\sigma \textbf{\textit{ENSURES}}\{\text{reconfigurationForNewAsteroidDone}\} \rightarrow \sigma'[err]} \; Err^a = \emptyset
$$

$$
(17) \quad \frac{ANTS \xrightarrow{Action(\text{reconfigureANTS})} ANTS'}{a \vdash_\sigma \textbf{\textit{ONERR\_TRIGGERS}}\{\text{reconfigurationForNewAsteroidDenied}\} \xrightarrow{Event(\text{reconfigurationForNewAsteroidDenied})} \sigma'} \; Err^a \neq \emptyset
$$

where a is the tier environment exposed by the *reconfigureANTS* action and Err^a is the finite set of errors produced by that action in a single performance of the $Action(\text{reconfigureANTS})$ transition operation. In addition, in rules 10 through 17 we use transition operations $Action(\dots)$ and $Event(\dots)$ to denote state transitions that occur during the evaluation of the action tier clauses. Moreover, we use the abstract function $perform(a)$ (see rules 10 and 11) to denote *continuation* of the *reconfigureANTS* action.

5.4 Self-healing

Figure 3 presents a partial specification of the self-healing policy for ANTS. In our approach, we assume that each worker sends, on a regular basis, heartbeat messages to the ruler [25]. The latter uses these messages to determine when a worker is not able to continue its operation, due to a crash or malfunction in its communication device or instrument. The specification snippet shows only fluents and mappings forming the

```
AE ANT_Worker {
    AESELF_MANAGEMENT {
        SELF_HEALING {
            FLUENT inCollision {
                INITIATED_BY { EVENTS.collisionHappen } TERMINATED_BY { EVENTS.instrumentChecked } }
            FLUENT inInstrumentBroken {
                INITIATED_BY { EVENTS.instrumentBroken } TERMINATED_BY { EVENTS.isMsgInstrumentBrokenSent
} }
            FLUENT inHeartbeatNotification {
                INITIATED_BY { EVENTS.timeToSendHeartbeatMsg } TERMINATED_BY { EVENTS.isMsgHeartbeatSent
} }
            MAPPING { // if collision then check if the instrument is still operational
                CONDITIONS { inCollision } DO_ACTIONS { ACTIONS.checkANTInstrument } }
            MAPPING { // if the instrument is broken then notify the group leader
                CONDITIONS { inInstrumentBroken } DO_ACTIONS { ACTIONS.notifyForBrokenInstrument } }
            MAPPING { // time to send a heartbeat message has come
                CONDITIONS { inHeartbeatNotification } DO_ACTIONS { ACTIONS.notifyForHeartbeat } }
        }
    }
    ....
    ACTIONS {
        ACTION IMPL checkInstrument { RETURNS { BOOLEAN } TRIGGERS { EVENTS.instrumentChecked } }
        ACTION checkANTInstrument {
            GUARDS { AESELF_MANAGEMENT.SELF_HEALING.inCollision }
            ENSURES { EVENTS.instrumentChecked }
            VARS { BOOLEAN canOperate }
            DOES { canOperate = CALL ACTIONS.checkInstrument }
            TRIGGERS { IF (not canOperate) THEN EVENTS.instrumentBroken END }
            ONERR_TRIGGERS { IF (not canOperate) THEN EVENTS.instrumentBroken END }
        }
    ....
    }
    ....
    EVENTS {
        EVENT collisionHappen {
            GUARDS { not METRICS.distanceToNearestObject }
            ACTIVATION { CHANGED { METRICS.distanceToNearestObject } } }
        EVENT timeToSendHeartbeatMsg { ACTIVATION { PERIOD { 1 min } } }
    }
    ....
    METRICS {
        METRIC distanceToNearestObject {
            METRIC_TYPE { RESOURCE }
            METRIC_SOURCE { AEIP.MANAGED_ELEMENTS.worker.getDistanceToNearestObject }
            THRESHOLD_CLASS { DECIMAL [0.001 ~ ) } }
    }// METRICS
} // ANT_Worker
```

Fig. 3. ASSL specification: self-healing

specification for the self-healing policy for an ANTS Worker. Here, the key features are:

- an *inCollision* fluent that takes place when the worker crashes into an asteroid or into another spacecraft, but it is still able to perform self-checking operations;
- an *inInstrumentBroken* fluent that takes place when the self-checking operation reports that the instrument is not operational anymore;
- an *inHeartbeatNotification* fluent that is initiated on a regular basis by a timed event to send the *heartbeat* message to the ruler;
- a *checkANTInstrument* action that performs operational checking on the carried instrument.
- a *distanceToNearestObject* metric that measures the distance to the nearest object in space (not presented here).
- a *collisionHappened* event prompted by the *distanceToNearestObject* metric when the latter changes its value and the same does not satisfy the metric's threshold class.

Operational Behavior

A self-management policy is evaluated as "held" if the policy is not in either one of its specified fluents, and as "not held" if there is at least one initiated fluent for that policy (the policy is currently in that fluent) [5, 6]. The **SELF_HEALING** policy (see Fig. 3) has three fluents: *inCollision*, *inInstrumentBroken*, and *inHeartbeatNotification*, i.e., the policy is evaluated as held when the policy is at least in one of these three fluents. Inference rules 18 through 48 enforce a definite strategy for evaluating the **SELF_-HEALING** policy. The policy clauses (fluents and mappings) are evaluated in the context π of the **SELF_HEALING** policy, and the actions, events, and metrics are evaluated in the context of the **ANT_Worker** autonomic element (see Fig. 3). Inference rule 18 presents the operational evaluation of the *timeToSendHeartbeatMsg* timed event initiating the *inHeartbeatNotification* fluent (see rules 22 through 25). Thus,

$$(18) \quad \frac{\sigma \vdash systemclock() \rightarrow t_{actv}}{ev \vdash_\sigma ACTIV\_TIME\{t_{actv}\} \xrightarrow{\quad Event(\text{timeToSendHeartbeatMsg}) \quad} \sigma'}$$

where *ev* is the tier environment exposed by the timed event, *systemclock()* is an abstract function returning the current time in the context σ, t_{actv} is the time at which the timed event is specified to occur.

Inference rules 19 through 21 present the operational evaluation of the *collisionHappened* event, which initiates the *inCollision* fluent (see rules 26–30). Thus,

$$(19) \quad \langle AE \rangle \frac{Metric(\text{distanceToNearestObject})}{ev \vdash_\sigma GUARDS\{\text{distanceToNearestObject}\} \rightarrow prompt(\text{collisionHappened})} \xrightarrow{} \langle AE \rangle' ev \vdash_\sigma \text{distanceToNearestObject} \rightarrow \textit{true}$$

$$(20) \quad \langle AE \rangle \frac{Metric(\text{distanceToNearestObject})}{ev \vdash_\sigma GUARDS\{\text{distanceToNearestObject}\} \rightarrow \neg prompt(\text{collisionHappened})} \xrightarrow{} \langle AE \rangle' ev \vdash_\sigma \text{distanceToNearestObject} \rightarrow \textit{false}$$

(21)
$$\frac{\langle AE\rangle \xrightarrow{\;Metric(\text{distanceToNearestObject})\;} \langle AE\rangle'}{ev\vdash_\sigma \textbf{\textit{CHANGED}}\{\text{distanceToNearestObject}\}\xrightarrow{Event(\text{collisionHappened})}\sigma'}$$

where *ev* is the tier environment exposed by the *collisionHappen* event. In rules 19 and 20 we use the transition operation *Metric*(distanceToNearestobject) to denote a state transition that occurs when the *distanceToNearestObject* metric changes its value, thus possibly prompting the *collisionHappened* event. Note that by operational semantic definition, an ASSL metric is evaluated as Boolean and is "true" only if the value it holds falls in the range determined by the metric's threshold class [5, 6] (see **THRESHOLD_CLASS** in Fig. 3). Here, rules 19 and 20 evaluate the **GUARDS {...}** clause, which verifies whether that metric is still valid after changing its value.

Inference rules 22 through 25 present the operational evaluation of the *inHeartbeatNotification* fluent together with the **MAPPING {...}** clause mapping that fluent to the *notifyForHeartbeat* action. Thus,

(22)
$$\frac{\langle AE\rangle \xrightarrow{\;Event(\text{timeToSendHeartbeatMsg})\;} \langle AE\rangle'}{f\vdash_{\sigma',\pi'} \textbf{\textit{INITIATED\_BY}}\{\text{timeToSendHeartbeatMsg}\}\xrightarrow{FluentIn(f,\text{timeToSendHeartbeatMsg})}\sigma',\pi}$$

(23)
$$\frac{\langle AE\rangle \xrightarrow{\;Event(\text{msgHeartbeatSent})\;} \langle AE\rangle'\pi\vdash_\sigma \text{inHeartbeatNotification}\rightarrow true}{f\vdash\sigma,\pi\,\textbf{\textit{TERMINATED\_BY}}\{\text{msgHeartbeatSent}\}\xrightarrow{FluentOut(f,\text{msgHeartbeatSent})}\sigma',\pi'}$$

(24)
$$\frac{f\vdash_{\sigma,\pi}\textbf{\textit{INITIATED\_BY}}\{\text{timeToSendHeartbeatMsg}\}\xrightarrow{FluentIn(f,\text{timeToSendHeartbeatMsg})}\sigma',\pi}{map\vdash_{\sigma',\pi'}\textbf{\textit{CONDITIONS}}\{\text{inHeartbeatNotification}\}\xrightarrow{ActionMap(f,\text{notifyForHeartbeat})}\sigma'',\pi''}$$

(25)
$$\frac{map\vdash_{\sigma',\pi'}\textbf{\textit{CONDITIONS}}\{\text{inHeartbeatNotification}\}\xrightarrow{ActionMap(f,\text{notifyForHeartbeat})}\sigma'',\pi''}{map\vdash_{\sigma'',\pi''}\textbf{\textit{DO\_ACTIONS}}\{\text{notifyForHeartbeat}\}\xrightarrow{Action(\text{notifyForHeartbeat})}\sigma''',\pi'''}$$

where *f* is the tier environment exposed by the *inHeartbeatNotification* fluent, π is the tier environment (and context) exposed by the **SELF_HEALING** policy, and *map* is the tier environment exposed by the **MAPPING {...}** clause (see Fig. 3).

Inference rules 26 through 30 present the operational evaluation of the *inCollision* fluent.

(26)
$$\frac{\langle AE\rangle \xrightarrow{\;Event(\text{collisionHappened})\;} \langle AE\rangle'}{f\vdash_{\sigma,\pi}\textbf{\textit{INITIATED\_BY}}\{\text{collisionHappened}\}\xrightarrow{FluentIn(f,\text{collisionHappened})}\sigma',\pi'}$$

(27)
$$\frac{\langle AE\rangle \xrightarrow{\;Event(\text{instrumentChecked})\;} \langle AE\rangle'\pi\vdash_\sigma \text{inCollision}\rightarrow true}{f\vdash_{\sigma,\pi}\textbf{\textit{TERMINATED\_BY}}\{\text{instrumentChecked}\}\xrightarrow{FluentOut(f,\text{instrumentChecked})}\sigma',\pi'}$$

(28)

$$\frac{\langle AE\rangle \xrightarrow{\;Event(\text{cannotCheckInstrument})\;} \langle AE\rangle'\; \pi\vdash_\sigma \text{inCollision} \;\rightarrow\; \boldsymbol{true}}{f\vdash_{\sigma,\pi} \boldsymbol{TERMINATED\_BY}\{\text{cannotCheckInstrument}\} \xrightarrow{\;FluentOut(f,\text{cannotCheckInstrument})\;} \sigma',\pi'}$$

(29)

$$\frac{f\vdash_{\sigma,\pi} \boldsymbol{INITIATED\_BY}\{\text{collisionHappened}\} \xrightarrow{\;FluentIn(f,\text{collisionHappened})\;} \sigma',\pi'}{map\vdash_{\sigma',\pi'} \boldsymbol{CONDITIONS}\{\text{inCollision }\} \xrightarrow{\;ActionMap(f,\text{checkANTInstrument})\;} \sigma'',\pi''}$$

(30)

$$\frac{map\vdash_{\sigma',\pi'} \boldsymbol{CONDITIONS}\{\text{inCollision }\} \xrightarrow{\;ActionMap(f,\text{checkANTInstrument})\;} \sigma'',\pi''}{map\vdash_{\sigma'',\pi''} \boldsymbol{DO\_ACTIONS}\{\text{checkANTInstrument}\} \xrightarrow{\;Action(\text{checkANTInstrument})\;} \sigma''',\pi'''}$$

Inference rules 31 through 34 present the operational evaluation of the *inInstrumentBroken* fluent (f is the tier environment exposed by that fluent).

(31)

$$\frac{\langle AE\rangle \xrightarrow{\;Event(\text{instrumentBroken})\;} \langle AE\rangle'}{f\vdash_{\sigma,\pi} \boldsymbol{INITIATED\_BY}\{\text{instrumentBroken}\} \xrightarrow{\;FluentIn(f,\text{instrumentBroken})\;} \sigma',\pi'}$$

(32)

$$\frac{\langle AE\rangle \xrightarrow{\;Event(\text{msgInstrumentBrokenSent})\;} \langle AE\rangle'\; \pi\vdash_\sigma \text{inInstrumentBroken} \;\rightarrow\; \boldsymbol{true}}{f\vdash_{\sigma,\pi} \boldsymbol{TERMINATED\_BY}\{\text{msgInstrumentBrokenSent}\} \xrightarrow{\;FluentOut(f,\text{msgInstrumentBrokenSent})\;} \sigma',\pi'}$$

(33)

$$\frac{f\vdash_{\sigma,\pi} \boldsymbol{INITIATED\_BY}\{\text{instrumentBroken}\} \xrightarrow{\;FluentIn(f,\text{instrumentBroken})\;} \sigma',\pi'}{map\vdash_{\sigma',\pi'} \boldsymbol{CONDITIONS}\{\text{inInstrumentBroken }\} \xrightarrow{\;ActionMap(f,\text{notifyForBrokenInstrument})\;} \sigma'',\pi''}$$

(34)

$$\frac{map\vdash_{\sigma',\pi'} \boldsymbol{CONDITIONS}\{\text{inInstrumentBroken }\} \xrightarrow{\;ActionMap(f,\text{notifyForBrokenInstrument})\;} \sigma'',\pi''}{map\vdash_{\sigma'',\pi''} \boldsymbol{DO\_ACTIONS}\{\text{notifyForBrokenInstrument}\} \xrightarrow{\;Action(\text{notifyForBrokenInstrument})\;} \sigma''',\pi'''}$$

Note that the *inInstrumentBroken* fluent is initiated by the *instrumentBroken* event (see Rule 31), which is triggered by the *checkANTInstrument* action (see Rule 40).

Inference rules 35 through 44 present the stepwise operational evaluation of the clauses of the *checkANTInstrument* action. Thus,

(35)

$$\frac{\langle AE\rangle \xrightarrow{\;Action(\text{checkANTInstrument})\;} \langle AE\rangle'\, a\vdash_\sigma \text{collisionHappend} \;\rightarrow\; \boldsymbol{true}}{a\vdash_\sigma \boldsymbol{GUARDS}\{\text{collisionHappend}\} \;\rightarrow\; \boldsymbol{perform}(\text{checkANTInstrument})}$$

(36)

$$\frac{\langle AE\rangle \xrightarrow{\;Action(\text{checkANTInstrument})\;} \langle AE\rangle'\, a\vdash_\sigma \text{collisionHappend} \;\rightarrow\; \boldsymbol{false}}{a\vdash_\sigma \boldsymbol{GUARDS}\{\text{collisionHappend}\} \;\rightarrow\; \boldsymbol{perform}(\text{checkANTInstrument})}$$

(37)

$$\frac{\langle AE\rangle \xrightarrow{\;Action(\text{checkANTInstrument})\;} \langle AE\rangle'}{a\vdash_\sigma \boldsymbol{DOES}\{\text{canOperate} = \boldsymbol{CALL}\text{CheckInstrument}\} \xrightarrow{\;Action(\text{checkInstrument})\;} \sigma'}$$

(38)

$$\frac{\langle AE\rangle \xrightarrow{\;Action(\text{checkANTInstrument})\;} \langle AE\rangle'}{a\vdash_\sigma \boldsymbol{DOES}\{\text{canOperate} = \boldsymbol{CALL}\text{ CheckInstrument}\} \xrightarrow{\;\neg Action(\text{checkInstrument})\;} \sigma'[err]}$$

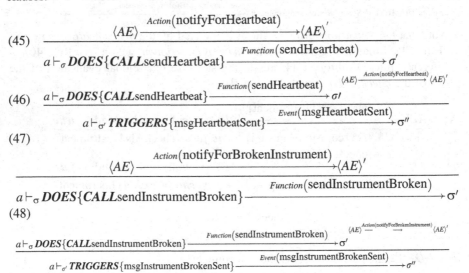

$$(39) \quad \langle AE \rangle \xrightarrow{Action(\text{checkANTInstrument})} \langle AE \rangle' \, {}^{\prime}a \vdash_{\sigma'} \textbf{\textit{DOES}} \{\text{canOperate} = \textbf{\textit{CALL}} \text{ CheckInstrument}\} \xrightarrow{Action(\text{checkInstrument})} \sigma'$$
$$a \vdash_{\sigma'} \textbf{\textit{ENSURES}} \{\text{instrumentChecked}\} \xrightarrow{Event(\text{instrumentChecked})} \sigma''$$

$$(40) \quad \langle AE \rangle \xrightarrow{Action(\text{checkANTInstrument})} \langle AE \rangle' \quad a \vdash_{\sigma'} \textbf{\textit{TRIGGERS}} \{\text{instrumentChecked}\} \xrightarrow{Event(\text{instrumentChecked})} \sigma'' \, a \vdash_{\sigma''} be \to \textbf{\textit{true}}$$
$$a \vdash_{\sigma''} \textbf{\textit{TRIGGERS}} \{IF \, be \, THEN \, \text{instrumentBroken} \, END\} \xrightarrow{Event(\text{instrumentBroken})} \sigma'''$$

$$(41) \quad a \vdash_{\sigma'} \textbf{\textit{TRIGGERS}} \{\text{instrumentChecked}\} \xrightarrow{Event(\text{instrumentChecked})} \sigma'' a \vdash_{\sigma''} be \to \textbf{\textit{false}} \qquad \langle AE \rangle \xrightarrow{Action(\text{checkANTInstrument})} \langle AE \rangle'$$
$$a \vdash_{\sigma''} \textbf{\textit{TRIGGERS}} \{IF \, be \, THEN \, \text{instrumentBroken} \, END\} \to \sigma''$$

$$(42) \quad \langle AE \rangle \xrightarrow{Action(\text{checkANTInstrument})} \langle AE \rangle' a \vdash_{\sigma} \text{instrumentChecked} \to \textbf{\textit{true}}$$
$$a \vdash_{\sigma} \textbf{\textit{ENSURES}} \{\text{instrumentChecked}\} \to \sigma$$

$$(43) \quad \langle AE \rangle \xrightarrow{Action(\text{checkANTInstrument})} \langle AE \rangle' a \vdash_{\sigma} \text{instrumentChecked} \to \textbf{\textit{false}}$$
$$a \vdash_{\sigma} \textbf{\textit{ENSURES}} \{\text{instrumentChecked}\} \to \sigma'[err]$$

$$(44) \quad \frac{\langle AE \rangle \xrightarrow{Action(\text{checkANTInstrument})} \langle AE \rangle'}{a \vdash_{\sigma} \textbf{\textit{ONERR\_TRIGGERS}} \{\text{cannotCheckInstrument}\} \xrightarrow{Event(\text{cannotCheckInstrument})} \sigma'} Err^a \neq \emptyset$$

where a is the tier environment exposed by the *checkANTInstrument* action and *be* states for a Boolean expression (evaluated in a single step). In addition, Err^a and *perform(a)* have the same meaning as in Sect. 5.3.1, but are addressed to the *checkANTInstrument* action.

Inference rules 45 through 46 and rules 47 through 48 present the operational evaluation of *notifyForHeartbeat* and *checkANTInstrument* actions respectively. Note, that 1) the ASSL specification of these actions is not presented in Fig. 3 due to space limitations; 2) we present only the evaluation of their **DOES {...}** and **TRIGGERS {...}** clauses.

$$(45) \quad \frac{\langle AE \rangle \xrightarrow{Action(\text{notifyForHeartbeat})} \langle AE \rangle'}{a \vdash_{\sigma} \textbf{\textit{DOES}} \{\textbf{\textit{CALL}}\text{sendHeartbeat}\} \xrightarrow{Function(\text{sendHeartbeat})} \sigma'}$$

$$(46) \quad a \vdash_{\sigma} \textbf{\textit{DOES}} \{\textbf{\textit{CALL}}\text{sendHeartbeat}\} \xrightarrow{Function(\text{sendHeartbeat})} \sigma' \quad \langle AE \rangle \xrightarrow{Action(\text{notifyForHeartbeat})} \langle AE \rangle'$$
$$a \vdash_{\sigma'} \textbf{\textit{TRIGGERS}} \{\text{msgHeartbeatSent}\} \xrightarrow{Event(\text{msgHeartbeatSent})} \sigma''$$

$$(47) \quad \frac{\langle AE \rangle \xrightarrow{Action(\text{notifyForBrokenInstrument})} \langle AE \rangle'}{a \vdash_{\sigma} \textbf{\textit{DOES}} \{\textbf{\textit{CALL}}\text{sendInstrumentBroken}\} \xrightarrow{Function(\text{sendInstrumentBroken})} \sigma'}$$

$$(48) \quad a \vdash_{\sigma} \textbf{\textit{DOES}} \{\textbf{\textit{CALL}}\text{sendInstrumentBroken}\} \xrightarrow{Function(\text{sendInstrumentBroken})} \sigma' \quad \langle AE \rangle \xrightarrow{Action(\text{notifyForBrokenInstrument})} \langle AE \rangle'$$
$$a \vdash_{\sigma'} \textbf{\textit{TRIGGERS}} \{\text{msgInstrumentBrokenSent}\} \xrightarrow{Event(\text{msgInstrumentBrokenSent})} \sigma''$$

Testing the Self-healing Behavior

In this example, we experimented with the Java generated code for the ASSL self-healing specification for ANTS [25]. Note that by default, any Java application generated with the framework generates run-time log records that show important state-transition operations ongoing in the system at runtime. Thus, we can easily trace the behavior of the generated system by following the log records generated by the same. In this test, we generated the Java application for the ASSL self-healing specification model for ANTS, compiled the same with Java 1.6.0, and ran the compiled code. The application ran smoothly with no errors.

First, it started all system threads as it is shown in the following log records. Note that starting all system threads first is a standard running procedure for all Java application skeletons generated with the ASSL framework.

Log Records "Starting System Threads"

```
***************************************************
********************* INIT ALL TIERS *********************
***************************************************

********************* START AS THREADS *********************
***************************************************
 1)   METRIC 'generatedbyassl.as.aes.ant_ruler.metrics.DISTANCETONEARESTOBJECT': started
 2)   EVENT 'generatedbyassl.as.aes.ant_ruler.events.INSTRUMENTLOST': started
 3)   EVENT 'generatedbyassl.as.aes.ant_ruler.events.MSGINSTRUMENTBROKENRECEIVED': started
 4)   EVENT 'generatedbyassl.as.aes.ant_ruler.events.SPACECRAFTCHECKED': started
 5)   EVENT 'generatedbyassl.as.aes.ant_ruler.events.TIMETORECEIVEHEARTBEATMSG': started
 6)   EVENT 'generatedbyassl.as.aes.ant_ruler.events.INSTRUMENTOK': started
 7)   EVENT 'generatedbyassl.as.aes.ant_ruler.events.MSGHEARTBEATRECEIVED': started
 8)   EVENT 'generatedbyassl.as.aes.ant_ruler.events.RECONFIGURATIONDONE': started
 9)   EVENT 'generatedbyassl.as.aes.ant_ruler.events.RECONFIGURATIONFAILED': started
10)   EVENT 'generatedbyassl.as.aes.ant_ruler.events.COLLISIONHAPPEN': started
11)   FLUENT 'generatedbyassl.as.aes.ant_ruler.aeself_management.self_healing.INHEARTBEATNOTIFICATION': started
12)   FLUENT 'generatedbyassl.as.aes.ant_ruler.aeself_management.self_healing.INCOLLISION': started
13)   FLUENT 'generatedbyassl.as.aes.ant_ruler.aeself_management.self_healing.INTEAMRECONFIGURATION': started
14)   FLUENT 'generatedbyassl.as.aes.ant_ruler.aeself_management.self_healing.INCHECKINGWORKERINSTRUMENT': started
15)   POLICY 'generatedbyassl.as.aes.ant_ruler.aeself_management.SELF_HEALING': started
16)   AE 'generatedbyassl.as.aes.ANT_RULER': started

***************************************************
17)   METRIC 'generatedbyassl.as.aes.ant_worker.metrics.DISTANCETONEARESTOBJECT': started
18)   EVENT 'generatedbyassl.as.aes.ant_worker.events.ISMSGHEARTBEATSENT': started
19)   EVENT 'generatedbyassl.as.aes.ant_worker.events.INSTRUMENTCHECKED': started
20)   EVENT 'generatedbyassl.as.aes.ant_worker.events.ISMSGINSTRUMENTBROKENSENT': started
21)   EVENT 'generatedbyassl.as.aes.ant_worker.events.COLLISIONHAPPEN': started
22)   EVENT 'generatedbyassl.as.aes.ant_worker.events.INSTRUMENTBROKEN': started
23)   EVENT 'generatedbyassl.as.aes.ant_worker.events.TIMETOSENDHEARTBEATMSG': started
24)   FLUENT 'generatedbyassl.as.aes.ant_worker.aeself_management.self_healing.INHEARTBEATNOTIFICATION': started
25)   FLUENT 'generatedbyassl.as.aes.ant_worker.aeself_management.self_healing.ININSTRUMENTBROKEN': started
26)   FLUENT 'generatedbyassl.as.aes.ant_worker.aeself_management.self_healing.INCOLLISION': started
27)   POLICY 'generatedbyassl.as.aes.ant_worker.aeself_management.SELF_HEALING': started
28)   AE 'generatedbyassl.as.aes.ANT_WORKER': started

***************************************************
29)   EVENT 'generatedbyassl.as.ants.events.SPACECRAFTLOST': started
30)   EVENT 'generatedbyassl.as.ants.events.EARTHNOTIFIED': started
31)   FLUENT 'generatedbyassl.as.ants.assself_management.self_healing.INLOSINGSPACECRAFT': started
32)   POLICY 'generatedbyassl.as.ants.assself_management.SELF_HEALING': started
33)   AS 'generatedbyassl.as.ANTS': started

***************************************************
**************** AS STARTED SUCCESSFULLY ****************
***************************************************
```

Here, records 1 through to 16 show the ANT_RULER autonomic element startup, records 17 through to 28 show the ANT_WORKER autonomic element startup, and records 29 through to 33 show the last startup steps of the ANTS autonomic system. After starting up all the threads, the system ran in idle mode for 60 s, when the timed event timeToSendHeartbeatMsg occurred. This event is specified in the *ANT_Worker* to run on a regular time basis every 60 s (see below). The occurrence of this event activated the self-healing mechanism as shown in the following log records.

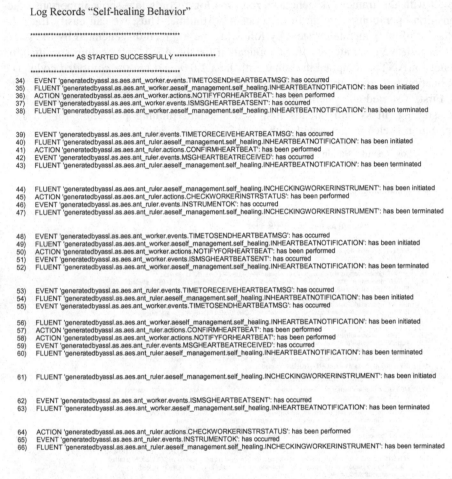

Log Records "Self-healing Behavior"

```
****************************************************************

*************** AS STARTED SUCCESSFULLY ***************

****************************************************************

34)  EVENT 'generatedbyassl.as.aes.ant_worker.events.TIMETOSENDHEARTBEATMSG': has occurred
35)  FLUENT 'generatedbyassl.as.aes.ant_worker.aeself_management.self_healing.INHEARTBEATNOTIFICATION': has been initiated
36)  ACTION 'generatedbyassl.as.aes.ant_worker.actions.NOTIFYFORHEARTBEAT': has been performed
37)  EVENT 'generatedbyassl.as.aes.ant_worker.events.ISMSGHEARTBEATSENT': has occurred
38)  FLUENT 'generatedbyassl.as.aes.ant_worker.aeself_management.self_healing.INHEARTBEATNOTIFICATION': has been terminated

39)  EVENT 'generatedbyassl.as.aes.ant_ruler.events.TIMETORECEIVEHEARTBEATMSG': has occurred
40)  FLUENT 'generatedbyassl.as.aes.ant_ruler.aeself_management.self_healing.INHEARTBEATNOTIFICATION': has been initiated
41)  ACTION 'generatedbyassl.as.aes.ant_ruler.actions.CONFIRMHEARTBEAT': has been performed
42)  EVENT 'generatedbyassl.as.aes.ant_ruler.events.MSGHEARTBEATRECEIVED': has occurred
43)  FLUENT 'generatedbyassl.as.aes.ant_ruler.aeself_management.self_healing.INHEARTBEATNOTIFICATION': has been terminated

44)  FLUENT 'generatedbyassl.as.aes.ant_ruler.aeself_management.self_healing.INCHECKINGWORKERINSTRUMENT': has been initiated
45)  ACTION 'generatedbyassl.as.aes.ant_ruler.actions.CHECKWORKERINSTRSTATUS': has been performed
46)  EVENT 'generatedbyassl.as.aes.ant_ruler.events.INSTRUMENTOK': has occurred
47)  FLUENT 'generatedbyassl.as.aes.ant_ruler.aeself_management.self_healing.INCHECKINGWORKERINSTRUMENT': has been terminated

48)  EVENT 'generatedbyassl.as.aes.ant_worker.events.TIMETOSENDHEARTBEATMSG': has occurred
49)  FLUENT 'generatedbyassl.as.aes.ant_worker.aeself_management.self_healing.INHEARTBEATNOTIFICATION': has been initiated
50)  ACTION 'generatedbyassl.as.aes.ant_worker.actions.NOTIFYFORHEARTBEAT': has been performed
51)  EVENT 'generatedbyassl.as.aes.ant_worker.events.ISMSGHEARTBEATSENT': has occurred
52)  FLUENT 'generatedbyassl.as.aes.ant_worker.aeself_management.self_healing.INHEARTBEATNOTIFICATION': has been terminated

53)  EVENT 'generatedbyassl.as.aes.ant_ruler.events.TIMETORECEIVEHEARTBEATMSG': has occurred
54)  FLUENT 'generatedbyassl.as.aes.ant_ruler.aeself_management.self_healing.INHEARTBEATNOTIFICATION': has been initiated
55)  EVENT 'generatedbyassl.as.aes.ant_worker.events.TIMETOSENDHEARTBEATMSG': has occurred

56)  FLUENT 'generatedbyassl.as.aes.ant_ruler.aeself_management.self_healing.INHEARTBEATNOTIFICATION': has been initiated
57)  ACTION 'generatedbyassl.as.aes.ant_ruler.actions.CONFIRMHEARTBEAT': has been performed
58)  ACTION 'generatedbyassl.as.aes.ant_ruler.actions.NOTIFYFORHEARTBEAT': has been performed
59)  EVENT 'generatedbyassl.as.aes.ant_ruler.events.MSGHEARTBEATRECEIVED': has occurred
60)  FLUENT 'generatedbyassl.as.aes.ant_ruler.aeself_management.self_healing.INHEARTBEATNOTIFICATION': has been terminated

61)  FLUENT 'generatedbyassl.as.aes.ant_ruler.aeself_management.self_healing.INCHECKINGWORKERINSTRUMENT': has been initiated

62)  EVENT 'generatedbyassl.as.aes.ant_worker.events.ISMSGHEARTBEATSENT': has occurred
63)  FLUENT 'generatedbyassl.as.aes.ant_worker.aeself_management.self_healing.INHEARTBEATNOTIFICATION': has been terminated

64)  ACTION 'generatedbyassl.as.aes.ant_ruler.actions.CHECKWORKERINSTRSTATUS': has been performed
65)  EVENT 'generatedbyassl.as.aes.ant_ruler.events.INSTRUMENTOK': has occurred
66)  FLUENT 'generatedbyassl.as.aes.ant_ruler.aeself_management.self_healing.INCHECKINGWORKERINSTRUMENT': has been terminated
```

As we see from the log records, the self-healing behavior correctly followed the specification model. Records 34 through to 38 show the initiation and termination of the INHEARTBEATNOTIFICATION fluent. This resulted in the execution of the NOTIFYFORHEARTBEAT action (see record 36) that sends a heartbeat message to *ANT_Ruler*[1] (see record 37). Records 39 through to 43 show how this message is handled by the *ANT_Ruler*. Records 44 through to 47 show how the INCHECK-INGWORKERINSTRUMENT fluent is handled by the system. This fluent is initiated by the MSGHEARTBEATRECEIVED event. Next the CHECKWORKERINSTR-STATUS action is performed (see record 45), which resulted into the

---

[1] The ASSL specification of ANT_Ruler is not presented here. The interested reader is advised to refer to [25].

INSTRUMENTOK event (see record 46). The latter terminated the INCHECK-INGWORKERINSTRUMENT fluent (see record 47). Records 48 through to 66 show that the system continued repeating the steps shown in records 34 though to 47. This is because the policy-triggering events are periodic timed events and the system did not encounter any problems while performing the executed actions, which could possibly branch the program execution.

This experiment demonstrated that the generated code had correctly followed the specified self-healing policy by reacting to the occurring self-healing events and, thus, providing appropriate self-healing behavior.

6 Formal Verification with ASSL

Due to the synthesis approach of automatic code generation, ASSL guarantees consistency between a specification and the corresponding implementation. Moreover, the framework provides mechanisms for formal verification of the ASSL specifications.

6.1 Consistency Checking

The ASSL Consistency Checker (see Fig. 3) is a framework mechanism for verifying ASSL specifications by performing exhaustive traversing. In general, the Consistency Checker performs two kinds of consistency-checking operations: (1) light - checks for type consistency, ambiguous definitions, etc.; and (2) heavy - checks whether the specification model conforms to special correctness properties. The ASSL correctness properties are special ASSL semantic definitions [5, 6] defining tier-specific rules that make it possible to reason about the properties of the specifications created with ASSL. They are expressed in First-Order Linear Temporal Logic (FOLTL)[2] [29], which allows for formalization of rules related to system evolution over time. An example of a semantic rule defined for the AS/AE *Self-management Policies Tier* (see Table 1) is related to policy initiation [5, 6]:

> *"Every policy is triggered by a finite non-empty set of fluents, and performs actions associated with these fluents".*

$$\forall \pi \in \Pi \bullet ((\mathcal{F} \neq \emptyset \land A \neq \emptyset) \Rightarrow (\forall f \in \mathcal{F} \bullet \exists a \in A \bullet (trigger(f, \pi) \Rightarrow perform(a))))$$

where:

- Π is the universe of self-management policies in the AS;
- $\mathcal{F}$ is a finite set of fluents specified by the policy π;
- A is a finite set of actions mapped to the fluents specified by the policy π.

---

[2] In general, FOLTL can be seen as a quantified version of linear temporal logic. FOLTL is obtained by taking propositional linear temporal logic and adding a first order language to it.

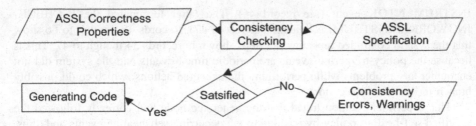

Fig. 4. Consistency checking with ASSL

It is important to mention that the consistency checking mechanism generates *consistency errors* and *warnings* (see Fig. 4). Warnings are specific situations, where the specification does not contradict the correctness properties, but rather introduces uncertainty as to how the code generator will handle it.

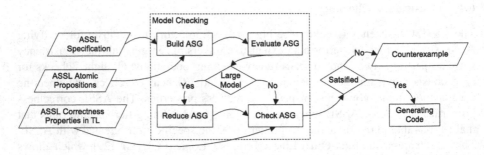

Fig. 5. Model checking with ASSL

6.2 Model Checking

Although the ASSL Consistency Checker tool takes care of syntax and consistency errors, it still cannot handle logical errors and thus, cannot assert safety (e.g., freedom from deadlock) or liveness properties. Therefore, to ensure the correctness of the ASSL specifications, and that of the generated ASs, at the time of writing, there was ongoing research on model checking with ASSL:

- The main trend influencing this research is on a *model-checking mechanism* that takes an ASSL specification as input and produces as output a *finite state-transition system* (called ASSL State Graph (ASG) or state machine) such that a specific correctness property in question is satisfied if and only if the original ASSL specification satisfies that property [30].
- Another research direction is towards mapping ASSL specifications to special service logic graphs, which support the so-called reverse model checking [31].

Figure 5 depicts the first approach to model checking in ASSL. As shown, the Model Checker tool builds the ASG for the AS in question by using its ASSL specification to derive the system states and associates with each derived state special atomic propositions (defined in FOLTL) true in that state [30].

The notion of state in ASSL is related to tiers. The *ASSL Operational Semantics* (see Sect. 4) considers a state-transition model where tier instances can be in different *tier states*. Formally, an ASG is presented as a tuple $(\mathbf{S}; \mathbf{Op}; \mathbf{R}; \mathbf{S}_0; \mathbf{AP}; \mathbf{L})$ [30] where: $\mathbf{S}$ is the set of all possible ASSL tier states; $\mathbf{Op}$ is the set of special ASSL state-transition operations (see Sect. 4.1); $\mathbf{R} \subseteq \mathbf{S} \times \mathbf{Op} \times \mathbf{S}$ are the possible transitions; $\mathbf{S}_0 \subseteq \mathbf{S}$ is a set of initial tier states; $\mathbf{AP}$ is a set of atomic propositions; $\mathbf{L} : \mathbf{S} \rightarrow 2^{\mathbf{AP}}$ is a labeling function relating a set $\mathbf{L(s)} \in 2^{\mathbf{AP}}$ of atomic propositions to any state $\mathbf{s}$, i.e., a set of atomic propositions that hold in that state. The ASSL model-checking mechanism uses *correctness properties* (see Sect. 6.1) to check if these are held over the system's $\mathbf{ASG}$ by matching for each state the correctness properties with the atomic propositions $\mathbf{AP}$. This helps the ASSL framework trace the execution state paths in ASG and produce counterexamples of such paths that lead to violation of the correctness properties. Moreover, the so-called state explosion problem [29] is considered when the size of the ASG must be reduced in order to perform efficient model checking [30].

7 Summary

This article has presented the formalism of ASSL (Autonomic System Specification Language) in terms of notation and operational semantics. ASSL is a domain-specific formal approach providing both formalism and tool support that help developers implement autonomic systems. It has been successfully used to develop prototype models for a variety of systems incorporating AC features and proven to be a valuable approach to problem formation, modeling, verification and implementation of autonomic systems. With ASSL, the formal specifications are automatically verified for consistency flaws and the provided synthesis approach of automatic code generation, guarantees consistency between a specification and the corresponding implementation. Moreover, to enhance the software verification capabilities of the framework, a model checking mechanism is under development.

ASSL implies a complex multi-tier hierarchy of *specification constructs* categorized as ASSL *tiers*, *sub-tiers* and *clauses*. Both *structural* and *functional relationships* form the semantic relations between the ASSL specification constructs. Whereas the ASSL multi-tier specification model imposes the structural relationships between tiers, sub-tiers and clauses, the ASSL operational semantics forms the functional relationships of the same. Conceptually, the ASSL operational semantics is driven by special state-transition operations and tier states. The operational evaluation of ASSL specifications is a stepwise evaluation of the specified ASSL tiers, sub-tiers and clauses, which are evaluated as state transition models where state-transition operations cause a current state to evolve to a new one.

Specifying with ASSL requires a good understanding of the ASSL formalism. This article tackles this problem by introducing the ASSL formalism from both structural and operational perspectives. In addition, to demonstrate the theoretical concepts and flavor of the ASSL formalism, case study examples have presented ASSL specifications and their operational evaluation.

In conclusion, it should be noted that ASSL provides the IT community with an extremely needed and powerful framework for development of autonomic systems. Overall, ASSL is sufficiently generic and adaptable to accommodate most of the AC development aspects.

Acknowledgement. This work was supported, in part, by Science Foundation Ireland grant 13/RC/2094 and co-funded under the European Regional Development Fund through the Southern & Eastern Regional Operational Programme to Lero - the Irish Software Research Centre (www.lero.ie).

References

1. Horn, P.: Autonomic computing: IBM's perspective on the state of information technology, Technical report, IBM T. J. Watson Laboratory, 15 October 2001
2. IBM Corporation: An architectural blueprint for autonomic computing, white paper, Fourth edition, IBM Corporation (2006)
3. Kephart, J.O., Chess, D.M.: The vision of autonomic computing. IEEE Comput. **36**(1), 41–50 (2003)
4. Murch, R.: Autonomic Computing: On Demand Series. IBM Press, Prentice Hall (2004)
5. Vassev, E.: Towards a framework for specification and code generation of autonomic systems, Ph.D. thesis, Department of Computer Science and Software Engineering, Concordia University, Montreal, Canada, November 2008
6. Vassev, E.: ASSL: autonomic system specification language - a framework for specification and code generation of autonomic systems, LAP Lambert Academic Publishing, Germany, November 2009
7. Vassev, E., Hinchey, M.: Modeling the image-processing behavior of the NASA Voyager mission with ASSL. In: Proceedings of the 3rd IEEE International Conference on Space Mission Challenges for Information Technology (SMC-IT 2009), pp. 246–253 IEEE Computer Society (2009)
8. Vassev, E., Hinchey, M., Paquet, J.: Towards an ASSL specification model for NASA swarm-based exploration missions. In: Proceedings of the 23rd Annual ACM Symposium on Applied Computing (SAC 2008) - AC Track, pp. 1652–1657. ACM (2008)
9. Vassev, E., Mokhov, S.A.: Towards autonomic specification of distributed MARF with ASSL: self-healing. In: Lee, R., Ormandjieva, O., Abran, A., Constantinides, C. (eds.) Software Engineering Research, Management and Applications 2010. Studies in Computational Intelligence, vol. 296, pp. 1–15. Springer, Heidelberg (2010). https://doi.org/10.1007/978-3-642-13273-5_1
10. Vassev, E., Hinchey, M., Nixon, P.: Prototyping home automation wireless sensor networks with ASSL. In: Proceedings of the 7th IEEE International Conference on Autonomic Computing and Communications (ICAC2010). IEEE Computer Society (2010 to appear)
11. Srivas, M., Miller, S.: Formal verification of the AAMP5 microprocessor: a case study in the industrial use of formal methods. In: Proceedings of the Workshop on Industrial-Strength Formal Specification Techniques (WIFT 1995), pp. 2–6. IEEE Computer Society (1995)
12. National Aeronautics and Space Administration: Formal Methods Specification and Analysis Guidebook for the Verification of Software and Computer Systems, I: Planning and Technology Insertion. NASA, Washington, DC (1998)

13. Kowalsky, R., Sergot, M.: A logic-based calculus of events. New Gener. Comput. **4**(1), 67–95 (1986)
14. IBM Corporation. Defining service-level objectives, Tivoli Software. IBM Tivoli. http:// publib.boulder.ibm.com/tividd/td/TDS390/SH19-6818-08/en_US/HTML/DRLM9mst27. htm. Accessed 19 Aug 2009
15. IBM Corporation: Policy Management for Autonomic Computing - Version 1.2, Tutorial. IBM Tivoli (2005)
16. The International Engineering Consortium, Specification and Description Language (SDL), Web ProForum Tutorials. http://www.iec.org. Accessed 2 Feb 2009
17. Cheng, S.W., Garlan, D., Schmerl, B.: Architecture-based self-adaptation in the presence of multiple objectives. In: Proceedings of ICSE 2006 Workshop on Software Engineering for Adaptive and Self-Managing Systems (SEAMS 2006), China (2006)
18. Read, D.: Utility theory from Jeremy Bentham to Daniel Kahneman, Working Paper No: LSEOR 04-64, Department of Operational Research, London School of Economics, London (2004)
19. Leavens, G.T., Cheon, Y.: Design by contract with JML, Technical report, Formal Systems Laboratory (FSL) at UIUC (2006)
20. Banatre, J.P., Fradet, P., Radenac, Y.: Programming self-organizing systems with the higher-order chemical language. Int. J. Unconv. Comput. **3**(3), 161–177 (2007)
21. Andrei, O., Kirchner, H.: A higher-order graph calculus for autonomic computing. In: Lipshteyn, M., Levit, Vadim E., McConnell, Ross M. (eds.) Graph Theory, Computational Intelligence and Thought. LNCS, vol. 5420, pp. 15–26. Springer, Heidelberg (2009). https:// doi.org/10.1007/978-3-642-02029-2_2
22. Corradini, A., Montanari, U., Rossi, F., Ehrig, H., Heckel, R., Lowe, M.: Algebraic approaches to graph transformation - Part I: basic concepts and double pushout approach. In: Rozenberg, G. (ed.) Handbook of Graph Grammars and Computing by Graph Transformations. Foundations, vol. 1, pp. 163–246. World Scientific, Singapore (1997)
23. Knuth, D.E.: Backus normal form vs. Backus Naur form. Commun. ACM **7**(12), 735–773 (1964)
24. Truszkowski, W., Hinchey, M., Rash, J., Rouff, C.: NASA's swarm missions: the challenge of building autonomous software. IT Prof. **6**(5), 47–52 (2004)
25. Vassev, E., Hinchey, M.: ASSL specification and code generation of self-healing behavior for NASA swarm-based systems. In: Proceedings of the 6th IEEE International Workshop on Engineering of Autonomic and Autonomous Systems (EASe 2009), pp. 77–86. IEEE Computer Society (2009)
26. Vassev, E., Hinchey, M., Paquet, J.: A self-scheduling model for NASA swarm-based exploration missions using ASSL. In: Proceedings of the 5th IEEE International Workshop on Engineering of Autonomic and Autonomous Systems (EASe 2008), pp. 54–64. IEEE Computer Society (2008)
27. Vassev, E., Hinchey, M.: ASSL specification of emergent self-adapting for NASA swarm-based exploration missions. In: Proceedings of the 2nd IEEE International Conference on Self-Adaptive and Self-Organizing Systems Workshops (SASOW 2008), pp. 13–18. IEEE Computer Society (2008)
28. Plotkin, G.D.: A structural approach to operational semantics, Report DAIMI FN-19, Computer Science Department, Aarhus University, Aarhus, Denmark (1981)
29. Baier, C., Katoen, J.-P.: Principles of Model Checking. MIT Press, Cambridge (2008)

30. Vassev, E, Hinchey, M., Quigley, A: Model checking for autonomic systems specified with ASSL. In: Proceedings of the First NASA Formal Methods Symposium (NFM 2009), pp. 16–25. NASA (2009)
31. Bakera, M., Wagner, C., Margaria, T., Vassev, E., Hinchey, M., Steffen, B.: Component-oriented behavior extraction for autonomic system design. In: Proceedings of the First NASA Formal Methods Symposium (NFM 2009), pp. 66–75. NASA (2009)

The Merits of Compositional Abstraction: A Case Study in Propositional Logic

Michael Huth[✉]

Department of Computing, Imperial College London, London SW7 2AZ, UK
m.huth@imperial.ac.uk

Abstract. We revisit a well-established and old topic in computational logic: algorithms – such as the one by Quine-McCluskey – that convert a formula of propositional logic into a semantically equivalent disjunctive normal form whose clauses are all prime implicants of that formula. This exercise in education is meant to honor Bernhard Steffen, who made important contributions in formal verification and its use of compositional abstraction, and who is a role model in transferring research insights into teaching addressed at students with varying skill levels. The algorithm we propose here is indeed compositional and can teach students about the value of compositional abstractions – making use of simple lattice-theoretic and semantic concepts.

Keywords: Propositional logic · Prime implicant · Compositionality

1 Introduction

Abstraction is a central principle in science and engineering alike. Computer Science and Computer Engineering, as relatively young disciplines, have progressed rapidly and made huge impact in no small part due to the use of abstractions and abstraction layers – e.g. in technology stacks, the development of programming languages and their compilers or the abstraction of signals into binary values.

Abstractions are especially powerful when they may be composed. For example, we would expect that two programs have the same behavior not just in terms of their own code but also when placed into other program contexts. Algebraically, concepts such as congruences and morphisms may be used to great advantage to capture such compositional aspects – drawing from tools of universal algebra, category theory and so forth.

This power of compositional abstraction often comes with a price: the composition of two abstractions of two respective systems may not be as "precise" as a sole and direct abstraction of the composition of those two systems. But in many settings the *curse of dimensionality* applies, meaning that the computation of abstractions directly from the composed systems does not scale in the number of systems. In fact, we may not even be able to build (faithful representations of)

T. Margaria et al. (Eds.): Steffen Festschrift, LNCS 11200, pp. 297–309, 2019.
https://doi.org/10.1007/978-3-030-22348-9_18

such large compositions of systems, prior to their abstraction. Thus, it is worth paying the price of less precision that results from resorting to compositional abstractions.

Mathematical Optimization, Formal Verification, and other research areas have made contributions in that regard, by developing such approaches and by also offering an understanding of how much precision may be lost by them. Bernhard Steffen and his collaborators have made important contributions in that area. For example, in [1] a method is developed that allows for the compositional computation of minimal state-transition systems that capture the semantics of a distributed system. The semantics is an abstraction: it is based on bisimulations but also on interface specifications that express global communication constraints. The correctness of this compositional abstraction is not affected by the choice of such interface specifications whereas its precision very well is.

Looking forward, we may need to draw from all of these research areas – including Mathematical Optimization and Formal Verification – in the development and verification of cyber-physical systems and systems of systems. This seems to be the case given that these types of systems combine physical (continuous mathematics) and logical (discrete mathematics) function. Achieving compositional and abstract reasoning for cyber–physical systems is particularly challenging: in these systems, physical state can influence logical state (as in conventional computers in which signals determine Boolean values), but also logical state can influence physical state – with potential feedback loops between physical and logical actions that may be hard to analyze, abstract or reason about compositionally. This seems to be a challenge for a broader community to tackle.

In this article, however, we will study a much simpler setting of compositional abstraction, a familiar problem in propositional logic: how to convert a formula into a disjunction of clauses that are all prime implicants of that formula. There are known heuristics and precise algorithms for computing such normal forms, for example the precise Quine-McCluskey algorithm [2,3] that solves a set-cover problem at its core.

We chose this particular setting since

- it seems well suited as an accessible educational piece that can teach students the value and potential limitation of compositional abstractions,
- the appreciation of its problem requires minimal background of students,
- it touches on two topics that are dear to Bernhard Steffen's heart in teaching and research: compositional abstraction and mathematical induction, and
- this case study will be integrated in a second volume of a trilogy *Foundations of Advanced Mathematics* (with first volume already published in [4]) – a project led by Bernhard Steffen and joined by the author of this paper.

This paper is meant to be an homage to Bernhard Steffen, whose passion of bringing research problems and solution methods into the undergraduate curriculum we admire.

Outline of Article: In Sect. 2, we present a lattice that forms the value space over which our algorithm for computing prime implicants will compute. Disjunctive normal forms, implicants, and prime implicants are reviewed in Sect. 3. In Sect. 4, we feature our algorithm, its description, and correctness proof. A discussion of how this algorithm could be used in teaching is given in Sect. 5 and the article concludes in Sect. 6.

2   A Lattice for Cartesian Abstraction

Let us define a familiar, finite lattice over which we will compute compositional abstractions that convert formulas into a normal form of prime implicants. We set

$$\mathbf{3} = \{?, \mathsf{t}, \mathsf{f}\} \qquad \mathbf{3}_\top^n = (\prod_{i=1}^n \mathbf{3}) \cup \{\top\} \tag{1}$$

The intuition is that we have formulas that contain up to n atomic Boolean propositions $x_1, \ldots, x_n$ that have truth values either t or f. The value ? denotes for x_i that we do not know (or do not care, depending on the use case) what the truth value of x_i is. For $n = 4$, for example, the element $(?, \mathsf{t}, ?, \mathsf{f})$ denotes that x_2 is true, x_4 is false, and we don't know or don't care about the truth value of x_1 and x_3. The special element $\top$ is there for computational reasons: we may want to merge the information that is represented in two such vectors, but these vectors may be inconsistent and then $\top$ denotes such inconsistency. We define an order $\preceq$ on $\mathbf{3}_\top^n$: for all x and y in $\mathbf{3}_\top^n$, we have $x \preceq y$ iff we have

$$(y = \top) \vee (x = y = \top) \vee ((\{x, y\} \cap \{\top\} = \emptyset) \wedge (\forall 1 \leq i \leq n: x_i \neq ? \Rightarrow x_i = y_i))$$

Let us unpack this definition. It says that we have $x \preceq y$ whenever y equals $\top$, and that $\top \leq y$ implies that y equals $\top$. In the remaining case, we have vectors x and y over $\mathbf{3}^n$ and all coordinates of x that have a truth value t or f force y to have that same truth value in that coordinate. For example, we have $(?, \mathsf{t}, ?, \mathsf{f}) \preceq (\mathsf{f}, \mathsf{t}, ?, \mathsf{f})$ but $(?, \mathsf{t}, ?, \mathsf{f}) \preceq (?, \mathsf{t}, ?, \mathsf{t})$ does not hold. Figure 1 shows the Hasse diagram of $\mathbf{3}_\top^2$.

We need to show that $(\mathbf{3}_\top^n, \preceq)$ is a lattice, for which we use a binary relation over $\mathbf{3}_\top^n \setminus \{\top\}$ that expresses whether two vectors are consistent with each other. For x and y in $\mathbf{3}_\top^n \setminus \{\top\}$, we define that x and y are *consistent with each other*, denoted by $x \uparrow y$, as follows:

$$x \uparrow y \text{ iff } \neg \exists i: (1 \leq i \leq n) \wedge (\{x_i, y_i\} = \{\mathsf{t}, \mathsf{f}\}) \tag{2}$$

In plain English, two vectors x and y are consistent if there is no coordinate at which they have a conflicting truth value, e.g. as in $x_2 = \mathsf{t}$ and $y_2 = \mathsf{f}$. We may generalize this to non-empty subsets X of $\mathbf{3}_\top^n \setminus \{\top\}$ by saying that singleton subsets X are consistent and subsets with more than 1 element are consistent iff all pairs from that set are consistent.

We recall the notion of a complete sup-lattice $(L, \leq)$, where $\leq$ is a partial order such that all subsets $X \subseteq L$ have a *supremum* s in $(L, \leq)$, i.e. where

- $x \leq s$ for all x in X, and
- $s \leq u$ for all u that satisfy $x \leq u$ for all x in X.

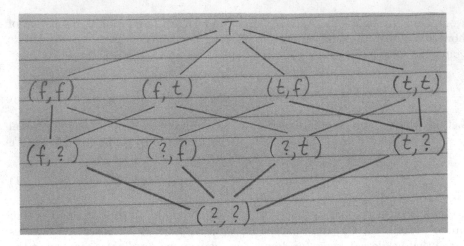

Fig. 1. Hasse diagram of the non-distributive lattice $(\mathbf{3}_\top^2, \preceq)$

In other words, s is an upper bound of X in $(L, \leq)$ and is also the *least* upper bound. We recall that such a complete sup-lattice is also a lattice: for all x and y in L

- their supremum is written $x \sqcup y$ as a binary operation, and
- there exists an element $x \sqcap y$, the *meet* of x and y, such that $x \sqcap y$ is the supremum of all lower bounds of $\{x, y\}$ in $(L, \leq)$.

Please recall that a lower bound of a set X is an element l with $l \leq x$ for all x in X.

We claim that $(\mathbf{3}_\top^n, \preceq)$ is a complete sup-semilattice. Let X be a subset of $\mathbf{3}_\top^n$:

- If X equals $\emptyset$, then $(?, \ldots, ?)$ is the least element in $(\mathbf{3}_\top^n, \preceq)$ which therefore is the supremum of $\emptyset$.
- If $\top$ is in X, then the supremum of X in $(\mathbf{3}_\top^n, \preceq)$ is clearly $\top$.
- If $\top$ is not in the non-empty X, we have two cases:
  - If X is a singleton, then clearly its supremum is its sole element.
  - If X contains at least two elements, we distinguish two cases:
    * If there are x and x' in X such that $x \uparrow x'$ does not hold, then the supremum of X is $\top$.
    * Otherwise, the supremum of X is the vector $(s_1, s_2, \ldots, s_n)$ where each s_i is defined as

$$s_i = \begin{cases} ? & \text{if } x_i = ? \text{ for all } x \text{ in } X \\ \mathsf{t} & \text{if } x_i = \mathsf{t} \text{ for some } x \text{ in } X \\ \mathsf{f} & \text{if } x_i = \mathsf{f} \text{ for some } x \text{ in } X \end{cases} \tag{3}$$

It is an instructive exercise to show that the definitions in the case when X has at least two elements do really render a desired supremum. In particular, this needs to reason that whenever x_i is t for some x in X that there cannot be some x' in X with $x'_i = $ f.

3 Disjunctive Normal Forms of Implicants

We now demonstrate how the lattice $(\mathbf{3}^n_\top, \preceq)$ can be used to compute a Disjunctive Normal Form (DNF) of a formula of propositional logic such that this computation is compositional in the structure of the formula and returns a DNF whose clauses are all minimal in a certain sense formalized below.

Here, we consider formulas ϕ of propositional logic, generated by finitely many atomic propositions $p_1, p_2, \ldots, p_n$. The BNF grammar for such formulas is:

$$\phi ::= p_1 \mid p_2 \mid \cdots \mid p_n \mid \neg\phi \mid \phi \wedge \phi \mid \phi \vee \phi \tag{4}$$

Although this grammar allows us to generate infinitely many formulas, they are all semantically equivalent to finitely many formulas since the grammar has only n atomic propositions. The BNF grammar for the corresponding DNFs is

$$
\begin{aligned}
L &::= p_1 \mid p_2 \mid \cdots \mid p_n \mid \neg p_1 \mid \neg p_2 \mid \cdots \mid \neg p_n \\
C &::= L \mid L \wedge C \\
D &::= C \mid C \vee D
\end{aligned}
\tag{5}
$$

Formulas generated by C are *clauses*. A DNF D is thus a disjunction of one or more clauses. Clause C is an implicant of a formula ϕ if the truth of C implies the truth of ϕ. We define implicants and their minimal versions formally. Recall that a formula is *valid* if it is true under all truth assignments.

Definition 1. *Let ϕ be a formula of propositional logic and C a clause. Then:*

1. *C is an* implicant *of ϕ iff $C \rightarrow \phi$ is valid*
2. *C is a* prime implicant *iff C is an implicant of ϕ and no clause C' obtained from C by removing one or more literals is an implicant of ϕ.*

It is useful to determine prime implicants of a formula ϕ such that the disjunction of these prime implicants is semantically equivalent to ϕ. For example, such a representation of ϕ may have an efficient implementation in hardware. For each formula ϕ, we therefore want to compute a DNF $\mathsf{PI}(\phi)$ such that

- $\mathsf{PI}(\phi)$ is semantically equivalent to ϕ, denoted by $\mathsf{PI}(\phi) \equiv \phi$, and
- all clauses in $\mathsf{PI}(\phi)$ are prime implicants of ϕ.

We also mean to compute such a representation *compositionally* in the structure of formula ϕ, since this will simplify algorithmic design and increase efficiency. But one obstacle we have is that we don't really know how to efficiently compute a DNF for $\neg\phi$ from a DNF for ϕ. We address this by computing, for each ϕ, *two* DNFs: one of prime implicants of ϕ that is semantically equivalent to ϕ, and another one of prime implicants of $\neg\phi$ that is semantically equivalent to $\neg\phi$.

We assume that the atomic propositions $p_1, p_2, \ldots, p_n$ are linearly ordered in this manner, as this allows us to represent the meaning of formulas in the lattice defined above. For an element x in $\mathbf{3}_\top^n \setminus \{\top\}$, the coordinate x_i therefore represents

- that p_i is true if $x_i = 1$
- that p_i is false if $x_i = 0$
- that the truth value of p_i is not known or not important if $x_i = \,?$.

The idea for computing the DNF of prime implicants $\mathsf{PI}(\phi)$ is that it returns a pair of DNFs which we can be represented as a pair (X, Y) where X and Y are finite subsets of $\mathbf{3}_\top^n \setminus \{\top\}$. We formalize this next:

Definition 2. *Let us write $\mathcal{P}$ for the set of all finite subsets of $\mathbf{3}_\top^n \setminus \{\top, (?, \ldots, ?)\}$. We then interpret each such element as a DNF in the above grammar as follows:*

$$\mathsf{DNF}(\emptyset) = p_1 \wedge \neg p_1 \tag{6}$$

$$\mathsf{DNF}(X) = \bigvee_{x \in X} \mathsf{Clause}(x) \qquad (X \neq \emptyset) \tag{7}$$

$$\mathsf{Clause}(x) = \Big(\bigwedge_{i \mid x_i = 1} p_i \Big) \wedge \Big(\bigwedge_{i \mid x_i = 0} \neg p_i \Big) \tag{8}$$

In particular, the empty set is represented by an unsatisfiable DNF and elements x determine their corresponding monomials $\mathsf{Clause}(x)$. Let us next introduce a unary operation on $\mathbf{3}_\top^n \setminus \{\top\}$:

Definition 3. *For all x in $\mathbf{3}_\top^n \setminus \{\top, (?, \ldots, ?)\}$ and i with $1 \leq i \leq n$ and $x_i \neq ?$, let $x_{@i}$ be the unique element z in $\mathbf{3}_\top^n \setminus \{\top\}$ with $z_i = \,?$ and $z_j = x_j$ for all $j \neq i$.*

This unary operation will be used on our algorithm to iteratively shrink implicants till they become prime implicants. We can now present the algorithm $\mathsf{PI}(\phi)$, depicted in Fig. 2, where $\sqcap$ and $\sqcup$ denote the respective lattice operations in $(\mathbf{3}_\top^n, \preceq)$.

4 Compositional Computation of Prime Implicants

The algorithm proceeds by mathematical induction over the structure of the input formula, and it is therefore compositional in that sense. For ϕ a positive literal, the result is immediate and returned: the first coordinate contains only a representation of p_i whereas the second one only represents $\neg p_i$.

For negation, we can simple call the algorithm on the unnegated input and then swap the resulting element of $\mathcal{P} \times \mathcal{P}$.

```
PI(φ) {
  Case {
    φ is pᵢ: return ({(?,...,?,1,?,...,?)},{(?,...,?,0,?,...,?)});
    φ is ¬ψ: return Swap(PI(ψ));
    φ is φ₁∧φ₂: return Conj(PI(φ₁),PI(φ₂));
    φ is φ₁∨φ₂: return PI(¬(¬φ₁∧¬φ₂));
  }
}

Swap((X,Y)) {
  return (Y,X);
}

Conj((X,Y),(U,V)) {
  P = {x⊔u | x∈X,u∈U}\{⊤};
  N = Y∪V;
  repeat {
    P' = P;  N' = N;
    P = Reduce(P',N');
    N = Reduce(N',P');
  } until ((P=P')∧(N=N'))
  return (P,N);
}

Reduce(X,Y) {
  Z = {(x,i)∈X×{1,...,n} | xᵢ≠?};
  Z = {(x,i)∈Z | ∀y∈Y: x@ᵢ⊔y=⊤};
  if (Z≠∅) {
    choose (x,i) from Z;
    R = {x@ᵢ}∪X\{w∈X | x@ᵢ≼w};
    return R;
  }
}
```

Fig. 2. Algorithm PI(ϕ) that returns a pair (X, Y) such that DNF(X) is semantically equivalent to ϕ and contains only prime implicants of ϕ; and DNF(Y) is semantically equivalent to $\neg\phi$ and contains only prime implicants of $\neg\phi$

For ϕ being a disjunction, we first transform that input into its De Morgan dual and call the algorithm on that transformed input.

In the remaining case, ϕ is a conjunction $\phi_1 \wedge \phi_2$. This is the case in which the algorithm does its "heavy lifting", within function Conj$((X, Y), (U, V))$. In that function, the meaning of the conjunction is first captured by the pair (P, N) where P consists of all consistent suprema from elements in X and U, respectively; and N is simply the union of Y and V. Then, a fixed-point iteration commences in which it is tested whether it is possible to change some element x in P to some $x_{@i}$ without changing the meaning of P. Similarly, it is testing whether there is such an element in N that can be changed without changing the meaning of N. When this is neither possible for P nor for N, the pair (P, N) is returned.

We stress that the representation (X, Y) of a pair of formulas $(\phi, \neg\phi)$ allows for a test, very efficient in the size of X and Y, of whether a clause $\mathsf{Clause}(x)$ is a prime implicant of ϕ: this is the case iff x is inconsistent with all elements of Y. We leave the proof of this fact as an easy exercise.

We now show the following claim by well-founded induction on ϕ:

"(**PI**) The call $\mathsf{PI}(\phi)$ returns a pair (X, Y) of finite sets of $\mathbf{3}^n_\top \setminus \{\top\}$ such that $\mathsf{DNF}(X) \equiv \phi$ and all clauses in $\mathsf{DNF}(X)$ are prime implicants of ϕ; and $\mathsf{DNF}(Y) \equiv \neg\phi$ and all clauses in $\mathsf{DNF}(Y)$ are prime implicants of $\neg\phi$."

First, we need to identify the well-founded order: we write d_ϕ, c_ϕ, and n_ϕ for the number of disjunction symbols, conjunction symbols, and negation symbols in formula ϕ. The well-founded order is then the lexicographical one of triples (d_ϕ, c_ϕ, n_ϕ) over $(\mathbb{N}, \leq)$. We write $(d_\psi, c_\psi, n_\psi) \prec (d_\phi, c_\phi, n_\phi)$ to denote that (d_ψ, c_ψ, n_ψ) is below (d_ϕ, c_ϕ, n_ϕ) in that well-founded order.

In proving (PI) for ϕ, we may therefore assume that (PI) holds for all ψ with $(d_\psi, c_\psi, n_\psi) \prec (d_\phi, c_\phi, n_\phi)$. We follow the case analysis of the code for $\mathsf{PI}(\phi)$.

1. Let ϕ be p_i. Then $\mathsf{PI}(\phi)$ returns (X, Y) such that $\mathsf{DNF}(X)$ equals p_i by construction. Clearly, $p_i \equiv p_i$, and p_i is a prime implicant of p_i since we cannot remove p_i from the clause (it would no longer be a clause). Also, $\mathsf{DNF}(Y)$ equals $\neg p_i$ by definition of $\mathsf{Clause}(\cdot)$. Now, $\neg p_i \equiv \neg p_i$ and $\neg p_i$ is a prime implicant of $\neg p_i$ as we cannot move any literal from that clause.

2. Let ϕ be $\neg\psi$. Then $\mathsf{PI}(\phi)$ returns (Y, X) where (X, Y) is the result computed by $\mathsf{PI}(\psi)$. Since ψ has as many disjunction symbols as ϕ, as many conjunction symbols as ϕ, but one less negation symbol than ϕ we have that $(d_\psi, c_\psi, n_\psi) \prec (d_\phi, c_\phi, n_\phi)$. By well founded induction, we know that (PI) holds for ψ. But then $\mathsf{DNF}(X) \equiv \psi$ and all clauses in $\mathsf{DNF}(X)$ are prime implicants of ψ. Now, $\psi \equiv \neg\neg\psi$, which is $\neg\phi$. Therefore, $\mathsf{DNF}(X) \equiv \neg\phi$ and all clauses of $\mathsf{DNF}(X)$ are prime implicants of $\neg\phi$. By well founded induction, we also know that $\mathsf{DNF}(Y) \equiv \neg\psi$, which equals ϕ, and all clauses of $\mathsf{DNF}(Y)$ are prime implicants of $\neg\psi$, i.e. of ϕ.

3. Let ϕ be $\phi_1 \vee \phi_2$. Then $\mathsf{PI}(\phi)$ returns (X, Y), the result of $\mathsf{PI}(\neg(\neg\phi_1 \wedge \neg\phi_2))$. Let us write ψ for $\neg(\neg\phi_1 \wedge \neg\phi_2)$. Then $(d_\psi, c_\psi, n_\psi) \prec (d_\phi, c_\phi, n_\phi)$ follows since ψ has one less disjunction symbol than ϕ. By well-founded induction, we get that $\mathsf{DNF}(X) \equiv \psi \equiv \phi$, and all clauses of $\mathsf{DNF}(X)$ are prime implicants of ψ, i.e. of ϕ as well. Similarly, we get that $\mathsf{DNF}(Y) \equiv \neg\psi \equiv \neg\phi$, and all clauses of $\mathsf{DNF}(Y)$ are prime implicants of $\neg\psi$, i.e. of $\neg\phi$ as well.

4. Let ϕ be $\phi_1 \wedge \phi_2$. It turns out that this is the most complex case, as it also involves reasoning in the lattice $(\mathbf{3}^n_\top, \preceq)$. Note that we have $(d_{\phi_i}, c_{\phi_i}, n_{\phi_i}) \prec (d_\phi, c_\phi, n_\phi)$ for $i = 1, 2$ since ϕ_i removes from ϕ at least one conjunction symbol, and possibly disjunction symbols and negation symbols. Let (X, Y) be the result of $\mathsf{PI}(\phi_1)$ and (U, V) the result of $\mathsf{PI}(\phi_2)$. Then (PI) holds for ϕ_1 with X and Y, and for ϕ_2 for U and V respectively.

Let us first assume that the call $\mathsf{Conj}((X, Y), (U, V))$ terminates (we prove this below). We claim that the body of this function satisfies the following invariant:

"**(CONJ)** We have $\mathsf{DNF}(P) \equiv \mathsf{DNF}(X) \wedge \mathsf{DNF}(U)$ and $\mathsf{DNF}(N) \equiv \mathsf{DNF}(U) \vee \mathsf{DNF}(V)$."

Next, we prove the above claim. Each assignment $\alpha: \{p_1, \ldots, p_n\} \to \{t, f\}$ corresponds to a lattice element $\mathsf{lat}(\alpha)$ where $\mathsf{lat}(\alpha)_i$ equals 0 if $\alpha(p_i) = f$, and $\mathsf{lat}(\alpha)_i$ equals 1 otherwise. Note that $\mathsf{lat}(\alpha)$ is a maximal element in the induced partial order $(\mathbf{3}_\top^n \setminus \{\top\}, \preceq)$. We can now define the lattice elements that make a formula true as

$$\mathsf{Lat}(\phi) = \{\mathsf{lat}(\alpha) \mid \alpha \models \phi\} \tag{9}$$

It easily follows that this representation is faithful in that any two formulas ψ and ν of propositional logic with atomic propositions from $\{p_1, \ldots, p_n\}$ are semantically equivalent iff $\mathsf{Lat}(\psi)$ equals $\mathsf{Lat}(\nu)$.

To show that $\mathsf{DNF}(P) \equiv \phi_1 \wedge \phi_2$, it therefore suffices to show that $\mathsf{Lat}(\mathsf{DNF}(P))$ equals $\mathsf{Lat}(\mathsf{DNF}(X) \wedge \mathsf{DNF}(U))$:

- Let $\mathsf{lat}(\alpha)$ be in $\mathsf{Lat}(\mathsf{DNF}(P))$. There is some x in X and u in U such that $\alpha \models \mathsf{Clause}(x \sqcup u)$. From this, we infer $\alpha \models \mathsf{Clause}(x)$ and $\alpha \models \mathsf{Clause}(u)$, which imply $\alpha \models \phi_1 \wedge \phi_2$, and so $\mathsf{lat}(\alpha)$ is in $\mathsf{Lat}(\phi_1 \wedge \phi_2)$.
- Let $\mathsf{lat}(\beta)$ be in $\mathsf{Lat}(\phi_1 \wedge \phi_2)$. Then $\beta \models \phi_1 \wedge \phi_2$, and so $\beta \models \phi_i$ for $i = 1, 2$. But then $\mathsf{lat}(\beta)$ is in $\mathsf{Lat}(\mathsf{DNF}(X))$ since $\mathsf{DNF}(X) \equiv \phi_1$. This means there is some x in X with $x \preceq \mathsf{lat}(\beta)$. In a similar manner, we reason that there is some u in U with $u \preceq \mathsf{lat}(\beta)$ since $\mathsf{DNF}(U) \equiv \phi_2$. But then $\mathsf{lat}(\beta)$ is an upper bound of x and u and so $x \sqcup u$ exists and is in P. Thus, $\mathsf{lat}(\beta)$ is in $\mathsf{Lat}(\mathsf{DNF}(P))$.

Now consider $\neg(\phi_1 \wedge \phi_2)$. We need to show that $\mathsf{DNF}(Y \cup V) \equiv \neg(\phi_1 \wedge \phi_2)$. It suffices to show $\mathsf{Lat}(\mathsf{DNF}(Y \cup V)) = \mathsf{Lat}(\neg(\phi_1 \wedge \phi_2))$:

- Let $\mathsf{lat}(\alpha)$ be in $\mathsf{Lat}(\neg(\phi_1 \wedge \phi_2))$. Then $\alpha \models \neg(\phi_1 \wedge \phi_2)$. Thus, there is an i in $\{1, 2\}$ such that $\alpha \models \neg\phi_i$. Without loss of generality, let i be 2. So $\mathsf{lat}(\alpha)$ is in $\mathsf{Lat}(\neg\phi_2)$, which equals $\mathsf{Lat}(\mathsf{DNF}(V))$ since $\mathsf{DNF}(V) \equiv \neg\phi_2$ by well-founded induction. But $\mathsf{Lat}(\mathsf{DNF}(V))$ is a subset of $\mathsf{Lat}(\mathsf{DNF}(Y \cup V))$.
- Let $\mathsf{lat}(\beta)$ be in $\mathsf{Lat}(\mathsf{DNF}(Y \cup V))$. Then $\beta \models \mathsf{DNF}(Y \cup V)$. Thus, there is some z in $Y \cup V$ such that $\beta \models \mathsf{Clause}(z)$. Without loss of generality, z is in Y. Then $\beta \models \neg\phi_1$ since $\mathsf{DNF}(Y) \equiv \neg\phi_1$ by well-founded induction. This implies $\beta \models \neg(\phi_1 \wedge \phi_2)$, form which we get $\mathsf{lat}(\beta) \in \mathsf{Lat}(\neg(\phi_1 \wedge \phi_2))$.

Finally, let us consider the *repeat*-statement and its assignments to P and N and prove that these assignments preserve the claim. It suffices to show that

"$\mathsf{Lat}(\mathsf{DNF}(P)) = \mathsf{Lat}(\mathsf{DNF}(P'))$ and $\mathsf{Lat}(\mathsf{DNF}(N)) = \mathsf{Lat}(\mathsf{DNF}(N'))$"

is an invariant, i.e. that the meanings of $\mathsf{DNF}(P)$ and $\mathsf{DNF}(N)$ won't change in these iterations. But this is pretty clear. For example, in the assignment to

P the only change is that some x in P is replaced with some $x_{@i}$ where $x_{@i}$ is inconsistent with all elements in N'. This means that $\mathsf{Clause}(x_{@i})$ is an implicant of P, and so the meaning of $\mathsf{DNF}(P)$ won't change if we remove any occurrence of p_i or $\neg p_i$ from $\mathsf{Clause}(x)$ in $\mathsf{DNF}(P)$. Note that we may also remove any elements from P if they are above $x_{@i}$ in the lattice ordering: this has no effect on the meaning of $\mathsf{DNF}(P)$ as $\mathsf{Clause}(x_{@i})$ will be a clause of that DNF. The reasoning for the assignments to N are dual and omitted.

From the above claim and well-founded induction, we have that

$$\mathsf{DNF}(P) \equiv \mathsf{DNF}(X) \wedge \mathsf{DNF}(U) \equiv \phi_1 \wedge \phi_2 = \phi$$
$$\mathsf{DNF}(N) \equiv \mathsf{DNF}(U) \vee \mathsf{DNF}(V) \equiv \neg\phi_1 \vee \neg\phi_2 = \neg(\phi_1 \wedge \phi_2) = \neg\phi$$

Since the final values of pair (P, N) are returned in this call, this proves that case provided we can show that all $\mathsf{Clause}(x)$ with x in P are prime implicants of ϕ, and all $\mathsf{Clause}(y)$ with y in N are prime implicants of $\neg\phi$. But this follows since the *repeat*-statement has terminated: for example, suppose that some $\mathsf{Clause}(x)$ with x in the final set P were not a prime implicant of ϕ. Then there would be some i such that $\mathsf{Clause}(x_{@i})$ is also an implicant of ϕ. But then $x_{@i}$ would be inconsistent with all y in N, and this would trigger another iteration of the *repeat*-statement, a contradiction.

Termination: Let ϕ be any formula. Then the call $\mathsf{PI}(\phi)$ terminates if all its calls $\mathsf{Conj}((X, U), (U, V))$ terminate. As variant for the *repeat*-statement in the body of $\mathsf{Conj}((X, U), (U, V))$, we use

$$v(P, N) = \sum_{x \in P \cup N} |\{i \mid x_i \neq ?\}| \tag{10}$$

It is clear that this is a non-negative natural number, and that each iteration of the *repeat*-statement decreases this variant by 1. This shows termination.

5   Exploring This Algorithm with Students

The algorithm that rendered this compositional abstraction has several variants that can be used to deepen the understanding of lattice theory, algorithmic concepts, and semantic issues. For the latter, e.g., students can learn about the Egli-Milner order. Then they can investigate and confirm that the method $\mathsf{Reduce}(X, Y)$ monotonically decreases the set X or Y with respect to that order, where the underlying partial order is that of the lattice $\mathbf{3}_{\top}^n$. Additional examples of such further understanding are given in Sect. A, as suggested exercises.

Of course, one should also discuss with students that there are formulas for which *any* semantically equivalent DNF yields an exponential blowup in formulas size. This can then also be compared with standard algorithms for converting a formula into DNF. Furthermore, it will be instructive for students to investigate and confirm that the above algorithm (or any of its variants) does not always compute a DNF in which the number of literals or the number of prime implicants for ϕ is the minimal possible one. There are known hardness results for such optimal computations, which could also be put into perspective here. For example, the decision problems for both minimal term size (number of clauses) and minimal literal size of a formula are both NP-complete in the size of the truth table of that formula [5]. Moreover, deciding whether the literal size of a formula is less than or equal to some k is Σ_2^P-complete.

Another aspect worth exploring is that the compositionality of this algorithms allows for *incremental* computations. For example, suppose that $\mathsf{PI}(\phi)$ has already been computed as (X, Y) and formula ϕ gets refined into $\psi = \phi \wedge C$ for some clause C. Then we only need to compute $\mathsf{PI}(C)$ as (U, V) and make one call $\mathsf{Conj}((X, Y), (U, V))$ to compute the output of $\mathsf{PI}(\psi)$.

It would also be of interest to let students experiment with different heuristics may implement our algorithm differently, e.g. by exploiting opportunities for parallelization presented in the choice of the element from Z.

Finally, it may be worth while to discuss the Tseitin encoding and to compare and contrast this with the approach we have presented here. The Tseitin encoding converts a formula ϕ into a *conjunctive* normal form ψ such that ψ and ϕ are equisatisfiable (ϕ is satisfiable iff ψ is satisfiable) but where ψ may contain additional propositional variables. This is a really important encoding for SAT solvers and formal methods that rely on them and, unfortunately, it is not broadly covered in undergraduate teachings of logic in computer science. Students may, e.g., explore how this encoding may be used to compute a DNF that is "equi-valid".

6   Conclusions

It is always worth while to investigate how complex research topics and methods can be presented in accessible and intuitive form to students. Doing this is hard work that requires passion, tenacity, and a feeling for the essence of research problems and solutions in order to be able to distill and render them in a form that a wider student body can appreciate. Bernhard Steffen seems blessed with possessing these qualities, and we hope that he will continue to exercise these skills by doing excellent research and by transferring these research outcomes into teaching in this manner. We send hereby our best wishes to him on the occasion of his sixtieth birthday.

A   Exercises

1. Let (X, Y) be such that $\mathsf{DNF}(X) \equiv \phi$ and $\mathsf{DNF}(Y) \equiv \neg\phi$. Show for all z in $3_{\top}^n \setminus \{\top\}$ that
   (a) $\mathsf{Clause}(z)$ is an implicant of ϕ iff z is inconsistent with all y in Y
   (b) $\mathsf{Clause}(z)$ is an implicant of $\neg\phi$ iff z is inconsistent with all x in X
2. Reconsider the algorithm $\mathsf{PI}(\phi)$ and the definition of $\mathsf{Reduce}(X, Y)$. The latter chose one element of a non-empty set Z to make a reduction. Discuss whether the algorithm $\mathsf{PI}(\phi)$ can be amended to make reductions for more than one or even all elements of set Z, concurrently or sequentially.

```
Reduce'(X, Y) {
    Z = {(x, x') ∈ X × X | x ≠ x', ∀y ∈
    Y: (x ⊓ x') ⊔ y = ⊤};
    if (Z ≠ ∅) {
        choose (x, x') from Z;
        R = {x ⊓ x'} ∪ X \ {w ∈ X | x ⊓ x' ⪯ w};
        return R;
    }
}
```

Fig. 3. Another implementation of function $\mathsf{Reduce}(X, Y)$ where ⊓ is the infimum operation in the lattice

3. Consider a different implementation of $\mathsf{Reduce}(X, Y)$ shown in Fig. 3 and let $\mathsf{PI}'(\phi)$ be the implementation of $\mathsf{PI}(\phi)$ that uses this new version $\mathsf{Reduce}'(X, Y)$ of $\mathsf{Reduce}(X, Y)$ instead.

   (a) Prove that $\mathsf{PI}'(\phi)$ terminates for all formulas ϕ that are legitimate input to $\mathsf{PI}(\phi)$.

   (b) Prove that $\mathsf{PI}'(\phi)$ satisfies the following:

   > **(PI')** The call $\mathsf{PI}(\phi)$ returns a pair (X, Y) of finite setsets of $3^n_\top \setminus \{\top\}$ such that $\mathsf{DNF}(X) \equiv \phi$ and $\mathsf{DNF}(Y) \equiv \neg\phi$."

   (c) Show that (PI') cannot be strengthened to the statement (PI) on page 8, i.e. the DNFs may not only contain prime implicants.

   (d) Consider a variant of $\mathsf{PI}(\phi)$ that uses both $\mathsf{Reduce}(X, Y)$ and $\mathsf{Reduce}'(X, Y)$ so that (PI) on page 8 will be satisfied of this variant. Discuss in which order these two types of reduction may have to be performed to guarantee (PI).

   (e) Let (X, Y) be the output of $\mathsf{PI}(\phi)$ for some formula ϕ. Show that the call to $\mathsf{Reduce}'(X, Y)$ will compute an empty set Z.

4. Consider another implementation of function $\mathsf{Conj}((X, Y), (U, V))$, in which P and N are still computed as in that function but where there is no *repeat* statement for function $\mathsf{Reduce}(X, Y)$. Instead, function $\mathsf{Reduce}(X, Y)$ calls another function $\mathsf{makePrime}(\emptyset, X, Y)$ with header $\mathsf{makePrime}(A, X, Y)$.

   The idea is that $\mathsf{makePrime}(A, X, Y)$ is a tail-recursive function that iteratively goes through each element of X, converts it into a prime implicant of $\mathsf{DNF}(X)$ that is below that x, adds that prime implicant to set A, and removes any elements from X that are above that new prime implicant. The desired output of $\mathsf{Reduce}(X, Y)$ is then the final value of set A.

   (a) Propose such an amended implementation of $\mathsf{Conj}(X, Y)$ and the methods it calls.

   (b) Prove that this still realizes an implementation that satisfies requirement (PI) on page 8.

References

1. Graf, S., Steffen, B., Lüttgen, G.: Compositional minimisation of finitestate systems using interface specifications. Form. Asp. Comput. **8**(5), 607–616 (1996). https://doi.org/10.1007/BF01211911
2. McCluskey, E.J.: Minimization of boolean functions. Bell Labs Tech. J. **35**, 1417–1444 (1956)
3. Quine, W.: The problem of simplifying truth functions. Am. Math. Mon. **59**, 521–531 (1952)
4. Steffen, B., Rüthing, O., Huth, M.: Mathematical Foundations of Advanced Informatics, Volume 1: Inductive Approaches. Springer, Cham (2018). https://doi.org/10.1007/978-3-319-68397-3
5. Umans, C.: The minimum equivalent DNF problem and shortest implicants. In: 39th Annual Symposium on Foundations of Computer Science, FOCS 1998, Palo Alto, California, USA, November 8–11, 1998, pp. 556–563 (1998). https://doi.org/10.1109/SFCS.1998.743506

JConstraints: A Library for Working with Logic Expressions in Java

Falk Howar[1], Fadi Jabbour[2], and Malte Mues[2(✉)]

[1] Dortmund University of Technology and Fraunhofer ISST, Dortmund, Germany
falk.howar@tu-dortmund.de
[2] Dortmund University of Technology, Dortmund, Germany
malte.mues@tu-dortmund.de

Abstract. In this paper we present JCONSTRAINTS, a constraint solver abstraction layer for JAVA. JCONSTRAINTS provides an object representation for logic expressions, unified access to different SMT and interpolation solvers, and useful tools and algorithms for working with logic formulas. The object representation enables implementation of algorithms on constraints by users. For deciding satisfiability of formulas, JCONSTRAINTS translates from its internal object representation to the format expected by constraint solvers or a format suitable for different analysis goals. We demonstrate the capabilities of JCONSTRAINTS by implementing a custom meta decision procedure for floating-point arithmetic that combines an approximating analysis over the reals with a proper floating-point analysis. The performance of the combined analysis is encouraging on a set of benchmarks: overall, a total reduction of time spent for constraint solving by 56% is achieved.

1 Introduction

Many problems in the analysis and formal verification of software can quite naturally be encoded as checking the satisfiability of a formula in some logic. Impressive advances in the past decades on the Boolean satisfiability problem and on satisfiability modulo theories (SMT) have made such encodings a viable approach in many cases. Today, there exists a plethora of tools and libraries that implement decision procedures with different profiles for a multitude of logics or fragments of logics [4].

For users of these decision procedures it is not easy to decide which implementation is particularly well-suited for a concrete analysis goal or problem instance. Moreover, most libraries have idiosyncratic native interfaces, making it hard to exchange one solver by another. The SMT-LIB Standard [3] mitigates this problem by defining a syntax for logic formulas that is supported by many solvers. A textual representation of formulas has some disadvantages, though: Encoded constraints are often specific to a domain: this can include structure of formulas, data types, and logic fragments. It is often beneficial to analyze, pre-process,

© Springer Nature Switzerland AG 2019
T. Margaria et al. (Eds.): Steffen Festschrift, LNCS 11200, pp. 310–325, 2019.
https://doi.org/10.1007/978-3-030-22348-9_19

and simplify constraints before submitting them to a constraint solver—as is, e.g., done by the Green tool, that implements canonization and caching on top of constraint solvers [34].

This paper, dedicated to Bernhard Steffen on the occasion of his 60th birthday, presents JCONSTRAINTS, a JAVA library for working with logic constraints. JCONSTRAINTS provides an object representation for logic expressions, native access to different SAT-, SMT- and interpolation-solvers, as well as useful tools and algorithms for working with logic constraints. The design philosophy behind JCONSTRAINTS is heavily influenced by works of Bernhard Steffen:

- Object representation and programming interface borrow many concepts from the design of domain-specific languages [32]. Logic expressions can be represented at a level that is semantically close to the application domain, allowing, e.g., logic and arithmetic expressions with JAVA language types.
- Analysis of expressions with off-the-shelf constraint solvers is achieved by translating constraints to a representation suitable for analysis by a concrete constraint solver, following the design principle of the electronic tool integration (ETI) platform [24,33].

This enables JCONSTRAINTS to maintain a representation and optimizations of constraints specific to the application domain (e.g., execution paths of Java programs) while utilizing the impressive performance and scalability of modern SMT solvers. It also allows the combination of different logic encodings and decision procedures. We demonstrate this feature by implementing a meta decision procedure, dubbed FEAL, for floating-point arithmetic that combines decision procedures for floating-point arithmetic and reals as back-ends. The performance of the combined analysis is encouraging on a set of benchmarks: overall, a total reduction of time spent for constraint solving by 56% is achieved.

Outline. We provide an overview of JCONSTRAINTS along with some examples of how the library can be used in Sect. 2. Section 3 details the meta decision procedure for floating-point arithmetic. Results from an evaluation on benchmarks from the literature are presented in Sect. 4. We discuss related work in Sect. 5 before concluding in Sect. 6.

2 The JConstraints Library

In this section, we first describe the architecture of JCONSTRAINTS and then give a brief overview of the transformation of expressions into the input language of concrete constraint solvers. We also provide some code examples that illustrate the use of JCONSTRAINTS. The code of JCONSTRAINTS is published under the Apache License (Version 2.0) and is hosted on GitHub.[1] The library was first publicly released in 2015 and is used by a number of projects. We provide a short description of projects that depend on JCONSTRAINTS for constraint representation and solver abstraction at the end of this section.

---

[1] https://github.com/psycopaths/jconstraints.

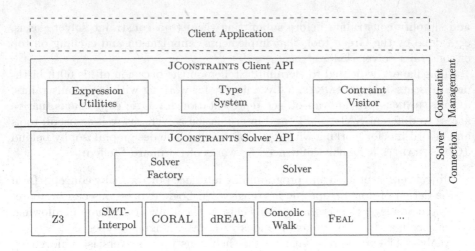

Fig. 1. The JCONSTRAINTS architecture.

Architecture. Figure 1 sketches the architecture of JCONSTRAINTS in detail: The upper part of the figure shows the client-side API, consisting of the basic library that provides an object representation for logic and arithmetic expressions and some basic utilities for working with expression objects (e.g., basic simplification, term replacement, and term evaluation). The object representation can be extended by custom types, and domain-specific algorithms on constraints that can be implemented using the visitor pattern. Utilities for building and reorganizing expressions are provided.

The lower part of the figure shows the solver-side API, consisting of solver factories for different solvers and a unified interface for interacting with different solvers. Plugins encapsulate the actual conversion from the general object representation into a solver input language and the necessary communication with the solver. Each of these plugins implements a solver factory and the unified solver interface for a specific constraint solver. Currently, JCONSTRAINTS provides plugins for Z3 [12], SMTInterpol [8], CORAL [31], dReal [14] and the Concolic Walk algorithm [13]. The work described in Sect. 3 adds FEAL, a meta-solver for floating-point problems.

Extending JCONSTRAINTS by a new solver is very easy: It is sufficient to implement a factory that instantiates a solver (satisfying the unified solver interface). The solver object has to take care of translating to and from the new solver. Changing or selecting solver back-ends in client applications can be done through a configuration value either programmatically or in a configuration file. Due to the separation into constraint representation layer and solver translation, benchmarking decision procedures of different solvers becomes exceptionally easy.

Type System and Evaluation JCONSTRAINTS manages variables as tuples of names and types. Out of the box, all JAVA types are supported. It is possible to define application-specific types. The example in line 1 of Listing 1.1

Listing 1.1. Example of JCONSTRAINTS usage.

```
1   Variable  x = create(BuiltinTypes.SINT32, "x");
2   Constant c5 = create(BuiltinTypes.SINT32, 5);
3
4   Expression<Integer> x_plus5 = plus(x, c5);
5
6   Expression<Boolean> test = eq(x_plus5 , c5);
7
8   Valuation val = new Valuation();
9   val.setValue(x, 0);
10
11  Integer i = x_plus5.evaluate(val);
12  Boolean b = test.evaluate(val);
13
14  Properties conf = new Properties();
15  conf.setProperty("symbolic.dp", "z3");
16  ConstraintSolverFactory factory =
17    new ConstraintSolverFactory(conf);
18  ConstraintSolver solver = factory.createSolver();
19
20  Valuation model = new Valuation();
21  Result r = solver.solve(test, model);
22  assert r == Result.SAT;
```

demonstrates the declaration of a variable of signed integer type with 32 bit width. Similar to the type system of JAVA, the addition of two integers creates a new integer (see line 4 of the same listing). Boolean operations are modeled in an analogous fashion (line 6). Given a value assignment for all variables in an expression (valuation), the evaluation of the expression using JAVA semantics is possible (line 11). Finally, a constraint solver can be instantiated and called for deciding satisfiability of the expression.

Inside the call to the `solve()` method, types of variables are translated into some native type provided by some logic in constraint solver. Similar to the *object-relational impedance mismatch* (e.g. [20,28]) where semantic differences between JAVA's object types and SQL's relational type system occur, the conversion from JAVA types to the corresponding logic type system is not always straightforward. Different plugins may provide different mappings. In general, a mapping from JAVA types to SMT-LIB [3] theories and types is the first step. The result sometimes needs some tailoring for the specific solver. JCONSTRAINTS aims at bridging this gap during SMT solver integration, so that a comparable development experience with using ORM system for database access is established. In case a solver supports the generation of models, the resulting valuation will be extracted for satisfiable expressions and transformed back to JAVA types (line 18 and line 21) of Listing 1.1. This model might be used to verify the solvers verdict using the evaluation functionality discussed above.

Instead of using JCONSTRAINTS, the problem from Listing 1.1 might have been expressed in the SMT-LIB constraint language, which is the standardized description language for SMT problems supported by many SMT-solvers. Listing 1.3 demonstrates how the constraints from Listing 1.1 might be described in the SMT-LIB language. When integrating SMT-LIB into JAVA, the same

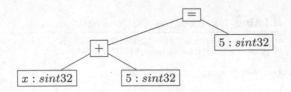

Fig. 2. Object representation of the expression from Listing 1.1.

difficulties arise that have been described in the past for the integration of SQL [28]: The resulting JAVA code consists of String concatenation instead of describing the real problem, which is now in the String content. Moreover, SMT-LIB uses prefix notation, while JAVA and most of handwritten problems are expressed in infix notation. As a consequence, transforming a problem into SMT-LIB format requires a mental shift during programming, mixing these two notation formats. JCONSTRAINTS supports parsing constraints from strings in infix notation avoiding this problem. The constraint from Fig. 2 could be parsed by JCONSTRAINTS from the string $(('x' : sint32 + 5) == 5)$.

Constraint Representation. Constraints are represented as trees of objects in JCONSTRAINTS. Figure 2 sketches the tree created for the expression from Listing 1.1: The expression **test** from line 6 decomposes into an addition on the left side of the expression and a single constant on the right side.

The constraint manipulation API of JCONSTRAINTS provides a set of default constraint visitors for traversing the tree representation. There is, e.g., a duplicating visitor, that duplicates a complete expression while traversing the tree. A visitor for renaming variables can easily be implemented by extending the behavior of the duplicating visitor to rename variables before cloning. Listing 1.2 demonstrates the code required. The method definition in line 5 overwrites the behavior of the duplicating visitor for nodes in the tree that represent variables.

Listing 1.2. Renaming Visitor.

```
1   class RenameVarVisitor extends
2       DuplicatingVisitor<Map<String, String>> {
3
4       @Override
5       public <E> Expression<?> visit(Variable<E> v,
6           Map<String, String> data) {
7           String newName = data.get(v.getName());
8           return Variable.create(v.getType(), newName);
9       }
10
11      public <T> Expression<T> rename(Expression<T> expr,
12          Map<String,String> renaming) {
13          return visit(expr, renaming).requireAs(expr.getType());
14      }
15  }
```

Listing 1.3. Example of SMT-LIB usage.

```
1   ...
2   String smtProblem = "(declare-fun x () Int)\n";
3   smtProblem += "(declare-fun tmp1 () Int)\n";
4   smtProblem += "(assert (= tmp1 (+ x 5)))\n";
5   smtProblem += "(assert (= tmp1 5))\n";
6   smtProblem += "(assert (= x 0))\n";
7   smtProblem += "(check-sat)\n";
8   ...
```

Listing 1.4. Translation to Z3.

```
1   @Override
2   public Expr visit(PropositionalCompound n, Void data) {
3     BoolExpr left = null, right = null;
4     try {
5       left = (BoolExpr)visit(n.getLeft(), null);
6       right = (BoolExpr)visit(n.getRight(), null);
7
8       switch(n.getOperator()) {
9       case AND:
10        return ctx.mkAnd(left, right);
11      case OR:
12        return ctx.mkOr(left, right);
13        ...
14    }
15    catch(Z3Exception ex) {...}
16  }
```

On the basis of these easily extensible visitors many analyses and transformation tasks can be broken down into local operations on tree nodes.

Constraint Solving. As discussed above, different constraint solvers can be used in JCONSTRAINTS as plugins. Translation from JCONSTRAINTS's object representation to solver-specific representations of constraints is based on the visitor pattern, too. Listing 1.4 shows an excerpt of the visitor that translates to Z3. The method in the listing handles object of type PropositionalCompund which is JCONSTRAINTS's expression sub-type for logical compounds (e.g., conjunctions). In this case, when encountering a conjunction in JCONSTRAINTS, a corresponding conjunction is created using Z3's native interface in line 10 of Listing 1.4. The two conjuncts left and right have already corresponding native Z3 representations (data type *BoolExpr*) in line 5 and line 6.

For most of the supported solvers JCONSTRAINTS currently relies on provided JNI interfaces. The dReal solver is an exception: it is connected using a visitor that translates to a subset of the SMT-LIB language.

Applications. JCONSTRAINTS is used in different applications. Historically, it has been developed along with JDART [23].

JDart. JDART is a concolic execution engine for JAVA based on JPF that can be used for generating test cases as well as the symbolic summaries for methods.

The tool executes Java programs with concrete and symbolic values at the same time and records symbolic constraints describing all the decisions along a particular path of the execution. These path constraints are then used to find new paths in the program. Concrete data values for exercising these paths are generated using a constraint solver. JCONSTRAINTS has been the central constraint management library and solver connector in this project.

RaLib. RALIB [7], an extension of LEARNLIB [21] for learning register automata [19], uses JCONSTRAINTS for representing transition guards of extended finite state machines and for finding concrete data values for executing sequences of guarded transitions.

Psyco. The PSYCO tool [16] generates and verifies symbolic behavioral interfaces for software components using a combination of multiple dynamic and static analysis techniques: active automata learning, concolic execution, static code analysis, symbolic search, predicate abstraction, and model-based testing. Especially the concolic execution, symbolic search and predicate abstraction modules depend on JCONSTRAINTS for representing constraints.

3   Feal: Multi-theory Solving for Floats

In this section we describe how JCONSTRAINTS can be used for defining meta-constraint solvers by integrating multiple decision procedures as back-ends. We demonstrate this capability by presenting a meta-analysis for floating-point expressions for which we combine an encoding and analysis over reals with one based on floating-point numbers. As we will show in the next section, the resulting meta-analysis improves the efficiency of dynamic symbolic execution over floating-point computations on a set of standard benchmarks.

Our meta-analysis is based on the observation that solving floating-point constraints after approximating them over reals is often more efficient than solving them over floating-point arithmetic. Such an analysis will find models in many cases. In some cases the models can be spurious (i.e., not be models when translated to floating point representation). Moreover, unsatisfiability verdicts may be spurious, too: e.g., due to rounding behavior the expression $a + b = a \land a \neq 0$ is satisfiable over floating point variables but trivially unsatisfiable over reals. Using an encoding over reals can serve as a fast generator for candidate models and verdicts, which then have to be validated using evaluation or analysis in floating point semantics.

The correctness of candidate models can be checked on the JCONSTRAINTS representation by evaluating obtained models on constraints using the actual JAVA floating-point implementation. In case a solution is correct (i.e., a model in floating-point semantics), we can save a call to a usually much more expensive floating-point decision procedure. This in turn reduces the total solving time and improves the run time of applications. In case a solution does not satisfy the constraints in floating-point arithmetic, we can still resort to a floating-point decision procedure.

On the other hand, if the decision procedure over reals concludes that a set of constraints is not satisfiable, this verdict has to be substantiated by a

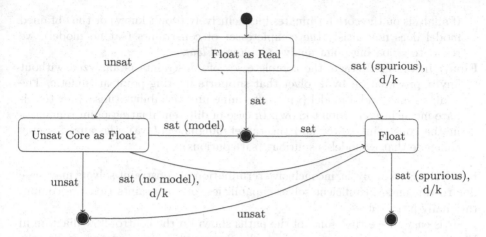

Fig. 3. Control-flow in the meta-analysis that combines solving over reals and solving in floating-point arithmetic.

floating-point decision procedure (cf. above example). We can, however, leverage the unsafisfiable core, i.e., a smallest unsatisfiable subset of the analyzed constraints, as a heuristic for optimizing the floating-point analysis: if this core proves unsatisfiable in floating-point arithmetic, we can circumvent analyzing the (possibly much larger) complete set of constraints in floating-point arithmetic.

The complete control-flow of the combined decision procedure is shown in Fig. 3. It can be divided into three stages:

Real: Floating-point constraints are approximated as constraints over rational numbers. A constraint solver that supports the real arithmetic theory is then used to check whether the resulting constraints are satisfiable. If this is the case, the solver will generate a model that satisfies the constraints over the reals. If the model can be validated over floating-point arithmetic (as described above), the decision procedure terminates with this model (sat). In case the model cannot be validated (spurious sat), or if the real analysis terminates inconclusively (don't know) we resort to a floating-point analysis in stage *Float*. If the constraints are found to be unsatisfiable by the real solver, we proceed to analyze the unsatisfiable core in stage *UnsatCore*.

UnsatCore: If the constraints are found to be unsatisfiable by the real analysis, an unsatisfiable core is obtained from the constraint solver. This core contains a subset of the original constraints, such that the conjunction of the constraints in this subset is still unsatisfiable. Satisfiability of this core is then checked using a floating-point decision procedure. If the core is unsatisfiable in floating-point arithmetic, the result of the first stage is substantiated and the analysis concludes (unsat). In case the core is satisfiable in floating-point arithmetic, a model can be obtained from the constraint solver. If this model of the core can be extended to a model that satisfies the complete set of constraints, this model is returned (sat model) and the analysis terminates.

If analysis on the core terminates inconclusively (don't know) or the obtained model does not satisfy the complete set of constraints (sat no model), we resort to a floating-point analysis in stage *Float*.

Float: In the final stage, the complete set of constraints is analyzed without any approximation by a solver that supports floating-point arithmetic. The analysis may find a model (sat), determine unsatisfiability (unsat), or terminate inconclusively (don't know). In case of different floating-point semantics in the constraint solver and the target language (Java), the analysis may conclude that a model is spurious (sat spurious).

In the sketched analysis, inconclusive termination of constraint solvers may arise due to timeouts, insufficient solver capabilities, or constraints that are computationally intractable.

It is easy to see that some of the paths shown in the control-flow diagram in Fig. 3 are more expensive than using a floating-point decision procedure directly. Hence, instead of using the floating-point analysis only as a last resort, we simply run the multi-step analysis sketched above in parallel with a floating-point analysis in our implementation. Whichever analysis terminates first determines result and analysis time of the meta-analysis.

The domain-specific type system of JCONSTRAINTS and the compilation-based approach to integrating constraint solvers in JCONSTRAINTS makes it easy to implement the necessary sequence of analysis steps and transformations as well as validation of obtained models in Java.

4   Experimental Evaluation

In this section we report the results of an experimental evaluation of the approach discussed in the previous section. We aim at evaluating the effectiveness and efficiency of the presented analysis.

Experimental Setup. We base our evaluation on the analysis of path constraints in the dynamic symbolic analysis framework JDART [23]. We compare the time spent on constraint solving when using our meta-analysis to the time spent when using a floating-point decision procedure. JDART is a suitable driver for our experiments as it uses JCONSTRAINTS internally and allows us to replace only the constraint solver while using identical setups otherwise. For every symbolic path in the analyzed program, we record the time spent for constraint solving and compare the two evaluated approaches. All experiments were performed on a laptop with Intel Core i5 2.3 GHz processor and 8 GB of RAM running macOS 10.13.2. For constrains solving Microsoft Z3 [12] version 4.6.0 was used with a timeout of 10 s per solver invocation.

Table 1. Performance improvement of FEAL over floating-point by constraint solver verdict.

Verdict	Instances [#]	FEAL/ FP per Path [%]	WCT FP [sec]	WCT FEAL [sec]	Optimized Paths [%]
unsat	358.00 (6.71)	72.22 (38.21)	3,843.65 (5,378.10)	1,202.81 (783.17)	55.49 (1.14)
sat	176.60 (4.16)	15.87 (8.82)	549.34 (515.09)	52.17 (17.54)	80.30 (5.85)
d/k	41.00 (1.73)	100.00 (0.00)	766.24 (1,294.46)	766.24 (1,294.46)	0.00 (0.00)
sat(sp.)	15.00 (2.24)	100.00 (0.00)	428.15 (928.08)	428.15 (928.08)	0.00 (0.00)

Selection of Benchmarks. A sample of benchmark functions was selected from multiple sources including open source projects on GitHub and other publications that focus on analysis of floating-point computations in programs [2, 26, 30]. In order to include some safety-critical methods in our analysis, we rewrote some C++ embedded software functions in Java (e.g., from TCAS [23]). Since JDART analyses methods for symbolic method parameters, we use only JAVA methods as benchmarks that contain floating-point computations depending on method parameters. We use a total of 15 benchmark methods.

Since symbolic execution engines for java programs are usually incapable of analyzing native implementation of mathematical functions (e.g., sqrt, sin, etc.), we replaced all calls to elementary mathematical functions in the benchmarks with calls to simpler versions written in Java that can be completely analyzed.

Experimental Results. Since the approach from Sect. 3 is designed to perform better or (in the worst case) only as good as a floating-point analysis, we report improvement (in runtime) over this baseline. We report averages and standard deviations from five runs for each benchmark.

On average, the cumulated wall clock time for all benchmarks was reduced by 56% from 5, 587 s (std. dev. 7, 428) to 2, 449 s (std. dev. 2, 076). For individual paths in programs (i.e., calls to the constraint solver) solving time was reduced by 28% on average (std. dev. 28%) and 57, 65% of paths (with a very low standard deviation of 1, 53%) were solved faster by FEAL than by the floating-point decision procedure.

Table 1 reports number of instances, average improvement over the baseline for individual paths, wall clock times for floating-point analysis and FEAL, as well as the average percentage of paths on which solving could be optimized for different possible verdicts of the decision procedure. Standard deviations are reported in parentheses. As the data shows, we observe improvements for constraint sets that are found satisfiable (84.13% reduction of runtime on average per path and 90.50% reduction of wall clock time) or unsatisfiable (27.78% reduction of runtime on average per path and 68.71% reduction of wall clock time). Together these cases account for 90.51% of analyzed path constraints and 78.62% of required runtime.

Table 2. Performance improvement of FEAL over floating-point by benchmark.

Benchmark	Paths [#]	WCT FP [sec]		WCT FEAL [sec]		Amenable Paths [%]	
generate_star	52.00 (0.00)	2,593.12	(5,648.60)	37.52	(1.67)	88,46	(0,00)
rgb_to_hsl	70.00 (0.00)	934.99	(1,292.98)	840.83	(1,291.55)	44,86	(2,17)
sv_newton	2.00 (0.00)	909.21	(769.34)	896.39	(782.15)	20,00	(44,72)
hsl_to_rgb	127.00 (0.00)	458.29	(929.61)	438.38	(928.48)	67,72	(0,79)
sm_sin	28.00 (2.24)	261.25	(536.32)	17.24	(0.92)	36,78	(5,87)
sv_arctan_Pade_true	12.00 (0.00)	203.79	(168.61)	93.67	(16.48)	56,67	(6,97)
getClosestPointOnSeg	19.00 (0.00)	104.96	(1.96)	25.57	(3.23)	62,11	(2,35)
interpolate_color	4.00 (0.00)	51.42	(1.76)	46.23	(1.52)	25,00	(0,00)
get_x_y	5.00 (0.00)	33.12	(3.35)	26.69	(15.24)	36,00	(35,78)
sv_exp_loop_true	200.20 (2.68)	17.53	(1.17)	11.52	(0.48)	53,51	(3,17)
e_adventure	6.00 (0.00)	11.56	(0.30)	10.01	(0.25)	33,33	(0,00)
sm_exp	38.40 (5.37)	5.13	(0.65)	3.87	(0.49)	32,50	(1,86)
sv_squer_2_var	3.00 (0.00)	2.24	(0.13)	1.34	(0.39)	40,00	(14,91)
sm_rint	10.00 (0.00)	0.59	(0.04)	0.07	(0.03)	98,00	(4,47)
sm_atan	14.00 (0.00)	0.19	(0.01)	0.04	(0.02)	88,57	(9,58)

Table 2 shows a more detailed analysis for individual benchmarks. It can be observed that FEAL is effective for every analyzed method. Performance gains range from 1.41% (for *sv_newton*) to 98.55% (for *generate_star*) reduction in wall clock time. All methods have a significant number of paths on which FEAL outperforms the floating-point analysis. As the reported standard deviations indicate, some paths are not consistently solved more efficiently by FEAL.

Table 3 shows performance improvements on different paths of the control-flow diagram shown in Fig. 3. Unsurprisingly, performance improvements can be observed in cases that only use stages *Real* and *UnsatCore* (79.31% of tree traversals). As the data shows, all control-flow paths are exercised by the benchmarks.

Threats to Validity. Generalizability of the observed performance improvements may be limited by two aspects of our experimental setup. First, our analysis can only show that there exists a potential for improvement for the sampled methods. We cannot estimate how representative our findings are for the set of all methods that contain floating-point computations. A second threat to the validity of the reported findings arises from the fact we replaced all calls to elementary mathematical functions with calls to versions written in JAVA. As a consequence, our analysis does not allow us to draw consequences about analyzing JAVA programs with floating-point computations in general.

5 Related Work

Constraint Libraries. There are several libraries for representing logic constraints and for providing a unified interface to constraint solvers. For JAVA, JavaSMT[2] provides constraint representation and unified access to multiple SMT solvers. The type system of JavaSMT mirrors types of the logics supported by solvers. JCONSTRAINTS, in contrast provides a flexible type system that allows to model types of target domains. For Python, PySMT [15] provides constraint representation and constraint solver abstraction. PySMT provides so-called *portfolio solving* (running multiple constraint solvers in parallel) but not the combination of solvers in more complex patterns.

Table 3. Performance improvement of FEAL over floating-point for stages and verdicts.

Stages	Verdict	Instances [#]	FEAL/ FP WCT [%]
Real	sat	142.60 (14.22)	1.33 (0.70)
Real, UnsatCore	unsat	325.80 (7.98)	56.66 (33.69)
Real, UnsatCore	sat	1.00 (0.00)	100.00 (0.00)
Real, Float	unsat	22.00 (4.47)	100.00 (0.00)
Real, Float	sat	32.00 (10.07)	100.00 (0.00)
Real, Float	d/k	38.20 (4.60)	100.00 (0.00)
Real, Float	sat (spurious)	8.00 (2.24)	100.00 (0.00)
Real, UnsatCore, Float	unsat	10.20 (3.35)	100.00 (0.00)
Real, UnsatCore, Float	sat	1.00 (0.00)	100.00 (0.00)
Real, UnsatCore, Float	d/k	2.80 (6.26)	100.00 (0.00)
Real, UnsatCore, Float	sat (spurious)	7.00 (0.00)	100.00 (0.00)

Analysis of Floating-Point Computations. The verification of floating point operations has a long history. First approaches, such as the one described by Aharoni et al. [1] used a combination of floating point constraints solving engines to solve data constraints on operands of individual instructions to generate test suites. Those suites aimed at the corner cases of floating-point operations for bug discovery. More recent test generators use symbolic execution to cover all possible execution branches and their intervals and use the symbolic execution output as input for the test case generation of the numeric floating point functions. Schumann et al. [29] build such a tool based on the KLEE tool [6] and generated test cases for an open source autopilot[3]. Liew et al. [22] extended KLEE towards a complete symbolic execution engine for floating-point programs based on constraint solving. This was achieved via using an of the shelf SMT solver that supports floating-point reasoning. Another symbolic execution engine

---

[2] https://github.com/sosy-lab/java-smt.
[3] https://github.com/ArduPilot/ardupilot.

for floating point C-programs that bundles various contribution in this area is FPSE first introduced by Botella et al. [5]. Their symbolic execution engine used a solver based on floating point interval propagation that is dedicated for floating point number.

Various abstract interpretation based methods have been proposed for verifying floating-point properties. Many of them focus the precision of the floating-point computations rather than potential run-time errors. Martel [25] introduced a concrete semantic for the propagation of round-off errors throughout the floating-point computations expressed in first order terms. Solving the combination of first order terms allows checking of eventual introduction of round-off errors. Gouboult and Putot implemented the tool FLUCTUAT [17,18,27] which uses abstract semantics and abstract domain for the static analysis of floating-point computations. Their approach is based on domains for bounding the ranges of the floating-point variables. These domains allow to analyze potential round-off errors during the floating-point computations.

Integrated Formal Analysis Methods. Though not directly related to the work we present here at a technical level there is a number of works that propose integration of multiple formal methods with different profiles with the purpose of optimizing effectiveness and efficiency: In context of analyzing software product lines, Damiani et al. present a meta decision procedure that decomposes the analyzed problem and computes results for sub-problems using multiple analysis methods with different profiles [10]. Cousot et. al. [9] combine different abstract domains during abstract interpretation and the work of Darulova and Kuncak [11] combines an exact SMT solver with affine and interval arithmetics.

6   Conclusion

In this paper, dedicated to Bernhard Steffen on the occasion of his 60th birthday, we have presented JCONSTRAINTS, a constraint solver abstraction layer for JAVA. JCONSTRAINTS provides an object representation for logic expressions, unified access to different SMT and interpolation solvers, and useful tools and algorithms for working with logic formulas. The design philosophy behind JCONSTRAINTS is heavily influenced by works of Bernhard Steffen: Object representation and programming interface borrow many concepts from the design of domain-specific languages [32]. Logic expressions can be represented at a level that is semantically close to the application domain, abstracting from the encoding constraint solvers support. Analysis of expressions with off-the-shelf constraint solvers is achieved by translating constraints to a representation suitable for analysis by a concrete constraint solver, following the design principle of the electronic tool integration (ETI) platform [24,33], allowing to generate and analyze views on a problem by translating to different back-ends.

We have demonstrated the capabilities of JCONSTRAINTS by implementing a custom meta decision procedure for floating-point arithmetic that combines an approximating analysis over the reals with a proper floating-point analysis. In a small evaluation in the context of symbolic execution, the meta decision procedure reduces time spent for constraint solving by 56%. As a next step, we plan to implement and evaluate several other meta decision procedures combining solvers with different profiles, e.g., one that does not provide models with one that does searches for models but cannot decide unsatisfiability.

Acknowledgments. JCONSTRAINTS has been developed as part of JDART and several people who worked on JDART have contributed ideas and code to JCONSTRAINTS. Notable contributions to JCONSTRAINTS have been made by Marko Dimjašević, Malte Isberner, and Kasper Luckow.

References

1. Aharoni, M., Asaf, S., Fournier, L., Koifman, A., Nagel, R.: FPgen-a test generation framework for datapath floating-point verification. In: Eighth IEEE International High-Level Design Validation and Test Workshop, 2003, pp. 17–22. IEEE (2003)
2. Bagnara, R., Carlier, M., Gori, R., Gotlieb, A.: Symbolic path-oriented test data generation for floating-point programs. In: 2013 IEEE Sixth International Conference on Software Testing, Verification and Validation (ICST), pp. 1–10. IEEE (2013)
3. Barrett, C., Fontaine, P., Tinelli, C.: The SMT-LIB standard: version 2.6. Technical report, Department of Computer Science, The University of Iowa (2017). www.SMT-LIB.org
4. Barrett, C.W., Sebastiani, R., Seshia, S.A., Tinelli, C.: Satisfiability modulo theories. In: Handbook of Satisfiability, pp. 825–885 (2009)
5. Botella, B., Gotlieb, A., Michel, C.: Symbolic execution of floating-point computations. Softw. Test. Verif. Reliab. **16**(2), 97–121 (2006)
6. Cadar, C., Dunbar, D., Engler, D.R., et al.: KLEE: unassisted and automatic generation of high-coverage tests for complex systems programs. In: OSDI, vol. 8, pp. 209–224 (2008)
7. Cassel, S., Howar, F., Jonsson, B., Steffen, B.: Learning extended finite state machines. In: Giannakopoulou, D., Salaün, G. (eds.) SEFM 2014. LNCS, vol. 8702, pp. 250–264. Springer, Cham (2014). https://doi.org/10.1007/978-3-319-10431-7_18
8. Christ, J., Hoenicke, J., Nutz, A.: SMTInterpol: an interpolating SMT solver. In: Donaldson, A., Parker, D. (eds.) SPIN 2012. LNCS, vol. 7385, pp. 248–254. Springer, Heidelberg (2012). https://doi.org/10.1007/978-3-642-31759-0_19
9. Cousot, P., et al.: Combination of abstractions in the ASTRÉE static analyzer. In: Okada, M., Satoh, I. (eds.) ASIAN 2006. LNCS, vol. 4435, pp. 272–300. Springer, Heidelberg (2007). https://doi.org/10.1007/978-3-540-77505-8_23
10. Damiani, F., Hähnle, R., Lienhardt, M.: Abstraction refinement for the analysis of software product lines. In: Gabmeyer, S., Johnsen, E.B. (eds.) TAP 2017. LNCS, vol. 10375, pp. 3–20. Springer, Cham (2017). https://doi.org/10.1007/978-3-319-61467-0_1
11. Darulova, E., Kuncak, V.: Sound compilation of reals. In: ACM SIGPLAN Notices, vol. 49, pp. 235–248. ACM (2014)
12. de Moura, L., Bjørner, N.: Z3: an efficient SMT solver. In: Ramakrishnan, C.R., Rehof, J. (eds.) TACAS 2008. LNCS, vol. 4963, pp. 337–340. Springer, Heidelberg (2008). https://doi.org/10.1007/978-3-540-78800-3_24

13. Dinges, P., Agha, G.: Solving complex path conditions through heuristic search on induced polytopes. In: Proceedings of the 22nd ACM SIGSOFT Symposium on Foundations of Software Engineering, Hong Kong, 16–21 November 2014. ACM (2014)

14. Gao, S., Kong, S., Clarke, E.M.: dReal: an SMT solver for nonlinear theories over the reals. In: Bonacina, M.P. (ed.) CADE 2013. LNCS (LNAI), vol. 7898, pp. 208–214. Springer, Heidelberg (2013). https://doi.org/10.1007/978-3-642-38574-2_14

15. Gario, M., Micheli, A.: PySMT: a solver-agnostic library for fast prototyping of SMT-based algorithms. In: SMT Workshop 2015 (2015)

16. Giannakopoulou, D., Rakamarić, Z., Raman, V.: Symbolic learning of component interfaces. In: Miné, A., Schmidt, D. (eds.) SAS 2012. LNCS, vol. 7460, pp. 248–264. Springer, Heidelberg (2012). https://doi.org/10.1007/978-3-642-33125-1_18

17. Goubault, E., Putot, S.: Static analysis of numerical algorithms. In: Yi, K. (ed.) SAS 2006. LNCS, vol. 4134, pp. 18–34. Springer, Heidelberg (2006). https://doi.org/10.1007/11823230_3

18. Goubault, E., Putot, S.: Static analysis of finite precision computations. In: Jhala, R., Schmidt, D. (eds.) VMCAI 2011. LNCS, vol. 6538, pp. 232–247. Springer, Heidelberg (2011). https://doi.org/10.1007/978-3-642-18275-4_17

19. Howar, F., Steffen, B., Jonsson, B., Cassel, S.: Inferring canonical register automata. In: Kuncak, V., Rybalchenko, A. (eds.) VMCAI 2012. LNCS, vol. 7148, pp. 251–266. Springer, Heidelberg (2012). https://doi.org/10.1007/978-3-642-27940-9_17

20. Ireland, C., Bowers, D., Newton, M., Waugh, K.: A classification of object-relational impedance mismatch. In: First International Conference on Advances in Databases, Knowledge, and Data Applications, DBKDA 2009, pp. 36–43. IEEE (2009)

21. Isberner, M., Howar, F., Steffen, B.: The open-source LearnLib. In: Kroening, D., Păsăreanu, C.S. (eds.) CAV 2015. LNCS, vol. 9206, pp. 487–495. Springer, Cham (2015). https://doi.org/10.1007/978-3-319-21690-4_32

22. Liew, D., Schemmel, D., Cadar, C., Donaldson, A.F., Zahl, R., Wehrle, K.: Floating-point symbolic execution: a case study in N-version programming. In: 2017 32nd IEEE/ACM International Conference on Automated Software Engineering (ASE), pp. 601–612. IEEE (2017)

23. Luckow, K., et al.: JDart: a dynamic symbolic analysis framework. In: Chechik, M., Raskin, J.-F. (eds.) TACAS 2016. LNCS, vol. 9636, pp. 442–459. Springer, Heidelberg (2016). https://doi.org/10.1007/978-3-662-49674-9_26

24. Margaria, T., Nagel, R., Steffen, B.: Remote integration and coordination of verification tools in JETI. In: 12th IEEE International Conference on the Engineering of Computer-Based Systems (ECBS 2005), Greenbelt, MD, USA, 4–7 April 2005, pp. 431–436 (2005)

25. Martel, M.: Propagation of roundoff errors in finite precision computations: a semantics approach. In: Le Métayer, D. (ed.) ESOP 2002. LNCS, vol. 2305, pp. 194–208. Springer, Heidelberg (2002). https://doi.org/10.1007/3-540-45927-8_14

26. Pasareanu, C., d'Amorim, M., Borges, M., Souza, M.: Coral: solving complex constraints for symbolic pathfinder (2010)

27. Putot, S., Goubault, E., Martel, M.: Static analysis-based validation of floating-point computations. In: Alt, R., Frommer, A., Kearfott, R.B., Luther, W. (eds.) Numerical Software with Result Verification. LNCS, vol. 2991, pp. 306–313. Springer, Heidelberg (2004). https://doi.org/10.1007/978-3-540-24738-8_18

28. Richly, K., Lorenz, M., Oergel, S.: S4J - integrating SQL into Java at compiler-level. In: Dregvaite, G., Damasevicius, R. (eds.) ICIST 2016. CCIS, vol. 639, pp. 300–315. Springer, Cham (2016). https://doi.org/10.1007/978-3-319-46254-7_24

29. Schumann, J., Schneider, S.-A.: Automated testcase generation for numerical support functions in embedded systems. In: Badger, J.M., Rozier, K.Y. (eds.) NFM 2014. LNCS, vol. 8430, pp. 252–257. Springer, Cham (2014). https://doi.org/10.1007/978-3-319-06200-6_20

30. Sherman, E., Dwyer, M.B.: Exploiting domain and program structure to synthesize efficient and precise data flow analyses (t). In: 2015 30th IEEE/ACM International Conference on Automated Software Engineering (ASE), pp. 608–618. IEEE (2015)

31. Souza, M., Borges, M., d'Amorim, M., Păsăreanu, C.S.: CORAL: solving complex constraints for symbolic pathfinder. In: Bobaru, M., Havelund, K., Holzmann, G.J., Joshi, R. (eds.) NFM 2011. LNCS, vol. 6617, pp. 359–374. Springer, Heidelberg (2011). https://doi.org/10.1007/978-3-642-20398-5_26

32. Steffen, B., Gossen, F., Naujokat, S., Margaria, T.: Language-driven engineering: from general purpose to purpose-specific languages. In: Steffen, B., Woeginger, G. (eds.) Computing and Software Science. LNCS, vol. 10000, pp. 311–344 (2019)

33. Steffen, B., Margaria, T., Braun, V.: The electronic tool integration platform: concepts and design. STTT 1(1–2), 9–30 (1997)

34. Visser, W., Geldenhuys, J., Dwyer, M.B.: Green: reducing, reusing and recycling constraints in program analysis. In: 20th ACM SIGSOFT Symposium on the Foundations of Software Engineering (FSE-20), SIGSOFT/FSE 2012, Cary, NC, USA, 11–16 November 2012, p. 58 (2012)

On the Expressiveness of Joining and Splitting

Thomas Given-Wilson$^{(\boxtimes)}$ and Axel Legay

Inria, Rennes, France
t.givenwilson@gmail.com

Abstract. An ongoing theme of the work of Bernhard Steffen has been the bringing together of different components in a coordinated manner and with a unified language. This paper explores this approach applied to process calculi that account for *coordination* of different kinds of workflows. Coordination here extends binary interaction to also account for *joining* of multiple outputs into a single input, and *splitting* from a single output to multiple inputs. The results here formalise which process calculi can and cannot be encoded into one another, and thus which language has the required expressiveness for given workflow properties. The combination of with other features of interaction allows for the representation of many systems and workflows in an appropriate calculus.

1 Introduction

An ongoing theme of the work of Bernhard Steffen has been the bringing together of different components in a functional and coordinated manner [12,14,42,55]. This ranges from early work on unifying models [8,55] to bringing together many components [37], to programming environments that combine components and workflows [14,42]. This theme has as its core finding common languages to express desirable behaviours, and approaches to unify these behaviours and workflows in a single language [8,12,14,37,42,44,55].

This paper explores languages based on process calculi in the style of π-calculus that focus on coordinating workflows and higher-order process modelling [44,45]. The expressiveness of process calculi based upon their choice of communication primitives has been explored before [9,16,21,23,28,49,58]. In [28] and [23] this is detailed by examining combinations of four features: synchronism, arity, communication medium, and pattern-matching, and formalising their relations via valid encodings [30]. These four features allow the representation of many languages and many kinds of constraints and typing on interaction [21,22]. However, recent work [27] has extended *binary* interaction to *joining* as a form of coordination that allows a single process to receive input from many workflow producers in a single interaction. This work generalises to also account for *splitting* where a single process may produce outputs for many workflows in a single interaction (the dual of joining).

© Springer Nature Switzerland AG 2019
T. Margaria et al. (Eds.): Steffen Festschrift, LNCS 11200, pp. 326–355, 2019.
https://doi.org/10.1007/978-3-030-22348-9_20

Along with the theme or Bernhard Steffen's works, this paper explores the common expressiveness of these languages, and shows which forms of interaction and workflow management can be represented in a single common process calculus. Similarly, the inability to express certain features of interaction is formalised, demonstrating which languages are required for which kinds of interaction and workflow behaviour.

The structure of the paper is as follows. Section 2 introduces the calculi considered here. Section 3 reviews the criteria used for comparing calculi. Section 4 considers encoding synchronism with coordination. Section 5 explores encoding arity via coordination. Section 6 presents results for encoding communication medium into coordination. Section 7 formalises that coordination cannot encode pattern-matching. Section 8 presents that coordination cannot be encoded by other features (i.e. synchronism, channel-names, pattern-matching). Section 9 considers relations between different forms of coordination. Section 10 concludes and discusses future work.

2   Calculi

This section defines the syntax, operational, and behavioural semantics of the calculi considered here. This relies heavily on the well-known notions developed for the π-calculus and adapts them when necessary to cope with different features. With the exception of the splitting this repeats many prior definitions from [27], although there are minor syntactic changes for clarity in this work.

Assume a countable set of names $\mathcal{N}$ ranged over by $a, b, c, \ldots$. *Name-match patterns* (denoted m, n), *input patterns (denoted p, q), and* terms *(denoted s, t) are defined according to the following grammar:*

$$
\begin{array}{rll}
m, n ::= & x & \textit{binding name} \\
& \mid \ulcorner a \urcorner & \textit{name-match} \\
p, q ::= & m & \textit{name-match pattern} \\
& \mid p \bullet q & \textit{(input pattern) compound} \\
s, t ::= & a & \textit{name} \\
& \mid s \bullet t & \textit{(term) compound.}
\end{array}
$$

The *name-match patterns* are used for input, with binding names doing binding, and name-matches testing equality. The input patterns generalise the name-match patterns to also include compounds that support structure. The terms are used for output, with names being the base and compounds adding structure. The free names and binding names for input patterns and terms are as expected, taking the union of sub-patterns for compounds. Note that an input pattern is linear if and only if all binding names within the pattern are pairwise distinct. The rest of this paper will only consider linear input patterns.

This paper considers the possible combinations of five features for communication in a language denoted $\mathcal{L}_{\alpha,\beta,\gamma,\delta,\epsilon}$ where:

$\alpha = A$ for asynchronous communication (output only prefoxes the empty process), and S for synchronous communication (output may prefix any process).

$\beta = M$ for monadic data (input or output only a single term), and P for polyadic data (input or output unbounded sequences of terms).

$\gamma = D$ for dataspace-based (interaction without named channels), and C for channel-based communications (interaction uses channel-names).

$\delta = NO$ for no-matching (inputs can only bind), NM for name-matching (inputs can test equality of names), and I for intensionality (inputs can test name equality and also term structure).

$\epsilon = B$ for binary (one input and one output interact), J for joining (one input may interact with many outputs), and L for splitting communication (one output may interact with many inputs).

For simplicity a dash $-$ will be used when the instantiation of a feature is unimportant. The (parametric) syntax for the languages is:

$$P, Q, R ::= \mathbf{0} \mid (\nu a)P \mid P|Q \mid *P \mid \text{if } s = t \text{ then } P \text{ else } Q$$
$$\mid \sqrt{} \mid OutProc \mid InProc.$$

Most of the process forms as as usual: $\mathbf{0}$ denotes the null process; restriction $(\nu a)P$ restricts the visibility of a to P; parallel composition $P|Q$ allows independent evolution of P and Q; and $*P$ represents replication of the process P. The **if** $s = t$ **then** P **else** Q represents conditional equivalence with **if** $s = t$ **then** P used when Q is $\mathbf{0}$ (like the name match of π-calculus, **if** $s = t$ **then** P **else** Q blocks either P when $s \neq t$ or Q when $s = t$). The $\sqrt{}$ is used to represent a success process or state, in other works a specific barb or name has been used, however here by isolating $\sqrt{}$ as a specific process it is easier to reason about encodings (as also in) [21,30]. Finally, different languages are obtained by replacing the output $OutProc$ and input $InProc$ with the various definitions in Fig. 1. The denotation $\widetilde{\cdot}$ represents a sequence of the form $\cdot_1, \cdot_2, \ldots, \cdot_n$ and can be used for names, terms, input patterns, etc. (also denote with $|\cdot|$ the size of a set, multiset, or sequence).

$$
\begin{array}{llll}
\mathcal{L}_{A,-,-,-,-} : & InProc ::= [\mathcal{I}] \triangleright P & OutProc ::= [\mathcal{O}] \triangleleft \\
\mathcal{L}_{S,-,-,-,-} : & InProc ::= [\mathcal{I}] \triangleright P & OutProc ::= [\mathcal{O}] \triangleleft P \\
\mathcal{L}_{-,-,-,-,B} : & \mathcal{I} ::= IN & \mathcal{O} ::= OUT \\
\mathcal{L}_{-,-,-,-,J} : & \mathcal{I} ::= IN \mid \mathcal{I} \mid \mathcal{I} & \mathcal{O} ::= OUT \\
\mathcal{L}_{-,-,-,-,L} : & \mathcal{I} ::= IN & \mathcal{O} ::= OUT \mid \mathcal{O} \mid \mathcal{O}
\end{array}
$$

$$
\begin{array}{llllll}
\mathcal{L}_{-,M,D,NO,-} : & IN ::= (x) & OUT ::= \langle a \rangle & \mathcal{L}_{-,M,D,NM,-} : & IN ::= (m) & OUT ::= \langle a \rangle \\
\mathcal{L}_{-,M,D,I,-} : & IN ::= (p) & OUT ::= \langle t \rangle & \mathcal{L}_{-,M,C,NO,-} : & IN ::= a(x) & OUT ::= \bar{a}\langle b \rangle \\
\mathcal{L}_{-,M,C,NM,-} : & IN ::= a(m) & OUT ::= \bar{a}\langle b \rangle & \mathcal{L}_{-,M,C,I,-} : & IN ::= s(p) & OUT ::= \bar{s}\langle t \rangle \\
\mathcal{L}_{-,P,D,NO,-} : & IN ::= (\tilde{x}) & OUT ::= \langle \tilde{a} \rangle & \mathcal{L}_{-,P,D,NM,-} : & IN ::= (\tilde{m}) & OUT ::= \langle \tilde{a} \rangle \\
\mathcal{L}_{-,P,D,I,-} : & IN ::= (\tilde{p}) & OUT ::= \langle \tilde{t} \rangle & \mathcal{L}_{-,P,C,NO,-} : & IN ::= a(\tilde{x}) & OUT ::= \bar{a}\langle \tilde{b} \rangle \\
\mathcal{L}_{-,P,C,NM,-} : & IN ::= a(\tilde{m}) & OUT ::= \bar{a}\langle \tilde{b} \rangle & \mathcal{L}_{-,P,C,I,-} : & IN ::= s(\tilde{p}) & OUT ::= \bar{s}\langle \tilde{t} \rangle
\end{array}
$$

Fig. 1. Syntax of Languages.

As usual $(\nu x)P$ and $[a(\ldots, x, \ldots)] \triangleright P$ and $[(x \bullet \ldots)] \triangleright P$ and $[\ldots \mid a(x) \mid \ldots] \triangleright P$ bind x in P. Observe that in $[a(\ldots, \ulcorner b \urcorner, \ldots)] \triangleright P$ and $[(\ldots \bullet \ulcorner b \urcorner)] \triangleright P$ neither a nor

b bind in P, both are free. The corresponding notions of free and bound names of a process, denoted $\mathsf{fn}(P)$ and $\mathsf{bn}(P)$, are as usual. Also note that α-equivalence, denoted $=_\alpha$ is assumed in the usual manner. Further, an input is linear if all binding names in that input occur exactly once (note that this is already assumed within an input pattern, here this is generalised to whole inputs). This paper shall only consider linear inputs. Finally, the structural congruence relation $\equiv$ is the smallest congruence such that the following hold:

$$P \mid \mathbf{0} \equiv P \qquad\qquad P \mid Q \equiv Q \mid P \qquad\qquad P \mid (Q \mid R) \equiv (P \mid Q) \mid R$$
$$P \equiv P' \text{ if } P =_\alpha P' \qquad\qquad *P \equiv P \mid *P \qquad\qquad (\nu a)\mathbf{0} \equiv \mathbf{0}$$
$$(\nu a)(\nu b)P \equiv (\nu b)(\nu a)P \qquad\qquad P \mid (\nu a)Q \equiv (\nu a)(P \mid Q) \text{ if } a \notin \mathsf{fn}(P).$$

Observe that $\mathcal{L}_{A,M,C,NO,B}$, $\mathcal{L}_{A,P,C,NO,B}$, $\mathcal{L}_{S,M,C,NO,B}$, and $\mathcal{L}_{S,P,C,NO,B}$ use the communication paradigm of the asynchronous/synchronous monadic/polyadic π-calculus [38,40,41]. The language $\mathcal{L}_{A,P,D,NM,B}$ uses the communication paradigm of LINDA[20]; the languages $\mathcal{L}_{A,M,D,NO,B}$ and $\mathcal{L}_{A,P,D,NO,B}$ the communication paradigm of the monadic/polyadic Mobile Ambients [11]; and $\mathcal{L}_{A,P,C,NM,B}$ that of μKLAIM [15] or semantic-π [13].

Due to the large number of intensional languages of the form $\mathcal{L}_{\alpha,\beta,\gamma,I,\epsilon}$ defined here, many do not match the communication paradigm of well-known calculi. However, the language $\mathcal{L}_{S,M,D,I,B}$ is the asymmetric concurrent pattern calculus of [22] and calculi with other communication paradigms that match some of those here have been mentioned in [21], as variations of Concurrent Pattern Calculus [21,25] (with their behavioural theory as a specialisation of [24]). Similarly, the language $\mathcal{L}_{S,M,C,I,B}$ uses the communication paradigm of Spi calculus [1,31] and Psi calculi (albeit with channel equivalence represented by equality and without the possibility of repeated binding names in patterns) [2]. There are also similarities between the communication paradigm of $\mathcal{L}_{S,M,C,I,B}$ and the polyadic synchronization π-calculus [10], although the intensionality in polyadic synchronization π-calculus is limited to the channel, i.e. inputs and outputs of the form $s(x).P$ and $\overline{s}\langle a \rangle.P$, respectively.

The joining languages have several similarities to existing calculi. The language $\mathcal{L}_{A,P,C,NO,J}$ uses a communication paradigm very close to an asynchronous π-calculus with joint input [43]. $\mathcal{L}_{S,P,C,NO,J}$ uses the communication paradigm of the general rendezvous calculus [4], and m-calculus [54], although the latter has higher order constructs and other aspects that are not captured within the features here. The language $\mathcal{L}_{S,M,C,NO,J}$ has a similar communication paradigm to the Quality Calculus [47,48], however the Quality Calculus has further conditions upon the inputs that cannot be represented by $\mathcal{L}_{S,M,C,NO,J}$. Despite these similarities to many languages related to Join Calculus, the Join Calculus itself is difficult to capture in the π-calculus based framework here. This is due to Join Calculus combining restriction, replication, and input into a single primitive [19]. There are no exact connections for the splitting languages. Although one might consider some similarity with broadcast calculus [53] and $b\pi$-calculus [18] that both allow a single output to communicate with multiple inputs, even the closest splitting language $\mathcal{L}_{S,M,C,NO,L}$ has a fundamentally different communication paradigm. The difference is that in the broadcast calculi the number of inputs required to interact with a broadcast is not fixed, while for $\mathcal{L}_{S,M,C,NO,L}$ the number of inputs is fixed.

Remark 1. The languages $\Lambda_{s,a,m,p}$ can be easily partially ordered; in particular $\mathcal{L}_{\alpha_1,\beta_1,\gamma_1,\delta_1,\epsilon_1}$ is a lesser language than $\mathcal{L}_{\alpha_2,\beta_2,\gamma_2,\delta_2,\epsilon_2}$ if it holds that $\alpha_1 \leq \alpha_2$ and $\beta_1 \leq \beta_2$ and $\gamma_1 \leq \gamma_2$ and $\delta_1 \leq \delta_2$ and $\epsilon_1 \leq \epsilon_2$, where $\leq$ is the least reflexive relation satisfying the following axioms:

$$A \leq S \quad M \leq P \quad D \leq C \quad NO \leq NM \leq I \quad B \leq J \quad B \leq L.$$

This can be understood as the lesser language variation being a special case of the more general language. Asynchronous communication is synchronous communication with all output followed by $\mathbf{0}$. Monadic communication is polyadic communication with all tuples of arity one. Dataspace-based communication is channel-based communication with all k-ary tuples communicating with channel name k. All name-matching communication is intensional communication without any compounds, and no-matching capability communication is both without any compounds and with only binding names in patterns. Lastly, binary communication is: joining communication with all joining inputs having only a single input pattern, and splitting communication with all splitting outputs having only a single output term.

The operational semantics of the languages is given here via reductions as in [23,33,38]. An alternative style is via a *labelled transition system* (LTS) such as [28]. Here the reduction based style is to simplify having to define here the (potentially complex) labels that occur when both intensionality, and joining/splitting is in play. The LTS style can be used for intensional languages [2,21,24]. Also, for the non-binary languages the techniques used in [5] can be used directly for the no-matching joining languages, and with the techniques of [5,24] to extend intensionality and other coordination forms.

Substitutions (denoted $\sigma, \rho, \ldots$) in non-pattern-matching and name-matching languages are mappings from names to names. For intensional languages substitutions are mappings from names to terms. Note that substitutions are assumed to have finite domain. The application of a substitution σ to a pattern p is defined as follows:

$$\sigma x = \sigma(x) \quad x \in \text{domain}(\sigma) \qquad \sigma x = x \quad x \notin \text{domain}(\sigma)$$
$$\sigma \ulcorner x \urcorner = \ulcorner (\sigma x) \urcorner \qquad \sigma(p \bullet q) = (\sigma p) \bullet (\sigma q).$$

Where substitution is as usual on names, and on the understanding that $\ulcorner (s \bullet t) \urcorner \overset{\text{def}}{=} \ulcorner s \urcorner \bullet \ulcorner t \urcorner$.

Given a substitution σ and a process P, denote with σP the (capture-avoiding) application of σ to P that behaves in the usual manner. Note that capture can always be avoided by exploiting α-equivalence, which can in turn be assumed [3,56].

The matching of terms $\widetilde{t}$ with patterns $\widetilde{p}$ is handled in two parts. First, the *match* rule $\{t /\!\!/ p\}$ of a term t with a pattern p to create a substitution σ:

$$\{t /\!\!/ x\} \stackrel{\text{def}}{=} \{t/x\} \qquad\qquad \{s \bullet t /\!\!/ p \bullet q\} \quad\stackrel{\text{def}}{=}\quad \{s /\!\!/ p\} \cup \{t /\!\!/ q\}$$
$$\{a /\!\!/ \ulcorner a \urcorner\} \stackrel{\text{def}}{=} \{\} \qquad\qquad \{t /\!\!/ p\} \text{ undefined otherwise.}$$

Any term t can be matched with a binding name x to generate a substitution from the binding name to the term $\{t/x\}$. A single name a can be matched with a name-match for that name $\ulcorner a \urcorner$ to yield the empty substitution. A compound term $s \bullet t$ can be matched by a compound pattern $p \bullet q$ when the components match to yield substitutions $\{s /\!\!/ p\} = \sigma_1$ and $\{t /\!\!/ q\} = \sigma_2$, the resulting substitution is the union of σ_1 and σ_2. (Observe that, since patterns are linear, the substitutions of components will always have disjoint domain). Otherwise the match is undefined.

The second part is then the *poly-match* rule $\text{MATCH}(\widetilde{t}; \widetilde{p})$ that determines matching of a sequence of terms $\widetilde{t}$ with a sequence of patterns $\widetilde{p}$, defined below.

$$\text{MATCH}(;) = \{\} \qquad\qquad \frac{\{s /\!\!/ p\} = \sigma_1 \qquad \text{MATCH}(\widetilde{t}; \widetilde{q}) = \sigma_2}{\text{MATCH}(s, \widetilde{t}; p, \widetilde{q}) = \sigma_1 \cup \sigma_2}.$$

The empty sequence matches with the empty sequence to produce the empty substitution. Otherwise, when there is a sequence of terms $s, \widetilde{t}$ and a sequence of patterns $p, \widetilde{q}$, the first elements are matched by $\{s /\!\!/ p\}$ and the remaining sequences use the poly-match rule. If both are defined and yield substitutions, then the union of substitutions is the result. (Like the match rule, the union is ensured to happen between substitutions with disjoint domain by linearity of inputs). Otherwise the poly-match rule is undefined, for example when a single match fails, or the sequences are of different arity.

There are now three base reduction rules, one for each of binary, joining, and splitting languages. The binary reduction rule is:

$$[\overline{s}\langle \widetilde{t} \rangle] \lhd P \mid [s(\widetilde{p})] \rhd Q \quad \longmapsto \quad P \mid \sigma Q \qquad \text{MATCH}(\widetilde{t}; \widetilde{p}) = \sigma$$

that states that the split $[\overline{s}\langle \widetilde{t} \rangle] \lhd P$ interacts with the join $[s(\widetilde{p})] \rhd Q$ to yield $P \mid \sigma Q$ when the channel name s is the same and the match $\text{MATCH}(\widetilde{t}; \widetilde{p})$ is defined and yields σ. Note that P is omitted in the asynchronous languages and the channel names s are omitted in the dataspace-based languages.

The joining reduction rule is:

$$[\overline{s_1}\langle \widetilde{t_1} \rangle] \lhd P_1 \mid \ldots \mid [\overline{s_i}\langle \widetilde{t_i} \rangle] \lhd P_i \mid [s_1(\widetilde{p_1}) \mid \ldots \mid s_i(\widetilde{p_i})] \rhd Q$$
$$\longmapsto \quad P_1 \mid \ldots \mid P_i \mid \sigma Q \qquad \text{MATCH}(\widetilde{t_1}, \ldots, \widetilde{t_i}; \widetilde{p_1}, \ldots, \widetilde{p_i}) = \sigma$$

that states that i splits $[\overline{s_i}\langle \widetilde{t_i} \rangle] \lhd P_i$ can interact with a single join when all of the outputs of the splits $\overline{s_i}\langle \widetilde{t_i} \rangle$ can be matched against the inputs of the join $\text{MATCH}(\widetilde{t_1}, \ldots, \widetilde{t_i}; \widetilde{p_1}, \ldots, \widetilde{p_i})$ to yield a substitution σ, and then reduce to the continuations of the splits $P_1 \mid \ldots \mid P_i$ in parallel with σQ.

The splitting reduction rule is the mirror of the joining rule:

$$[\overline{s_1}\langle \widetilde{t_1} \rangle \mid \ldots \mid \overline{s_i}\langle \widetilde{t_i} \rangle] \lhd P \mid [s_1(\widetilde{p_1})] \rhd Q_1 \mid \ldots \mid [s_i(\widetilde{p_i})] \rhd Q_i$$
$$\longmapsto \quad P \mid \sigma_1 Q_1 \mid \ldots \mid \sigma_i Q_i \qquad \text{MATCH}(\widetilde{t_j}; \widetilde{p_j}) = \sigma_j \quad j \in \{1, \ldots, i\}$$

where all the outputs of a single split $[\overline{s_1}\langle \widetilde{t_1}\rangle \mid \ldots \mid \overline{s_i}\langle \widetilde{t_i}\rangle] \lhd P$ match $\textsc{Match}(\widetilde{t_j}; \widetilde{p_j})$ with separate joins $[s_j(\widetilde{p_j})] \rhd Q_i$ to yield σ_j and reduce to $P \mid \sigma_1 Q_1 \mid \ldots \mid \sigma_i Q_i$ for all $j \in \{1, \ldots, i\}$.

The general reduction relation $\longmapsto$ for all languages also includes:

$$\frac{P \longmapsto P'}{P \mid Q \longmapsto P' \mid Q} \qquad \frac{P \longmapsto P'}{(\nu a)P \longmapsto (\nu a)P'} \qquad \frac{P \equiv Q \quad Q \longmapsto Q' \quad Q' \equiv P'}{P \longmapsto P'}$$

$$\frac{s = t \qquad P \mid Q \longmapsto S}{P \mid \textbf{if } s = t \textbf{ then } Q \textbf{ else } R \longmapsto S} \qquad \frac{s \neq t \qquad P \mid R \longmapsto S}{P \mid \textbf{if } s = t \textbf{ then } Q \textbf{ else } R \longmapsto S} \quad .$$

The reflexive transitive closure of $\longmapsto$ is denoted by $\Longmapsto$.

Lastly, for each language let $\simeq$ denote a reduction-sensitive behavioural equivalence for that language. A *reduction-sensitive* behavioural equivalence $\simeq$ is one where it holds that $P \simeq P'$ and $P' \longmapsto$ imply $P \longmapsto$ as in Definition 5.3 of [30] (observe that this rules out weak bisimulations for example). For the non-intensional languages these are mostly already known, either by their equivalent language in the literature, such as asynchronous/synchronous monadic/polyadic π-calculus or Join Calculus, or from [28]. For the intensional languages the results in [24] can be used. For the joining languages that reflect those of the literature the techniques used in [5] apply. For other combinations of joining, and splitting, as well as the addition of intensionality to non-binary languages, adaptations of [5,24] should prove adequate.

3 Encodings

This section recalls the definition of valid encodings as well as some useful results (details in [30]) for formally relating process calculi.

The choice of valid encodings here is to align with prior works [23,28,30] and where possible reuse prior results. These valid encodings are those used, sometimes with mild adaptations, in [21,25,26,29,30,46] and have also inspired similar works [34,35,57]. However, there are alternative approaches to encoding criteria or comparing expressive power [6,10,17,50,57]. Further arguments in favour of, or against, the valid encodings here can be found in [26,29,30,51,57].

An *encoding* of a language $\mathcal{L}_1$ into another language $\mathcal{L}_2$ is a pair $([\![\cdot]\!], \varphi_{[\![]\!]})$ where $[\![\cdot]\!]$ translates every $\mathcal{L}_1$-process into an $\mathcal{L}_2$-process and $\varphi_{[\![]\!]}$ maps every name (of the source language) into a tuple of k names (of the target language), for $k > 0$. In doing this, the translation may fix some names to play a precise rôle or may translate a single name into a tuple of names, this can be obtained by exploiting $\varphi_{[\![]\!]}$.

To aid in the following definition and the results later in the paper, a process P is defined to be at *top-level* when P may be under any combination of restrictions, conditionals, or replications, but that none of these can prevent reduction or interaction by P. For example, P is top-level in $(\nu n)P$ and $*P$ and $\textbf{if } s = s \textbf{ then } P \textbf{ else } Q$ and $\textbf{if } s = t \textbf{ then } Q \textbf{ else } P$ where $s \neq t$ and $(\nu n)\textbf{if } s = s \textbf{ then } * (P \mid Q) \textbf{ else } R$.

Now consider only encodings that satisfy the following properties. Let a k-ary context $C(\cdot_1; \ldots; \cdot_k)$ be a process with k holes. Denote with $\longmapsto^\omega$ an infinite sequence of reductions. Let $P \Downarrow$ mean there exists P' such that $P \Longmapsto P'$ and P' has an instance of $\sqrt{}$ at top-level, that is the process P eventually exhibits the success process $\sqrt{}$. Moreover, let $\simeq$ denote the reference behavioural equivalence. Finally, to simplify reading, let S range over processes of the source language (viz., $\mathcal{L}_1$) and T range over processes of the target language (viz., $\mathcal{L}_2$) and let the notation of a language $\mathcal{L}_i$ be subscripted by i, e.g. $\simeq_i$, $\longmapsto_i$, etc.

Definition 1 (Valid Encoding). *An encoding $([\![\cdot]\!], \varphi_{[\![\,]\!]})$ of $\mathcal{L}_1$ into $\mathcal{L}_2$ is valid if it satisfies the following five properties:*

1. Compositionality: *for every k-ary operator op of $\mathcal{L}_1$ and for every subset of names N, there exists a k-ary context $C_{\mathsf{op}}^N(\cdot_1; \ldots; \cdot_k)$ of $\mathcal{L}_2$ such that, for all $S_1, \ldots, S_k$ with $\mathsf{fn}(S_1, \ldots, S_k) = N$, it holds that $[\![\mathsf{op}(S_1, \ldots, S_k)]\!] = C_{\mathsf{op}}^N([\![S_1]\!]; \ldots; [\![S_k]\!])$.*
2. Name invariance: *for every S and substitution σ, it holds that $[\![\sigma S]\!] = \sigma'[\![S]\!]$ if σ is injective and $[\![\sigma S]\!] \simeq_2 \sigma'[\![S]\!]$ otherwise where σ' is such that $\varphi_{[\![\,]\!]}(\sigma(a)) = \sigma'(\varphi_{[\![\,]\!]}(a))$ for every name $a \in N$.*
3. Operational correspondence: *for all $S \Longmapsto_1 S'$, it holds that $[\![S]\!] \Longmapsto_2 \simeq_2 [\![S']\!]$; and for all $[\![S]\!] \Longmapsto_2 T$, there exists S' such that $S \Longmapsto_1 S'$ and $T \Longmapsto_2 \simeq_2 [\![S']\!]$.*
4. Divergence reflection: *for every S such that $[\![S]\!] \longmapsto_2^\omega$, it holds that $S \longmapsto_1^\omega$.*
5. Success sensitiveness: *for every S, it holds that $S \Downarrow_1$ if and only if $[\![S]\!] \Downarrow_2$.*

The existence of encodings $[\![\cdot]\!]_1$ from $\mathcal{L}_1$ into $\mathcal{L}_2$ and $[\![\cdot]\!]_2$ from $\mathcal{L}_2$ into $\mathcal{L}_3$ does not ensure that $[\![[\![\cdot]\!]_1]\!]_2$ is a valid encoding from $\mathcal{L}_1$ into $\mathcal{L}_3$ [29]. However, compositionality can be ensured by respecting the below definition of compositional valid encodings. All encodings considered in this paper satisfy this restriction, and therefore are compositional and may be used as such in later proofs.

Definition 2 (Compositional Valid Encodings). *An encoding $([\![\cdot]\!], \varphi_{[\![\,]\!]})$ of $\mathcal{L}_1$ into $\mathcal{L}_2$ is compositional if it satisfies the properties 1,2,4 and 5 from Definition 1 and the following properties:*

- Operational Correspondence revisited: *for all $S \Longmapsto_1 S'$, it holds that $[\![S]\!] \Longmapsto_2 [\![S']\!] \mid T$, for some $T \simeq_2 \mathbf{0}$; and for all $[\![S]\!] \Longmapsto_2 T$, there exists S' such that $S \Longmapsto_1 S'$ and $T \Longmapsto_2 [\![S']\!] \mid T'$, for some $T' \simeq_2 \mathbf{0}$.*
- preserves the equivalence class of $\mathbf{0}$: *for every $S \simeq_1 \mathbf{0}$, $[\![S]\!] \simeq_2 \mathbf{0}$.*
- is homomorphic w.r.t. $\mid$: *for every S_1, S_2, $[\![S_1 \mid S_2]\!] = [\![S_1]\!] \mid [\![S_2]\!]$.*

The following three results are here recalled from prior works as they are useful for later proofs.

Proposition 1 (Proposition 5.5 from [30]). *Let $[\![\cdot]\!]$ be a valid encoding; then, $S \longmapsto\!\!\!\!/\,\,$ implies that $[\![S]\!] \longmapsto\!\!\!\!/\,\,$.*

Proof. By contradiction, assume that $[\![\,S\,]\!] \longmapsto T$, for some $S \longmapsto\!\!\!\!\!/\,$. By operational correspondence, there exists an S' such that $S \Longrightarrow S'$ and $T \Longrightarrow T' \simeq [\![\,S'\,]\!]$; but the only such S' is S itself. Since $\simeq$ is reduction-sensitive and since $[\![\,S'\,]\!] = [\![\,S\,]\!] \longmapsto$, then $T' \longmapsto T''$. Again by operational correspondence $T'' \Longrightarrow T''' \simeq [\![\,S\,]\!]$, and so on; thus, $[\![\,S\,]\!] \longmapsto T \Longrightarrow T' \Longrightarrow T'' \Longrightarrow T''' \longmapsto \ldots$, in contradiction with divergence reflection (since $S \longmapsto\!\!\!\!\!/\,$ implies $S \longmapsto\!\!\!\!\!/\,^{\omega}$).

The following two results (and a few later in the paper) exploit the notation $block(S)$ that denotes the process $(\nu n)(\nu m)\mathbf{if}\ n = m\ \mathbf{then}\ S$ where $n, m \notin \mathsf{fn}(S)$.

Proposition 2 (Proposition 5.6 from [30]). *Let $[\![\,\cdot\,]\!]$ be a valid encoding; then for every set of names N, it holds that $\mathcal{C}_{|}^{N}(\cdot_1, \cdot_2)$ has both its holes at top-level.*

Proof. Fix a set of names N and a process S with $\mathsf{fn}(S) = N$. Now consider $S' = \sqrt{}\ |\ block(S)$. By Proposition 1 it must be that $[\![\,S'\,]\!] \longmapsto\!\!\!\!\!/\,$, since $S' \longmapsto\!\!\!\!\!/\,$. By compositionality we must have $[\![\,S'\,]\!] = \mathcal{C}_{|}^{N}([\![\,\sqrt{}\,]\!], [\![\,block(S)\,]\!])$. By success sensitiveness it must be that $[\![\,S'\,]\!] \Downarrow$ since $S' \Downarrow$. All these facts entail that the top-level occurrence of $\sqrt{}$ in $[\![\,S'\,]\!]$ is exhibited: either by the translating context and so $\mathcal{C}_{|}^{N}(\cdot, \cdot) \Downarrow$; or by $[\![\,\sqrt{}\,]\!]$, but this implies that $\mathcal{C}_{|}^{N}(\cdot, \cdot)$ has the first hole $\cdot$ at top-level. Indeed, it is not possible that $\sqrt{}$ is exhibited by $[\![\,block(S)\,]\!]$ since $block(S) \not\Downarrow$. However, the first case is not possible otherwise $[\![\,block(S)\ |\ block(S)\,]\!] \Downarrow$, whereas $block(S)\ |\ block(S) \not\Downarrow$. To show that the second hole in $\mathcal{C}_{|}^{N}(\cdot, \cdot)$ is at top-level it suffices to reason in the very same way using $S' = block(S)\ |\ \sqrt{}$.

Proposition 3 (Adapted from Proposition 5.7 from [30]). *Let $[\![\,\cdot\,]\!]$ be a valid encoding; if there exist two processes S_1 and S_2 such that $S_1\ |\ S_2 \Downarrow$, with $S_i \not\Downarrow$ and $S_i \longmapsto\!\!\!\!\!/\,$ for $i = 1, 2$, then $[\![\,S_1\ |\ S_2\,]\!] \longmapsto$.*

Proof. By success sensitiveness $[\![\,S_1\ |\ S_2\,]\!] \Downarrow$ and by Proposition 2 $\mathcal{C}_{|}^{N}([\![\,S_1\,]\!], [\![\,S_2\,]\!])$ has both $[\![\,S_1\,]\!]$ and $[\![\,S_2\,]\!]$ at top-level. However, since none of $[\![\,S_1\,]\!]$, $[\![\,S_2\,]\!]$, and $[\![\,block(S_1)\ |\ block(S_2)\,]\!]$ can report success, it must be the case that $[\![\,S_1\ |\ S_2\,]\!] \longmapsto$. This can only happen by interaction between $[\![\,S_1\,]\!]$ and $[\![\,S_2\,]\!]$. If this was not the case, we would have $[\![\,S_1\ |\ block(S_2)\,]\!] \longmapsto$ or $[\![\,block(S_1)\ |\ S_2\,]\!] \longmapsto$ or $[\![\,block(S_1)\ |\ block(S_2)\,]\!] \longmapsto$, in violation of Proposition 1: indeed $S_1\ |\ block(S_2) \longmapsto\!\!\!\!\!/\,$ because $S_1 \longmapsto\!\!\!\!\!/\,$, $block(S_2) \longmapsto\!\!\!\!\!/\,$ and $block(S_2)$ cannot interact with S_1. Similar reasoning holds for $block(S_1)\ |\ S_2$ and $block(S_1)\ |\ block(S_2)$.

The general way to prove the lack of a valid encoding is as follows. By contradiction assuming there is a valid encoding $[\![\,\cdot\,]\!]$. Find a pair of processes P and Q that satisfy Proposition 3 such that $P\ |\ Q \longmapsto$ and $[\![\,P\ |\ Q\,]\!] \longmapsto$. From Q obtain some Q' such that $P\ |\ Q' \longmapsto\!\!\!\!\!/\,$ and $[\![\,P\ |\ Q'\,]\!] \longmapsto$. Conclude by showing this in contradiction with some properties of the encoding or Proposition 1.

The following result is a consequence of the choices of languages and encoding criteria, which corresponds to formalising Remark 1.

Theorem 1. *If a language $\mathcal{L}_1$ is a lesser language than $\mathcal{L}_2$ (by the $\leq$ relation of Remark 1) then there exists a (compositional) valid encoding $[\![\,\cdot\,]\!]$ from $\mathcal{L}_1$ into $\mathcal{L}_2$.*

Proof. The encoding $[\![\,\cdot\,]\!]$ is as described in Remark 1. The proof is then straight-forward and ensured by definition of the rule for the base reduction. For a detailed example of the proof technique see Theorem 2.

4   Coordination and Synchronism

This section considers the relation between coordination and synchronism. It turns out that coordination is unable to encode synchronism unless it could otherwise be encoded by other features.

In general synchronous communication can be encoded into asynchronous communication when the target language includes: channel names; name-matching and polyadicity; or intensionality. Thus it is sufficient to consider the languages $\mathcal{L}_{A,M,D,NO,-}$ and $\mathcal{L}_{A,P,D,NO,-}$ and $\mathcal{L}_{A,M,D,NM,-}$ since the other asynchronous languages can encode their synchronous joining counterparts in the usual manner [7,32]. This can be adapted in the obvious manner for $\mathcal{L}_{S,M,C,NO,J}$ into $\mathcal{L}_{A,M,C,NO,J}$ as follows

$$[\![\,[\overline{n}\langle a\rangle] \vartriangleleft P\,]\!] \stackrel{\text{def}}{=} (\nu z)([\overline{n}\langle z\rangle] \vartriangleleft \mid [z(x)] \vartriangleright ([\overline{x}\langle a\rangle] \vartriangleleft \mid [\![\,P\,]\!]))$$

$$[\![\,[n_1(a_1) \mid \ldots \mid n_i(a_i)] \vartriangleright Q\,]\!] \stackrel{\text{def}}{=} (\nu x_1,\ldots,x_i)[n_1(z_1) \mid \ldots \mid n_i(z_i)] \vartriangleright$$
$$([\overline{z_1}\langle x_1\rangle] \vartriangleleft \mid \ldots \mid [\overline{z_i}\langle x_i\rangle] \vartriangleleft$$
$$\mid [x_1(a_1) \mid \ldots \mid x_i(a_i)] \vartriangleright [\![\,Q\,]\!]).$$

The idea for binary languages is that the encoded output creates a fresh name z and sends it to the encoded input. The encoded input creates a fresh name x and sends it to the encoded output along channel name z. The encoded output now knows it has communicated and evolves to $[\![\,P\,]\!]$ in parallel with the original a sent to the encoded input along channel name x. When the encoded input receives this it can evolve to $[\![\,Q\,]\!]$. The joining version is similar except the join synchronises with all the encoded outputs at once, sends the fresh names x_j in parallel, and then synchronises on all the a_j in the last step.

The encoding above is shown for $\mathcal{L}_{S,M,C,NO,J}$ into $\mathcal{L}_{A,M,C,NO,J}$ and is the identity on all other process forms. This can be proven to be a valid encoding.

Lemma 1. *If $P \equiv Q$ then $[\![P]\!] \equiv [\![Q]\!]$. Conversely, if $[\![P]\!] \equiv Q$ then $Q \equiv [\![P']\!]$ for some $P' \equiv P$.*

Proof. The only non-trivial cases are the join and split as the others are translated homomorphically. The join and split are also straightforward as the only non-trivial parts are the possible renaming of new restricted names introduced in the translation.

Lemma 2. *Given a $\mathcal{L}_{S,M,C,NO,J}$ join P and split Q then $[\![P]\!] \mid [\![Q]\!] \longmapsto$ if and only if $P \mid Q \longmapsto$.*

Proof. Both parts can be proved by induction on the height of the proof tree for the judgements $[\![P \mid Q]\!] \longmapsto$ and $P \mid Q \longmapsto$. The base case is ensured by k applications of the poly-match rule when P is of the form $[n_1(x_1) \mid \ldots \mid n_k(x_k)] \triangleright P'$. Note that Lemma 1 is used for structural congruence.

Lemma 3. *The translation* $[\![\cdot]\!]$ *from* $\mathcal{L}_{S,M,C,NO,J}$ *into* $\mathcal{L}_{A,M,C,NO,J}$ *preserves and reflects reductions. That is: if* $P \longmapsto P'$ *then there exists* Q *such that* $[\![P]\!] \longmapsto^k Q$ *and* $Q = [\![P']\!]$; *and if* $[\![P]\!] \longmapsto Q$ *then there exists* Q' *such that* $Q \longmapsto^{k-1} Q'$ *and* $Q' = [\![P']\!]$ *for some* P' *such that* $P \longmapsto P'$.

Proof. Both parts can be proved by straightforward induction on the judgements $P \longmapsto P'$ and $[\![P]\!] \longmapsto Q$, respectively. In both cases, the base step is the most interesting and follows from Lemma 2, for the second case the step $Q \longmapsto Q'$ is ensured by the definition of the translation and match rule. The size of k (the number of target steps required to simulate one source step) in both cases is $2 + i$ where i is the number of inputs of the join involved in $P \longmapsto P'$. The inductive cases where the last rule used is a structural one rely on Lemma 1.

Theorem 2. *There is a valid encoding from* $\mathcal{L}_{S,M,C,NO,J}$ *into* $\mathcal{L}_{A,M,C,NO,J}$.

Proof. Compositionality and name invariance hold by construction. Operational correspondence (with structural equivalence in the place of $\asymp$) and divergence reflection follow from Lemma 3. Success sensitiveness can be proved as follows: $P \Downarrow$ means that there exists P' and $k \geq 0$ such that $P \longmapsto^k P'$ and P' has $\sqrt{}$ at top-level; by exploiting Lemma 3 k times and Lemma 1 obtain that $[\![P]\!] \longmapsto^j [\![P']\!]$ and P' has $\sqrt{}$ at top-level and where j can be determined from the instantiations of Lemma 3, i.e. that $[\![P]\!] \Downarrow$. The converse implication can be proved similarly.

Splitting can be adapted in a similar manner, e.g. consider the encoding from $\mathcal{L}_{S,M,C,NO,L}$ into $\mathcal{L}_{A,M,C,NO,L}$

$$[\![\, [\overline{n_1}\langle a_1 \rangle \mid \ldots \mid \overline{n_i}\langle a_i \rangle] \triangleleft P \,]\!] \overset{\text{def}}{=} (\nu z_1, \ldots, z_i)([\overline{n_1}\langle z_1 \rangle \mid \ldots \mid \overline{n_i}\langle z_i \rangle] \triangleleft \mid$$
$$[z_1(x_1)] \triangleright \ldots \triangleright [z_i(x_i)] \triangleright$$
$$([\overline{x_1}\langle a_1 \rangle \mid \ldots \mid \overline{x_i}\langle a_i \rangle] \triangleleft \mid [\![P]\!]))$$
$$[\![\, [a(b)] \triangleright Q \,]\!] \overset{\text{def}}{=} (\nu x)[a(z)] \triangleright ([\overline{z}\langle x \rangle] \triangleleft \mid [x(b)] \triangleright [\![Q]\!])$$

The use of fresh names z and x is as before. The splitting version is similar except the split synchronises with all the encoded inputs at once, sending fresh names z_j in parallel, then collects all the responses with fresh names x_j, and then splits sending all the original names a_i at once in the last step.

The encoding above for $\mathcal{L}_{S,M,C,NO,L}$ into $\mathcal{L}_{A,M,C,NO,L}$ is the identity on all other process forms. This can similarly be proven to be a valid encoding.

Theorem 3. *There is a valid encoding from* $\mathcal{L}_{S,M,C,NO,L}$ *into* $\mathcal{L}_{A,M,C,NO,L}$.

Proof. The same proof technique as Theorem 2 applies here.

Corollary 1. *If there exists a valid encoding from $\mathcal{L}_{S,\beta,\gamma,\delta,B}$ into $\mathcal{L}_{A,\beta,\gamma,\delta,B}$ then there exists a valid encoding from $\mathcal{L}_{S,\beta,\gamma,\delta,\epsilon}$ into $\mathcal{L}_{A,\beta,\gamma,\delta,\epsilon}$.*

Proof. Theorems 2 and 3 provide the foundation for all the channel-based results. For the other encodings where channels are not available in the target language, the target language can already encode channel-based communication and so the above results can still be used. For the polyadic and name-matching languages this holds by Proposition 4.1 of [28], otherwise for the intensional languages this holds by Theorem 6.4 of [23].

These results confirm that the ability to encode synchronous communication into asynchronous communication is not impacted by changes to coordination. Any encoding that holds from a binary synchronous language into a binary asynchronous language also holds when both languages are instead joining, or splitting. Thus no expressiveness is lost by changing from binary languages to other coordination forms, and existing results can easily be transferred.

The following results formalise that there exist no new encodings from a synchronous languages into an asynchronous languages as a result of shifting from both languages being binary, to both languages being joining or splitting. That is, if there exists no valid encoding from $\mathcal{L}_{S,\beta_1,\gamma_1,\delta_1,B}$ into $\mathcal{L}_{A,\beta_2,\gamma_2,\delta_2,B}$, then there exists no valid encoding from $\mathcal{L}_{S,\beta_1,\gamma_1,\delta_1,\epsilon}$ into $\mathcal{L}_{A,\beta_2,\gamma_2,\delta_2,\epsilon}$. The impossibility of encoding $\mathcal{L}_{S,M,D,NM,J}$ into $\mathcal{L}_{A,M,D,NM,J}$ is detailed as it illustrates the key proof technique. The other results are either simpler variations (i.e. without name-matching) or straightforward adaptations to consider splitting.

Theorem 4. *There exists no valid encoding from $\mathcal{L}_{S,M,D,NM,J}$ into $\mathcal{L}_{A,M,D,NM,J}$.*

Proof. The proof is by contradiction. Consider two processes $P = [(x)] \rhd$ **if** $x = b$ **then** $\sqrt{}$ and $Q = [\langle a \rangle] \lhd Q'$ where $a \neq b$ and $Q' \not\Downarrow$. Because $P \mid Q \longmapsto$ by validity of the encoding and Proposition 3 it follows that $[\![P \mid Q]\!] \longmapsto$ and this must be between some $R_1 = [\langle m \rangle] \lhd$ (for some m) and R_2. (This can be obtained by induction over the derivation tree for $[\![P \mid Q]\!] \longmapsto R$). Observe that $R_1 \mid R_2$ cannot be a parallel component of either $[\![P]\!]$ or $[\![Q]\!]$ because then by Proposition 1 either P or Q would reduce and this is not the case.

If R_1 is a top-level component of $[\![P]\!]$ then $[\![P]\!]$ must also include a join because otherwise there would be no join in $[\![P]\!]$ that can bind some name(s) to $\varphi_{[\![ ]\!]} x = \tilde{x}$ and name invariance or success sensitiveness would be shown to fail (i.e. $P \mid Q \longmapsto$ **if** $a = b$ **then** $\sqrt{} \mid Q'$ and $\{b/a\}$**if** $a = b$ **then** $\sqrt{} \mid Q' \Downarrow$ while $\mathcal{C}_{\mid}^{N}([\![P]\!], [\![Q]\!]) \Longmapsto$ does no inputs on any part of $[\![P]\!]$ and so must always or never succeed regardless of interaction with $[\![Q]\!]$). Because the target language is asynchronous, no output can block any join and so $[\![P]\!]$ must contain an unblocked join that must include an input pattern $(\ulcorner n \urcorner)$ for some $n \neq m$. Otherwise if the join was only $[(x_1) \mid \ldots \mid (x_i)] \rhd R'$ for some R' then $[\![P \mid \ldots \mid P]\!]$ for i instances of P would reduce while $P \mid \ldots \mid P$ does not, contradicting Proposition 1. It follows that $[\![Q]\!]$ must include both some $\langle n \rangle$ as part of some split, and some $(\ulcorner m \urcorner)$ where $m \neq n$ (this can be name-matches for any number of names $\neq n$, but assume one for simplicity) as part of some join. Otherwise the join must be of the form $[(z_1) \mid \ldots \mid (z_j) \mid (\ulcorner n \urcorner) \mid \ldots \mid (\ulcorner n \urcorner)] \triangleright S$ for k instances of $(\ulcorner n \urcorner)$ and it follows that $j + k$ instances of Q_1 in parallel would reduce when encoded $[\![Q_1 \mid \ldots \mid Q_1]\!] \longmapsto$ while $j + k$ instances of Q_1 in parallel do not reduce unencoded $Q_1 \mid \ldots \mid Q_1 \not\longmapsto$ violating Proposition 1. Thus, observe that $[\![Q]\!]$ must be able to send at least one name to $[\![P]\!]$ via an output $\langle d \rangle$ for some d (this could be any number of names sent via different outputs, but assume 1 here for simplicity). Now consider the name d.

1. If $d \neq m$ and $d \neq n$ then consider $[\![P \mid Q \mid P]\!]$. After at least the reduction $R_1 \mid R_2 \longmapsto$ then $\langle d \rangle$ must be available from the reduct R of $[\![P \mid Q]\!]$. Now consider $\mathcal{C}_1^N([\![P \mid Q]\!], [\![P]\!])$ after the reduction $[\![P \mid Q]\!] \longmapsto R$ and the two top-level outputs: $\langle d \rangle$ available from R, and $\langle m \rangle$ from $[\![P]\!]$. Clearly the join that would bind d to some name in $\widetilde{x}$ (to be tested in the conditional **if** $x = b$) cannot ensure binding to d and could instead bind to m. Conclude because $d \neq m$ and without the name d being communicated to $[\![P]\!]$ the conditional **if** $x = b$ can be made to be false when it should be true via substitutions such as $\{a/b\}$ and this contradicts either name invariance or success sensitiveness.
2. If $d = n$ then this fails name invariance or success sensitiveness (by $P \mid Q \longmapsto$ **if** $a = b$ **then** $\checkmark \mid Q'$ and $\{b/a\}$**if** $a = b$ **then** $\checkmark \mid Q' \Downarrow$); or d must be bound to some name in $\widetilde{x}$ as in the previous case.
3. If $d = m$ then consider where $\langle d \rangle$ appears in $[\![Q]\!]$.
   - If $\langle d \rangle$ is top-level in $[\![Q]\!]$ then there exist some k such that k instances of Q_1 in parallel would reduce if encoded $[\![Q_1 \mid \ldots \mid Q_1]\!] \longmapsto$ while k instances of Q_1 in parallel unencoded do not reduce $Q_1 \mid \ldots \mid Q_1 \not\longmapsto$ and this violates Proposition 1.
   - If $\langle d \rangle$ is not top-level in $[\![Q]\!]$, instead $\langle d \rangle$ is top-level in some S where $[\![P \mid Q]\!] \Longmapsto S$. Conclude in the same manner as in the first case.

If R_1 is a top-level component of $[\![Q]\!]$ then $[\![Q]\!]$ must also include a top-level join because otherwise if $Q' = \Omega$ (where Ω is a divergent process) then $[\![Q]\!]$ would always diverge or never diverge regardless of interaction with $[\![P]\!]$ and this contradicts divergence reflection or operational correspondence. Thus $[\![Q]\!]$ must include a top-level join and further it must include an input pattern $(\ulcorner n \urcorner)$ for some $n \neq m$ (reasoning as above for R_1 in $[\![P]\!]$). Otherwise if the join was only $[(z_1) \mid \ldots \mid (z_i)] \triangleright R'$ for some $\widetilde{z}$ and R' then $[\![Q \mid \ldots \mid Q]\!]$ for i instances of Q would reduce while $Q \mid \ldots \mid Q$ does not contradicting Proposition 1. Consider when $Q' = $ **if** $a = b$ **then** Ω and the substitution $\sigma = \{b/a\}$. Clearly $P \mid \sigma Q \mid Q \longmapsto S$ where either: $S \longmapsto^\omega$ and $S \Downarrow$; or $S \not\longmapsto^\omega$ and $S \Downarrow$. Now consider the reduction $[\![P \mid \sigma Q \mid Q]\!] \longmapsto R'$ that must be between some component of $[\![P]\!]$ and either a component of $[\![\sigma Q]\!]$ or $[\![Q]\!]$ (because if $[\![P]\!]$ was not involved then $\mathcal{C}_1^N(\mathcal{C}_1^N([\![(\nu n)[(\ulcorner n \urcorner)] \triangleright [\langle b \rangle] \triangleleft \mathbf{0}]\!], [\![\sigma Q]\!]), [\![Q]\!])$ would reduce which contradicts Proposition 1). If this reduction is the initial one between $[\![P]\!]$ and $[\![\sigma Q]\!]$ then the output $\langle n \rangle$ must now be available in R' because otherwise the reduct of $[\![\sigma Q]\!]$ would be unable to reduce further and this would contradict operational correspondence (because $P \mid \sigma Q \longmapsto^\omega$ while $R' \not\longmapsto^\omega$). However, this

$\langle n \rangle$ can now reduce with $[\![Q]\!]$ instead of $[\![\sigma Q]\!]$, which leads to $R' \Downarrow$ and $R' \longmapsto\!\!\!\!\!/ \;^\omega$ which contradicts operational correspondence via lack of divergence of R'.

Theorem 5. *There exists no valid encoding from $\mathcal{L}_{S,M,D,NM,L}$ into $\mathcal{L}_{A,M,D,NM,L}$.*

Proof. This is proved in a very similar manner to Theorem 4.

Corollary 2. *If there exists no valid encoding from $\mathcal{L}_{S,\beta_1,\gamma_1,\delta_1,B}$ into $\mathcal{L}_{A,\beta_2,\gamma_2,\delta_2,B}$, then there exists no valid encoding from $\mathcal{L}_{S,\beta_1,\gamma_1,\delta_1,\epsilon}$ into $\mathcal{L}_{A,\beta_2,\gamma_2,\delta_2,\epsilon}$.*

Proof. The techniques in Theorems 4 and 5 apply to all monadic joining and splitting languages, respectively. Monadic no-matching languages are simpler variants of the same proof technique, while polyadic no-matching (because polyadic name-matching can encode synchronous communication into asynchronous) is a simple generalisation of the above proofs.

That joining or splitting do not allow for an encoding of synchronous communication alone is not surprising, because there is no control in the input of which outputs are interacting with (without some other control such as channel names or pattern-matching). Thus, being able to consume more outputs or inputs in a single interaction does not capture synchronous behaviours.

This formalizes that there is no change to results within languages grouped by their coordination form. Separation results between coordination forms, and that synchronism and coordination are orthogonal are concluded in Sect. 8.

5 Coordination and Arity

This section considers the relation between non-binary coordination and arity. Although there appears to be some similarities in that both have a base case (monadic or binary), and unbounded cases (polyadic or joining/splitting, respectively), these cannot be used to encode arity into coordination unless they could be encoded otherwise.

The interesting results here are the separation results that ensure no new encodings or expressiveness. The proof technique is clearly illustrated by the following result for the joining setting.

Theorem 6. *There exists no valid encoding from $\mathcal{L}_{A,P,D,NO,B}$ into $\mathcal{L}_{A,M,D,NO,J}$.*

Proof. The proof is by contradiction, assume there exists a valid encoding $[\![\cdot]\!]$. Consider the $\mathcal{L}_{A,P,D,NO,B}$ processes $P = [\langle a, b \rangle] \lhd$ and $Q = [(x, y)] \rhd \sqrt{}$. Clearly it holds that $P \mid Q \longmapsto \sqrt{}$ and so $[\![P \mid Q]\!] \Downarrow$ and $[\![P \mid Q]\!] \longmapsto$ by validity of the encoding and Proposition 3. Now consider the reduction $[\![P \mid Q]\!] \longmapsto$.

The reduction must be of some top-level component of $[\![P]\!]$ and $[\![Q]\!]$ (because of Proposition 2) of the form $[\langle a_1 \rangle] \lhd \mid \ldots \mid [\langle a_i \rangle] \lhd \mid [(x_1) \mid \ldots \mid (x_i)] \rhd R'$ for some $\tilde{a}$ and $\tilde{x}$ and i and R'. Now consider the process whose encoding produces $[(x_1) \mid \ldots \mid (x_i)] \rhd R'$ at top-level, assume Q although the results do not rely on this assumption. Observe that no $[\langle a_j \rangle] \lhd$ are also from the encoding of Q because it follows that the encoding of i instances of Q in parallel will reduce, i.e. $[\![Q \mid \ldots \mid Q]\!] \longmapsto$, while $Q \mid \ldots \mid Q \longmapsto\!\!\!\!/$ and this yields contradiction. Now consider two fresh processes $S = [\langle c_1, \ldots, c_k \rangle] \lhd$ and $T = [(z_1, \ldots, z_k)] \rhd$ $\mathbf{0}$ where $k \neq 2$. By validity of the encoding, since $S \mid T \longmapsto \mathbf{0}$ and $S \longmapsto\!\!\!\!/$ and $T \longmapsto\!\!\!\!/$, it follows that $[\![S \mid T]\!] \longmapsto$ (by Proposition 3) and $[\![S]\!] \longmapsto\!\!\!\!/$ and $[\![T]\!] \longmapsto\!\!\!\!/$. As above, the reduction $[\![S \mid T]\!] \longmapsto$ must be of the form $[\langle d_1 \rangle] \lhd$ $\mid \ldots \mid [\langle d_k \rangle] \lhd \mid [(z_1) \mid \ldots \mid (z_k)] \rhd T'$ for some $\tilde{d}$ and $\tilde{z}$ and k and T'. Again, assume that $[\![T]\!]$ has $[(z_1) \mid \ldots \mid (z_k)] \rhd T'$ at top-level (although the result does not rely on this assumption). Now $[\![S]\!]$ must contain at least one $[\langle d_j \rangle] \lhd$ (since otherwise $[\![T]\!] \longmapsto$ in violation of Proposition 1), and this must be at top-level by Proposition 2. Conclude by showing that $[\![S \mid \ldots \mid S \mid Q]\!] \longmapsto$ while $S \mid \ldots \mid S \mid Q \longmapsto\!\!\!\!/$ for i instances of S in contradiction with Proposition 1.

The splitting result is very similar with only minor adaptations to the proof.

Theorem 7. *There exists no valid encoding from* $\mathcal{L}_{A,P,D,NO,B}$ *into* $\mathcal{L}_{A,M,D,NO,L}$.

Proof. A straightforward adaptation of Theorem 6.

Corollary 3. *If there exists no valid encoding from* $\mathcal{L}_{\alpha_1,P,\gamma_1,\delta_1,B}$ *into* $\mathcal{L}_{\alpha_2,M,\gamma_2,\delta_2,B}$, *then there exists no valid encoding from* $\mathcal{L}_{\alpha_1,P,\gamma_1,\delta_1,\epsilon}$ *into* $\mathcal{L}_{\alpha_2,M,\gamma_2,\delta_2,\epsilon}$.

Proof. The techniques in Theorems 6 and 7 apply to all joining and splitting languages, respectively. Name-matching requires only a small change of $Q = [(x, y)] \rhd$ if $a = x$ then $\sqrt{}$ to then ensure binding occurs and not only name-matching; this is then proved via contradiction of name invariance and success sensitiveness like in Theorem 5. The techniques in Theorem 11 more elegantly show that channel-based communication is insufficient, so they are omitted here.

Thus any form of non-binary coordination does not allow for encoding a polyadic language into a monadic language unless it could already be encoded by some other means.

The other main results are to show that existing encodings between binary languages can be reproduced in other forms of coordination. This turns out to be a straightforward adaptation of the usual techniques.

Consider the usual encoding of $\mathcal{L}_{S,P,D,NO,B}$ into $\mathcal{L}_{S,M,C,NO,B}$ [39]:

$$[\![[\langle \tilde{a} \rangle] \lhd P]\!] \overset{\text{def}}{=} (\nu c)[\overline{n}\langle c \rangle] \lhd [\overline{c}\langle a_1 \rangle] \lhd \ldots \lhd [\overline{c}\langle a_n \rangle] \lhd [\![P]\!]$$
$$[\![[(\tilde{x})] \rhd Q]\!] \overset{\text{def}}{=} [n(z)] \rhd [z(x_1)] \rhd \ldots \rhd [z(x_n)] \rhd [\![Q]\!]$$

where c is not in the free names of $[\langle \tilde{a} \rangle] \lhd P$, and z is not in the free names of $[(\tilde{x})] \rhd Q$ or $\tilde{x}$. Also n is derived from $\tilde{a}$ since $\tilde{a} = a_1, \ldots, a_n$ (and similarly for $\tilde{x}$). Thus when an output and input agree upon their arity n then they interact with the output sending a fresh name c used for sending the n names $\tilde{a}$.

This can be adapted in the obvious manner, shown below for the encoding of $\mathcal{L}_{S,P,D,NO,J}$ into $\mathcal{L}_{S,M,C,NO,J}$.

$$[\![[\langle \tilde{a} \rangle] \lhd P]\!] \overset{\text{def}}{=} (\nu c)[\overline{n}\langle c \rangle] \lhd [\overline{c}\langle a_1 \rangle] \lhd \ldots \lhd [\overline{c}\langle a_n \rangle] \lhd [\![P]\!]$$
$$[\![[(\widetilde{x1})] \mid \ldots \mid (\widetilde{xk})] \rhd Q]\!] \overset{\text{def}}{=} [n1(z_1) \mid \ldots \mid nk(z_k)] \rhd [z_1(x1_1)] \rhd \ldots \rhd [z_1(x1_{n1})] \rhd$$
$$\ldots \rhd [z_k(xk_1)] \rhd \ldots \rhd [z_k(xk_{nk})] \rhd [\![Q]\!]$$

where the restrictions on z are here extended to distinct $z_1, \ldots, z_k$ for each input.

Theorem 8. *There is a valid encoding from $\mathcal{L}_{S,P,D,NO,J}$ into $\mathcal{L}_{S,M,C,NO,J}$.*

Proof. The proof technique is identical to Theorem 2.

This illustrates the key ideas for the following general result, that requires only straightforward adaptations of the proofs in the obvious manner. It is worth noting that all such results rely on the use of a channel-name, or an equivalent pattern match of some form to detect compatible arity and then ensure the right processes communicate. This is clearly available when adding channel-based communication, or when exploiting intensionality.

Theorem 9. *If there exists a valid encoding from $\mathcal{L}_{\alpha_1,P,\gamma_1,\delta_1,B}$ into $\mathcal{L}_{\alpha_2,M,\gamma_2,\delta_2,B}$ then there exists a valid encoding from $\mathcal{L}_{\alpha_1,P,\gamma_1,\delta_1,\epsilon}$ into $\mathcal{L}_{\alpha_2,M,\gamma_2,\delta_2,\epsilon}$.*

This confirms that encodings in the binary setting still exist in different coordination settings. Thus no expressiveness differences between languages are lost by changing coordination form, and existing results can be transferred.

6   Coordination and Communication Medium

This section considers the relation between coordination and communication medium. In general coordination is unable to encode communication medium unless it could otherwise be encoded by other features. This is proved by two main results: that if there is no valid encoding from a channel-based binary language to a dataspace-based binary language then there is no encoding when replacing binary with joining or splitting; and that if there exists a valid encoding from a channel-based binary language into a dataspace-based binary language then there exists an encoding with binary replaced by joining or splitting.

The base result for joining is illustrated in the following theorem, generalised in the corollary that follows.

Theorem 10. *There exists no valid encoding from $\mathcal{L}_{A,M,C,NO,B}$ into $\mathcal{L}_{A,M,D,NO,J}$.*

Proof. The proof is by contradiction and uses a very similar to that of Theorem 6. The differences are to use the $\mathcal{L}_{A,M,C,NO,B}$ processes $P = [\overline{a}\langle b\rangle]\lhd$ and $Q = [a(x)] \rhd \sqrt{}$ initially, and then $S = [\overline{c}\langle b\rangle]\lhd$ and $T = [c(z)] \rhd 0$ where $c \neq a$.

Theorem 11. *There exists no valid encoding from* $\mathcal{L}_{A,M,C,NO,B}$ *into* $\mathcal{L}_{A,M,D,NO,L}$.

Proof. The proof is by contradiction and very similar to that of Theorem 7, the main differences are to consider the $\mathcal{L}_{A,M,C,NO,B}$ processes $P = [\overline{a}\langle b\rangle]\lhd$ and $Q = [a(x)] \rhd \sqrt{}$, and then $S = [\overline{c}\langle d\rangle]\lhd$ and $T = [c(z)] \rhd 0$.

Corollary 4. *If there exists no valid encoding from* $\mathcal{L}_{\alpha_1,\beta_1,C,\delta_1,B}$ *into* $\mathcal{L}_{\alpha_2,\beta_2,D,\delta_2,B}$, *then there exists no valid encoding from* $\mathcal{L}_{\alpha_1,\beta_1,C,\delta_1,\epsilon}$ *into* $\mathcal{L}_{\alpha_2,\beta_2,D,\delta_2,\epsilon}$.

Proof. The technique in Theorems 10 and 11 apply to all monadic languages (the addition of name-matching can be proved using the techniques as in Theorem 4). For the polyadic no-matching setting the results above holds by observing that the arity must remain fixed for an encoding, i.e. $[\![\,[\overline{a}\langle b_1,\ldots,b_i\rangle]\lhd\,]\!]$ is encoded to inputs/outputs all of some arity j. If the arity is not uniform then the encoding fails either Proposition 1 (by showing that the reduction $[\![\,[a(x)] \rhd 0 \mid [\overline{a}\langle b_1,b_2\rangle]\lhd\,]\!] \longmapsto$ must occur) or divergence reflection (by showing that $[\![\,[a(x)] \rhd 0 \mid [\overline{a}\langle b_1,b_2\rangle]\lhd\,]\!] \longmapsto\Longmapsto [\![\,[a(x)] \rhd 0 \mid [\overline{a}\langle b_1,b_2\rangle]\lhd\,]\!]$ and so $[\![\,[a(x)] \rhd 0 \mid [\overline{a}\langle b_1,b_2\rangle]\lhd\,]\!] \longmapsto^\omega$).

Thus any form of non-binary coordination does not allow for encoding channels in a dataspace-based language unless it could already be encoded.

The positive encoding results are the typical adaptations of the positive encoding results in the binary setting. The adaptation of the usual encoding for $\mathcal{L}_{S,P,C,NM,J}$ into $\mathcal{L}_{S,P,D,NM,J}$ is the obvious one as below.

$$[\![\,[\overline{a}\langle\widetilde{c}\rangle] \lhd P\,]\!] \stackrel{\text{def}}{=} [\langle a,\widetilde{c}\rangle] \lhd [\![P]\!]$$

$$[\![\,[a_1(\widetilde{x1}) \mid \ldots \mid a_k(\widetilde{xk})] \rhd Q\,]\!] \stackrel{\text{def}}{=} [(\ulcorner a_1\urcorner,\widetilde{x1}) \mid \ldots \mid (\ulcorner a_k\urcorner,\widetilde{xk})] \rhd [\![Q]\!]$$

For the each channel-based output $\overline{a}\langle\widetilde{c}\rangle$ the channel name a is moved to the first position of the dataspace-based output $\langle a,\widetilde{c}\rangle$ in the encoding. The same is done for each channel-based input $a(\widetilde{x})$ becoming a dataspace-based input $(a,\widetilde{x})$.

Theorem 12. *There is a valid encoding from* $\mathcal{L}_{S,P,C,NM,J}$ *into* $\mathcal{L}_{S,P,D,NM,J}$.

Proof. The proof technique is identical to Theorem 2 (albeit simpler since each reduction in the source language corresponds to exactly one reduction in the target language and vice versa).

This illustrates the key ideas for the following general result, that requires only straightforward adaptations of the proofs in the obvious manner. Again all such results rely upon the use of pattern-matching, either via name-matching or intensionality, to represent the channel.

Theorem 13. *If there exists a valid encoding from $\mathcal{L}_{\alpha_1,\beta_1,C,\delta_1,B}$ into $\mathcal{L}_{\alpha_2,\beta_2,D,\delta_2,B}$ then there exists a valid encoding from $\mathcal{L}_{\alpha_1,\beta_1,C,\delta_1,\epsilon}$ into $\mathcal{L}_{\alpha_2,\beta_2,D,\delta_2,\epsilon}$.*

This confirms that encodings of channel-based communication into dataspace-based communication in the binary setting still exist in different coordination settings. Thus no expressiveness differences between languages are lost by changing coordination form, and existing results can be transferred.

7 Coordination and Pattern-Matching

This section considers the relations between coordination and pattern-matching. Intensionality cannot be encoded into a name-matching (or no-matching) language by exploiting joining or splitting. Similarly name-matching cannot be encoded into a no-matching language by exploiting joining or splitting.

To assist with the below theorem, define the *maximal interaction patterns* $\mathrm{MIP}(P)$ of a process P as follows:

$$\mathrm{MIP}(\mathbf{0}) = 0 \quad \mathrm{MIP}((\nu a)P) = \mathrm{MIP}(P) \quad \mathrm{MIP}(*P) = \mathrm{MIP}(P) \quad \mathrm{MIP}(\sqrt{}) = 0$$

$$\left.\begin{array}{r}\mathrm{MIP}(P \mid Q) \\ \mathrm{MIP}(\mathbf{if}\ s = t\ \mathbf{then}\ P\ \mathbf{else}\ Q)\end{array}\right\} = \begin{cases} \mathrm{MIP}(P)\ \text{if}\ \mathrm{MIP}(P) > \mathrm{MIP}(Q) \\ \mathrm{MIP}(Q)\ \text{otherwise}\end{cases}$$

$$\mathrm{MIP}([\langle \widetilde{t_1}\rangle \mid \ \ldots \ \mid \langle \widetilde{t_i}\rangle] \lhd P) = \textstyle\sum_{j=0,\ldots,i} |\widetilde{t_j}|$$

$$\mathrm{MIP}([\overline{s_1}\langle \widetilde{t_1}\rangle \mid \ \ldots \ \mid \overline{s_i}\langle \widetilde{t_i}\rangle] \lhd P) = i + \textstyle\sum_{j=0,\ldots,i} |\widetilde{t_j}|$$

$$\mathrm{MIP}([(\widetilde{p_1}) \mid \ \ldots \ \mid (\widetilde{p_i})] \rhd P) = \textstyle\sum_{j=0,\ldots,i} |\widetilde{p_j}|$$

$$\mathrm{MIP}([a_1(\widetilde{p_1}) \mid \ \ldots \ \mid a_i(\widetilde{p_i})] \rhd P) = i + \textstyle\sum_{j=0,\ldots,i} |\widetilde{p_j}|.$$

The intuition is that $\mathrm{MIP}(P)$ indicates the maximum number of patterns that can be matched by any single split or join of P (i.e. any single *OutProc* or *InProc*). For the null process, restriction, parallel composition, replication, conditional, and success process this is straightforward, the only non-trivial case is the conditional **if** $s = t$ **then** P **else** Q where both P and Q can be considered (this is to allow flexibility when substitutions may allow either P or Q to be possible). For the splits (resp. joins), when the language is dataspace-based then this is the sum of the arities of all outputs in the split (resp. inputs in the join), and when the language is channel-based the maximum interaction patterns also counts the channel terms ($i+$ above).

Lemma 4. *Given a process P (for any language), for all substitutions σ it holds that $\mathrm{MIP}(P) = \mathrm{MIP}(\sigma(P))$.*

Proof. The proof is straightforward by induction on the structure of P.

Observe that in name-matching languages, for any process P then $\mathrm{MIP}(P)$ is the upper bound on the number of names that can be matched in any split or join of P. For no-matching languages the upper bound is at most $\frac{\mathrm{MIP}(P)}{2}$ (when the maximum arity of any output in a split or input in a join is 1), although this is less significant to the result below. (For intensional languages there is no upper bound, related to $\mathrm{MIP}(P)$ or otherwise, however since the goal is to use $\mathrm{MIP}(P)$ to reason about non-intensional languages, this is not relevant).

The first result is to prove that intensionality cannot be encoded by coordination. Recall that since intensionality alone can encode all other features aside from coordination, it is sufficient to consider $\mathcal{L}_{A,M,D,I,B}$.

Theorem 14. *There exists no valid encoding from $\mathcal{L}_{A,M,D,I,B}$ into $\mathcal{L}_{-,-,-,\delta,J}$ where $\delta \neq I$.*

Proof. The proof is by contradiction. Assume there exists a valid encoding $[\![\cdot]\!]$ from $\mathcal{L}_{A,M,D,I,B}$ into $\mathcal{L}_{\alpha,\beta,\gamma,\delta,J}$ for some α and β and γ and δ where $\delta \neq I$. Consider the encoding of the processes $P = [(\ulcorner a\urcorner)] \triangleright P'$ and $Q = [\langle a \rangle] \triangleleft$. Because $P \mid Q \longmapsto$ then by Proposition 3 $[\![P \mid Q]\!] \longmapsto$. Now define $k = \mathrm{MIP}([\![P \mid Q]\!])$ and define $\sigma = \{b_1 \bullet \ldots \bullet b_{k+1}/a\}$. Observe that $\sigma(P \mid Q) \longmapsto$ and so $[\![\sigma(P \mid Q)]\!] \longmapsto$ by Proposition 3, and that the reduction $[\![\sigma(P \mid Q)]\!] \longmapsto$ can match at most k names because $k \geq$ the maximum possible patterns of any join in $[\![\sigma(P \mid Q)]\!]$ by Lemma 4 and $\delta \neq I$. Therefore, there must exist at least one name b_j (but assume only b_j for simplicity here) that is not being tested for equality either by a name match or channel name in the reduction $[\![\sigma(P \mid Q)]\!] \longmapsto$. Define $P' = [\langle m \rangle] \triangleleft$ and $\rho = \{m/b_j, b_j/m\}$. Now since b_j is not tested for equality in the reduction $[\![\sigma P \mid \sigma Q]\!] \longmapsto$ it follows that $[\![\rho \sigma P \mid \sigma Q]\!] \longmapsto$. Conclude by showing that $*(\rho \sigma P \mid \sigma Q)$ does not reduce (or diverge) while because $[\![\rho \sigma P \mid \sigma Q]\!] \longmapsto$ it follows that $[\![*(\rho \sigma P \mid \sigma Q)]\!] \longmapsto^{\omega}$ in violation of divergence reflection.

Theorem 15. *There exists no valid encoding from $\mathcal{L}_{A,M,D,I,B}$ into $\mathcal{L}_{-,-,-,\delta,L}$ where $\delta \neq I$.*

Proof. The same technique as in Theorem 14 can be applied for splitting.

Corollary 5. *If there exists no valid encoding from $\mathcal{L}_{\alpha_1,\beta_1,\gamma_1,I,B}$ into $\mathcal{L}_{\alpha_2,\beta_2,\gamma_2,\delta,B}$, then there exists no valid encoding from $\mathcal{L}_{\alpha_1,\beta_1,\gamma_1,I,\epsilon}$ into $\mathcal{L}_{\alpha_2,\beta_2,\gamma_2,\delta,\epsilon}$.*

Proof. The joining case is by Theorem 14 and the splitting by Theorem 15.

It follows that any form of coordination cannot represent intensionality in a language that does not have intensionality already (including name-matching or no-matching languages).

The next results show that coordination is insufficient to encode name matching. Unlike Theorem 14, these need to be separated into two results due to the encoding from $\mathcal{L}_{A,M,D,NM,B}$ into $\mathcal{L}_{A,M,C,NO,B}$ [28].

Theorem 16. *There exists no valid encoding from $\mathcal{L}_{A,M,D,NM,B}$ into $\mathcal{L}_{\alpha,\beta,D,NO,J}$.*

Proof. The proof is by contradiction, assume there exists a valid encoding $[\![\cdot]\!]$. Consider the $\mathcal{L}_{A,M,D,NM,B}$ processes $P = [\langle a \rangle] \triangleleft$ and $Q = [(\ulcorner a\urcorner)] \triangleright ([\langle b \rangle] \triangleleft \mid \sqrt{})$.

Observe that $P \mid Q \longmapsto$ and $P \mid Q \Downarrow$ and so $[\![\, P \mid Q \,]\!] \longmapsto$ and $[\![\, P \mid Q \,]\!] \Downarrow$ by Proposition 3 and validity of the encoding. Now consider the substitution $\sigma = \{c/a\}$, it follows that $P \mid \sigma Q \longmapsto\!\!\!\!\!/\,$ and so $[\![\, P \mid \sigma Q \,]\!] \longmapsto\!\!\!\!\!/\,$ by Proposition 1. Now if there is no blocking via an **if** $a_1 = a_2$ **then** S_1 **else** S_2 then this yields a contradiction in the usual manner (see Theorem 4) via either: $[\![\, P \mid \sigma Q \,]\!] \Downarrow$ while $P \mid \sigma Q \Downarrow\!\!\!\!\!/\,$, or $[\![\, \sigma(P \mid Q) \,]\!] \Downarrow\!\!\!\!\!/\,$ while $\sigma(P \mid Q) \Downarrow$. Therefore there must be a conditional **if** $a_1 = a_2$ **then** S_1 **else** S_2 that prevents reduction (there may be many, but assume one for simplicity). Further, this must be in $[\![\, Q \,]\!]$ because otherwise this would violate compositionality and success sensitivity with $\mathcal{C}^N_{|}([\![\, P \,]\!], \cdot)$ replacing $\cdot$ with $[\![\, Q \,]\!]$ or $[\![\, \sigma Q \,]\!]$. It must be that $a_1 \neq a_2$ in $[\![\, Q \,]\!]$ because otherwise if $a_1 = a_2$ then no substitution σ' (defined by name invariance $\sigma'[\![\, \cdot \,]\!] = [\![\, \sigma(\cdot) \,]\!]$) could make $\sigma' a_1 \neq \sigma' a_2$ when $a_1 = a_2$. Therefore, it must be that $\sigma' a_1 = \sigma' a_2$, however by considering the substitution $\rho = \{a/c\}$ (and associated ρ' from name invariance) it must be that $\rho' \sigma'[\![\, Q \,]\!] \simeq [\![\, Q \,]\!]$, yet ρ' cannot induce inequality in $\sigma' a_1 = \sigma' a_2$ and because no other mechanism can prevent interaction then because $[\![\, P \mid \rho \sigma Q \,]\!] \longmapsto$ (by Proposition 3) it follows that $[\![\, P \mid \sigma Q \,]\!] \longmapsto$ in violation of Proposition 1.

Theorem 17. *There exists no valid encoding from* $\mathcal{L}_{A,P,D,NM,B}$ *into* $\mathcal{L}_{\alpha,\beta,\gamma,NO,J}$.

Proof. The proof is by contradiction, assume there exists a valid encoding $[\![\, \cdot \,]\!]$. If $\gamma = D$ then the proof of Theorem 16 applies, so the rest of this proof shall assume $\gamma = C$. Consider the $\mathcal{L}_{A,P,D,NM,B}$ processes $P = [\langle a, b \rangle] \lhd$ and $Q = [(\ulcorner a \urcorner, \ulcorner b \urcorner)] \rhd Q'$. Observe that $P \mid Q \longmapsto$ and so $[\![\, P \mid Q \,]\!] \longmapsto$ by Proposition 3 and validity of the encoding. The reduction $[\![\, P \mid Q \,]\!] \longmapsto$ must be of the form $[\overline{c_1}\langle \widetilde{m_1} \rangle] \lhd \mid \ldots \mid [\overline{c_i}\langle \widetilde{m_i} \rangle] \lhd \mid [c_1(\widetilde{z_1})] \mid \ldots \mid c_i(\widetilde{z_i})] \rhd R'$ for some $\widetilde{c}$ and $\widetilde{m}$ and $\widetilde{z}$ and i and R'. Now consider the substitutions $\sigma = \{c/a\}$ and $\rho = \{d/b\}$ (and their associated substitutions on encoded processes σ' and ρ' determined by name invariance and validity of the encoding). Observe that because $\sigma P \mid Q \longmapsto\!\!\!\!\!/\,$ it follows that $\mathcal{C}^N_{|}(\sigma'[\![\, P \,]\!], [\![\, Q \,]\!]) \longmapsto\!\!\!\!\!/\,$ by Proposition 1. The reduction can only be prevented by either a conditional or the changing of a channel name via the substitution σ'. (Observe that conditionals may introduce or remove splits and joins accounting for missing components or changes in arity, and so the only other possibility for preventing reduction is by changing the channel name). If the reduction is prevented due to a conditional then contradiction can be achieved as in Theorem 16, so it must be that $\sigma'(c_j) \neq c_j$ for some $j \in \{1, \ldots, i\}$. The same can be shown for $\rho P \mid Q$ and some c_k such that $\rho'(c_k) \neq c_k$. Further, by exploiting the inverse substitutions denoted $\mathrm{inv}(\sigma)$ for the inversve of σ (defined in the obvious manner) it must be that $j \neq k$, because otherwise $\mathrm{inv}(\sigma')\rho'(c_j) = c_j$ and contradiction could be shown because $\mathrm{inv}(\sigma)\rho P \mid Q \longmapsto\!\!\!\!\!/\,$. Finally, because the join and all the splits involved in the reductions $[\![\, P \mid Q \,]\!] \longmapsto$ must be at top-level by Proposition 2, conclude by observing that $[\![\, \sigma P \mid \rho P \mid Q \mid \rho \sigma Q \,]\!] \longmapsto$ because all the components required for interaction are at top-level and because $[\![\, Q \mid \rho \sigma Q \,]\!]$ provides all the outputs (or inputs) required for the inputs (or outputs) of σP and ρP. However, because $\sigma P \mid \rho P \mid Q \mid \rho \sigma Q \longmapsto\!\!\!\!\!/\,$ this contradicts Proposition 1.

The next two results are the splitting version of the two theorems above.

Theorem 18. *There exists no valid encoding from* $\mathcal{L}_{A,M,D,NM,B}$ *into* $\mathcal{L}_{\alpha,\beta,D,NO,L}$.

Proof. The same technique as in Theorem 16 can be applied here.

Theorem 19. *There exists no valid encoding from* $\mathcal{L}_{A,P,D,NM,B}$ *into* $\mathcal{L}_{\alpha,\beta,\gamma,NO,L}$.

Proof. The same technique as in Theorem 17 can be applied here.

Corollary 6. *If there exists no valid encoding from* $\mathcal{L}_{\alpha_1,\beta_1,\gamma_1,NM,B}$ *into* $\mathcal{L}_{\alpha_2,\beta_2,\gamma_2,\delta,B}$, *then there exists no valid encoding from* $\mathcal{L}_{\alpha_1,\beta_1,\gamma_1,NM,\epsilon}$ *into* $\mathcal{L}_{\alpha_2,\beta_2,\gamma_2,\delta,\epsilon}$.

Proof. The joining cases are covered by Theorems 16 and 17 and the splitting by Theorems 18 and 19.

Thus coordination does not allow for encoding name-matching into a no-matching language unless it could already be encoded by some other means.

For the positive results that remain it is straightforward to adapt the existing encodings in the same manner as for Corollary 1, and Theorems 9 and 13.

Theorem 20. *If there exists a valid encoding from* $\mathcal{L}_{\alpha,\beta,\gamma,\delta_1,B}$ *into* $\mathcal{L}_{\alpha,\beta,\gamma,\delta_2,B}$ *where* $\delta_1 \leq \delta_2$ *then there exists a valid encoding from* $\mathcal{L}_{\alpha,\beta,\gamma,\delta_1,\epsilon}$ *into* $\mathcal{L}_{\alpha,\beta,\gamma,\delta_2,\epsilon}$.

Proof. The same techniques as Corollary 1, and Theorems 9 and 13 can be applied.

Finally, the positive results that preserve encodings when changing the coordination feature can be combined into a single general result.

Corollary 7. *If there exists a valid encoding from* $\mathcal{L}_{\alpha_1,\beta_1,\gamma_1,\delta_1,B}$ *into* $\mathcal{L}_{\alpha_2,\beta_2,\gamma_2,\delta_2,B}$ *then there exists a valid encoding from* $\mathcal{L}_{\alpha_1,\beta_1,\gamma_1,\delta_1,\epsilon}$ *into* $\mathcal{L}_{\alpha_2,\beta_2,\gamma_2,\delta_2,\epsilon}$.

Proof. By combining Corollary 1, and Theorems 9, 13, and 20.

8   Coordination and Other Features

This section considers the expressive power gained by coordination. It turns out that coordination adds expressive power that cannot be represented by binary languages regardless of other features.

The expressive power gained by joining or splitting can be captured by the concept of the *coordination degree* of a language $\mathcal{L}$, denoted $\mathrm{CD}(\mathcal{L})$, as the least upper bound on the number of processes that must coordinate to yield a particular reduction in $\mathcal{L}$. For example, all the binary languages $\mathcal{L}_{-,-,-,-,B}$ have coordination degree 2 since their reduction axiom is only defined for two processes. By contrast, the coordination degree of the non-binary languages is ∞ since there is no bound on the number of inputs that can be part of a join, or outputs that can be part of a split.

Theorem 21. *If* $\text{CD}(\mathcal{L}_1) > \text{CD}(\mathcal{L}_2)$ *then there exists no valid encoding* $[\![\cdot]\!]$ *from* $\mathcal{L}_1$ *into* $\mathcal{L}_2$.

Proof. By contradiction, assume there is a valid encoding $[\![\cdot]\!]$. Fix N and pick i processes S_1 to S_i where $i = \text{CD}(\mathcal{L}_2) + 1$ and $N = \bigcup \text{fn}(S_j)$ for $j \in \{1, \ldots, i\}$ such that all these processes must coordinate to yield a reduction and yield success. That is: $S_1 \mid \ldots \mid S_i \longmapsto \sqrt{}$ but not if any S_j (for $1 \leq j \leq i$) is replaced by $block(S_j)$. By validity of the encoding and Proposition 3 it must be that $[\![S_1 \mid \ldots \mid S_i]\!] \Downarrow$ and $[\![S_1 \mid \ldots \mid S_i]\!] \longmapsto$.

By compositionality of the encoding $[\![S_1 \mid \ldots \mid S_i]\!] = \mathcal{C}_S = \mathcal{C}_{|}^N([\![S_1]\!],$ $\mathcal{C}_{|}^N(\ldots, \mathcal{C}_{|}^N([\![S_{i-1}]\!], [\![S_i]\!])))$. Now consider the reduction $[\![S_1 \mid \ldots \mid S_i]\!] \longmapsto$ that can be at most between $i - 1$ processes by the coordination degree of $\mathcal{L}_2$. If the reduction does *not* involve some process $[\![S_j]\!]$ then it follows that $[\![S_1 \mid \ldots \mid S_{j-1} \mid block(S_j)]\!] \mid S_{j+1} \mid \ldots \mid S_i \longmapsto$ (by replacing the $[\![S_j]\!]$ in the context $\mathcal{C}_S$ with $[\![block(S_j)]\!]$). By construction of $S_1 \mid \ldots \mid S_i$ and $\text{CD}(\mathcal{L}_2) < i$ there must exist some such S_j. However, this contradicts the validity of the encoding since $S_1 \mid \ldots \mid S_{j-1} \mid block(S_j) \mid S_{j+1} \mid \ldots \mid S_i \not\longmapsto$. The only other possibility to prevent reduction of $[\![S_1 \mid \ldots \mid S_{j-1} \mid block(S_j) \mid S_{j+1} \mid \ldots \mid S_i]\!]$ is if $[\![block(S_j)]\!]$ blocks the reduction by blocking some $[\![S_k]\!]$. This can only occur when $[\![S_k]\!]$ is either underneath an interaction primitive (e.g. $[\overline{s}\langle \tilde{t} \rangle] \lhd [\![S_k]\!]$) or inside a conditional (e.g. **if** $s = t$ **then** $[\![S_k]\!]$ where $s \neq t$). Both require that $[\![S_k]\!]$ not be top-level in $\mathcal{C}_S$, which can be proven contradictory by Proposition 2.

The above may not appear intuitive when some implementations of n-ary coordination are achieved by 2-ary coordination. However, the result shows that such implementations must have conditions under which they begin coordination when the coordination cannot be completed and so either: become stuck waiting for further coordination; or must roll-back to a prior state. The first case would here invalidate the encoding by blocking an alternative valid coordination, while the second case would here indicate an infinite reduction sequence again invalidating the encoding.

Corollary 8. *There exists no valid encoding from* $\mathcal{L}_{-,-,-,-,\epsilon}$ *into* $\mathcal{L}_{-,-,-,-,B}$ *where* $\epsilon \neq B$.

In the other direction the result is ensured by Remark 1. Thus for any languages $\mathcal{L}_{\alpha,\beta,\gamma,\delta,\epsilon_1}$ and $\mathcal{L}_{\alpha,\beta,\gamma,\delta,\epsilon_2}$ where $\epsilon_1 < \epsilon_2$ then it holds that $\mathcal{L}_{\alpha,\beta,\gamma,\delta,\epsilon_2}$ is strictly more expressive than $\mathcal{L}_{\alpha,\beta,\gamma,\delta,\epsilon_1}$. That is, joining or splitting languages are strictly more expressive than binary languages.

Thus coordination turns out to be orthogonal to all other features, since from the prior sections coordination cannot encode any other feature, and here it is proven that other features cannot encode coordination.

9 Within Coordination

This section considers relations between different forms of coordination. It turns out that there are some encodings from joining languages into splitting languages and vice versa, however most joining and splitting languages are unrelated.

A joining (resp. splitting) language without matching capabilities can be encoded into a splitting (resp. joining) language. For example, consider the encoding from $\mathcal{L}_{S,M,C,NO,J}$ to $\mathcal{L}_{S,M,C,NO,L}$ that is the identity on all forms except the output and join as follows:

$$[\![\, [\overline{a}\langle b\rangle] \lhd P \,]\!] \overset{\mathrm{def}}{=} [a(c)] \rhd [\overline{c}\langle b\rangle] \lhd [\![\, P \,]\!]$$

$$[\![\, [a_1(x_1)] \mid \ldots \mid a_i(x_i)] \rhd Q \,]\!] \overset{\mathrm{def}}{=} (\nu\widetilde{c})([\overline{a_1}\langle c_1\rangle \mid \ldots \mid \overline{a_i}\langle c_i\rangle] \lhd$$
$$[c_1(x_1)] \rhd \ldots \rhd [c_i(x_i)] \rhd [\![\, Q \,]\!])$$

where c is not b or in the free names of P; and $\widetilde{c}$ does not intersect with $\widetilde{a}$ or $\widetilde{x}$ or the free names of Q. The key idea is that the direction of communication is reversed; splits become joins (with outputs becoming inputs), and joins become splits (with inputs becoming outputs), a fresh name c is transmitted to be used for then sending the original name b from the output to the encoded join. Thus the requirement that all inputs of a join interact at once is maintained by all the outputs of the split. Observe that this is similar in concept to the encoding of synchrony into asynchrony by Honda and Tokoro [32].

Theorem 22. *The encoding from $\mathcal{L}_{S,M,C,NO,J}$ into $\mathcal{L}_{S,M,C,NO,L}$ is valid.*

Proof. The proof technique is identical to Theorem 2.

The same approach can be used to encode $\mathcal{L}_{S,M,C,NO,L}$ into $\mathcal{L}_{S,M,C,NO,J}$ with adjustments to the split and join as follows:

$$[\![\, [\overline{a_1}\langle b_1\rangle \mid \ldots \mid \overline{a_i}\langle b_i\rangle] \lhd P \,]\!] \overset{\mathrm{def}}{=} [a_1(c_1) \mid \ldots \mid a_i(c_i)] \rhd$$
$$[\overline{c_1}\langle b_1\rangle] \lhd \ldots \lhd [\overline{c_i}\langle b_i\rangle] \lhd [\![\, P \,]\!]$$

$$[\![\, [a(x)] \rhd Q \,]\!] \overset{\mathrm{def}}{=} (\nu c)[\overline{a}\langle c\rangle] \lhd [c(x)] \rhd [\![\, Q \,]\!]$$

$\widetilde{c}$ does not intersect $\widetilde{b}$ or free names of P; and c is not a or in free names of Q.

Theorem 23. *The encoding from $\mathcal{L}_{S,M,C,NO,L}$ into $\mathcal{L}_{S,M,C,NO,J}$ is valid.*

Proof. The proof technique is identical to Theorem 2.

Interestingly there are encodings that do not require channel names for the language that are dataspace-based and no-matching. Consider the following encoding from $\mathcal{L}_{S,M,D,NO,J}$ to $\mathcal{L}_{S,M,D,NO,L}$ that is the identity of all forms except the split and join as follows:

$$[\![\, [\langle a\rangle] \lhd P \,]\!] \overset{\mathrm{def}}{=} [(x)] \rhd [\langle a\rangle] \lhd [\![\, P \,]\!]$$

$$[\![\, [(x_1)] \mid \ldots \mid (x_i)] \rhd Q \,]\!] \overset{\mathrm{def}}{=} (\nu\widetilde{c})([\langle c_1\rangle \mid \ldots \mid \langle c_i\rangle] \lhd$$
$$[(x_1)] \rhd \ldots \rhd [(x_i)] \rhd [\![\, Q \,]\!])$$

where x is not a or in the free names of $[\![\, P \,]\!]$; and $\widetilde{c}$ does not intersect the free names of $[\![\, Q \,]\!]$. Again the key idea is to reverse the direction of communication, only now no attempt is made to maintain the relation of which encoded process initiated communication with which. This turns out not to be a concern since the split that represents the encoded join ensures sufficient encoded outputs are available before reduction, although the actual binding of names may not match that initial reduction. For example, $[\![[\langle a \rangle] \vartriangleleft \mid [\langle b \rangle] \vartriangleleft]\!]$ may begin a reduction with $[\![[(x) \mid (y)] \vartriangleright P]\!]$, i.e. $[\![[\langle a \rangle] \vartriangleleft \mid [\langle b \rangle] \vartriangleleft \mid [(x) \mid (y)] \vartriangleright P]\!] \longmapsto S$ and similarly, $[\![[\langle c \rangle] \vartriangleleft]\!]$ and $[\![[(z)] \vartriangleright Q]\!]$ may begin with a reduction $[\![[\langle c \rangle] \vartriangleleft [(z)] \vartriangleright Q]\!] \longmapsto T$. Despite these initial reductions, it is still possible for $S \mid T \Longmapsto \{b/x, c/y\}P \mid \{a/z\}Q$. This may seem unusual, but despite this lack of control over where the actual names are communicated after the initial reductions of an encoded join, this still meets the criteria for a valid encoding.

Theorem 24. *The encoding from $\mathcal{L}_{S,M,D,NO,J}$ into $\mathcal{L}_{S,M,D,NO,L}$ is valid.*

Proof. The proof technique is identical to Theorem 2.

Theorem 25. *There exists a valid encoding from $\mathcal{L}_{S,M,D,NO,L}$ into $\mathcal{L}_{S,M,D,NO,J}$.*

Proof. The same approach is used as in Theorem 23.

The same techniques can be applied to the asynchronous and polyadic variations of the above languages.

Theorem 26. *The languages $\mathcal{L}_{-,\beta,\gamma,NO,J}$ and $\mathcal{L}_{-,\beta,\gamma,NO,L}$ can validly encode each other.*

Proof. The proof technique is identical to Theorem 2.

However there are usually not encodings between joining and splitting languages. This can be illustrated by considering attempts to encode any sort of name-matching from either joining or splitting into the other.

Theorem 27. *There exists no valid encoding from $\mathcal{L}_{A,M,D,NM,J}$ into $\mathcal{L}_{-,-,-,-,L}$.*

Proof. The proof is by contradiction. (Note that the proof assumes channels in the target language as this is more general, they are simply omitted for the data-space based languages). Consider the processes $P = [(\ulcorner a \urcorner) \mid (\ulcorner b \urcorner)] \vartriangleright P'$ and $Q_1 = [\langle a \rangle] \vartriangleleft$ and $Q_2 = [\langle b \rangle] \vartriangleleft$. Because $P \mid Q_1 \mid Q_2 \longmapsto \sqrt{}$ by instantiating $P' = \sqrt{}$, then by validity of the encoding and Proposition 3 $[\![P \mid Q_1 \mid Q_2]\!] \longmapsto$, now consider this reduction. It must be between $R_1 = [\overline{s_1}\langle \widetilde{t_1} \rangle \mid \ldots \mid \overline{s_i}\langle \widetilde{t_i} \rangle] \vartriangleleft R'_1$ and R_2 for some $\widetilde{s}$ and $\widetilde{t}$ and R'_1 and R_2 such that $R_1 \mid R_2 \longmapsto$. Observe that $R_1 \mid R_2$ cannot be a parallel component of $[\![P \mid Q_1 \mid \mathbf{0}]\!]$ or $[\![P \mid \mathbf{0} \mid Q_2]\!]$ or $[\![\mathbf{0} \mid Q_1 \mid Q_2]\!]$ because this would contradict Proposition 1.

If R_1 is a top level component of $[\![Q_1]\!]$ or $[\![Q_2]\!]$ then $[\![P]\!]$ must exhibit some join $[s(\widetilde{p})] \vartriangleright R'_2$ that interacts with R_1 because otherwise $[\![\mathbf{0} \mid Q_1 \mid Q_2]\!] \longmapsto$ which contradicts Proposition 1. Now by Proposition 3 and considering the substitution $\sigma = \{c/a, c/b\}$ it must be that $[s(\widetilde{p})] \vartriangleright R'_2$ tests equality of some translated names of both $\varphi_{[\![}(a)$ and $\varphi_{[\![}(b)$ because otherwise one of $[\![\,P \mid \sigma Q_1 \mid Q_2\,]\!]$ or $[\![\,P \mid Q_1 \mid \sigma Q_2\,]\!]$ or $[\![\,P \mid \sigma Q_1 \mid \sigma Q_2\,]\!]$ would reduce in contradiction with Proposition 1. Further, because $[s(\widetilde{p})] \triangleright R_2'$ must test names from both $[\![\,Q_1\,]\!]$ and $[\![\,Q_2\,]\!]$ then R_1 must come from only the encoding $[\![\,Q_1 \mid Q_2\,]\!]$ and not from either of $[\![\,Q_1\,]\!]$ and $[\![\,Q_2\,]\!]$ alone. However, by considering $S = [(x)] \triangleright S_1 \mid [(y)] \triangleright S_2$ and the fact that $S \mid Q_1 \mid Q_2 \longmapsto$ and $S \mid Q_1 \mid 0 \longmapsto$ and $S \mid 0 \mid Q_2 \longmapsto$ it follows that either: both $[\![\,Q_1\,]\!]$ and $[\![\,Q_2\,]\!]$ must exhibit a top-level split, or $[\![\,Q_1 \mid Q_2\,]\!]$ must exhibit more than one top-level split. In both cases this yields a contradiction via $[\![\,S \mid P \mid Q_1 \mid Q_2\,]\!]$ with $S_1 = \surd$ and $P' = \Omega$ by violating either success sensitiveness or operational correspondence (as in concluding Theorem 4).

Therefore, it must be that R_1 is a top-level component of $[\![\,P\,]\!]$, so consider the process $S = [(z)] \triangleright S'$ such that $Q_1 \mid S \longmapsto$ and $[\![\,Q_1 \mid S\,]\!] \longmapsto$ (by instantiating $S' = \surd$ and Proposition 3). Observe that $[\![\,Q_1\,]\!]$ interacts with $[\![\,P\,]\!]$ via some $[s_j(\widetilde{p})] \triangleright Q_1'$ (there may be many such, but assume one for simplicity because the following can be proved for all of them). Now consider the reduction $[\![\,Q_1 \mid S\,]\!] \longmapsto$:

- If it is via the same $[s_j(\widetilde{p})] \triangleright Q_1'$ that interacts with $[\![\,P\,]\!]$ then there must be some $[\ldots \mid \overline{s_j}\langle \widetilde{t}\rangle \mid \ldots] \triangleleft T'$ in $[\![\,S\,]\!]$ such that $\mathrm{MATCH}(\widetilde{t}, \widetilde{p})$ is defined. Observe that this must not rely on equality/matching of any names that depend upon a because otherwise the substitution $\sigma = \{c/a\}$ would prevent the reduction of $[\![\,Q_1 \mid \sigma S\,]\!]$ yet $Q_1 \mid \sigma S \longmapsto$ and so this yields contradiction via Proposition 3. However, because no name in $[s_j(\widetilde{p})] \triangleright Q_1'$ depends upon a it follows that $[\![\,P \mid \sigma Q_1 \mid Q_2\,]\!] \longmapsto$ which contradicts Proposition 1.
- Otherwise it must be that the reduction is via some different input or output in $[\![\,Q_1\,]\!]$. However, then contradiction can be achieved via success sensitiveness or divergence reflection in a similar manner to the conclusion of Theorem 4 by instantiating $P' = \surd$ and $S' = \mathbf{if}\ z = a\ \mathbf{then}\ \Omega$ and considering $[\![\,P \mid Q_1 \mid Q_2 \mid S \mid \sigma Q_1\,]\!]$.

Theorem 28. *There exists no valid encoding from* $\mathcal{L}_{A,M,D,NM,L}$ *into* $\mathcal{L}_{-,-,-,-,J}$.

Proof. The proof is by contradiction in a similar manner to Theorem 27 by starting with the processes $P = [(a) \mid (b)] \triangleleft$ and $Q_1 = [(\ulcorner a \urcorner)] \triangleright Q_1'$ and $Q_2 = [(\ulcorner b \urcorner)] \triangleright Q_2'$.

These results show that once name-matching (or intensionality) is in play it is no longer possible for splitting or joining languages to encode one another.

Corollary 9. *There exists no valid encoding from* $\mathcal{L}_{A,M,D,I,J}$ *into* $\mathcal{L}_{-,-,-,-,L}$.

Corollary 10. *There exists no valid encoding from* $\mathcal{L}_{A,M,D,I,L}$ *into* $\mathcal{L}_{-,-,-,-,J}$.

Thus although there are some languages where a difference only of joining or splitting prove equally expressive, in general different forms of coordination usually indicate differences in expressive power.

10   Conclusions

In the theme of Barnhard Steffen's work this paper demonstrates expressiveness of different approaches to workflow coordination and their relation to other language features. This paper formalises that increases in coordination always correspond to increases in expressive power: both joining and splitting languages are strictly more expressive than binary languages. However, this expressive power does not allow coordination to encode other aspects of communication; increasing coordination does not allow encoding of other features unless they could already be encoded.

This formalizes that languages using Join Calculus style joins such as general rendezvous calculus, and m-calculus cannot be validly encoded into binary languages, regardless of other features. Although there exist approaches to encoding from these kinds of languages into π-calculus, these often do not meet the criteria for a *valid encoding* used here. A common approach [19] used in such encodings is to encode joins by $[\![\, [m(x) \mid n(y)] \rhd P \,]\!] = m(x).n(y).[\![\, P \,]\!]$, however this can easily fail operational correspondence, or success sensitivity. For example consider $P_1 = [c_1(w) \mid c_2(x)] \rhd \sqrt{}$ and $P_2 = [c_2(y) \mid c_1(z)] \rhd \Omega$ and $Q = \overline{c_1}\langle a \rangle \mid \overline{c_2}\langle b \rangle$. Together $P_1 \mid P_2 \mid Q$ can either report success or diverge, but their encoding $[\![\, P_1 \mid P_2 \mid Q \,]\!]$ can deadlock. Even ordering the channel names to prevent this can be shown to fail under substitutions. However, there are different forms of encodings between such calculi and π-calculi that do not meet the criteria used here [19,51]. The interesting cases are where joining calculi are encoded into π-calculi. Those in [19] still suffer the problem above for the criteria used here although they are not an issue for the full abstraction result obtained. In [51] the author asserts the existence of an encoding from Join Calculus into a π-calculus with the same communication paradigm as $\mathcal{L}_{A,M,C,N,B}$ here. However, they choose a different instantiation of Gorla's encoding criteria to here, opting for a non-reduction-sensitive equivalence relation. These different choices in the formal relations mean the results do not quite conflict with those here, instead illustrating the impact of different encoding criteria. This aligns with other results [52] where it is shown that the communication primitives of joins cannot be encoded into the communication primitives of π-calculi under different definitions of encoding.

That a language with coordination degree n cannot be encoded into a language with coordination degree less than n aligns with some recent results. Laneve and Vitale considered "synchronization" from a perspective that appears similar but is in fact rather different [36]. They consider languages to have *n-join* forms where n is the number of inputs a process can have. Thus, $[a_1(x_1) \mid \ldots \mid a_i(x_i)] \rhd P$ has an i-join. They then show that an n-join language cannot be encoded into an $(n-1)$-join language, this agrees with the results here. (Indeed, the results here generalise this by considering both joining and splitting). They further show that if mixed "joins" are allowed that can contain both inputs and outputs (e.g. $[a(x) \mid \overline{b}\langle c \rangle] \rhd P$) then any n-join language can be encoded into a 3-join language. However, in doing this the number of processes that must coordinate to perform the encoded reduction increases, i.e. the coordination degree must increase. This further reinforces the results here.

References

1. Abadi, M., Gordon, A.D.: A calculus for cryptographic protocols: the spi calculus. In: Proceedings of the 4th ACM Conference on Computer and Communications Security, CCS 1997, pp. 36–47. ACM, New York (1997)
2. Bengtson, J., Johansson, M., Parrow, J., Victor, B.: Psi-calculi: a framework for mobile processes with nominal data and logic. Log. Methods Comput. Sci. 7(1) (2011)
3. Bengtson, J., Parrow, J.: Formalising the pi-calculus using nominal logic. Log. Methods Comput. Sci. 5(2), 63–77 (2009)
4. Bocchi, L., Wischik, L.: A process calculus of atomic commit. Electron. Notes Theor. Comput. Sci. 105, 119–132 (2004). Proceedings of the First International Workshop on Web Services and Formal Methods (WSFM 2004)
5. Boreale, M., Fournet, C., Laneve, C.: Bisimulations in the Join-Calculus. In: Gries, D., de Roever, W.-P. (eds.) Programming Concepts and Methods PROCOMET '98. ITIFIP, pp. 68–86. Springer, Boston, MA (1998). https://doi.org/10.1007/978-0-387-35358-6_9
6. Boudol, G.: Notes on algebraic calculi of processes. In: Apt, K.R. (ed.) Logics and Models of Concurrent Systems. NATO ASI Series (Series F: Computer and Systems Sciences), vol. 13, pp. 261–303. Springer, Heidelberg (1985). https://doi.org/10.1007/978-3-642-82453-1_9
7. Boudol, G.: Asynchrony and the pi-calculus. Rapport de Recherche 1702 (1992)
8. Burkart, O., Caucal, D., Steffen, B.: Bisimulation collapse and the process taxonomy. In: Montanari, U., Sassone, V. (eds.) CONCUR 1996. LNCS, vol. 1119, pp. 247–262. Springer, Heidelberg (1996). https://doi.org/10.1007/3-540-61604-7_59
9. Busi, N., Gorrieri, R., Zavattaro, G.: On the expressiveness of linda coordination primitives. Inf. Comput. 156(1–2), 90–121 (2000)
10. Carbone, M., Maffeis, S.: On the expressive power of polyadic synchronisation in π-calculus. Nord. J. Comput. 10(2), 70–98 (2003)
11. Cardelli, L., Gordon, A.D.: Mobile ambients. In: Nivat, M. (ed.) FoSSaCS 1998. LNCS, vol. 1378, pp. 140–155. Springer, Heidelberg (1998). https://doi.org/10.1007/BFb0053547
12. Cassel, S., Howar, F., Jonsson, B., Merten, M., Steffen, B.: A succinct canonical register automaton model. J. Log. Algebr. Meth. Program. 84(1), 54–66 (2015)
13. Castagna, G., De Nicola, R., Varacca, D.: Semantic subtyping for the pi-calculus. Theor. Comput. Sci. 398(1–3), 217–242 (2008)
14. de Lara, J., Zisman, A. (eds.): FASE 2012. LNCS, vol. 7212. Springer, Heidelberg (2012). https://doi.org/10.1007/978-3-642-28872-2
15. De Nicola, R., Ferrari, G.L., Pugliese, R.: KLAIM: a kernel language for agents interaction and mobility. IEEE Trans. Softw. Eng. 24(5), 315–330 (1998)
16. De Nicola, R., Gorla, D., Pugliese, R.: On the expressive power of Klaim-based calculi. Theor. Comput. Sci. 356(3), 387–421 (2006)
17. de Simone, R.: Higher-level synchronising devices in Meije-SCCS. Theor. Comput. Sci. 37, 245–267 (1985)
18. Ene, C., Muntean, T.: A broadcast-based calculus for communicating systems. In: International Parallel and Distributed Processing Symposium, vol. 3, p. 30149b. IEEE Computer Society (2001)

19. Fournet, C., Gonthier, G.: The reflexive CHAM and the join-calculus. In: Proceedings of the 23rd ACM Symposium on Principles of Programming Languages, pp. 372–385. ACM Press (1996)
20. Gelernter, D.: Generative communication in LINDA. ACM Trans. Program. Lang. Syst. **7**(1), 80–112 (1985)
21. Given-Wilson, T.: Concurrent Pattern Unification. Ph.D. thesis, University of Technology, Sydney, Australia (2012)
22. Given-Wilson, T.: An intensional concurrent faithful encoding of turing machines. In: Lanese, I., Lluch-Lafuente, A., Sokolova, A., Vieira, H.T. (eds.) Proceedings 7th Interaction and Concurrency Experience, ICE 2014, Berlin, Germany, 6th June 2014. EPTCS, vol. 166, pp. 21–37 (2014)
23. Given-Wilson, T.: On the expressiveness of intensional communication. In: Combined 21th International Workshop on Expressiveness in Concurrency and 11th Workshop on Structural Operational Semantics, Rome, Italie, September 2014
24. Given-Wilson, T., Gorla, D.: Pattern matching and bisimulation. In: De Nicola, R., Julien, C. (eds.) COORDINATION 2013. LNCS, vol. 7890, pp. 60–74. Springer, Heidelberg (2013). https://doi.org/10.1007/978-3-642-38493-6_5
25. Given-Wilson, T., Gorla, D., Jay, B.: Concurrent pattern calculus. In: Calude, C.S., Sassone, V. (eds.) TCS 2010. IAICT, vol. 323, pp. 244–258. Springer, Heidelberg (2010). https://doi.org/10.1007/978-3-642-15240-5_18
26. Given-Wilson, T., Gorla, D., Jay, B.: A concurrent pattern calculus. Log. Methods Comput. Sci. **10**(3) (2014)
27. Given-Wilson, T., Legay, A.: On the expressiveness of joining. In: 8th Interaction and Concurrency Experience (ICE 2015), Grenoble, France, June 2015
28. Gorla, D.: Comparing communication primitives via their relative expressive power. Inf. Comput. **206**(8), 931–952 (2008)
29. Gorla, D.: A taxonomy of process calculi for distribution and mobility. Distrib. Comput. **23**(4), 273–299 (2010)
30. Gorla, D.: Towards a unified approach to encodability and separation results for process calculi. Inf. Comput. **208**(9), 1031–1053 (2010)
31. Haack, C., Jeffrey, A.: Pattern-matching spi-calculus. Inf. Comput. **204**(8), 1195–1263 (2006)
32. Honda, K., Tokoro, M.: An object calculus for asynchronous communication. In: America, P. (ed.) ECOOP 1991. LNCS, vol. 512, pp. 133–147. Springer, Heidelberg (1991). https://doi.org/10.1007/BFb0057019
33. Honda, K., Yoshida, N.: On reduction-based process semantics. Theor. Comput. Sci. **152**, 437–486 (1995)
34. Lanese, I., Pérez, J.A., Sangiorgi, D., Schmitt, A.: On the expressiveness of polyadic and synchronous communication in higher-order process calculi. In: Abramsky, S., Gavoille, C., Kirchner, C., Meyer auf der Heide, F., Spirakis, P.G. (eds.) ICALP 2010. LNCS, vol. 6199, pp. 442–453. Springer, Heidelberg (2010). https://doi.org/10.1007/978-3-642-14162-1_37
35. Lanese, I., Vaz, C., Ferreira, C.: On the expressive power of primitives for compensation handling. In: Gordon, A.D. (ed.) ESOP 2010. LNCS, vol. 6012, pp. 366–386. Springer, Heidelberg (2010). https://doi.org/10.1007/978-3-642-11957-6_20
36. Laneve, C., Vitale, A.: The expressive power of synchronizations. In: 2010 25th Annual IEEE Symposium on Logic in Computer Science (LICS), pp. 382–391. IEEE (2010)

37. Margaria, T., Steffen, B.: Middleware: just another level for orchestration. In: Proceedings of the Workshop on Middleware for Next-Generation Converged Networks and Applications, MNCNA 2007, Newport Beach, California, USA, 26 November 2007, p. 4. ACM (2007)
38. Milner, R.: The polyadic π-calculus: a tutorial. In: Bauer, F.L., Brauer, W., Schwichtenberg, H. (eds.) Logic and Algebra of Specification. NATO ASI Series (Series F: Computer & Systems Sciences), vol. 94, pp. 203–246. Springer, Heidelberg (1993). https://doi.org/10.1007/978-3-642-58041-3_6
39. Milner, R.: Communicating and Mobile Systems - the Pi-Calculus. Cambridge University Press, Cambridge (1999)
40. Milner, R., Parrow, J., Walker, D.: A calculus of mobile processes, I. Inf. Comput. **100**(1), 1–40 (1992)
41. Milner, R., Parrow, J., Walker, D.: A calculus of mobile processes, II. Inf. Comput. **100**(1), 41–77 (1992)
42. Naujokat, S., Lamprecht, A., Steffen, B.: Tailoring process synthesis to domain characteristics. In: Perseil, I., Breitman, K.K., Sterritt, R. (eds.) 16th IEEE International Conference on Engineering of Complex Computer Systems, ICECCS 2011, Las Vegas, Nevada, USA, 27–29 April 2011, pp. 167–175. IEEE Computer Society (2011)
43. Nestmann, U.: On the expressive power of joint input. Electron. Notes Theor. Comput. Sci. **16**(2), 145–152 (1998)
44. Neubauer, J., Steffen, B.: Plug-and-play higher-order process integration. IEEE Comput. **46**(11), 56–62 (2013)
45. Neubauer, J., Steffen, B., Margaria, T.: Higher-order process modeling: product-lining, variability modeling and beyond. In: Banerjee, A., Danvy, O., Doh, K., Hatcliff, J. (eds.) Semantics, Abstract Interpretation, and Reasoning about Programs: Essays Dedicated to David A. Schmidt on the Occasion of his Sixtieth Birthday, Manhattan, Kansas, USA, 19–20th September 2013. EPTCS, vol. 129, pp. 259–283 (2013)
46. Nielsen, L., Yoshida, N., Honda, K.: Multiparty symmetric sum types. In: Proceedings of the 17th International Workshop on Expressiveness in Concurrency (EXPRESS 2010), pp. 121–135 (2010)
47. Nielson, H.R., Nielson, F., Vigo, R.: A calculus for quality. In: Păsăreanu, C.S., Salaün, G. (eds.) FACS 2012. LNCS, vol. 7684, pp. 188–204. Springer, Heidelberg (2013). https://doi.org/10.1007/978-3-642-35861-6_12
48. Nielson, H.R., Nielson, F., Vigo, R.: A calculus of quality for robustness against unreliable communication. J. Log. Algebr. Methods Program. **84**(5), 611–639 (2015)
49. Palamidessi, C.: Comparing the expressive power of the synchronous and asynchronous pi-calculi. Math. Struct. Comput. Sci. **13**(5), 685–719 (2003)
50. Parrow, J.: Expressiveness of process algebras. Electron. Notes Theor. Comput. Sci. **209**, 173–186 (2008)
51. Peters, K.: Translational expressiveness: comparing process calculi using encodings. Ph.D. thesis, Technische Universität Berlin, Fakultät IV - Elektrotechnik und Informatik, Germany (2012)
52. Peters, K., Nestmann, U., Goltz, U.: On distributability in process calculi. In: Felleisen, M., Gardner, P. (eds.) ESOP 2013. LNCS, vol. 7792, pp. 310–329. Springer, Heidelberg (2013). https://doi.org/10.1007/978-3-642-37036-6_18
53. Prasad, K.V.: A calculus of broadcasting systems. Sci. Comput. Program. **25**(2), 285–327 (1995)

54. Schmitt, A., Stefani, J.: The M-calculus: a higher-order distributed process calculus. In: Conference Record of POPL 2003: The 30th SIGPLAN-SIGACT Symposium on Principles of Programming Languages, New Orleans, Louisisana, USA, 15–17 January 2003, pp. 50–61 (2003)
55. Steffen, B.: Unifying models. In: Reischuk, R., Morvan, M. (eds.) STACS 1997. LNCS, vol. 1200, pp. 1–20. Springer, Heidelberg (1997). https://doi.org/10.1007/BFb0023444
56. Urban, C., Berghofer, S., Norrish, M.: Barendregt's variable convention in rule inductions. In: Pfenning, F. (ed.) CADE 2007. LNCS (LNAI), vol. 4603, pp. 35–50. Springer, Heidelberg (2007). https://doi.org/10.1007/978-3-540-73595-3_4
57. van Glabbeek, R.J.: Musings on encodings and expressiveness. In: Proceedings of EXPRESS/SOS. EPTCS, vol. 89, pp. 81–98 (2012)
58. van Glabbeek, R.J.: On the validity of encodings of the synchronous in the asynchronous π-calculus. Inf. Process. Lett. **137**, 17–25 (2018)

Fast Verified BCD Subtyping

Jan Bessai[1]([✉]), Jakob Rehof[1], and Boris Düdder[2]

[1] Technische Universität Dortmund,
Otto-Hahn-Straße 12, 44227 Dortmund, Germany
{jan.bessai,jakob.rehof}@tu-dortmund.de
[2] University of Copenhagen, Universitetsparken 5, 2100 Copenhagen, Denmark
boris.d@di.ku.dk

Abstract. A decision procedure for the Barendregt-Coppo-Dezani subtype relation on intersection types ("BCD subtyping") is presented and formally verified in Coq. Types are extended with unary, covariant, distributing, preordered type constructors and binary products. A quadratic upper bound on the algorithm runtime is established. The formalization can be compiled to executable OCaml or Haskell code using the extraction mechanism of Coq.

Keywords: Intersection types · Subtyping · Coq · BCD

1 Introduction

The subtyping relation of Barendregt, Coppo, and Dezani [4] is a natural, semantically motivated notion of subtyping on intersection types. The relation, often referred to as BCD subtyping for short, is important within the theory of intersection types, and many variants of the intersection type system are associated with theories of subtyping which are contained in the theory of BCD subtyping (see [3] for an overview). The present paper concerns the formal verification, by means of theorem proving, of an efficient (quadratic time) decision procedure for the BCD subtyping relation: Given two intersection types A and B, does $A \leq B$ hold (where $\leq$ denotes the BCD subtyping relation)? Decidability of the subtyping relation is probably most easily established by first performing a pre-processing step called normalization following Hindley [14]. However, since this step may cause exponential blow-up in type size, it only gives rise to a computationally suboptimal algorithm. In fact, a quadratic time algorithm time is known for deciding BCD subtyping [10], and quadratic time is in all likelihood asymptotically optimal for the problem. But efficient algorithms for the problem tend to get complicated, in part due to the necessity of organizing rather intricate case analyses under recursive descent over type expressions. When the relation is further extended with type constants for applications, correctness of efficient implementations becomes even more of an issue of interest (see Sect. 2 for further discussion). From the perspective of formal verification it is a topic of

© Springer Nature Switzerland AG 2019
T. Margaria et al. (Eds.): Steffen Festschrift, LNCS 11200, pp. 356–371, 2019.
https://doi.org/10.1007/978-3-030-22348-9_21

more general interest to see how far we can get towards verification of correctness of algorithms under given complexity bounds.

In this paper a decision procedure for the BCD subtype relation on intersection types is presented and formally verified in Coq. Types are extended with unary, covariant, distributing, preordered type constructors and binary products. A quadratic upper bound on the algorithm runtime is established. The formalization can be compiled to executable OCaml or Haskell code using the extraction mechanism of Coq. The accompanying Coq proofs for this paper are available online[1].

This paper is organized as follows: Related work on decision procedures for the BCD subtype rules is discussed in Sect. 2. This discussion is also used to pinpoint novel contributions made here. Section 3 contains the definition of intersection types and the subtype relation on them. The decision procedure is presented and proven correct in Sect. 4. An upper bound on its runtime is proven in Sect. 5. Finally, Sect. 6 provides some concluding remarks and ideas for future work.

2   Related Work and Contribution

Pierce [22] provides an algorithm for deciding the BCD subtype relation under a set of additional constraints on type variables. No asymptotic runtime bound is established. Damm [8,9] reduces the problem of deciding subtyping for intersection types extended with recursive types and a union operator to regular tree expressions, resulting in a non-deterministic exponential time algorithm. Kurata and Takahashi [18] provide an algorithm for intersection types without additional extensions. It needs a pre-computation step to normalize (see [14]) types, which requires exponential runtime. Rehof and Urzyczyn [23] first established an algorithm with an $O(n^4)$ upper bound on its runtime. Their memoization-based formalization is manual. Practical experience from the (CL)S-Framework [5] has shown that implementing the required memoization techniques is possible but error prone. Also within the context of (CL)S, the algorithm implementation was experimentally extended with distributing covariant n-ary type-constructors. Subsequently, Statman [24] presented a rewriting-based $O(n^5)$ algorithm for which no implementation or computer supported verification exists yet. His presentation includes some insights about factorizations of intersection types, which were then picked up in [10], where a simpler $O(n^2)$ algorithm is sketched. This algorithm uses a preprocessing step, which can in contrast to [18] be performed in linear time. Additionally, the insights of [24] led to the development of the first theorem prover verified algorithm by Bessai et al. [6]. The algorithm is based on purely mathematical principles (ideals and filters) and can be extracted to OCaml and Haskell. Throughout the formalization, high-level mathematical concepts are accessed via the Coq tactics language, which hides algorithmic aspects and makes reasoning about runtime (except for guaranteed termination) difficult. Hence, while practical experiments hint at an $O(n^4)$ upper bound, this result has never been formally established. The development in [6] sparked at least two

---

[1] https://github.com/JanBessai/SubtypeMachine.

more formalization efforts. Honsell et al. [16] extend the type system with union types, basing their work on a fork of the original formalization. Laurent [20] extends intersection types with n-ary co- and contra-variant constructors and translates the subtype rules into a syntax-driven sequent-calculus. The translation is proven correct in Coq, but its algorithmic aspects remain unstudied. Similarly, Dunfield [11] earlier proposed an extension with union types presentable in sequent-calculus form. Bi et al. [7] go back to the algorithm presented in [22] and propose an extension with records and coercions. They do not study runtime complexity. A theorem proven Coq formalization and a manual translation of their syntax directed rules into a Haskell implementation are provided. The formalization effort led to the discovery of a mistake in the original manual proof in [22].

The contribution of this paper is to describe a Coq-formalized subtype decision procedure for intersection types extended with unary, co-variant, distributing, preordered type constructors and binary products. An $\mathbb{O}(n^2)$ upper bound on the runtime is formally established. The decision procedure does not require any preprocessing steps on the input types, no translation into another calculus, and no imperative programming language features such as memoization. Extraction of the Coq formalization into Haskell and OCaml is possible. Besides the improvements over prior attempts, the formalization can serve as an example application for a technique recently presented by Larchey-Wendling and Monin [19]. The goal of this technique is to decompose termination proofs from fixpoint definitions and thereby make reasoning more compositional. The quest for compositional proof methods is an old topic, which can also be found in earlier work by Steffen and Cleaveland [25] in the context of model-checking. This contribution can be seen as a very detailed study of an improved algorithm for a particular problem, as well as a larger example scenario of applying a proof compositionality technique in a theorem prover.

3   Types and Subtyping

Intersection types A, B are formed over the following syntax:

$$\mathbb{T} \ni A, B ::= \omega \mid c(A) \mid (A \times B) \mid (A \to B) \mid (A \cap B)$$

where $c \in \mathbb{C}$ is a type constructor drawn from a countable set $\mathbb{C}$. Intuitively, ω is a universal type and supertype of every other type. Constants are encoded by type constructors and may appear nested inside type expressions. This allows for types such as $\texttt{List}(A)$, $\texttt{List}(\texttt{List}(A))$. Instead of assigning an arity to each constructor, all constructors take exactly one argument. This restriction avoids lots of index sets, adds uniformity to proofs and does not affect the runtime complexity of subtyping. Atomic types, often modeled by constructors without arguments, can still be represented using ω as argument: types such as $\texttt{bool}$ or $\texttt{int}$ are formally written as $\texttt{int}(\omega)$ and $\texttt{bool}(\omega)$. Multiple arguments can be passed to a type constructor by wrapping them into the product type $(A \times B)$, e.g. $\texttt{Graph}(N \times E)$ for a graph with nodes of type N and edges of type E.

Function types are written as $(A \to B)$ and the presence of products allows to choose between curried $(A \to (B \to C))$ and un-curried $((A \times B) \to C)$ representations. Finally, the intersection type operator $(A \cap B)$ encodes the greatest lower bound of two types. In contrast to the pair $(A \times B)$, which is used to assign two types to two components, the intersection $(A \cap B)$ is used to assign two types to a single component. In the rest of this paper, superfluous parentheses in types are omitted by following the convention that arrows and intersections associate to the right, products associate to the left, and intersections bind stronger than products, which bind stronger than arrows.

The subtype relation $A \leq B$ is the least relation closed under the rules:

$$\frac{c \leq_c d \qquad A \leq B}{c(A) \leq d(B)} \text{ (CAx)} \qquad \frac{}{c(A) \cap c(B) \leq c(A \cap B)} \text{ (CDist)}$$

$$\frac{}{A \leq \omega} \ (\omega) \qquad \frac{}{\omega \leq \omega \to \omega} \ (\to \omega)$$

$$\frac{B_1 \leq A_1 \qquad A_2 \leq B_2}{A_1 \to A_2 \leq B_1 \to B_2} \text{ (Sub)} \qquad \frac{}{(A \to B_1) \cap (A \to B_2) \leq A \to B_1 \cap B_2} \text{ (Dist)}$$

$$\frac{A_1 \leq B_1 \qquad A_2 \leq B_2}{A_1 \times A_2 \leq B_1 \times B_2} \text{ (ProdSub)}$$

$$\frac{}{(A_1 \times A_2) \cap (B_1 \times B_2) \leq A_1 \cap B_1 \times A_2 \cap B_2} \text{ (ProdDist)}$$

$$\frac{A \leq B_1 \qquad A \leq B_2}{A \leq B_1 \cap B_2} \text{ (GLB)} \quad \frac{}{B_1 \cap B_2 \leq B_1} \text{ (LUB}_1) \quad \frac{}{B_1 \cap B_2 \leq B_2} \text{ (LUB}_2)$$

$$\frac{A \leq B \qquad B \leq C}{A \leq C} \text{ (Trans)} \qquad \frac{}{A \leq A} \text{ (Refl)}$$

Rules (CAx), (CDist), (ProdSub) and (ProdDist) are extensions, while the other rules are standard [10, 24] and equivalent [2] to the rules originally presented by Barendregt, Coppo and Dezani [4]. In rule (CAx) constructors are compared using an externally defined relation $c \leq_c d$, which can be instantiated according to application specific use-cases and has to be transitive and reflexive. A potential application are nominal comparisons between type-constructors according to a class-table: to model a Java-like type-system $\text{ArrayList} \leq_c \text{List}$ can be added, which would allow using instances of ArrayList whenever List is required. Rule (CDist) allows to distribute intersections over constructors. If something is simultaneously a list of A and a list of B, it is a list of things which are simultaneously A and B: $\text{List}(A) \cap \text{List}(B) \leq \text{List}(A \cap B)$. Note, that the converse direction is derivable from (CAx) and (GLB). Rules (ProdSub) and (ProdDist) are analogous to the constructor rules, allowing to compare products and again to distribute intersections. The chosen extensions are conservative over the original BCD-system, which only supports atoms: choosing

$c \leq_{\mathbb{C}} d$ iff $c = d$ and encoding atom a as $a(\omega)$ collapses rule (CDist) into an instance of (LUB$_1$), and (CAx) into (Refl).

There are several functions on types which are useful throughout the entire formalization. The arity of a type is the arity of its outermost operation or constructor:

$$\text{arity}(A) = \begin{cases} \mathbb{1} & \text{if } A = \omega \\ \mathbb{T} & \text{if } A = c(A') \\ \mathbb{T} \times \mathbb{T} & \text{otherwise} \end{cases}$$

where $\mathbb{1}$ is the (meta-logical) unit set $\{\emptyset\}$, and $\mathbb{T} \times \mathbb{T}$ is the Cartesian product of the set of types with itself (not to be confused with the product type operator). For $(A, B) \in \mathbb{T} \times \mathbb{T}$, the first and second projections are defined as $(A, B).1 = A$ and $(A, B).2 = B$. The size, depth, length and breadth of a type are useful measures for runtime-complexity and termination of algorithms:

$$\text{size}(A) = \begin{cases} 1 & \text{if } A = \omega \\ 1 + \text{size}(B) & \text{if } A = c(B) \\ 1 + \text{size}(B) + \text{size}(C) & \text{if } A = B \to C, A = B \times C, \text{ or } A = B \cap C \end{cases}$$

$$\text{depth}(A) = \begin{cases} 1 & \text{if } A = \omega \\ 1 + \text{depth}(B) & \text{if } A = c(B) \\ 1 + \max\{\text{depth}(B), \text{depth}(C)\} & \text{if } A = B \to C, \text{ or } A = B \times C \\ \max\{\text{depth}(B), \text{depth}(C)\} & \text{if } A = B \cap C \end{cases}$$

$$\text{length}(A) = \begin{cases} 1 + \text{length}(A_2) & \text{if } A = A_1 \to A_2 \\ \text{length}(A_1) + \text{length}(A_2) & \text{if } A = A_1 \cap A_2 \\ 1 & \text{otherwise} \end{cases}$$

$$\text{breadth}(A) = \begin{cases} \text{breadth}(A_1) + \text{breadth}(A_2) & \text{if } A = A_1 \cap A_2 \\ 1 & \text{otherwise} \end{cases}$$

From now on $\text{size}(A)$ will be abbreviated as $\|A\|$. Following the definition of Ω in [4], a type can be identified as subtype-equal to ω ($A \leq \omega$ and $\omega \leq A$) in $\mathbb{O}(\text{length}(A))$ by:

$$\text{isOmega}(A) = \begin{cases} \text{true} & \text{if } A = \omega \\ \text{isOmega}(B) & \text{if } A = A' \to B \\ \text{false} & \text{otherwise} \end{cases}$$

The intersection of a list of n types is computed in n steps by

$$\text{intersect}(\Delta) = \begin{cases} \omega & \text{if } \Delta = [::] \\ A & \text{if } \Delta = [::A] \\ A \cap \text{intersect}(\Delta') & \text{if } \Delta = [::A \;\&\; \Delta'] \end{cases}$$

where $[::]$ is the empty list, $[::A]$ is a list with one element A and $[::A \text{ \& } \Delta']$ is the list constructed by inserting A before list Δ'. In the following, $\bigcap_{A_i \in \Delta} M$ will serve as a shorthand notation for $\text{intersect}(\text{map}(\lambda A_i.M, \Delta))$, where map is defined as usual by $\text{map}(\lambda A_i.M, [::]) = [::]$ and $\text{map}(\lambda A_i.M, [::A \text{ \& } \Delta]) = [::M[A_i := A] \text{ \& } \text{map}(\lambda A_i.M, \Delta)]$.

4   Decision Procedure

While elegant and concise, the axiomatic relational presentation of $\leq$ is inherently non-algorithmic and therefore ill-suited for the construction of executable decision programs. This becomes obvious, considering the cut-type B in the transitivity rule (TRANS) and cycles which can arise, e.g. by instantiating A to ω in rule (ω) and proceeding with rule $(\rightarrow \omega)$. This motivates the rest of the paper. Following the approach in [19], the decision procedure is designed in three phases. First, the algorithm is defined by means of its relational semantics. Then, the semantical relation is shown to be functional. Finally, a termination certificate is designed to turn the relational semantics into an executable denotational equivalent. Soundess of the functional interpretation with respect to the relational description is enforced by its type. Correctness of the algorithm is proven by showing that the relation is equivalent to the subtype relation. This way, the termination proof is effectively separated from the correctness proof. Also, bounds on the runtime are established by bounding the number of transitive steps in the semantical relation. An additional benefit is to establish a mental model of a subtype machine executing instructions in a step-wise fashion. Each of these steps can be understood and reasoned about independently, while the usual presentation of abstract pseudo code does not allow this kind of mental specification debugging. The instruction set $\mathcal{I}$ of the subtype machine contains two instructions: $[\text{ subty } A \text{ of } B]$ and $[\text{ tgt\_for\_srcs\_gte } A \text{ in } \Delta]$ for types A, B, and a list Δ which contains pairs $(A_n, B_n) \in \mathbb{T} \times \mathbb{T}$. The first instruction advises the machine to check if A is a subtype of B, while the second instruction collects all types B_n in Δ, for which A is a subtype of the corresponding A_n. Outputs $\mathcal{O}$ are $[\text{ Return } b]$ and $[\text{ check\_tgt } \Delta]$ for a boolean value b and a list of collected types Δ. The functions defined in the last section are taken as meta-operations usable during the machine specification. All of these functions could have been specified together with the relational machine semantics, but since none of them have interesting termination or runtime behavior, this would have been unnecessarily complicated. Another meta-function, cast, is needed before defining the semantical relation:

$$\text{cast}_B(A) = \begin{cases} [::\omega] & \text{if } B = \omega \\ [::(\omega, \omega)] & \text{if } B = B_1 \rightarrow B_2 \text{ and isOmega}(B_2) \\ \text{cast}'_B(A, [::]) & \text{otherwise} \end{cases}$$

$$\text{cast}'_B(A, \Delta) = \begin{cases} [::A' \;\&\; \Delta] & \text{if } A = c(A'), B = d(B') \text{ and } c \leq_C d \\ [::(A_1, A_2) \;\&\; \Delta] & \text{if } A = A_1 \to A_2 \text{ and } B = B_1 \to B_2 \\ [::(A_1, A_2) \;\&\; \Delta] & \text{if } A = A_1 \times A_2 \text{ and } B = B_1 \times B_2 \\ \text{cast}'_B(A_1, \text{cast}'_B(A_2, \Delta)) & \text{if } A = A_1 \cap A_2 \\ \Delta & \text{otherwise} \end{cases}$$

The range of function cast_B is $\text{arity}(B)$ and collects all relevant components of A for recursive comparison with B. If B is subtype equal to ω, comparison can proceed with ω components, otherwise cast' loops over all parts of A, filtering those which are irrelevant. Note that cast' collects components in an accumulator argument Δ rather than using list concatenation. This way the runtime of cast' is linear in $\text{breadth}(A)$ (all cases except for intersection are in $\mathbb{O}(1)$ and the intersection is in $\mathbb{O}(\text{breadth}(A))$). List concatenation in the intersection case would have caused quadratic runtime if cast' were to be implemented using functional programming and immutable lists with concatenation in $\mathbb{O}(n)$. Overall the runtime of cast is in $\mathbb{O}(\text{breadth}(A) + \text{length}(B))$ and the output of cast will be a list of size less or equal to $\text{breadth}(A)$. Now the subtype machine execution semantics $\leadsto$ is defined to be the least relation closed under the following rules, where annotations in boxes indicate runtime bounds and can be ignored until Sect. 5:

$$\frac{}{[\text{ subty } A \text{ of } \omega] \leadsto [\text{ Return true}] \quad \boxed{\mathbb{O}(1)}} \; (\text{STEP}_\omega)$$

$$\frac{[\text{ subty } \bigcap_{A_i \in \text{cast}_{c(B)}(A)} A_i \text{ of } B] \leadsto [\text{ Return } b] \quad \boxed{n}}{[\text{ subty } A \text{ of } c(B)] \leadsto [\text{ Return } \text{cast}_{c(B)}(A) \neq [::] \wedge b]} \; (\text{STEP}_\text{CTOR})$$
$$\boxed{(\mathbb{O}(\text{breadth}(A) + \text{length}(c(B))) + \mathbb{O}(\text{breadth}(A)) + \mathbb{O}(1)) + n}$$

$$\frac{[\text{ tgt\_for\_srcs\_gte } B_1 \text{ in } \text{cast}_{B_1 \to B_2}(A)] \leadsto [\text{ check\_tgt } \Delta] \quad \boxed{m}}{[\text{ subty } \bigcap_{A_i \in \Delta} A_i \text{ of } B_2] \leadsto [\text{ Return } b] \quad \boxed{n}}{[\text{ subty } A \text{ of } B_1 \to B_2] \leadsto [\text{ Return } \text{isOmega}(B_2) \vee b]} \; (\text{STEP}_\to)$$
$$\boxed{\begin{array}{c}(\mathbb{O}(\text{breadth}(A) + \text{length}(B_1 \to B_2)) + \mathbb{O}(\text{breadth}(A)) + \mathbb{O}(\text{length}(B_2)) + \\ \mathbb{O}(1)) + m + n\end{array}}$$

$$\frac{[\text{ subty } B \text{ of } A.1] \leadsto [\text{ Return } b] \quad \boxed{m}}{[\text{ tgt\_for\_srcs\_gte } B \text{ in } \Delta] \leadsto [\text{ check\_tgt } \Delta'] \quad \boxed{n}}{[\text{ tgt\_for\_srcs\_gte } B \text{ in } [::A \;\&\; \Delta]] \leadsto} \; (\text{STEP}_\text{CHOOSETGT})$$
$$[\text{ check\_tgt if } b \text{ then } [::A.2 \;\&\; \Delta'] \text{ else } \Delta'] \quad \boxed{\mathbb{O}(1) + m + n}$$

$$\frac{}{[\text{ tgt\_for\_srcs\_gte } B \text{ in } [::]] \leadsto [\text{ check\_tgt } [::]] \quad \boxed{\mathbb{O}(1)}} \; (\text{STEP}_\text{DONETGT})$$

$$\frac{\begin{array}{l} [\text{ subty } \bigcap_{A_i \in \text{cast}_{B_1 \times B_2}(A)} A_i.1 \text{ of } B_1] \rightsquigarrow [\text{ Return } b_1] \quad \boxed{m} \\ [\text{ subty } \bigcap_{A_i \in \text{cast}_{B_1 \times B_2}(A)} A_i.2 \text{ of } B_2] \rightsquigarrow [\text{ Return } b_2] \quad \boxed{n} \end{array}}{[\text{ subty } A \text{ of } B_1 \times B_2] \rightsquigarrow [\text{ Return } \text{cast}_{B_1 \times B_2}(A) \neq [::] \wedge b_1 \wedge b_2]} (\text{STEP}_\times)$$

$$\boxed{(\mathbb{O}(\text{breadth}(A) + \text{length}(B_1 \times B_2)) + 2 \cdot \mathbb{O}(\text{breadth}(A)) + \mathbb{O}(1)) + m + n}$$

$$\frac{\begin{array}{l} [\text{ subty } A \text{ of } B_1] \rightsquigarrow [\text{ Return } b_1] \quad \boxed{m} \\ [\text{ subty } A \text{ of } B_2] \rightsquigarrow [\text{ Return } b_2] \quad \boxed{n} \end{array}}{[\text{ subty } A \text{ of } B_1 \cap B_2] \rightsquigarrow [\text{ Return } b_1 \wedge b_2] \quad \boxed{\mathbb{O}(1) + m + n}} (\text{STEP}_\cap)$$

Rules (STEP_ω) and $(\text{STEP}_\cap)$ are immediate implementations of the (GLB) and (ω) subtype rules. Similarly, $(\text{STEP}_{\text{CTOR}})$ and $(\text{STEP}_\times)$ can be thought of as implementations combinations of (CAx) with (CDist), and (PRODSUB) with (PRODDIST). In both cases cast projects A to relevant components, which are intersected (distribution axioms) and recursively compared. If no relevant components are present, A cannot be a subtype. This is in contrast to the rule for arrows $(\text{STEP}_\rightarrow)$, which allows B_2 to be ω in which case no restrictions have to be imposed on A because of the subtype rule $(\rightarrow \omega)$. The contra-variant nature of arrow sources requires $(\text{STEP}_\rightarrow)$ to additionally filter relevant components using $(\text{STEP}_{\text{CHOOSETGT}})$ and $(\text{STEP}_{\text{DONETGT}})$. This can be illustrated by showing $(A_1 \rightarrow B_1) \cap (A_2 \rightarrow B_2) \leq (A_1 \cap A_2) \rightarrow (B_1 \cap B_2)) \not\leq A_1 \rightarrow B_1 \cap B_2$ for $A_1 \not\leq A_2$.

The next part of the formalization, Lemma 1, is to prove that $\rightsquigarrow$ is functional.

Lemma 1 (Functionality). *For all instructions $i \in \mathcal{I}$ and outputs $o_1, o_2 \in \mathcal{O}$, if $i \rightsquigarrow o_1$ and $i \rightsquigarrow o_2$ then $o_1 = o_2$.*

Proof. Induction on the proof of $i \rightsquigarrow o_1$ followed by case analysis on $i \rightsquigarrow o_2$. □

The final step in obtaining an algorithm is to design a termination certificate for each instruction. The certificate Dom is inductively defined by the rules:

$$\frac{}{[\text{ subty } A \text{ of } \omega] \in \text{Dom}} \qquad \frac{\boxed{1} [\text{ subty } \bigcap_{A_i \in \text{cast}_{c(B)}(A)} A_i \text{ of } B] \in \text{Dom}}{[\text{ subty } A \text{ of } c(B)] \in \text{Dom}}$$

$$\frac{\begin{array}{l} \boxed{1} [\text{ tgt\_for\_srcs\_gte } B_1 \text{ in } \text{cast}_{B_1 \rightarrow B_2} A] \in \text{Dom} \\ \boxed{2} \text{ for all } \Delta, \text{ if } [\text{ tgt\_for\_srcs\_gte } B_1 \text{ in } \text{cast}_{B_1 \rightarrow B_2} A] \rightsquigarrow [\text{ check\_tgt } \Delta] \\ \text{ then } [\text{ subty } \bigcap_{A_i \in \Delta} A_i \text{ of } B_2] \in \text{Dom} \end{array}}{[\text{ subty } A \text{ of } B_1 \rightarrow B_2] \in \text{Dom}}$$

$$\frac{\boxed{1} [\text{ subty } B \text{ of } A.1] \in \text{Dom} \qquad \boxed{2} [\text{ tgt\_for\_srcs\_gte } B \text{ in } \Delta] \in \text{Dom}}{[\text{ tgt\_for\_srcs\_gte } B \text{ in } [::A \& \Delta]] \in \text{Dom}}$$

$$[\text{ tgt\_for\_srcs\_gte } B \text{ in } [::]] \in \text{Dom}$$

$$\frac{\boxed{1}[\text{ subty } \bigcap_{A_i \in \text{cast}_{B_1 \times B_2}(A)} A_i.1 \text{ of } B_1] \in \text{Dom} \qquad \boxed{2}[\text{ subty } \bigcap_{A_i \in \text{cast}_{B_1 \times B_2}(A)} A_i.2 \text{ of } B_2] \in \text{Dom}}{[\text{ subty } A \text{ of } B_1 \times B_2] \in \text{Dom}}$$

$$\frac{\boxed{1}[\text{ subty } A \text{ of } B_1] \in \text{Dom} \qquad \boxed{2}[\text{ subty } A \text{ of } B_2] \in \text{Dom}}{[\text{ subty } A \text{ of } B_1 \cap B_2] \in \text{Dom}}$$

Analyzing Dom yields a new termination certificate for each recursive call needed by the subtype machine. In Coq, Dom is defined as an inductive datatype, which ensures that termination certificates for recursive calls are structurally smaller in each step. In the following text for a proof $p : i \in$ Dom function inv_k is used to obtain premise $\boxed{i}$ of the proof.

The denotational interpretation is defined in Fig. 1 and exactly follows each step of the subtype relation. The range restriction $\{o \in \mathcal{O} \mid i \leadsto o\}$ ensures soundness wrt. the relational semantics. On paper it has to be checked manually, while in Coq a Σ-type is used to attach proofs of $i \leadsto p$ to each function result. Completeness follows from Lemmas 1 and 2, which ensures that every possible instruction gives rise to an instance of the termination certificate.

Lemma 2 (Totality). *For all instructions $i \in \mathcal{I}$, $i \in$ Dom.*

Proof. Induction on B to obtain $[\text{ subty } \omega \text{ of } B] \in$ Dom.
Then for $[\text{ subty } A \text{ of } B]$ induction on the maximal depth of A and B followed by induction on the structure of B. Either cast decreases the depth of compared components, or it returns an empty list or a list only containing ω or (ω, ω). In the first case, an induction hypothesis can be used and in the second case $[\text{ subty } \omega \text{ of } B] \in$ Dom can be used. Using the prior result, for $[\text{ tgt\_for\_srcs\_gte } B \text{ in } \Delta]$ simple induction on the length of list Δ is sufficient. □

When extracting the above specification from Coq to OCaml or Haskell, the termination certificate $i \in$ Dom and the soundness proof $i \leadsto o$ are automatically erased, because these languages do not require termination certificates or proofs. Also uses of cast are surrounded by type-casts in the target language (Obj.magic, unsafeCoerce) since neither OCaml nor Haskell can natively express the type dependency between the input and output of cast which is encoded by function arity. In all other aspects, the extracted code exactly follows the specification up to syntax, which is why we elide it here and refer to the online sources.

It remains to show, that the machine specification is correct wrt. the BCD subtype relation. First, some properties of $\leq$ are established in Lemma 3.

Lemma 3 (Properties of the BCD-Relation).

1. $\text{intersect}(\text{map}(\lambda A_i.M, [::A_1 \ \& \ [::A_2 \ \& \ \dots [::A_n \ \& \ \Delta]]])) \leq$
   $\text{intersect}(\text{map}(\lambda A_i.M, [::A_1 \ \& \ [::A_2 \ \& \ \dots [::A_n \ \& \ [::]]]])) \ \cap$
   $\text{intersect}(\text{map}(\lambda A_i.M, \Delta))$

2. $\text{isOmega}(B)$ *implies* $A \leq B$

3. $\text{cast}_{c(B)}(A) \neq [::]$ *implies* $A \leq c(\bigcap_{A_i \in \text{cast}_{c(B)}(A)} A_i)$

4. $A \leq \bigcap_{A_i \in \text{cast}_{B_1 \to B_2}(A)}(A_i.1 \to A_i.2)$

5. $A \leq \bigcap_{A_i \in \text{cast}_{B_1 \times B_2}(A)}(A_i.1 \times A_i.2)$

6. $(A_1 \to B_1) \cap (A_2 \to B_2) \leq (A_1 \cap A_2) \to (B_1 \cap B_2)$

$\text{subtypes}(i \in \mathcal{I}) : i \in \text{Dom} \to \{p \in \mathcal{O} \mid i \rightsquigarrow p\}$

$\text{subtypes}(i)(p) =$
$\begin{cases}
[\ \text{Return } true] \text{ if } i = [\ \text{subty } A \text{ of } \omega] \\[4pt]
[\ \text{Return } \text{cast}_{c(B)}(A) \neq [::] \wedge b] \\
\quad \text{if } i = [\ \text{subty } A \text{ of } c(B)] \text{ and} \\
\quad \text{for } A' := \bigcap_{\text{cast}_{c(B)}(A)} A_i \\
\quad \text{subtypes}([\ \text{subty } A' \text{ of } B])(\text{inv}_1(p)) = [\ \text{Return } b] \\[4pt]
[\ \text{Return } \text{isOmega}(B_2) \vee b] \\
\quad \text{if } i = [\ \text{subty } A \text{ of } B_1 \to B_2] \text{ and} \\
\quad \text{for } A_1 := \text{cast}_{B_1 \to B_2}(A) \\
\quad \text{subtypes}([\ \text{tgt_for_srcs_gte } B_1 \text{ in } A_1])(\text{inv}_1(p)) = \\
\qquad [\ \text{check_tgt } \Delta] \text{ and} \\
\quad \text{for } A_2 := \bigcap_{A_i \in \Delta} A_i \\
\quad \text{subtypes}([\ \text{subty } A_2 \text{ of } B_2])(\text{inv}_2(p)) = [\ \text{Return } b] \\[4pt]
[\ \text{Return } \text{cast}_{B_1 \times B_2}(A) \neq [::] \wedge b_1 \wedge b_2] \\
\quad \text{if } i = [\ \text{subty } A \text{ of } B_1 \times B_2] \text{ and} \\
\quad \text{for } A_1 := \bigcap_{A_i \in \text{cast}_{B_1 \times B_2}(A)} A_i.1 \\
\quad \text{subtypes}([\ \text{subty } A_1 \text{ of } B_1])(\text{inv}_1(p)) = [\ \text{Return } b_1] \text{ and} \\
\quad \text{for } A_2 := \bigcap_{A_i \in \text{cast}_{B_1 \times B_2}(A)} A_i.2 \\
\quad \text{subtypes}([\ \text{subty } A_2 \text{ of } B_2])(\text{inv}_2(p)) = [\ \text{Return } b_2] \\[4pt]
[\ \text{Return } b_1 \wedge b_2] \\
\quad \text{if } i = [\ \text{subty } A \text{ of } B_1 \cap B_2] \text{ and} \\
\quad \text{subtypes}([\ \text{subty } A \text{ of } B_1])(\text{inv}_1(p)) = [\ \text{Return } b_1] \text{ and} \\
\quad \text{subtypes}([\ \text{subty } A \text{ of } B_2])(\text{inv}_2(p)) = [\ \text{Return } b_2] \\[4pt]
[\ \text{check_tgt } \text{ if } b \text{ then } [::A.2 \ \& \ \Delta'] \text{ else } \Delta'] \\
\quad \text{if } i = [\ \text{tgt_for_srcs_gte } B \text{ in } [::A \ \& \ \Delta]] \text{ and} \\
\quad \text{subtypes}([\ \text{subty } B \text{ of } A.1])(\text{inv}_1(p)) = [\ \text{Return } b] \text{ and} \\
\quad \text{subtypes}([\ \text{tgt_for_srcs_gte } B \text{ in } \Delta])(\text{inv}_2(p)) = \\
\qquad [\ \text{check_tgt } \Delta'] \\[4pt]
[\ \text{check_tgt } [::]] \text{ if } i = [\ \text{tgt_for_srcs_gte } B \text{ in } [::]]
\end{cases}$

Fig. 1. Interpreter for the subtype machine

7. $\bigcap_{A_i \in \Delta} (A_i.1 \times A_i.2) \leq (\bigcap_{A_i \in \Delta} A_i.1) \times (\bigcap_{A_i \in \Delta} A_i.2)$ *if* $\Delta \neq [::]$

Proof. Easy induction and case analysis.   □

Now soundness, which is the easier part of the correctness proof, can be shown.

Lemma 4 (Soundness). *Relation* $\rightsquigarrow$ *is sound wrt. relation* $\leq$, *i.e.*
[subty A of B] $\rightsquigarrow$ [Return true] *implies* $A \leq B$.

Proof. First induction on the depth maximum of the depths of types A and B. Then induction on the derivation of [subty A of B] $\rightsquigarrow$ [Return true]. The induction hypotheses generated by the second induction are strong enough to solve the cases when B is ω, $c(B)$, $B_1 \times B_2$, and $B_1 \cap B_2$ with the help of Lemma 3. For rule (STEP$_\rightarrow$) with $B = B_1 \rightarrow B_2$, the outer induction hypothesis is required to allow for the covariant position of B_1. The proof requires using a transitive step with an intersection of arrows selected by executing [tgt_for_srcs_gte $B1$ in cast$_{B_1 \rightarrow B_2} A$] as the center element. It then succeeds using Lemmas 3.4, 3.6, the induction hypotheses and an extra case-analysis for isOmega(B_2), and cast$_{B_1 \rightarrow B_2} A = [::]$.   □

The converse direction, completeness, is more difficult to prove. It follows from Lemma 5, the sub-cases of which should be proven in the order they are presented.

Lemma 5 (Properties of the subtype machine).

1. isOmega(B) *implies* [subty A of B] $\rightsquigarrow$ [Return true]
2. [tgt_for_srcs_gte $B1$ in Δ] $\rightsquigarrow$ [check_tgt Δ'] *implies*
   $\Delta' \sqsubseteq$ map($\lambda A_i.A_i.2, \Delta$).
3. [tgt_for_srcs_gte B_1 in cast$_{B_1 \rightarrow B_2} A$] $\rightsquigarrow$ [check_tgt Δ] *and*
   isOmega(A) *implies* isOmega(A_i) *for all* A_i *in* Δ
4. [subty A of B] $\rightsquigarrow$ [Return true] *and* isOmega(A) *implies* isOmega(B)
5. $\Delta_2 \sqsubseteq \Delta_1$ *and* [tgt_for_srcs_gte B_1 in Δ_1] $\rightsquigarrow$ [check_tgt Δ'_1] *and*
   [tgt_for_srcs_gte B_1 in Δ_2] $\rightsquigarrow$ [check_tgt Δ'_2] *implies* $\Delta'_2 \sqsubseteq \Delta'_1$
6. $\Delta \sqsubseteq \Delta'$ *and* [subty $\bigcap_{A_i \in \Delta} A_i$ of A] $\rightsquigarrow$ [Return true] *implies*
   [subty $\bigcap_{B_i \in \Delta'} B_i$ of A] $\rightsquigarrow$ [Return true]
7. $\Delta_1 = [::A_1 \& [::A_2 \& \dots [::A_n \& [::]]]]$ *for* $n \geq 0$ *and*
   [subty A of $\bigcap_{A_i \in \Delta_1} A_i$] $\rightsquigarrow$ [Return b_1] *and*
   [subty A of $\bigcap_{A_i \in \Delta_2} A_i$] $\rightsquigarrow$ [Return b_2] *implies*
   [subty A of $\bigcap_{A_i \in \Delta_3} A_i$] $\rightsquigarrow$ [Return $b_1 \wedge b_2$] *for*
   $\Delta_3 = [::A_1 \& [::A_2 \& \dots [::A_n \& \Delta_2]]]$
8. [subty A of B] $\rightsquigarrow$ [Return true] *implies*
   [subty $\bigcap_{A_i \in \text{cast}_{c(C)} A} A_i$ of $\bigcap_{B_i \in \text{cast}_{c(C)} B} B_i$] $\rightsquigarrow$ [Return true]
9. [tgt_for_srcs_gte B in $[::(\omega, A)]$] $\rightsquigarrow$ [check_tgt Δ] *implies* $\Delta = [::A]$
10. [subty A of A] $\rightsquigarrow$ [Return true]

11. $\Delta_1 = [::A_1 \,\&\, [::A_2 \,\&\, \ldots [::A_n \,\&\, [::]]]]$ *for* $n \geq 0$ *and*
    $\Delta'_1 = [::A'_1 \,\&\, [::A'_2 \,\&\, \ldots [::A'_m \,\&\, [::]]]]$ *for* $m \geq 0$ *and*
    [tgt_for_srcs_gte A in Δ_1] $\rightsquigarrow$ [check_tgt Δ'_1] *and*
    [tgt_for_srcs_gte A in Δ_2] $\rightsquigarrow$ [check_tgt Δ'_2] *implies*
    [tgt_for_srcs_gte A in Δ_3] $\rightsquigarrow$ [check_tgt Δ'_3] *for*
    $\Delta_3 = [::A_1 \,\&\, [::A_2 \,\&\, \ldots [::A_n \,\&\, \Delta_2]]]$ *and*
    $\Delta'_3 = [::A'_1 \,\&\, [::A'_2 \,\&\, \ldots [::A'_m \,\&\, \Delta'_2]]]$
12. [subty A of $B_1 \cap B_2$] $\rightsquigarrow$ [Return true] *implies* [subty A of B_1] $\rightsquigarrow$
    [Return true] *and* [subty A of B_2] $\rightsquigarrow$ [Return true]
13. $C = c(C')$ *or* $C = C_1 \times C_2$ *and* cast$_C B \neq [::]$ *and* [subty A of B] $\rightsquigarrow$
    [Return true] *implies* cast$_C A \neq [::]$
14. [subty A of B] $\rightsquigarrow$ [Return true] *and*
    [subty B of C] $\rightsquigarrow$ [Return true] *implies*
    [subty A of C] $\rightsquigarrow$ [Return true]
15. [subty $a(A_1) \cap a(A_2)$ of $a(A_1 \cap A_2)$] $\rightsquigarrow$ [Return true]
16. [subty $A \cap A$ of A] $\rightsquigarrow$ [Return true]

where list Δ *is a sublist of* Δ', $\Delta \sqsubseteq \Delta'$, *if* $\Delta' = [::A_1 \,\&\, [::A_2 \,\&\, \ldots [::A_n \,\&\, [::B_1 \,\&\, [::B_2 \,\&\, \ldots [::B_m \,\&\, \Delta'']]]]]]$ *and* $\Delta = [::B_1 \,\&\, [::B_2 \,\&\, \ldots [::B_m]]]$ *for some* $n, m \geq 0$.

Proof. Mostly straightforward induction, case-analysis, and applying the previously proven facts. The weakening property expressed in 6 is inspired by [20] and is crucial for the proof of the reflexivity property 10 in the case for $A = A_1 \cap A_2$. Just as in sequent calculus, the proof of the transitivity property 5 is complicated. Similar to the proof of Lemma 4 it needs nested induction on the maximal depth of types A and C, and then on the structure of C. The cases for constructors, products, and targets of arrows need an additional nested induction on the left proof. The case for collecting sources needs an additional induction on the casted type A.   □

Lemma 6 (Completeness). *Relation* $\rightsquigarrow$ *is complete wrt. relation* $\leq$, *i.e.* $A \leq B$ *implies* [subty A of B] $\rightsquigarrow$ [Return true].

Proof. By induction on the proof of $A \leq B$. The cases are either immediate, or, like (TRANS) follow from Lemma 5 and the induction hypothesis.   □

Logical properties of the semantic relation also hold for the interpreter, allowing to proof that subtypes of Fig. 1 really is a decision procedure for the BCD subtype relation.

Theorem 1 (Correctness). *Function* subtypes *of Fig. 1 is a correct decision procedure for BCD subtyping, i.e.: for all types* A *and* B, *there exists a proof* p : [subty A of B] $\in$ Dom *and* $A \leq B$ *if and only if* subtypes([subty A of B])$(p) = $ [Return true].

Proof. The termination certificate p always exists because of Lemma 2. Elements r in the image of subtypes([subty A of B])(p) are those which satisfy

[subty A of B] $\leadsto r$. This implies $A \leq B$ by Lemma 4. Lemma 6 allows to deduce [subty A of B] $\leadsto r$ from $A \leq B$. Lemma 1 implies that r is equal to subtypes([subty A of B])(p). □

5   Quadratic Runtime

The termination certificate Dom ensures that function subtypes does not loop and can also be used to put an upper bound on the function runtime. To this end, Dom is indexed with the size of its proof. Formally:

$$p \in \mathrm{Dom}_{1+n_1+n_2} \text{ iff } p \in \mathrm{Dom} \text{ and for } k = 1, 2 :$$
$$\mathrm{inv}_k(p) \in \mathrm{Dom}_{n_k} \text{ or } \mathrm{inv}_k(p) \text{ does not exist and } n_k = 0.$$

It is easy to check by induction, that every termination certificate $p : i \in \mathrm{Dom}$ is also valid for Dom_n and the opposite holds by definition. For a termination certificate $p : i \in \mathrm{Dom}_n$, subtypes can perform no more than n recursive steps: all recursive calls are started with the result of inv_k and every certificate is only used once. The next lemma establishes a bound on n for any instruction i.

Lemma 7 (Domain size). *For any i, n: if $p : i \in \mathrm{Dom}_n$ exists, then $n \leq$ cost(i), where*

$$\mathrm{cost}(i) = \begin{cases} 2 \cdot \|A\| \cdot \|B\| \ \textit{if } i = [\text{ subty } A \text{ of } B] \\ 1 + \|B\| \cdot \sum_{i=1}^k (1 + 2 \cdot \|A_i.1\|) \\ \quad \textit{if } i = [\text{ tgt\_for\_srcs\_gte } B \text{ in } [::A_1 \ \& \ [::A_2 \ \& \ [::\ldots \ \& \ [::A_k]]]]] \end{cases}$$

Proof. By induction and case-analysis on casted types, their size is less or equal to the size before casting. The only exception is the case cast$_{B_1 \to B_2}A$ if isOmega($B2$) is true and the size of A is less than 3. Now the lemma follows by induction on p, taking care of the special case by observing that its minimal value for cost is 3, which is enough to bound the proof-tree. □

Bounding the size of Dom is the most fine-grained analysis possible in a formally verified way. In the present formalization this only limits the number of recursive steps, but not the amount of time spent on "primitive" operations such as cast. In future work, these could be removed and their stepwise execution made part of the instruction set. For now, the cost-annotations on the (STEP)-rules allow for a more detailed, albeit manual, analysis. Every rule has overhead and recursive costs. Overhead costs are stated in $\mathbb{O}$-Notation and recursive costs are given as variables m and n. If present, the recursive costs can grow up to $\mathbb{O}(\|A\| \cdot \|B\|)$ by the prior argument about Dom. This always dominates over the overhead costs, which are constant or bound by the sum of the breadth and length of the types, since breadth(A) $\leq \|A\|$ and length(B) $\leq \|B\|$. Hence, $\mathbb{O}(\|A\| \cdot \|B\|)$ is an upper bound on the runtime of the presented algorithm.

6   Conclusion and Future Work

A procedure to decide the BCD subtyping relation of intersection types has been presented and formalized. The BCD relation is at the core of countless extended subtype systems [7,8,11,16]. Advances in formalized procedures for its decision may one day help to deal with the current undecidability issues in the type systems of modern programming languages [12,17]. The formalization is based on the Coq theorem-prover and makes use of a technique newly introduced by Larchey-Wendling and Monin [19]. The asymptotic complexity of the algorithm is in $\mathbb{O}(n^2)$ and thereby on a par with the currently best known result presented by Dudenhefner et al. in 2017 [10]. In contrast to the former algorithm it does not require preprocessing types. This avoids redundant work if types are large and requests fails early, which is often the case during proof search. It makes it a candidate for future integration into the (CL)S framework [5]. The formalization can be extracted to purely functional executable OCaml or Haskell code, which closely matches its specification. The key properties of soundness and completeness wrt. the BCD subtype relation could be proven without referring to any termination arguments. Additionally, a formalized proof for a bound on the number of recursive calls was enabled by the technique. Proving asymptotic bounds with theorem provers is an active field of study [1,13,15]. The relatively easy established bound on recursive calls might be interesting for its further development. In reverse, the $\mathbb{O}(n^2)$ runtime result could be proven in Coq using one of the aforementioned results. All current attempts without adding another heavy weight framework were hindered by the tediousness of solving inequations performing rewrite steps (especially for associativity) in the theorem prover by hand. Here, clearly more automation would help. The currently experimental early stage project of making to the existing automation compatible with the mathematical components library [21], which was employed in the proof, has great potential benefit.

Acknowledgments. The authors would like to thank Olivier Laurent, as well as Andrej Dudenhefner, Tristan Schäfer, Anna Vasileva, and Jan Winkels for the prior work, and patient as well as enlightening discussions without which the results in this paper would have been impossible.

References

1. Avigad, J., Donnelly, K.: Formalizing O notation in Isabelle/HOL. In: Basin, D., Rusinowitch, M. (eds.) IJCAR 2004. LNCS (LNAI), vol. 3097, pp. 357–371. Springer, Heidelberg (2004). https://doi.org/10.1007/978-3-540-25984-8_27
2. van Bakel, S.: Complete restrictions of the intersection type discipline. Theor. Comput. Sci. **102**(1), 135–163 (1992). https://doi.org/10.1016/0304-3975(92)90297-S
3. Barendregt, H.P., Dekkers, W., Statman, R.: Lambda Calculus with Types. Perspectives in logic. Cambridge University Press (2013). http://www.cambridge.org/de/academic/subjects/mathematics/logic-categories-and-sets/lambda-calculus-types

4. Barendregt, H., Coppo, M., Dezani-Ciancaglini, M.: A filter lambda model and the completeness of type assignment. J. Symb. Log. **48**(4), 931–940 (1983). https://doi.org/10.2307/2273659

5. Bessai, J., Dudenhefner, A., Düdder, B., Martens, M., Rehof, J.: Combinatory logic synthesizer. In: Margaria, T., Steffen, B. (eds.) ISoLA 2014. LNCS, vol. 8802, pp. 26–40. Springer, Heidelberg (2014). https://doi.org/10.1007/978-3-662-45234-9_3

6. Bessai, J., Dudenhefner, A., Düdder, B., Rehof, J.: Extracting a formally verified Subtyping algorithm for intersection types from ideals and filters. Types (2016)

7. Bi, X., Oliveira, B.C.d.S., Schrijvers, T.: The essence of nested composition. In: 32nd European Conference on Object-Oriented Programming, ECOOP 2018, Amsterdam, The Netherlands, 16–21 July 2018, pp. 22:1–22:33 (2018). https://doi.org/10.4230/LIPIcs.ECOOP.2018.22

8. Damm, F.M.: Subtyping with union types, intersection types and recursive types. In: Hagiya, M., Mitchell, J.C. (eds.) TACS 1994. LNCS, vol. 789, pp. 687–706. Springer, Heidelberg (1994). https://doi.org/10.1007/3-540-57887-0_121

9. Damm, F.M.: Subtyping with union types, intersection types and recursive types II. Ph.D. thesis, INRIA (1994)

10. Dudenhefner, A., Martens, M., Rehof, J.: The algebraic intersection type unification problem. Log. Methods Comput. Sci. **13**(3) (2017). https://doi.org/10.23638/LMCS-13(3:9)2017

11. Dunfield, J.: A unified system of type refinements. Ph.D. thesis, Carnegie Mellon University (2007)

12. Grigore, R.: Java generics are turing complete. In: Proceedings of the 44th ACM SIGPLAN Symposium on Principles of Programming Languages, POPL 2017, Paris, France, 18–20 January 2017, pp. 73–85 (2017). http://dl.acm.org/citation.cfm?id=3009871

13. Guéneau, A., Charguéraud, A., Pottier, F.: A fistful of dollars: formalizing asymptotic complexity claims via deductive program verification. In: Ahmed, A. (ed.) ESOP 2018. LNCS, vol. 10801, pp. 533–560. Springer, Cham (2018). https://doi.org/10.1007/978-3-319-89884-1_19

14. Hindley, J.R.: The simple semantics for Coppo-Dezani-Sallé types. In: Dezani-Ciancaglini, M., Montanari, U. (eds.) Programming 1982. LNCS, vol. 137, pp. 212–226. Springer, Heidelberg (1982). https://doi.org/10.1007/3-540-11494-7_15

15. Hoffmann, J., Das, A., Weng, S.: Towards automatic resource bound analysis for OCaml. In: Proceedings of the 44th ACM SIGPLAN Symposium on Principles of Programming Languages, POPL 2017, Paris, France, 18–20 January 2017, pp. 359–373 (2017). http://dl.acm.org/citation.cfm?id=3009842

16. Honsell, F., Liquori, L., Stolze, C., Scagnetto, I.: The Delta-framework. CoRR abs/1808.04193 (2018). http://arxiv.org/abs/1808.04193

17. Kennedy, A., Pierce, B.C.: On decidability of nominal subtyping with variance. In: International Workshop on Foundations and Developments of Object-Oriented Languages (FOOL/WOOD), January 2007

18. Kurata, T., Takahashi, M.: Decidable properties of intersection type systems. In: Dezani-Ciancaglini, M., Plotkin, G. (eds.) TLCA 1995. LNCS, vol. 902, pp. 297–311. Springer, Heidelberg (1995). https://doi.org/10.1007/BFb0014060

19. Larchey-Wendling, D., Monin, J.F.: Simulating induction-recursion for partial algorithms. In: TYPES (2018)

20. Laurent, O.: Intersection subtyping with constructors. In: Pagani, M. (ed.) Proceedings of the Ninth Workshop on Intersection Types and Related Systems (2018)

21. Magaud, N.: Transferring arithmetic decision procedures (on Z) to alternative representations. In: CoqPL 2017: The Third International Workshop on Coq for Programming Languages (2017)

22. Pierce, B.C.: A decision procedure for the subtype relation on intersection types with bounded variables. Citeseer (1989)

23. Rehof, J., Urzyczyn, P.: Finite combinatory logic with intersection types. In: Ong, L. (ed.) TLCA 2011. LNCS, vol. 6690, pp. 169–183. Springer, Heidelberg (2011). https://doi.org/10.1007/978-3-642-21691-6_15

24. Statman, R.: A finite model property for intersection types. In: Proceedings Seventh Workshop on Intersection Types and Related Systems, ITRS 2014, Vienna, Austria, 18 July 2014, pp. 1–9 (2014). https://doi.org/10.4204/EPTCS.177.1

25. Steffen, B., Cleaveland, R.: When is "partial" adequate? A logic-based proof technique using partial specifications. In: Proceedings of the Fifth Annual Symposium on Logic in Computer Science (LICS 1990), Philadelphia, Pennsylvania, USA, 4–7 June 1990, pp. 440–449 (1990). https://doi.org/10.1109/LICS.1990.113768

Composition: A Fresh Look
at an Old Topic

Wolfgang Reisig[(✉)]

Humboldt-Universität zu Berlin, 10099 Berlin, Germany
`reisig@informatik.hu-berlin.de`

Abstract. Composing separate components is a fundamental design principle for concurrent systems. Composition $A_1 \cdot A_2$ of two components A_1 and A_2 is mostly modeled by "gluing" according elements of the *interfaces* of A_1 and A_2. Composition of *many* components is usually assumed to be *associative* (i.e. $(A_1 \cdot A_2) \cdot A_3 = A_1 \cdot (A_2 \cdot A_3)$). In this paper we suggest such a composition operator for any kind of graph based structures. The central and new idea exploits the observation that in a composed system $A_1 \cdot \ldots \cdot A_n$, every component A_i ($2 \leq i \leq n-1$) has a *left* partner A_{i-1} and a *right* partner A_{i+1}. The interface of A_i hence canonically partitions into the *left* and the *right port* of A_i. To gain $A_1 \cdot A_2$, elements of the right port of A_1 are glued with corresponding elements of the left port of A_2. We present two instantiations of this framework, modeling *synchronous* and *asynchronous* composition, respectively, of components with local states.

1 Introduction

1.1 Composing Components

Large systems are usually composed of (smaller) *components*. A component typically operates autonomously to some extent, and is equipped with an *interface* to establish some kind of cooperation with other components. Cooperating components may asynchronously exchange messages, or jointly perform steps. In a more technical setting, cooperation of two components A and B is frequently organized as some kind of *composition*, $A \cdot B$, such that $A \cdot B$ is again a component. A system is then just a component that may be composed of some (more elementary) components. A lot of modeling techniques employ the principle of composition to inductively construct system models. Pertaining examples include process algebras, statecharts, and special classes of (e.g. "open") Petri Nets.

1.2 The Quest for Associativity

In general, more than two components are to be composed. For example, a business supply chain may be composed of an ore producer C_1, steel works C_2, metal wholesale C_3, cutlery factory C_4, retailer C_5 etc., yielding a system shaped

© Springer Nature Switzerland AG 2019
T. Margaria et al. (Eds.): Steffen Festschrift, LNCS 11200, pp. 372–389, 2019.
https://doi.org/10.1007/978-3-030-22348-9_22

$$C_1 \cdot \ldots \cdot C_n. \tag{1}$$

Composition is assumed to be associative (i.e. $C_i \cdot (C_{i+1} \cdot C_{i+2}) = (C_i \cdot C_{i+1}) \cdot C_{i+2}$); therefore brackets can be skipped in (1). Associativity is indeed required in most areas where more than two components are composed. But many modeling techniques struggle with this requirement. For example LOTOS and I/O-Automata do with composition operators that are associative in special cases only.

1.3 Property Preservation

With n and m the number of states of two systems A and B, the number of states of a composed system $A \cdot B$ is in the order of $n \cdot m$. Hence, proving a property of $A \cdot B$ is usually much more costly than proving a property of A and of B separately. Therefore, interesting and relevant properties are those that are *preserved* under composition: If A and B both have property p, so has $A \cdot B$.

1.4 Interface Based Composition

Behavioural system models are frequently based on graphs. Nodes and arcs of such a graph are partitioned into *inner* and *interface* elements. Composition of two such systems is then gained by unifying (gluing, overlying, identifying) "according" interface elements. Examples include various versions of process algebras, data flow graphs, bigraphs, control flow graphs, network layouts, automata, BPMN-models, open Petri Nets, etc. As outlined above, associativity of composition of such systems is highly desirable.

In this paper we suggest a notion of composition, applicable to this kind of system models, that we proved to be associative. We furthermore show two instantiations of this principle of composition, an *asynchronous* and a *synchronous* version, depending only on the shape of the interface. For both versions we show special subclasses of models, for which composition preserves important properties.

The forthcoming composition operator is motivated by the observation that a component C_i ($2 \le i \le n - 1$) as in (1) has a *left* and a *right* partner, C_{i-1} and C_{i+1}, respectively. These partners frequently play different *roles* for C_i: In a business supply chain, C_{i-1} and C_{i+1} may be supplier and customer, provider and requester, buy side and sell side, predecessor and successor, respectively, of C_i. So, it is overly intuitive to assume the interface of a component C be partitioned into two *ports*, the *left port* $^*C$ and the *right port* C^*. Composition $C \cdot D$ of two components C and D then means to glue the elements of the right port C^* of C with the corresponding elements of the left port $^*D$ of D. This is a fundamental concept. Its consequences and some applications will be studied in the rest of this paper.

2   The General Framework

As explained above, it is overly intuitive to partition the interface of a component into its left and its right port. Here we introduce an abstract framework for such components, and we suggest a composition operator for components that reflects and exploits this structure. We denot this kinds of structures as *interface graphs*. Technically, an interface graph is a graph C together with two subsets of labeled nodes, the *left port* and the *right port* of C. The remaining nodes are the *inner nodes* of C.

2.1   Index Labeled Sets

The labeling of the ports of an interface graph exhibits a particular structure: Each node of a port carries a label from a globally given set L of labels, as well as a number (its "index") that is the node's position in the set of equally labeled nodes in the port. Labels and indices of nodes together constitute the port's *index label*.

For the sake of simplicity, in the rest of this paper we assume

$$\text{a set } L \text{ of labels.} \tag{2}$$

Definition 1. *Let A be a set and let $\lambda : A \longrightarrow L$.*

(i) For $l \in L$, let $\#(l, A) =_{def} |\lambda^{-1}(l)|$.
(ii) Let $\delta : A \longrightarrow \mathbb{N}$ such that for each $l \in L$ and each $1 \leq i \leq \#(l, A)$ there exists exactly one $a \in A$ with $\lambda(a) = l$ and $\delta(a) = i$.

Then δ is an index *for λ, and (λ, δ) is an* index label *for A. A is said to be* index labeled *by λ and δ. The index labeling of an index labeled set A is usually written λ_A and δ_A.*

Observation 1. *Let A, l, δ and $\#(l, A)$ be as in Definition 1.*

(i) The number of l-labeled elements of A is given by $\#(l, A)$.
(ii) The indices of the l-labeled elements of A are pairwise different and range between 1 and $\#(l, A)$.

2.2   Interface Graphs

We are now prepared to define the fundamental notion of this paper. As outlined above already, an *interface graph* is just a graph C with two distinguished subsets $^*C$ and C^* of nodes. Both these subsets are assumed to be index labeled:

Definition 2. *Let A be a finite set and let $Q \subseteq A \times A$.*

(i) $C =_{def} (A, Q)$ is a graph.
(ii) Let $^*C, C^* \subseteq A$ both be index labeled. Then C together with $^*C$ and C^* is an interface graph.
A and Q are the nodes *and* edges *of C. $^*C$ and C^* are the* left *and the* right port *of C. inner$(C) =_{def} A \setminus (^*C \cup C^*)$ is the set of* inner nodes *of C.*

2.3   Composing Interface Graphs

To prepare the notion of composition $C \cdot D$ of two interface graphs C and D, we introduce the notation $C \sqcap D$ for the set of elements of C^* and $^*D$ with equal labels and equal indices:

Definition 3. *Let C and D be disjoint interface graphs. Let $C \sqcap D =_{def}$ $\{(c, d)|c \in C^*, d \in^* D, \lambda_{C^*}(c) = \lambda_{*D}(d)$ and $\delta_{C^*}(c) = \delta_{*D}(d)\}$.*

Upon composing two interface graphs C and D, each $(c, d) \in C \sqcap D$ is a new inner element of $C \cdot D$, replacing $c \in C$ and $d \in D$. The inner elements of C and D turn unchanged into inner elements of $C \cdot D$. The remaining elements of $^*D$ go to $^*(CD)$ "on top" of $^*C$, and the remaining elements of C^* go to $(CD)^*$ "on top" of D^*. All arcs of C and of D remain in $C \cdot D$, up to the above outlined replacement of nodes c and d in $(c, d) \in C \sqcap D$. Figure 1 outlines this construct. Notice that $\sqcap$ is not commutative, i.e., in general, $C \sqcap D \neq D \sqcap C$.

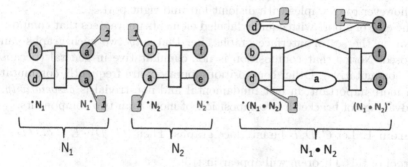

Fig. 1. Interface graphs N_1, N_2 and $N_1 \bullet N_2$ Left ports: ; right ports: . Indices of equally labelled elements: (index "1" is mostly skipped). The inner nodes of N_1 and N_2 are sketched as boxes.

Definition 4. *Let C and D be interface graphs. Then the interface graph $C \cdot D$ is given by*

(i) inner$(C) =_{def}$ inner$(C) \cup$ inner$(D) \cup (C \sqcap D)$
(ii) $x \in^* (CD)$ *iff*

- *(a)* $x \in {}^*C$, *with* $\lambda_{*(C \cdot D)}(x) = \lambda_{*C}(x)$ *and* $\delta_{*(C \cdot D)}(x) = \delta_{*C}(x)$,
  or
- *(b)* $x \in^* D \setminus pr_2(C \sqcap D)$, *where with* $l =_{def} \lambda_{*D}$ *holds:* $\lambda_{*(C \cdot D)}(x) = l$ *and* $\delta_{*(C \cdot D)}(x) = \#(l, {}^*C) + \delta_{*D}(x) - \#(l, C \sqcap D)$

(iii) $x \in (CD)^*$ *iff*

- *(a)* $x \in D^*$, *with* $\lambda_{(C \cdot D)^*}(x) = \lambda_{C^*}(x)$ *and* $\delta_{(C \cdot D)^*}(x) = \delta_{C^*}(x)$,
  or
- *(b)* $x \in D^* \setminus pr_1(C \sqcap D)$, *where with* $l =_{def} \lambda_{C^*}$ *holds:* $\lambda_{(C \cdot D)^*}(x) = l$ *and* $\delta_{(C \cdot D)^*}(x) = \#(l, D^*) + \delta_{C^*}(x) - \#(l, C \sqcap D)$

(iv) Each arc (x, y) of C and of D with $x, y \notin pr_1(C \sqcap D) \cup pr_2(C \sqcap D)$ is an arc of $C \cdot D$, where for $i = 1, 2$, pr_i denotes the projection to the i-th component.

(v) For each $(c, d) \in C \sqcap D$ and each node a of C and D holds:
   $(a, (c, d))$ is an arc of $C \cdot D$ iff (a, c) is an arc of C or of D,
   $((c, d), a)$ is an arc of $C \cdot D$ iff (c, a) is an arc of C or of D.

Figure 1 shows an example.

Observation 2. (i) $^*C \subseteq {}^* (C \cdot D)$ and $D^* \subseteq (C \cdot D)^*$.
(ii) If $^*C \cap C^* = {}^* D \cap D^* = \emptyset$, then $^*(C \cdot D) \cap (C \cdot D)^* = \emptyset$.

Observation 2 (ii), implies that the set of interface graphs with disjoint ports is closed under composition.

The above definition does not require $^*C$ and C^* be disjoint. In fact, they may even be identical. Even more, for an element c in $^*C \cap C^*$, the label and the index of c in $^*C$ may differ from the label and the index of c in C^*. Some instantiations of interface graphs exploit this technical option. In this paper we stick however to examples with disjoint left and right ports.

The case of a port with equally labeled elements guarantees that composition is total on the set of interface graphs, i.e. that *any* two such graphs can be composed. Notice that composition is not commutative in general (because $\sqcap$ is not commutative). Other composition operators are frequently commutative. Much more important, in fact fundamental and non-trivial is *associativity*, i.e. the advantage of bracket-free composition of more than two components:

Theorem 1. Let C, D, E be interface graphs. Then $(C \cdot D) \cdot E = C \cdot (D \cdot E)$.

Proof of this Theorem will appear in [13].

3   Synchronous and Asynchronous Composition

Here we consider two *instantiations* of interface graphs, i.e. classes of components with two distinguished ports. Each component exhibits discrete, dynamic behavior, i.e. some kind of *steps*. Such systems are usually designed as transition systems. For two transition systems C_i with k_i states ($i = 1, 2$), any kind of composition $C_1 \cdot C_2$ usually yields a transition system with an amount of states in the order of $k_1 \cdot k_2$. Hence the number of states grows exponentially for transition systems shaped $C_1 \cdot \ldots \cdot C_n$. This well-known state explosion problem can be overcome by means of system models that do not explicitly represent all reachable states. Examples of such system models include Process algebras, Petri nets, statecharts, etc.

Synchronously and asynchronously communicating systems can conveniently be modeled by means of Petri nets. A Petri net together with two index labeled subsets of elements (i.e. places and transitions) is an *interface net*. An interface net can be conceived as an interface graph, as studied in Sect. 2. Composition of interface nets can then be inherited from interface graph composition, and thus

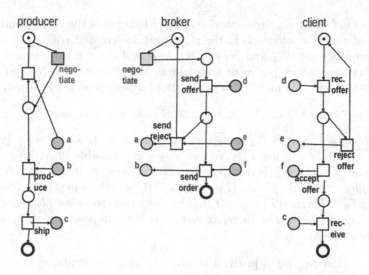

Fig. 2. Three interface nets. As in Fig. 1, elements of left and right port are colored blue and red, respectively.

is guaranteed to be associative. In general, a port of an interface net N may contain places as well as transitions. Figure 2 shows intuitive examples.

In the sequel we recall some fundamental notions and notations of Petri nets as e.g. given in [12] , and define the special class of *interface nets*, *workflow nets* and *sound workflow nets*.

3.1   Interface Nets

The static structure of a Petri Net N, together with two index labeled subsets, yields an interface net. Each interface net is obviously an interface graph. As usual, we define:

Definition 5. *Let P and T be finite, disjoint sets, and let $F \subseteq (P \times T) \cup (T \times P)$.*

(i) $N = (P, T, F)$ *is a* net structure. *The elements of P, T and F are places, transitions and* arcs, *respectively.*
(ii) For $x \in P \cup T$, let $^*x =_{def} \{y | (y, x) \in F\}$ and $x^* =_{def} \{y | (x, y) \in F\}$.

A net structure, equipped with two index labeled subsets of its elements, is an interface net, and canonically an interface graph:

Definition 6. *Let $N = (P, T, F)$ be a net structure, let $^*N, N^* \subseteq P \cup T$ both be index labeled.*

(i) N together with $^*N$ and N^* is an interface net.
(ii) $(P \cup T, F)$ together with $^*N$ and N^* is an interface graph, *the* interface graph *of N, written $\overline{N}$.*

Figure 2 in fact shows three interface nets. Elements of the corresponding left port are colored *blue*; elements in the right port are colored *red*.

Two interface nets N_1 and N_2 can be *composed* iff each two elements to be "glued" both are either places or transitions. More technically N_1 and N_2 are composable iff no tuple in $N_1^* \sqcap^* N_2$ consists of a place and a transition:

Definition 7. *For* $i = 1, 2$ *let* $N_i = (P_i, T_i, F_i)$ *be interface nets.*

(i) *Let* $P =_{def} \{(x, y) \in \overline{N_1} \sqcap \overline{N_2} | x \in P_1 \text{ and } y \in P_2\}$. *Let* $T =_{def} \{(x, y) \in \overline{N_1} \sqcap \overline{N_2} | x \in T_1 \text{ and } y \in T_2\}$. N_1 *and* N_2 *are composable iff* $\overline{N_1} \sqcap \overline{N_2} = P \cup T$.

(ii) *Assume* N_1 *and* N_2 *be composable, with* P *and* T *in (i). Let* N *be the interface net with places* $(P_1 \cup P_2 \cup P) \backslash (pr_1(P) \cup pr_2(P))$, *transitions* $(T_1 \cup T_2 \cup T) \backslash (pr_1(T) \cup pr_2(T))$, *and arcs and ports as obviously inherited from* $\overline{N_1} \cdot \overline{N_2}$. *The interface net* N *is the* composition *of* N_1 *and* N_2, *written* $N_1 \cdot N_2$.

The notation $N_1 \cdot N_2$ is justified by the following observation:

Observation 3. Let N_1, N_2 be two composable interface nets. Then $\overline{N_1 \cdot N_2} = \overline{N_1} \cdot \overline{N_2}$.

Figure 2 shows three interface nets. Together they represent a business case where a producer and a broker synchronously (e.g. by phone) agree on an offer. The broker sends the offer to the client. If the client rejects the offer, a new offer is prepared and sent to the client. Producer and broker, as well as broker and client, are composable (producer and client are also composable, but their composition does not make much sense). Notice that (producer·broker)*, as well as *(broker · client) contains a c-labeled place: The producer ships the produced goods directly to the client, bypassing the broker.

The two ports of an interface net frequently include either only transitions of only places. We consider two special classes of interface nets in the sequel, fostering synchronous and asynchronous composition, respectively. In both classes, any two interface nets are composable, and the resulting interface net remains in the class.

Definition 8. *Let* N *be an interface net.*

(i) N *is* synchronous *iff its two ports* *N *and* N* *include only transitions of* N.
(ii) N *is* asynchronous *iff its two ports* *N *and* N* *include only places of* N.

In Fig. 2, the *client* interface net is asynchronous. The other two interface nets are neither synchronous nor asynchronous. Forthcoming Fig. 7 shows two synchronous interface nets, N_1 and N_2: The interface nets in Figs. 8 and 10 are all asynchronous.

Theorem 2. Let N_1 and N_2 be synchronous interface nets

(i) N_1 and N_2 are composable.
(ii) $N_1 \cdot N_2$ is again an synchronous interface net.

Proof. By Definition 3 and Definition 12, all tuples $(x, y) \in \overline{N_1} \sqcap \overline{N_2}$ consist of transitions x and y. Proposition (i) then follows from Definition 9. Proposition (ii) follows from Definition 4.

Theorem 3. *Let N_1 and N_2 be asynchronous interface nets.*

(i) *N_1 and N_2 are composable.*
(ii) *$N_1 \cdot N_2$ is again an asynchronous interface net.*

This theorem can be proven in analogy to the proof of Theorem 2.

3.2 Dynamic Behavior

This subsection compiles the well-known concepts of dynamic behavior of Petri nets.

Definition 9. *Let $N = (P, T, F)$ be a net structure.*

(i) *For $x \in P \cup T$, let $y \in {}^\bullet x$ iff $(y, x) \in F$, and $y \in x^\bullet$ iff $(x, y) \in F$.*
(ii) *A mapping $M : P \longrightarrow \mathbb{N}$ is a* marking *of N.*
(iii) *A marking M'* exceeds *a marking M (written $M' > M$) iff for all places p of N, $M'(p) \geq M(p)$ and $M' \neq M$.*
(iv) *A marking M is* 1-bounded *iff $M(p) \leq 1$ for all $p \in P$. By abuse of notation, M occasionally denotes the set $\{p \in P | M(p) = 1\}$.*
(v) *A marking M* enables *a transition t iff $M(p) \geq 1$ for all $p \in {}^\bullet t$.*

Definition 10. *Let N be a net structure.*

(i) *Two markings M and M', and a transition t of N form a* step, *written $M \xrightarrow{t} M'$, if M enables t, and for each $p \in P$*
$$M'(p) = \begin{cases} M(p) - 1 & \text{iff } p \in {}^\bullet t \setminus t^\bullet \\ M(p) + 1 & \text{iff } p \in t^\bullet \setminus {}^\bullet t \\ M(p), & \text{otherwise} \end{cases}$$
(ii) *Steps $M_{i-1} \xrightarrow{t_i} M_i (i = 1, ..., n)$ form a* sequential run *from M_0 to M_n, written $M_0 \xrightarrow{t_1} M_1 \xrightarrow{t_2} ... \xrightarrow{t_n} M_n$.*
(iii) *A marking M' is* reachable *from M in N iff there exists a sequential run from M to M'.*
(iv) *For two markings M and M' of N, the marking $M + M'$ of N is defined by $(M + M')(p) =_{def} M(p) + M'(p)$, for each place p of N.*

3.3 Workflow Nets

A *workflow net* is a net structure N together with two distinguished markings, start_N and stop_N. The idea is to focus on sequential runs from start_N to stop_N, and to define the semantics of such nets as the set of sequential runs from start_N to stop_N. The original definition of workflow nets in [15] is much more restrictive, assuming places p, q with $\text{start}_N(p) = \text{stop}_N(q) = 1$, and all other places unmarked.

Definition 11. *Let N be a net structure and let start$_N$ and stop$_N$ be markings of N. Then*

(i) N together with start$_N$ and stop$_N$ is a workflow net.

(ii) A sequential run $M_0 \xrightarrow{t_1} M_1 \xrightarrow{t_2} ... \xrightarrow{t_n} M_n$ with $M_0 = start_N$ and $M_n = stop_N$ is a run of N.

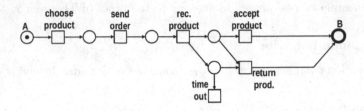

Fig. 3. Non-sound work net: a client of an internet shop

Fig. 3 shows a workflow net. The initial marking has a token on A; the final marking has a token on B.

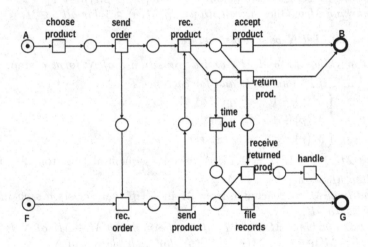

Fig. 4. Sound workflow net: client and internet shop

Figure 4 extends Fig. 3 to a workflow net with initial and final markings, each of which includes *two* places. As a general rule, the initial marking of a workflow net is represented by black dots (tokens), as usual in Petri nets. The places including final markings are boldfaced. This is unique in case, the final marking is 1-bounded (as in all our examples).

The notion of *soundness* characterizes semantically reasonable, well structured systems: each transition can be enabled, each sequential run can be finished, the final markings is reached without leaving tokens behind, and a token of a final marking can not be used to fire another transition. It will furthermore turn out useful to assume the start- and stop marking be 1-bounded:

Definition 12. *Let N be a workflow net. N is sound if and only if*

(i) *$start_N$ and $stop_N$ are 1-bounded.*

(ii) *For each transition t of N there exists a marking M that is reachable from $start_N$ and enables t.*

(iii) *$stop_N$ is reachable from each reachable marking in N.*

(iv) *No marking $M > stop_N$ is reachable from $start_N$.*

(v) *For each place p with $stop_N(p) = 1$ holds: $p^\bullet = \emptyset$.*

This definition corresponds to van der Aalst' definition of soundness (modulo the slightly more general start- and stop markings.) The workflow net as in Fig. 3 is not sound: it violates requirement (iv). Figure 4 is sound.

4   Interface-Workflow-Nets

This section brings the core of this paper: The combination of interface nets with workflow nets:

4.1   The Notion of Iw-Nets

Interface nets are equipped with initial and final markings. (The same said differently: workflow nets are equipped with left and right ports.) In the sequel we denote such nets as *interface-workflow-nets*.

Definition 13. *Let N be an interface net as well as an workflow net. Then N is an* interface-workflow-net *(iw-net, for short).*

The three nets in Fig. 2 are in fact iw-nets. The ports *producer and client* are empty. Elements belonging to the left port, the right port, the initial marking and the final marking are colored blue, red, marked by a token and are boldfaced, respectively. In fact, all Figures of this paper with the exception of Fig. 1, can be conceived as iw-nets, some with empty ports.

Composition of iw-nets N_1 and N_2 should yield again an iw-net $N_1 \cdot N_2$. This rises the quest of fixing the initial and the final marking $start_{N_1 \cdot N_2}$ and $stop_{N_1 \cdot N_2}$. We are not interested in a "most general" definition of $start_{N_1 \cdot N_2}$ and $stop_{N_1 \cdot N_2}$. Instead, we strive for classes of iw-nets that are closed under composition, and where composition preserves important properties. In particular, criteria would be useful that guarantee $N_1 \cdot N_2$ be sound, provided N_1 and N_2 both are sound. For the two classes of synchronous and asynchronous interface nets, as defined in Sect. 3, we derive such criteria in the sequel.

4.2   Parallel Composition of Iw-Nets

Composition $N_1 \cdot N_2$ of two composable iw-nets is often ment to execute N_1 and N_2 in parallel, where N_1 and N_2 communicate or synchronize along N_1^* and $^*N_2$. Initial and final marking of $N_1 \cdot N_2$ is in this case just the sum of the corresponding markings of N_1 and N_2:

Definition 14. *Let N_1 and N_2 be two composable iw-nets.*

(i) Let $start_{N_1 \cdot N_2} =_{def} start_{N_1} + start_{N_2}$, *and* $stop_{N_1 \cdot N_2} =_{def} stop_{N_1} + stop_{N_2}$.
(ii) $N_1 \cdot N_2$ together with $start_{N_1 \cdot N_2}$ and $stop_{N_1 \cdot N_2}$ as in (i) is the parallel composition of N_1 and N_2.

Obviously, $N_1 \cdot N_2$ is again an iw-net.

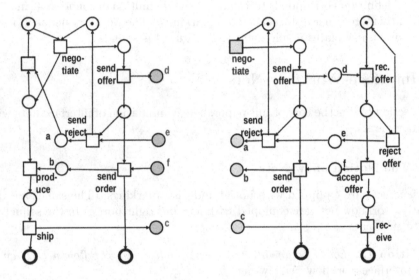

Fig. 5. Producer • broker, and broker • client

Figures 5 and 6 show the parallel composition of components of Fig. 1. All involved nets are iw-nets, though some with empty ports. In particular, both ports $^*N$ and N^* of the iw-net N in Fig. 6 are empty. So, N can be conceived as a workflow net. In fact, this workflow net is sound.

With the definition of workflow nets as in [15], with initial and final markings restricted to a single place, parallel composition of iw-nets would yield no workflow net (and hence no iw-net). So, our slightly generalized definition turns out quite useful.

One can not expect this general setting of composition to preserve any relevant property, in particular not the soundness property. However, soundness is preserved in the special case, where

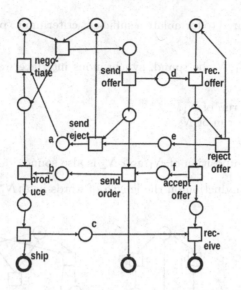

Fig. 6. Producer ● broker ● client

- N_1 and N_2 communicate synchronously,
- each nondeterministic choice inside N_1 and N_2 is "observed" by N_1^* and $^*N_2$, respectively, and
- the projections of the runs of N_1 and N_2 to the labeled transitions of N_1^* and $^*N_2$, coincide

Formulated more intuitively, we say a marking M "chooses" two or more transitions, if M enables them all. A port A "observes" this choice iff all those transitions belong to A.

A sequential run as in Definition 14 (ii) defines a sequence of transition occurrences. Transitions belonging to a port A yield a subsequence $u_1 \cdots u_n$ of transitions $u_i \in A$. Replacing u_i by its index label yields a sequence $< \lambda(u_1), \delta(u_1) > \cdots < \lambda(u_n), \delta(u_n) >$. Those sequences constitute the language $\mathcal{L}(A)$ of A:

Definition 15. *Let N be an iw-net, let A be a port of N, and let $w = M_0 \xrightarrow{t_1} M_1 \xrightarrow{t_2} \dots \xrightarrow{t_n} M_n$ be a sequential run of N.*

(i) A observes w iff for all $1 \leq i \leq n$ holds: If M_{i-1} enables some $t \neq t_i$, then $t, t_i \in A$.

(ii) With $w' = M_0 \xrightarrow{t_1} M_1 \xrightarrow{t_2} \dots \xrightarrow{t_{n-1}} M_{n-1}$,

$$let\ A(w) = \begin{cases} \epsilon & if\ n = 0 \\ A(w') < \lambda(w_n), \tau(w_n) > & if\ t_n \in A \\ A(w') & if\ t_n \notin A \end{cases}$$

(iii) Let $\mathcal{L}(A) =_{def} \{A(w) \mid w \text{ is a run of } N\}$

We are now prepared to formulate a sufficient criterium to preserve soundness of synchronous iw-nets:

Theorem 4. Let N_1, N_2 be sound, synchronous interface workflow nets, such that

- N_1^* observes each run of N_1,
- $^*N_2$ observes each run of N_2,
- $\mathcal{L}(N_1^*) = \mathcal{L}(^*N_2)$.

Then the parallel composition of N_1 and N_2 is also sound.

Proof follows by induction on the length of words in $\mathcal{L}(N_1^*)$ and in $\mathcal{L}(^*N_2)$.

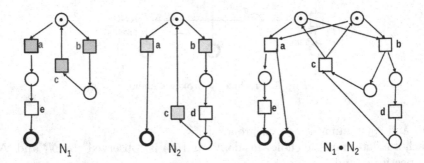

Fig. 7. Two sound, synchronous interface workflow nets, N_1 and N_2. By construction, $N_1 \bullet N_2$ is also a sound, synchronous interface workflow net (with empty ports).

As an example, N_1 and N_2 in Fig. 7 are sound, synchronous iw-nets, and meet the three properties. (with $\mathcal{L}(N_1^*) = (bc)^*a \cup (bc)^\infty$). Hence $N_1 \cdot N_2$ (as in Fig. 7) is sound by Theorem 19.

4.3 Sequential Composition of Iw-Nets

Asynchronous composition couples iw-nets more loosely than synchronous composition. Property preservation hence requires stricter requirements in this case.

In the sequel we consider asynchronous iw-nets with the left port used for input and the right port for output. In view of workflows it is worthwile to identify the left port with the initial marking and the right port with the final marking (by abuse of notation we identify 1-bounded markings M with $\{p \mid M(p) = 1\}$). This kind of nets is denoted as "i/o-interfaced". Figure 8 shows a very simple example of an i/o-interfaced net N, as well as composition of 2 or 3 instances of this kind of nets.

Composition of i/o-interfaced iw-nets is essentially sequential composition. However, in $N_1 \cdot N_2$, some transitions of N_2 may occur already before all transitions of N_1 occurred. This kind of iw-nets has beautiful properties. They are closed under composition, and composition preserves soundness.

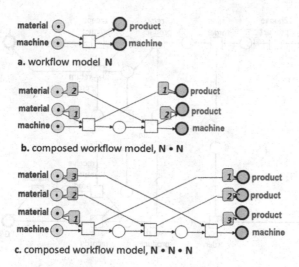

a. workflow model N

b. composed workflow model, N • N

c. composed workflow model, c. N • N • N

Fig. 8. Model **N** of a simple workflow, transforming material into products by help of a machine, together with **N • N** and **N • N • N**

Definition 16. *Let N be an asynchronous iw-net with 1-bounded markings $start_N$ and $stop_N$. N is i/o-interfaced iff $start_N =^* N$ and $stop_N = N^*$.*

The set of i/o-interfaced iw-nets is closed under composition:

Theorem 5. Let N_1, N_2 be i/o-interfaced nets. Then $N_1 \cdot N_2$ is also an i/o-interfaced net.

This follows from the definition of composition and of i/o-interfaced nets.

As a final example we consider the above models of an internet shop and its client. The iw-net N_1 in Fig. 9 extends the workflow net model of a client as in Fig. 3, with a right interface.

The iw-net N_2 in Fig. 9 models the behavior of an internet shop. The workflow net in Fig. 5 is the composed iw-net $N_1 \cdot N_2$, with empty ports $^*(N_1 \cdot N_2)$ and $(N_1 \cdot N_2)^*$. Hence, $N =_{def} N_1 \cdot N_2$ is a workflow net. It is simple (but out of scope of this paper) to show that N is sound. Now we conceive N as i/o-interfaced, with some re-labeling of the final places, as sketched in Fig. 10a.

Figure 10b shows the composition $N \cdot N$ of two instances of N. Notice that the client (upper line) may choose his second product and order it, while the internet shop (lower line) is still pending for the delivery timeout of the first product. According to Theorem 10, $N \cdot N$ is sound (as N is sound).

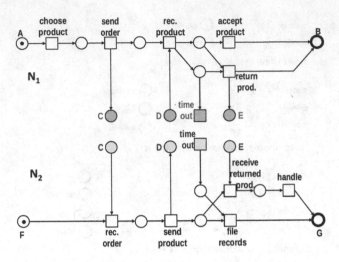

Fig. 9. Two interface workflow nets, N_1 and N_2, modeling a client and an internet shop.

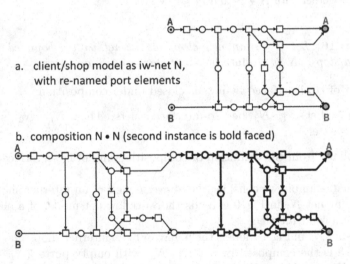

a. client/shop model as iw-net N, with re-named port elements

b. composition N • N (second instance is bold faced)

Fig. 10. Sequential composition of two instances of the internet shop and its client

5 Related Work

During the last decades, many ideas have been published as how to model components and their composition. Some are based on automata [6], [8]. The FOCUS-approach specifies the semantics of a component as a relation over streams of symbols, together wirh a fully-fledged software development method, e.g. [4] or the recent [3]. The REO framework [1] composes components by means of specialized channels and fitting connectors [5]. Generalizes this approach to component networks. Composition of components is a central concern of software architecture languages (cf. [9]) and [14] In fact, many software architecture languages can be embedded into our framework. In particular, microservice architectures fit in our framework, by composing *many* small components [10].

A number of related contributions construct variants of process algebras, e.g. [7], [17]. Define a π -calculus like formalism to represent service-based systems [11]. Considers questions similar to ours, and develop a π -calculus based formalism.

A couple of Petri net based formalisms define building blocks and several composition operators in an algebraic style, such as the box calculus [2], [16]. Identifies a class of "distributable" Petri nets, and shows that any distributable nets may be implemented on a network of asynchronously communicating components.

6   Conclusion

We suggest a composition operator for components with a number of important aspects:

1. The operator is particularly structured: among the many suggestions to model components and their composition by help of "glueing" interface elements, none partitions the interface elements into "right" and "left", and defines the composition $A \cdot B$ of two components A and B, by composing the right interface elements of A with the left interface elements of B.
2. The operator is universal in the sense that any kind of composition in any network of components can be represented: Properties p of a specific composition $A \cdot B$, including those mentioned in the relades work section, can be modeled by help of a mediator (adapter) C, such that $A \cdot C \cdot B$ guarantees p. Any network with components $A_1, \ldots, A_n$ can be represented by $A_1 \cdot \ldots \cdot A_n$, with interface elements properly discriminated as left and right: if for indices i and j with $i < j$, the interface element e_i of A_i is to be glued with e_j from A_j, select e_i as right and e_j as left. This also shows there is no need for three or more kind of interface elements: two ("left" and "right") suffice.
3. The operator can easily be implemented: Only a minimum of computational infrastructure is required because the aspect of composition is maximally detached from the inner structure of components: The interface elements are linked by a relation to any kind of internal elements of components. All semantical aspects are hidden from the mechanics of composition.

Acknowledgements. Holger Hermann's remarks and questions on a previous version of this paper significantly improved its contents. I am also grateful for the referee's comments.

References

1. Arbab, F.: Reo: a channel-based coordination model for component composition. Math. Struct. Comput. Sci. **14**(3), 329–366 (2014)
2. Best, E., Devillers, R.R., Koutny, M.: Petri Net Algebra. Monographs in Theoretical Computer Science. Springer, Heidelberg (2001). https://doi.org/10.1007/978-3-662-04457-5
3. Broy, M.: A logical approach to systems engineering artifacts: semantic relationships and dependencies beyond traceability - from requirements to functional and architectural views. Softw. Syst. Model. **17**(2), 365–393 (2018)
4. Broy, M., Stølen, K.: Specification and Development of Interactive Systems - Focus on Streams, Interfaces, and Refinement. Monographs in Computer Science. Springer, New York (2001). https://doi.org/10.1007/978-1-4613-0091-5
5. Dastani, M., Arbab, F., de Boer, F.S. Coordination and composition in multiagent systems. In 4th International Joint Conference on Autonomous Agents and Multiagent Systems (AAMAS 2005), pp. 439–446, Utrecht, The Netherlands, 25–29 July 2005 (2005)
6. de Alfaro, L., Henzinger, T.A. Interface automata. In: Tjoa, A.M., Gruhn, V. (Eds.) Proceedings of the 8th European Software Engineering Conference held Jointly with 9th ACM SIGSOFT International Symposium on Foundations of Software Engineering 2001, Vienna, Austria, 10–14 September 2001. ACM, pp. 109–120 (2001)
7. Garavel, H., Sighireanu, M.: A graphical parallel composition operator for process algebras. In: Formal Methods for Protocol Engineering and Distributed Systems, FORTE XII / PSTV XIX 1999, IFIP TC6 WG6.1 Joint International Conference on Formal Description Techniques for Distributed Systems and Communication Protocols (FORTE XII) and Protocol Specification, Testing and Verification (PSTV XIX), pp. 185–202, 5–8 October 1999, Beijing, China (1999)
8. Lynch, N.A., Tuttle, M.R.: Hierarchical correctness proofs for distributed algorithms. In: Proceedings of the Sixth Annual ACM Symposium on Principles of Distributed Computing, pp. 137–151, Vancouver, British Columbia, Canada, 10–12 August 1987 (1987)
9. Medvidovic, N., Taylor, R.N.: A classification and comparison framework for software architecture description languages. IEEE Trans. Software Eng. **26**(1), 70–93 (2000)
10. Nadareishvili, I., Mitra, R., McLarty, M., Amundsen, M.: Microservice Architecture: Aligning Principles, Practices, and Culture. O'Reilly, Newton (2016)
11. Nierstrasz, Oscar, Achermann, Franz: A calculus for modeling software components. In: de Boer, Frank S., Bonsangue, Marcello M., Graf, Susanne, de Roever, Willem-Paul (eds.) FMCO 2002. LNCS, vol. 2852, pp. 339–360. Springer, Heidelberg (2003). https://doi.org/10.1007/978-3-540-39656-7_14
12. Reisig, W.: Understanding Petri Nets - Modeling Techniques, Analysis Methods, Case Studies. Springer, Heidelberg (2013)
13. Reisig, W.: Associative composition of components with double-sided interfaces. submitted to Acta Informatica (2018)
14. Rostami, N.H., Kheirkhah, E., Jalali, M.: An optimized semantic web service composition method based on clustering and an colony algorithm. CoRR abs/1402.2271 (2014)
15. van der Aalst, W.M.P., van Hee, K.M., ter Hofstede, A.H.M., Sidorova, N., Verbeek, H.M.W., Voorhoeve, M., Wynn, M.T.: Soundness of workflow nets: classification, decidability, and analysis. Formal Asp. Comput. **23**(3), 333–363 (2011)

16. van Glabbeek, R.J., Goltz, U., Schicke-Uffmann, J.: On distributability of petri nets - (extended abstract). In: Foundations of Software Science and Computational Structures - 15th International Conference, FOSSACS 2012, Held as Part of the European Joint Conferences on Theory and Practice of Software, ETAPS 2012, 24 March - 1 April 2012, Tallinn, Estonia, Proceedings, pp. 331–345 (2012)

17. Vieira, Hugo T., Caires, Luís, Seco, João C.: The conversation calculus: a model of service-oriented computation. In: Drossopoulou, Sophia (ed.) ESOP 2008. LNCS, vol. 4960, pp. 269–283. Springer, Heidelberg (2008). https://doi.org/10.1007/978-3-540-78739-6_21

Benchmarks for Automata Learning and Conformance Testing

Daniel Neider[1], Rick Smetsers[2], Frits Vaandrager[2(✉)], and Harco Kuppens[2]

[1] Max Planck Institute for Software Systems, Kaiserslautern, Germany
[2] Institute for Computing and Information Sciences, Radboud University,
Nijmegen, The Netherlands
`F.Vaandrager@cs.ru.nl`

Abstract. We describe a large collection of benchmarks, publicly available through the wiki `automata.cs.ru.nl`, of different types of state machine models: DFAs, Moore machines, Mealy machines, interface automata and register automata. Our repository includes both randomly generated state machines and models of real protocols and embedded software/hardware systems. These benchmarks will allow researchers to evaluate the performance of new algorithms and tools for active automata learning and conformance testing.

1 Introduction

Active automata learning (or model learning) aims to construct black-box state machine models of software and hardware systems by providing inputs and observing outputs. State machines are crucial for understanding the behavior of many software systems, such as network protocols and embedded control software, as they allow us to reason about communication errors and component compatibility. Model learning is emerging as a highly effective bug-finding technique, and is slowly becoming a standard tool in the toolbox of the software engineer [35,68]. Bernhard Steffen has been (and still is) the main intellectual driving force behind this important development, and together with his students and coworkers he has made numerous important contributions to the theory and application of model learning, see e.g., [9,14,15,34,35,37,38,63]. His ideas have been implemented in the open source automata learning framework LearnLib [49,55,56], which has become the most prominent tool in this area.

Many model learning algorithms have been proposed in the literature, for instance by Angluin [8], Rivest and Schapire [57], Kearns and Vazirani [40], Shahbaz and Groz [61], Bollig et al. [10], Howar [33], Isberner et al. [37], Aarts et al. [1], Cassel et al. [14,15], and Moerman et al. [50]. Often variations of algorithms exist for different classes of models, e.g., DFAs, Mealy machines, Moore machine, interface automata, and various forms of register automata.

R. Smetsers—Supported by NWO/EW project 628.001.009 (LEMMA).
F. Vaandrager—Supported by NWO project 13859 (SUMBAT).

Active automata learning is closely related to conformance testing [9]. Whereas automata learning aims at constructing hypothesis models from observations, conformance testing checks whether a system under test conforms to a given model. Conformance test tools play a crucial role within active automata learning, as a way to determine whether a hypothesis model is correct or not. Also in the literature on conformance testing many algorithms have been proposed for different model classes, for surveys see [23,43,44,67].

Although there has been some experimental work on evaluating algorithms for model learning and conformance testing, see e.g., [3,12,23,24], the number of realistic benchmarks is rather limited, and different papers use different models and/or black-box implementations. Often the benchmarks used are small, academic, or randomly generated. Small, academic benchmarks are useful during tool development, but do not say much about the performance on industrial cases. The performance of algorithms on randomly generated benchmarks is often radically different from performance on benchmarks based on real systems that occur in practice. A mature field is characterized by the presence of a rich set of shared benchmarks, used to evaluate the efficiency of algorithms and tools, and as challenges for pushing the state-of-the-art.

In this article, we describe a large collection of benchmarks, publicly available through the wiki repository `automata.cs.ru.nl`, that includes both randomly generated state machines and models of real protocols and embedded software/hardware systems. Our benchmarks will allow researchers to compare the performance of algorithms and tools for learning and conformance testing, to check whether tools and methods advance, and to demonstrate that new methods are effective.

We are aware of a few other repositories with benchmarks for model learning and/or conformance testing. The ACM/SIGDA benchmark dataset [12,24] contains behavioral models for testing, logic synthesis and optimization of circuits. We have included Mealy machine versions of these benchmarks in our repository. The goal of the GitHub repository AutomatArk [19] is to collect benchmark problems for different models of automata, transducers, and related logics. In particular, AutomatArk contains NFAs that are adapted from a few verification case studies. The RERS challenges [38], www.rers-challenge.org, aim to provide realistic benchmarks that allow researchers to compare different software validation techniques, e.g., static analysis, model checking, symbolic execution and (model-based) testing. Benchmarks of previous challenges are still available via the website. The StaMinA competition [71], `stamina.chefbe.net`, focused on the complexity of learning with respect to the alphabet size. The competition is closed, but the website still hosts all of its benchmarks, a total of 100. Finally, we mention the Very Large Transition Systems (VLTS) benchmark suite, http://cadp.inria.fr/resources/vlts/, which has been set up by CWI and INRIA to support the evaluation of algorithms and tools for explicit state verification. Whereas the benchmarks in our repository model the behavior of individual components with at most a few thousand states, the VLTS benchmarks typically describe the behavior of concurrent systems that are composed of multiple components and that have a global state space with milions of states. Most VLTS benchmarks are completely out of reach for state-of-the-art learning and testing tools.

The remainder of this article is organized as follows. In Sect. 2, we discuss the different types of automata frameworks that are supported in our repository (DFAs, Moore machines, Mealy machines, interface automata, and register automata) and behavior preserving translations between these frameworks. Even though most of the definitions are standard, and most of the translations are folklore, this is the first time all these definitions and translations are presented together in a comprehensive manner, using consistent terminology and notation. The translations play a crucial role in our automata repository, since they allow us to transfer benchmarks from one framework to another, and thus obtain many benchmarks "for free". Section 3 gives an overview of the network protocols, embedded controllers, circuits, and other realistic applications for which models have been included in our benchmark collection. Section 4 discusses algorithms for generating the random automaton models that we have included in our repository. Finally, Sect. 5 draws some conclusions.

2   State Machine Frameworks

Below we recall the definitions of the different types of state machines for which we have collected benchmarks, discuss data formats to represent different model classes, define the corresponding notions of behavioral equivalence, and describe behavior preserving translations between types of state machines.

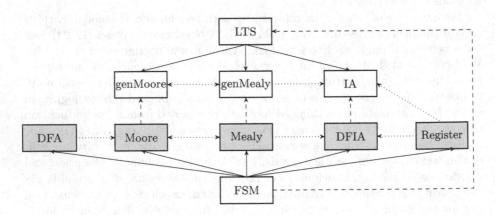

Fig. 1. Overview of state machine frameworks.

Figure 1 presents an overview of the different state machine frameworks that we will discuss, and their relationships. For the finite state frameworks indicated with red boxes, benchmark models have been included in our repository: *DFAs, Moore machines, Mealy machines, deterministic finite interface automata*

(DFIAs), and *register automata.* For some frameworks, more general (nondeterministic and infinite state) variants have been studied in the literature: *generalized Moore machines, generalized Mealy machines,* and *interface automata (IAs).* All finite state frameworks have an underlying *finite state machine (FSM),* and all infinite state frameworks have an underlying *labeled transition system (LTS).* In Fig. 1, a regular arrow indicates that one framework is a substructure of another, a dashed arrow that one framework is a special case of another, and a dotted arrow that a behavior preserving translation exists.

2.1   Labeled Transition Systems

All the state machines that we consider are labeled, directed graphs, equipped with some extra structure. Following standard terminology, we refer to the underlying graphs as *labeled transition systems* [41].

Definition 1 (Labeled transition systems). *A* labeled transition system (LTS) *is a tuple* $S = \langle Q, Q_0, A, \rightarrow \rangle$, *where*

- *Q is a non-empty set of* states,
- *$Q_0 \subseteq Q$ is a non-empty set of* initial states,
- *A is a set of* actions, *and*
- *$\rightarrow \subseteq Q \times A \times Q$ is a* transition relation.

We write $q \xrightarrow{a} q'$ if $(q, a, q') \in \rightarrow$. An LTS S is deterministic *if Q_0 is a singleton set, and for each state $q \in Q$ and each action $a \in A$, there is at most one state $q' \in Q$ such that $q \xrightarrow{a} q'$. An action $a \in A$ is* enabled *in state $q \in Q$, notation $q \xrightarrow{a}$, if there exists a state $q' \in Q$ such that $q \xrightarrow{a} q'$. An LTS S is* completely specified *(or* complete*) if each action is enabled in each state. An LTS S is* finite *and is called a* finite-state machine (FSM) *if sets Q and $\rightarrow$ are both finite.*

For a sequence of actions $\sigma = a_1 a_2 \cdots a_m \in A^*$ and states $q, q' \in Q$, we write $q \xRightarrow{\sigma} q'$ if there exist states $q_0, \ldots, q_m \in S$ such that $q_0 = q$, $q_m = q'$, and $q_{j-1} \xrightarrow{a_j} q_j$ for all $1 \leq j \leq m$.

FSMs and the various extensions that we will review below are syntactically represented in our repository using the graph description language DOT [28]. Scripts are provided to translate between DOT and other common formats for representing state machines. Figure 2 shows the graphical representation of a simple FSM (left) and its representation in DOT (right). The graphical representation follows the usual conventions for representing graphs. Initial states are indicated by a small incoming edge. The DOT representation first lists all the states, then the start states, and then the transitions. In order to mark the initial states, an auxiliary "invisible" node is created with edges to all the start states. Actions are indicated as labels of transitions.

Definition 2 (Bisimulation). *Let $S_1 = \langle Q_1, Q_0^1, A, \rightarrow_1 \rangle$, $S_2 = \langle Q_2, Q_0^2, A, \rightarrow_2 \rangle$ be LTSs. A* bisimulation *between S_1 and S_2 is a relation $R \subseteq Q_1 \times Q_2$ that satisfies:*

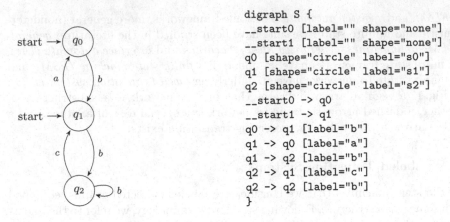

```
digraph S {
__start0 [label="" shape="none"]
__start1 [label="" shape="none"]
q0 [shape="circle" label="s0"]
q1 [shape="circle" label="s1"]
q2 [shape="circle" label="s2"]
__start0 -> q0
__start1 -> q1
q0 -> q1 [label="b"]
q1 -> q0 [label="a"]
q1 -> q2 [label="b"]
q2 -> q1 [label="c"]
q2 -> q2 [label="b"]
}
```

Fig. 2. An FSM and its representation in DOT.

1. for every $q_1 \in Q_0^1$ there exists a $q_2 \in Q_0^2$ such that $(q_1, q_2) \in R$,
2. for every $q_2 \in Q_0^2$ there exists a $q_1 \in Q_0^1$ such that $(q_1, q_2) \in R$,
3. for every $q_1, q_1' \in Q_1$, $a \in A$ and $q_2 \in Q_2$ with $(q_1, q_2) \in R$ and $q_1 \xrightarrow{a} q_1'$, there exists a $q_2' \in Q_2$ such that $q_2 \xrightarrow{a} q_2'$ and $(q_1', q_2') \in R$,
4. for every $q_2, q_2' \in Q_2$, $a \in A$ and $q_1 \in Q_1$ with $(q_1, q_2) \in R$ and $q_2 \xrightarrow{a} q_2'$, there exists a $q_1' \in Q_1$ such that $q_1 \xrightarrow{a} q_1'$ and $(q_1', q_2') \in R$.

We say that S_1 and S_2 are **bisimilar**, and write $S_1 \simeq S_2$, if there exists a bisimulation between S_1 and S_2.

2.2 Finite Automata

A finite automaton [32] extends an FSM by identifying some states as accepting.

Definition 3 (Finite automaton). *A* (nondeterministic) finite automaton (or NFA) *is a tuple* $\mathcal{A} = \langle Q, Q_0, \Sigma, \rightarrow, F \rangle$, *where* $\langle Q, Q_0, \Sigma, \rightarrow \rangle$ *is an FSM and* $F \subseteq Q$ *is a set of* final (or accepting) *states. Elements of* Σ *are referred to as* input symbols. *A deterministic finite automataton (DFA) is an NFA for which the underlying FSM is deterministic and complete.*

In the DOT format, accepting states of a finite automaton are denoted by a double circle, following the standard convention:

```
digraph g {
  ...
  q [shape="doublecircle"]
  ...
}
```

Definition 4 (Equivalence of NFAs). *A finite sequence (or word)* $w \in \Sigma^*$ *is* accepted *by NFA* $\mathcal{A}$ *iff there exists an initial state* $q \in Q_0$ *and a final state* $q' \in F$ *such that* $q \overset{w}{\Rightarrow} q'$. *If* w *is not accepted then we say it is* rejected. *The language* $L(\mathcal{A})$ *of* $\mathcal{A}$ *is the set of all words accepted by* $\mathcal{A}$. *Two NFAs* $\mathcal{A}$ *and* $\mathcal{B}$ *are* equivalent, *notation* $\mathcal{A} \approx \mathcal{B}$, *if they have the same set of input symbols and* $L(\mathcal{A}) = L(\mathcal{B})$.

2.3   Moore Machines

A (generalized) Moore machine [51] extends an LTS by assigning an output to each state.

Definition 5 (Generalized Moore machine). *A generalized Moore machine (or genMoore) is a tuple* $\mathcal{M} = \langle Q, Q_0, \Sigma, \Gamma, \rightarrow, \omega \rangle$, *where* $\langle Q, Q_0, \Sigma, \rightarrow \rangle$ *is an LTS,* Γ *is a set of* output symbols, *and* $\omega : Q \rightarrow \Gamma$ *is an* output function. *We call elements of* Σ input symbols. *A* Moore machine *is a genMoore for which the underlying LTS is deterministic, complete and finite.*

In the DOT representation of a Moore machine, the value o of the output function in state q is listed after a "|" in the label of state q:

```
digraph g {
  ...
  q [shape="record", style="rounded", label="{ q | o }"]
  ...
}
```

Definition 6 (Equivalence of genMoores). *Suppose* $w = i_1 i_2 \cdots i_m \in \Sigma^*$, $q_0 \in Q_0$, *and* $q_1, \ldots, q_m \in Q$ *with* $q_{j-1} \overset{i_j}{\longrightarrow} q_j$ *for all* $1 \leq j \leq m$. *Then the sequence* $\omega(q_1) \cdots \omega(q_m) \in \Gamma^*$ *is an* output *of genMoore* $\mathcal{M}$ *in reponse to* w.[1] *The* output function *of* $\mathcal{M}$ *is the function* $\lambda_{\mathcal{M}}$ *that assigns to each input word* $w \in \Sigma^*$ *the set of all outputs of* $\mathcal{M}$ *in response to* w. *Two genMoores* $\mathcal{M}$ *and* $\mathcal{N}$ *are* equivalent, *notation* $\mathcal{M} \approx \mathcal{N}$, *if they have the same input symbols and* $\lambda_{\mathcal{M}} = \lambda_{\mathcal{N}}$.

A DFA $\mathcal{A} = \langle Q, Q_0, \Sigma, \rightarrow, F \rangle$ can be translated to a Moore machine $\mathsf{DFA2Moore}(\mathcal{A}) = \langle Q, Q_0, \Sigma, \Gamma, \rightarrow, \omega \rangle$ by associating to each state $q \in Q$ an output that indicates whether or not q is final [32]. That is, we define $\Gamma = \{0, 1\}$ and

$$\omega(q) = \begin{cases} 1 \text{ if } q \in F, \\ 0 \text{ otherwise.} \end{cases}$$

Suppose $\mathcal{A}$ and $\mathcal{B}$ are DFAs with $\epsilon \in L(\mathcal{A}) \Leftrightarrow \epsilon \in L(\mathcal{B})$. Then $\mathcal{A} \approx \mathcal{B}$ iff $\mathsf{DFA2Moore}(\mathcal{A}) \approx \mathsf{DFA2Moore}(\mathcal{B})$. Thus, the translation $\mathsf{DFA2Moore}$ preserves the behavior of DFAs. The counterexample of Fig. 3 shows that if we lift translation

---

[1] Following Hopcroft and Ullman [32], we ignore the initial output in order to obtain equivalence of Moore and Mealy machines.

Moore to NFAs, the behavior is no longer preserved: $\mathcal{A} \approx \mathcal{B}$ since $L(\mathcal{A}) = L(\mathcal{B}) = \{a, aa\}$, but $\mathsf{DFA2Moore}(\mathcal{A}) \not\approx \mathsf{DFA2Moore}(\mathcal{B})$ since $\lambda_{\mathsf{DFA2Moore}(\mathcal{A})}(a) = \{0, 1\}$ and $\lambda_{\mathsf{DFA2Moore}(\mathcal{B})}(a) = \{1\}$.

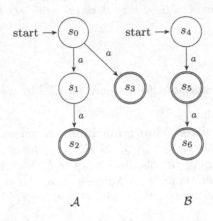

$\mathcal{A}$ $\mathcal{B}$

Fig. 3. Two NFAs $\mathcal{A}$ and $\mathcal{B}$ with $\mathcal{A} \approx \mathcal{B}$ and $\mathsf{DFA2Moore}(\mathcal{A}) \not\approx \mathsf{DFA2Moore}(\mathcal{B})$.

2.4   Mealy Machines

A (generalized) Mealy machine [48] is an LTS in which the labels of transitions are input/output pairs.

Definition 7 (Generalized Mealy machine). *A generalized Mealy machine (genMealy) is a tuple* $\mathcal{M} = \langle Q, Q_0, \Sigma, \Gamma, \rightarrow \rangle$, *where* $\langle Q, Q_0, \Sigma \times \Gamma, \rightarrow \rangle$ *is an LTS. We refer to elements of* Σ *as* input symbols *and to elements of* Γ *as* output symbols. *We write* $q \xrightarrow{i/o} q'$ *if* $(q, (i, o), q') \in \rightarrow$. *We say that* $\mathcal{M}$ *is* input enabled *if, for each state* q *and input symbol* i, *there exists an output symbol* o *and a state* q' *such that* $q \xrightarrow{i/o} q'$. *We call* $\mathcal{M}$ deterministic *if* Q_0 *is a singleton set, and for each state* q *and each input* i, *there is exactly one output* o *and one state* q' *such that* $q \xrightarrow{i/o} q'$. *We call* $\mathcal{M}$ finite *if its underlying LTS is finite, and a* Mealy machine *if it is input enabled, deterministic, and finite.*

In the DOT encoding of a Mealy machine, inputs and outputs are separated by a "/" in the definition of transitions:

```
digraph g {
  ...
  q1 -> q2 [label="i/o"]
  ...
}
```

Definition 8 (Equivalence of genMealys). *Suppose* $w = i_1 i_2 \cdots i_m \in \Sigma^*$ *and* $u = o_1 o_2 \cdots o_m \in \Gamma^*$. *Then* u *is an* output *of genMealy* $\mathcal{M}$ *in response to* w *if there exists* $q \in Q_0$ *and* $q' \in Q$ *such that* $q \stackrel{z}{\Rightarrow} q'$, *where* $z = (i_1, o_1)(i_2, o_2) \cdots (i_m, o_m)$. *The* output function $\lambda_{\mathcal{M}}$ *of* $\mathcal{M}$ *assigns to each input word* $w \in \Sigma^*$ *the set of outputs of* $\mathcal{M}$ *in response to* w. *Generalized Mealy machines* $\mathcal{M}$ *and* $\mathcal{N}$ *are* equivalent, *notation* $\mathcal{M} \approx \mathcal{N}$, *if they have the same input symbols and* $\lambda_{\mathcal{M}} = \lambda_{\mathcal{N}}$.

Equivalence of deterministic genMealys can alternatively be characterized using bisimulations. Call genMealy's $\mathcal{M}$ and $\mathcal{N}$ *bisimilar*, written $\mathcal{M} \simeq \mathcal{N}$, if they have the same input symbols and their underlying LTSs are bisimilar. Then the following proposition holds:

Proposition 1. *Let* $\mathcal{M}$ *and* $\mathcal{N}$ *be deterministic genMealys. Then* $\mathcal{M} \approx \mathcal{N}$ *iff* $\mathcal{M} \simeq \mathcal{N}$.

Each generalized Moore machine $\mathcal{M} = \langle Q, Q_0, \Sigma, \Gamma, \rightarrow, \omega \rangle$ can be translated to a generalized Mealy machine $\mathsf{Moore2Mealy}(\mathcal{M}) = \langle Q, Q_0, \Sigma, \Gamma, \rightarrow' \rangle$ by moving the output symbol of each state to all of the incoming transitions of that state. Thus, for each transition $q \stackrel{i}{\rightarrow} q'$ of $\mathcal{M}$, $\mathsf{Moore2Mealy}(\mathcal{M})$ has a transition $q \xrightarrow{i/\omega(q')}{}' q'$. Then we have $\lambda_{\mathcal{M}} = \lambda_{\mathsf{Moore2Mealy}(\mathcal{M})}$ (see e.g., [32]). This implies that genMoores $\mathcal{M}$ and $\mathcal{N}$ are equivalent iff $\mathsf{Moore2Mealy}(\mathcal{M})$ and $\mathsf{Moore2Mealy}(\mathcal{N})$ are equivalent. The reader may check that if we take a Moore machine and apply translation $\mathsf{Moore2Mealy}$, the result is a Mealy machine.

Example 1. Figure 4 shows a Moore machine and its associated Mealy machine.

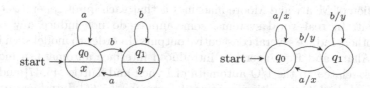

Fig. 4. A Moore machine (left) and its translation to a Mealy machine (right).

Conversely, a generalized Mealy machine $\mathcal{M} = \langle Q, Q_0, \Sigma, \Gamma, \rightarrow \rangle$ can be translated to a generalized Moore machine $\mathsf{Mealy2Moore}(\mathcal{M}) = \langle Q', Q_0', \Sigma, \Gamma, \rightarrow', \omega \rangle$ by taking the output of a state to be equal to the output of the preceding transition. For initial states we pick an arbitrary output $o_0 \in \Gamma$. Formally:

- $Q' = \Gamma \times Q$,
- $Q_0' = \{(o_0, q) \mid q \in Q_0\}$, where o_0 is an arbitrarily element of Γ,[2]

---

[2] If $\Gamma = \emptyset$ then also $\rightarrow = \emptyset$, which means that $\mathcal{M}$ is equivalent to $\mathcal{M}$ with Γ replaced by an arbitrary set. Thus, we may assume w.l.o.g. that $\Gamma \neq \emptyset$.

- $\rightarrow'$ is the smallest set such that $o \in \Gamma$ and $q \xrightarrow{i/o'} q'$ implies $(o, q) \xrightarrow{i} '(o', q')$,
- $\omega((o, q)) = o$.

Then we have $\lambda_{\mathcal{M}} = \lambda_{\mathsf{Mealy2Moore}(\mathcal{M})}$ (see e.g., [32]). This implies that generalized Mealy machines $\mathcal{M}$ and $\mathcal{N}$ are equivalent iff $\mathsf{Mealy2Moore}(\mathcal{M})$ and $\mathsf{Mealy2Moore}(\mathcal{N})$ are equivalent. The reader may check that if we take a Mealy machine and apply translation $\mathsf{Mealy2Moore}$, the result is a Moore machine.

Example 2. Figure 5 shows a Mealy machine and its associated Moore machine.

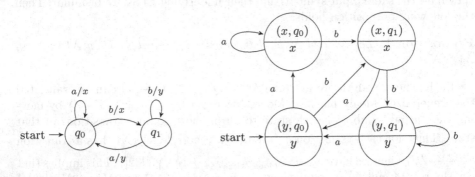

Fig. 5. A Mealy machine (left) and its translation to a Moore machine (right).

2.5   Interface Automata

A restriction of Mealy and Moore machines is that each input generates exactly one output. In real-world systems, some inputs do not induce any output, whereas others induce several consecutive outputs. In order to model such behaviors, De Alfaro and Henzinger [21] introduced interface automata, a modeling framework related to the I/O automata of Lynch and Tuttle [46,47] and Jonsson [39], and the I/O transition systems of Tretmans [65,66]. Interface automata extend LTSs by declaring actions to be either inputs or outputs.

Definition 9. (Interface automata). *An* interface automaton (IA) *is a tuple* $\mathcal{T} = \langle Q, Q_0, \Sigma, \Gamma, \rightarrow \rangle$, *where* $\langle Q, Q_0, \Sigma \cup \Gamma, \rightarrow \rangle$ *is an LTS and* $\Sigma \cap \Gamma = \emptyset$. *We refer to elements of* Σ *as* input symbols *and to elements of* Γ *as* output *symbols. An interface automaton is* deterministic *(resp. finite) if its underlying LTS is deterministic (resp. finite). We refer to a finite deterministic interface automaton as a* DFIA.

Figure 6 shows the graphical representation of a simple DFIA (left) and its representation in DOT (right). The DFIA has inputs $\Sigma = \{a, b\}$ and outputs $\Gamma = \{x, y\}$. There are three states: an initial idle state q_0, a state q_1 in which output x is produced, and a state q_2 in which output y is produced. From each state,

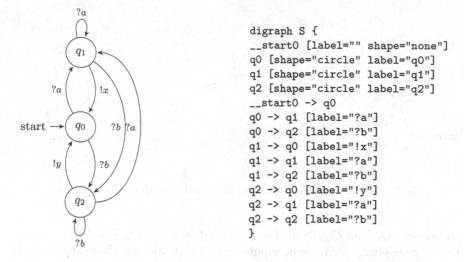

```
digraph S {
__start0 [label="" shape="none"]
q0 [shape="circle" label="q0"]
q1 [shape="circle" label="q1"]
q2 [shape="circle" label="q2"]
__start0 -> q0
q0 -> q1 [label="?a"]
q0 -> q2 [label="?b"]
q1 -> q0 [label="!x"]
q1 -> q1 [label="?a"]
q1 -> q2 [label="?b"]
q2 -> q0 [label="!y"]
q2 -> q1 [label="?a"]
q2 -> q2 [label="?b"]
}
```

Fig. 6. A DFIA and its representation in DOT.

input a brings the DFIA to state q_1 and input b brings it to state q_2. In DOT format, input symbols of an IA are of the form ?a, whereas output symbols are of the form !x.

Various preorders have been advocated for IAs: Lynch and Tuttle propose inclusion of (fair) traces [47], De Alfaro and Henzinger alternating refinement [21], Tretmans [65] the IOCO conformance relation, and Volpato and Tretmans [69] UIOCO conformance. For deterministic automata all these relations coincide, and their kernel coincides with bisimulation equivalence. Therefore, since our benchmark repository focuses on deterministic IAs, we only consider bisimulation as behavioral equivalence on IAs.

Definition 10. (Equivalence of IAs). *Interface automata T and U are bisimilar, written $T \simeq U$, if they have the same input symbols and their underlying LTSs are bisimilar.*

Suppose $M = \langle Q, Q_0, \Sigma, \Gamma, \rightarrow \rangle$ is a generalized Mealy machine with disjoint input and output symbols. Then M can be translated to an interface automaton Mealy2IA(M) by adding states $\Gamma \times Q$, and splitting each transition $q \xrightarrow{i/o} q'$ of M into a pair of consecutive transitions $q \xrightarrow{i} (o, q')$ and $(o, q') \xrightarrow{o} q'$. Note that if M is a Mealy machine, Mealy2IA(M) is a DFIA. Figure 7 shows a Mealy machine and its associated DFIA.

Proposition 2. *Let M and N be deterministic genMealys. Then $M \approx N$ iff Mealy2IA(M) $\simeq$ Mealy2IA(N).*

For any generalized Mealy machine M, Mealy2IA(M) has a specific form in which inputs and outputs alternate: (a) the set of states can be partitioned

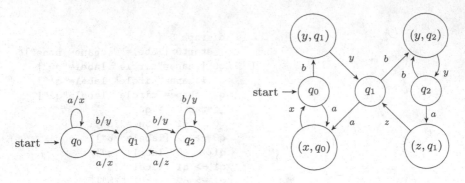

Fig. 7. A Mealy machine (left) and its translation to a DFIA (right).

into two sets Q_{in} and Q_{out}, with $Q_0 \subseteq Q_{in}$, (b) states in Q_{in} enable no outputs, whereas states in Q_{out} enable no inputs, (c) all transitions go from states in Q_{in} to states in Q_{out}, or from states in Q_{out} to states in Q_{in} (i.e., the underlying graph is bipartite). We call an IA $\mathcal{T}$ that satisfies properties (a)–(c) *Mealy-like*. Any Mealy-like IA $\mathcal{T}$ can be translated to a generalized Mealy machine IA2Mealy($\mathcal{T}$) by taking Q_{in} as set of states, Q_{in} as the set of initial states, and merging each pair of consecutive transitions $q \xrightarrow{i} q' \xrightarrow{o} q''$ of $\mathcal{T}$ into a single transition $q \xrightarrow{i/o} q''$. Note that if $\mathcal{T}$ is a Mealy-like DFIA with each input enabled in each state from Q_{in} and a single output enabled in each state of Q_{out}, IA2Mealy($\mathcal{T}$) is a Mealy machine. Also note that IA2Mealy ∘ Mealy2IA is the identity function, whereas Mealy2IA ∘ IA2Mealy is not. However, we do have the following proposition:

Proposition 3. *Let $\mathcal{T}$ and $\mathcal{U}$ be Mealy-like deterministic IAs. Then $\mathcal{T} \simeq \mathcal{U}$ iff IA2Mealy($\mathcal{T}$) $\approx$ IA2Mealy($\mathcal{U}$).*

2.6   Register Automata

Register automata extend FSMs with data values that may be communicated, stored and tested. Below we recall the definition of register automata from [15], slightly adapted to the setting of interface automata. Register automata are parameterized on a vocabulary that determines how data can be tested, which in our setting is called a structure.[3] A *(relational) structure* is a pair $\langle \mathcal{D}, \mathcal{R} \rangle$ where $\mathcal{D}$ is an unbounded domain of *data values*, and $\mathcal{R}$ is a collection of *relations* on $\mathcal{D}$. Relations in $\mathcal{R}$ can have arbitrary arity. Known constants can be represented by unary relations. Examples of simple structures include:

- $\langle \mathbb{N}, \{=\} \rangle$, the natural numbers with equality; instead of the set of natural numbers, we could consider any other unbounded domain, e.g., the set of strings (representing passwords or usernames).
- $\langle \mathbb{R}, \{<\} \rangle$, the real numbers with inequality: this structure also allows one to express equality between elements.

---

[3] In [15] this is called a *theory*, but we prefer the standard terminology from logic [18].

Operations, such as increments, addition and subtraction, can in this framework be represented by relations. For instance, addition can be represented by a ternary relation $p_1 = p_2 + p_3$. In the following definitions, we assume that some structure $\langle \mathcal{D}, \mathcal{R} \rangle$ has been fixed.

We assume a set of *registers* $\mathcal{V} = \{x_1, x_2, \ldots\}$, and we assume that actions carry a single formal data parameter $p \notin \mathcal{V}$.[4] A *guard* is a conjunction of negated and unnegated relations (from $\mathcal{R}$) over the formal parameter p and the registers. We use Φ to denote the set of guards. An *assignment* is a partial function in $\mathcal{V} \rightharpoonup (\mathcal{V} \cup \{p\})$. We use Υ to denote the set of assignments. A *valuation* is a partial function in $(\mathcal{V} \cup \{p\}) \rightharpoonup \mathcal{D}$.

Definition 11 (Register automaton). *A register automaton (RA) is a tuple* $\mathcal{A} = \langle L, L_0, \mathcal{X}, \Sigma, \Gamma, \rightarrow \rangle$, *where* $\langle L, L_0, (\Sigma \cup \Gamma) \times \Phi \times \Upsilon, \rightarrow \rangle$ *is an FSM, we refer to elements of L as* locations, $\Sigma \cap \Gamma = \emptyset$, $\mathcal{X}$ *maps each location $l \in L$ to a finite set $\mathcal{X}(l)$ of registers, and for each transition $\langle l, a, g, \pi, l' \rangle \in \rightarrow$, g is a guard over $\mathcal{X}(l) \cup \{p\}$ and π is a mapping from $\mathcal{X}(l')$ to $\mathcal{X}(l) \cup \{p\}$. Function π specifies, for each register x from target state l', the parameter or register from source state l whose value will be assigned to x.*

Within the Tomte and RALib tools, XML formats have been defined for representing register automata syntactically. We will not discuss these formats here but refer to the tool websites http://tomte.cs.ru.nl/ and https://bitbucket.org/learnlib/ralib/ for more details.

Example 3. Figure 8 shows a register automaton over structure $\langle \mathbb{N}, \{=\} \rangle$ that models a FIFO-set with capacity two, similar to an example in [34]. A FIFO-set is a queue in which only different values can be stored. The automaton has an input Push that tries to insert a value in the queue, and an input Pop that tries to retrieve a value from the queue. Push triggers an output NOK if the input value is already in the queue or if the queue is full. Pop triggers an output NOK if the queue is empty, and otherwise an output Out with as parameter the oldest value from the queue. We write $x := y$ for the function that maps x to y, and acts as the identity for the other variable in the target state. We omit guards true, trivial assignments, and parameters that not occur in the guard and are not touched by the assignment. Thus we write, for instance, Pop instead of Pop(p). Function $\mathcal{X}$ assigns variable set $\emptyset$ to locations l_0 and l_3, variable set $\{v\}$ to locations l_1, l_4 and l_6, and variable set $\{v, w\}$ to locations l_2, l_5 and l_7.

Example 4. By just a minor change of the register automaton of Example 3, we may define a priority queue with capacity 2. This register automaton over the structure $\langle \mathbb{R}, \{<\} \rangle$ is identical to the register automaton of Fig. 8, except that the two outgoing Push-transitions of l_1 have been replaced by transitions

$$l_1 \xrightarrow{\text{Push}, p < v, v := p; w := v} l_2 \qquad\qquad l_1 \xrightarrow{\text{Push}, p \geq v, w := p} l_2$$

---

[4] Actually, our repository supports actions with zero or more data parameters, but this assumption simplifies the presentation.

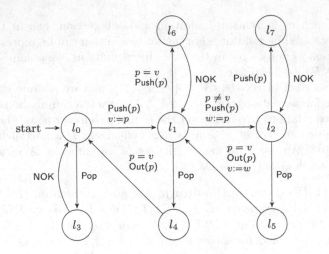

Fig. 8. FIFO-set with capacity 2.

This ensures that in location l_2, the value in register v is less than or equal to the value in register w. As a result, output Out will return the smallest value in the queue.

Semantically, a register automaton is just a finite representation of an infinite interface automaton.

Definition 12 (Semantics register automata). *Let* $\mathcal{A} = \langle L, L_0, \mathcal{X}, \Sigma, \Gamma, \rightarrow \rangle$ *be a register automaton. The interface automaton* $RA2IA(\mathcal{A})$ *is the tuple* $\langle Q, Q_0, \Sigma \times \mathcal{D}, \Gamma \times \mathcal{D}, \rightarrow' \rangle$, *where*

1. Q *is the set of pairs* $\langle l, \nu \rangle$ *with* $l \in L$ *and* $\nu : \mathcal{X}(l) \rightarrow \mathcal{D}$.
2. Q_0 *is the set of pairs* $\langle l, \nu \rangle \in Q$ *with* $l \in L_0$.
3. $\langle l, \nu \rangle \xrightarrow{a(d)}' \langle l', \nu' \rangle$ *iff* $\mathcal{A}$ *has a transition* $l \xrightarrow{a,g,\pi} l'$ *such that* g *is satisfied in* l *and by parameter* d *(i.e.,* $\iota \models g$, *where* $\iota = \nu \cup \{(p, d)\}$*), and* $\nu' = \iota \circ \pi$.

Two register automata $\mathcal{A}$ *and* $\mathcal{A}'$ *are* bisimilar *iff their associated interface automata are bisimilar, i.e.,* $RA2IA(\mathcal{A}) \simeq RA2IA(\mathcal{A}')$. *Similarly, we call register automaton* $\mathcal{A}$ deterministic *iff its associated interface automaton* $RA2IA(\mathcal{A})$ *is deterministic.*

The interface automaton associated to the register automaton of Fig. 8 is deterministic and, for instance, has the following sequence of transitions:

$$\langle l_0, \emptyset \rangle \xrightarrow{\text{Push}(4)} \langle l_1, \{(v, 4)\} \rangle \xrightarrow{\text{Push}(5)} \langle l_2, \{(v, 4), (w, 5)\} \rangle \xrightarrow{\text{Pop}} \langle l_5, \{(v, 4), (w, 5)\} \rangle$$

$$\xrightarrow{\text{Out}(4)} \langle l_1, \{(v, 5)\} \rangle \xrightarrow{\text{Push}(5)} \langle l_6, \{(v, 5)\} \rangle \xrightarrow{\text{NOK}} \langle l_1, \{(v, 5)\} \rangle.$$

Register automata over structure $\langle \mathbb{N}, \{=\} \rangle$ can be translated to a finite interface automaton by restricting the data domain $\mathcal{D}$ to a finite set. Let $RA2IA_n(\mathcal{A})$ be the finite interface automaton obtained by replacing $\mathcal{D}$ by $\{0, \ldots, n-1\}$ in the definition of RA2IA($\mathcal{A}$), for any $n \in \mathbb{N}$. Heidarian [22, Chapter 8] showed that two register automata $\mathcal{A}$ and $\mathcal{A}'$ are bisimilar iff RA2IA$_n(\mathcal{A}) \simeq$ RA2IA$_n(\mathcal{A}')$, for large enough n. Via the translations RA2IA$_n$, each deterministic register automaton benchmark can be used to generate an infinite number of DFIA benchmarks, in which the numbers of states and transitions grow unboundedly. In several of our register automata benchmarks, inputs and outputs alternate. As a result, the DFIAs obtained via translations RA2IA$_n$ are Mealy-like, and can subsequently be converted to Mealy machines via translation IA2Mealy from Sect. 2.5.

Thus far, all the register automaton benchmarks in our repository are deterministic register automata over structure $\langle \mathbb{N}, \{=\} \rangle$, but we are planning to include register automata benchmarks over different structures, such as the models described in [25].

3   Benchmarks Derived from Applications

Our repository automata.cs.ru.nl contains four types of benchmarks: (1) randomly generated automata, (2) small toy examples, (3) benchmarks derived from realistic applications, and (4) benchmarks obtained via the translations from Sect. 2. In this section, we focus on the benchmarks derived from realistic applications, and briefly pay attention to some of the smaller "toy" models that have been included in the repository. All the benchmarks in this section are either Mealy machines or register automata. In the next Sect. 4, we discuss algorithms for generating random automata, and a collection of randomly generated DFAs and Moore machines that we have included in the repository.

3.1   Mealy Machines

The large majority of the Mealy machine benchmarks in our repository has fewer than 100 states, fewer than 20 inputs, and fewer than 50 outputs. For a detailed listing of the numbers of states, inputs and outputs of all the benchmarks we refer to automata.cs.ru.nl/Table.

Toy Examples. We included several toy Mealy machines, such as a simple model of a coffee machine used as running example in [63], a trivial three state model used to explain L* in [68], and some instructive examples from [44,52].

Circuits. The logic synthesis workshops (LGSynth89, LGSynth91 and LGSynth93) provided 59 behavioral models for testing, logic synthesis and optimization of circuits, see [12,24]. These models can be viewed as Mealy machines in several ways. We provide four interpretations of each model as a Mealy machine. If two or more interpretations give equivalent results, we have included only one of them in the repository. The circuit benchmarks have been used recently for Mealy machine testing by Hierons & Türker [31].

TCP. The Transmission Control Protocol (TCP) is a widely used transport layer protocol that provides reliable and ordered delivery of a byte stream from one computer application to another. The authors of [26] combined model learning and model checking in a case study involving Linux, Windows and FreeBSD implementations of TCP. Model learning was used to infer models of different software components and model checking was applied to fully explore what may happen when these components (e.g., a Linux client and a Windows server) interact. The analysis revealed several instances in which TCP implementations do not conform to their RFC specifications.

TLS Protocol. TLS, short for Transport Layer Security, is a widely used protocol that aims to provide privacy and data integrity between two or more communicating computer applications, for example in HTTPS. The authors of [58] analyzed both server- and client-side implementations of TLS with a test harness that supports several key exchange algorithms and the option of client certificate authentication. Using LearnLib, they succeeded to learn Mealy machine models of a number of TLS implementations. They showed that this approach can catch an interesting class of flaws that is apparently common in security protocol implementations: in three of the TLS implementations that were analyzed (GnuTLS, the Java Secure Socket Extension, and OpenSSL), new security flaws were found. This indicates that model learning is a useful technique to systematically analyze security protocol implementations. As the analysis of different TLS implementations resulted in different and unique state machines for each one, the technique can also be used for fingerprinting TLS implementations.

SSH Protocol. SSH, short for Secure Shell, is a cryptographic network protocol that is widely used to interact securely with remote machines. The authors of [27] applied model learning to three SSH implementations (OpenSSH, Bitvise and DropBear) to infer Mealy machine models, and then used model checking to verify that these models satisfy basic security properties and conform to the RFCs. The analysis showed that all tested SSH server models satisfy the stated security properties. However, several violations of the standard were uncovered.

ABN AMRO e.dentifier2. The e.dentifier2 is a hand-held smart card reader with a small display, a numeric keyboard, and OK and Cancel buttons. Customers of the Dutch ABN AMRO bank use it for Internet banking in combination with a bank card and a PIN code. The authors of [16] showed that model learning can be successfully used to reverse engineer the behavior of the e.dentifier2, by using a Lego robot to operate the devices. The Mealy machines that were automatically inferred by the robot revealed a security vulnerability in the e.dentifier2, that was previously discovered by manual analysis, and confirmed the absence of this flaw in an updated version of this device.

EMV Protocol. Bank cards (debit cards) are smart cards used for payment systems. Most smart cards issued by banks or credit cards companies adhere to the EMV (Europay-MasterCard-Visa) protocol standard, which is defined on top of ISO/IEC 7816. In [6], LearnLib and some simple abstraction techniques were used to learn Mealy machine models of EMV applications on bank cards issued by several Dutch banks (ABN AMRO, ING, Rabobank), one German bank (Volksbank), and one MasterCard credit cards issued by Dutch and Swedish banks (SEB, ABN AMRO, ING) and of one UK Visa Debit card (Barclays). These models provide a useful insight into decisions (or indeed mistakes) made in the design and implementation, and would be useful as part of security evaluations—not just for bank cards but for smart card applications in general—as they can show unexpected additional functionality that is easily missed in conformance tests.

MQTT Protocol. The Message Queuing Telemetry Transport (MQTT) protocol is a lightweight publish/subscribe protocol that is well-suited for resource-constrained environments such as the Internet of Things (IoT). The authors of [64] used model learning to obtain Mealy machine models of five freely available implementations of MQTT brokers (included in Apache ActiveMQ 5.13.3, emqttd 1.0.2, HBMQTT 0.7.1, Mosquitto 1.4.9 and VerneMQ 0.12.5p4). Examining these models, the authors found several violations of the MQTT specification. In fact, all but one of the considered implementations showed faulty behavior.

ESM Printer Controller. The Engine Status Manager (ESM) is a software component that is used in printers and copiers of Oce. Using a combination of LearnLib and a novel conformance testing algorithm, the authors of [62] succeeded to learn a Mealy machine model of this component fully automatically. Altogether, around 60 million queries were needed to learn a model of the ESM with 77 inputs and 3.410 states. They also constructed a model by flattening a Rational Rose Real-Time description from which the ESM software was generated, and established equivalence with the learned model.

An Interventional X-ray System. Model learning and equivalence checking are used by [60] to improve a new implementation of a legacy control component. Model learning is applied to both the old and the new implementation of the Power Control Service (PCS) of an interventional X-ray system. The resulting models are compared using an equivalence check of a model checker. The authors report about their experiences with this approach at Philips. By gradually increasing the set of input stimuli, they obtained implementations of the PCS for which the learned behavior is equivalent.

From Rhapsody to Dezyne. In his PhD thesis, Schuts [59, Chapter 8] describes a case study, carried out at Philips, in which models created with a legacy tool (Rhapsody) are transformed to models that can be used by another tool (Dezyne). The transformation is established by means of a DSL for the legacy models. Model learning was applied to increase confidence in the correctness of the generated code. Two versions of state-machine code, generated by Rhapsody and Dezyne, were stimulated by all possible inputs and the resulting outputs were examined by LearnLib. The two models constructed by LearnLib were compared by the equivalence checker of the mCRL2 tool set. With this approach two errors were found in the Dezyne models that were not detected by the existing regression test set.

3.2   Register Automata

Toy examples. We included several toy models in the repository: the sender and receiver of the well-known Alternating Bit Protocol, a simple login protocol, an automaton that test whether a list of numbers is a palindrome or a repdigit, and a river crossing puzzle.

SIP. The Session Initiation Protocol (SIP) is a signalling protocol used for initiating, maintaining, and terminating real-time sessions that include voice, video and messaging applications. In [4], an abstract Mealy machine model was inferred that describes the SIP Server entity when setting up connections with a SIP Client. The model was obtained by connecting LearnLib with the protocol simulator ns-2, and generated a model of the SIP component as implemented in ns-2. Using a (manually constructed) mapper component, concrete SIP messages were converted into abstract input and output symbols. Even though no implementation errors were found, the work of [4] showed the feasibility of the approach for inferring models of implementations of realistic communication protocols. In [2], the Mealy machine model of [4] was converted into a register automaton model that is included in the repository.

Data Structures. As observed by Howar et al. [34], register automata with input and output events can be used to represent semantic interfaces of simple data structures such as stacks, queues, and FIFO-sets with fixed capacities. Since they are parametrized by their capacity, these data structures provide excellent benchmarks for model learning tools, see e.g., [3].

Biometric Passport. The biometric passport is an electronic passport provided with a computer chip and antenna to authenticate the identity of travelers. Examples of used protocols are Basic Access Control (BAC), Active Authentication (AA) and Extended Access Control (EAC) [13]. Official standards are documented in the International Civil Aviation Organisation's (ICAO) Doc 9303 [36]. In [7], LearnLib was used to automatically generate a model of fragments of these protocols as implemented on an authentic biometric passport. The data on the chip could be accessed via a smart card reader with JMRTD serving as API. A simple mapper component serves as an intermediary between the SUT and LearnLib.

Bounded Retransmission Protocol. The Bounded Retransmission Protocol (BRP) is a well-known benchmark case study from the verification literature [20,30]. The BRP is a variation of the classical alternating bit protocol that was developed by Philips to support infrared communication between a remote control and a television. In [5], a reference implementation of the protocol is described, as well as six faulty mutants of this implementation. The authors use a combination of model learning, model-based testing and verification to detect behavioral differences between the mutants and the reference implementation.

4 Random Generation of Benchmarks

As argued throughout this paper, high-quality benchmarks are an integral part of the evaluation of (automata learning) algorithms. In this context, synthetic, i.e., randomly generated, automata play an important role due to their relevancy to average case analyses and their usually high Kolmogorov complexity [17,45]. Contrary to what one might think, however, randomly generating automata is not a trivial task: automata carry a semantics (in form of the accepted language) and, hence, properties such as connectedness and minimality with respect to the accepted language are of great importance. In fact, estimating the number of pairwise non-equivalent automata of a certain size is already a challenging problem [17,29].

In this section, we survey three popular algorithms for generating random DFAs, taken both from the literature and from automata learning competitions:

1. the algorithm used in the Abbadingo DFA learning competition [42], which we present in Sect. 4.1;
2. the algorithm used in the Stamina DFA learning competition [70,71] (based on the forest-fire algorithm [45] for generating random graphs), which we present in Sect. 4.2; and
3. Champarnaud and Paranthoën's method [17], which we present in Sect. 4.3.

Methods for generating other types of state machines (such as NFAs, Mealy and Moore machines, etc.) exists as well, but are often ad-hoc approaches and far less studied.

In Sect. 4.4, we briefly describe a series of random DFAs and random Moore machines, which we have generated on the occasion of Bernhard Steffen's 60th birthday. In this section, we also sketch a simple method for randomly generating Moore machines.

For the following description, recall from Sect. 2.2 that a DFA is a tuple $\mathcal{A} = \langle Q, Q_0, \Sigma, \rightarrow, F \rangle$ where $\langle Q, Q_0, \Sigma, \rightarrow \rangle$ is a complete and deterministic FSM and $F \subseteq Q$ is a set of final states. Moreover, let $n = |Q|$ denote the desired size, i.e., the number of states, of the DFA to be generated.

4.1 Abbadingo Competition Random DFA Algorithm

The Abbadingo random DFA algorithm [42] is a simplistic algorithm, which constructs a DFA with n states ($n > 0$) in four steps:

1. It creates n states, say $Q = \{q_1, \ldots, q_n\}$.
2. For each pair of state $p \in Q$ and input symbol $a \in \Sigma$, it chooses a destination state $q \in Q$ uniformly at random and adds the transition $p \xrightarrow{a} q$.

3. It chooses a state $q_0 \in Q$ uniformly at random and marks it as the initial state, i.e., $Q_0 = \{q_0\}$.
4. For each state $q \in Q$, it determines whether q is a final state by flipping a fair coin, i.e., it adds q to F with probability $1/2$.

Clearly, a major drawback of this simple approach is the neglect of any structural property of the generated DFA—except for the fact that the resulting automaton is deterministic. In particular, the algorithm neither guarantees that the resulting DFA is *accessible*, i.e., that all its states are reachable from the initial state, nor that it is minimal. For this reason, the Abbadingo competition used the following procedure: in order to obtain a DFA of size roughly n, a DFA of size $1.2n$ is generated and all states that are not reachable from the initial state are removed. Although this additional step ensures that the resulting DFA is accessible, it might still not produce minimal DFAs.

4.2   Stamina Competition Random DFA Algorithm

The algorithm used in the Stamina competition [70] has been designed to produce random DFAs that are representative of software models. Its basis is the forest-fire algorithm by Leskovec, Kleinberg, and Faloutsos [45], which produces directed graphs that resemble complex networks arising in a variety of domains. The forest-fire algorithm is an iterative algorithm (each iteration adds one new vertex as well as edges from and to this vertex) that takes three parameters as input: a number $N > 0$ of vertices, a *forward burning probability* $p \in [0,1]$, and a *backward burning ratio* $r \in [0,1]$.

The forest-fire algorithm proceeds in N rounds. In the first round, it initializes the graph with a single vertex. In each subsequent round, it performs the following four steps (Step 1 inserts a new vertex, while Steps 2, 3, and 4 insert new edges):

1. The algorithm creates a new vertex v. Moreover, it initializes an auxiliary set $U = \emptyset$, which is used to mark vertices that have been visited by the algorithm in the current round.
2. It picks a vertex $w \neq v$, called *ambassador vertex*, uniformly at random and adds the edge $v \to w$. Moreover, it adds w to U, marking w as visited.
3. It draws a random number $x \in \mathbb{N}$ from a geometric distribution with mean $p/(1-p)$ and a second random number $y \in \mathbb{N}$ from a geometric distribution with mean $rp/(1-rp)$. Then, it selects
   - x incoming edges of w, say $v_1 \to w, \ldots, v_x \to w$, and
   - y outgoing edges of w, say $w \to v'_1, \ldots, w \to v'_y$,
   uniformly at random such that $\{v_1, \ldots, v_x, v'_1, \ldots, v'_y\} \cap U = \emptyset$, i.e., none of the vertices $v_1, \ldots, v_x$ and $v'_1, \ldots, v'_y$ have been visited in this iteration; if not enough edges are available, the algorithm selects as many as possible.
4. It adds the edges $v \to v_1, \ldots, v \to v_x, v \to v'_1, \ldots, v \to v'_x$ and then applies Step 2 recursively with each of the vertices $v_1, \ldots, v_x, v'_1, \ldots, v'_y$ as ambassador vertex. Note that this procedure stops eventually as vertices cannot be visited more than once.

To generate a DFA (rather than a directed graph), the algorithm used in the Stamina competition takes three additional parameters as input: a set Σ of input symbols, a *self-loop probability* $l \in [0,1]$, and a *parallel-edge probability* $e \in [0,1]$. (Note that the forest-fire algorithm can neither create self-loops nor parallel edges.) Based on these additional parameters, the forest-fire algorithm is adapted as follows:

- The initial state is chosen uniformly at random, and each vertex has the probability $1/2$ of being a final state.
- In order to make sure that each state is reachable, edges added in Step 2 are added in the reverse direction, i.e., $w \to v$.
- Whenever the forest-fire algorithm adds an edge in Step 4, with probability l this edge gets instead redirected to form a self-loop.
- Whenever the forest-fire algorithm inserts an edge, the edge is turned into a transition that is labeled with an input symbol $a \in \Sigma$. The input symbol a is drawn uniformly at random from the set Σ such that the automaton remains deterministic, i.e., symbols that are already used in an outgoing transition from the state in question are not considered. If all symbols from Σ already occur on an outgoing transition, then no transition is added.
- Finally, every time a transition is inserted, a second, parallel transition is added with probability e. The second transition is labeled using the labeling rule described above.

Although this algorithm produces accessible DFAs, it does not guarantee that these DFAs are minimal. To account for this, the DFAs used in the Stamina competition have been generated slightly larger than desired and have subsequently been minimized. The parameters used to generate the competition DFAs were $\Sigma = \{1, \ldots, a\}$ for $a \in \{2, 5, 10, 20, 50\}$, $n = 50$ (the actual value N has been chosen slightly larger than 50 due to the subsequent minimization process), $f = 0.31$, $r = 0.385$, $l = 0.2$, and $e = 0.2$.

4.3 Champarnaud and Paranthoën's Method

Champarnaud and Paranthoën's method [17] is a generalization of an algorithm proposed by Nicaud [53], which randomly generates accessible DFAs over two input symbols. An interesting property of Nicaud's algorithm is that it generates minimal DFAs with a probability of about $4/5$. Champarnaud and Paranthoën's method shares this property when generating DFAs over two input symbols, while an experimental evaluation with over a million DFAs has shown that nearly all generated DFAs were minimal if the number of input symbols was chosen greater than two [17]. Hence, should a minimal DFA be required, a viable approach is to simply repeat Champarnaud and Paranthoën's method until the resulting DFA is minimal.

Champarnaud and Paranthoën's method is a fairly complex algorithm, which is based on two ideas:

- The FSM $\langle Q, Q_0, \Sigma, \rightarrow \rangle$ underlying any DFA can be represented by a Σ-labeled tree of arity $m = |\Sigma|$ with $n = |Q|$ inner nodes, i.e., a tree of arity m with n inner nodes whose edges are labeled with symbols from Σ.
- Labeled trees can be encoded by a special type of tuples over the natural numbers, which Champarnaud and Paranthoën call *generalized tuples*.

Hence, one can generate a random DFA by first randomly generating a generalized tuple, then constructing the corresponding tree, and finally deriving a DFA from the tree. Although an in-depth description of this procedure is out of the scope of this paper, the remainder of this section sketches the main steps of the algorithm.

At the heart of Champarnaud and Paranthoën's method lies the observation that every Σ-labeled tree is determined (up to isomorphism) by one of its *prefix traversals*. More precisely, a complete m-ary tree with n inner nodes—and, therefore, $s = n(m - 1) + 1$ leaf nodes—can be encoded by the tuple

$$(k_1, \ldots, k_{s-1}) \in \{1, \ldots, n\}^{s-1},$$

where the i-th entry k_i corresponds to the number of inner nodes visited during a prefix traversal of the tree prior to the visit of the i-th leaf (note that there is no need to store this information for the last leaf as this number is n). The set of all generalized tuples of length $l + 1$ can be constructed recursively from the set of generalized tuples of length l, and Champarnaud and Paranthoën give an algorithm to draw such tuples randomly. Once a generalized tuple of length $s - 1$ has been generated, the corresponding tree with n inner nodes can be constructed effectively.

The tree generated in the previous step represents a deterministic transition structure that serves as template for a number of (non-isomorphic) n-state DFAs. Constructing a DFA from such a template involves two steps: first, edges to leaf nodes need to be redirected to inner nodes (so as to be able to produce a DFA that is complete and accepting an infinite language); second, final states have to be selected. However, edges cannot be redirected arbitrarily as this might result in the same DFA being generated from two different generalized tuples. In order to prevent this from happening, Champarnaud and Paranthoën's method redirects edges only to inner nodes that have been visited earlier during the prefix traversal. The final DFA is then obtained by setting the initial state to be the root node and choosing uniformly at random one possibility of inserting back edges and selecting final states. Note that this implies in particular that the probability of a state being final is $1/2$.

4.4 Random DFAs and Moore Machines Dedicated to Bernhard Steffen's 60th Birthday

On the occasion of Bernhard Steffen's 60th birthday, we have included four sets of randomly generated DFAs and Moore machines in our repository:

1. 60×60 DFAs with $1\,000$ states each over the alphabet $\Sigma = \{0, 1, \ldots, 19\}$;

2. 60×60 DFAs with $2\,000$ states each over the alphabet $\Sigma = \{0, 1, \ldots, 9\}$;
3. 60×60 Moore machines with $1\,000$ states each over the input alphabet $\Sigma = \{0, 1, \ldots, 19\}$ and output alphabet $\Gamma = \Sigma$; and
4. 60×60 Moore machines with $2\,000$ states each over the input alphabet $\Sigma = \{0, 1, \ldots, 9\}$ and output alphabet $\Gamma = \Sigma$.

The number of states and the number of elements in the input/output alphabets of these automata were chosen to be challenging, though still manageable for state-of-the-art algorithms.

All DFAs were generated using libalf's [11] off-the-shelf implementation of Champarnaud and Paranthoën's method. To generate Moore machines, we used the following two-step process: first, we randomly generated a DFA using Champarnaud and Paranthoën's method, which serves as the LTS underlying our Moore machines; second, we assigned to each state an output symbol that was drawn uniformly at random from the output alphabet. Note that the second step is in fact a generalization of the way Champarnaud and Paranthoën select final states, which is essentially by flipping a fair coin for each state. As with all methods described in this section, however, our DFAs and Moore machines are accessible but might not be minimal.

5   Conclusions

Many of the benchmark models in our repository have clear practical relevance, e.g., they helped to reveal standard violations in network protocols and eliminate bugs in industrial software. Nevertheless, the benchmarks are surprisingly small: several models have less than ten states and our largest models only have a few thousand states. A possible explanation is that model learning and testing typically focus on a single component (e.g., a TCP server) and there is already some implicit abstraction in the selection of the interface. This should be contrasted with benchmarks used for explicit model checking, which typically focus on the behavior of networks of components, and have millions of states.

Even though our benchmarks are small, they still pose enormous challenges for state-of-the-art automata learning and conformance testing tools. In practice, conformance testing algorithms often have difficulties to find subtle bugs in implementations for models with more than say a hundred states and a dozen inputs. For instance, with 3.410 states and 77 inputs the ESM printer controller model is at the limit of what current algorithms can handle [62]. In particular, state-of-the-art techniques are unable to learn models of the printer controller for slightly different configurations of the same software. Also, input/output interactions and resets of software and hardware often take a significant amount of time. For instance, in the case study of the interventional X-ray system [60], it took up to 9 hours to learn models with up to 9 states and 12 inputs. This was because running a single test sequence took on average about 10 seconds and a reset of the implementation took about 5 seconds. This means that any reduction of the number of queries needed for learning and testing reliable models has immediate practical relevance. Clearly, a comprehensive evaluation of existing learning and testing algorithms on our benchmarks is an important direction for future research.

Finally, we would like to encourage all our colleagues to contribute new benchmarks to the repository! Our automata wiki is built using the PmWiki software, which makes it easy to add new benchmarks.

Acknowledgements. This article was initiated at the Dagstuhl Seminar 16172 "Machine Learning for Dynamic Software Analysis: Potentials and Limits" organized by Amel Bennaceur, Reiner Hähnle, and Karl Meinke. We thank Fides Aarts, Petra van den Bos, Alexander Fedotov, Paul Fiterău-Broştean, Falk Howar, Joshua Moerman, Erik Poll, and Joeri de Ruiter for helping with the repository. Many thanks to Pierre van de Laar and the anonymous reviewers for their suggestions on an earlier version of this paper.

References

1. Aarts, F., Fiterau-Brostean, P., Kuppens, H., Vaandrager, F.: Learning register automata with fresh value generation. In: Leucker, M., Rueda, C., Valencia, F.D. (eds.) ICTAC 2015. LNCS, vol. 9399, pp. 165–183. Springer, Cham (2015). https://doi.org/10.1007/978-3-319-25150-9_11
2. Aarts, F., Heidarian, F., Kuppens, H., Olsen, P., Vaandrager, F.: Automata learning through counterexample guided abstraction refinement. In: Giannakopoulou, D., Méry, D. (eds.) FM 2012. LNCS, vol. 7436, pp. 10–27. Springer, Heidelberg (2012). https://doi.org/10.1007/978-3-642-32759-9_4
3. Aarts, F., Howar, F., Kuppens, H., Vaandrager, F.: Algorithms for inferring register automata. In: Margaria, T., Steffen, B. (eds.) ISoLA 2014. LNCS, vol. 8802, pp. 202–219. Springer, Heidelberg (2014). https://doi.org/10.1007/978-3-662-45234-9_15
4. Aarts, F., Jonsson, B., Uijen, J.: Generating models of infinite-state communication protocols using regular inference with abstraction. In: Petrenko, A., Simão, A., Maldonado, J.C. (eds.) ICTSS 2010. LNCS, vol. 6435, pp. 188–204. Springer, Heidelberg (2010). https://doi.org/10.1007/978-3-642-16573-3_14
5. Aarts, F., Kuppens, H., Tretmans, G.J., Vaandrager, F.W., Verwer, S.: Improving active Mealy machine learning for protocol conformance testing. Mach. Learn. **96**(1–2), 189–224 (2014)
6. Aarts, F., de Ruiter, J., Poll, E.: Formal models of bank cards for free. In: IEEE International Conference on Software Testing Verification and Validation Workshop, Los Alamitos, CA, USA, pp. 461–468. IEEE Computer Society (2013)
7. Aarts, F., Schmaltz, J., Vaandrager, F.: Inference and abstraction of the biometric passport. In: Margaria, T., Steffen, B. (eds.) ISoLA 2010. LNCS, vol. 6415, pp. 673–686. Springer, Heidelberg (2010). https://doi.org/10.1007/978-3-642-16558-0_54
8. Angluin, D.: Learning regular sets from queries and counterexamples. Inf. Comput. **75**(2), 87–106 (1987)
9. Berg, T., Grinchtein, O., Jonsson, B., Leucker, M., Raffelt, H., Steffen, B.: On the correspondence between conformance testing and regular inference. In: Cerioli, M. (ed.) FASE 2005. LNCS, vol. 3442, pp. 175–189. Springer, Heidelberg (2005). https://doi.org/10.1007/978-3-540-31984-9_14

10. Bollig, B., Habermehl, P., Kern, C., Leucker, M.: Angluin-style learning of NFA. In: Boutilier, C. (ed.) Proceedings of IJCAI 2009, pp. 1004–1009 (2009)
11. Bollig, B., Katoen, J.-P., Kern, C., Leucker, M., Neider, D., Piegdon, D.R.: libalf: The automata learning framework. In: Touili, T., Cook, B., Jackson, P. (eds.) CAV 2010. LNCS, vol. 6174, pp. 360–364. Springer, Heidelberg (2010). https://doi.org/10.1007/978-3-642-14295-6_32
12. Brglez, F.: ACM/SIGDA benchmark dataset (1996). http://people.engr.ncsu.edu/brglez/CBL/benchmarks/Benchmarks-upto-1996.html. Accessed 14 Aug 2018
13. BSI: Advanced security mechanisms for machine readable travel documents - extended access control (EAC) - version 1.11. Technical report TR-03110, German Federal Office for Information Security (BSI), Bonn, Germany (2008)
14. Cassel, S., Howar, F., Jonsson, B., Merten, M., Steffen, B.: A succinct canonical register automaton model. J. Log. Algebr. Meth. Program. **84**(1), 54–66 (2015)
15. Cassel, S., Howar, F., Jonsson, B., Steffen, B.: Active learning for extended finite state machines. Formal Asp. Comput. **28**(2), 233–263 (2016)
16. Chalupar, G., Peherstorfer, S., Poll, E., de Ruiter, J.: Automated reverse engineering using Lego. In: Proceedings WOOT 2014, Los Alamitos, CA, USA. IEEE Computer Society, August 2014
17. Champarnaud, J.-M., Paranthoën, T.: Random generation of DFAs. Theor. Comput. Sci. **330**(2), 221–235 (2005)
18. van Dalen, D.: Logic and Structure. Springer, London (1983)
19. D'Antoni, L.: AutomatArk. https://github.com/lorisdanto/automatark. Accessed 14 Aug 2018
20. D'Argenio, P.R., Katoen, J.-P., Ruys, T.C., Tretmans, J.: The bounded retransmission protocol must be on time!. In: Brinksma, E. (ed.) TACAS 1997. LNCS, vol. 1217, pp. 416–431. Springer, Heidelberg (1997). https://doi.org/10.1007/BFb0035403
21. de Alfaro, L., Henzinger, T.A.: Interface automata. In: Proceedings ESEC/FSE-01, Software Engineering Notes, vol. 26, pp. 109–120. ACM Press, New York, September 2001
22. Heidarian Dehkordi, F.: Studies on verification of wireless sensor networks and abstraction learning for system inference. Ph.D. thesis, Radboud University Nijmegen, July 2012
23. Dorofeeva, R., El-Fakih, K., Maag, S., Cavalli, A.R., Yevtushenko, N.: FSM-based conformance testing methods: a survey annotated with experimental evaluation. Inf. Softw. Technol. **52**(12), 1286–1297 (2010)
24. Fiser, P.: Collection of digital design benchmarks. https://ddd.fit.cvut.cz/prj/Benchmarks/. Accessed 14 Aug 2018
25. Fiterău-Broştean, P., Howar, F.: Learning-based testing the sliding window behavior of TCP implementations. In: Petrucci, L., Seceleanu, C., Cavalcanti, A. (eds.) FMICS/AVoCS -2017. LNCS, vol. 10471, pp. 185–200. Springer, Cham (2017). https://doi.org/10.1007/978-3-319-67113-0_12
26. Fiterău-Broştean, P., Janssen, R., Vaandrager, F.: Combining model learning and model checking to analyze TCP implementations. In: Chaudhuri, S., Farzan, A. (eds.) CAV 2016. LNCS, vol. 9780, pp. 454–471. Springer, Cham (2016). https://doi.org/10.1007/978-3-319-41540-6_25
27. Fiterău-Broştean, P., Lenaerts, T., Poll, E., de Ruiter, J., Vaandrager, F., Verleg, P.: Model learning and model checking of SSH implementations. In: Proceedings SPIN Symposium, SPIN 2017, pp. 142–151. ACM, New York (2017)
28. Gansner, E.R., North, S.C.: An open graph visualization system and its applications to software engineering. Softw. Pract. Exper. **30**(11), 1203–1233 (2000)

29. Harary, F., Palmer, E.M.: Enumeration of finite automata. Inf. Control. **10**(5), 499–508 (1967)
30. Helmink, L., Sellink, M.P.A., Vaandrager, F.W.: Proof-checking a data link protocol. In: Barendregt, H., Nipkow, T. (eds.) TYPES 1993. LNCS, vol. 806, pp. 127–165. Springer, Heidelberg (1994). https://doi.org/10.1007/3-540-58085-9_75
31. Hierons, R.M., Türker, U.C.: Incomplete distinguishing sequences for finite state machines. Comput. J. **58**(11), 3089–3113 (2015)
32. Hopcroft, J.E., Ullman, J.D.: Introduction to Automata Theory, Languages and Computation. Addison-Wesley, Boston (1979)
33. Howar, F.: Active learning of interface programs. Ph.D. thesis, University of Dortmund, June 2012
34. Howar, F., Isberner, M., Steffen, B., Bauer, O., Jonsson, B.: Inferring semantic interfaces of data structures. In: Margaria, T., Steffen, B. (eds.) ISoLA 2012. LNCS, vol. 7609, pp. 554–571. Springer, Heidelberg (2012). https://doi.org/10.1007/978-3-642-34026-0_41
35. Howar, F., Steffen, B.: Active automata learning in practice. In: Bennaceur, A., Hähnle, R., Meinke, K. (eds.) Machine Learning for Dynamic Software Analysis: Potentials and Limits. LNCS, vol. 11026, pp. 123–148. Springer, Cham (2018). https://doi.org/10.1007/978-3-319-96562-8_5
36. ICAO: Doc 9303 - machine readable travel documents - part 1–2. Technical report, International Civil Aviation Organization, Sixth edition (2006)
37. Isberner, M., Howar, F., Steffen, B.: The TTT algorithm: a redundancy-free approach to active automata learning. In: Bonakdarpour, B., Smolka, S.A. (eds.) RV 2014. LNCS, vol. 8734, pp. 307–322. Springer, Cham (2014). https://doi.org/10.1007/978-3-319-11164-3_26
38. Jasper, M., et al.: The RERS 2017 challenge and workshop (invited paper). In: Proceedings SPIN Symposium, pp. 11–20. ACM (2017)
39. Jonsson, B.: Modular verification of asynchronous networks. In: PODC 1987 [54], pp. 152–166
40. Kearns, M.J., Vazirani, U.V.: An Introduction to Computational Learning Theory. MIT Press, Cambridge (1994)
41. Keller, R.M.: Formal verification of parallel programs. Commun. ACM **19**(7), 371–384 (1976)
42. Lang, K.J., Pearlmutter, B.A., Price, R.A.: Results of the Abbadingo one DFA learning competition and a new evidence-driven state merging algorithm. In: Honavar, V., Slutzki, G. (eds.) ICGI 1998. LNCS, vol. 1433, pp. 1–12. Springer, Heidelberg (1998). https://doi.org/10.1007/BFb0054059
43. Lee, D., Yannakakis, M.: Testing finite-state machines: state identification and verification. IEEE Trans. Comput. **43**(3), 306–320 (1994)
44. Lee, D., Yannakakis, M.: Principles and methods of testing finite state machines — a survey. Proc. IEEE **84**(8), 1090–1123 (1996)
45. Leskovec, J., Kleinberg, J.M., Faloutsos, C.: Graph evolution: densification and shrinking diameters. TKDD **1**(1), 1–41 (2007). https://doi.org/10.1145/1217299.1217301
46. Lynch, N.A.: Distributed Algorithms. Morgan Kaufmann Publishers Inc., San Fransisco (1996)
47. Lynch, N.A., Tuttle, M.R.: Hierarchical correctness proofs for distributed algorithms. In: PODC 1987 [54], pp. 137–151. A full version is available as MIT Technical Report MIT/LCS/TR-387
48. Mealy, G.H.: A method for synthesizing sequential circuits. Bell Syst. Tech. J. **34**(5), 1045–1079 (1955)

49. Merten, M., Steffen, B., Howar, F., Margaria, T.: Next generation LearnLib. In: Abdulla, P.A., Leino, K.R.M. (eds.) TACAS 2011. LNCS, vol. 6605, pp. 220–223. Springer, Heidelberg (2011). https://doi.org/10.1007/978-3-642-19835-9_18

50. Moerman, J., Sammartino, M., Silva, A., Klin, B., Szynwelski, M.: Learning nominal automata. In: Proceedings POPL 2017, pp. 613–625. ACM (2017)

51. Moore, E.F.: Gedanken-experiments on sequential machines. In: Automata Studies. Annals of Mathematics Studies, vol. 34, pp. 129–153. Princeton University Press (1956)

52. Naik, K.: Efficient computation of unique input/output sequences in finite-state machines. IEEE/ACM Trans. Netw. **5**(4), 585–599 (1997)

53. Nicaud, C.: Étude du comportement en moyenne des automates finis et des langages rationnels. Ph.D. thesis, Université Paris 7 (2000)

54. Proceedings of the 6th Annual ACM Symposium on Principles of Distributed Computing, August 1987

55. Raffelt, H., Steffen, B., Berg, T.: LearnLib: a library for automata learning and experimentation. In: Proceedings FMICS 2005, pp. 62–71. ACM Press, New York (2005)

56. Raffelt, H., Steffen, B., Berg, T., Margaria, T.: LearnLib: a framework for extrapolating behavioral models. STTT **11**(5), 393–407 (2009)

57. Rivest, R.L., Schapire, R.E.: Inference of finite automata using homing sequences. Inf. Comput. **103**(2), 299–347 (1993)

58. de Ruiter, J., Poll, E.: Protocol state fuzzing of TLS implementations. In: Proceedings USENIX Security 15, pp. 193–206. USENIX Association, August 2015

59. Schuts, M.: Industrial experiences in applying domain specific languages for system evolution. Ph.D. thesis, Radboud University Nijmegen, September 2017

60. Schuts, M., Hooman, J., Vaandrager, F.: Refactoring of legacy software using model learning and equivalence checking: an industrial experience report. In: Ábrahám, E., Huisman, M. (eds.) IFM 2016. LNCS, vol. 9681, pp. 311–325. Springer, Cham (2016). https://doi.org/10.1007/978-3-319-33693-0_20

61. Shahbaz, M., Groz, R.: Inferring Mealy machines. In: Cavalcanti, A., Dams, D.R. (eds.) FM 2009. LNCS, vol. 5850, pp. 207–222. Springer, Heidelberg (2009). https://doi.org/10.1007/978-3-642-05089-3_14

62. Smeenk, W., Moerman, J., Vaandrager, F., Jansen, D.N.: Applying automata learning to embedded control software. In: Butler, M., Conchon, S., Zaïdi, F. (eds.) ICFEM 2015. LNCS, vol. 9407, pp. 67–83. Springer, Cham (2015). https://doi.org/10.1007/978-3-319-25423-4_5

63. Steffen, B., Howar, F., Merten, M.: Introduction to active automata learning from a practical perspective. In: Bernardo, M., Issarny, V. (eds.) SFM 2011. LNCS, vol. 6659, pp. 256–296. Springer, Heidelberg (2011). https://doi.org/10.1007/978-3-642-21455-4_8

64. Tappler, M., Aichernig, B.K., Bloem, R.: Model-based testing IoT communication via active automata learning. In: Proceedings ICST 2017, pp. 276–287. IEEE Computer Society (2017)

65. Tretmans, J.: Test generation with inputs, outputs, and repetitive quiescence. Softw. Concepts Tools **17**, 103–120 (1996)

66. Tretmans, J.: Model based testing with labelled transition systems. In: Hierons, R.M., Bowen, J.P., Harman, M. (eds.) Formal Methods and Testing. LNCS, vol. 4949, pp. 1–38. Springer, Heidelberg (2008). https://doi.org/10.1007/978-3-540-78917-8_1

67. Utting, M., Pretschner, A., Legeard, B.: A taxonomy of model-based testing approaches. Softw. Test. Verif. Reliab. **22**(5), 297–312 (2012)

68. Vaandrager, F.W.: Model learning. Commun. ACM **60**(2), 86–95 (2017)
69. Volpato, M., Tretmans, J.: Towards quality of model-based testing in the ioco framework. In: Proceedings JAMAICA 2013, pp. 41–46. ACM, New York (2013)
70. Walkinshaw, N., Bogdanov, K., Damas, C., Lambeau, B., Dupont, P.: A framework for the competitive evaluation of model inference techniques. In: Proceedings MIIT 2010, pp. 1–9. ACM (2010)
71. Walkinshaw, N., Lambeau, B., Damas, C., Bogdanov, K., Dupont, P.: STAMINA: a competition to encourage the development and assessment of software model inference techniques. Empir. Softw. Eng. **18**(4), 791–824 (2013)

Synchronous or Alternating?
LTL Black-Box Checking of Mealy Machines by Combining the LearnLib and LTSmin

Jaco van de Pol[(✉)] and Jeroen Meijer

Formal Methods and Tools, University of Twente, Enschede, The Netherlands
{j.c.vandepol,j.j.g.meijer}@utwente.nl

Abstract. Mealy machines transduce inputs to outputs, based on finite memory. They are often used to model reactive systems. The requirements on their behaviour can be specified by formulas in Linear-time Temporal Logic. We will study two interpretations of LTL for Mealy machines: the synchronous semantics, where inputs and outputs occur simultaneously; and the alternating semantics, where inputs and outputs strictly alternate. We define and study Mealy-robust LTL properties, which are insensitive to which of these interpretations is chosen.

The motivating application is in the context of black-box checking: Given the interface to some reactive system, one would like to test that a particular LTL property holds. To this end, we combine active automata learning with model checking into sound black-box checking. Here the LTL properties are already checked on intermediate hypotheses, in order to speed up the learner. Finally, we perform an experiment on the Mealy machines provided by the RERS challenge (Rigorous Examination of Reactive Systems). We investigate how many LTL properties from the RERS challenges in 2016 and 2017 are actually robust.

1 Introduction

The problem of black-box checking is to verify (or test) that a reactive system satisfies a number of properties. Here the system is provided as black-box, accessible through its input/output interface only. Assuming that the reactive system has a finite number of states, it can be modeled by a Mealy machine [10]. The properties on the system's behaviour can be specified in Linear-time Temporal Logic (LTL [13]). A solution to the black-box checking problem can be obtained by combining active automata learning [1,6,17] and model checking [2].

A realisation of the black-box checking approach is provided by integrating LearnLib[1] [7,15] with LTSmin[2] [9]. The yearly RERS challenge[3] (Rigorous Evaluation of Reactive Systems [5,8]) provides an excellent testbed

---

[1] The LearnLib: https://learnlib.de.

[2] LTSmin: ltsmin.utwente.nl and https://github.com/utwente-fmt/ltsmin.

[3] RERS challenge: http://rers-challenge.org.

© Springer Nature Switzerland AG 2019
T. Margaria et al. (Eds.): Steffen Festschrift, LNCS 11200, pp. 417–430, 2019.
https://doi.org/10.1007/978-3-030-22348-9_24

for checking properties on reactive systems. The combination of LearnLib + LTSmin has been applied on the problems in the RERS Challenge 2017, as reported in [11].

1.1 Motivating Context: Sound Black-Box Checking

The sound approach to black-box checking is illustrated in Fig. 1. A naive approach to black-box checking would be to first learn a Mealy machine that models the System Under Learning (SUL) and to subsequently check the properties on that automaton. Learning proceeds according to the Angluin-style active automata-learning paradigm [1,6], adapted to Mealy machines in [17]. Here the learner proceeds by performing I/O sequences (membership queries $\in$) on the system. When it believes that it has complete information, it generates a hypothesis automaton (H). This hypothesis is validated on the system using a

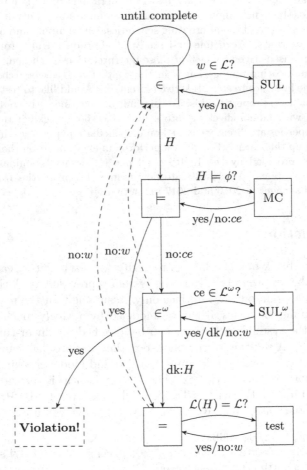

Fig. 1. Sound black-box checking procedure, adapted and simplified from [11]

model-based tester (=); this is an expensive step, involving many queries. This procedure is iterated as long as testing reveals a counterexample (w). The final hypothesis can be used to check the LTL properties, for instance using the Nested Depth-First Search algorithm [3].

A smarter approach to black-box checking [12] applies the model checker (MC) already on the intermediate hypotheses ($\vDash$). If the model checker provides a counter-example (ce) to the property, this is tested on the reactive system. If the counter-example can be simulated on the system, we found a violation of the property. If not, a prefix of the counter example (w) is provided to the learner, saving one expensive test-procedure.

A complication is that the counter-example provided by the model checker is an infinite path, presented by a lasso xy^{ω}. In principle, one can only check finite unrollings xy^{n} on the system. However, this yields an unsound method, unless one knows an upperbound on the number of states of the reactive system.

A sound approach to black-box checking was proposed in [11]. We adapt the check for infinite words ($\in^{\omega}$), by assuming that one can additionally save states and check their equivalence. So we test the word and save intermediate states $x(s_0)y(s_1)y(s_2), \ldots, y(s_n)$. As soon as we find that $s_k = s_j$ for some $0 \leq k < j \leq n$, we definitely know that xy^{ω} is a valid counterexample, and report a violation. If the path cannot be continued, we have a found a finite prefix w for the learner. Otherwise, we don't know if xy^{ω} holds, and we proceed to the tester.

The adapted procedure is sound, in the sense that it only reports true violations. However, it may miss some violations, so it is incomplete: First, the final hypothesis may still not reflect all system behaviour. Second, the model checker may have detected a lasso that could not be confirmed within the bound. Note that the state recording facility could in principle be used for a full model check.

1.2 Problem Statement and Contribution

This paper, dedicated to Bernhard Steffen on the occasion of his 60th birthday, is devoted to taking a closer look at the precise LTL semantics for Mealy machines. In particular, we study the difference between the *synchronous* semantics and the *alternating* semantics. The RERS organisers clearly stipulate that LTL properties are interpreted in the *alternating* semantics, i.e. interpreted over alternating traces of the form $i, o, i, o, \ldots$ However, in the first RERS attempt in 2012 [14], LTSmin used the *synchronous* semantics, interpreted over synchronous traces of the form $i/o, i/o, \ldots$

Surprisingly, this discrepancy leads to only very few wrong answers. When applying sound black-box learning (Fig. 1) to the first 4 problems of the RERS 2017 challenge, with 100 LTL formulas each, we detect the following number of LTL violations for the alternating, resp. synchronous semantics. So there is only a 0.5% deviation! We will show a deviating LTL property from RERS 2017 in Example 4.

We will try to explain this, by studying the class of *Mealy-robust LTL properties*, which are insensitive to choosing the synchronous or alternating LTL seman-

Semantics	Problem 1	Problem 2	Problem 3	Problem 4
Alternating	52	46	54	69
Synchronous	50	46	54	69

tics. In Sect. 2, we formally define (partial) Mealy machines, the synchronous and alternating semantics of LTL properties, and the set of Mealy-robust LTL properties. Section 3 studies Robust LTL in more detail; we restrict ourselves to properties in LTL\X. To this end, we need to introduce a number of finer distinctions (α-, α^1-, σ and σ^1-robustness). A Prolog program summarises *and* automates the derivation rules for robustness. Its correctness depends on the lemmas proved in Appendix A. Section 4 performs a small experiment on the problems of the RERS challenge, checking how many of them we can detect to be robust. Finally, we conclude with some problems left for future research.

2   Preliminaries: LTL Interpretations for Mealy Machines

A (partial) Mealy machine $M = (S, s_0, I, O, \delta)$ consists of a finite set of states S, initial state $s_0 \in S$, nonempty finite disjoint sets of input symbols (I) and output symbols (O), and a partial transition function $\delta : S \times I \hookrightarrow O \times S$. An example is provided in Fig. 2. We will distinguish its *synchronous traces* and *alternating traces*. In a synchronous trace, inputs and outputs happen simultaneously, for example $a/x, a/y, a/x, a/y, b/z, b/z, \ldots$. In an alternating trace, inputs and outputs happen in strict alternation, as in $a, x, a, y, a, x, a, y, \ldots$.

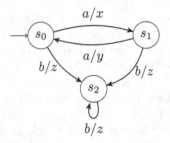

Fig. 2. Mealy machine M with $I = \{a, b\}$ and $O = \{x, y, z\}$.

An (infinite) sequence over A is a function $\mathbb{N} \to A$. Given a sequence π, we write π_i for the i-th element (so $\pi = \pi_0, \pi_1, \ldots$) By π^i we denote the suffix $\pi^i, \pi^{i+1}, \pi^{i+2}, \ldots$.

We formally define the set of synchronous traces $Tr_s = \mathbb{N} \to I \times O$ over I and O, and the set of alternating traces $Tr_a = \pi : \mathbb{N} \to I \cup O$, with $\pi_i \in I \iff \pi_{i+1} \in O$. The latter can be split in Tr_{ai} (starting with an input: $\pi_0 \in I$) and Tr_{ao} (starting with an output: $\pi_0 \in O$). With $Tr_s(M)$ (resp. $Tr_a(M)$) we denote the synchronous (resp. alternating) traces that start in s_0 and follow transitions in M. Note that $Tr_a(M) \subseteq Tr_{ai}$. For $\pi \in Tr_{ai}$, we write $\sigma(\pi)$ for the corresponding synchronous trace. For $\pi \in Tr_s$, $\alpha(\pi)$ denotes the corresponding alternating trace. Note that $\sigma = \alpha^{-1}$ forms a bijection between Tr_s and Tr_{ai}. However, traces in Tr_{ao} still arise as suffixes.

Example 1. Let M be the Mealy machine in Fig. 2. Define the synchronous trace $\pi := a/x, a/y, a/x, a/y, \ldots$ and the alternating trace $\rho := a, x, a, y, b, z, b, z, \ldots$. Indeed, $\pi \in Tr_s(M)$ and $\rho \in Tr_a(M)$. In particular, $\rho \in Tr_{ai}$ and $\rho^1 \in Tr_{ao}$. Finally, $\alpha(\pi) = a, x, a, y, a, x, a, y, \ldots$, while $\sigma(\rho) = a/x, a/y, b/z, b/z, \ldots$ However, $\sigma(\rho^1)$ is not defined.

The distinction between synchronous and alternating traces may seem a small technical detail, but it does have a crucial impact on the corresponding LTL semantics. Let us first define action-based LTL formulas with atomic properties in $I \cup O$, using the following grammar (U is *until*; X is *next*):

$$\Phi ::= I \mid O \mid \neg \Phi \mid \Phi \wedge \Phi \mid \Phi \, \mathsf{U} \, \Phi \mid \mathsf{X} \Phi$$

We permit the usual abbreviations $\phi \vee \psi := \neg(\neg\phi \wedge \neg\psi)$, $\mathsf{F}\phi := \mathsf{true} \, \mathsf{U} \, \phi$ (future), $\mathsf{G}\phi := \neg\mathsf{F}\neg\phi$ (globally), $\phi \mathsf{R} \psi := \neg(\neg\phi \mathsf{U} \neg\psi)$ (release), and $\phi \mathsf{WU} \psi := (\phi \, \mathsf{U} \, \psi) \vee (\mathsf{G}\phi)$ (weak until). We also introduce conveniently defined atomic properties: $\mathsf{false} := i_0 \wedge \neg i_0$ (with $i_0 \in I$ arbitrary), $\mathsf{true} := \neg\mathsf{false}$, $\mathsf{input} := \bigvee_{i \in I} i$, $\mathsf{output} := \bigvee_{o \in O} o$, which hold for none, all, all input, and all output actions, respectively.

Next, we define the LTL semantics over both synchronous and alternating traces, i.e. $\vDash \subseteq (Tr_s \cup Tr_a) \times \Phi$, by induction over ϕ:

$$\pi \vDash i \iff \pi_0 \in \{i/o, i\}, \text{ for some } o \in O$$
$$\pi \vDash o \iff \pi_0 \in \{i/o, o\}, \text{ for some } i \in I$$
$$\pi \vDash \neg\phi \iff \pi \nvDash \phi$$
$$\pi \vDash \phi \wedge \psi \iff \pi \vDash \phi \text{ and } \pi \vDash \psi$$
$$\pi \vDash \phi \, \mathsf{U} \, \psi \iff \exists j : (\forall k < j : \pi^k \vDash \phi) \text{ and } \pi^j \vDash \psi$$
$$\pi \vDash \mathsf{X}\phi \iff \pi^1 \vDash \phi$$

We are now ready to define the synchronous and alternating semantics of LTL. Note that the following definition discards finite executions of the Mealy machine, even when they lead to a deadlock. The motivation for handling *partial* Mealy machines, but ignoring finite traces, is simply to abide to the rules of the RERS challenge.

Definition 2 (LTL semantics). *For a Mealy machine M and LTL formula ϕ, we define:*

- $M \vDash_s \phi$ *if and only if for all synchronous traces* $\pi \in Tr_s(M)$, $\pi \vDash \phi$
- $M \vDash_a \phi$ *if and only if for all alternating traces* $\pi \in Tr_a(M)$, $\pi \vDash \phi$

The *alternating* semantics is the official LTL semantics of the RERS challenge. Indeed, it supports the intuition that the current state and the input determine, so should precede, the next state and the output. However, when mapping this to a standard LTS for model checking, one typically introduces an "intermediate state" between an input and its subsequent output, which seems unnatural and superfluous. This would lead to $|S| \cdot |I|$ extra states, which makes model checking less efficient. The *synchronous* semantics avoids introducing intermediate states, so it would lead to a more efficient model checking procedure. This is in particular useful when applying brute-force white-box model checking to the RERS problems, for which LTSmin has traversed state spaces of over 5.10^9 states and 5.10^{10} transitions [14], but it is also convenient in the black-box checking scenario.

So the main question is: when is using the synchronous semantics justified? We will call LTL properties that are insensitive to choosing the synchronous or alternating semantics *Mealy-robust*.

Definition 3 (Mealy-Robust LTL properties). *We call LTL formula ϕ Mealy-robust if for all Mealy machines M, it holds that $M \vDash_s \phi \iff M \vDash_a \phi$.*

Example 4. Property 2 of Problem 1 of the RERS challenge 2017 is:

   (false R (! ((oY & ! iC) & (true U iC)) | (! oU U (iB | iC))))

In standard notation: $G(\neg o_Y \vee i_C \vee (G \neg i_C) \vee (\neg o_U \cup (i_B \vee i_C)))$. This happens to be one of the examples from the Introduction (Sect. 1) where the alternating and synchronous semantics differ, so it is not robust.

Example 6 will introduce some simpler robust and non-robust formulas.

3   Mealy-Robust LTL Properties

We will now investigate the following question: *Which LTL formulas ϕ are Mealy-robust?* We start by defining a number of fine-grained robustness notions on paths. Subsequently, we will prove preservation of robustness by LTL operators. This will yield a procedure to identify a class of robust LTL properties.

3.1   Robustness Notions

Note that to prove robustness of ϕ, we can focus on the robustness for individual paths. We need preservation in two directions, leading to the notions of α- and σ-robustness. However, for the alternating semantics we also need to consider the situation between an input and output action. Hence the notions of α^1- and σ^1-robustness, which consider traces that start with an output action.

Definition 5 (Robustness w.r.t. paths).

- ϕ *is α-robust if* $\forall \pi \in Tr_s : \pi \vDash \phi \implies \alpha(\pi) \vDash \phi$
- ϕ *is σ-robust if* $\forall \pi \in Tr_{ai} : \pi \vDash \phi \implies \sigma(\pi) \vDash \phi$
- ϕ *is α^1-robust if* $\forall \pi \in Tr_s : \pi \vDash \phi \implies \alpha(\pi)^1 \vDash \phi$
- ϕ *is σ^1-robust if* $\forall \pi \in Tr_{ai} : \pi^1 \vDash \phi \implies \sigma(\pi) \vDash \phi$
- ϕ *is input-universal (ι) if* $\forall \pi \in Tr_{ai} : \pi \vDash \phi$

The last notion states that a property holds universally on traces starting with input (for instance: $\neg o_1$ is input-universal). This will sometimes be needed to "fill the gap" between two outputs.

Example 6. Recall the traces $\pi \in Tr_s(M)$ and $\alpha(\pi) \in Tr_{ai}(M)$ of Example 1: $\pi = a/x, a/y, a/x, a/y, \ldots$ and $\alpha(\pi) = a, x, a, y, a, x, a, y, \ldots$. Let $\phi := G(x \cup y)$. Clearly, $\pi \vDash \phi$, but $\alpha(\pi) \nvDash \phi$, since in the first alternating action "a", neither x nor y holds. So ϕ is not α-robust.

On the other hand, let $\psi = G(\neg z \cup y)$. Then both $\pi \vDash \psi$ and $\alpha(\pi) \vDash \psi$. Indeed, it will turn out that ψ is robust.

3.2 Robustness Preservation by LTL\ X Operators

We will now first check how robustness is preserved by the Boolean connectives conjunction and disjunction, and establish a duality for negation. Subsequently, we will discuss robustness of the atomic properties (cf. Fig. 3). Finally, we will investigate the robustness properties of the until-operator. Robustness of the neXt-operator is left for future research.

	α	σ	α^1	σ^1	ι	M
i	✓	✓	✗	✓	✗	✓
$\neg i$	✓	✓	✓	✗	✗	✓
o	✗	✓	✓	✓	✗	✗
$\neg o$	✓	✗	✓	✓	✓	✗
false	✓	✓	✓	✓	✗	✓
true	✓	✓	✓	✓	✓	✓
input	✓	✓	✗	✓	✓	✓
output	✗	✓	✓	✓	✗	✗

Fig. 3. $\alpha/\alpha^1/\sigma/\sigma^1$-robustness, input-universality and Mealy-robustness for atomic formulas.

All lemmas in this section are summarised in Fig. 4, in the form of a Prolog program. This program can actually be run. For a formula P, if `robust(P)` succeeds, then robustness is guaranteed. However, if the query fails, the property may still be robust. We do not claim that our derivation rules are complete. The soundness of all rules is proved in detail in Appendix A.

First, we establish that α-robustness and σ-robustness are dual, and so are α^1- and σ^1-robustness. Next, all notions of robustness are preserved by $\wedge$ and $\vee$. Also, we claim compositionality of input-universality for $\wedge$ and $\vee$.

Lemma 7 (Boolean connectives).

1. ϕ is α-robust, if and only if $\neg\phi$ is σ-robust.
2. ϕ is α^1-robust, if and only if $\neg\phi$ is σ^1-robust.
3. If ϕ, ψ are $\alpha/\sigma/\alpha^1/\sigma^1$-robust, then so are $\phi \wedge \psi$ and $\phi \vee \psi$.
4. If ϕ and ψ is input-universal, then so is $\phi \wedge \psi$. If either of ϕ or ψ is input-universal, then also $\phi \vee \psi$ is.

Next, we check the robustness of atomic properties and their negations. These results are also tabulated in Fig. 3. We also show whether the atomic properties are input-universal, and Mealy-robust.

Lemma 8 (Robustness of atomic properties).

1. Let $i \in I$. Then i and $\neg i$ are α-robust and σ-robust.
2. Let $o \in O$. Then o and $\neg o$ are α^1-robust and σ^1-robust.
3. Let $i \in I$. Then i is σ^1-robust and $\neg i$ is α^1-robust.
4. Let $o \in O$. Then o is σ-robust and $\neg o$ is α-robust.
5. Let $o \in O$. Then $\neg o$ is input-universal.
6. Let $i \in I$. Then i and $\neg i$ are Mealy-robust.

Obviously, o is not α-robust, since it holds in $i/o, \pi$ but not in $i, o, \alpha(\pi)$. Similarly, i is not α^1-robust, since it holds in $i/o, \pi$, but not in $o, \alpha(\pi)$.

```
:- op(500,xfx,[until,and,or]).        % define infix LTL operators
:- op(450,fy,not).                    % define prefix LTL operators
:- op(400,fx,[in,out]).               % define atomic input, output


robust(X) :- alpha(X), sigma(X).      % main predicate

alpha(X) :- member(X,[false,true,input,in _]).
alpha(not X) :- sigma(X).
alpha(X and Y) :- alpha(X), alpha(Y).
alpha(X or Y) :- alpha(X), alpha(Y).
alpha(X until Y) :- alpha(X), alpha1(X), alpha(Y).
alpha(X until Y) :- alpha1(X), iota(X), alpha1(Y).

sigma(X) :- member(X,[false,true,input,output,in _,out _]).
sigma(not X) :- alpha(X).
sigma(X and Y) :- sigma(X), sigma(Y).
sigma(X or Y) :- sigma(X), sigma(Y).
sigma(X until Y) :- sigma(X), sigma(Y), sigma1(Y).
sigma(X until Y) :- sigma1(X), sigma(Y), sigma1(Y).

alpha1(X) :- member(X,[false, true, output, out _]).
alpha1(not X) :- sigma1(X).
alpha1(X and Y) :- alpha1(X), alpha1(Y).
alpha1(X or Y) :- alpha1(X), alpha1(Y).
alpha1(X until Y) :- alpha(X), alpha1(X), iota(X), alpha1(Y).

sigma1(X) :- member(X,[false,true,input,output,in _,out _]).
sigma1(not X) :- alpha1(X).
sigma1(X and Y) :- sigma1(X), sigma1(Y).
sigma1(X or Y) :- sigma1(X), sigma1(Y).
sigma1(X until Y) :- sigma1(X), sigma(Y), sigma1(Y).

iota(X) :- member(X,[true,not false,input,not out _]).
iota(not not X) :- iota(X).
iota(X and Y) :- iota(X), iota(Y).
iota(X or Y) :- iota(X) ; iota(Y).
iota(X until Y) :- iota(Y).
```

Fig. 4. Prolog program for deriving robustness of LTL properties. This program can be viewed as a summary of Lemmas 7–11.

π	i_0/o_0	i_1/o_1	i_2/o_2	i_3/o_3	$\cdots$
$\pi \vDash \phi \cup \psi$	ϕ	ϕ	ϕ	ψ	$\cdots$

$\alpha(\pi)$	i_0	o_0	i_1	o_1	i_2	o_2	i_3	o_3	$\cdots$
Case 1:	ϕ	ϕ	ϕ	ϕ	ϕ	ϕ	ψ	?	$\cdots$
Case 2:	ϕ	ϕ	ϕ	ϕ	ϕ	ϕ	ϕ	ψ	$\cdots$

Lemma 9

π	i_0	o_0	i_1	o_1	i_2	o_2	i_3	o_3	$\cdots$
Case 1:	ϕ	ϕ	ϕ	ϕ	ϕ	ϕ	ψ	?	$\cdots$
Case 2:	ϕ	ϕ	ϕ	ϕ	ϕ	ϕ	ϕ	ψ	$\cdots$

$\sigma(\pi)$	i_0/o_0	i_1/o_1	i_2/o_2	i_3/o_3	$\cdots$
$\sigma(\pi) \vDash \phi \cup \psi$	ϕ	ϕ	ϕ	ψ	$\cdots$

Lemma 10

Fig. 5. Illustration of subcases of Lemmas 9 and 10

We now get to the main lemmas, first providing the criteria for the α-robustness of until-formulas (cf. Fig. 5, left):

Lemma 9 (α-Robustness of Until-formulas).

1. Let ϕ be α-robust and α^1-robust; let ψ be α-robust. Then $\phi \cup \psi$ is α-robust.
2. Let ϕ be α^1-robust and input-universal; let ψ be α^1-robust. Then $\phi \cup \psi$ is α-robust and α^1-robust.

We will now apply Lemmas 8 and 9 to derive α-robustness of basic Until formulas (see also Fig. 6). From Lemma 8 we obtain that $\neg i$ and $\neg o$ are α- and α^1-robust. Also, we obtain that i, $\neg i$ and $\neg o$ are α-robust ($\forall i \in I, o \in O$). Hence, by Lemma 9, Case 1, the first six shapes below are α-robust. Furthermore, by Lemma 8, $\neg i$, o and $\neg o$ are α^1-robust. Note that $\neg o$ is input-universal, since $i\pi \vDash \neg o$ ($\forall o \in O, i \in I, \pi \in Tr_{ao}$). Hence by Lemma 9, Case 2, we obtain that last three shapes below are α-robust. In total this gives 7 α-robust shapes. Only the last three are guaranteed to be α^1-robust.

$$\neg i_1 \cup i_2 \mid \neg i_1 \cup \neg i_2 \mid \neg i_1 \cup \neg o_2 \mid \neg o_1 \cup i_2 \mid \neg o_1 \cup \neg i_2 \mid \neg o_1 \cup \neg o_2 \mid \neg o_1 \cup o_2$$

Recall that this means that whenever a synchronous trace π satisfies one of those formulas, the corresponding alternating trace $\alpha(\pi)$ satisfies it as well. The last three are even satisfied by $\alpha(\pi)^1$.

We continue with σ-robustness of Until-formulas (cf. Fig. 5, right).

Lemma 10. σ-Robustness of Until-formulas

1. Let ϕ be σ-robust. Let ψ be both σ-robust and σ^1-robust. Then $\phi \cup \psi$ is σ-robust.
2. Let ϕ be σ^1-robust. Let ψ be both σ-robust and σ^1-robust. Then $\phi \cup \psi$ is σ-robust and σ^1-robust.

Note that if ϕ is just σ-robust and ψ is both σ- and σ^1-robust, it is not necessary that $\phi \cup \psi$ is σ^1-robust. For instance, take $\pi = o_1, i_2, o_2, \ldots \in Tr_{ao}$. Then $\pi \vDash \neg i_1 \cup o_1$. However, we don't have $i_1/o_1, i_2/o_2, \ldots \vDash \neg i_1 \cup o_1$.

Since i, $\neg i$, o and $\neg o$ are all σ- or σ^1-robust, and since only i and o are σ^1-robust, we obtain the following 8 σ-robust basic Until formula shapes. Since $\neg i$ is not σ^1-robust, only the last six are also σ^1-robust.

$$\neg i_1 \cup i_2 \mid \neg i_1 \cup o_2 \mid i_1 \cup i_2 \mid i_1 \cup o_2 \mid o_1 \cup i_2 \mid o_1 \cup o_2 \mid \neg o_1 \cup i_2 \mid \neg o_1 \cup o_2$$

Lemma 11 (Input-universal Until). *If ψ is input-universal, then $\phi \cup \psi$ is input-universal.*

Theorem 12 (Correctness). *If the Prolog program in Fig. 4 derives the goal* robust(ϕ), *then ϕ is Mealy-robust.*

Figure 6 indicates the robustness of basic until formulas without nesting. Here ✓ means that robustness can be proved using previous theorems. ✗ only means that the property cannot be proved, but these might still hold for special cases. The last row deserves some attention: If $o_1 = o_2$, then $\neg o_1 \cup \neg o_2 = \neg o_1$, which is really not σ-robust. However, if $o_1 \neq o_2$, then $\neg o_1 \cup \neg o_2 = \text{true}$, since the first action cannot be both o_1 and o_2, so this is σ-robust. Also, $\forall \pi \in Tr_{ai}: \pi \vDash \phi \cup \neg o_2$. So $\phi \cup \neg o_2$ is trivially α-robust. Finally, note that $\text{input} \cup \text{output}$ is input-universal, but not recognized by our derivation rules.

All theorems in this section are proved in Appendix A. The theorems in this section can be turned into derivation rules, as presented in the Prolog program in Fig. 4. Given an LTL property P, it tries to derive robust(P) by applying the rules, proving α/σ-robustness where necessary. However, this program may fail on some robust formulas since we don't guarantee completeness. Also, it cannot handle formulas that contain the neXt-operator.

Until	α	α^1	σ	σ^1	ι	M
$i_1 \cup i_2$	✗	✗	✓	✓	✗	✗
$i_1 \cup \neg i_2$	✗	✗	✗	✗	✗	✗
$i_1 \cup o_2$	✗	✗	✓	✓	✗	✗
$i_1 \cup \neg o_2$	✗	✗	✗	✗	✓	✗
$\neg i_1 \cup i_2$	✓	✗	✓	✗	✗	✓
$\neg i_1 \cup \neg i_2$	✓	✗	✗	✗	✗	✗
$\neg i_1 \cup o_2$	✗	✗	✓	✗	✗	✗
$\neg i_1 \cup \neg o_2$	✓	✗	✗	✗	✓	✗
$o_1 \cup i_2$	✗	✗	✓	✓	✗	✗
$o_1 \cup \neg i_2$	✗	✗	✗	✗	✗	✗
$o_1 \cup o_2$	✗	✗	✓	✓	✗	✗
$o_1 \cup \neg o_2$	✗	✗	✗	✗	✓	✗
$\neg o_1 \cup i_2$	✓	✗	✓	✓	✗	✓
$\neg o_1 \cup \neg i_2$	✓	✓	✗	✗	✗	✗
$\neg o_1 \cup o_2$	✓	✓	✓	✓	✗	✓
$\neg o_1 \cup \neg o_2$	✓	✓	✗	✗	✓	✗

Fig. 6. $\alpha/\alpha^1/\sigma/\sigma^1$-robustness and input-universality for simple until-properties. The last column concludes whether the property is robust for all Mealy machines.

4   Experiment: Robustness of RERS Constraints

We applied our Prolog program to the constraints of the sequential LTL properties from the RERS 2016 and 2017 problems [4, 8] (after a syntactic transformation). Both years featured 9 problems, with 100 LTL properties each. We first filtered out the properties that contain the X-operator. For each property P, we ran the query robust(P) in Prolog. The results are displayed in Fig. 7. Here #\X shows the number of X-free formulas; #R shows the number of LTL formulas proven robust.

Apparently, 30% of the formulas was X-free. From these formulas 38% could be established robust. We conclude that this result only partly explains why applying an "alternating model checker" to the "synchronous RERS problems" resulted in a couple of errors only. Either, some formulas are robust

Problem	2016		2017	
	#\X	#R	#\X	#R
1	35	9	37	15
2	35	9	30	14
3	34	13	26	8
4	31	11	28	16
5	32	11	28	8
6	35	17	28	6
7	18	9	30	16
8	23	9	28	9
9	25	9	30	12
%	30%	37%	29%	39%

Fig. 7. Experiments on the LTL properties from RERS 2016 and RERS 2017.

but are not recognized by our

method, or they are not robust, but the Mealy machines corresponding to these problems don't distinguish the two interpretations.

5   Conclusion

We introduced *robustness* of LTL properties, which indicates that they are insensitive to their interpretation over *synchronous* or *alternating* traces. We proved a number of derivation rules for robust properties, implemented them in Prolog, and tested them on the RERS 2016 and 2017 challenges. We found that 38% of the X-free LTL properties could be proven robust.

Of course, the model checker should be correct in all cases. We have solved this in RERS 2017 [11] by transforming the Mealy machine M to an incomplete DFA M', introducing an extra state for each edge, in between an input and the subsequent output. On M' we can apply the standard model checking procedure. For the transformed M', we have: $M \vDash_a \phi \iff M' \vDash \phi$. An alternative procedure could be to transform formula ϕ instead, such that $M \vDash_a \phi \iff M \vDash_s \phi'$. We leave the study of the feasibility of this approach for future research.

Future work also includes a complete (precise) characterisation and decision procedure for robust properties. This would also require a study of the neXt-operator. Maybe previous work on stutter-invariant LTL properties can be useful [16]. Another line would be to extend to input-output systems without strict alternation, like I/O-automata. Finally, it would be interesting to consider the robustness of model checking under general action refinement.

Acknowledgement. The authors are supported by the 3TU.BSR project and the TTW project SUMBAT, grant 13859. We thank Mirja van de Pol for carefully reading a preliminary version of this document. We also profited from the numerous suggestions by the anonymous reviewers. Finally, we thank Bernhard Steffen and his team, for their wonderful work in designing, maintaining and sharing the LearnLib, and organising the RERS challenge series.

A   Full Soundness Proofs for Robustness Derivation Rules

Lemma 7 (Boolean connectives)

1. ϕ is α-robust, if and only if $\neg\phi$ is σ-robust.
2. ϕ is α^1-robust, if and only if $\neg\phi$ is σ^1-robust.
3. If ϕ, ψ are $\alpha/\sigma/\alpha^1/\sigma^1$-robust, then so are $\phi \wedge \psi$ and $\phi \vee \psi$.
4. If ϕ and ψ is input-universal, then so is $\phi \wedge \psi$. If either of ϕ or ψ is input-universal, then also $\phi \vee \psi$ is.

Proof. 1. $\Rightarrow$. Let ϕ be α-robust. Let $\pi \in Tr_{ai}$ and assume $\pi \vDash \neg\phi$, so $\pi \nvDash \phi$. Note that $\pi = \alpha(\sigma(\pi))$. By α-robustness and contraposition, $\sigma(\pi) \nvDash \phi$, so $\sigma(\pi) \vDash \neg\phi$. Hence $\neg\phi$ is σ-robust.

$\Leftarrow$: Similar, by noting that for $\pi \in Tr_s$, $\pi = \sigma(\alpha(\pi))$.

2. $\Rightarrow$: Let ϕ be α^1-robust. Let $\pi \in Tr_{ai}$. Assume $\pi^1 \models \neg\phi$, so $\pi^1 \not\models \phi$. Note that $\pi^1 = \alpha(\sigma(\pi))^1$ By α^1-robustness and contraposition, $\sigma(\pi) \not\models \phi$, so $\sigma(\pi) \models \neg\phi$. Hence $\neg\phi$ is σ^1-robust.

$\Leftarrow$: Similar, by noting that for $\pi \in Tr_s$: $\pi = \sigma(\alpha(\pi))$.

3. Holds obviously for $\phi \wedge \psi$ by inspecting the LTL semantics. It follows for $\phi \vee \psi$ by dualities.

4. Trivial.

Lemma 8 (Robustness of atomic properties)

1. Let $i \in I$. Then i and $\neg i$ are α-robust and σ-robust.
2. Let $o \in O$. Then o and $\neg o$ are α^1-robust and σ^1-robust.
3. Let $i \in I$. Then i is σ^1-robust and $\neg i$ is α^1-robust.
4. Let $o \in O$. Then o is σ-robust and $\neg o$ is α-robust.
5. Let $o \in O$. Then $\neg o$ is input-universal.
6. Let $i \in I$. Then i and $\neg i$ are Mealy-robust.

Proof. 1. Let $i \in I$. Let $\pi = i_0/o_0, \pi'$. Note that $\alpha(\pi) = i_0, o_0, \alpha(\pi')$. Then $\pi \models i \iff i = i_0 \iff \alpha(\pi) \models i$.

2. Let $o \in O$. Let $\pi = i_0/o_0, \pi'$. Note that $\alpha(\pi)^1 = o_0, \alpha(\pi')$. Then $\pi \models o \iff o = o_0 \iff \alpha(\pi)^1 \models o$.

3. Let $i \in I$ and $\pi \in Tr_{ao}$. Then $\pi = o, \pi'$, so $\pi \not\models i$. So i is trivially σ^1-robust, and $\neg i$ is α^1-robust by Lemma 7.

4. Let $o \in O$ and $\pi \in Tr_{ai}$. Assume $\pi = i_0, o_0, \pi'$. Then $\pi \not\models o$ (since I and O are disjoint). So o is trivially σ-robust. Hence $\neg o$ is α-robust by Lemma 7.

5. Any trace in Tr_{ai} is of the form i, o, π', so $\pi \models \neg o$.

6. These formulas are both α- and σ-robust, so they agree on the synchronous and alternating traces from any Mealy machine.

Lemma 9 (α-Robustness of Until-formulas)

1. Let ϕ be α-robust and α^1-robust; let ψ be α-robust. Then $\phi \, \mathsf{U} \, \psi$ is α-robust.
2. Let ϕ be α^1-robust and input-universal; let ψ be α^1-robust. Then $\phi \, \mathsf{U} \, \psi$ is α-robust and α^1-robust.

Proof. 1. (cf. case 1 in Fig. 5, left) Let ϕ be α- and α^1-robust and let ψ be α-robust. Let $\pi \in Tr_s$; assume $\pi \models \phi \, \mathsf{U} \, \psi$. Then $\exists j : (\forall k < j : \pi^k \models \phi) \wedge \pi^j \models \psi$. Note that $\forall k : \alpha(\pi^k) = \alpha(\pi)^{2k}$. By α-robustness of ψ, $\alpha(\pi)^{2j} \models \psi$. By α- and α^1-robustness of ϕ, for each $k < j$, $\alpha(\pi)^{2k} \models \phi$ and $\alpha(\pi)^{2k+1} \models \phi$. Hence, for $j' = 2j$, we obtain: $\exists j' : (\forall k < j' : \alpha(\pi)^k \models \phi) \wedge \alpha(\pi)^{j'} \models \psi$, so $\alpha(\pi) \models \phi \, \mathsf{U} \, \psi$.

2. (cf. case 2 in Fig. 5, left) The proof is similar, but now for $j' = 2j + 1$ we obtain $\alpha(\pi)^{j'} \models \psi$. For $k' = 2k < j'$, we derive ϕ because it is input-universal. For $k' = 2k+1 < j'$, we derive ϕ because it is α^1-robust. Hence, $\alpha(\pi) \models \phi \, \mathsf{U} \, \psi$. In this case, α^1-robustness follows as well (even if $j = 0$).

Lemma 10 (σ-Robustness of Until-formulas)

1. Let ϕ be σ-robust. Let ψ be both σ-robust and σ^1-robust. Then $\phi \, \mathsf{U} \, \psi$ is σ-robust.

2. Let ϕ be σ^1-robust. Let ψ be both σ-robust and σ^1-robust. Then $\phi \cup \psi$ is σ-robust and σ^1-robust.

Proof. We first prove the conclusions on σ-robustness, then σ^1-robustness.

- σ-robustness: Let ϕ be σ- or σ^1-robust; let ψ be σ- and σ^1-robust. Let $\pi \in Tr_{ai}$ be given, with $\pi \vDash \phi \cup \psi$. Then $\exists j : (\forall k < j : \pi^k \vDash \phi) \land \pi^j \vDash \psi$. Note that $\sigma(\pi)^k = \sigma(\pi^{2k})$. If $j = 2j'$ (case 1 in Fig. 5, right), then $\sigma(\pi)^{j'} \vDash \psi$ because ψ is σ-robust. If $j = 2j' + 1$ (case 2 in Fig. 5, right), then $\sigma(\pi)^{j'} \vDash \psi$ because ψ is σ^1-robust. In both cases, for $k' < j'$, we obtain $\sigma(\pi)^{k'} \vDash \phi$ either from $\pi^{2k'}$ (if ϕ is σ-robust), or from $\pi^{2k'+1}$ (if ϕ is σ^1-robust). So indeed $\sigma(\pi) \vDash \phi \cup \psi$.
- σ^1-robustness: Similar, but we start with $\pi \in Tr_{ao}$ with $\pi \vDash \phi \cup \psi$. We now need σ^1-robustness of ϕ to infer ϕ at the first state of $\sigma(\pi)$.

Lemma 11. If ψ is input-universal, then $\phi \cup \psi$ is input-universal.

Proof. Trivial: If $\pi \vDash \psi$ then $\pi \vDash \phi \cup \psi$ (at π_0).

Theorem 12 (Correctness). If the Prolog program in Fig. 4 derives the goal robust(ϕ), then ϕ is Mealy-robust.

Proof. Note that α- and σ-robustness imply robustness. All other rules of the program correspond to previous lemmas.

References

1. Angluin, D.: Learning regular sets from queries and counterexamples. Inf. Comput. **75**(2), 87–106 (1987)
2. Clarke, E.M., Henzinger, T.A., Veith, H., Bloem, R. (eds.): Handbook of Model Checking. Springer, Cham (2018). https://doi.org/10.1007/978-3-319-10575-8
3. Courcoubetis, C., Vardi, M.Y., Wolper, P., Yannakakis, M.: Memory-efficient algorithms for the verification of temporal properties. Formal Meth. Syst. Des. **1**(2/3), 275–288 (1992)
4. Geske, M., Jasper, M., Steffen, B., Howar, F., Schordan, M., van de Pol, J.: RERS 2016: parallel and sequential benchmarks with focus on LTL verification. In: Margaria, T., Steffen, B. (eds.) ISoLA 2016. LNCS, vol. 9953, pp. 787–803. Springer, Cham (2016). https://doi.org/10.1007/978-3-319-47169-3_59
5. Howar, F., Isberner, M., Merten, M., Steffen, B., Beyer, D., Pasareanu, C.S.: Rigorous examination of reactive systems - the RERS challenges 2012 and 2013. STTT **16**(5), 457–464 (2014)
6. Isberner, M., Howar, F., Steffen, B.: The TTT algorithm: a redundancy-free approach to active automata learning. In: Bonakdarpour, B., Smolka, S.A. (eds.) RV 2014. LNCS, vol. 8734, pp. 307–322. Springer, Cham (2014). https://doi.org/10.1007/978-3-319-11164-3_26
7. Isberner, M., Howar, F., Steffen, B.: The open-source LearnLib. In: Kroening, D., Pǎsǎreanu, C.S. (eds.) CAV 2015. LNCS, vol. 9206, pp. 487–495. Springer, Cham (2015). https://doi.org/10.1007/978-3-319-21690-4_32
8. Jasper, M., et al.: The RERS 2017 challenge and workshop (invited paper). In: 24th ACM SIGSOFT IS SPIN on Model Checking of Software (SPIN 2017), pp. 11–20 (2017)

9. Kant, G., Laarman, A., Meijer, J., van de Pol, J., Blom, S., van Dijk, T.: LTSmin: high-performance language-independent model checking. In: Baier, C., Tinelli, C. (eds.) TACAS 2015. LNCS, vol. 9035, pp. 692–707. Springer, Heidelberg (2015). https://doi.org/10.1007/978-3-662-46681-0_61

10. Mealy, G.H.: A method for synthesizing sequential circuits. Bell Syst. Tech. J. **34**(5), 1045–1079 (1955)

11. Meijer, J., van de Pol, J.: Sound black-box checking in the LearnLib. In: Dutle, A., Muñoz, C., Narkawicz, A. (eds.) NFM 2018. LNCS, vol. 10811, pp. 349–366. Springer, Cham (2018). https://doi.org/10.1007/978-3-319-77935-5_24

12. Peled, D.A., Vardi, M.Y., Yannakakis, M.: Black box checking. J. Automata Lang. Comb. **7**(2), 225–246 (2002)

13. Pnueli, A.: The temporal logic of programs. In: 18th AS on Foundations of Computer Science (FOCS 1977), pp. 46–57 (1977)

14. van de Pol, J., Ruys, T.C., te Brinke, S.: Thoughtful brute-force attack of the RERS 2012 and 2013 challenges. STTT **16**(5), 481–491 (2014)

15. Raffelt, H., Steffen, B., Berg, T., Margaria, T.: LearnLib: a framework for extrapolating behavioral models. STTT **11**(5), 393–407 (2009)

16. Ben Salem, A.E., Duret-Lutz, A., Kordon, F., Thierry-Mieg, Y.: Symbolic model checking of stutter-invariant properties using generalized testing automata. In: Ábrahám, E., Havelund, K. (eds.) TACAS 2014. LNCS, vol. 8413, pp. 440–454. Springer, Heidelberg (2014). https://doi.org/10.1007/978-3-642-54862-8_38

17. Steffen, B., Howar, F., Merten, M.: Introduction to active automata learning from a practical perspective. In: Bernardo, M., Issarny, V. (eds.) SFM 2011. LNCS, vol. 6659, pp. 256–296. Springer, Heidelberg (2011). https://doi.org/10.1007/978-3-642-21455-4_8

Author Index

Printed in the United States
By Bookmasters